Meeting Physical and Health Needs of Children with Disabilities

Teaching Student Participation and Management

KATHRYN WOLFF HELLER
Georgia State University

PAULA E. FORNEY
Ga. PINES Program

PAUL A. ALBERTO
Georgia State University

MORTON N. SCHWARTZMAN
Children's Rehabilitation Network

TRUDY M. GOECKEL
Gwinnett County Schools

Wadsworth
Thomson Learning™

Australia • Canada • Mexico • Singapore • Spain • United Kingdom • United States

Education Editor: Dianne Lindsay
Assistant Editor: Tangelique Williams
Editorial Assistant: Keynia Johnson
Marketing Manager: Becky Tollerson
Project Editor: Trudy Brown
Print Buyer: April Reynolds
Permissions Editor: Joohee Lee

Production Service: Penmarin Books
Copy Editor: Laura Larson
Illustrator: Elizabeth Morales
Cover Designer: Yvo Riezebos
Cover Printer: Webcom, Ltd.
Compositor: The PRD Group
Printer: Webcom, Ltd.

For permission to use material from this text,
contact us by
Web: http://www.thomsonrights.com
Fax: 1-800-730-2215 **Phone:** 1-800-730-2214

For more information, contact
Wadsworth/Thomson Learning
10 Davis Drive
Belmont, CA 94002-3098
USA
http://www.wadsworth.com

International Headquarters
Thomson Learning
International Division
290 Harbor Drive, 2nd Floor
Stamford, CT 06902-7477
USA

UK/Europe/Middle East/South Africa
Thomson Learning
Berkshire House
168-173 High Holborn
London WC1V 7AA
United Kingdom

Asia
Thomson Learning
60 Albert Street, #15-01
Albert Complex
Singapore 189969

Canada
Nelson Thomson Learning
1120 Birchmount Road
Toronto, Ontario M1K 5G4
Canada

Library of Congress Cataloging-in-Publication Data
On file
ISBN: 0534-34837-8

With gratitude to all the children, families, teachers, and university students from whom we have learned so much over the years and with love to our own children and grandchildren: Daniel Bryan, Megan Caitlin, Rhonda Beth, Paula Renee, Jon David, Harold Steven, Marissa Leigh, Ari Michael, Lauren Michele, Alicia Renee, Ashten Nicole, Daniel William, Matthew Brendan, and Philip Patrick, who make life a continuous learning process. Also, special thanks to the Tumlin family: Beth, Bill, Jennifer, Tracy, and Natalie. Our journey together over the past 15 years has meant so much.

Contents

PART II PHYSICAL AND MANAGEMENT SKILLS

5   Lifting, Carrying, and Transferring

15   Oxygen Management   364

16   Ventilator Management   382

Preface

This textbook is designed to provide crucial information on physical management skills and specialized health care procedures for students with disabilities. It contains specific strategies for addressing such physical management areas as lifting, transferring, positioning, and mobility. Step-by-step procedures are also provided for implementation of health care procedures, such as tube feeding and clean intermittent catheterization, as well as information on what to do if a problem occurs. Since these health care procedures fall under the category of self-help skills, special emphasis has been placed on teaching students with disabilities to perform or participate in their physical management and health care procedures.

Since a team of individuals are needed to educate students properly in these areas, a team of individuals wrote this book. Collectively, our backgrounds include education, medicine, nursing, physical therapy, occupational therapy, parent of a child with severe health impairments, and grandparent of a child with a severe physical disability.

This book is divided into four major parts. The first part, which contains Chapters 1 through 4, lays a foundation for the rest of the book. Chapter 1 provides an overview of the health problems and their impact on students with orthopedic impairments, health impairments and multiple disabilities. Guidelines and legal implications of performing physical health care procedures are addressed, as well as other safety considerations such as infection control. This first chapter provides explanations regarding the use of equipment, assistive strategies, and instructional strategies that are provided in each chapter to help the reader perform or teach each skill or procedure. Explanations and guidelines of IHPs (individualized health plans) and IEPs (individualized educational programs) are found in this first chapter, and examples are given in each of the book chapters.

The remaining chapters in Part I provide vital information that can be utilized in other sections of the book. Chapter 2, "Promoting Independence through the Use of Instructional Strategies," provides systematic strategies for assessment and instruction that are to be used for teaching the content of the book to students, whether this be teaching students to assist with positioning or their own tube feeding. Descriptions of data collection and a sample form is included that can be used for the procedures in the book. Chapter 3, "Communication for Physical and Health Needs," provides an overview of augmentative communication and specifically targets the vocabulary students need to address their specific health needs. This includes vocabulary needed to express a health or physical concern, vocabulary to perform health care procedures, and vocabulary for hospital settings. Chapter 4, "Medications and Procedures for Administration," provides content knowledge and skills for administering medication. However, this chapter also provides information on permission forms and documentation for medication and physical health care procedures that are pertinent for each chapter of the book.

Part II deals with physical management skills.

Chapter 5, "Lifting, Carrying, and Transferring," provides handling considerations prior to lifting, principles of basic body mechanics, adapted equipment for lifting, and strategies for performing the various lifts. A section is also provided on teaching students how to lift objects properly—a skill many students will need in various community-based vocational instructional sites. Chapter 6, "Proper Handling and Positioning," provides information on various handling techniques, as well as techniques for prone, supine, side-lying, sitting, and standing positions. This chapter also has information on proper positioning of instructional materials to promote easy access by students with physical impairments. Chapter 7, "Mobility," describes a range of mobility skills and strategies for promoting mobility from rolling to walking or wheeling a wheelchair.

The third part of the book addresses basic self-help skills and related health procedures. Chapter 8, "Eating and Feeding Techniques," begins by describing various factors affecting eating and feeding and then provides a range of strategies to address feeding and eating problems. For students who are unable to take food by mouth, the next chapter, "Tube Feeding," explains different types of tube-feeding routes and formula delivery, as well as specific procedures for providing nutrition or medication through a tube. Chapter 10, "Toilet Training," contains specific information on general techniques for toilet training, as well as trip-training and bowel-training methods. Students who require urinary catheterization or the use of urinary collection devices will find specific strategies and information on this topic in Chapter 11. The last chapter in this section, Chapter 12, provides information and strategies for the management of colostomies and other types of ostomies.

Part IV provides information on a range of respiratory procedures that students may need during the school day. This includes tracheostomy care (Chapter 13), suctioning and other forms of secretion management (Chapter 14), oxygen management (Chapter 15), and ventilator management (Chapter 16). Each of these areas addresses specific strategies for managing and teaching these important health areas.

ACKNOWLEDGMENTS

We are grateful to the many people who assisted us in the preparation of this textbook. We want to thank Lee Wolff and Elisabeth Cohen who are coauthors on the medication and toileting chapters, respectively. We want to extend a special thanks to the following individuals who assisted in reviewing select chapters, taking photographs, and providing support: Edward Heller, Larry Forney, Marilyn Schwartzman, Chris Goeckel, Michael Carroll, Stefanie Case, John O'Connor, Laura Fredrick, Cindy Terry, Kathie Rush, Lori Shapell, Eileen Wolff, and Virgil Wolff.

We also would like to thank our reviewers, who were selected by our editor and who provided meaningful feedback to assist us in providing a comprehensive textbook. These reviewers are Sherwood J. Best, California State University, Los Angeles; Dennis L. Cates, Cameron University; Donald Cross, University of Kentucky; Mary Kay Dykes, University of Florida; and Mary Jane K. Rapport, University of Colorado Health Sciences Center.

Finally, we would like to thank all the graduate students who took our course on "Physical and Health Management of Students with Disabilities." The writing of this textbook was prompted by the students' need to have a book that described not only physical and health management issues, but the instruction of them. These students' feedback on draft chapters over the past 2 years have assisted us in providing an understandable and meaningful textbook that we hope will provide crucial knowledge and skills to teachers educating students with physical, health, and multiple disabilities.

Kathryn Wolff Heller
Paula E. Forney
Paul A. Alberto
Morton N. Schwartzman
Trudy M. Goeckel

About the Authors

Kathryn Wolff Heller, R.N., Ph.D., an associate professor of educational psychology and special education at Georgia State University, coordinates graduate programs in physical/health impairments (orthopedic impairments) and visual impairments. She also directs several projects including the Bureau for Students with Physical and Health Impairments, a statewide technical assistance project, and the Georgia Deafblind Project, which also provides statewide assistance to students, teachers, and families.

Dr. Heller is a registered nurse with experience in pediatric medicine, who worked for 5 years in intensive care units, and then went on to obtain master's and doctoral degrees in special education. She has worked as a classroom teacher of students with orthopedic impairments, mental retardation, traumatic brain injury, and visual impairments. In addition, Dr. Heller provided technical assistance to nine states and territories in the area of deafblindness as part of a national technical assistance grant. She has made numerous presentations and has served on several advisory boards. Dr. Heller has also coauthored textbooks, monographs, and numerous articles pertaining to students with physical impairments, sensory impairments, and/or mental retardation. One of her primary interests is the provision of effective educational instruction and health care for students with physical, sensory, and health impairments.

Paula E. Forney, RPT, M.M.Sc., a therapy coordinator for the Ga. PINES Program in Atlanta, Georgia, trains and supervises physical and occupational therapists throughout Georgia to provide home-based technical assistance services to families of young children with multiple disabilities including sensory impairments. Ms. Forney has a B.S. degree in physical therapy from Simmons College in Boston, an M.M.Sc. degree in pediatric physical therapy from Emory University in Atlanta, and is certified in both pediatric neurodevelopmental treatment and sensory integration assessment and treatment. In addition, she has over 25 years of experience in pediatric physical therapy, including development of school therapy and early intervention programs.

Ms. Forney has coauthored the INSITE and AHEAD curricula as well as a textbook and several articles on children with multiple disabilities, developed instructional videotapes on children with motor impairments, and taught numerous courses and workshops on pediatric physical therapy, early intervention, and children with sensory impairments. She is also extensively involved with local and state interagency councils that service young children with special needs and their families. Ms. Forney's major interest is in collaborative training to provide optimal services to children with multiple disabilities and their families.

Paul A. Alberto, Ph.D., a professor of educational psychology and special education at Georgia State University, coordinates the teacher training program in multiple and severe disabilities. He also directs the Bureau for Students with Multiple and Severe Disabilities, a project funded to provide technical assistance on instruction and curriculum to students, teachers, parents, and administrators; and the Center for Collaborative Education, a project funded to facilitate the least restrictive placement for students with disabilities. Previously, he was a classroom teacher of students with mental retardation.

Dr. Alberto has coauthored a college textbook on applied behavior analysis for teachers and has written numerous chapters and articles concerning the education of students with moderate, severe, and profound mental retardation. In addition, he has directed funded projects for the development of community-based instruction, secondary and transition programs, and instruction of students with profound disabilities. His primary interest is the provision of effective instructional strategies for students with severe disabilities from a behavioral perspective.

Morton N. Schwartzman, M.D., P.A.A.P., F.C.C.P., a pediatrician who specializes in pulmonary diseases, is the medical director of the Cystic Fibrosis Center affiliated with the Joe DiMaggio Children's Hospital at Memorial, Hollywood, Florida. Dr. Schwartzman, whose previous experience includes working as a private practitioner for 29 years, was a medical consultant for the Health Rehabilitative Service Agency, Miami-Dade County, Florida. His responsibilities included caring for infants, children, and adolescents with chronic diseases, such as neurological disorders, muscular dystrophy and myopathies, and pulmonary diseases. He also was involved with the care and treatment of children with special needs, who resided in various group homes. He has served as a medical director for a prescribed pediatric extended care facility for children with medical and physical impairments. He also has served on many advisory boards, medical boards, and boards of directors, including the American Lung Association of South Florida, and of the state of Florida. Dr. Schwartzman is a past president of the medical staff at Miami Children's

Hospital in Miami, Florida, and is a past president of the American Lung Association of Dade and Monroe Counties of South Florida. He also has been associated with the Cystic Fibrosis Center of the University of Miami.

Dr. Schwartzman has lectured to local university students, civic groups, and professional organizations, and has coauthored several articles published in various journals. His interest lies in creating new avenues to improve care for children and adolescents with medical needs and with physical and mental impairments.

Trudy M. Goeckel, OTR, BCP, an occupational therapist for Gwinnett County Public Schools in metro Atlanta, provides school-based occupational therapy services for children ages 3 through 21 to assist children in gaining the functional skills required for the school environment. She serves children with physical, sensory, and multiple disabilities by collaborating in the development of programs that will assist the child in gaining daily living skills such as eating, dressing, and personal hygiene, as well as educational living skills such as written communication, organizing materials, and manipulating materials. Ms. Goeckel also serves as therapy consultant for an early intervention program providing services for families with physical and sensory impairments. She is board certified in pediatrics by the American Occupational Therapy Association. In addition, she has 9 years experience in pediatric occupational therapy and has received extensive training in sensory integration and feeding disorders.

Ms. Goeckel regularly lectures to graduate students at a local university and has supervised occupational therapy students. She also enjoys speaking with parents' support groups, teachers, and therapists about strategies to develop feeding, writing, and other skills in the home and school environment. One of her primary interests is to collaboratively develop individualized programs that have effective strategies to assist the child in accomplishing functional tasks in multiple environments.

Part I

Instructional and Health Issues

1

Promoting Health in Students with Disabilities

Everyone encounters illness, disease, or injury sometime during their lifetime. Children with physical or health disabilities tend to encounter additional health concerns depending on the nature of their medical condition. These students need to learn how to manage their health, including how to monitor their condition, perform certain physical management interventions or health care procedures, and follow specific restrictions or precautions. To meet these children's needs, teachers need to help their students learn to manage their own care. Teachers also must learn how to promote a safe and healthy environment for their students by learning to monitor students' health effectively and intervene if significant problems occur.

Several different types of physical and health disabilities can adversely affect students' general health. Physical and health disabilities can be divided into three main categories: orthopedic impairments, other health impairments (including students with complex health care needs and students who are technology-dependent), and mul-

tiple disabilities (in which a physical or health impairment is present) (see Table 1-1). A student is considered to have an **orthopedic impairment** when this impairment adversely affects the student's educational performance. The term includes

> impairments caused by congenital anomalies (e.g., club foot, absence of some body part, etc.), impairments caused by disease (e.g., poliomyelitis, bone tuberculosis, etc.), and impairments from other causes (e.g., cerebral palsy, amputations, and fractures or burns that cause contractures) (Department of Education, 1992, p. 44802).

Orthopedic impairments typically result in limitations in motor movement and mobility, which in turn can have negative effects on the major systems of the body and increase health problems.

Other health impairment refers to "having limited strength, vitality, or alertness, due to chronic or acute health problems such as heart

Table 1-1 Defining Physical/Health Impairments

Orthopedic impairments	Other health impairments	Multiple disabilities
Orthopedic impairments caused by congenital anomalies	Chronic or acute health problems	Concomitant impairments, with one impairment being an orthopedic or health impairment
Orthopedic impairments caused by disease	Complex health care needs	
Orthopedic impairments caused by other causes	Technology-dependent	

condition, tuberculosis, rheumatic fever, nephritis, asthma, sickle cell anemia, hemophilia, epilepsy, lead poisoning, leukemia, or diabetes that adversely affects a child's educational performance" (Department of Education, 1992, p. 44802). The term *other health impairments,* can also include students who are technology assisted or who have complex health care needs. These students may be dependent on such technology as mechanical ventilators, oxygen, and tube feeding (Knight & Wadsworth, 1994). By the very definition of other health impairments, these students are at risk of developing health problems unless proper monitoring and treatment occur.

Multiple disabilities describes individuals who have two or more disabilities that significantly affect their ability to function in educational and community environments. The combination usually results in an interactional, multiplicative effect, rather than a simple additive one (Hart, 1988; Alberto & Heller, 1995). *Multiple disabilities* refers to concomitant impairments (e.g., mental retardation-orthopedic impairment), "the combination of which causes such severe educational problems that they cannot be accommodated in special education programs solely for one of the impairments" (Department of Education, 1992, p. 44802).

Multiple disabilities include a broad range and multiple combinations of conditions. In this book, the term *multiple disabilities* will refer to disabilities with a physical or health component as one of the impairments.

DESCRIPTION OF HEALTH PROBLEMS AND THEIR IMPACT

Health may be defined as a state of optimal mental, social, and physical well-being, not merely the absence of disease and infirmity (*Dorland's Illustrated Medical Dictionary,* 1994). Students with physical and health impairments, just as any student, may have any number of health concerns such as depression, poor socialization skills, and poor physical fitness. However, unique concerns can arise because of their disabilities. In the area of mental health, learned helplessness is a concern; in the area of social health, ineffective communication systems can be a problem; and in the area of physical health, specific problems can result from the student's physical or health impairment.

Mental Health Issues

Part of the definition of *health* is a state of mental well-being. One of the threats to the health of students with physical and health impairments is the development of learned helplessness (Heller, Alberto, & Meagher, 1996). **Learned helplessness** is the lack of persistence at tasks that can be mastered. Typically, a student with learned helplessness behaves as if he or she is not capable of performing certain tasks and relies on others to perform the task instead. As a result, the student does not learn critical skills necessary to be as independent as possible, and feelings of self-worthlessness and helplessness may ensue. Learned helplessness can occur when well-meaning school system personnel and/or parents provide more assistance to the student than is necessary. For example, some students with physical impairments may not learn to feed themselves because they are always fed by someone. For the student who requires tube feeding, the student may never learn to do the procedure or participate in helping with the procedure because the child has never been expected to learn it. Learned helplessness can be avoided, or combated, by having reasonable expectations, using systematic teaching techniques, implementing modifications, and using adapted equipment as needed. Throughout this book, we will discuss instructional strategies to teach students to perform the skill as independently as possible, thus preventing learned helplessness. We will describe not only physical management but also basic self-help or independent living skills (which include health care procedures).

Social Health Issues

Students' mental, physical, and social well-being may be affected when the student has an ineffective communication system. Many students with severe physical impairments, such as cerebral palsy, are unable to speak effectively and need alternative and augmentative forms of communication. Frustration or depression may occur when effective augmentative communication is missing or inadequately provided. To promote social well-being, therefore, the student needs a communication system that will allow the student to convey thoughts and needs and to maintain social interaction. Having a way to communicate with others decreases frustration and increases social interactions. The teacher must thus be sure that an appropriate communication system(s) is available to the student with sufficient vocabulary and the student is taught the communication system using effective instructional strategies. The communication system should also have the appropriate

vocabulary to allow students to communicate health needs in order to promote physical well-being as well. (Because of the large breadth of this topic, Chapter 3 will specifically target communication for physical and health needs.)

Physical Health Issues

The largest category of health concerns for students with physical and health impairments is how the disability itself can adversely impact physical health. The following sections will separately describe the impact of orthopedic impairments, health impairments, and multiple disabilities on health. This is followed by sections on how these issues can be addressed and where they are discussed in depth in this textbook. The chapter concludes with specific management issues pertaining to individualized education programs, individualized health plans, educational teams, guidelines for performance of procedures, training issues, and infection control.

Impact of Orthopedic Impairments on Health. Children without disabilities who are confined to bed due to illness or injury are usually active enough to avoid developing complications of immobility. However, when a person is unable to move well because of a physical impairment (e.g., cerebral palsy, muscular dystrophy), problems can result affecting most major systems of the body, including the musculoskeletal, integumentary (skin), sensory, respiratory, immune, and gastrointestinal systems, in addition to other body systems (e.g., renal, cardiovascular, and immune systems).

Musculoskeletal System. The musculoskeletal system is affected when a person has a condition resulting in a lack of normal muscle tone and movement. This state may vary from a lack of range of motion in one or more joints to conditions resulting in increased or low tone, to a complete lack of ability to move a limb. This inability to move a part of the body, or to move it completely, can worsen over time. Inactive muscles lose strength and muscle mass can decrease, resulting in atrophy of muscles with lessening strength and endurance. Besides further affecting the ability to move, lack of muscle strength may affect internal structures by preventing the muscles from effectively holding certain body structures in place. The spinal column (backbone), for example, can begin to curve abnormally when the muscles surrounding it are unable to support it properly, which in turn can negatively affect other body systems (Lovell & Winter, 1986; Westcott, Dynes, Remer, Donaldson, & Dias, 1992).

For students with an inability to move or conditions resulting in high muscular tone, normal structural stretching and movement of the limbs may be absent. When this occurs, the collagen fibers of the joints undergo changes that can result in permanent shortening of the muscles, known as **contractures** (Wong, 1995). Contractures can result in a further loss of range of motion of the joint. Contractures of the elbows, for example, can impact on functional arm use needed during such tasks as eating. Those affecting the hips and knees can interfere with sitting or walking.

Bone growth and bone density are adversely affected by a lack of motion. There is a delicate balance in the body between normal bone formation and bone reabsorption. Movement and weight bearing (e.g., standing) stimulates bone growth. When movement is restricted and weight bearing is decreased (e.g., in conditions affecting the ability to stand), bone formation decreases while bone absorption continues. An imbalance between bone formation and absorption then occurs, resulting in a depletion of bone calcium and thus less dense, weaker bones. Minimal stress on these weakened bones can then result in fractures, which would not have occurred if the bones had been healthy (Wong, 1995). Also, a lack of weight bearing during the growing years can result in decreased height of the person. Use of positioning equipment, special positioning and handling

techniques, and physical and occupational therapy will be needed to maximize the health of the musculoskeletal system.

Integumentary System (Skin). The integumentary system of students with orthopedic impairments is at risk for developing **decubitus ulcers** (also known as *pressure sores*). With less movement and inactivity, the circulation to the skin is decreased. When pressure is applied to these areas, the skin may break down, causing a decubitus ulcer. This is especially the case where the skin covers bony areas of the body. Prolonged sitting, for example, can place pressure on the skin over the sacrum, or a poorly fitting ankle-foot orthosis (AFO) can place pressure over the ankle area.

A decubitus ulcer is forming when there is prolonged redness over an area (over 30 minutes). Other signs may be increased temperature, swelling, blistering, or dark black areas (Wong, 1995). If appropriate treatment is not provided, this pressure area can worsen, as the cells of the skin die and the skin breaks. Decubitus ulcers may initially appear small, but they are typically cone shaped with much larger damage occurring under the surface of the skin. This ulceration can extend to the bone. If it is left untreated, local and then systemic infection may result. In extreme cases, an individual can die from the systemic infection resulting from the infected decubitus ulcer. Fortunately, these are preventable when proper positioning and frequent position changes occur.

Sensory System. The sensory system can also be affected, indirectly, by the student's inability to move. Improper body positioning or a poorly applied orthoses can trigger pressure on the nerves and blood vessels that can result in nerve degeneration and affect the ability to feel pressure or touch. Also, in some physical conditions, such as spinal cord injury, there may be a lack of feeling below the level of the injury. Students who lack sensation are at risk for developing injuries, perhaps inadvertently burning or otherwise hurting themselves without realizing it. Skin breakdown (decubitus ulcer) may occur without the student feeling the area. Splints or orthoses may rub against the skin without the student realizing it. Proper positioning of the student and carefully checking to be sure that the skin is not being hurt are important to prevent injury.

Respiratory System. The respiratory system can also be affected in students who are unable to move around normally. Respirations may be more shallow due to less demand for oxygen or decrease in strength of some of the muscles used in breathing. This may result in a decreased expansion of the chest, as well as a weak cough. Normal lung secretions may collect in the lungs rather than be expelled. This provides an environment for growth of bacteria and can result in respiratory infection and pneumonia (Graff, Ault, Guess, Taylor, & Thompson, 1990). Use of special respiratory procedures (e.g., postural drainage) may be needed to help prevent illness.

Immune System. Students with physical disabilities tend to have a higher frequency of colds, influenza, and other infections that result in increased absenteeism and/or medical attention. Conditions like these indicating a weakened immune system may be due to the impact of physical impairments on the respiratory system and decreased hygiene (Schupf, Ortiz, & Kapell, 1995). Students with reduced immunity, or a propensity to acquire infections because of some aspect of their physical or health impairment, can more easily acquire an infection from another student or school staff. It is therefore essential that sick students or personnel be sent home. It is equally important that infection control procedures be implemented in the school to prevent the spread of infection and promote a healthy environment.

Gastrointestinal System. Students with physical impairments are also at risk of having gastrointestinal difficulties involving nutrition and

elimination. Lack of movement can result in reduced energy requirements, diminished appetite, and, subsequently, less ingestion of nutrients. Also, physical conditions such as severe spastic cerebral palsy may have several associated oral motor problems (e.g., chewing problems, tongue movement abnormalities) that negatively impact on the ability to take in sufficient quantities of food and liquids. Improper nutritional status may occur for those reasons. Therefore, proper feeding and eating techniques to promote adequate eating are essential.

Elimination may also be affected by a lack of activity. Inactivity due to motor tone problems, weakness, paralysis, or various physical impairments can affect the normal smooth muscle and skeletal muscle activity that acts on the movement of feces through the intestines. Slowing of the feces as they travel through the intestines results in the feces becoming harder, which can lead to constipation or an impaction. This condition is further compounded if the muscles used for defecation (abdominal muscles and diaphragm) are weak, making elimination more difficult. Promoting activity and assisting students to take medications for elimination then becomes important to promote the health of the gastrointestinal system.

Other Bodily Functions. The cardiovascular system and renal system, as well as the student's general alertness, may be affected by limitations in activity from a physical impairment. Significant immobility results in an increased likelihood that some individuals may develop blood clots. The renal system can develop kidney stones because of a lack of movement, especially if the body is kept in a somewhat horizontal position. Students with severe physical impairments who have limited ability to move may expend a great deal of energy to make the movements they can make. Expending this energy can result in fatigue and decreased attention. If the fatigue persists, it can affect the student's general health and well-being (Gaff et al., 1990; Wong, 1995). A careful balance between promoting movement and allowing for breaks is important to promote health.

Impact of Other Health Impairments on Health. By the very nature of the disability, specific health impairment can adversely affect the health of the student. Health conditions require an understanding of the specific health impairment, proper management of the condition (e.g., medication, restrictions, modifications), proper monitoring of the student, and steps to take in event of an emergency. As seen in Table 1-2, there are specific modifications and skills required for many of these conditions. Teachers should be thoroughly familiar with these when they have a student with a health impairment. Information regarding specific disabilities can be obtained from a variety of agencies. Detailed information of these health impairments are beyond the scope of this book, and the reader is referred to "Understanding Physical, Sensory, and Health Impairments" (Heller, Alberto, Forney, & Schwartzman, 1996) for specific information.

Another area of health impairments includes students who have complex health care needs that require health care procedures. Some of the most common procedures that teachers will encounter include tube feeding, urinary catheterization (and urinary collection devices), colostomies/ileostomies, tracheostomies, suctioning (and other procedures to manage respiratory secretions), oxygen management, and ventilator management. Each of these requires specialized training and careful monitoring on the part of all school personnel, family members, and the student to detect whether there is a problem. As seen in Table 1-3, severe health problems and complications may occur with these procedures (Heller, Fredrick, & Rithmire, 1997). Each of these will be discussed in detail in their respective chapter in this book.

Impact of Multiple Disabilities on Health. Students who have multiple disabilities with a physical or health component will also be at risk for health problems, in the same fashion as students who only have a singular orthopedic or health problem. However, because of the combination of disabilities, health prevention may be more difficult. For example, students with severe mental retardation and cerebral palsy may have difficulty learning to wash their hands after using the restroom owing to both physical and cognitive impairments. Several aspects of a multiple disability may interfere with regimen compliance or task completion. Some of these include memory deficits, sequencing deficits, inattention, attending to irrelevant or incorrect aspects of the task, difficulty generalizing pertinent information between tasks, and motor problems interfering with the ability to perform a task easily. Because of the complexity of multiple disabilities, as well as the multifaceted nature of singular physical or health disabilities, a team approach is needed to meet the health needs of these students.

Team Approach. The education of students with physical and health disabilities requires the coordinated effort of an educational team. To implement and teach students the various physical management and self-help procedures correctly (including health care procedures) discussed in this book, a collaborative effort is required among all team members. The educational team may have several members, depending on the student's needs and the type of objective being considered. Some teams may include any combination of the following: the parent, student, special education teacher, regular education teacher, administrators, physical therapist, occupational therapist, paraprofessional, adapted physical education teacher, speech and language pathologist, community service provider, nurse, physician, psychologist, social worker, nutritionist, and others (Heller, Alberto, Forney, et al., 1996). See Table 1-4 for a description of possible educational team members.

Different professionals may take the lead of the educational team, depending on the type of objective being considered. For example, the physical therapist would most likely take the lead in positioning and handling techniques, but the other team members will need to provide their

Table 1-2 Potential Classroom Modifications and Teacher Skill Requirements

Chronic condition	Potential modifications	Skills required
Asthma	Avoidance of allergens	CPR
	Participation in physical activity	Recognition of signs and symptoms of respiratory stress
	Administration of medication as needed	Recognition of medication side effects
Congenital heart disease	Participation in physical activity	CPR
	Administration of medication as needed	Recognition of signs and symptoms of heart failure
	Diet and/or fluids	Recognition of medication side effects
Diabetes	Diet, bathroom frequency, availability of snacks, and source of sugar	Recognition of signs and symptoms of hypoglycemia (rapid onset)
	Balance of exercise and food	Recognition of signs and symptoms of hyperglycemia (slow onset)
Leukemia	Participation in physical activity	Recognition of signs and symptoms of infection
	Avoid exposure to communicable diseases	Recognition of signs and symptoms of bleeding
Seizure disorder	Participation in physical activity	Seizure management
	Environment	Recognition of signs and symptoms of distress during and after seizure
	Administration of medications as needed	Recognition of medication side effects
Spina bifida	Participation in physical activity	Recognition of signs and symptoms of shunt blockage
	Environment to accommodate mobility and movement	Recognition of signs and symptoms of urinary infections
	Diet and/or fluids	Recognition of signs and symptoms of skin breakdowns
	Movement to prevent pressure sore	Use of equipment and mobility devices
	Bathroom availability	
Sickle cell	Participation in physical activity	Recognition of signs and symptoms of impending crisis
	Fluids	
Juvenile rheumatoid arthritis	Participation in physical activity	Recognition of signs and symptoms of increased inflammation
	Environment, i.e., stairs	Recognition of broken bones
	Administration of medication as needed	
	Frequency of movement	
	Classroom activities, i.e., writing, carrying books	
Hemophilia	Physical activity	Recognition of signs and symptoms of bleeds
		Management of bleeding, i.e., cuts and scrapes
Cystic fibrosis	Physical activity	Recognition of signs and symptoms of respiratory distress
	Administration of medication as needed	Management of oxygen therapy and respiratory treatments
	Diet	Recognition of medication side effects
Kidney disease	Physical activity	Recognition of signs and symptoms of fluid retention
	Diet and fluids	Recognition of medication side effects
	Bathroom privileges	
	Medication administration	

SOURCE: Reprinted by permission of the publisher from *Community Provider's Guide: An Information Outline for Working with Children with Special Needs*, eds. Terry Heintz Caldwell et al. (New Orleans, LA: Children's Hospital, 1986).

Note: This table contains general information. Individualized health care plans are recommended.

Table 1-3 Select Complications of Special Health Care Procedures

Procedure	Complications
Tube feeding	Flow of formula stopping
	Displacement of tube
	Severe cramping
	Redness, drainage, tenderness, bleeding around stoma
	Abdominal distention, nausea, vomiting, diarrhea
	Choking
	Aspiration of formula
	Pneumonia from aspiration
	Respiratory arrest from aspiration
Colostomy care	Changes in stoma
	Skin problems around stoma
	Problems with fecal elimination
	Blockage of stoma (may result in cramping, abdominal distention, vomiting, decreased circulation, and emergency situation due to tissue death)
Urinary catheterization	Infection
	Tissue damage
	Permanent damage to urinary system if done incorrectly
Suctioning	Respiratory infections
	Skin irritation and infection
	Respiratory distress
	Respiratory arrest if unable to clear secretions blocking trachea
Ventilator management	Incorrectly responding to alarms, resulting in distress
	Respiratory distress and arrest if managed incorrectly
Medication	Medication side effects and toxic effects
	Allergic reaction to medication
	Choking on medication

Table 1-4 Examples of Educational Team Members

Member	Role
General education teacher	Brings important information regarding age-appropriate curricular activities and social interactions
Nurse	Has knowledge of students' physical and medical conditions and is trained to perform health care procedures
Nutritionist	Has knowledge of proper nutrition; adjusts caloric intake; designs special diets
Occupational therapist	Provides information about optimal physical function in age-appropriate activities, particularly as they relate to fine-motor skills, visual-motor skills, and self-care activities
Parents	Have the most knowledge regarding their son or daughter
Physical therapist	Provides information about optimal physical functioning in age-appropriate activities, particularly as they relate to gross-motor skills and mobility
Physician	Provides appropriate medical information and treatments
Psychologist	Primarily evaluates student's intellectual and adaptive abilities
Student	Provides information regarding goal and objective selection
Special education teacher	Works cooperatively with students, family members, and other team members to identify age-appropriate, functional activities and academic skills for instruction and provides information on appropriate instructional strategies and adaptations
Speech language pathologist	Provides information on communication programming in age-appropriate functional activities and augmentative communication devices

input regarding timing of the positioning and techniques to teach the student to indicate when a position change is needed. In the area of health care procedures (e.g., tube feeding, urinary catheterization), the nurse would most likely describe how the physical health care procedures are to be done, while the teacher would provide information on teaching techniques to help others instruct the student on how to perform them. Several school-based team members would also need to learn the procedure and pertinent information so they can be ready to act if a problem occurs. The specific team members and types of equipment, assistive strategies, and instructional strategies used to promote health are discussed in detail in each chapter.

EQUIPMENT, ASSISTIVE STRATEGIES, AND INSTRUCTIONAL STRATEGIES

To meet the health and educational needs of students with physical, health, or multiple disabilities, the educational team will need to use specialized equipment, assistive strategies, and systematic instructional strategies. The aim is to provide students with the proper assistance and instruction to help them become as independent as possible in managing their own health needs. Each type of physical and health management area has its own specific equipment, assistive strategies, and instructional strategies. A general overview is presented here, with specific equipment and strategies addressed in each chapter of this book.

Equipment and Adaptive Equipment to Address Health Concerns

Students will often need specialized equipment to meet their health care needs. This may take the form of typical equipment (e.g., soap for hand washing or a colostomy bag for elimination) or **adaptive equipment** (e.g., a positioning device). Adaptive equipment consists of specialized devices used to help the student perform some function. Adaptive equipment may assist in preventing the effects of immobility or impaired movement and promoting better positioning and mobility. Adaptive equipment falls into two general broad categories: (a) those that assist in providing proper positioning, (including provision of weight bearing and preventing injury due to periods of immobility) and (b) those that assist in providing mobility, movement, or support. Equipment and/or adaptive equipment can be examined across physical management and self-help skills (including health care procedures).

Promoting Physical Management with Adaptive Equipment. Several types of equipment are made to assist individuals to maintain proper position and to allow for weight bearing. For example, wheelchairs and adaptive chairs are made with specific inserts to help promote proper positioning and decrease abnormal stress on certain body locations that could otherwise result in contractures, decubitus ulcers, and other problems. One type of insert is an **abductor** pad (a pad that goes between the knees) for individuals who have contractures or tightness causing the knees to be drawn together. This abductor pad can help prevent certain contractures and decubitus ulcers from forming on the knees. Other types of pads may be necessary to bring the legs inward or help keep the trunk in an upright position. Inserts in the seat can help promote proper hip flexion. Support may also be given at the head, chest, shoulders, hips, and/or feet to promote optimal alignment.

Other types of positioning equipment may promote weight bearing and muscle use. For example, some adaptive equipment (e.g., prone standers) positions students in an upright position, promoting weight bearing, bone growth, and functioning of the major systems of the body. Other positioning equipment (e.g., side-lyers) allows students to be positioned on their side, allowing gravity to help bring the students' hands together to more easily manipulate an object. Positioning equipment is described in depth in Chapter 6, "Proper Handling and Positioning."

Adaptive equipment may also be used to promote mobility and movement. Some adaptive equipment is used to move oneself (e.g., wheelchairs, walkers, scooter boards, adaptive bicycles) and to help promote arm movement and access (e.g., a mechanical feeding device, an augmentative communication device with alternative access, an adapted slanted surface to promote access to material). Each type of adaptive equipment is discussed in Chapter 3 ("Communication for Physical and Health Needs"), Chapter 6 ("Proper Handling and Positioning"), and Chapter 7 ("Mobility").

Promoting Self-Help Skills and Health Care Procedures with Adaptive Equipment. In the area of health impairments, an array of equipment or adaptive equipment may be required to implement a self-help skill or health care procedure. Certain types of equipment to provide medications may be needed, such as a nebulizer for breathing treatments (see Chapter 4, "Medications and Procedures for Administration"). Specialized feeding equipment may be necessary to promote independent eating or eating with assistance (see Chapter 8, "Eating and Feeding Techniques"). Adaptive toilets may be required to position a child properly to use the toilet (see Chapter 10, "Toilet Training"). Health care procedures use a variety of equipment (e.g., syringe barrels for tube feeding, colostomy bags) as described in each chapter pertaining to health care procedures.

Teachers' Role Using Equipment and Adaptive Equipment. Teachers will need to gain a thorough understanding of the equipment and adaptive equipment their students are using. Teachers may be involved in (a) assessing the need for adaptive equipment and evaluating adaptive equipment use, (b) monitoring equipment and its use, (c) assisting the student in using the adaptive equipment, and (d) cleaning and caring for the equipment.

In regard to assessing the need for adaptive equipment and evaluating its use, a teacher may determine the need for an **augmentative and alternative communication (AAC)** device (a device to promote communication through symbols, pictures, or words) to express health problems. In this example, the teacher may play a primary role in determining the feasibility of the AAC device and how well the selected device meets the student's needs. This role may be carried out jointly with the speech language pathologist.

Teachers may also monitor a student's use of certain equipment, such as a prone stander (a piece of adaptive equipment used to help promote standing). In this example, the teacher may be taught by the physical therapist how to position the student properly in the equipment and how to monitor the student while the equipment is in use. A photograph of the student correctly positioned in the equipment may be helpful for later reference.

In another situation, the teacher may be responsible for assisting the student to use the equipment or cleaning the equipment. For example, a student with a physical impairment may require an adapted spoon. The occupational therapist and teacher may work jointly together in teaching the student how to use it correctly. The teacher may also be responsible for caring for certain equipment. For example, a teacher may be taught by the nurse to empty and clean a student's colostomy bag. Having an understanding of the equipment, its use, precautions, and care will help promote a student's physical health.

Assistive Strategies to Address Health Concerns

Assistive strategies are techniques that another person performs to help the student do some task. Just like a piece of adaptive equipment can assist a student to perform a task (e.g., use of an adapted spoon for feeding), an assistive strategy provides the same type of support but is provided by a person (e.g., a teacher holding the student's jaw to promote chewing). Assistive strategies are also used when the student's physical impairment interferes with or makes performance of a step of the task unfeasible without some type of support. For example, in tube feeding, fluids and food formulas are poured into a tube that goes directly into the stomach. A student may lack the motor control to pour the liquid but may be able to do so with an assistive strategy of an adult giving elbow support.

When students have severe physical impairments, they may be unable to participate physically in the procedure. In these instances, adults may perform most of the physical management or health care procedure as an assistive strategy. As discussed later in this chapter, if the student is to be taught part or all of the procedure, instructional strategies are needed. Assistive strategies provide teachers and parents with techniques that will help students and promote health across physical management and health care areas.

Assistive Strategies Promoting Physical Management.

Several types of assistive strategies can promote physical management. Frequent position changes are important for the health of the musculoskeletal, gastrointestinal, integumentary, respiratory, cardiovascular, and renal systems. Proper lifting, carrying, and transferring procedures when implementing position changes will help promote the safety and health of the student. Facilitating and encouraging movement and stretching of the joints can help improve range of motion and muscle mass. Encouraging mobility by providing support to prevent falling is an important assistive strategy as well. Most of these techniques and strategies are important components in providing proper positioning and handling, lifting and assisting with movement, and promoting mobility as discussed in Chapters 5, 6, and 7.

Assistive Strategies Promoting Self-Help Skills and Health Procedures.

Assistive strategies may be used to promote self-help skills and health care procedures. Examples for assistive strategies for self-help skills may include providing jaw support to facilitate chewing to partially lifting the student's arm to facilitate spoon use. Assistive strategies for health care procedures may vary widely as to the degree of assistance given. In some situations, teachers may use assistive strategies in which they help the student hold a piece of equipment steady (e.g., syringe barrel for tube feeding) so that the student can carry out the rest of the steps of the procedure. In other situations, more extensive assistive strategies may be necessary in which the teacher (or designated person) performs almost all of the steps of the health care procedure and the student participates by setting up or putting away the needed equipment. How extensive the assistive strategies need to be depend on the student's capabilities. Each health care procedure in this book provides information on assistive strategies and on how and why procedures are performed.

Teachers' Role in Using Assistive Strategies.

When dealing with physical management issues, such as positioning, handling, and mobility, teachers are typically shown by a physical therapist the proper assistive strategies to use with individual students. Teachers need to learn proper positioning, handling, and mobility techniques to help each student access the educational environment. Without proper positioning and handling, many students with physical impairments will be unable to do many tasks and educational activities otherwise possible if the student were positioned correctly or provided certain types of assistance. (See Part II of this book for more information.)

In regard to traditional self-help skills, teachers have often used various assistive strategies to help students perform such activities as eating or learning to use a toilet. Therapists will often work collaboratively with the teacher on proper implementation of assistive strategies in such areas.

Some students require various health care procedures, and whether teachers should perform some of these is a subject of debate across the nation. Decisions regarding who should perform procedures are based on each state's Nurse Practice Act, legal decisions, state policy, and local guidelines. Even when a teacher is not responsible for performing the health care procedure, there are several areas related to the health care procedures for which the teacher should be responsible. The teacher should:

1. promote a safe, healthy environment by monitoring students for any specific problems or emergencies resulting from the health care procedure;

2. have sufficient knowledge and skill to know what to do should a problem or emergency arise; and

3. assist with teaching the student the health care procedure utilizing appropriate instructional strategies, as any other type of self-help (or independent living) skill (DPHD Critical Issues and Leadership Committee, 1999).

Teachers' role should be clearly delineated by the school system's guidelines. (See the subsection on guidelines and legal implications under the "Management Issues" section later in this chapter for more information.) Specific suggestions regarding monitoring health and infection control are delineated next.

Assistive Strategies in Monitoring Health Conditions. Students should learn how to monitor their own health. However, teachers and other school personnel must also know what to look for and how to act appropriately should a problem occur; each chapter discusses these topics in more detail. (Refer back to Table 1-2 for a brief overview of some major health conditions and needed skills.) Teachers and school personnel should also have current training in cardiopulmonary resuscitation (CPR) and first aid to help any child should the need arise. Training in infection control is also important.

Assistive Strategies Promoting Infection Control. All personnel assisting students with physical and health management should promote proper infection control measures at all times. Proper hand-washing procedures should be followed at all times since improper hand washing contributes to the spread of infection between school personnel and students and among students. Prior to every self-help procedure, including health care procedures, hand washing should occur. If at all possible, the student should also be taught proper hand washing. Equally important is the cleaning of environmental surfaces and proper disposal of wastes. Understanding how to prevent the spread of infection is crucial for helping maintain a safe, healthy environment. (See the "Management Issues" section.)

Instructional Strategies for Physical Management, Self-Help, and Health Procedures

Instructional strategies are techniques used to teach a student to perform a skill, learn targeted information, or apply critical thinking skills. As discussed in Chapter 2, multiple teaching techniques may be used with students with physical and health impairments. Teaching strategies range from those traditionally used with students with severe or profound mental retardation to those for students with normal intelligence or gifted abilities. However, when there are severe physical impairments affecting speech and motor movement, most of these strategies can be adapted to accommodate the lack of movement or speech.

One way to promote health in students with physical and health impairments is to assist students to be responsible for their own health and care as much as possible. All students, regardless of age, should not be allowed to be passive and expect others to wait on them. They must be taught to request position changes and know the schedule for using different adaptive equipment. Students should also learn to check whether they are properly positioned on adaptive equipment and whether different adaptive equipment is correctly applied. Self-help skills such as toileting and eating are typically taught to children with physical disabilities to perform as independently as possible.

Since health care procedures such as tube feeding, catheterization, colostomy/ileostomy care, and respiratory procedures are the domain of self-help skills, the educational team will determine whether the student will partially or fully participate in self-performing the health care procedure. When students are to learn the procedure, or aspects of it, this skill should be included as an educational goal on the IEP. When this is the case, the nurse and teacher will need to work closely together. If the student has mental retardation or a learning problem, the nurse often lacks knowledge on appropriate instructional strategies to use to teach a procedure to students with these cognitive or learning impairments. The special education teacher can work together with the nurse to task analyze the procedure and provide the most appropriate instructional strategy, such as time delay, systems of least prompts and maximum prompts, graduated guidance, learning strategies, modeling, demonstration-guided practice, and/or antecedent prompts (including self-operated picture or auditory prompts). If the student has a physical impairment, the physical and occupational therapists may provide information on the body or arm positioning to help promote participation or independence in performing the procedure.

Some students may have such severe physical impairments that they are unable to perform the health care procedure themselves. In these situations, the teacher may instruct the student on how to direct someone else to perform the procedure. This approach still allows the student to participate actively and have some control over the implementation of the procedure. Having the ability to direct another person's performance is especially critical when the person helping with the procedure has questions or needs some guidance. For students who use augmentative communication systems, the teacher, along with the speech therapist, must assure that the proper vocabulary is in place to allow a student to direct another's performance of the procedure and an-

swer questions (see Chapter 3, "Communication for Physical and Health Needs"). Also, having the vocabulary to explain if something is wrong is very important. Teachers will need to teach students how to communicate information effectively regarding the procedure and any problems. This will promote mental, social, and physical health through fostering independence, combating learned helplessness, and providing a safe, healthy environment.

MANAGEMENT ISSUES

IHP and IEP

Each student eligible for special education services who has a physical and/or health disability should have an **individualized health (care) plan (IHP)** and an **individualized educational program (IEP).** IHPs are designed to provide information on the student's medical status and on the student's specific prescribed health care procedure or physical management area. Although IHPs are not required, it is recommended that the educational team construct one for each student who has health care procedures or physical management techniques being performed at school. IHPs serve as an important guide and reference regarding the student's specific health care procedure or physical management areas. It provides written, precise information regarding what to do if specific problems arise from the health care procedure or physical management technique.

Each IHP contains general and specialized information. The general information includes student information and history, diagnosis, and assessment data that include the procedure the student needs, goals of care, expected outcomes, and interventions (e.g., training of school personnel involved with the student) (Haas, 1993). Specialized information is procedure-specific. For example, Figure 1-1 lists several specialized areas to include for tube feeding (a procedure in which fluids and nutritional formulas are placed through

Student Information and History

Sally is a 6-year-old girl with severe spastic quadriplegia cerebral palsy. She had a gastrostomy inserted at 4 years of age because of severe gag reflex and inability to take in enough nutrition. Oral feedings have been contraindicated owing to aspiration.

Diagnosis and Assessment Data

Sally is determined to have appropriate weight for her height. She is not receiving any oral feedings at present as ordered by her gastroenterologist, Dr. Green. She is currently tolerating her feedings well and has appropriate bowel elimination. Her diagnosis consists of impaired swallowing, resulting in an inability to eat independently. This has resulted in the need for tube feedings. See specialized information for more details regarding the procedures.

Goal of Care

To administer gastrostomy feedings as primary form of nutrition.

Interventions

1. Nurse will instruct special education teacher, paraprofessional, and one other teacher on how to administer tube feeding and document training.
2. Nurse will supervise staff administering feedings on a regular basis.
3. Nurse and teacher will collaboratively teach student to self-administer tube feedings.

Expected Outcomes

1. Student will receive adequate nutrition through tube feeding.
2. Staff will demonstrate competence in tube feeding, documentation, and what to do if complications occur.
3. Student will learn to partially or fully participate in tube feeding herself.

Emergency Information and Contacts

Dr. Green (404) 651-2222; Sally's mom (404) 394-1111

Specialized Information

Tube-feeding route: gastrostomy tube

Type of tube feeding: Bolus method

Formula: 1 can Ensure, 1 can dry baby food with water, extra water as needed for flushing tube

Preparation of formula: add amount of water specified on baby food box

Schedule of feeding: every four hours (8:30 A.M., 12:30 P.M.)

Child-specific procedure attached: yes

Directions for feeding problems and emergencies: (Directions would be given for the following problems: aspiration, tube displacement, nausea, vomiting, cramping, diarrhea, infection, leaking of stomach contents, clogged tube.)

FIGURE 1-1 Sample IHP form for tube feeding

a tube going into the student's stomach instead of by mouth). The specialized information includes the type of feeding route, type of tube feeding, type of formula, how to prepare the formula, schedule of feeding, and directions for feeding problems and emergencies. Any restrictions or precautions should also be noted. By having di-

rections for problems and emergencies (as well as restrictions or precautions), the teacher and educational team have the necessary information as to the appropriate action if a problem occurs. This information is invaluable. Each chapter in this book on health care procedures will provide possible problems and emergencies to include in an

IHP for each procedure. Also discussed is specific specialized information that can serve as a guide when constructing the student's IHP. General child-specific procedures are suggested in each chapter that can be approved (or modified) by the physician and should be attached to the IHP.

An IEP is designed to specify the educational goals for the student that will be targeted for instruction. Each student in special education is required to have an IEP in place. The IEP is developed by the educational team, and the student may be included as part of the team. Physical management skills and self-help skills (including health care procedures) may constitute part of the student's goals and objectives on the IEP. They typically follow under the area of self-help skills or independent living skills (especially if the student is older).

The student's IEP objectives for health care procedures or physical management skills may be divided into four categories: (a) independent performance of the task, (b) partial performance of the task, (c) directing the task, and (d) knowledge of the task (see Figure 1–2 for examples for tube feeding). Objectives targeting the independent performance of the task are aimed at having the student perform the skill independently, such as learning to tube-feed himself. Some students because of physical or multiple disabilities are unable to complete the targeted task independently but could partially participate. In this case, objectives are written with the intent that the student would participate in the task, thus having some control over the procedure and promoting some independence. For example, the student may help with some component of tube feeding. Some student's physical impairment is so severe that the student cannot physically assist with the task. In these situations, the student may be taught to direct another person to perform the task, such as describing the steps of the procedure. In the last category, knowledge of the task, the student may learn more in-depth information about the task and its implications (including emergency care).

Independent Performance of Task
The student will independently gather supplies and self-perform the tube-feeding procedure according to the prescribed step-by-step procedure with 100% accuracy for 2 weeks.

Partial Performance of Task
When given the equipment for tube feeding, the student will prepare the formula for tube feeding with 100% accuracy for 2 weeks.
The student will assist with performing the tube feedings by holding the syringe barrel at the proper height when adult is pouring the formula with 100% accuracy for 1 week.

Directing the Task
The student will direct another person in gathering the correct materials listed on

a checklist for tube feeding with 100% accuracy for 1 week.
The student will direct another person to perform each step of the prescribed procedure for tube feeding with 100% accuracy for 2 weeks.

Knowledge of the Task
The student will list the signs of infection at the tube-feeding site with 80% accuracy for four consecutive sessions.
When asked what to do if he has nausea or abdominal cramping, the student will demonstrate how he will use his AAC device to alert another person to these problems with 100% accuracy in 10 of 10 opportunities.

FIGURE 1-2 Sample IEP objectives across categories for tube feeding

For example, students may be taught about the digestive system or how to identify infection at the tube-feeding site. The objective category (or categories) that the educational team selects will depend on the student's cognitive status and physical ability.

Guidelines and Legal Implications

Personnel Responsible for the Implementation of the Procedures. Legislation supports the provision of health care procedures during the school day as a "related service" (Rapport, 1996). Since the Supreme Court decision in *Irving Independent School District v. Tatro* (1984), schools have been obligated to provide appropriate health services if (a) the child requires special education, (b) the health care procedure is necessary during the school day (and without the procedure the student cannot participate in school), and (c) a physician is not required to perform the procedure, but the procedure could be performed by a nurse or other qualified person (Rapport, 1996). The ruling in this case has led to the distinction that services requiring a physician are medical services (or medical procedures) that the school does not have to provide, while those that can be done without a physician are health services (or health procedures) for which the school is responsible. In the case of *Irving Independent School District v. Tatro,* clean intermittent catheterization (CIC) was considered a school health service that the school had to provide as a related service. Following the same line of reasoning, other health services have been interpreted as related services and thus required in schools. Other federal court cases have ruled in favor of the school districts providing health care procedures as related service (e.g., *Department of Education, Hawaii v. Katherine D.,* 1983; *Macomb County Intermediate School District v. Joshua S.,* 1989). In certain cases, health care procedures have been considered beyond the school districts responsibility when they have been very extensive and complex (e.g., *Neeley v. Rutherford County Schools,* 1995; *Detsel v. Board of Education of the Auburn Enlarged City School District,* 1986). However, in

a more recent Supreme Court decision, *Cedar Rapids Community School District v. Garret, F.* (1999), health care procedures were again ruled as supportive services that were the responsibility of the school system in this case of a boy who had a physical disability, used a ventilator, and was receiving one-on-one nursing care.

The decision regarding who will provide the health care service is based on each state's Nurse Practice Act, state regulations, state and local guidelines, and the decision of the nurse and educational team as to whether care should be provided by a nurse or delegated to a qualified person (Heller et al., 1997). Because of shortages of school nurses and caseloads that can be in the thousands, some states' Nurse Practice Act allows nurses to delegate certain procedures to unlicensed personnel provided they have appropriate training and supervision. In these situations, unlicensed personnel such as teachers and paraprofessionals work under the nurse's supervision, and the nurse is accountable for the appropriateness of delegating the specialized health care procedure (National Council of State Boards of Nursing, 1995). Some health care procedures may not be appropriate to delegate, given the condition of the student or the invasiveness of the procedure.

In some states, certain procedures cannot be delegated, while in other states they can. This provision can vary not only across states but also across school districts. In Atlanta, for example, one school district has nurses perform all the tube-feeding procedures, and in a neighboring school district teachers and paraprofessionals have been trained by nurses to perform almost all of the students' tube feedings. Regardless of who performs each procedure, it is important that all team members understand the procedure and know what to do in an emergency to promote a safe, healthy environment. In situations where the nurse performs the procedure, the teacher must also learn it to help teach the student to learn the procedure as much as possible.

The staff in each school district must be familiar with the regulations in their state. In situations where there are no state guidelines, it is important that policy and guidelines are developed within each school district to determine who can provide health care procedures and under what circumstances. In situations where there are no students receiving health care procedures, it is important that guidelines be developed so the school district staff will be ready when a student requiring a health care procedure does enter the district. Guidelines typically include how the decision is made to determine who will perform these procedures, who can perform the procedures given appropriate training, how the procedures are to be performed, and who performs the training and how often (McDonald, Wilson, Turner, & Mulligan-Ault, 1988; Mulligan-Ault, Guess, Struth, & Thompson, 1988). Some school systems establish a medical review board to determine responsibility of care on an individual basis, while others have only written procedures to guide decision making.

Permission. Another important guideline is obtaining physician and parent permission for the procedure to be performed at school. A permission form should include the student's name, birth date, address, type of procedure, time schedule and/or indications for procedure, precautions, and possible reactions and interventions, who will be performing the procedure, how long the procedure is to be continued, and a place for the signature of the physician and parent. (See "Medication and Health Care Procedure Permission Form" in Chapter 4.) Also, it is important to have the physician sign off on the steps of the procedure (especially if this is not provided by the physician). Typically, the procedure can be copied from this book and followed by these choices for the physician: (a) "I reviewed and approved this procedure as written," (b) "I reviewed and approved this procedure with the attached modification," or (c) "I do not approve the procedure and have attached an alternate written procedure." The physician would check one of these and then add his or her signature and date, along with any necessary addenda.

Documentation. Documentation of compliance with required health care procedures is important. Entries in an appropriate log or data sheet not only provide written proof that the procedures are being performed but also can decrease the likelihood of an error. When more than one person is responsible for performing a procedure (e.g., a teacher and paraprofessional), documentation that the procedure was performed should immediately be done to decrease the likelihood of the procedure being repeated by the second person (e.g., tube feeding provided twice around 10:00 A.M.). One possible data form is found in Figure 1-3 (Heller et al., 1992). More than one procedure or medication can be documented on this form. The health care procedures and/or medications are written in the first column. The times the procedure is to be performed are written in the next designated area. At the beginning of each day, the times the procedure is to be performed that day are written under that day of the week. When a procedure is performed that day, the time is crossed out and the initials of the person who performed the procedure are written beside the time. If the procedure was not performed for some reason, the time is circled. If the procedure was performed at a different time, the original time is circled, and the time it was performed is recorded. See Figure 1-4 for a completed form.

Training Issues

The performance of health care procedures requires competency and expertise. Although the health care procedures themselves may be simple to perform, the persons carrying them out need to have a thorough knowledge base that should include (a) the rationale and correct implementation of each step of the procedure; (b) the ability to identify early subtle signs of side effects, problems, or complications; (c) knowledge of appropriate intervention when side effects, problems, or complications occur; (d) knowledge of emergency procedures; and (e) knowledge of universal precautions appropriate for the intervention (Heller, Alberto, Forney, et al., 1996).

When a nurse is performing the procedure, it should not be assumed that the nurse is familiar

MONTHLY MEDICATION/PROCEDURE REPORT

Student's name _____   Month _____

Directions: Write the medications/procedures, dates and times for each week. At the beginning of each day, write in the times for that day. When procedure is performed, cross out time and initial. If not done, circle time. If done at different time, circle time and record new time.

Meds/Procedure	Dates	Time(s)	Mon.	Tues.	Wed.	Thurs.	Fri.

Meds/Procedure	Dates	Time(s)	Mon.	Tues.	Wed.	Thurs.	Fri.

Meds/Procedure	Dates	Time(s)	Mon.	Tues.	Wed.	Thurs.	Fri.

Meds/Procedure	Dates	Time(s)	Mon.	Tues.	Wed.	Thurs.	Fri.

Comments:

FIGURE 1-3 Monthly medication/procedure report

MONTHLY MEDICATION/PROCEDURE REPORT

Student's name   _Joe Smith_   Month   _February_

Directions: Write the medications/procedures, dates and times for each week. At the beginning of each day, write in the times for that day. When procedure is performed, cross out time and initial. If not done, circle time. If done at different time, circle time and record new time.

Meds/Procedure	Dates	Time(s)	Mon.	Tues.	Wed.	Thurs.	Fri.
Dilantin 5mg oral	2/1 - 2/5	10	10 KH	10 KH			
Tube feed	2/1 - 2/5	9 12	9 KH 12 KH	9 KH 1:30 (12)KH			
Suction	2/1 - 2/5	p.r.n.	10 KH 2:30 KH	9 KH 12:45 KH			

Meds/Procedure	Dates	Time(s)	Mon.	Tues.	Wed.	Thurs.	Fri.

Meds/Procedure	Dates	Time(s)	Mon.	Tues.	Wed.	Thurs.	Fri.

Meds/Procedure	Dates	Time(s)	Mon.	Tues.	Wed.	Thurs.	Fri.

Comments:

FIGURE 1-4 Completed monthly medication/procedure report

with the procedure since nurses specialize in different areas. If the student requires a procedure with which the nurse is unfamiliar, then the nurse must receive appropriate training to perform it.

When procedures are to be performed by teachers or paraprofessionals, training with routine supervision and updating should occur with the appropriate health personnel in the local school district (Graff et al., 1990). Although other teachers and parents may be familiar with the procedures, a health care professional is needed to provide training due to their expertise in the area. This training is also considered nongeneralizable. In other words, when a teacher has learned to perform a tube-feeding procedure on Mary, the teacher will need to be trained again to perform the tube-feeding procedure on Joe. Individuals have differences that make such student-specific training necessary. Also, the student's IHP should be in place, and the person performing the procedure should be familiar with it.

Training with an appropriate health personnel should consist of several guided practice sessions and close supervision. If the teacher being trained is not comfortable with performing the procedure, the training should continue until the teacher demonstrates competency and confidence. The teacher should not be checked off as being able to perform the procedure until the teacher feels ready. Once the teacher has demonstrated competence and feels comfortable with the procedure, the teacher is ready to perform the procedure without the guided assistance of the nurse.

Documentation should note that the teacher has completed this training. Documentation will often include (a) the name of the teacher who was trained, (b) the name of the procedure, (c) the specific student the teacher was trained to do the procedure with, (d) the name of the health personnel who trained the teacher, and (e) the dates the procedure was trained. Subsequent training updates or checks to ensure that the procedure is still being performed correctly are also typically performed and documented.

Infection Control

Maintaining proper infection control in the schools is the responsibility of all school personnel. To help prevent the spread of infection, the classroom teacher, school personnel, parent, and child can implement a number of preventative measures. These procedures are derived from a group of standards, referred to as **universal precautions**. Universal precautions encompass a method of preventing the transmission of contact infections. They were originally developed for hospital use to minimize the health care worker's contact with blood and body fluids, lessen the likelihood of transmission of infection between health care workers and patients, and decrease the risk of patients' acquiring infections in the hospital (Skale, 1992). These precautions include hand washing, using personal protective equipment (e.g., gloves, gowns), taking personal hygiene precautions, following decontamination procedures (e.g., cleaning environmental surfaces), and disposing of waste (e.g., items contaminated with infectious material, syringes) (Medcom Trainex, 1993). These precautions are instituted with all patients, since there is no way to know for sure who is infected and who is not.

Universal precautions have been adapted and instituted into school settings (Kerr, 1991). Not only do teachers implement infection control procedures, but students need to be taught them as well. Some of these infection control procedures for the school include hand washing, using gloves, taking personal hygiene precautions, and instituting environmental infection control procedures.

Hand Washing. The single most preventive measure to prevent the spread of infection is proper hand washing. Practicing hand washing when and where it is needed is important in order for hand washing to become routine (Loumiet & Levack, 1993). To decrease the spread of infection, it is essential that hands are washed before preparing food, before eating, after using the restroom, and before taking medications. Making hand washing a required part of daily routines reinforces its importance to students.

To teach hand washing effectively to a student with physical or multiple disabilities, it is important that it be broken down into steps. Figure 1-5 presents a task analysis of each of the steps. Unlike what is commonly done when hand washing, it is important that the student dry hands first, and then turn off the water by using a paper towel on the faucet handles. This prevents recontamination of the hands by not directly touching the handles that were touched when hands were contaminated. Also, it is important to note how long hand washing should occur; typically the process of scrubbing hands with soap should last 10 to 15 seconds (Smith, 1992; Medcom Trainix, 1993).

Hand washing can be a difficult task to implement for students with severe physical impairments, because of decreased range of motion, limited arm and hand movement, as well as limited accessibility to the sink and other items. Such problems can be resolved by having sinks that wheelchairs can roll under, installing various types of handle adaptations, teaching proper positioning to the student, or providing physical support at the shoulder or elbow to assist the

student's ability to reach the sink. Students with physical disabilities who cannot rotate their hands upward (supinate) may use an adapted method of hand washing. In this instance, the student pumps the soap with the palm of the left hand, on the back of the right hand. The student then pumps the soap with the palm of the right hand, on top of the left hand. The student rubs the hands together by placing the right hand over the left and moving back and forth, then vice versa. Rinsing then proceeds by placing the hands under running water. In some instances, sponges may be set up to rub against, or two soap dispensers can be positioned for ease of use. Pump soap is not only easier for many students to access but more hygienic.

Glove Use. Typically, students performing a procedure on themselves do not wear gloves. However, gloves should be worn by personnel who are assisting students and coming in contact with bodily secretions. Using gloves when assisting with toileting, clean intermittent catheterization, or suctioning, for example, would be very appropriate. This practice decreases the risk of transmission of infection, as well as being more appropriate in personal hygiene activities. However, the student should still engage in hand washing even if they only partially participated in the activity. It is also important that the person using gloves always wash their hands after taking off the gloves. It is always possible that some infectious agent penetrated the gloves, and washing hands will rid the skin of any contaminate.

Latex Allergy Alert. Some individuals are allergic to latex gloves, and so the type of glove being used needs careful consideration. An allergic reaction may occur the first time gloves are used or much later. Reactions to latex may range from a mild reaction of contact dermatitis to a severe reaction of cardiovascular collapse (McLaughlin, Murray, VanZandt, & Carr, 1996). Students who are allergic to latex should have this included on their IHP, and personnel assisting the student

---

1. Recognized need for washing hands.
2. Go to designated area to wash.
3. Position body for hand washing.
4. Turn on faucet.
5. Adjust water temperature.
6. Thoroughly wet hands.
7. Put soap on hands.
8. Rub hands together, creating lather.
9. Continue rubbing; count to 15 slowly.
10. Rinse soap off hands thoroughly.
11. Dry hands.
12. Turn off faucet with paper towel.

FIGURE 1-5 Task analysis for hand washing

with self-help skills (e.g., hygiene skills, health care procedures) should be aware of this allergy and only use nonlatex (i.e., plastic) gloves.

Personal Hygiene Precautions. Students should be taught personal hygiene procedures to decrease the risk of infection. Some of these include brushing teeth, brushing hair, face washing, using Band-Aids and tissues, covering the mouth when coughing, and changing menstrual pads. Although these are beyond the scope of this book, teachers can task-analyze the steps to these procedures and apply systematic teaching strategies to teach these areas (see Chapter 2). In the area of infection control, it is important that there is no sharing of personal care items.

Environmental Infection Control. The environmental surfaces in the classroom setting can be exposed to a wide range of infectious organisms. For example, respiratory secretions can be transmitted to a table from a sneeze or cough, or saliva may get on a toy from a child's mouthing the toy or drooling on the table. In all of these examples, other individuals may acquire an infection if they get the organism on their hand after touching a contaminated surface and then place their hand in their mouth or eyes. Therefore, proper cleaning of environmental surfaces becomes important to prevent the spread of infection.

Environmental surfaces should be cleaned on a daily basis and after being exposed to bodily fluids. Surfaces should be cleaned with 1 part chlorine bleach to 10 parts water. For ease of delivery, the mixture may be placed in a spray bottle. A new mixture should be made each day. Paper towels used for cleaning, as well as other disposable wastes such as facial tissues and diapers, should be discarded in an appropriately plastic lined receptacle.

SUMMARY

Students with physical, health, and multiple disabilities are at risk of developing health problems. A team of individuals must plan collaboratively how the student's health needs will be optimally addressed. This includes reconceptualizing health care procedures as self-help skills that many students can be taught to perform independently or participate in to the greatest extent possible. Responsibility of performing the procedure, training issues, establishment of school district guidelines, development of the IEP and IHP, and documentation will all need to be addressed. In the following chapters, each physical or health procedure will be explored in regard to effective implementation and student training.

2

Promoting Independence through the Use of Instructional Strategies

Students with physical impairments, health impairments, or multiple disabilities will require instruction in a broad range of skills to allow them to be as independent as possible. One major area in which these students will require assistance, unless they learn to perform the tasks themselves, is physical and health management. This area primarily falls under self-help skills or independent living skills. This skill area includes basic skills such as learning how to position and move themselves correctly and position the materials around them. Also, students with physical impairments will need to learn to use assistive technology and adaptive devices to perform such common self-help skills as eating, hand washing, and toileting. In addition to the more commonly thought of self-help skills, many of these students will need to learn such self-help skills as tube feeding, ostomy care, urinary catheterization, and respiratory procedures. Without proper instruction, these students will have to rely on others for their care in these areas.

Designing instruction and developing the supporting environment in which instruction takes place requires contributions from many educational team members. Although the teacher must serve as the central manager of a student's education plan, all team members contribute their expertise to provide an environment that is physically supportive of the student, who must access and take full advantage of the instruction being provided. Learning for students with physical, health, and multiple disabilities does not occur without considerable effort on the part of the student and the educational team. It does not occur simply by osmosis or by a demonstration for the student to imitate. Students must be provided systematic instruction and physical and/or sensory support so that they may access the instruction provided.

The various professional members of the education team each provide particular supportive expertise (see Chapter 1). The occupational therapist must identify, plan, and facilitate a motor response that enables the student to manipulate materials to practice and demonstrate information and skill mastery through manual or adapted responses. The physical therapist must design environmental support for body control in various positions that enables the student to access the instructional plane and mobility within school, community, and home environments. The speech-language pathologist must identify, design, and assist in implementing a communication system that enables the student to demonstrate information mastery through a language response and to communicate functional and social wants and needs. The vision and hearing consultant must identify the student's visual and auditory strengths and weaknesses so that the classroom environment, instructional plan, and materials are prepared to enhance opportunities for the student to visually access the learning environment and the learning materials. The nurse must provide information regarding the student's health and physical status and information, supervision, and/or instruction regarding specific procedures that pertain to health care.

These professionals provide services that facilitate the work of the student and the teacher. Their work is learning and instruction. The focus of this chapter is the teacher's expertise in managing content and instruction. It is the teacher who has the expertise in the selection, analysis, and sequencing of content. It is the teacher who has the expertise in selection and delivery of instructional strategies that enable mastery of content. Even when a nurse is the person responsible for performing the health care procedure, the nurse will have limited knowledge on how to teach a student the procedure when the student has a cognitive impairment. It is the teacher who has the pedagogical expertise to work collaboratively with the nurse in teaching students to perform health care procedures in these situations. This type of collaboration also applies to all school personnel and team members. The teacher has the responsibility for coordinating the expertise of all the education team members to provide the student with the most efficient and effective educational experience.

ASSESSMENT AND CONTENT SELECTION

The curriculum content for students with physical, health, and multiple disabilities will vary based on the student's cognitive abilities and needs. Students with physical disabilities have seven different curriculum options: (a) general grade-level appropriate curriculum without modifications, (b) general education curriculum with modifications to accommodate for the physical impairments, (c) general advanced or above grade-level academic curriculum with or without modifications for the physical impairment, (d) parallel curriculum that uses the general education curriculum but at a reduced level of complexity, (e) lower grade-level curriculum that targets lower grade-level objectives, (f) functional academic curriculum that unlike the general education curriculum has an applied skills focus and targets functional academics, and (g) functional curriculum that targets life management skills including such areas as daily living skills, social skills, vocational skills, and leisure skills (Bigge, 1991).

Often the student with physical disabilities will require functional skills to be included within standard academic curriculum tracks. The disabilities of these students require that teachers look beyond standard curricula and consider the additional requirements of the student to learn, apply information, and function as independently as possible across life skills. These physical impairments create different and significant challenges due to the need for the students to learn how to manage equipment, technology, and health issues in addition to other curriculum requirements.

Regardless of which curriculum option the student is following, the physical and health impairments of these students result in a need for self-management skills, regardless of the student's cognitive level. These students require instruction in specialized physical and health management skills to function competently in school, community, and home environments. These skills are not part of the general education curriculum and are often omitted in typical functional curricula. Teachers and other members of the student's educational team must critically examine the student's curriculum and determine whether these functional physical/health management skills should be addressed.

If the teacher is to use a strategy for developing functional educational objectives, guidelines must be developed delineating what makes an activity or skill functional. The following points may assist in determining whether a skill is functional:

1. It increases the student's independence in current environments in which the student operates.

2. It provides the student access to a future environment.

3. It increases the number of activities and tasks in which the student can perform independently or with partial participation, reducing dependence on others.

4. It expands the student's control over the environment.

5. It increases the number of environments in which the student can function.

6. It adds opportunities for, and the number of, social interactions for the student.

7. It reduces stigmatization.

Students' ability to perform their own physical and health management will typically meet most of these criteria.

To determine what functional goals are appropriate for the student, the teacher engages in a three-step process. First, needed tasks and skills must be identified. This is known as developing an ecological inventory (Brown et al., 1979; Falvey, 1989; Wolery, Ault, & Doyle, 1992). Second, a student's capability to perform the identified tasks and skills must be assessed. This is known as discrepancy analysis. (Sometimes the combination of an ecological inventory and a discrepancy analysis is referred to as an ecological assessment.) Finally, the teacher must determine whether the task or skill should be taught directly, with an adaptation, or through an alternative performance strategy.

Ecological Inventory

The process by which the teacher identifies the functional or specialized skills that should be a part of a student's education plan is the development of an **ecological inventory.** An ecological inventory is a listing of sequences of behaviors that reflect skills necessary for the student to participate within the community, home, or school. It is a top-down approach to identifying curriculum content. Rather than looking at developmental sequences and identifying isolated skills the student cannot perform, this process determines activities within an environment in which the student must or wants to participate and then defines the tasks and skills that enable this participation.

An ecological inventory is developed for each of four broad curriculum domains: personal and domestic domain, community domain, leisure domain, and vocational domain. The ecological inventory itself entails a five-step sequence: (a) listing current and future student environments, (b) identifying the relevant subenvironments within each environment, (c) listing the priority activities that occur within each subenvironment, (d) identifying the priority skills needed to engage in the activities, and (e) prioritizing among the activities and skills for placement on the individualized education program (IEP). Table 2-1 depicts an overview of this process with sample activities and skills. Each step is further described as follows.

Listing Current and Future Environments. Through interviews with the student, parents, and the other education team members, the teacher identifies current school, home, and community environments in which the student must or wants to function; next, environments in which the student must function (e.g., specialty rooms in the school, the next school to which the student will attend, parental desired community settings in

Table 2-1 Ecological Inventory

Domain: Personal/Domestic

Environment	Subenvironment	Activity	Skills
	Drop-off area	Moving from drop area to classroom	Going up incline
			Propelling self to room
School	Lunchroom/snack area	Tube feeding	Opening door
			Gathering equipment
			Preparing feeding
	Gym	Dressing	Assembling equipment
	Bathroom	Washing hands	Performing procedure
		Catheterization	Cleaning equipment
		Brushing hair	Putting on gym clothes
			Inspecting hair in mirror
			Obtaining adapted brush
			Brushing hair so it is neat
			Returning brush

which the student does not currently participate); and, as the student advances to transition planning, postschool environments in which the student may participate, including postsecondary education, vocational, residential, and leisure settings.

School environments might include general education and special education classrooms and labs, bathrooms, the cafeteria, specialty rooms such as home living units, the nurse's room, the gymnasium, hallways (corners, doorways), stairwells, elevators, the school yard (land contours, play equipment), and the surrounding neighborhood streets. Community environments might include fast-food and cafeteria-style restaurants, large and small department stores, groceries, drug stores, card shops, laundromats, medical services, public bathrooms, malls, and parking lots.

Identifying Relevant Subenvironments. Subenvironments are areas, rooms, or departments within an environment where different activities take place. For example, in the home each room (e.g., the kitchen, bedroom, and bathroom) is a subenvironment because different activities are performed in each. In a grocery the entrance way, the delicatessen counter, the produce section, and the checkout are each a subenvironment.

Listing Priority Activities. Within each selected subenvironment the teacher identifies the activities or functions that take place. For example, in fast-food restaurants there are the activities of entering through the front door, locating and approaching the counter, waiting in turn to order, ordering and paying, locating supplies (napkins, straws, etc.), dispensing a drink, locating and moving to an empty seat, seating, eating, disposing of tray and trash, and exiting.

Identifying Priority Skills. Within each activity the teacher identifies the communication, motor, mobility, social, self-help, and cognitive/academic tasks and skills required to perform the activity. For example, for eating at school or home, some students cannot eat through their mouth and have a gastrostomy button, which is a small device going directly into the stomach. An extension tube and syringe barrel are connected to it, and the child's liquefied food or formula is directly poured into the syringe barrel and travels through the barrel, extension tube, and gastrostomy button, directly into the stomach (see Figure 2-1). For performing tube feeding, the student must be able to gather the equipment, prepare the formula, assemble the

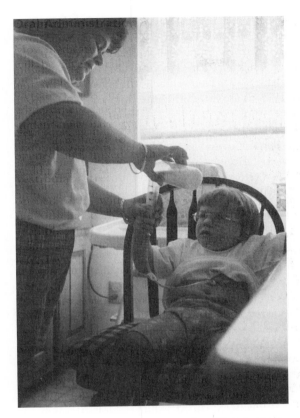

FIGURE 2-1 Student learning to assist with tube feeding by holding up syringe barrel

equipment, give the formula, and dissemble and clean the equipment.

Prioritizing among Activities and Skills for the IEP. Over time the results of an ecological inventory will yield more content than can possibly be done simultaneously or possibly even within a given school year. Therefore, the education team must use some mechanism for prioritizing among the various potential learning objectives (Brown et al., 1980; Nietupski & Hamre-Nietupski, 1987). A collaborative approach to this prioritizing is the most effective, taking into account each member's opinions. First, the team decides on the variables that should be considered in this process, such as student preferences, parent preferences, teacher preferences, safety concerns, frequency of occurrence of the skill across environments, social significance, age appropriateness, access to a future environment, time availability, material, and appropriate setting for instruction. As seen in Table 2-2, the team may list the potential activities and skills and then apply a simple rating system for each variable selected. Adding the ratings for each activity yields a numerical ranking. This is not meant to be an absolute ranking; rather, it is an additional

Table 2-2 Rating Form for Prioritizing Activities

Activity	Parent preference	Student preference	Practitioner preference	Frequency of occurrence	Safety concerns	Social significance	Total
1. Moving independently	2	3	2	1	2	2	12
2. Tube feeding	3	3	3	3	2	3	17
3. Dressing	2	1	3	2	1	3	12
4. Washing hands	2	1	2	2	3	3	13
5. Catheterizing	3	2	3	3	2	3	16
6. Brushing hair	1	2	1	2	1	3	10

3 = high preference/frequency/safety/social

2 = medium preference/frequency/safety/social

1 = low preference/frequency/safety/social

SOURCE: Adapted from V. A. Nietupski and S. M. Hamre-Nietupski, "An Ecological Approach to Curriculum Development." In L. Goetz, D. Guess, and K. Stremel-Campbell, eds., *Innovative Program Design for Individuals with Sensory Impairments.* (Baltimore, MD: Brookes, 1987).

piece of information for the team to consider when developing the IEP.

Discrepancy Analysis

Once the objectives have been identified, an analysis of the student's current capability must be performed to determine the areas requiring instruction and/or adaptation. This form of analysis is known as a **discrepancy analysis.** A discrepancy analysis is a direct measure of a student's performance capability. It entails observing the student performing the targeted skill in the environment in which he or she will have to perform it and noting which components cannot be done and so will require instruction.

A discrepancy analysis consists of four steps: (a) delineating the steps of the activity by performing a task analysis, (b) observing and scoring the student's performance of the tasks/skills, (c) recording the student errors and doing a performance discrepancy, and (d) determining whether the tasks/skills that the student is unable to perform should be taught directly or whether the student will need and an adaptation or alternative performance strategy (see Figure 2-2).

Performing a Task Analysis

In the first step, the activity needs to be broken down into small measurable steps, also referred to as a **task analysis.** The steps are initially written as a nondisabled peer or person would perform the steps in the targeted activity or task. One way to do this is for the teacher to perform the activity him- or herself or to watch someone else perform the skill, listing each functional or motor movement the person performs in the first column of the form (see Figure 2-3 for an example of a completed discrepancy analysis form). For certain students with physical impairments, such as students in wheelchairs, certain additional or alternative steps to a task analysis are immediately evident; for others, they come to attention during

the later performance discrepancy phase. For example, for toileting there are certain steps that a nondisabled individual would perform in a different manner than a person in a wheelchair (see Table 2-3). The principles of developing a task analysis are listed in Figure 2-4.

Observing and Scoring Performance

Once the steps have been delineated and written on the form, the student is asked to perform the steps, preferably in at least one setting in which performance is required. The student is verbally directed to perform the task, and then to perform each step. In the second column, the teacher notes whether the student is able to perform the step. Because of the possible effect of the student's physical impairment, it is important to give assistance when needed to determine whether the student has difficulty with the step because of not knowing how to do it or because of a problem with physically manipulating the material. To help make this determination, the student is first observed to see whether he knows the next step and can do it independently. If not, the next step is verbally explained. If he is unable to follow the verbal direction, he is given physical assistance to perform the step to assess his range of motion and ability to move his arms (or whatever) in certain ways to perform the task. For best results, the step may be physically guided, but then the student is encouraged to repeat the required motion motorically. This is because it is possible that the teacher can physically guide the student through a step and yet the student is unable to physically perform the step on his own due to his different motor pattern movements and constraints of his active range of motion (ability to move on his own, rather than be passively moved by another).

Based on the student's performance, the teacher indicates how the student performed each step. In the second column, the teacher puts an *I* if the student does the step totally independently. A *V* is placed for any verbal prompt or description and a *P* for any other type of prompt. For

Student: _____   Teacher: _____   Date: _____
Domain: _____   Environment: _____   Subenvironment: _____

Task Analysis (Nondisabled person inventory) for activity of:	Score I = Independence V = Verbal prompt P = Prompt	Student Error	Performance Discrepancy L = Learning P = Physical H = Health (endurance) S = Sensory C = Communication M = Motivation	Adaptation or Alternative Performance Strategies
1.				
2.				
3.				
4.				
5.				
6.				
7.				
8.				
9.				
10.				

FIGURE 2-2 Discrepancy analysis form

Student: _____
Domain: _____

Teacher: _____
Environment: _____

Date: _____
Subenvironment: _____

Task Analysis (Nondisabled person inventory) for activity of: Tube Feeding	Score I = Independence V = Verbal prompt P = Prompt	Student Error	Performance Discrepancy L = Learning P = Physical H = Health S = Sensory C = Communication M = Motivation	Adaptation or Alternative Performance Strategies
1. Wash hands	I			
2. Prepare equipment	P	Unsure how it goes	L	
3. Clamp/kink tube	P	Difficulty manipulating	P	Provide more practice
4. Remove plug	P	Unsure how	L	
5. Attach syringe barrel	P	Unsure how	L	
6. Pour formula	P	Cannot align formula can with barrel	P	Provide funnel
7. Hold barrel	P	Barrel held sideways	P	Provide elbow support, for now
8. Allow formula flow	V	Unsure how	L	
9. Add more formula before it empties	V	Difficulty knowing when to pour	L	Put red line on barrel to indicate when should begin pouring
10. Continue to add	V	Unsure how	L	

FIGURE 2-3 Example of a completed discrepancy analysis form for tube feeding

Table 2-3 Task Analysis for Toileting for Children with and without a Physical Impairment

Ambulatory child	Physical impairment—Wheelchair User
1. Request to use restroom	1. Request to use restroom
2. Go into restroom into stall	2. Move into restroom and stall
	2.1. Position chair
	2.2. Lock brakes
	2.3. Undo seat belt
	2.4. Move to edge of seat
	2.5. Assist with assisted standing
	2.6. Hold onto handrail
3. Unfasten pants and pull down	3. Help unfasten pants and pull down
3.1. Unfasten belt	
3.2. Undo zipper	
3.3. Pull down pants	
3.4. Pull down underwear	
4. Sit on toilet	4. Sit on toilet
5. Urinate	5. Urinate
6. Wipe self	6. Call for assistance to wipe
6.1. Take toilet paper	
6.2. Pull off roll	
6.3. Wipe self from front to back	
7. Stand up	7. Request assistance to stand
	7.1. Hold handrail and assist with standing
8. Pull up clothing	8. Assist in pulling up pants and fastening
8.1. Pull up underwear	
8.2. Pull up pants	
8.3. Zip up zipper	
8.4. Fasten belt	
9. Reach for handle and flush	9. Move into chair and reach for handle
	9.1. Assist with turning and sitting on wheelchair seat
	9.2. Move back into seat
	9.3. Put on seatbelt
	9.4. Unlock brakes
	9.5. Move wheelchair near handle and push to flush
10. Flush and go wash hands	10. Flush and go wash hands

certain activities, such as those in the physical/health category, performance may be partially simulated to avoid injury to the student. In the example of tube feeding, the student is observed performing the steps, but the teacher partially controls the flow of the formula by kinking the tube herself to avoid the student incorrectly infusing the formula and getting air in the feeding tube.

Recording Student Errors and Doing a Performance Discrepancy

When the student does not perform the step independently, the **error** or response of the student is recorded. On the discrepancy form, this information can be placed under the third column entitled "Student Error." Information in

1. Using the results of an ecological inventory, select an individually functional skill for the particular student.
2. Define the skill simply. Include a description of the materials required for performance.
3. Observe peers or adults performing the task using the chosen materials in at least one natural setting. Write down each motor movement as a step. Each step results in a visible change in the students body, the process, or the material; therefore, steps are stated in terms of observable behavior.
4. Adapt the steps to suit the specific student's disabilities and skill strengths. Some steps may require further "slicing" into smaller elements. Some may need further adaptation to the sequence of steps or the materials and devices being used. Employ the principle of partial participation as needed.
5. Validate the task analysis by observing the student performing the task, providing assistance on steps that are unknown so that all steps can be observed. Revise the task analysis as needed, after finishing the discrepancy analysis.
6. Write the steps of the task analysis on a data collection form. See the section on data collection later in this chapter for a sample data form and a procedure to fill it out and analyze the data.

FIGURE 2-4 Principles of developing a task analysis

this column will help in analyzing why the error occurred.

The teacher or team members will next decide why the student was unable to perform the step without assistance. More specifically, is the problem performing the step due to learning (or cognitive), physical (or motor), health (or endurance), sensory, communication, or motivational reasons? As seen in the example in Figure 2-3, the reason is written into the fourth column. For example, the student is unable to hold the syringe barrel straight (step 7) because of his physical disability. Another motor problem was found in pouring the formula into the barrel since it was difficult for him to pour the formula into such a small container. Difficulty manipulating the clamp or kinking the tube was thought to be a motor problem as well. The other missed steps were attributed to learning problems in need of instruction. Sometimes it is difficult to determine the reason for lack of performance, so specific observations are necessary. Further manipulation of the material or the student's positioning and movements may be needed, especially to determine whether a physical or learning problem exists. Consultation with the occupational therapist may be needed in certain instances. Care must be taken that the student is motivated to try his best to perform the task. Reinforcement or discussion with the student about the task should be used to ensure that the student understands to try to complete the task to the best of his or her ability.

Providing Instruction, Adaptations, or Alternate Performance Strategies

In the final step, the team must determine which performance options should be used for the missed steps: (a) teach as performed by a nondisabled person, (b) make adaptations and teach, or (c) develop an alternative performance strategy and teach. The first choice is to teach in the same way as would occur for someone without a physical disability. Adaptations and assistive devices should not be used unless required. The student should learn the tasks without supports if possible. Teaching without unneeded adaptations will avoid potential difficulties if the adaptations or devices are not available in a different setting or situation. In other situations students will require adaptation to perform the activity or task.

Adaptations and Alternative Performance Strategies. If teaching the student in the same manner as a person without physical disabilities is

Table 2-4 Types of Adaptations and Examples

Type of adaptation	Examples
Adapting existing material	Built-up fork handle
	Velcro
	Relevant dimensions highlighted on material
Using adaptive materials and devices	Switches
	Augmentative/alternative communication
	Picture prompts for sequences
	Prone stander
Using assistive strategies	Support for mobility
	Elbow held in position for accessibility
	Jaw control for eating
Adapting a skill sequence	Inability to open flip end of toothpast tube so instead end of tube is hit on edge of table to open
Adapting rules	More time between classes to allow for mobility issues
	More swings for T-ball
Adapting physical environment	Wider aisles for wheelchair mobility
	Materials relocated within student's reach

not an effective option, the team must determine whether an adaptation in the material or task will promote task performance. If so, then the student is taught to perform the task or step using the adaptation, as noted with examples in Table 2-4. Possible adaptations include (a) adapting existing materials, (b) using adaptive materials and devices (including assistive technology), (c) using assistive strategies (in which a person assists the student instead of an adaptive device), (d) adapting a skill sequence, (e) adapting rules governing performance, or (f) making adaptations to the physical environment that would allow student performance. In our example on tube feeding, material was adapted by adding a funnel to the syringe barrel. A red line was also placed on the syringe barrel (as an antecedent prompt) to cue the student as to when he should start pouring more fluid. It should be noted that if making an adaptation is the chosen option, certain cautions should be observed:

1. Be sure the adaptation is needed and the student cannot be taught the skill.

2. Any adaptation must be individualized to the specific student. Even a commercial product may need further adaptation.

3. Communication regarding the adaptation and its use should be communicated across personnel and noted on data collection sheets.

4. Systematic instruction must be used to teach the student how to use the adaptation.

5. Adaptations must be continually evaluated for efficacy and modification, or fading. This is especially needed as the student becomes more proficient at performance.

In some cases adaptations may not be sufficient. If the team concludes that the existing manner in which a task is performed cannot be practically, efficiency, or effectively adapted, then they must create an **alternative performance strategy** in which the student can perform to achieve the same functional outcome (Wilcox & Bellamy, 1982). Alternative performance strategies are common in the classrooms and homes of students with physical impairments (see Table 2-5). For example, in lieu of writing with a pen, students use computers for written communication; instead of verbal communication, students employ an augmentative communication device; and catheterization is a health procedure alternative for normal urination.

Table 2-5 Examples of Alternative Performance Strategies

Teach nondisabled performance	Teach adaptation strategy	Teach alternative performance
Teaching feeding skill	Using adaptive spoon	Tube feeding
Buttoning shirt	Using button hook	Wearing pullover shirts
	Using Velcro	Wearing plastic pants
Using urinal	Holding handrail at toilet	Sitting on toilet
Washing hands	Operating elongated faucet handles	Using waterless cleansing liquid
Sitting with classmates on floor in a circle	Sitting in adaptive chair with classmates in a circle	Lying over wedge beside classmates in a circle

The most divergent alternative strategy, which should be avoided if possible because of the dependency involved in its use, is the use of a personal assistant for activities such as dressing and eating. However, even when an individual must employ another person to engage in an activity, the team must consider and provide instruction for **partial participation.** That is, to the manner and extent possible, the student will partially participate in the activity (Baumgart et al., 1982).

For those students with the most significant physical and cognitive impairments, ways may be devised so they are in some way a part of an activity. Such partial participation may take a variety of forms. For example, a student may participate communicatively indicating initiation, continuation, or termination of an activity. Another communication example would be indicating pleasure or displeasure with an event or material. A student may participate cognitively by indicating yes/no answers in some manner or communicate socially by facial or tonal changes. Or a student may participate motorically by performing just a basic skill within an entire chain of steps, such as rolling the toilet paper, rolling to the side during dressing, or just laying a hand on that of the person feeding the student.

Students with severe physical impairments and mild to no cognitive impairments may participate in an activity in additional ways. The student may direct another person in the activity or monitor the physical/health management procedure and how he feels afterward, indicating specific problems and courses of action. (See Chapter 3 on communication for more information in this area.)

INSTRUCTIONAL STRATEGIES

Instruction is the arrangement of learning materials and the systematic presentation of opportunities for student response. It is presented in a systematic manner to promote student understanding of what is being asked, foster skill acquisition of the task being presented, and provide systematic information and assistance that enables student mastery of content.

The elemental unit of instruction, the dynamics of which the teacher must understand and manipulate, is known as a *trial*. A trial is an opportunity for the student to perform a requested skill or task. The components of a trial are the behavior(s) being requested, the materials and information being presented to the student that inform and set up performance of the behavior (*antecedents*), and the environmental results of the behavior having occurred (*consequences*). For example, for the behavior of drinking milk from a cup, the antecedents may include a glass filled with milk (with a straw, modified handle, or modified cup lip) and the natural antecedent of thirst, the instructional cue of "Daniel, drink your milk," or a combination of the two; the consequences may include the natural reinforcement of the taste of the milk, the quenching of Daniel's thirst, and the verbal praise by the teacher for correct performance. The selection of behaviors, antecedents, and consequences, and their arrangements and manipulations, are the basics of instruction. These instructional basics are addressed through the use of systematic **instructional strategies.** Some of the major instructional strategies used to teach physical management and self-help skills (including health care procedures) are antecedent prompts, learning strategies, response prompts (including time delay, system of maximum prompts, system of least prompts, and graduated guidance), and demonstration-guided practice–independent practice model.

Antecedent Prompts

Antecedents are the materials and instructions presented to a student for performance of a behavior. If the natural appearance of antecedents is not sufficient to initiate performance, the teacher uses **antecedent prompts.** These are alterations of, or additions to, the instructional material to focus student attention on the natural cue(s) for making correct responses.

Effective antecedent prompting is characterized by the following guidelines (Alberto, Sharpton, Sternberg, & Bowen, 1994):

1. Prompts should focus student attention on the natural cue, not distract from it (e.g., an antecedent prompt such as placing a small red circle on a shirt tag to draw attention to this natural cue and to teach the direction the shirt should face while dressing; placing something on the front of the shirt does not teach the natural cue).

2. Prompts should be as weak as possible. The use of strong prompts when weak ones will do is inefficient and may unnecessarily prolong instruction (e.g., if a small red

circle on the shirt tag is effective, having a large neon circle that glows and has an auditory component would be unnecessary and could make it more difficult to fade the prompt).

3. Prompts should be faded as rapidly as possible. Continuing to prompt longer than necessary may result in artificial dependence on the prompt rather than on the natural cues. However, abrupt removal of prompts may result in termination of the desired behavior. *Fading* is conducted by progressively and systematically providing less frequent, intrusive, or intense prompts over the course of instruction (e.g., cutting the red circle smaller and smaller until it is no longer present).

4. Unplanned prompts should be avoided. A teacher may be unaware that students are being prompted by facial expression or vocal inflection. Consider the example of a teacher involved in teaching a student to select a fork. The teacher may be unaware that his or her facial expression, as the student reaches for the utensil, may be prompting the student's correct selection rather than the shape of the utensil.

A number of types of antecedent prompts are available: expanded feature prompts, relevant feature prompts, proximity prompts, associative prompts, modeling, match-to-sample prompts, self-operated picture or auditory prompts, and learning strategies. Each one is described next.

Expanded Feature Prompts. Expanded feature prompts provide added components or elaboration to the natural antecedent cue that adds information to assist the student in determining the appropriate response. A common use of expanded feature prompts occurs when a student is learning to write her name. She is first taught to trace the name or connect dots that result in it. The lines to be traced or the dots to be connected are added information that enable the student to perform the task. Similarly, when the student is being taught to set the table for lunch, outlines of the dish, glass, and utensils may initially be placed in appropriate places on the table to provide added information to the student.

Relevant Feature Prompts. Relevant feature prompts are those by which the teacher highlights the feature of the task materials on which the student should focus to make the correct response. The most common method of relevant feature prompting is color coding. The teacher adds a noticeable color to the part of the material on which the student should focus. For example, when teaching a student how to put on a sweater or T-shirt, the natural cue for determining front from back is the label at the back of the neck. Therefore, the teacher may assist the student in focusing on this by placing a red circle or piece of ribbon on the label. As the student has repeated success in putting on the sweater correctly, the red circle or ribbon is faded so that the natural cue becomes sufficient information. Similarly, when more formula should be added to the syringe barrel for tube feeding, a color mark may be added to the syringe barrel. This mark helps the student identify when more formula should be added. Over time, the mark may be faded.

Proximity Prompts. Proximity prompts are employed by changing the placement of materials on the table in front of the student (Lovaas, 1981). If the student is being taught to discriminate a fork from a spoon (with fork the correct response), during initial instructional trials, the two utensils are placed such that the fork is immediately in front of the student, with the spoon a number of inches away. The proximity of the fork highlights it for the student during selection. Over trials, the distance between the two materials would be reduced until they are finally presented in parallel fashion.

Associative Prompts. Associative prompts are one of the most common strategies used by teachers. They entail the presentation of an abstract concept paired with a more concrete representation. In essence these are flash cards on which, for example, the word *fork* is initially paired with a picture of a fork or the number *6* paired with six dots. During repeated presentations, the student associates the abstract word or number with the more concrete representation of the picture or dots. Over successive learning opportunities (trials), the picture or dots are faded so that the student is "reading" just the word or number. Similarly, when the teacher and student prepare a daily schedule of activities, the word for each activity is paired with a picture of the activity. Over the course of the school year, the pictures are faded so the student is reading their schedule in words alone.

Modeling. Modeling as an antecedent prompt comes before asking the student to perform a response. An individual demonstrates the behavior to allow for student imitation. For example, the student might watch the teacher put toothpaste on a toothbrush and then be asked to imitate the process. For antecedent modeling to be effective, some basic guidelines should be followed (Baer, Peterson, & Sherman, 1967; Bandura, 1969). First, the teacher must gain the student's attention before presenting the model. The instructional cue for student imitation should be a simple generalizable phrase, such as "Do this." During modeling the student must have a clear view of the demonstration and be made aware of the position of any materials and how they are manipulated. The pace of the demonstration should be such that the student can clearly discriminate the order and interdependence of each step. When initially modeling a series of actions, the individual should keep the length or complexity short and simple; extensions may be added as successful imitation occurs. Finally, when directionality of the response is important, as in tying a shoe, both the teacher and the student should face the same direction. When tying a shoe, for example, the teacher would sit behind the student, bring his arms around, and tie the shoe in front of the student.

Match-to-Sample Prompt. Sometimes a sample item is provided for the student to follow. This practice is referred to as a match-to-sample prompt. It is similar to modeling, but an item is used for the student to follow instead of a person. The sample item may be in its completed form, or shown as the series of steps leading to the final form. For example, in Figure 2-5, the student is putting together his nebulizer for a breathing treatment by following the sample in front of him.

Self-Operated Picture or Auditory Prompts.
Self-operated prompts provide a student additional and *ongoing* direction for performance of a task (Alberto, Sharpton, Briggs, & Stright, 1986; Connis, 1979; Martin, Rusch, James, Decker, & Trytol, 1982; Wacker & Berg, 1984). They are most often used to assist students in performing multistep tasks. These types of antecedent prompts provide the student information on performance of the task and on the sequence in which the steps are to be done to result in a successful outcome. Such prompts may be used during initial instruction, or for students with significant cognitive deficits, they may be used each time the student performs the task.

Self-operated picture prompts provide the student with a visual cue for the sequence of a task's steps. The preparation of picture prompts is a simple sequence:

1. Prepare a written task analysis with any needed adaptations the student requires for performing the task to accommodate physical or health impairments.

2. Decide on the type of pictures the student will use. Each student may be more adept at reading different types of pictures. Pictures may be color or black-and-white photographs, line drawings, magazine pictures, or, for communication board users, the symbol system on their board.

3. Prepare a picture for each motor step of the task analysis. Under teacher direction, the student performs the entire task, and each step is photographed. Extra people, materials,

and other distractions should be kept to a minimum and not clutter the picture. These pictures are then put in sequence in one of the various formats. For example, they may be put in a linear array on a single piece of board. This method is usually used in a classroom or workstation. The pictures may be put on a ring to be attached to a belt or wheelchair to increase their portability. The pictures may be put in a small photo album so that the student turns a page for each step. If using an album, attach a picture to the cover that indicates which task is enclosed. This picture will also serve as a cue to the student as to where to begin. A "finished" card should be included at the end of the booklet so the student knows the task is terminated and not to repeat the procedure.

4. If specific materials are needed to perform a task or a particular step, a picture of the materials should be included. For example, if the student is going to be dusting the classroom or a motel room, a picture of a dust rag and polish should appear as the first picture in the sequence. If materials are needed for one particular step, they should be depicted in an isolated area near the top of the page above the picture of the "action" step.

5. Someone other than the student should perform the task, using the picture prompts to check the completeness, accuracy, sequence, and clarity of the pictures before the student uses the prompt.

6. At the end of the series of picture steps, place a page indicating access to a reinforcer—for example, a picture of a radio, the next activity in a series of activities, or an indicator of break time. A way of formatting frequent (denser) reinforcer delivery is to place a token on the bottom of each photo page (attached with Velcro) so that the student may take the token when he has completed the step. This reinforcement may be decreased (thinned) as the student acquires

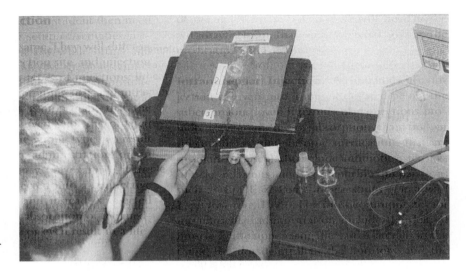

FIGURE 2-5 Using a match-to-sample prompt to put together a nebulizer

the skill by placing the token on every other page, then every three pages, and so on.

Self-operated auditory prompts provide the student a recorded auditory cue of the step of a task they are to perform. The ordering of the verbal directions provide the student with an auditory cue as to the sequence in which the steps are to be performed. As with picture prompts, auditory prompts can be prepared with a few basic steps:

1. Prepare a written task analysis. Have a person perform the task according to the steps you have listed to check their accuracy.

2. Prepare a tape recording (for a portable device such as a Walkman) of each directional statement for each motor step of the task analysis. Be sure to allow enough time between directions for student motor planning and performance. Also, use vocabulary that is in the student's receptive understanding.

3. At the end of the task sequence provide a reinforcer such as verbal praise, music, or a direction to engage in some preferred leisure activity.

4. Test the audiotape by having a naive listener perform the task while listening to the tape

to confirm its accuracy, sequence, clarity, and the length of time allowed for performance. The time allowance between steps will need to be adjusted for a particular student with a physical disability.

5. Following about each third or fourth step, directions should be included for self-evaluation and correction. For example, after doing several of the steps for preparing a sandwich, a direction should be included in which the student is asked what is in front of him or her—for instance, "Do you have a plate, bread, a jar of peanut butter, a jar of jelly, and a knife?" The student is then directed, "If not, raise your hand."

The basics of picture and auditory prompts preparation and use have been outlined. Each requires additional instruction, which might include teaching students to read pictures, operate a tape player, or self-correct. The reader is encouraged to review various articles that detail such instruction.

Learning Strategies

Learning strategies are a collection of strategies that focus on how the student learns rather than the specific content. They are primarily used with students with mild or no cognitive impairment. Learning strategies are defined as "behaviors and thoughts that a learner engages in during learning and that are intended to influence the learner's encoding process" (Weinstein & Mayer, 1986, p. 315). They consist of describing the strategy, modeling the strategy, engaging the student in verbal rehearsal of the strategy, providing practice in the strategy use, and orienting the student where the strategy can be applied (Ellis & Sabornie, 1986; Polloway & Patton, 1993).

Several types of learning strategies have been developed for specific areas that support efficient learning, such as note taking, listening to lecture, and studying texts. Learning strategies can also be used for teaching physical and health needs. Many of them involve teaching the student a mnemonic in which each letter stands for a particular part of the strategy. For example, a general strategy for each physical and health management learning task is teaching the mnemonic "You need to have ESP" (*E,* know the equipment; *S,* know the steps; *P,* know the problems and what to do). A more specific mnemonic may be used for each type of procedure; for example, for teaching tube feeding, "Feeding is the 4 *F*s" (*f*lush the tube; *f*ood goes in the tube; *f*ill the tube before it's empty; *f*lush the tube when you are done).

Instead of a mnemonic, some learning strategies teach the relevant content or task in terms of a saying. Learning strategies may also use a rhythmic structure such as a melody in the form of a jingle, tune, or rap to learn specific content. Others may use mental imagery, specific outlines, or special figures or images to teach students to learn to associate and remember content.

Response Prompts

Behavior targeted for instruction is either absent from the student's repertoire or incompletely performed. Therefore, to teach and shape the behavior, instruction involves providing guidance and assistance in the actual performance of the behavior. This guidance and assistance take the form

of **response prompts.** Response prompts are used to help the student initiate a motor response, provide guided practice of a motor response, and inhibit the student from practicing errors. They can also reinforce correct performance to increase the probability of continued performance, shape an approximation of the response, or correct an incorrect response.

From the most to the least intrusive assistance, the five basic types of response prompts are full physical prompt, partial physical prompt, model prompt, gesture prompt, and verbal prompt.

1. A *full physical prompt* provides total assistance to the student. The teacher actually moves the student, hand over hand, through the entire motor behavior, thereby providing assistance for each movement necessary for successful performance. This degree of teacher control leaves little opportunity for student error.

2. A *partial physical prompt* is physical assistance to initiate or provide direction for performance. When the teacher feels the student engaging in the response or is redirecting their movement, the prompt is terminated.

3. A *model prompt* is a response prompt when the model is presented concurrently with student performance, thereby occasioning coactive imitation by the student. The teacher says, "Do this with me." The teacher may then model for the student the entire response or a part of the response with which the student is having particular difficulty.

4. A *gesture prompt* is a gesture or signal given to the student to indicate he should perform the behavior, or to redirect his movement. This can be seen when a teacher raises her hands while telling a student to get out of his chair, or pointing to or tapping the materials to be manipulated.

5. A *verbal prompt* is assistance provided beyond the initial verbal instruction. Verbal prompts can take the form of direct assistance as in restating the instructional cue or providing a

procedure's description ("Turn the faucet") or indirect assistance by asking questions ("How do you connect your extension tube to your gastrostomy button?"), offering encouragement ("You are doing very well"), or providing a rule to be followed ("We cross the street when the light is ___?"). Some individuals will differentiate between a verbal prompt, referring to providing a step in the procedure as a verbal cue and further description of what to do as verbal description.

To provide consistent, predictable patterns of assistance to students, a systematic use of response prompts should be used. Guidelines for the systematic use of response prompts have been researched for the use of just one type of prompt at a time and for the coordinated use of several prompts. The systematic use of a single response prompt is known as time delay. The systematic use of multiple response prompts is the system of maximum prompts, the system of least prompts, or graduated guidance. All four will be discussed in the following subsections.

Time Delay. A teacher may give an instructional cue such as "Daniel, pull up your pants,"

and then wait for the student to perform the response. After waiting, if the student does not respond, the teacher helps him perform the task. The time delay procedure is an approach that uses only one type of help or prompt and systematizes the amount of time the teacher waits before providing the prompt (Snell & Gast, 1981).

At initial instruction the teacher begins each trial of an instructional session at a 0-second delay; that is, the teacher gives the instruction and the prompt simultaneously. The response prompt selected is the least intrusive type of prompt for which the student has a history of successful response. The simultaneous presentation of the instruction and the prompt allows the student to associate the instructional cue and the nature of the response being requested while providing immediate assistance. After a session at 0-second delay, the teacher begins to give the student time to respond before delivering the prompt (Table 2-6). The teacher usually allows approximately 4 seconds for the student to respond before delivering the prompt. For students with physical impairments, this 4-second delay is lengthened to the amount of time the particular student requires for motor planning and performance. The goal is for the student to perform the correct response before the need for the teacher to deliver

Table 2-6 Time Delay

Antecedent (A)	Delay (D)	Prompt (P)	Behavior (B)	Consequence (C)
Natural/environmental	0 seconds	(1 prompt)	Performs skill	Reinforcement
Instructional cue		Full physical		
Material		Partial physical		
Setting	4 seconds	Model		
		Gesture		
		Verbal description		
		Verbal		
Example of dressing after toileting				
"Daniel, pull up your pants" (instructional cue)	Wait 4 seconds	*If no response:* After 4 seconds, provide gesture	Pulls up pants	Verbal praise
		If response:	Pulls up pants	Verbal praise

the response prompt. If the student waits for the prompt before performing the response, continued practice is necessary. If the student continually performs incorrectly before the prompt, a temporary return to a 0-second delay is required. If the student continually performs incorrectly after the teacher has delivered the prompt, this indicates the need for a more intrusive prompt during instruction.

System of Maximum Prompts. To use this multiprompt system, the teacher begins by providing the student the most assistance possible. Gradually, the amount of assistance is reduced. The intrusiveness of the prompt is faded as the student's independence increases over sessions. Instruction begins with a full physical prompt, where the teacher physically assists the student through the entire response while restating the instructional cue. The teacher performs the task hand over hand with the student, providing errorless practice. After one or more sessions of full physical assistance, the teacher begins the next session at a reduced amount of assistance, such as a partial physical prompt (see Figure 2-6). If the student can perform the response at this reduced level of prompting, the teacher continues the session with that prompt. If the student is unable to perform correctly, the teacher returns to the full physical prompt. The teacher continues this sequence of instruction and testing at a lesser level of prompt, systematically reducing the level of response prompt across sessions. The goal is for the student to perform the response without any assistance when given an instructional cue.

System of Least Prompts. The system of least prompts operates from the opposite perspective of the system of maximum prompts (see Figure 2-7). Instead of beginning instruction with the greatest amount of assistance, the teacher begins by providing the student with the least amount of assistance. The student has the opportunity to perform at his or her highest level of independence on each trial before assistance is increased

Instructional Sessions

Session 1—Delivery of full physical prompt
Session 2—Probe two trials at partial physical prompt

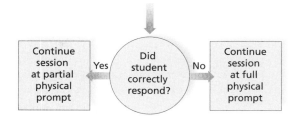

FIGURE 2-6 System of maximum prompts

within the trial (Doyle, Wolery, Ault, & Gast, 1988).

The trial begins with presentation of the materials and the instructional cue. If the response is not initiated after 3 to 5 seconds, the teacher repeats the instructional cue and increases the prompt level. The prompt continues to increase within the trial until the student correctly performs the response or until the teacher makes use of the most intrusive prompt, a full physical prompt. At each subsequent request for performance (the beginning of each new trial), the teacher again begins at the instructional cue and progressively increases assistance as needed.

In both the system of maximum prompts and the system of least prompts, it is not necessary for the teacher to employ all types of response prompts. Instead, the teacher should select the response prompts most appropriate for each student. For example, if a student's cognitive or physical impairment gives them minimal ability to imitate, the use of a model would not be included within the hierarchy of response prompts selected for instruction.

Graduated Guidance. Graduated guidance is an extension of full physical prompting. It provides an amount of continuous physical contact by the teacher necessary for the student to complete a response correctly (Foxx, 1981). The amount of physical contact can be adjusted

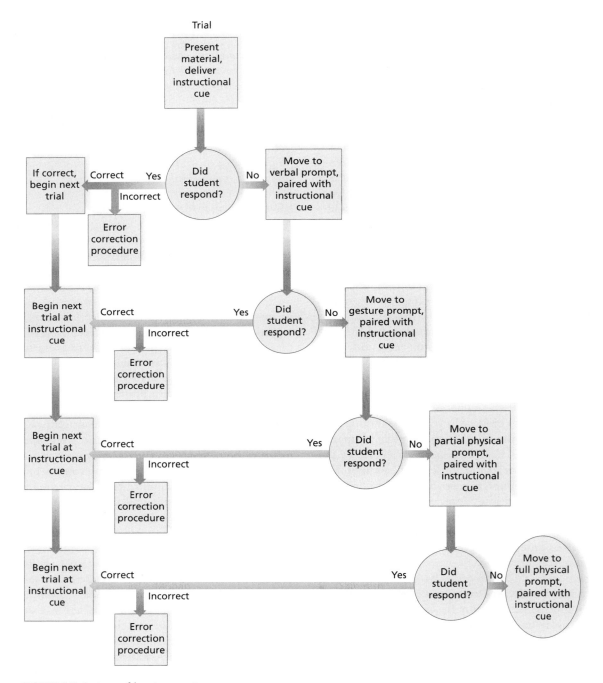

FIGURE 2-7 System of least prompts

throughout the trial depending on the student's performance.

Instruction begins with full graduated guidance, which is the same as a full physical prompt. The teacher's hands remain in full contact with the student's, performing the task together hand over hand. The teacher continues to put the student through the entire behavior until the student offers no resistance to the movement or begins to initiate or lead the movement on his or her own. At this point partial graduated guidance is offered, in one of two ways. Continual full contact by the teacher may be moved up the student's arm to the wrist, then the elbow, then the upper arm, and finally the shoulder. Alternatively, the teacher may lie only the thumb and forefinger on the student's hand or wrist to assist and guide movement. In both approaches the student begins to take more responsibility for the actions. If the action is not initiated by the student, if resistance is felt, or if an incorrect action is started, the teacher may return to full graduated guidance.

Once the student is reliably performing the behavior with minimal assistance, the teacher may use **shadowing.** With this procedure, the teacher does not touch the student but rather keeps his or her hand within an inch of the student's hand throughout the trial until the behavior is completed. Therefore, if assistance is needed, it can easily be provided. As the student continues to perform the behavior, the teacher may move farther away, thereby allowing for more independent movement.

Demonstration-Guided Practice-Independent Practice Model

This instructional strategy is frequently used with students with mild to no cognitive impairments. It consists of three parts: demonstration, guided practice, and independent practice (Polloway & Patton, 1993). In the first part, the teacher explains the skill to be taught and demonstrates the skill. As with other strategies, the steps of the procedure are task-analyzed into small steps. The teacher may demonstrate a few steps of a physical or health management skill then move on to the student practicing these steps until mastery, or the teacher may demonstrate the entire skill and have the student learn it all at once. Depending on the student's skill and ability, the demonstration may initially be done with a model to familiarize the student with the equipment and minimize errors. In this instance, the student would be taught to practice, say, tube feeding with the equipment on a model, and after the student has learned the task, the teacher would demonstrate the student's own tube feeding. Demonstration would then move to the student tube-feeding him- or herself. However, students who have difficulty generalizing skills from models to themselves should not be taught with models initially.

The second part in the demonstration-guided practice-independent practice model consists of allowing the student to practice the skill while the teacher monitors the student and provides immediate guidance and feedback. In this step, the teacher's role is to prevent, redirect, and correct errors. The teacher may provide antecedent or response prompts to help the student correctly master a step of the task. If a particular step is difficult for the student to perform, some additional repeated practice on this step (mass practice) or some adaptation due to physical limitations may be necessary. As the student learns the task, less and less teacher guidance is provided.

The last part in this strategy is independent practice. Students practice the skill without assistance or guidance but still receive feedback from the teacher as needed. For skills such as putting on a coat or brushing hair, the teacher can leave the student to give directions to another student and return to give the student feedback. However, this approach is not recommended when the student is performing health care procedures (e.g., catheterization, tube feeding, suctioning) or mobility goals (e.g., learning to use a walker), because these skills can result in injury or problems if done incorrectly. It is important that the teacher continues to supervise the student in this case should a problem arise calling for intervention. The type of feedback that the student should receive is twofold: motivational feedback, such as positive statements of their performance, and corrective feedback to help teach the student how to improve performance.

COLLECTING DATA

Collecting data on the student's performance of a task is important for several reasons. The collection and display of data on student performance provide documentation that the skill is being systematically taught and that progress, or lack thereof, is being made. The data will allow the teacher to monitor student progress and identify which steps the student is having difficulty learning and reveal any consistent pattern of error. The data for these difficult steps will allow them to be targeted for isolated practice (mass practice), an alteration in the antecedent or response prompt being used, and/or the need to reevaluate the adaptive equipment or assistive strategy being used.

Numerous data sheets may be used to record data depending on the information the data sheet will provide, its ease of use, the readability to others, and the teacher's preference. One possible data sheet that may be used for multiple-step tasks (such as those in this book) is presented in Figure 2-8. On the top of the data sheet, the teacher writes in the student's name and the procedure to be performed. The type of instructional strategy is written in the space as well as any antecedent prompts, assistive strategies, and special adaptive equipment. The teacher places the steps in ascending order of the skill, with the first step at the bottom of the page. If the student is not targeting any steps at this time, a *T* is placed next to the step to indicate that the teacher is completing the step without student participation, and a line is drawn through the adjacent squares since no data will be taken on this step. The date is placed at the top of the column as indicated. Each step receives

a code as to the level of prompt used for the student's response. Errors are noted at the end of the column under "Error Analysis." If a change is made to correct the error (e.g., adding an antecedent prompt or a new assistive strategy or adaptive equipment), a line is drawn when it starts and a notation is made at the bottom of the form indicating the change.

The completed data sheet (Figure 2-9) shows example strategies and prompts used for instruction. Because of the student's prior partial participation in this task of indicating when more food should be poured into the syringe barrel, an antecedent prompt of placing a red line on the syringe barrel to indicate when more food should be poured in was continued. This prompt will be faded soon. Besides the typical equipment used in tube feeding, the student also has a funnel on the end of the syringe barrel to allow him to pour the formula without spilling. In this example, step 2 of preparing the formula is not being targeted at this time, as indicated by the *T* for the teacher performing the step and the line through the adjacent boxes.

To monitor how the student is performing, many data sheets can be graphed. In the example data sheet, each independent score is counted for each date. Under 4/1, for example, there is one *I*. A mark is made in the upper-right corner of the first square. On 4/2, there are three *I*s. A mark is made in the upper-right corner of the third square (not counting the step that the teacher is performing). The two marks are connected, showing that the student went from completing one step to three steps independently. On 4/3, the student again did three steps independently, so the third box from the bottom (skipping the box with the line through it) is marked. This continues for each date. The marks are connected as the student completes each session to create the learning curve. When the graph line remains at the same level for a period of time or is decreasing, a problem is indicated. A graph line that is going upward indicates that the student is learning.

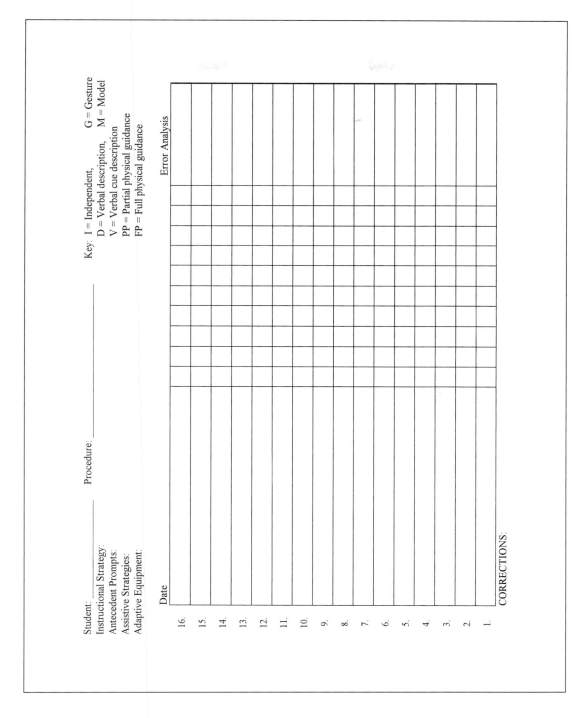

FIGURE 2-8 Sample data sheet

Student: *Joe Smith* Procedure: *Intermittent Tube Feeding*
Instructional Strategy: *Least prompts*
Antecedent Prompts: *Red line on syringe barrel*
Assistive Strategies: *Support left elbow to hold barrel straight*
Adaptive Equipment: *Funnel on syringe barrel*

Key: I = Independent, G = Gesture
D = Verbal description, M = Model
V = Verbal cue description
PP = Partial physical guidance
FP = Full physical guidance

	Date	4/1	4/2	4/3	4/4	4/5	4/8	Error Analysis
16.								
15.	Put plug in tube	PP	PP	V	V	V	V	
14.	Take off syringe barrel	PP	PP	PP	I	V	I	
13.	Kink/clamp tube before water empties from barrel	FP	FP	FP	PP	M	G	can't kink clamp
12.	Add water when formula near bottom of barrel	D	V	V	V	V	Y	
11.	Continue to add formula until all is added	G	G	G	D	I	I	
10.	Add more formula before completely empties	FP	FP	FP	FP	FP	D	too slow adding
9.	Allow formula to flow by gravity	D	D	I	I	I	I	
8.	Hold barrel 6 inches above stomach	D	D	D	D	D	I	
7.	Pour prepared fluid/formula into barrel	D	D	D	V	I	I	
6.	Attach syringe barrel	D	I	I	I	I	I	
5.	Remove plug	PP	PP	D	I	I	I	
4.	Clamp or kink tube	FP	FP	FP	M	M	D	can't kink clamp
3.	Prepare equipment	PP	PP	G	D	D	V	
(T) 2.	Prepare formula -----------------	---	---	---	---	---	---	
1.	Wash hands	I	I	I	I	I	I	
	CORRECTIONS:							

New clamp (4, 13)

Change to clamp then add (10)

FIGURE 2-9 Completed data sheet

ERROR CORRECTION AND ANALYSIS

Error Correction

The basic consequence for correct performance or an approximation of correct performance is reinforcement. Basic reinforcement procedures are detailed in any introductory text on applied behavior analysis. During instruction, the consequence for an incorrect performance is a correction procedure, of which three basic types are possible: trial and error, corrective feedback, and error interruption.

1. In trial and error, the teacher ignores errors made during student performance but does not allow the error to be repeated (which would provide practice of the error). The teacher's feedback is the encouragement "Try another way." This feedback continues until the student performs correctly.

2. With corrective feedback, the teacher provides additional information after the error has occurred. After saying, "No, that is not correct," the teacher may give more verbal information or direction, engage in corrective modeling in which the correct performance is modeled with step-by-step explanation, increase the level of the response prompt, or offer a trial of full physical assistance.

3. In error interruption, the teacher interrupts performance before the student actually commits the error and redirects the student response either verbally and/or physically.

Error Analysis

Regardless of the type of instructional strategy used, it is important that the teacher does an error analysis on the steps the student is missing or showing little progress on. An error analysis is a close examination for a pattern in the type of **er-**

ror the student is making in order to correct it. It should occur on an ongoing basis for quick intervention. Several types of errors can occur, including learning errors, physical errors, sensory errors, motivational errors, and others. As with a discrepancy analysis, when in doubt as to which type of error the student is making after close observation, the teacher should first assume it is physical (or sensory) and adapt accordingly.

Learning Errors. Learning errors are mistakes due to some difficulty understanding (or learning) a step (or steps) in the procedure. These types of errors are corrected by (a) providing further instruction on the step, (b) giving more practice of the step (mass practice), (c) breaking the step further (further task analysis), or (d) using an additional or different instructional strategy (e.g., adding an antecedent prompt or using a mnemonic to help remember a missed step).

Physical Errors. Physical errors occur because of some physical limitation resulting from the student's physical disability. These errors can be corrected by (a) changing how the student manipulates the material, (b) altering the steps in the procedure (by adding steps or changing how it is done) to make performance possible within the parameters of the student's physical abilities, (c) providing an assistive strategy (which is the least desirable since it affects the student's independence), or (d) adding a piece of adapted equipment. In the example data sheet, the student had a previous learning error of when to pour fluid into the barrel, so the antecedent prompt of having a red line was used. The student's discrepancy analysis and initial error analysis showed that he required support under his left elbow to hold the syringe barrel upright and a funnel was needed to help with pouring. The error shown on the data sheet of difficulty clamping or kinking the tube was determined to be a physical error. It was remediated by adding a different type of clamp to the tube that was easier to manipulate.

Sensory Errors. Many students with physical or multiple disabilities have visual impairments and so may miss steps requiring close examination of an item. To correct this, the teacher may (a) provide sharp contrast of the area by using bold lines or coloring in some aspect of the task; (b) enlarge the problem area, if possible; or (c) give tactile cues allowing the student to access the material correctly without the use of sight. Consultation with the vision teacher will help in determining changes in this area.

Sensory errors may also occur when the student has a hearing impairment. Correction usually consists of finding an alternative method of having the student attend to what is making the sound needed for a step. Such alternatives will vary depending on the task. A common example is the use of flashing light when the telephone rings. Most physical management and basic self-help skills, including health care procedures, do not have necessary auditory components.

Motivational Errors. Motivational errors may occur when the student is not interested in learning the activity. Depending on the student, motivational types of errors may be corrected by (a) reexplaining the importance of the task, (b) providing stronger or more frequent reinforcement, (c) discussing the problem with the student to come up with a solution, and/or (d) changing the materials used in the task when feasible (e.g., using a purple toothbrush instead of a white one for a child whose favorite color is purple).

It is important to offer students an understanding of the function and importance of the task before beginning to teach it. However, some students may not have received sufficient explanation and require further discussion of why they are learning the task. Clarifying the relevance of a physical/health management task can assist with compliance and motivation to learn it.

The student may not be motivated because of a lack of effective reinforcement. Changing the type or frequency of reinforcement may re-

sult in improved performance and motivation to perform the task. The type of reinforcement will depend on student interests and tastes. Reinforcement may occur after the task, such as the immediate delivery of a treat, or with the use of a token economy or a behavioral contract. (Refer to books on applied behavioral analysis for more information such as Alberto & Troutman's [1999] *Applied Behavior Analysis for Teachers.*)

Sometimes there may be a problem regarding the student's ideas or beliefs regarding the procedure. For example, a girl learning to self-catheterize herself using clean intermittent catheterization procedure may not be motivated to learn because she was initially taught that she should not touch her genital area. In such a case, the teacher and parents need to work collaboratively to solve the problem, discussing the task with the student and offering encouragement.

Other Errors: Health and Communication Errors. Various types of additional errors may occur during the learning process. Some may happen from fatigue and lack of endurance, which are examples of health errors. In these instances, more frequent breaks may be needed, or the student may require an easier or different position from which to work. Communication errors may occur when the student is not understood. This type of error is corrected by providing appropriate augmentative communication (see Chapter 3).

EXPANDING INSTRUCTION

Instruction of tasks in the physical or health management area, as well as other areas, requires that the student learn the task across several stages. These **stages of learning** are entry level, acquisition, proficiency, maintenance, generalization, and application (or adaptation) (Bos & Vaughn, 1998; Mercer & Mercer, 1998).

Entry Level

Entry level is the level of performance the student has of the targeted task prior to instruction. Having an understanding of what the student is able to perform can assist in planning instruction.

Acquisition

Initially, instruction is provided at the acquisition level. At this level, the emphasis of instruction is on accuracy. The student needs to perform the skill accurately at a high level of performance. For example, when the student can correctly perform each step of the task-analyzed tube-feeding skill, he has achieved acquisition of the task.

Proficiency

The next level is proficiency, in which the target behavior is performed with high accuracy and fluency. *Fluency* refers to the rate at which the student is able to provide the correct response or behavior. In the tube-feeding example, for proficiency the student would be able to complete the tube-feeding process (including preparing the formula and cleaning up afterward) at an acceptable rate and accuracy.

Fluency is typically taught after acquisition of the task, but in some cases it may be taught simultaneously. In the tube-feeding example (Figure 2-9), step 10 asks the student to add more formula to the syringe barrel before it is completely emptied from the syringe barrel. This particular step requires fluency and accuracy to be correctly performed. When this step is accomplished, fluency may be taught simultaneously while the other steps continue on acquisition level. Later, the fluency of the entire task may be targeted to decrease the amount of time the procedure takes.

Maintenance

Maintenance focuses on continued proficient performance of the task over time. Unless the student continues to participate actively in the task, he or she may forget parts of it. The teacher thus needs to continue to have the student perform the task to aid in retention. Since tasks regarding physical management and self-help skills (including health care procedures) occur throughout the day, it is assumed that such continual practice would occur.

Generalization

Generalization is the phase in which the student is expected to perform the skill in settings with materials or persons not included during initial acquisition instruction. Unless the skill can be generalized, it has not really been functionally learned. If the student can only perform urinary catheterization in the school bathroom, for example, and cannot do it in her home or in the bathroom at the mall, the student's independence will be severely limited. Learning to perform some of the procedures in this book in alternate locations can be a challenge owing to differences in space and material (e.g., the lack of a table). The skill should initially be taught with these differences in mind to avoid problems with generalization. For example, if a child who catheterizes herself uses a table in the toilet stall to hold her equipment, she will be limited when going to other bathrooms. An alternative arrangement, such as the wheelchair seat or a special bag to hold equipment a certain way, can be used from the start to allow the student to generalize the skill to other locations.

Application

Application is when the student applies the acquired skill to new situations. For example, when a student who has learned to wash his hands prior to eating washes his hands before tube feeding without ever having been told to do so, he is applying his knowledge of infection control to a new situation.

SUMMARY

The instruction of students with physical impairments, health impairments, or multiple disabilities requires the collaborative expertise and efforts of all members of the educational team. While serving as the central manager of a student's educational plan, the teacher's primary expertise is on the systematic management of instruction that leads to student learning. This management uses the various elements of instructional technology such as the organization of content; the use of antecedent prompts, response prompts, and learning strategies; and the collection and analysis of data for determining learning progress and error patterns. The framework for instructional decisions is one in which the educational team must determine whether the student will be taught to perform tasks directly as a nondisabled individual performs them or whether adaptations, adaptive equipment, and/or alternative performance strategies will be needed.

3

Communication for Physical and Health Needs

Students with physical and health impairments need a way to communicate their health needs, especially when there is a combined problem with effective communication and physical/health concerns. Students with severe speech impairments or who are nonspeaking are estimated to comprise less than 1% of the total school-age population in the United States and between 4% and 6% of the special education population (Glennen & DeCoste, 1997). These students typically have severe physical disabilities. In one study 31.5% of the sampled population who were nonverbal had cerebral palsy (Lafontaine & DeRuyter, 1987), and another study found 47.3% of its sample had multiple disabilities (Matas, Mathy-Laikko, Beukelman, & Legresley, 1985). Other physical diseases may adversely affect communication such as genetic disorders (e.g., CHARGE syndrome, Angelman syndrome), inborn errors of metabolism (e.g., Lesch-Nyhan), and progressive neuromuscular diseases (e.g., Duchenne muscular dystrophy). Students may also have severe health impairments requiring the use of tracheostomies or ventilators

that interfere with speech production (Glennen & DeCoste, 1997). The ability to communicate about health or physical concerns will allow their needs to be met more effectively.

Students who use augmentative and alternative communication (AAC) to communicate with others have varying communication systems that range in form (type), function (intent of the communicative message), and content (vocabulary). Communication takes numerous forms, including sign language, nonelectronic and electronic devices (using symbols, pictures, objects, and/or words), and nonsymbolic communication (e.g., gestures, behaviors with communicative intent). Students may use one or a combination of systems to express one or many different functions. Some students may only be able to do the communicative function of making a request, such as "I need to be suctioned." Other students may be able to make comments, greetings, refusals, and questions with their AAC system. Each student's communication system will also differ in the amount and type of content he or she can communicate. For example, some students may be able to communicate only basic wants and needs, while others have a wide breadth of content, allowing them to engage in long social interactions and academic discussions. AAC systems are tailored to the student's needs and abilities.

Regardless of the type of AAC system the student uses, consideration should be given regarding whether the communication can address the student's health needs in three major areas: (a) informing another person of a health problem, (b) instructing someone else in a health procedure, and (c) communicating needs in a health setting. The area of augmentative communication is very broad, so this chapter will only provide a general discussion of the types of augmentative communication systems, means of accessing them, and strategies specific to the three major areas regarding communication for health.

DESCRIPTION OF AUGMENTATIVE COMMUNICATION

Augmentative and alternative communication (AAC) is the combination of all methods of communication available to an individual including any speech, vocalization, gestures, and communication behaviors as well as specific communication strategies and communication aids (Doster & Politano, 1996). Nonsymbolic forms of communication such as facial expressions and behaviors are just as vital for complete communication as the symbolic types of communication that use signs, pictures, or voice output. The three types of augmentative communication that will be discussed here include nonsymbolic communication, nonaided communication, and aided communication.

Nonsymbolic Communication

Nonsymbolic communication consists of the behaviors, basic gestures, and/or expressions that a person displays that do not have a direct symbolic meaning but do have communicative meaning. Everyone communicates using nonsymbolic forms of communication. However, this form of communication may be easily overlooked. When it is the primary way a student with severe physical impairments communicates and is overlooked, then communication is lost. It is important that teachers and other persons interacting with students with physical impairments closely observe their facial and body expressions in regard to the current task. Signs of stress or discomfort can often be seen when a student demonstrates increased tension in facial and upper-body muscles. Respiration and heart rates may quickly change with stress or decrease with attention. This is especially true for students who have a problem with one of their many body systems (circulatory, respiratory, neurological). A student may also physically pull his or her body away from the instructor or materials as a sign of discomfort. This type of communication may be suitable for the people who know this student well, but it can be misinterpreted in some situations. Thus, a more formalized symbolic system will often need to be developed in order for the child to communicate with less familiar people. More formalized systems consist of nonaided or aided symbolic forms of communication.

Nonaided Symbolic Communication

Nonaided AAC is a communication system in which meaning has been assigned to some type of consistent movement the person makes. It is symbolic when the communication represents, or stands for something else (e.g., signing "ball" represents an actual ball). Nonaided symbolic forms of communication include manual sign languages, gestures, and/or individualized communication behaviors with symbolic meaning. These forms of communication may range from making simple movements such as one blink for yes and two blinks for no, to using specific hand positions with arm movements to indicate colors, actions, names, needs, and so forth. Students who have the ability to individualize finger movements and perform a sequence of meaningful movements may use sign language to express their needs. However, students with gross- and fine-motor problems may have difficulty using formalized traditional sign language, but they may be able to use sign approximations. However, these may be highly idiosyncratic and unrecognizable to trained personnel.

Whatever the selected form of nonaided communication, it is important that the student has the ability to display different types of movements and display them consistently, to establish readable messages. For this system to be effective, the user of a nonaided communication system will need to combine cognitive and motor skills by being able to (a) remember the meaning and the sequence of the movements, (b) execute the movement motorically, and (c) perform the movement at the appropriate time (Doster & Politano, 1996).

Aided Symbolic Communication

Aided AAC includes any device that students may use beyond their bodies to communicate to another person. These devices may be nonelectronic (low-tech) (e.g., paper and pencil, a picture board) or electronic (high-tech) communication devices (e.g., Wolf communication board, Liberator). They usually use some form of symbol set for students to communicate their meaning. These symbol sets usually encompass the use of objects, parts of the objects, miniatures, photographs, line drawings, pictures, rebus, the alphabet, or other symbols (Doster & Politano, 1996). The type and size of the symbol will depend on the student's sensory, motor, and cognitive skills. A young child, for example, may use a spoon to indicate hunger, while an older, more advanced child may use a line drawing of a sandwich, milk carton, and banana to indicate what he would prefer for lunch. For students who recognize letters and words, the communication system may include words, phrases, sentences, or letters to form words.

It is important to remember that AAC devices must be individually selected based on the student's needs. Students vary in their ability to use certain devices because of physical or cognitive demands. Not all devices are suitable for all students. Also, communication devices should be selected that are usable for the student in current environments with consideration as to its feasibility in future environments. When an electronic communication device is selected, a nonelectronic system should also be devised to serve as a backup when the electronic device is low on energy, out for repair, or not available for quick access during change of the student's position or activity. Consideration should also be given regarding the effect of the communication system on communicative interactions. Some students will be able to use their communication systems well but very slowly. Additional training will be required to encourage the communication partner to wait and for the student to understand why someone might walk away in the middle of the student constructing a message.

EQUIPMENT AND ADAPTIVE EQUIPMENT FOR AAC

Several types of nonelectronic and electronic communication devices are available (see Figure 3-1). Nonelectronic communication systems can be handmade and commercially bought. They include such devices as eye gaze boards, communication books, communication cards, and any other item that can hold symbols used for communication. These communication systems may use plastic-coated boards of various sizes for stick-and-peel picture symbols, transparent boards for eye gazing, notebooks to categorize communication groups, or wallet-size booklets. The size of the device will depend on the type of symbols used, the user's visual and motor skills, and the situational environment.

Many commercially available nonelectronic communication systems may be used with students. The B-H Communicator, for example, is a communication card that uses a letter- and number-scanning system whereby an assistant

FIGURE 3-1 Examples of nonelectronic and electronic communication devices (clockwise from top right: Liberator, Blackhawk, Big Mac, nonelectronic symbol board, and object communications notebook)

runs his or her finger across the top of the symbols until the student uses some type of motor or verbal signal (eye blinking, head nodding, sound) to indicate selection. Another type is the Eye Transfer (E-Tran) Communication System manufactured by Zygo Industries Inc. This is a clear plastic board on which symbols may be placed on both sides. It has an open area in the center so that the communication partner can sit opposite the student to follow his eye gaze. The student then communicates by gazing at the desired symbol, then looks back at the partner to indicate the last symbol looked at was the selected symbol.

Electronic communication devices have become more prominent with students with physical and health needs since the 1980s. These devices can be separated into two categories:

dedicated communication devices and computer-based communication systems. Dedicated communication devices are usually portable units designed specifically for communication (Struck, 1996). They usually contain all the components within one unit. Some dedicated communication devices allow more that one input option and usually include a synthesized voice output. Some offer print output and keyboard emulation for use with computers. Computer-based communication systems usually consist of a computer with a method for input, communication software, and speech synthesizer. These systems have become increasingly more portable with the use of laptop computers. Input methods may vary depending on the student's skills and needs if the student is unable to access the system using the standard

keyboard (see Chapter 6 on positioning of materials). Another advantage of computer-based systems is that the computer may be used to provide other computer-accessed academic materials.

Some examples of electronic communication devices that are dedicated include the Big Mac, Alpha Talker, Macaw, Wolf, Dynavox, Liberator, and Walker Talker. The Big Mac is a simple one-message, dedicated communication device that may be used to initiate the use of a frequently used single command for communication. A large switch records a short message that may be activated by the student touching the item or a connecting switch (see Figure 3-1). This device has limited usage, but the student may use it at least to indicate "I need help" or "I am finished" as part of physical and health needs. Other simple-message dedicated systems may consist of a rocker switch with two to eight messages. Some of these devices may even scan the messages by lighting the choice panel. The student chooses the correct message by activating a switch when the desired choice lights up.

The Alpha Talker, Macaw, and Blackhawk are examples of dedicated communication devices that may use icons or picture symbols for the student to choose a message. The Alpha Talker can have a keyboard of 32 locations (i.e., 32 symbols can be displayed at one time), or it can be configured with 4 or 8 locations. It includes icon prediction that lights up possible keys related to the topic to help locate the next word in a message. The Macaw can have 32 or 128 locations but can be configured to as few as one large location. As many as 32 levels (overlays) are available. The student can select a programmed message through direct select by pressing on a symbol on the keyboard or through the visual or auditory scanning method for individuals with fine-motor deficits. The Blackhawk is a less sophisticated device that can display up to 16 symbols at once with four different levels (overlays), for a total of 64 messages (see Figure 3-1).

The Dynavox is a dedicated augmentative communication system with a color or black-and-white active display and voice output. This device is accessed by touching the screen. The pictures, symbols, and/or words are displayed on the screen, and with a touch on the screen, new screens appear. For example, the student may touch a symbol for food, and then the screen can automatically change to display a new screen showing different selections of foods. The grid size and the screen's intensity and contrast can be changed by the touch of a button with the built-in toolbox.

The Liberator is a sophisticated portable dedicated communication system that can provide several different age and gender voices (see Figure 3-1). This system uses Minspeak, which is an icon-based system in which multiple meanings may be derived from one icon. For example, a picture of an apple may indicate *apple, red, snack, school,* or *George Washington.* The message is dependent on the series of selection. The Liberator can also display the message on an eight-line display screen; this message can then be printed. The Liberator can be accessed through direct select and scanning (visual and auditory). Icon sequence prediction, a math scratch pad, a calculator, a clock, and a calendar are additional features. The Liberator may also be used to control computers and environmental control units. As with most AAC devices, the Liberator can be mounted on a wheelchair (see Figure 3-2).

For students who are mobile and/or ambulatory, the Walker Talker is a communication device that can be housed in a waist belt. The device is removed from a pouch when used. It may have more than 100 words, phrases, or sentences with the extended memory program. This device also uses Minspeak for encoding.

Computer-based communication systems are often used when a student needs a computer and communication system in one. Many types of systems are available and can be looked up on the Internet (by using such systems as ABLEDATA at www.abledata.com/). Speaking Dynamically is a computer program compatible for MacIntosh computers. It uses a symbolic system that can customize a multilevel picture or word communication board. The student has access through direct

FIGURE 3-2 A student using a mounted board on her wheelchair

select via TouchWindow or a scanning system. By making a selection, the student can either make it talk and/or change screens. This system can be used for interacting with individuals or for recording academic work.

ASSISTIVE STRATEGIES TO PROMOTE COMMUNICATION

Accessing Communication Boards and Devices

The first consideration for accessing a communication board or device is proper positioning of the student. Positioning devices may be required in certain environments to position the communication system for the student with motor or

visual impairments to access it. For example, a student may be able to access a communication board at the desk without a positioning device but may need to have an alternative position for the communication aid in the bathroom. These positioning devices may include slant boards, wheelchair lap trays, or adjustable desk tabletops (see Chapter 6). Pointing devices may also be required for the student to indicate the appropriate symbol for communication. These devices may include head pointers, mouth sticks, supportive arm splints, or light beams. An occupational therapist should be consulted to assist with determining appropriate positioning and pointing devices.

The communication devices previously described will also require some sort of method for the student to make a selection of a picture, symbol, or letter-and-number symbol. The method used to access the communication device will depend on the student's physical, sensory, and cognitive skills. Physical skills include the student's ability to move the body, timing of the movement, and accuracy of the movement. Cognitive skills affect the type of symbol system the student can use (e.g., objects, pictures, icons, or letters/numbers) and entail the student's ability to recall the meaning and sequence of the symbol. There are three main types of access for ACC devices: direct select, scanning, and encoding.

Direct Select. Direct select is a method in which the student touches or points to the symbol used for communication. It is preferred for students with the gross- and fine-motor abilities to touch or point. Cognitively, direct select is the easiest system to learn of the three methods, as the student does not have any intermediate steps before the selection (Struck, 1996). It is also the quickest method of access. For students who do not have the hand skills to direct select with the use of the index finger, other adaptations such as head pointers, mouth sticks, optical indicators, joysticks, mice and trackballs, or keyboards may be used.

Direct select may be used with nonelectronic or electronic devices. It may consist of a single display or multiple displays. For students unable to turn pages, a message/picture may be used for the student to point at to indicate that the message is on a different page and the student needs assistance getting to it. Ideally, it would be best if the student could access the other pages independently. To obtain more independent access, different devices (e.g., page turner, tabs to lift pages) can be experimented with. Some electronic devices will automatically change the screen to a new display when a category or certain symbol is selected.

Scanning. Scanning is an indirect method used to access ACC devices. The student must use an intermediate step to make a selection on the communication device (Struck, 1996). Scanning uses a single switch-type activation in order for the student to make a selection. There are four types of scanning: automatic scanning, inverse scanning, step scan, and directed scan (Doster & Politano, 1996). The student's cognitive and physical abilities will determine which of these types is most suitable.

Automatic scanning occurs when choices are highlighted visually and/or auditorially in a serial fashion, and a switch is activated when the given choice is highlighted. With inverse scanning, the switch is held down to advance the scan and released when a selection is to be made. Step scanning occurs by activating the switch each time the cursor moves. A second switch may then be used to select the item of choice, or the choice is activated waiting for a preset acceptance time. Direct scanning uses multiple switches (or a joystick switch), with four or five switches indicating choices up, down, left, or right. The fifth switch may be used to make the selection.

Not only do scanning systems for ACC have different techniques to activate the scan, as described earlier, but they also may be arranged in four different patterns: linear, circular, row-column, and group row-column. With linear scanning, the items are usually set up in a line from left to right or top to bottom. This usually is the first method used for developmentally young students (Doster & Politano, 1996). A circular scanning pattern is when the items are scanned in a circular clock-type pattern. In row-column scanning, each row as a whole is scanned until the student selects the row that has the correct symbol. Then scanning in a left-to-right progression on that selected row occurs. This system is more complex as more steps are involved prior to the final selection. With group row-column scanning, there may be two or more groups (e.g., top half of the rows and bottom half of the rows, or topics) to choose from prior to attempting row-column scanning. This method is more complex but can increase speed.

Scanning can also be done without the use of an electronic system. The communication partner can slowly point to each symbol on the communication device, and the user indicates when the partner's finger is pointing to the correct selection. Care must be taken that the board is held in the optimal position for the user to see it and the speed of the finger movement is not too fast. Typically, it is best to verify that the correct selection has been chosen.

Encoding. Encoding is the third method that is often used to access communication devices. Encoding is a method that uses codes by combining symbols, numbers, colors, or letters to represent words or messages. It includes formalized systems such as Morse code, abbreviation expansion, or Minspeak or any system that uses combinations of letters, numbers, pictures, or colors to symbolize a message (Doster & Politano, 1996).

Morse code is an international system of a sound or symbol code of dots and dashes to represent letters, numbers, and punctuation. It may be used with controlled activation of a pressure switch or sip-and-puff switch. This method requires good consistent control of movement or breath and cognitive skills.

Abbreviation expansion is a method that uses a small number of letter combinations to represent longer phrases or sentences. For example, *EMD* may stand for "I want to eat at McDonald's." This method may decrease the amount of motor output needed to express thoughts, but it requires the cognitive skills to retrieve the codes from memory or memory aids. When the abbreviation is entered in some devices, the entire unabbreviated message is visually displayed or spoken with voice output.

Minspeak (trademark of Prentke Romich Company) is an encoding system that uses pictures or icons in a sequence to relate words, phrases, and sentences. By selecting a limited number of pictures in various series, the student has many possible messages. This system is used in several electronic voice-output devices.

Encoding systems may also be established for nonelectronic communication devices. The student may choose colors, pictures, or number/letter series to indicate prechosen messages. A display of the codes and messages for quick reference is typically required for others to decode the message (see Figure 3-3). For example, the student may look at the letter *C* then back at the communication partner to indicate a choice was made, and then look at the number *3* and back at the communication partner. The communication partner would look on a display for "C3" and find the message "I feel OK." These types of systems are typically placed on eye gaze boards with the center cut out to reduce glare and increase personal contact. The symbols (pictures, letters, numbers, etc.) may be arranged around the board with adequate spacing to easily determine where the student is looking.

Vocabulary Selection

The vocabulary selected to address physical and health needs will vary greatly depending on the student's cognitive abilities and physical and health needs. Selection of vocabulary should be based individually since individualized vocabulary selection is typically more effective and efficient than standard word lists (Yorkstone, Smith, & Beukelman, 1990). Vocabulary should be selected to (a) express health or physical needs, (b) instruct another person in performing a health procedure, and (c) address needs in hospital settings.

Selection of the vocabulary for physical and health needs follows an eight-step process:

1. The instructional team brainstorms the vocabulary necessary to indicate health or physical needs, with the student who will be using the system being involved in the process whenever possible (Beukelman, McGinnis, & Morrow, 1991).

2. A list of all the possible physical/health concerns is made that pertains to the student. This would include comments such as "sick" as well as additional communicative functions such as demands (e.g., "Call my mother; I want to go home"), questions (e.g., "Can I have my medicine?"), or requests (e.g., "Please check my colostomy bag").

3. Vocabulary is prioritized based on importance to health.

4. Vocabulary is selected as to which messages are feasible for the student to currently learn based on cognitive status.

5. Possible future targets are identified at this time.

6. The picture, sign, gesture, icon, or word(s) for each vocabulary word or message is selected. If the communication system has verbal output and a phrase is being used, peer input can provide age-appropriate vocabulary and phrases. For example, instead of a message that says, "I'm nauseous," a peer may suggest, "I'm going to throw up."

7. Vocabulary is arranged for ease to access. If, for example, the student on a ventilator wanted to communicate he was having some difficulty breathing, he should have a quick and easy way of indicating this. Vital messages should be quick, easy to execute, and understandable.

8. Vocabulary is dynamic as health conditions change. Vocabulary and its usefulness should be continually evaluated for changes.

Vocabulary to Express Health and Physical Needs. Vocabulary to express health and physical needs should be selected based on the basic,

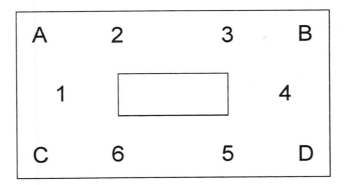

FIGURE 3-3 Eye gaze board with encoding display for a hospital setting

A. Medical/Questions
1. Tell me how I am doing.
2. Tell me about my medical treatment.
3. Can I sit in the chair now?
4. What's happening?
5. When can I leave the hospital?
6. Who are you?

B. Needs
1. I hurt. Can I have some medicine?
2. I can't breathe well.
3. I'm nauseous.
4. I'm hot/cold.
5. I'm hungry/thirsty.
6. I want my mom or dad.

C. Feelings
1. I feel worse.
2. I feel better.
3. I feel OK.
4. Leave me alone.
5. I'm scared or sad.
6. I love you.

D. Miscellaneous.
1. I want to spell something, get my spelling board.
2. Please stay.
3. Thanks.
4. I want the TV/radio/book/flowers/etc.
5. You don't understand what I'm trying to say.
6. I can't see the board/material.

general messages concerning health, as well as specialized messages pertaining to the particular physical and health procedures the student has performed. General messages regarding health may include basic vocabulary such as "hurt" and "sick," to a more specific general vocabulary including "headache," "stomachache," "nausea," "dizzy," and "tired." Sometimes a stick picture of a person is provided for the student to point to which part of the body hurts. A pain gauge is also sometimes supplied on which the student would indicate the severity of the pain, ranging from a little (1) to a lot (10), with happy and sad faces over the numbers. Additional vocabulary may indicate what the student wants done about the problem, such as "Call parent," "Need medication," "See nurse," "Go home," or "Lie down."

Specialized vocabulary pertains to the student's physical or health procedures. Students who use positioning equipment may have vocabulary such as "Time to go in the stander," "I'm tired in this position," or "Please help me out of my chair." Students who receive tube feedings may have vocabulary such as "Please check my tube," "My skin hurts near my tube," and "I feel too full." For ostomies, the student may have vocabulary to communicate "My colostomy bag needs to be changed," "My bag is leaking," "Please check the skin beside my colostomy bag," and "I'm having cramps." One helpful way to pinpoint the vocabulary for physical/health needs is to examine the procedure itself as well as possible problems and emergencies that can occur for each procedure. (See subsequent chapters for how procedures are carried out and the sections on problems and emergencies.)

Vocabulary that needs to be accessed in a hurry, such as "Suction me," should be the most easily accessible. For direct selection, these messages should be the easiest to reach. For scanning devices, these types of messages are usually the first message to be encountered. For encoding, they are also typically the first messages to encounter, such as various single digits (for those using a number encoding system) representing the critical messages. As mentioned previously, gestures, nonsymbolic behaviors, and additional forms of communication may also be targeted for their speed and ease of use. It is critical that the meaning of these forms of communication be easily understandable to all communication partners, and the meanings should be written down and in plain view (e.g., on the wheelchair) for others to interpret should the need arise.

Vocabulary for Performing Health Care Procedures. Some students with physical disabilities will be unable to physically perform a health care procedure because of physical restraints. In these instances, the student may learn how to direct another person to perform the procedure. Although the school personnel performing the procedure will have been thoroughly trained, the student should be taught to direct the individual to provide the student some independence and control over his or her environment. Also, the student may be in an environment where the person performing the procedure is not very well trained and the student could provide assistance. The vocabulary needed for performing a health procedure would include the supplies, the steps of the procedure, and directional phrases.

The vocabulary to include for communicating how to perform a procedure is easily taken from a task analysis. The student may have a series of phrases or pictures (with words written for the person performing the procedure) indicating the steps. Sign language or gestures may be used for the steps (with a card indicating the meaning of the sign/gesture).

Directional phrases are also necessary and must be selected by the team. This vocabulary is meant to provide additional instructions or directions to the person performing the procedure. For example, it could include such phrases as "Stop—you are doing it wrong," "The food is going in too quickly," or "The barrier for the colostomy is cut too large."

Depending on the type of communication system the student uses, this type of vocabulary may be placed on its own topic page or parts of it integrated on the student's main page (when using an aided form of communication). Often students will have pages or separate communication boards set up for special topics. The steps of how to perform the procedure are often placed on that task's own page. It is important, therefore, that the student always has access to it. Problems arising from the procedure may be placed on the student's main page for ease of access.

Vocabulary for Hospital Settings. Students with physical and health impairments can encounter several hospitalizations for different types of surgeries, treatments, and/or emergency care.

Thus, they will need the means to communicate in the hospital setting as well as any specialized vocabulary. Although these students may already have a communication system in place, the form of communication they use at school and home may not be feasible in the hospital because of difficulty accessing the system in a hospital bed or lack of energy to do so. Additional forms of communication are often necessary, and having some preparation for the event of a hospitalization will help make the transition easier to this setting.

Several considerations need to be made when preparing for hospitalization. First, the student's team must evaluate all the methods the student uses to communicate. Are there different ways that may be easier to use when in a hospital setting, especially if the student will be on bed rest? If the student uses a communication device and it is not thought to be feasible in a hospital, can the student access an alternative communication board with vital vocabulary?

Research has confirmed the need for multiple means of communication in acute care settings (Dowden, Beukelman, & Lossing, 1986; Fried-Oken, Howard, & Stewart, 1991). An approach encompassing a yes/no response, gestures, a simple communication board, and the student's typical system provides flexibility and increases the chances that effective communication will occur. Since hospital staff are typically not familiar with augmentative communication, written explanations should be available as well as demonstrations of how the student communicates. Clear, concise written directions are vital because of a large turnover of personnel working various shifts.

When a communication board/device is being used, a second consideration is determining placement of the board/device for easy access (Fried-Oken et al., 1991). It must be placed in an easy location for the student to use and the hospital staff to notice to promote its use. If the communication board needs to be held, a sign indicating that the board is beside the bed and where it should be positioned when in use can be helpful.

A third consideration is determining how long the output will take since hospital personnel are extremely busy and may not be able to attend to all parts of the message (Dowden et al., 1986). Systems that require minimal listener training then become important (Beukelman & Mirenda, 1992). If the student uses gestures or signs, a chart explaining what these mean so that hospital staff will understand is necessary. Also, if encoding or scanning is used, simple directions for hospital personnel to help the communication system be effective is vital.

Specific vocabulary to be used in a hospital setting also needs careful evaluation. A reliable motor response indicating yes/no is important and may initially be all that is necessary for communication to take place when the student is quite ill. This can be in terms of a thumb up or down, eye blinks, raised fingers, a hand squeeze, or other consistent movement (Glennen & DeCoste, 1997). Expansion of the vocabulary is usually necessary to address wants and needs, questions about what is going on, and requests for items and others.

The content of communication boards will vary depending on the individual. Some communication systems may center around a few choices indicating basic health needs (e.g., giving words and/or pictures for pain, nausea, "I want Mom," better, not better), while others may have several categories (as in Figure 3-3) (Mitsuda, Baarsiag-Benson, Hazel, & Therriault, 1992). Sometimes, separate topic pages or topic communication boards are developed especially for use in the hospital setting in addition to the student's regular communication. In other situations, such vocabulary is integrated into the student's existing system.

Regardless of the type of communication system selected for hospital use, the vocabulary and communication system can be learned before hospitalization occurs so that the student will be prepared to communicate using it. As seen in the example in Figure 3-3, the vocabulary is general enough to meet the needs for many different hospitalization situations. More specific vocab-

---

Communication Protocol for: _____ *Mary Smith* _____

1. Mary uses CHIN MOVEMENTS to answer YES/NO questions.

   Yes = Moves chin up and down (open and close mouth)
   No = Moves chin sideways motion (back and forth)

2. Mary uses a COMMUNICATION BOARD to communicate basic WANTS.

   Point to each choice, and Mary will indicate yes or no with her chin movements.

3. Mary can SPELL using page 2 of her COMMUNICATION BOARD.

   Point to each row of letters for her to select the row the letter is on with her Yes/No.

   Then point to each individual letter on that row, and she will indicate yes with her chin movement when you are pointing to the correct letter.

Specific directions are on back of the communication board.

Communication board is on the table on the right side of the bed. Please return it there when finished.

For information or questions call:
   Jackie Marsh   or   Sherry Miller
   Speech Language Pathologist   Special Education Teacher
   Briarwood School   Briarwood School
   (404) 651-1111   (404) 651-1111
   (404) 773-2190 beeper

FIGURE 3-4 Sample communication protocol for the hospital setting

ulary can be added if planning for a specific scheduled hospitalization or after an unexpected hospital admission. For example, a student being scheduled for surgery may want to include "Sign my cast." If the student was hospitalized in an emergency, vocabulary such as "I want off the ventilator" may be desired.

Depending on the hospitalized student's communication system, a communication protocol should be in place that provides instructions to other medical staff about the communication system and its uses (Glennen & DeCoste, 1997). This protocol is usually placed in front of the patient's medical chart and by the bedside (see Figure 3-4 for a sample of a communication protocol).

INSTRUCTIONAL STRATEGIES FOR AAC

Students who have physical and health needs and require an augmentative communication system will need to be systematically taught how to use the system. Typically, the AAC system is taught on an ongoing basis and integrated into natural daily activities (Glennen & DeCoste, 1997). The student should have continual access to his or her communication system, and communication opportunities should be planned throughout the day. Situations may be set up at snack time when the student is to request a tube feeding, for example, or to request getting out of the wheelchair to stretch out on the floor. No communicative attempt should be ignored, and responses to the student's attempts at communication should be consistent and predictable. Continual use of the communication system across activities, people, and environments is crucial for learning to use the device effectively and efficiently.

Multiple techniques can teach the student how to use the system. Students may be prompted (using a system of least prompts, maximal prompts, or time delay) to touch a symbol, make a gesture, or look at a picture and immediately receive the context of the symbol (e.g., student touches a picture of crackers and receives the cracker, which is reinforcing for the student). Some students may learn by direct instruction and modeling in which the instructor teaches the use of the system and a communication partner uses the student's AAC system to converse with the student. This can help teach the student how to use the communication system and appropriate use of the vocabulary, as well as help with comprehension by pairing the symbol with the spoken word (Light, 1997; Romski & Sevcik, 1996).

Students need to be taught both the vocabulary as well as the type(s) of communication systems. The methodology used to teach the student their communication system will be nearly the same as that used to teach the communication system for health and physical concerns. The difference deals with the topic and the frequency with which some topics may occur.

In regard to health needs and wants, students need to understand the differences among *pain, sick,* and *nauseous,* if these terms are to be used as part of their AAC system. Students of normal intelligence who have heard these terms as applied to people may comprehend them and only need to learn the symbol, word, or sign that corresponds to them. These terms can also be introduced when the student displays symptoms of pain, feeling poorly, or nausea/vomiting. Instruction is more difficult when the student does not comprehend a term's meaning. Students may indicate that something is wrong through behaviors such as crying or facial expressions of discomfort. Such nonverbal means may be considered the most reliable form of communication to use in these situations. Another option is for the student to learn a symbol meaning generally "feel bad" and then how to access this symbol (e.g., on a communication device) or to make a sign and receive assistance.

Students learning to direct their own care would be taught to do so when the procedure is being performed. They would learn to select each phrase, word, gesture, or symbol indicating each step of the procedure, then it would be carried out. Unlike teaching other communicative functions in which the communicative partner carries out what is selected even if it is incorrect (to teach the relationship between what is selected and what happens), the person doing the procedure would correct the student so that the procedure would not be done improperly. Steps of the procedure may be arranged in a particular order to help retain the sequence of steps. The teacher can assess for comprehension and teach appropriate vocabulary use by starting to do a step out of sequence or something incorrect for the student to use such vocabulary as "You are doing it wrong." Of course, the procedure must never be done incorrectly since it could be injurious to the student.

Students who may be preparing to go to the hospital cannot practice the use of the communication system in the natural environment. Instead, some preparatory teaching and practice are necessary. Since it is often important to have multiple forms of communication available, especially to meet the student's needs in the hospital setting, students should be taught multiple ways to communicate. Often parallel training is used in which the student simultaneously learns different forms of communication. The student may learn a gesture for "yes," "no," "Bathroom," and "Help me" and use a communication board for other target vocabulary, in addition to an electronic communication device. This system allows the student to communicate using several modalities and will prepare the student for effective communication when the electronic communication device is not available or accessible, such as in some hospital settings. When teaching multiple forms of communication, it is sometimes helpful to keep training activities distinctly separate (Glennen & DeCoste, 1997). For example, the student may use the encoding technique when out of the wheelchair, the electronic device when in the wheelchair, and gestures when engaging in certain activities.

Another aspect of training is being sure that the student's communication partners are trained in how to communicate with the student (Heller, Alberto, & Bowdin, 1995). If school system personnel are unfamiliar with how the student communicates, the student's messages may be misunderstood or ignored. All personnel in contact with the student should thus receive training. This also applies to staff in the hospital who will come in contact with the student if hospitalization occurs. One study found that patients using AAC considered inservice training of hospital staff with AAC techniques important for effective communication to occur (Fried-Oken et al., 1991). Family members play a major role in offering such training as well as selecting vocabulary, as do the student's teachers, the student, and other team members.

SUMMARY

Students who are unable to speak effectively may have any number of different AAC systems to meet their needs. Besides addressing academic and social needs, the student also must be able to communicate health issues, including specific health needs, vocabulary to direct someone in performing the student's health care procedure, and means to communicate in a hospital setting. Through a team approach, decisions can be made regarding the system, vocabulary, means of access, as well as the appropriate vocabulary for addressing each student's particular health needs.

4

Medications and Procedures for Administration

KATHRYN WOLFF HELLER,
LEE WOLFF,
PAULA FORNEY,
PAUL ALBERTO,
MORTON SCHWARTZMANN,
AND TRUDY GOECKEL

It is not uncommon for school-age children to require medication during school hours. For students with physical and health impairments, it becomes even more likely. Medications may range from those taken daily for a chronic or acute disorder (e.g., a seizure disorder or respiratory infection) to medication taken on the onset of certain symptoms (e.g., medication taken for an asthma attack). In each instance, the medication will need to be taken correctly and with knowledge regarding the purposes and effects of the medication.

Several individuals may be involved in administering medication at school—the teacher, school nurse, paraprofessional, secretary, and the student (Graff et al., 1990). In one study (Heller et al., 1997), 59% of the teachers were responsible solely or in combination with another person for medication administration. The nurse was the second most likely person responsible for giving medications.

Teachers and other school personnel need to have knowledge about the effects of their students' medication, regardless of who is responsible for administering it, for two reasons. First, the effects of the medication may interfere with the student's optimal performance on school tasks. Medication has been identified as one of the major variables that can affect school performance (Heller, Alberto, Forney, et al., 1996). Although medication is used to manage many conditions effectively, all medications have potential side effects that may interfere with student performance. For example, many medications taken to control seizures may cause fatigue, and some asthma medications may result in tremors, jitteriness, and decreased ability to concentrate on tasks (Pellock, 1984; *Physicians' Desk Reference,* 1999). A student's ability to perform the tasks described in this book, for example, could be affected by her medications. By knowing the side effects of medications, teachers may target certain times of day as more ideal for instruction and identify variance in performance due to medication effects. Measures can often be taken to minimize effects, such as scheduling when medications are taken (along with the physician) or providing breaks. (Side effects are further discussed in this chapter under "Problems and Emergencies.")

A second reason for being knowledgeable about medication is to be able to report the medication's effectiveness and side effects. Physicians and parents will rely on school personnel to be alert for the effects of the medication and to report their observations. Often medication changes will be necessary if the side effects interfere too much with the student's activities or if the medication does not appear to be effective.

Prior to learning about specific medications, it is helpful to have some understanding of basic pharmacology, the study of the action of chemical substances on living tissue. Where such action is primarily beneficial, the field is termed *therapeutics;* if the action is primarily harmful, the field is termed *toxicology.* People receive therapeutic drugs to (a) treat disease (e.g., antibiotics for bacterial infections), (b) prevent disease (e.g., vaccine to prevent rubella), and (c) aid in diagnosis of disease (e.g., TB tests).

For a medication to have an effect, it must be absorbed into the body and distributed to the significant parts of the body for which the medication is intended. For the effect of the medication to be terminated, the medication must be broken down into inactive substances that are excreted from the body (Gadow, 1986). This four-part process of absorption, distribution, biotransformation, and excretion plays a vital role in proper medication management.

Absorption refers to the manner in which the medication enters the body. Medication is made to be absorbed in a certain manner. Some medications are swallowed, while others are inhaled. Others may be absorbed through the skin, eyes, ears, or nose, or rectum. Still others are injected. Some drugs are made in a variety of absorption routes. For example, Imitrex (for migraines) is made in tablet, injection, and nasal spray forms. The nasal spray is absorbed the fastest, followed by injection, then oral administration. How fast the medication is absorbed will depend on the route of administration as well as individual factors. Typically, taking medication by injection will result in a much faster absorption rate than taking medication orally. Drugs that are taken by mouth are dissolved by the fluids in the stomach and intestine and then travel through the cell lining of the stomach and intestines into the body's blood vessels. How quickly and how well the medication is absorbed may be influenced by the chemical composition of the drug, presence of other drugs or foods, acidity of the stomach, illness, and other individual differences. Some of these factors can be controlled, such as the presence of other drugs or foods. It is important to know when these factors can affect absorption. For example, knowing that a drug needs to be taken 1 hour before or 2 hours after eating due to the possible interference of absorption with food will determine the optimal time to give the medication.

Distribution is the movement of the drug throughout the body. The drug's composition will determine the main sites of distribution and how concentrated the drug will be at those sites. Upon entering the bloodstream, a percentage of the drug molecules will bind to the circulating plasma proteins. Plasma-bound molecules will be unable to pass from the bloodstream because of their size and will exert no effect on the body. Those that do not bind (unbound drugs) will pass from the bloodstream and bind to receptor sites in various tissues to exert an effect. Some bound molecules will become unbound as the body tries to maintain an even ratio of bound and unbound drug molecules. The distribution of the drug can also vary from one person to another because of differences in the amount of proteins and binding sites available, the influence of pathological and physiological conditions, the presence of substances that can compete for protein binding, and body weight and age (affecting protein-binding characteristics, hemodynamic factors, and composition and size of body water compartments) (Behrman, 1992). Distribution is thus one of the areas that will affect dosage.

The body also protects the brain from the distribution of many drugs. A blood-brain barrier exists that refers to the ability of the brain's capillaries to prevent certain classes of drugs from entering the brain. This protects the nervous system from alteration from many chemicals in the food we eat and many prescribed medications. A specific class of drugs, termed *psychotropic drugs,* are designed to traverse the blood-brain barrier to exert an effect.

The last two processes that occur to drugs are metabolism (also known as *biotransformation*) and excretion. *Metabolism* refers to the process of breaking down the drugs into typically inactive compounds that can be removed from the body. The liver is primarily responsible for breaking down the drugs. *Excretion* is the process of eliminating the metabolized drug out of the body, which primarily occurs through the kidneys. Drugs vary in how quickly they are metabolized and excreted. Some drugs are metabolized in a fraction of a second, resulting in no clinical usefulness. Others may be metabolized in a few minutes, a few hours, days, or weeks. The duration of action can be modified by the route of administration; drugs given intravenously, for example, often have a shorter duration of action than those given orally. The rate a drug is metabolized and excreted can be affected by the presence of another drug or chemical as well as genetic factors (Behrman, 1992; Gadow, 1986). Therefore, the duration of a drug's action can vary so that some individuals may experience the effect of a drug for a longer or shorter period of time than others.

Absorption, distribution, metabolism, and excretion all play a part in medication management, and people's bodies vary as to how they react to drugs and how they carry out these four processes. With such differentiation in mind, to obtain the correct dosage of certain drugs, a small dose is first given, then it is gradually increased until the desired effect occurs. This is called **titration.** Titration is especially apparent in the antiseizure medications in which the amount of a medication administered has little to do with the amount in the bloodstream. Dosages can therefore greatly vary among students, and monitoring blood levels of the drug is necessary to assess proper dosage.

Drug interactions may occur between medications. One way drugs interact is through an alteration in absorption, distribution, metabolism, and excretion of one drug by another. Some drugs or compounds may partially block the absorption of another, such as drinking milk and taking the antibiotic drug tetracycline. Distribution of a drug may be affected if one drug primarily binds to the plasma protein, leaving an increase of the other drug unbound. This condition in turn can result in a rapid increase in the second drug's effects. One drug could also affect the metabolism and excretion of another, resulting in longer effect of the drug and unwanted side effects or a more pronounced therapeutic effect. Although some drugs may be prescribed together to enhance an effect, care must be taken that certain drug combinations are avoided because of the interference of one drug or the possibility of an additive effect between two drugs. For example, taking alcohol and barbiturates in the same time frame results in an additive effect that could be lethal (Gadow, 1986). Precautions and contraindications exist with certain medications to prevent these undesirable effects, and the person administering the medication should know and understand what drugs (or foods) cannot be taken with the student's medication.

DESCRIPTION OF MEDICATIONS AND ADMINISTRATION CONSIDERATIONS

Some of the categories of medications commonly prescribed for students with physical developmental disabilities include (a) antiepileptic (antiseizure) medication (for treatment of seizures), (b) antispasticity (to decrease spasticity in such conditions as cerebral palsy), (c) antireflux (to decease the backing up of stomach contents into the esophagus as found in gastroesophageal reflux), (d) antibiotic (to fight bacterial infections), (e) mood or psychotropic drugs (to modify mood and disruptive behaviors, such as antidepressants, CNS stimulants, and sedatives), (f) skin medications (to treat skin ulcers, allergic reactions, rashes, etc.), and (g) respiratory medications (to improve breathing and air exchange) (Batshaw et al., 1996). Table 4-1 presents some examples of these medications.

Students with significant health impairments may receive many other types of medications. Some of these additional medications include (a) cardiovascular medications (to treat heart and circulation conditions), (b) insulin (to treat diabetes) or other endocrinologic medications (to treat other endocrine conditions such as thyroid problems), (c) clotting factors (to treat hemophilia), (d) antineoplastic agents (chemotherapy, to treat cancer), (e) pain medication (to treat injuries, sickle-cell anemia crisis, juvenile rheumatoid arthritis, and others), and (f) fluid and electrolyte preparations (for treatment of end-stage renal disease and others). It is important that the person administering the medication—and the student, when possible—know the name of the medication and what it is to treat.

Some students may receive **prescription drugs,** which require a physician's order. In some cases, less potent drugs that serve in the treatment of many minor medical conditions may be used that do not require a physician's order. These are referred to as **over-the-counter (OTC) drugs.** It is important to note that drug interactions may

occur between two drugs regardless of whether they are prescription drugs, so a physician or pharmacist should be consulted when multiple drugs are being taken.

Both prescription and OTC drugs may be referred to by their **trade** or **generic name.** The trade name is the name of the drug given by the pharmaceutical company who patented the drug. After the patent of the drug ends with the original pharmaceutical company, other pharmaceutical companies can manufacture the drug. These other manufacturers sell the drug under the drug's generic name, which is the name of the drug's chemical compound. Generic drugs have the same chemical composition as their trade name counterpart but typically cost less. In a few instances, some physicians will insist that the trade name drug be taken over the generic name drug, due to possible slight differences in absorption rates between certain drugs or slight differences in making the medication. Most drug reference books will indicate both the trade and generic names.

Permission to Administer Medication at School

Both prescription and OTC drugs require permission from the parent and/or physician to be given at school (Urbano, 1992). This point should not be taken lightly, because a drug given by even well-meaning school personnel without permission may react with a medication the student is receiving at home or may be contraindicated given the student's condition. The student may have a dangerous reaction as a result. For example, giving a child on seizure medication certain cold remedies could result in additive drowsiness or diminish the effect of the seizure medication. Giving a child with a certain type of asthma an aspirin may result in a serious asthma attack.

Depending on school policy, a current prescription label on the medication bottle may be acceptable in addition to the parent's written request. If the medication is an OTC drug, the school still needs approval to be certain that the medication is not contraindicated owing to the stu-

Table 4-1 Medications Commonly Prescribed for Students with Physical and Developmental Disabilities

Antiepileptic	Antispasticity	Antireflux	Antibiotic	Mood	Skin	Respiratory
ACTH (Corticotropin)	Alprazolam (Xanax)	Cimetidine (Tagamet)	Acyclovir (Zovirax)	*CNS Stimulants*	Benzoyl peroxide (Clearasil, Oxy, Fostex, Desquam X)	Albuterol (Ventolin, Proventil)
Carbamazepine (Tegretol)	Baclofen, intrathecal	Cisapride (Propulsid)	Amoxicillin (Amoxil)	Adderall	Calcium undecylenate 10% (Caldesene powder)	Beclomethasone (Beclovent, Vanceril)
Clonazepam (Klonopin)	Baclofen, oral (Lioresal)	Famotidine (Pepcid)	Amoxicillin + clavulanic acid (Augmentin)	Clonidine hydrochloride (Catapres)	Cetyl alcohol (Cetaphil)	Cromolyn (Intal)
Ethosuximide (Zarontin)	Clonazepam (Klonopin)	Magnesium hydroxide + aluminium hydroxide (Maalox)	Cefixime (Suprax)	Dextroamphetamine sulfate (Dexedrine)	Chloroxine 2% (Capitrol)	Flunisolide (Aerobid)
Felbamate (Felbatol)	Dantrolene sodium (Dantrium)	Metoclopramide (Reglan)	Cefuroxime (Ceftin)	Methylphenidate hydrochloride (Ritalin)	Clindamycin (Cleocin-T)	Ipratropium bromide (Atrovent)
Gabapentin (Neurontin)	Diazepam (Valium)	Ranitidine (Zantac)	Cephalexin (Keflex)	Nortriptyline (Pamelor)	Clotrimazole 1% (Lotrimin, Mycelex)	Metaproterenol (Alupent, Metaprel)
Lamotrigine (Lamictal)			Cephradine (Velosef)	Pemoline (Cylert)	Colloidal oatmeal (Aveeno)	Prednisone and methylprednisolone (Solu-Medrol, Medrol)
Phenobarbital (Luminal)			Clarithromycin (Biaxin)	Sertraline (Zoloft)	Crotamiton (Eurax)	Salmeterol (Serevent)
Phenytoin (Dilantin)			Cloxacillin (Tegopen)	*Antidepressants*	Erythromycin 2% (T-Stat)	Terbutaline (Brethine, Azmacort)
Primidone (Mysoline)			Dicloxacillin (Pathocil)	Amitriptyline hydrochloride (Elavil)	Griseofulvin (Fulvicin)	Theophylline (Theo-Dur, Slo-Bid, Uniphyl, Aerolate)
Valproic acid (Depakene, Depakote)			Erythromycin (various brands)	Desipramine hydrochloride (Norpramin)	Hydrocortisone (Caldecort Cort-Dome, Hytone)	Triamcinolone (Azmacort)
			Nystatin (Mycostatin)	Fluoxetine (Prozac)	Hydrocortisone + Polymyxin B + Neomycin (Cortisporin)	
			Penicillin (Pen Vee K)	Imipramine (Janimine, Tofranil)	Lanolin oil (Balmex)	
			Sulfisoxazole (Gantrisin)	*Antipsychotics*	Lanolin (A & D ointment)	
			Trimethoprim + sulfamethoxazole (Bactrim, Septra)	Chlorpromazine hydrochloride (Thorazine)	Lindane (Kwell)	
				Haloperidol (Haldol)	Miconazole 2% (Monistat)	
				Thioridazine (Mellaril)	Mineral oil (Lubriderm, Nivea)	
				Thiothixene (Navane)	Mineral oil (Alpha Keri)	
					Mupirocin 2% (Bactroban)	
					Nystatin (Mycostatin)	
					Permethrin 5% (Elimite)	
					Permethrin 1% (Nix)	
					Petrolatum (Eucerin)	
					Retinoic acid derivative (Accutane)	
					Selenium sulfide 2.5% (Selsun Blue)	
					Tetracycline (Sumycin)	
					Tolnaftate (Tinactin)	
					Triamcinolone (Kenalog, Aristocort)	
					Zinc oxide (Caldesene ointment)	

SOURCE: Reprinted with permission from Kurtz et al., *Handbook of Developmental Disabilities: Resources for Interdisciplinary Care*, p. 401, © 1996, Aspen Publishers, Inc.

dent's medical condition or adverse reactions with other medications the student is currently taking.

As seen in Figure 4-1, the physician's permission form contains the student's name, address, date of birth, name of medication (or procedure), dose, and times of administration. The medication will usually be specified to be taken at a certain time, often to permit a constant level of the medication in the bloodstream (Urbano, 1992). However, in some cases the medication may be ordered to be taken **p.r.n.,** or as needed. For example, a student may use his inhaler with a bronchodilator when he has an asthma attack. The form should specify when a p.r.n. drug should be taken as well as any other special instructions or precautions. The reason for the medication and possible side effects should also be specified, as well as the course of action should these side effects occur. The beginning and ending dates of the medication are important to include. Finally, the physician's name, telephone number, address, and signature should also be on the form.

A parent's (or guardian's) permission form is similar to the physician's form and may be included on the same form (see Figure 4-1). It contains the physician's name and phone number and a statement giving authorization for the school to give medication (or perform a health care procedure) in the school setting (Urbano, 1992). There should be a statement specifying that the parent will notify the school of any changes in the student's medication or dosage. Some forms also state that the parent is responsible for ensuring the medication arrives at school and for getting refills of the medication. There is also a place for the parent to sign.

Receiving and Storing Medication

Medication should only be accepted by the school when it is accompanied with a permission form. School personnel cannot give medication if a permission form is not signed. Also, the expiration date should be checked upon receiving the medication. If it has expired, the medication should not be given and the parent should be immediately contacted.

Medication should only be accepted in its original container along with the student's name on the container, name of medication, dosage, and frequency of administration. Prescription drugs should display the prescription label on the container as well as the dates of prescription and expiration. These provisions are important to assure the proper medication is given. The pharmacy's and physician's phone numbers should be on the label so they can be easily contacted if any questions arise. Parents should be informed that pharmacists will gladly supply a second prescription bottle with the relevant information when asked. In that way, the parent can divide up the medication between the two bottles to keep some at school and some at home.

School personnel who receive the medication should first check how the medication should be stored. Some medication should not be exposed to light, while others require refrigeration. Medication should be stored in its original container and placed in a locked storage area or a designated place in a secure refrigerator. Refrigerated medications are usually placed in a box in the refrigerator, and the box should be locked if students have access to the refrigerator. The medication should never be stored in the refrigerator door, since frequent opening of the refrigerator may not keep that portion of the refrigerator cool enough for the medication (Heller et al., 1992).

Safety Precautions for Administration

Several safety precautions need to be followed prior to administering the medication. First, the integrity of the medication needs to be checked. The person administering the medication should check the medication's expiration date, not only upon receiving the medication but prior to administering it. Sometimes medication only specifies the month and year of expiration, instead of a full date. When only a month is given, that means that the medication expires at the end of the month, not the beginning. If a medication has expired, the parent should be contacted immediately and the medication should not be given.

Authorization to Administer Medication or Health Care Procedure to a Student While in School

Student_____ Date of birth_____

Address_____

Physician's Authorization

Name of medication or procedure_____

Dosage of medication_____

Time(s) medication (or procedure) is to be given during the school day_____

Expected duration of administration of medication (or procedure)_____

Steps of health care procedure with approval or modifications attached? (yes/no)

Possible side effects and actions to take_____

Special directions:

_____   _____   _____
(Physician's signature)   (Please print physician's name)   (Date)

Physician's phone number_____

Physician's address_____

Parent's or Guardian's Authorization

I hereby request Toon's Public School System, through its designated authority, to administer to my child the medication (or perform the health care procedure) herewith provided according to the instructions contained on the attached physician's statement. I understand I am responsible for notifying the school of any changes in the medication or health care procedure. I understand that administration of the medication or performance of the health care procedure will terminate at the end of the school year and a new form will need to be submitted by the beginning of the next school year. Also, I understand that all medication must be sent in the prescription bottle or it will not be given. I understand that a nurse or a trained teacher will be giving the medication or performing the health care procedure.

_____   _____
Parent's/guardian's signature   Date

FIGURE 4-1 Sample medication/health care procedure permission form

MONTHLY MEDICATION/PROCEDURE REPORT

Student's name _____   Month _____

Directions: Write the medications/procedures, dates and times for each week. At the beginning of each day, write in the times for that day. When procedure is performed, cross out time and initial. If not done, circle time. If done at different time, circle time and record new time.

Meds/Procedure	Dates	Time(s)	Mon.	Tues.	Wed.	Thurs.	Fri.

Meds/Procedure	Dates	Time(s)	Mon.	Tues.	Wed.	Thurs.	Fri.

Meds/Procedure	Dates	Time(s)	Mon.	Tues.	Wed.	Thurs.	Fri.

Meds/Procedure	Dates	Time(s)	Mon.	Tues.	Wed.	Thurs.	Fri.

Comments:

FIGURE 4-2 Monthly medication/procedure report

Medication should also be checked to be sure it has not "gone bad." If it has changed in odor, color, or consistency, it should be withheld and the parent contacted immediately. If the person giving the medication is unsure about its condition, he or she should contact the pharmacist.

If a new medication has been prescribed, the parent should be the first to give the dose and observe for adverse effects, since such effects or an allergic reaction is always possible. Although the student's teachers and person administering the medication should be knowledgeable regarding the possible effects of the medication and should observe for them, it is the parent's responsibility to give the first dose.

The person administering the medication should check the Five *R*s: (a) right student, (b) right drug, (c) right dose, (d) right route, and (e) right time (Ashcroft & Smith, 1993; Skale, 1992). In addition, any precautions should be noted, such as whether the medication needs to be taken with food. Typically, the medication label should be read three times to prevent accidental administration: when taking it out of storage, before giving it, and before returning it to storage (Heller et al., 1992).

Documentation of Administration

A record of administration needs to be kept that specifies when medications are given in the school setting. This is important for several reasons. First, it can help prevent medication errors. As discussed later in the chapter under "Problems and Emergencies," prompt documentation that the medication was given at a specific time will prevent inadvertent readministration by another person or omission of a dose. Also, having a form to document that the medication was given can serve as a legal document showing that the school followed doctor's orders for administration of a medication. A medication record noting important information such as length of time medication has been given and frequency of administration may be needed at a later date.

There are several different types of medication forms. The monthly form discussed in Chapter 1 can combine not only health care procedures but medications as well. As seen in Figure 4-2, the medication (or health care procedure) is specified in the first blank and should include the dosage and route. Dates and times for administration of the medication are placed in the next designated area. The times the medication is to be given that day are written out at the beginning of the day. When a medication is given, the time is crossed out under the appropriate day of the week and the initials of the person giving it are written beside the medication. If the medication was not given for some reason, the time is circled. If it was given at a different time, the original time is circled, and the time it was given is recorded. (See Chapter 1 for an example of a completed form.)

EQUIPMENT AND ASSISTIVE STRATEGIES FOR MEDICATION ADMINISTRATION

Certain principles should be followed when helping a student with a physical or health impairment take medication. First, the student should never be given a choice as to taking the medication or not. The medication is ordered and must be given. Second, some other choices *should* be given to allow the student some control over the situation, such as the type of juice to take the medication with or the place the injection occurs. Third, the student should never be lied to. For example, to tell the student that the medicine tastes good when in fact it does not merely makes the student distrustful. Also, to say that there is no medication in the food being served when the medication has been crushed and put into pudding may only result in the student's refusing to eat. Fourth, always give a brief explanation as to what is about to occur (Skale, 1992).

Medication can be given in several different ways (routes). Some of the most common ways encountered in the school setting include orally, with a feeding tube, topically (on the skin), via the respiratory route, via the nasal route, in the eyes (eye drops), in the ears (ear drops), rectally, by injection, and with a pump. Although all of these differ in the necessary body position of the student and the exact steps in administration, some steps are common across all routes and comprise the standard procedure for medication administration. The standard procedure to give the medication should include the following steps:

Steps in the Procedure for Standard Administration	Rationale
1. Wash hands.	This will help prevent the spread of infection.
2. Collect any equipment needed to administer the medication.	This will vary depending on the route (e.g., spoon, eye dropper, nebulizer, syringe).
3. Check the medication data sheet for administration. Get the medication. Medication label should be read three times: when taking it out of storage, before giving it, and before returning it to storage.	This will help prevent accidental administration of the wrong medication, wrong dose, wrong route, or missing any precautions.
4. Be certain you have the correct student, and provide a brief explanation of what you are going to do.	If you are unfamiliar with the student, ask the student his name. If the student is nonverbal, ask the teacher or aide. Each year, a picture of the student can be taken to be put on the permission form and/or medication form for a substitute's reference.
5. Position the student to be given the medication. Most medications will be given in a sitting or elevated position. See the following sections for optimal positions for each administration route.	The student should never be placed flat on his back because of the possibility of choking and vomiting. A physical therapist can help with positioning needs.
6. Give the medication. This will differ depending on how the medication is delivered (e.g., orally, topically). See the next sections for specific information.	Medication needs to be given in accordance to the physician and the procedures specific to the ordered route.
7. Stay with the student until you are sure it is all taken.	Some students may spit out the medication when the caregiver leaves.
8. Document that medication has been given.	This will help prevent errors and provide written proof of administration.
9. Observe the student for any side effects.	Many medications have side effects, but some effects will necessitate the medication or its dosage being changed. All side effects should be reported.

Oral Administration

Most medications that students will take at school will be given orally (also referred to as *p.o.* in medical terms), in a tablet, capsule, or liquid form. Certain tablets are designed to be swallowed, while others can be chewed. In some instances, students may have swallowing difficulties and the tablet may need to be crushed or the capsule opened and mixed with such things as water, pudding, apple sauce, syrup, or soft food. It is important that tablets are crushed or capsules opened only with the physician's permission since doing so may change the absorption. For example, time-released medications in capsule form can be altered if chewed instead of swallowed whole.

Oral medication, especially in liquid form, may use several different types of containers to give the medication. As seen in Figure 4-3, most containers will have a place to measure the medication and then may be administered by tilting up the container or slowly depressing a plunger to draw the medication into the plunger. A special brush is often included for cleaning.

The method of administration will depend on the student's oral-motor abilities and the ease of administration. The standard procedure for administering medication is followed (as described earlier) with specific directions regarding position and procedure for oral medications as follows:

Steps in the Procedure for Oral Medications	*Rationale*
Steps 1–4 same as those for the standard procedure for medication administration.	
5. Position the student for oral medication, in a sitting or elevated position.	The student should never be placed flat on his or her back, due to the possibility of choking and vomiting. A physical therapist can help with positioning needs.
6. Place the medication in the student's mouth. A dropper or syringe (without a needle) is placed along the side of the mouth and given slowly.	Medication is given slowly to prevent choking.
Place a tablet to be swallowed on the middle of the tongue and provide water.	Most individuals will need water or other liquid to swallow the tablet.
Place the medication mixed with food on the middle of the tongue.	If the student uses assistive feeding techniques to help with eating and swallowing, these would also be used here. (See Chapter 8 on feeding techniques.)
7. Stay with the student until you are sure it is all taken.	Some students may spit out medication when the adult leaves.
8. Follow standard procedure for documentation and observation.	

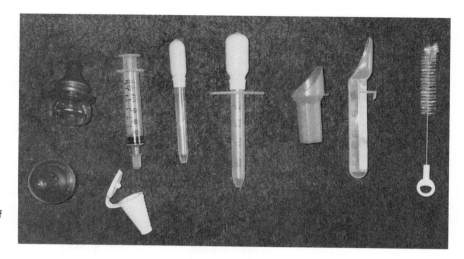

FIGURE 4-3 Examples of oral dosage containers and cleaning brush

Feeding Tube Administration

Some students have a G-tube (gastrostomy tube), gastrostomy button, or other type of tube going directly into their stomach or intestines. (See Chapter 9, "Tube Feeding," for a discussion of the types of tubes.) Medication may be prescribed to be given through the feeding tube (or other similar tube). This can be accomplished with liquid medications or medications that have been thoroughly crushed and mixed with a small amount of water, formula, milk, or juice. The amount of water or liquid it is being mixed with should be checked with the physician, especially if the student's treatment entails any liquid restrictions.

When medication is being given through the feeding tube, it should not be mixed with the student's food or formula to reduce the possibility of a blockage. Although blockages can be undone, the student may receive an incomplete dose since some medication may be lost in the process of unblocking the tube. The tube should always be flushed before and after administration. The feeding may occur before or after giving the medication or at a different time, depending on the frequency of administration and whether the medication should be taken with food. The procedure is as follows:

Steps in the Procedure for Feeding Tube	*Rationale*
Steps 1–4 same as those for the standard procedure for medication administration.	
5. Position the student for feeding tube administration. The student should be in an elevated position.	The student should never be placed flat on his back, because of the possibility of vomiting, then aspirating the medication.
6. Flush the feeding tube with water.	Flushing the feeding tube will assure patency.

Steps in the Procedure for Feeding Tube	*Rationale*
7. Give the medication through the feeding tube.	Follow standard procedures as discussed in Chapter 9 on tube feeding.
8. Flush the G-tube with water.	Flushing the tube with water will assure that all medication goes into the body rather than adhering to the sides of the tube.
9. If the student has food or formula to be given, it can be given after the medication is flushed.	Medication should be given separate from the student's food (nutrients) either before or after feeding or at a different time to avoid having any clogging of medication.
10. Document that the medication has been given, and observe for any side effects as discussed under the standard procedure.	Documentation will help prevent errors and provide written proof of administration. Side effects should be observed for and reported if they occur.

Topical Administration

Sometimes students may need a medication applied topically (i.e., on the skin). These medications may be supplied as creams and ointments. Creams and ointments should be applied sparingly in thin layers, unless otherwise specified. Use disposable gloves (remember to check whether the student has a latex allergy) in removing the medication from its container to avoid contamination of the medication as well as inadvertent medication absorption on the person applying it. Some creams will have an applicator or use a Q-tip for application. If the cream or ointment has dissolved, separated, or hardened, it should not be used. Creams and ointments should also not be applied to broken or infected skin.

Another method of topical administration is a transdermal patch, which is the application of medication by a skin patch. Patches are constructed so that the medication contained in the upper layers of the patch seep through a specifically designed membrane on the surface of the skin. From there, the medication continues to seep through the layers of the skin into the capillary bed where it enters the bloodstream. The patches are adhesive backed and are applied by placing on the specific location recommended by the manufacturer or physician. Generally, sites are rotated to minimize skin irritation (from adhesive backing), but patches should be placed where hair growth is minimal.

The procedure for using creams, ointments, or transdermal patches follows steps 1 through 4 and 7 through 9 as given in the standard procedure. However, the topical administration should follow the physician's orders of the specific location and amount of medication to administer.

Respiratory Administration

Some students, especially those with asthma, cystic fibrosis, and other respiratory illnesses, will require medication through the respiratory route. Although there are several methods of medication administration through the respiratory route, the most common methods found at school are through metered–dose inhalers and nebulizers.

A metered–dose inhaler is a small device that delivers medication in a premeasured amount. The physician specifies how many puffs or depressions of the medication is to be administered.

There are different techniques of administering the medication, depending on the physician's orders. In one method, the person places his or mouth over the opening of the inhaler (closed-mouth method), and in another method the person holds the inhaler 1 to 1½ inches in front of the open mouth (open-mouth method). A third method is using a spacer between the inhaler and the mouth (see Figure 4-4). A spacer may be used between the inhaler and the mouth to filter out small particles. It also serves as a reminder not to inhale too quickly, since many brands make a noise to indicate when the person breathes the medication in too fast.

The procedure for administering a metered-dose inhaler follows the standard procedure. However, the student must also do the following to assure that the medication is properly given:

FIGURE 4-4 Using an inhaler with a spacer

Steps in the Procedure for Inhaler Administration	Rationale
Steps 1–4 same as those for the standard procedure for medication administration.	
5. Position the student in an upright position, usually sitting.	Usually the student is to sit up to help lung expansion.
6. Shake the inhaler for 2 to 5 seconds (and put on the spacer if ordered).	Shaking mixes the medication.
7. Position the inhaler with the mouthpiece on the bottom and canister on the top. The index finger is usually on the top and the thumb on the bottom.	This allows for easy operation of the inhaler.
8. Have the student exhale normally to the end of breath.	Exhaling first will allow the student to take a deep breath in when inhaling the medication.
9. Place the inhaler in proper position using either closed- or open-mouth technique. a. *Closed-mouth technique:* Place the inhaler (with or without a spacer, as ordered) between the student's teeth, with the mouth closed around the mouthpiece.	The physician will determine the proper technique to use.

Steps in the Procedure for Inhaler Administration	*Rationale*

b. *Open-mouth technique:* Place the inhaler 1 to 1½ inches in front of the student with the student's mouth open (Nix, 1991c).

10. Administer the medication by firmly pushing down the canister toward the mouthpiece, which will deliver a "puff" of medication.

    a. *Closed-mouth technique:* Administer the puff first, then have student breathe slowly.

    b. *Open-mouth technique:* Have the student begin to breathe through the mouth first, then administer medication.

It is important that the medication is coordinated with the breathing. In the open-mouth technique, some medication may be lost if the student does not begin breathing first.

The student should breathe in slowly and as deeply as possible to get the medication to the lungs.

11. Have the student hold breath for approximately 10 seconds after breathing in, then exhale.

Holding the breath after slowly breathing in maximizes the amount of medication deposited in the lungs (Traver & Martinez, 1988).

12. If a second puff of medication is to be given, the student should wait 2 to 10 minutes (follow the physician's or drug manufacturer's instructions) before giving the second dose.

The time delay will allow the first dose time to dilate the airways and result in the second dose having a greater effect (Dunlap & Marchionno, 1983).

13. When completed, the student should rinse her mouth.

Rinsing helps prevent fungal infections.

14. Continue with the last steps of the standard procedure: documentation and observation.

The inhaler should be cleaned with warm water daily and taken apart to air dry. It should also be periodically checked to determine how full the canister is. This is accomplished by putting the canister in water and seeing whether it sinks (full) or floats (empty). A canister floating in a vertical position is half empty (see Figure 4–5).

A nebulizer is an aerosol machine that provides the medication in a mist that is inhaled through a mouth- or nosepiece. Although nebulizers come in different styles and sizes, all have (a) an air compressor; (b) tubing; (c) a nebulizer (medication) chamber; (d) a T-piece, spacer, or other attachment; and (e) a mouthpiece or mask

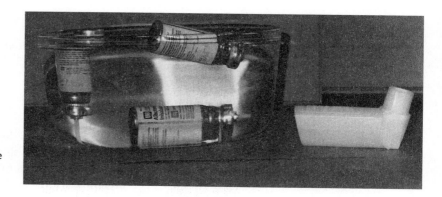

FIGURE 4-5 Canisters are taken out of their plastic holders (on the right) and placed in water to determine whether they float, which indicates they are empty.

(see Figure 4-6). Each of these fit easily together. The person administering the medication will need to be familiar with the equipment and how it is put together. A procedure for using a nebulizer is as follows:

Steps in the Procedure for Nebulizer	Rationale
Steps 1–4 same as those for the standard procedure for medication administration.	
5. Position the student in an upright position, usually sitting.	Usually the student is to sit up to help lung expansion.
6. Verify that the power switch is in the off position, and plug the nebulizer into a wall outlet.	
7. Assemble the equipment, placing the medication as ordered into the nebulizer (medication) chamber. Follow precise amounts of dosages ordered.	The assembly and type of medication chamber will vary. Figure 4-6 shows typical construction of one type of nebulizer.
8. Have the student put on the mask or mouthpiece. The mouthpiece fits between the teeth with the tongue below the mouthpiece.	For a mouthpiece to be effective, the student must have it properly placed and breathe only through the mouth, not the nose.
9. Instruct the student to breathe deeply.	Deep breathing will help the distribution of the medication in the lungs.
10. Turn on the nebulizer, and observe that mist is forming.	A fine, steady mist indicates the nebulizer is working.
11. Occasionally, the sides of the nebulizer chamber should be gently tapped.	Tapping allows any medication clinging to the sides of the chamber to drain to the bottom and be delivered into the mouth.

Steps in the Procedure for Nebulizer	*Rationale*
12. When the nebulizer chamber is empty and no mist is seen, turn off the nebulizer.	
13. Continue with observation and documentation as described in the standard procedure.	

The nebulizer chamber, T-tube, and mouthpiece or mask should be rinsed under warm tap water for at least 30 seconds to remove any excess medication after each use and air dried (Mackay,

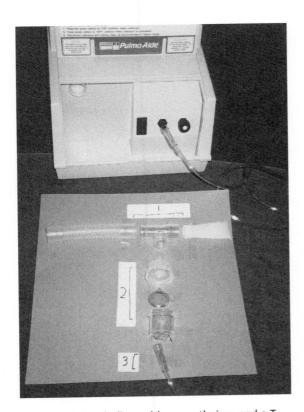

FIGURE 4-6 A nebulizer with a mouthpiece and a T-piece (identified as #1), medication chamber (identified as #2), connecting tube (indicated as #3), and the air compressor (the machine at the top of the photo).

1991). Once a day, this nebulizer equipment should be soaked in warm soapy water and then disinfected with a solution of one part vinegar and two parts water. After soaking the parts in this disinfectant, they need to be rinsed with tap water and allowed to air dry. The air tubing does not need to be cleaned since only compressed air goes through it. The air filter, located on the compressor, should be changed when it turns gray or on a monthly basis.

Nasal Administration

Medication given nasally in spray or dropper form may be prescribed for many conditions, ranging from simple decongestants for nasal congestion caused by infection or allergies to medications given for migraine headaches. Some of these medications (e.g., decongestants) target the nasal airways, while others (e.g., migraine medications) use the nasal airways as a rapid means of absorption to the blood vessels of the brain.

Nasal sprays will differ in their administration. Some sprays instruct the person to tilt the head back and breathe in while spraying the medication (e.g., Imitrex for migraines), while others direct the person not to tilt back the head or inhale while administering the medication (e.g., Migranal for migraines). It is very important that the precise method of nasal administration closely follow the manufacturer's or physician's orders. Some manufacturers will include a picture-prompting system of how to prepare the medication and administer it, especially when several steps are involved.

Steps in the Procedure for Nose Drops	*Rationale*
Steps 1–4 same as those for the standard procedure for medication administration.	
5. The position of the student is usually with the head tilted back and secure.	It is important that the head does not move about to prevent possible damage to the delicate lining of the nose.
6. Withdraw the prescribed amount of medication into the dropper (if necessary).	Most droppers will have markings on them indicating the amount. Some medications will come predrawn.
7. Insert the tip of the nose dropper slightly into the nose in an upward direction.	Care must be taken that the tip does not touch the sides of the nose to prevent contamination of the dropper.
8. Give the medication by depressing the dropper.	
9. The head should remain tilted back for 1 minute.	This time will promote absorption of the medication (Nix, 1991a).
10. Continue with documentation and observation of the student as described in the standard procedure.	

Ocular Administration
(Eye Drops and Eye Ointments)

Medications given in the form of eye drops or eye ointments are used to treat a variety of eye infections (e.g., conjunctivitis) and diseases (e.g., glaucoma). They are typically applied through the use of an eye dropper or are squeezed directly out of a tube into the eye.

Steps in the Procedure for Eye Medication	*Rationale*
Steps 1–4 same as those for the standard procedure for medication administration.	
5. Position the student with the head tilted back and slightly turned to the same side as the eye receiving the medication.	This position will help with proper absorption.
6. Instruct the student to look up.	Looking up will prevent spasms of the eyelid muscles.
7. The person administering the eye drops or ointment should place an index finger of the nondominant hand under the lower eyelid and gently pull the lid down.	This step will expose the conjunctival cul-de-sac in which the medication is given (see Figure 4-7a).

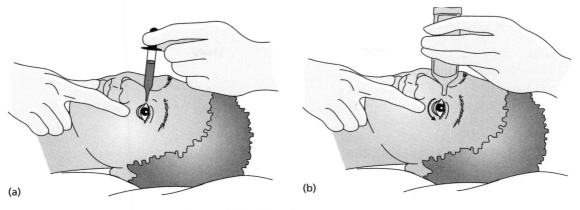

(a)   (b)

FIGURE 4-7 Administering (a) eye drops and (b) ointment

Steps in the Procedure for Eye Medication	*Rationale*

8. Give the medication:
  a. *Eye drops:* Squeeze the correct number of drops into the exposed area (i.e., the conjunctival cul-de-sac).
  b. *Eye ointments:* Squeeze a ½ inch into the exposed area (e.g., conjunctival cul-de-sac), beginning inward on the side near the nose and moving outward (toward the ear) (Figure 4-7b; Nix, 1991a).
	The eye dropper should not touch any part of the eye or face to avoid injury and/or contamination of the eye dropper. Blurring of vision may occur, especially after ointments.

9. After receiving eye drops or eye ointments, the student should keep the eyes closed for a few seconds or blink.	This helps distribute the medication.
10. Follow with documentation and observation as delineated in the standard procedure.	

Otic Administration (Ear Drops)

Ear drops are commonly prescribed for certain types of outer ear infections involving fungus or bacteria. Care must be taken that when ear drops are given, they are given at room temperature since cold ear drops can cause vertigo, pain, and/or nausea, and drops that are too warm can burn the ear (Nix, 1991a).

Steps in the Procedure for Ear Drops	*Rationale*

Steps 1–4 same as those for the standard procedure for medication administration.

5. Position the student with the head turned to one side.

   If drops are given in both ears, always start on the same side each time to avoid confusion if stopped in the middle of the procedure.

6. If the student is under 3 years old, pull the auricle (pinna) down and back (Figure 4-8a). If the student is older than 3, pull the auricle up and back (Figure 4-8b).

   This will allow the ear canal to be straightened to allow better entry of the medication.

7. Hold the dropper above the ear canal and administer the number of prescribed drops (Figure 4-8c).

   The dropper should not touch any part of the ear to avoid contamination of the dropper or injury to the ear.

8. Massage the area anterior to the ear for approximately 30 seconds (Figure 4-8d).

   This motion will help move medication down the ear canal to the ear drum (tympanic membrane).

9. Have the student remain on the side for 5 minutes. If cotton balls are ordered, place after 5 minutes into canal opening (not into canal).

   This will allow time for the ear drops to move into position and start becoming absorbed.

10. Repeat with the other ear, if ordered.

11. Continue with documentation and observation as specified under the standard procedure.

(a)

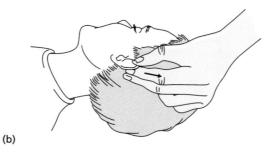

(b)

FIGURE 4-8 Administering ear drops. A student under 3 years of age needs the ear pulled downward (a) for correct administration, whereas a student over 3 years old needs the ear pulled upward (b). The dropper should not touch the ear (c), and the ear is massaged afterward (d).

Rectal Administration

Rectal administration may be used to allow local effects of the medication (e.g., suppository for constipation) or when the medication cannot be given orally (e.g., medication for migraine accompanied with nausea and vomiting). The most common form of rectal medication given in the school setting is typically suppositories. These are usually bullet shaped for ease of administration and designed to dissolve with body heat. This type of medication administration should occur in a private location with dignity and respect for the student.

Steps in the Procedure for Rectal Suppositories	*Rationale*
Steps 1–4 same as those for the standard procedure for medication administration.	
5. Position the student on her side.	An alternate position is on the stomach.
6. If indicated, lubricate the suppository with a water-soluble gel (e.g., K-Y Jelly).	Some suppositories are already lubricated or do not require lubrication.
7. With a gloved hand (check for a latex allergy) or finger cot, gently insert the suppository into the rectum, without inserting the finger farther than ½ inch past the rectal muscle. Remove finger.	Suppository administration should be done gently and without inserting a finger too far up the rectum to avoid injury.
8. Hold the buttocks together for 5 to 10 minutes (Skale, 1992).	This will help prevent expulsion of the medication.
9. Remove the glove and wash hands.	
10. Continue with documentation and observation as described under the standard procedure.	

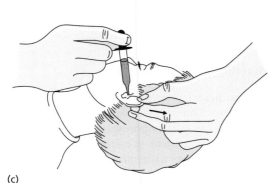

(c)

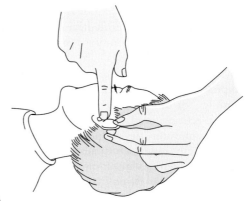

(d)

FIGURE 4-8 *(continued)*

Administration by Injection

All injections are not the same. They will differ in types of needles used, injection site, and injection type. There are four main types of injections: intradermal, subcutaneous, intramuscular, and intravenous (Elliott, 1991). It is important that the correct injection type is given with the ordered medication, since using the wrong type can result in ineffective medication administration or, in some cases, significant injury. For example, if the medication should be injected into a connective tissue layer of the body and instead is injected into a vein, the very rapid absorption of the medication could cause injury or even result in a life-threatening emergency.

Intradermal Injection. An intradermal injection is given within the dermal layer of the skin, just under the top (epidermal) layer of skin. It is a very shallow injection used for allergy testing, tuberculin skin testing, and other similar uses. It is usually given on the forearms, although the shoulder blade area, upper chest, and inner thigh have also been used. When properly given, a small bleb (raised or bubble-like area) forms.

Subcutaneous Injection. A subcutaneous injection is given into the connective tissues, directly below the dermal skin layer. Medication may be given subcutaneously when the medication cannot be taken by mouth (because of the student's inability to take medication that route or the medication's inability to withstand gastric juices of the stomach). It also provides a more rapid absorption than oral administration. Examples of medications given subcutaneously are insulin (for diabetes), epinephrine (for severe allergic reactions), and Imitrex (for migraines). The most common sites include the outer side of the upper arm, lower abdomen, and the top of the thighs. When giving a subcutaneous injection, it is important to pull back on the syringe plunger (aspirate) to determine whether a vein has been hit by mistake. If blood is seen, the end

of the needle is in a vein and will need to be withdrawn from that area to avoid giving the medication intravenously.

Intramuscular Injection. An intramuscular injection is given into a muscle, located below the subcutaneous level. Intramuscular injections provide a faster means of absorption than oral or subcutaneous routes. Some medications that are given intramuscularly include antibiotics, steroids, muscle relaxants, and epinephrine preparations such as Epi E-Z Pen for bee stings (*Physicians' Desk Reference,* 1999). The most common sites for intramuscular administration include the deltoid muscle in the upper arm, the vastus lateralis in the thigh, the dorsogluteal in the buttocks, and the ventrogluteal in the muscle on the side of the hip. When giving an intramuscular injection, it is important to pull back on the syringe plunger (aspirate) to determine whether a vein has been hit by mistake. If blood is seen, the end of the needle is in a vein and will need to be withdrawn from that area to avoid giving the medication intravenously.

Intravenous Injection. An intravenous injection is the administration of medication into a vein. This method provides the fastest means of absorption of all the injections. Many types of medications are given intravenously. One of the most commonly encountered intravenous medications in the school setting are clotting factors given to students with hemophilia when they have a bleed. Considerable skill and care must be taken that the medication is injected into a vein rather than intramuscularly or subcutaneously.

Indwelling Continuous Pumps

Some medications are infused over a continuous time frame. One of the ways this is done is through the use of continuous pumps that are partially or completely indwelling. One type of pump that teachers may encounter are *continuous subcutaneous insulin infusion (CSII) pumps,* also referred to as *insulin pump therapy.* These pumps consist of an external pumping device that is attached to tubing linked to a needle (or plastic catheter) that stays inside the person and is typically placed in the abdominal subcutaneous tissue. The pump is programmed to deliver specific amounts of insulin over time. The pump is often carried in a pocket or special pouch. Care must to taken that the tubing is not accidentally pulled.

Another type of pump is an *intrathecal baclofen infusion pump*. The programmable pump, about 3 inches in diameter, is surgically placed in the subcutaneous tissue and infuses baclofen into the superficial layers of the spinal cord. Its use is to relieve spasticity in the legs in conditions such as cerebral palsy, spinal cord injuries, and multiple sclerosis (Albright, 1995). The teacher should be aware of the location of the pump and any precautions that need to be taken.

INSTRUCTIONAL STRATEGIES

Students who take medications should participate in their treatment regime as much as possible. They should be taught what their medication is, when it should be taken, what the medication is for, and how it is to be delivered. Teaching this self-help skill will increase the student's independence.

Students may keep a picture schedule or a daily planner that indicates when it is time for their medication. They may then participate by asking for the medication at the appropriate time, which helps make them responsible for their own care.

Some students take their own medication under supervision. For some students this may consist of opening a package to get a tablet to swallow, while others may need to learn how to assemble a nebulizer and correctly inhale the medication. These skills may be task-analyzed and systematically taught (see an example of a task analysis in Figure 4-9). Some students, due to the severity of their physical impairment, may not be able to take their medication independently. In these instances, students may at least partially participate in the task by performing the steps they are capable of doing. Some students' physical disability is so great, however, that it is not possible for them physically to perform the steps. In these instances, the students can learn to direct another person in administering the medication. This scenario could be as simple as a boy telling another person it is time for his seizure medication, the tablet needs to be placed on his tongue, and he needs to be given plenty of water. It could be as complex as a girl directing someone through each step of providing medication through her feeding tube. Such instruction can be performed orally or through the use of augmentative communication (see Chapter 3 on communication).

Several types of medication containers can be used in instruction to help the student keep track of taking medication. Some containers are divided by the day; others have specific times. Some of these are also easier to manipulate and open than traditional containers. If the student is going to be taught to use these, it is important to be sure

1. Identify that it is time to take medication.
2. Wash hands.
3. Retrieve the inhaler medication.
4. Shake inhaler for 5 seconds.
5. Attach the spacer.
6. Exhale.
7. Put the mouth around spacer.
8. Push down on the inhaler canister.
9. Slowly breathe (so no sound is heard from spacer).
10. Hold breath for 10 seconds, then exhale.
11. Take apart the inhaler from the spacer.
12. Put the medication away.

FIGURE 4-9 Task analysis of administering inhaler medication

that the container is suitable for the medication ordered, since some medication requires containers that block light or are air-tight. A second consideration is the specification that medications need to be in their original containers at school. This requisite can usually be dealt with by taping the original container to the daily or weekly container.

PROBLEMS AND EMERGENCIES

Side Effects

Most drug treatments have side effects, also referred to as *untoward reactions, adverse reactions,* and *adverse drug reactions.* Side effects may range in severity from very mild and trivial to serious health concerns. The presentation of side effects will depend on the person's internal makeup. Most of the time, the possible side effects are predictable and well documented in any pharmacology book. (See Table 4-2 for examples of medications and potential side effects.) In some instances, the side effects go away after a short time or may continue throughout the duration of administration of the medication.

Side effects are sometimes unavoidable if adequate doses of the medication are given. The selection of the medication takes into account the possible side effects against the therapeutic value of the medication. However, if side effects significantly interfere with the person's daily living, the medication may need to be adjusted, or a different one may be prescribed in its place. For example, a child may be excessively drowsy from a seizure medication. The teacher may assume this behavior is due to fatigue when it is actually an unwanted side effect of the medication that may warrant changing. It is important that school personnel look up possible side effects that can arise with the student's medication and document any occurrence of them. If a side effect is suspected, the school personnel should contact the parent and physician to determine whether the next dose of medication should be given or whether a decrease in dosage is needed.

Allergic Reaction

A student may develop an allergic reaction to a medication at any time, even if she has been taking the medication for years. Allergic reactions may be mild and primarily consist of a rash or hives with itching. In some instances, there may be vomiting and irritability. Severe allergic reactions include difficulty or even cessation of breathing. In these more severe instances, CPR may need to be initiated and the paramedics called. School personnel should be ready to give the paramedics a card that lists the medications the student takes at school (along with dosage, times, and route). If the physician confirms an allergic reaction, the medication should never be given to the student again (Urbano, 1992). The school should have documented on the health record all allergies.

Tolerance

Medication dosages typically need to be increased as a child grows. They may also need to be increased because of the body developing a tolerance to the medication. **Tolerance** refers to the loss of the characteristic effect of the medication after repeated administrations. In some instances, this is a metabolic tolerance. A metabolic tolerance occurs when repeated administrations of the drug results in the drug being metabolized faster. The drug is then actively working in the body for a shorter time. Cellular (pharmacodynamic) tolerance may also occur in which the targeted cells actually adjust to the presence of the medication (Gadow, 1986). In both types of tolerance, the drug dosage will need to be increased to achieve the same therapeutic effect as before tolerance occurred.

Physical Dependence

Repeated use of medications may result in physical dependence. *Physical dependence* occurs when

Table 4-2 Sample Medications and Their Side Effects

Class	Drug	Problems associated with use (by class)[a]
Antacids	Amphogel Gelusil Maalox Mylanta	■ Most drugs in this class are constipating ■ Antacids containing aluminum salts can interfere with absorption of calcium and phosphorus
Antianxiety drugs	Ativan Buspar Librium Tranxene Valium Xanax	■ Sedation ■ Weakness/dizziness ■ Restlessness ■ Hearing loss ■ Blurred vision ■ Difficulty swallowing
Anticholinergics	Artane Cogentin Urecholine	■ Often used with psychotropic medication to prevent dyskinesia or extrapyramidal signs ■ Dry mouth, nose ■ Constipation ■ Slow stomach emptying, contributing to gastro-esophageal reflux ■ Sleepiness, lethargy ■ Rapid heart rate ■ Uncoordinated movement ■ Urinary retention ■ Decreased control of temperature regulation
Antidepressants[b]	Elavil Norpramin Pamelor Sinequan Tofranil Triavil	■ Extrapyramidal effects ■ Sun-sensitive skin ■ Headaches ■ Loss of appetite ■ Blurred vision ■ Constipation ■ Lowering of seizure threshold ■ Neck stiffness ■ High blood pressure
Antiemetics/GE reflux control agents	Emetrol Phenergan Reglan	■ Reglan lowers seizure threshold, possibly increasing seizure frequency ■ Nausea and vomiting ■ See other classes for specific effects
Antiepileptics	Thorazine Depakene Depakote Dilantin Klonopin Mysoline Phenobarbital Tegretol	■ Toxicity; lethargy or drowsiness ■ Constipation ■ Gingival hypertrophy ■ Poor appetite ■ Nausea or vomiting ■ Elevated liver enzymes or liver failure ■ Anemias

(continued)

Table 4-2 (*continued*)

Class	Drug	Problems associated with use (by class)[a]
Antiepileptics	Zarontin	■ Osteoporosis (These vary by medication: for specific effects of medications, see individual medications)
Bronchodilators	SioPhyllin Theo-Dur Theophylline	■ Stomach irritation/nausea ■ Arrhythmias/tachycardia ■ Insomnia ■ Jitteriness ■ Seizures ■ Relaxation of smooth muscle, including the lower esophageal sphincter, which may lead to gastroesophageal reflux
Histamine blockers	Tagamet Zantac	■ Constipation ■ Drowsiness ■ Slowing of gastric emptying due to decreased secretion of acid and enzymes (stomach pH must be sufficiently low for emptying to occur)
Laxatives/cathartics and bowel preparations	Castor oil Colace Dulcolax Fleet enema Glycerine suppositories Metamucil Modane Senokot Surfak	■ Dependence (for any bowel flow) ■ Abdominal cramping ■ Rectal irritation and sloughing of mucosa ■ Loss of electrolytes
Muscle relaxants	Dantrium Lioresal Valium	■ Weakness/tiredness/difficulty with voluntary movements, including swallowing ■ Severe respiratory failure ■ Increased sun sensitivity ■ Irritability
Psychotropics	Ativan Haldol Inderal Lithium Mellaril Moban Navane Prolixin Ritalin Seretil Stelazine	■ Blurred vision ■ Constipation ■ Increased appetite ■ Dry mouth ■ Nasal stuffiness ■ Skin rash ■ Increased sun sensitivity ■ Orthostatic hypotension ■ Extrapyramidal effects/tardive dyskinesia ■ Jaundice or skin discoloration
Stimulants	Cylert Dexedrine	■ High blood pressure ■ Tachycardia

(*continued*)

Table 4-2 (*continued*)

Class	Drug	Problems associated with use (by class)[a]
Stimulants	Ritalin	▪ Insomnia
		▪ Nausea or vomiting
		▪ Headache
		▪ Weight loss
		▪ Arrythmias
		▪ Restlessness
		▪ Skin rashes

SOURCE: L. Barks, L. Capozzi, C. Smith, and C. Tencza, *Health Building: Medications Reference Manual,* produced for the Oklahoma Department of Human Services (Winter Park, FL: Therapeutic Concepts, 1991). Reprinted by permission of Developmental Health, Inc.

[a]*Note:* Not every medication in each class is associated with the effects listed; see individual drug information.

[b]*Note:* Monoamine oxidase inhibitors (MAOIs) are also antidepressants. When taken with some other medications and foods, MAOIs can cause hypertension, liver damage, and death. MAOIs are usually not used for people with developmental disabilities.

the drug alters the physiological state of the body, and to prevent withdrawal symptoms, the person must receive continued administration of the drug. Another term for this situation is *addiction.* Physical dependence only occurs with certain drugs (e.g., nicotine, barbiturates). The symptoms of withdrawal are associated with the area targeted by the drug and may result in symptoms opposite of the drug effect. For example, suddenly stopping an antiseizure medication (e.g., phenobarbital) may result in a seizure. It is crucial that the dosage of certain drugs are slowly lowered over a period of time before discontinuing a drug to prevent withdrawal effects.

Missed Dosage and Overmedication

Medication may be given improperly, resulting in a missed dose or overmedication. A missed dose may occur owing to forgetfulness or a lack of compliance with the drug regime. For drugs that require a certain blood level to be effective, several missed dosages may result in the drug being ineffective for a period of time until a steady blood level can again be secured. Also, if several doses are missed or the drug is suddenly stopped, the student may have a severe withdrawal reaction.

Medication should be given as ordered. If the parent wants to discontinue the drug, the parent should inform the physician and ask how to do so safely. If school personnel forget to give a dose of medication, they should not just go ahead and give it when they think of it since it may be given too close to the next dose, resulting in overmedication. The school personnel should have on their IHP what action to take for a missed dose. This information can be obtained from the parent, pharmacist, and/or physician. In some instances, if the mistake is found within 1 or 2 hours of when the medication was scheduled, the school personnel are directed to go ahead and give the next dose and inform the parent so that the timing of the next dose can be adjusted. In other circumstances, the dose may be skipped, owing to the frequency of the drug administration and the closeness to the next dose.

Overmedication may occur in two different situations. In one, the caregiver may not understand the mechanism of the drug and decide to give more of the medication in the erroneous belief that it will be more effective. This could have fatal results. Overmedication may also result when two doses are given too close together (Urbano, 1986). This can happen when someone is trying to make up for a missed dose or when two people are giving medication and miscommunicate as to when the doses were given.

To help prevent omissions and overmedication, documentation of medication administration should occur at school. Documentation should be done directly after the medication is given. Looking at the documentation prior to giving the medication will prevent errors. Also, only one person should be responsible each day for the administration of the medication.

Incomplete Administration

Some medications may not be completely administered or completely taken, such as when the student vomits some of the medication, spits some out, or some inadvertently spills. If this occurs, it is important to know ahead of time whether the dose should be repeated. Sometimes it is harmful repeating the dose since the individual can receive more medication than should be taken. Not repeating the dose can also be harmful since an incomplete dose may be ineffective. Knowing ahead of time by consulting with parents, physician, and/or pharmacist is important to know how to address this situation. An incomplete dose should be noted on the medication sheet.

Wrong Medication or Dose

If the wrong medication or dose is given, the parent and physician should be notified to determine the effects of the medication given. It will be important to know what medication was given and the amount. In some instances, the student will need to be observed; in others, he or she may require an antidote or medication to induce vomiting. An incident report should be completed detailing what was incorrectly given, who was contacted, and what action was taken.

Proper precautions should prevent the wrong medication or dose being given. If the medication protocol is followed, it is unlikely that such an error will occur. This precaution includes storing

the medication in a safe place, checking the label three times, being sure to have the correct student, and carrying out proper documentation. (See the standard procedure for medication administration earlier in this chapter.)

Choking

Students with physical impairments may have difficulty swallowing liquid or tablet forms of medication. To prevent possible choking or aspiration, the student needs to be properly positioned, sitting in an upright position (the physical therapist on the team may assist with proper positioning techniques). A special feeding technique may be used if the student requires jaw or lip support or other assistance to swallow the medication (see Chapter 8, "Eating and Feeding Techniques"). If the student is tactually defensive, the team may develop a program of relaxation and desensitization, as well as provide suggestions for medication administration. The person administering the medication should be trained in the Heimlich maneuver in case choking occurs.

MANAGEMENT ISSUES

Individualized Health Plan and Individualized Educational Program

An individualized health plan (IHP) for a student should contain the typical information discussed in Chapter 1, as well as information about the medication the student is taking at school. This would include the type, dosage, route of administration, description of what it is for, potential side effects, and any precautions. Any student-specific guidelines for administration of the medication should be included in the IHP. A copy of the permission form will typically be attached to the IHP. The IHP should also contain guidelines for the following problems or emergencies: side effects, allergic reactions, missed dosages, incomplete dosages, and wrong dosages. A sample of the specialized infor-

Type of medication: _____

Dosage: _____

Frequency of administration: _____

Route of administration: _____

Purpose of medication: _____

Potential side effects: _____

Precautions and contraindications: _____

_____

Directions for problems and emergencies

Missed dose: _____

Incomplete dosage: _____

Wrong dosage: _____

Wrong time: _____

Wrong medication: _____

Overmedication: _____

Allergic reaction: _____

FIGURE 4-10 Specialized information to include on an IHP for administering medication

mation to include in the IHP for medication administration is provided in Figure 4-10.

The student's IEP should address what aspects of medication administration the student is learning. Areas of instruction may include (a) identifying times for medication administration, (b) knowing the names of medications and what they are for, (c) knowing the route of administration, (d) demonstrating how to take the medication, and (e) knowing the potential problems and emergencies and how to treat them. Objectives for this area may be divided into independent performance of task, partial performance of task, directing the task, and knowledge of the task (see Figure 4-11 for sample objectives).

Medications Taken as Needed (p.r.n.)

Some medications are taken on a p.r.n. (as-needed) basis. In some instances, these medica-

Independent Performance of Task

When provided with an hourly medication container, the student will tell the adult when it is time to take his medication and correctly select and take the medication with 100% accuracy for 2 weeks.

The student will properly assemble the nebulizer, place the correct amount of medication in the nebulizer, and correctly breathe into the nebulizer to self-administer his asthma medication with 100% accuracy for 2 weeks.

Partial Performance of Task

When told it is time for the student's ear drops, the student will assume the correct position with 80% accuracy for four consecutive sessions.

When taking medication through a nebulizer, the student will hold the mouthpiece in place and take deep, easy breaths, when reminded by an adult, with 100% accuracy for 1 week.

Directing the Task

When given a checklist, the student will direct another person in the steps for putting together the nebulizer with the appropriate medication with 100% accuracy for five consecutive sessions.

When given a schedule, the student will direct another person to get her medication when it is time to take it with 90% accuracy for 2 weeks.

Knowledge of the Task

The student will be able to state the name of the medication he is taking, what the medication is for, and possible side effects with 80% accuracy for five consecutive sessions.

The student will tell an adult with his AAC device when the medication is almost finished and the pharmacy needs to be contacted for more medication on 8 out of 10 occasions.

FIGURE 4-11 Sample IEP objectives for taking medications

tions are taken when a certain set of symptoms arise and need to be taken immediately. This is typically the case with medications for an asthma attack, severe allergic reactions (e.g., to bee stings), and a hemophilic bleed. These types of medications must be placed in a location that allows for quick attainment. Determining the best location can often become difficult when the student goes to multiple places. If the student leaves the school for community-based instruction, for example, the medication will need to be taken to these distant sites. In some instances, the parents and student may prefer that certain medication remains with the student (e.g., an inhaler for asthma) because of the benefits of quick administration. The educational team, in conjunction with school administration, will need to determine when medications can be kept with a student.

SUMMARY

Many students with physical impairments will take medications at school for a variety of conditions. It is important that persons administering the medication be familiar with the medication, its potential side effects, and procedures for administration. Medication may be administered in the school setting in many ways: orally, with a feeding tube, topically, in the eyes (optic administration), in the ears (otic administration), nasally, via respiratory administration, rectally, through injections, or by a pump. Each of these routes have various considerations regarding position and proper technique. Students should know about their medication as much as possible and participate in its administration, both to learn a vital self-help skill and to increase their independence.

Part II

Physical Management Skills

5

Lifting, Carrying, and Transferring

Some students with severe physical disabilities will need partial or complete assistance in moving from one area to another. Parents and school personnel who are lifting and/or carrying students should have a good foundation in the basics of proper body mechanics and principles of lifting and carrying. The student's physical or occupational therapist (PT and OT, respectively) or the school nurse is a good source for learning proper techniques for individual students. This chapter will discuss general principles related to lifting, carrying, and transferring students from one area to another, including potential assistive technology, assistive strategies, and instructional strategies.

Lifting and carrying even a small student can cause severe back pain if done improperly. Some back injuries can be permanent, resulting in long-term disability and/or the need for surgery. Eight out of 10 individuals can expect some degree of lower-back pain during their adult life, mainly due to poor posture and incorrect lifting and carrying (Klein, 1990). By using the strong leg muscles to do the work of lifting and by protecting the weaker back muscles, through proper body mechanics, individuals working with students with physical disabilities can position themselves and move in ways that avoid personal injury and also ensure greater safety and security for the students being moved.

To correctly lift and carry students with physical disabilities, and place them on a piece of equipment (e.g., adapted chair), it is important to know the principles of proper handling and positioning. This chapter will address specific strategies to promote proper handling of students when lifting, carrying, and transferring. However, a PT or OT may suggest specialized techniques to increase or decrease the student's muscle tone or to position the student in a way that prepares the body to be moved most safely and easily. For some students these techniques may be used prior to lifting and/or before motorically engaging in activities. The student's PT or OT would need to determine which of the suggested strategies would be most appropriate for that particular student. (See Chapter 6 for more information on handling and positioning of students with physical disabilities.)

The ultimate mobility goal for any student should be for the student to become as independent as possible in moving about the environment (see Chapter 7, "Mobility"). To achieve optimum independence, the student may need to use various assistive technology devices that facilitate transferring from one place to another. Such devices can also help optimize safety and efficiency when the assistance of another person(s) is required to help the student to move. These devices will be covered in the "Assistive Strategies" section in this chapter.

Besides needing to be taught to the greatest extent possible to move from place to place on their own, students with physical disabilities who have the motor skills also need to be taught how to optimally lift and handle items themselves. These areas will be covered in this chapter under "Instructional Strategies for Lifting."

DESCRIPTION OF LIFTING, CARRYING, AND TRANSFERRING

Proper lifting, carrying, and transferring are basic skills team members should possess when working with students with physical disabilities. *Lifting* refers to the act of picking up the student and *transferring* refers to moving the student from one place to another. School personnel should be checked for proper lifting and carrying techniques to be sure they do not injure themselves or the student with a physical disability.

One of the most common problems when lifting and carrying students with physical disabilities arises in determining whether one or more persons are needed to complete the transfer safely. Trying to lift the student alone when more than one person is needed will increase the risk of back injury for the adult and of dropping and injuring the student. How to determine whether a one- or two-person lift is needed will be covered in a later section, under "Assistive Strategies."

When lifting the student, the location that support is given on the student's body can also be an important factor for the adult to consider to prevent student injury. These key points are close to the center of the student's body, usually at the trunk, shoulders, or hips. When lifting, carrying, or transferring a student, to prevent injury such as dislocations of shoulders or hips, the student's body should be supported close to the center of mass. The student's arms or legs should never be used as "handles" to lift the weight of the body.

Proper planning prior to actually lifting or assisting the student to transfer is also needed to prepare the environment adequately to facilitate the transfer. Several different plans may need to be devised by the student's team (i.e., the student, parents, and all professionals working with the student), depending on the various locations the student is being moved or is moving himself to/from. Assistive devices and strategies that may be used in these instances will be covered in the next two sections.

EQUIPMENT AND ADAPTIVE EQUIPMENT FOR LIFTING AND TRANSFERRING

Mechanical Lifts

For adults or older students who are very large, very heavy, or severely physically disabled, use of a person or even several people to lift the individual may put all parties at too much physical risk. In these cases, a **mechanical lift** may be used to transfer the individual.

Several types of mechanical lifts are available. Most mechanical lifts for home or school use are hydraulically operated. Figure 5-1a illustrates a hydraulic lift in action. The student is first positioned on the slings as he lies on his back. The slings are adjusted under the student so that they will sup-

(a)

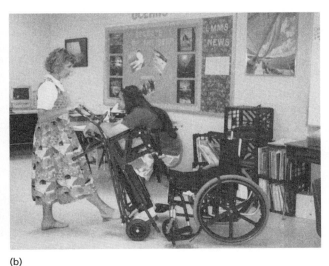

(b)

FIGURE 5-1 Students being transferred by a hydraulic mechanical lift (a) and a Cindy lift (b)

port him as needed when the lift is activated. Some students require full support behind the head and trunk, while others with some degree of head control require only support behind the trunk. Chains are then attached, one end to the slings and the other end to the lift's suspension system. When a handle on the lift is turned by hand, a hydraulic pump operates a lever arm that lifts the suspension system up into the air. As the suspension system lifts, it pulls on the chains, also lifting the slings and the individual supported within. Once the student is off the supporting surface, the lift can be wheeled to the place of transfer.

Another type of lift uses simple mechanics to lift and move a student. A Cindy lift, for example, looks like a hand truck with padding (see Figure 5-1b). The student is strapped into this lift and tilted forward on it. It is very easy to maneuver and has a braking mechanism for safety. However, care must be taken that the student is correctly positioned and a Cindy lift may not be appropriate for students with severe contractures.

Although mechanical lifts are valuable assistive devices, their use must be prescribed and monitored by a physical therapist to ensure the student's safety. Students must also be prepared and gradually trained in the procedure, since use of such a device requires a great deal of trust on the student's part.

Assistive Transfer Devices

When the student with physical disabilities is able to assist somewhat with transferring, a number of commercially available devices can be used to facilitate the process. This includes a transfer board, transfer disc, belts, straps, and other devices. These need to be evaluated for the individual student for their usefulness and safety.

To be able to safely and efficiently transfer in and out of a wheelchair independently, some students will need to be taught how to use a transfer board or transfer disc. A transfer board is a lightweight, smooth board, usually with tapered ends, which is typically made out of wood or plastic. The board is used to "bridge the gap" between the wheelchair and a bed, chair, or other item. To use the board, the individual places one end of the board under her buttock or thigh and the other end on the surface onto which she wants to transfer. Smaller, safer, more controlled sideways movements of the body can then be made to transfer over the gap between the wheelchair and another area. Some transfer boards have a movable piece that the student sits on and moves along the board (see Figure 5-2a).

Transfer discs are also available to assist in transferring the student who can bear some weight on his legs. These discs have rubberized surfaces to prevent slipping. After the student's feet are positioned on the disc and he is assisted to bring his body weight onto his feet, the student can be slowly pivoted on the disc to the desired position to complete the transfer (see Figure 5-2a).

A number of different belts or straps also may be used in the transfer process. A student can wear a belt that assists the adult who is helping with the transfer to grasp the student's body more safely while lifting. Various straps are also some-

times used to assist the student to lift their own legs manually off or onto various surfaces, if they do not have the muscle strength to do so otherwise.

Another item to help with transfers are changing tables. A table may be placed in a large stall to help transfer the student from the wheelchair to the toilet and vice versa. This allows the adult to pull pants and underwear down prior to placing student on the toilet (or pull up prior to placing in wheelchair). A changing table has the advantage of being an appropriate height for the adult to easily assist the student without danger of injuring her back. These tables are typically needed in situations where the student is heavy, cannot bear weight, and has severe physical impairments.

Other devices may be used to help the student lift and transfer objects. Some students who are primarily using a wheelchair for mobility may also need to be taught to use a reacher to enable

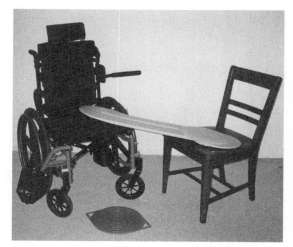

(a)

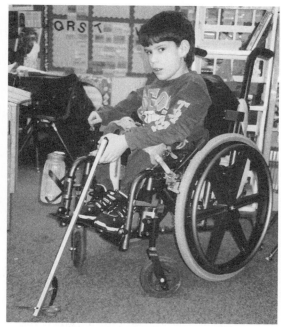

(b)

FIGURE 5-2 A transfer board between two chairs with a transfer disc on the floor (a) and a student using a reacher to grab a pair of scissors (b)

them to retrieve and lift objects from the floor. A reacher typically has a pistol grip handle that operates jaws at the end of a long pole (usually 18 to 30 inches in length). The jaws are opened by the handle and can be used to grip small objects and bring them to the individual. Reachers are especially useful for students who have limited strength or decreased range of motion that would affect reaching away from the body. Figure 5-2b illustrates a reacher in use.

ASSISTIVE STRATEGIES FOR LIFTING, CARRYING, AND TRANSFERRING

Handling Considerations Prior to Lifting

Several handling techniques may be used to prepare the student's body to make lifting, carrying, and transferring easier. First, the student may be prepared for lifting through the use of handling techniques that alter muscle tone. These techniques are usually used to prepare the student's body before movement but should be used as needed throughout the movement activity to optimize function. Generally, movement activities that are slow, smooth, and repetitive and have low levels of sensory stimulation are inhibitory to muscle tone that is too high (e.g., gentle and slow rocking, deep pressure, and regular rhythms of voice or music). Generally, movement activities that are fast, irregular, and repetitive and have high-level sensory stimulation are facilitory to muscle tone that is too low (e.g., swinging, bouncing, stretching to a muscle, and tapping over a muscle). Any handling technique used to assist in lifting, carrying, or transferring the student from one place to another needs to be done under the direction of the student's physical or occupational therapist and needs to be performed the same way by all adults assisting the student. (See Chapter 6 for more information on these techniques.)

A second guideline is that the student should be lifted and handled using "key points." These key points are close to the center of the body. Handling close to the center of the body allows the person facilitating the student's movements to provide support most accurately. This results in the greatest effect on the student's movement. When positioning a student prior to movement, guiding the student's body in typical patterns of movement will facilitate completing the lifting, carrying, or transferring procedure. Typical patterns of movement tend to be symmetrical, with both sides of the body being positioned similarly, and toward the midline (or center) of the body.

A third guideline is to remember that handling techniques should be used to prepare and guide the student with physical disabilities to move in typical, functional ways. Care must be taken that they are not overused. The ultimate goal of handling should be to have the student learn to move functionally, gradually fading out the handling support and requiring more independent movement as the student attempts to assist with transferring.

Lifting Considerations

If there is any doubt about whether a student is too heavy to be safely lifted by a single individual, a two-person lift should be used. The following is a good rule of thumb to use in determining whether a student is too heavy for an adult to lift: If the student weighs more than 35% of the adult's body weight, the adult should not attempt to lift the student alone. For example, if the adult weighs 120 pounds, she should not lift a student who weighs more than 42 pounds by herself. If the adult weighs 185 pounds, the student weight limit for a one-person transfer would be 65 pounds (Klein, 1990).

Planning prior to actually lifting the student is a step that adults frequently leave out and, by doing so, they put themselves and the student at risk for injury. Before actually lifting the student, the adult should determine how much assistance the student can provide in moving, if the assistance of another adult is needed to lift the student, what handling techniques should be done to normalize the student's muscle tone in preparation for lifting, what position the student should be in before being lifted, and how the environment needs to be adapted to facilitate the transfer (Orelove & Sobsey, 1996).

For the last consideration, the environment should be arranged to minimize the distance the adult must carry the student. This may mean that the student first moves himself, if he has the physical skills, to the area where lifting will need to occur (e.g., a young student may crawl to a changing table). If the student is in a wheelchair, he may wheel himself, or his chair may be wheeled close to the transfer area. If the student is being lifted into a piece of equipment, the equipment may be brought close to the student prior to lifting. All equipment necessary for positioning the student following the transfer should also be brought to the transfer area before lifting. Finally, the path between the student and the transfer area should be free of obstacles to ensure a safe transfer.

Body Mechanics for Proper Lifting

When all handling and planning considerations have been met, the adult should inform the student that she will be lifted. It is important to enlist the student's participation in the movement to whatever degree possible. For some students, this may mean reaching for and holding onto the adult's shoulders and bearing some weight on their feet as they are transferred. For other students, this may mean remaining relaxed while they are being lifted. Enlisting the student's participation not only decreases the risk of the adult being injured but also provides instructional opportunities to maximize the student's independence in moving from place to place.

It is important that the lift itself, as well as carrying and transfer, incorporate good body mechanics to avoid back injury. These principles are as follows:

1. Before lifting, take your time and think about what you are doing, where you are going, and what muscles you should be using.

2. Prior to lifting, establish a broad base of support, with one foot slightly ahead of the other and feet apart.

3. Use good body posture, with your back straight and stomach muscle tightened.

4. Lifting should entail using the large muscles of the thighs, arms, and legs, and not the small back muscles.

5. If lifting the student (or object) from a lower level, kneel or squat while keeping the back straight. Bend at the knees; do not bent at the waist.

6. While lifting, keep the student as close to your body as possible as you straighten at the knees. Use the large muscles of your arms and legs to lift the student, not the small muscles of the back. Keep your back straight; do not twist your upper body. Instead, turn by moving your feet, keeping your whole body straight (i.e., your feet should always face in the same direction as your body to prevent twisting at the spine, with potential resulting injury).

7. While lifting, support the student's body at "key points" close to the student's center of mass. Support at the student's trunk, shoulders, and/or hips, as instructed by the student's therapist. Never grasp the student's arms or legs at points distant from the center of the body (e.g., at hands or feet), and never pull on the arms and legs to lift the student.

8. If it is necessary to carry the student for any distance, follow the instructions of the student's physical therapist in terms of how to hold the student for carrying. Keep the student close to your body, and support the student's body where instructed. For example, some students with high muscle tone will be easier to carry when held with arms and legs in flexion, bent in toward the body. Students with low muscle tone will probably require their head and trunk to be supported against the adult's body.

9. When completing the lift/transfer, placing

the student on the surface or in the equipment, do not bend at the waist. Keep the back straight, bend at the knees, and keep the student close to your body until his weight is on the support surface.

There are some basic maneuvers to avoid when lifting to prevent injury to the student or to the lifter. First, the student's arms and legs should never be used as handles. Second, never lift a student under the armpits. Instead, inward pressure against the student's sides should be used. Third, you should never twist your back; instead rotate your entire body. Your feet and back should point in the same direction. Fourth, never lift with your back; use your legs instead. Fifth, never move a student by yourself when two or three people or a mechanical lift is needed.

Types of Lifting

Several types of lifting may be used to move a student from one location to another. The types differ primarily in terms of the number of adults involved in performing the lift. The strategies described in this section are examples of different lifts that can be used with students with physical disabilities. They are described as being done from the floor since this is the most difficult lift to perform. It is usually easier to lift a student from an elevated surface than from the floor. Adaptations may have to be made to the manner in which the lifts are performed, based on the individual student's physical needs, and will need to be adapted according to the student's therapist's direction.

One-Person Lift. A one-person lift involves lifting the student by oneself. Adults typically injure their backs performing this lift if they (a) do not bring the student into a sitting position before lifting them; (b) do not use proper body mechanics, as described earlier; or (c) carry the student far from their body. The following procedure outlines assistive strategies for performing a one-person lift from the floor (Heller, Alberto, Forney et al., 1996), and Figure 5-3 illustrates the strategies.

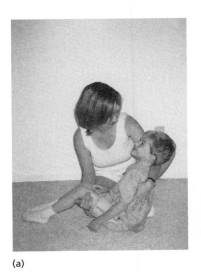  

(a) (b) (c)

FIGURE 5-3 In this one-person lift, the adult brings the student to a sitting position (a), begins to come to a standing position with the student held securely and close to the adult's body (b), and (c) comes to a standing position while keeping her back straight.

Steps in the Procedure for the One-Person Lift	*Rationale*
1. Bring the wheelchair or other equipment as close to the student as possible or have the student move as close to the area of transfer as possible.	This will make carrying easier since there will be not as far to go.
2. Kneel on one knee with the opposite foot planted firmly on the floor (i.e., half-kneeling position) next to the student, as close as possible.	This is the most stable position, although full kneeling or squatting could be used in special circumstances.
3. Bring the student into a sitting position, as instructed by the student's therapist. Be sure you are keeping your back straight during this procedure. Move your body at the hips and legs, not at the waist.	For a large student, the lifter may place her knee behind the student to prevent him from falling backward while she gets in position. The student should always be placed in a sitting position first to avoid injuring one's back.
4. Place one arm under the student's thighs and the other arm around the student's back below the armpits. (Some adults may prefer to be behind the student, placing their arms under the student's arms and grasping the student's thighs with both hands. The student's therapist can determine whether this is an appropriate lifting position.)	Some students with high muscle tone who tend to extend their bodies in a total pattern may benefit from this more flexed or bent position as provided by the lifter positioning herself behind the student.
5. Bring your body close to the student's body.	Lifting close to the center of gravity prevents lifting injuries.
6. Communicate to the student when you are going to lift him by using a touch cue or count of "One, two, three, lift," for example.	Whatever is used to communicate this to the student should be the same each time the lift is done and used by all adults lifting the student.
7. Come to a standing position using the large leg muscles, keeping your back straight.	The lifter should not bend her back since that will result in using the small back muscles that are easily injured.
8. Slowly carry the student to the equipment/support surface and lower the student, keeping the back straight and bending at the knees. The student's body should be at or below the adult's waist and held close to the adult's body.	The student should be held during carrying as instructed by the student's therapist.
9. When lowering the student onto equipment, do not bend at the back but again bend at the knees. Properly position the student in equipment or at transfer site, as instructed by the student's therapist.	The tendency to bend at the back when lowering a student will result in back injury.

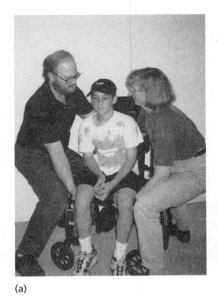
(a)

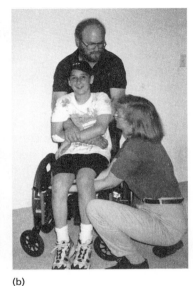
(b)

FIGURE 5-4 Two-person lifts may be used to lift a student from a wheelchair using a side-to-side method (a) or a top-bottom method (b)

Two-Person Lift. A two-person lift is used when it is determined that the student is too heavy to be safely lifted by one person alone. There are two basic types of two-person lifts: a side-to-side lift and a top-bottom lift (see Figure 5-4). In a side-to-side lift, two adults stand on either side of the student, thereby taking equal weight of the student during the lift. In the top-bottom lift, one adult lifts the upper half of the student's body while the other adult lifts the lower half. Since more of the student's body weight will be concentrated in the upper half of the body, the taller or larger adult usually performs the top part of this lift. The following procedure is followed when performing two-person lifts when lifting from the floor to a wheelchair.

Steps in the Procedure for the Two-Person Lift	*Rationale*
1. Bring the wheelchair or other equipment as close to the student as possible or have the student move as close to the area of transfer as possible.	This will make carrying easier since there will be not as far to go.
2A. Side-to-Side Method	
a. Two adults kneel on either side of the student, as close as possible to the student and with one foot on the floor (half-kneeling).	Alternate positions may be used in certain circumstances, but this one is the most stable.
b. Bring the student into a sitting position, as instructed by the student's therapist. Be sure you are keeping your back straight during this procedure. Move your body at the hips and legs, not at the waist.	For large students, the lifter may place her knee behind the student to prevent him from falling backward while she gets in position. The student should always be placed in a sitting position first to avoid injuring one's back.

Steps in the Procedure for the Two-Person Lift	*Rationale*
c. One adult places one arm under the student's thigh and the other arm around the student's back. The second adult does the same on the opposite side.	This results in the adult crossing arms behind the student.
2B. Top-Bottom Method	
a. One adult kneels at the top of the student, as close as possible to the student's head, and the other adult kneels as close as possible at the student's feet.	The taller adult should be at the student's head since that will be the heavier portion and also the more elevated side.
b. Bring the student into a sitting position, as instructed by the student's therapist. Be sure you are keeping your back straight during this procedure.	Move your body at the hips and legs, not at the waist to prevent back injury.
c. The adult at the top brings his arms under the student's arms and around to the front of the student's chest, holding the student's crossed arms close to the student's chest.	Inward pressure will be applied along the student's sides while lifting.
d. The adult at the bottom places his hands/forearms on the student's thighs behind the student's knees.	Be sure the adult is not bending at the back to avoid back injury.
3. Communicate to the student and the other adult when you are going to lift the student by using a count. For example, the adult at the top says, "Lift on three. One, two, three."	The adult at the top usually calls the count because he has the heavier end of the student's body.
4. Together lift student straight up, keeping student close to the adults' bodies.	If this step is not timed well, the student can feel as though he is being pulled in two directions, especially during the side-to-side transfer.
5. Come to a standing position using the large leg muscles, keeping the back straight.	This will prevent back injury.
6. Slowly carry the student to the equipment/support surface and lower the student, keeping the back straight and bending at the knees.	Care should be taken when lowering the student that the bending is done at the knees, not the back, to prevent injury.
7. Properly position the student in equipment or at the transfer site, as instructed by the student's therapist.	

Three-Person Lift. A three-person lift may sometimes be necessary if the student is very large or very heavy or if he has severe physical disabilities that require precise support at points on the body to control body movements. The student's physical therapist would need to direct the specific lifting procedure in these cases. One way of performing a three-person lift entails stationing a person at the head/upper body position, having the second person at the hip area, and the last person at the legs. The adults may be positioned all on one side of the student, especially if the student is going onto a table, or they may be positioned on alternating sides. These lifts require precise timing and coordination of efforts among the adults performing the lifts so that the student being lifted does not feel insecure and as if he is being pulled in several directions. Often the person at the head/upper body is in charge of counting to three to lift the student.

Transfer Considerations

The aforementioned assistive strategies are for transfers to and from the floor. As already stated, transfers to and from an elevated surface are usually easier to assist the student with, because less lifting is required by the adult. The following section will describe some additional considerations for lifting in other circumstances/environments. It will also discuss transfers from the wheelchair when the student can assist, by bearing weight and standing, and when the student is unable to do this.

Wheelchair Transfers. When transferring a student to and from a wheelchair, several additional considerations need to be made. The brakes should always be on so that the wheelchair does not roll and result in injury. All straps and seat belts should be removed, being careful to hold the student so that he does not suddenly extend out of position or fall. In some instances, the legrests may be removed or swung away to allow better positioning for transferring. If the student is going to be slid onto a parallel surface (e.g., from a wheelchair to a bed), the wheelchair's armrest

may be removed. The adult should move the student as close to the front of the seat as possible before lifting the student. For a one-person transfer, the adult usually stands close to the side of the wheelchair, although with small students it may also be possible to stand behind the wheelchair. Guidelines for a one-person transfer from the floor, as outlined earlier, are then followed, except that the adult bends his knees, keeping his back straight, as the student is lifted. For a two-person transfer, the adults may stand at the sides of the chair or at the top and bottom of the chair (refer back to Figure 5-4). A side-to-side or top-bottom transfer may then be performed, following guidelines for proper body mechanics, as outlined earlier, being careful to bend knees and keep back straight as the student is being lifted.

Toilet Transfers. Some students with physical disabilities may be able to assist in transferring from a wheelchair to a toilet using partial weight bearing and a pivot transfer with an adult's help, and others may be able to utilize a transfer board to transfer independently onto the toilet (see "Instructional Strategies," later). However, many students with more severe physical disabilities may require full assistance to transfer onto and off of the toilet. One important consideration is the relatively small space to which these transfers are usually confined to (e.g., bathrooms or bathroom stalls). Usually the student with severe physical disabilities is also transferring onto a toilet adapted with special seating supports, making the transfer even more difficult.

The student will need to be transferred with the legs bent and apart and positioned so that she has adequate trunk support, foot support, and support to keep the legs separated. After assuring proper positioning on the toilet, the student with high muscle tone may have difficulty remaining relaxed enough to urinate or defecate. Using techniques that inhibit high tone and promote relaxation may help the student, such as having soft music playing or low lighting. The physical therapist will be able to give ideas on how to further promote relaxation. (See Chapter 6 for further discussions on inhibition techniques to promote or decrease muscle tone and enhance relaxation.)

The adult or adults transferring the student onto the toilet will need to be especially vigilant about proper body mechanics. In a small space, it is easy to forget to keep the back straight and the body in good alignment while helping the student transfer, but in a bathroom environment, with its small, usually angular space and hard, sometimes slippery floor, good body mechanics are even more important for the safety of the adult and the student as well.

Bathtub Transfers. Transferring a student into a bathtub entails the same considerations as in toilet transfers in that the space is small and angular and the floor is hard and slippery, but, in addition, the adult is having to transfer the student to/from almost floor level, and the student and tub are wet. It is helpful to have all the towels and clothes ready and near the tub. To place the student in the tub, once you have the student in your arms, face the tub and kneel as close to it as you can. When lifting the student out of the tub, first place a towel on the edge of the tub and lift the student onto the towel. Then, move the student onto the floor or into the wheelchair by moving your whole body as a unit, rather than using your upper body only. Do not twist your body; instead, keep all parts of your body facing in the same direction. Since lifting from a somewhat elevated surface is easier than lifting from floor level, try using a folding, child-sized lawn chaise without arms (for the smaller child) or a commercial bath chair in the tub to elevate the tub's resting surface.

Assisted Standing Transfer

When a student can assist by standing, there are several differences in promoting transferring as opposed to when the student cannot assist. The following describes a transfer from a wheelchair to another chair or platform when the student is able to stand and bear weight:

Steps in the Procedure for Assisted Transfer	Rationale
1. Place the wheelchair at a 45- to 90-degree angle to the transfer surface. The student's stronger side should be toward the chair or mat.	Placing the wheelchair in this position will make it easier to help rotate the student into position.
2. The brakes should be engaged first to provide a stable surface off or onto which to transfer the student.	Having the brakes on is an important safety measure.
3. All straps and seat belts should be removed prior to moving the students. In addition, legrests may be removed or swung away. In some cases, a sliding transfer to the side may be made from the wheelchair to an elevated surface such as a bed. The wheelchair's armrest would have to be removed to allow this type of transfer.	Removing legrests may allow better position of the chair for transfer.
4. Move the student as close to the front of the seat as possible before lifting the student.	By moving the student forward, lifting will be made easier. How the student is brought forward will depend on how much the student can participate.

Steps in the Procedure for Assisted Transfer	*Rationale*
a. If the student can move her hips: The adult holds under the shoulder and assists the student to shift weight from one side to another. b. If the student cannot move her hips forward, move the student forward by holding under the hips and shifting the student's weight from one side to the other as one hip then the other is brought forward.	
5. After the student is positioned at the end of the chair, be sure your knees are against the student's knees forming a knee lock (see Figure 5-5). Typically one of the lifter's feet is between the student's feet and the other is between the student's leg and the surface that the student is being transferred. The student's legs should also be firmly on the floor, with legs bent.	A knee lock prevents the student from collapsing to the floor or her feet from sliding against the floor, resulting in a fall. If the student collapses, the knee lock will result in the adult being able to bring the student back down into the chair in a controlled manner. If the student is not able to stand, a one- or two-person lift should be used, not an assisted transfer lift.
6. Place your hands on the student's sides and slowly rock the student forward and back, saying on three "Stand up." On the count of three, push the student up into a standing position. (If the student can assist by pushing down on the arm-rests, she is instructed to do so.)	For this to be effective, the adult needs to be positioned low, with knees bent so the leg and arm muscles are being used, not the back muscles.
7. While standing, pivot your body and the student's body until the student is standing with the transfer surface behind her. This may be done by moving feet or using a pivot disc.	It is important that the adult and student do not use a twisting motion but move their feet as they pivot. This most frequently results in back injury when done incorrectly.
8. Slowly lower the student onto the transfer surface. If the student can hold the surface as she is being lowered, this is encouraged.	
9. The student's hips are moved into the back of the chair (or surface) in the same manner as step 4, and then any straps or belts are applied.	

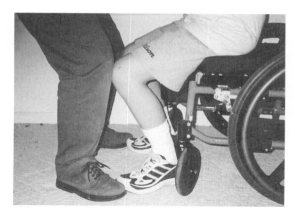

FIGURE 5-5 The standing knee lock

INSTRUCTIONAL STRATEGIES FOR LIFTING

Teaching Students to Perform Independent Transfers/Task Analysis

To teach a student with physical disabilities to perform assisted or independent transfers, the student's team will need to determine what motor skills are necessary to perform the transfer through task analysis of the transfer process. Then, the team will have to determine what necessary movements the student can make on his own, what movements he can be taught to make, and what adaptive technology, if any, is needed to facilitate moving through the transfer.

Students will range in their capability to do transfers, with some students being totally independent and others providing some small movements that help with the process. If the student is unable to participate motorically in the transfer because of the severity of the physical impairment, then the student should learn to request changes in position. Also, some students may have preferences regarding which type of two-person lift they feel more secure with and communicate that to the persons doing the lifting. An example of a task analysis of a student learning to transfer from a wheelchair to a mat table is in Figure 5-6. The steps of the task analysis should be taught to the

student sequentially, initially using visual, verbal, or tactile cues and/or physical prompts or physical assistance as needed by the student to achieve partial or total independence in each step. As the student gains independence, prompts should be faded (gradually removed) when possible. The same transfer procedure can also be used for transferring out of the wheelchair onto a bed, couch, school chair, and so forth, but the student would need to be checked

1. The student retrieves a transfer board from the storage space, placing it in her lap.
2. The student wheels up to the mat table with the right side of her chair at a 45-degree angle to the mat table. (The team has pre-determined that the student's right side is stronger, so transfer to this side is preferred.)
3. The student removes the right chair arm and places it beside the wheelchair.
4. The student lifts her legs off the legrests and swings them out of the way. (The team has pre-determined that the legrests get in the way of a smooth transfer if left in place.)
5. The student removes the seat belt.
6. The student shifts her weight to the left side and places the transfer board under her right buttock.
7. The student safely positions the transfer board to bridge the gap between the wheelchair and the mat table.
8. The student lifts her weight off the seat (using her arms) and shifts her body to the right.
9. The student repeats step 8 until she is sitting on the mat table.
10. The student removes the transfer board and places it on the floor near the mat table to use later when transferring back into the chair.

FIGURE 5-6 A task analysis of transferring from a wheelchair to a mat table using a transfer board

out in these different activities using the procedure before generalization of skills would be assumed.

Teaching Students to Lift and Handle Items

One area that is usually not covered when instructing adults or students in lifting, carrying, and transferring strategies is how to teach the student with physical disabilities how to lift items safely and efficiently. A critical first step in teaching these skills would be to discuss with the student's team (a) what kinds of lifting the student is physically capable of doing; (b) what types of things the student can and cannot be expected to lift, based on the student's physical skills as well as environmental demands (e.g., a work situation); (c) what kinds of assistive technology devices may be needed to support the lifting skills; and (d) a task analysis of the lifting procedure.

For some students who are primarily mobilizing in a wheelchair, this step may be as simple as procuring a reacher device for the student (see the earlier section "Assistive Strategies") and teaching him in its use when lifting light objects from the floor while in the wheelchair. For other students who walk and can kneel to pick up an item, instruction may first target teaching the student to determine what objects are too heavy or too large to lift alone (e.g., during community-based vocational instruction, the student is taught to identify types or sizes of objects that should not be lifted alone). Additional instruction for these students would be in the area of using good body mechanics while lifting, as described earlier. Some students may be required to wear support belts while lifting to keep the low back in a good position (although the student must still know proper body mechanics for the support belts to be effective).

When instructing a student with physical disabilities how to lift safely and efficiently, the steps required should first be written out by the student's physical therapist, including any necessary special adaptations, devices, or restrictions. The student should then be taught the steps, through demonstration, practice, role playing, and so forth. Prompts may initially be used to remind the student of the steps, but should eventually be faded

(phased out) if the student is to be independent in lifting. These steps should be written down in the student's IHP so that adults working with the student can assist, as necessary. For some students, it may also be necessary to have written or illustrated steps posted at the student's work site if lifting occurs frequently as part of the job. Figure 5-7

---

1. The student determines whether the object can be lifted alone (i.e., predetermined and listed or pictured by size, category, etc.).

2. The student puts on a support belt, if necessary.

3. The student faces the object to be lifted with body straight.

4. The student assumes a position with feet apart, one foot slightly ahead of the other.

5. The student bends at the knees, keeping the back straight.

6. The student firmly grasps the object to be lifted, with its weight distributed equally in each arm. (Some students may need to vary this step, depending on their specific physical disability. For example, a student with hemiparesis, exhibiting weakness on one side of the body, may need to rely on the stronger arm to do more of the lifting and stabilize with the weaker side. The student's therapist should determine this during initial task analysis.)

7. The student brings himself close to the object to be lifted.

8. The student lifts the object, using leg muscles by straightening the knees, and keeps his back straight.

9. The student carries the object close to his body, keeping his body aligned.

10. The student sets the object down by moving close to the supporting surface, bending at his knees and keeping his back straight as he lowers the object onto the surface.

FIGURE 5-7 A task analysis for a student lifting objects at a work site

is a sample task analysis of a student lifting objects at a work site.

LIFTING PROBLEMS AND EMERGENCIES

Dropping a Student

Every precaution should be taken that a student is not dropped when being lifted and carried. First, the person lifting the student should be sure that she is not trying to lift a student who is too heavy for her. Second, the adult should not lift the student if there is any doubt as to the ability to lift a student due to size, movements, or the lifter's own ability to lift and carry. Students who are participating in their transfers should be closely watched, and the adult should be readily available to stop or break a fall. All adults lifting and transferring should be trained on the best way this should be done, including how to implement correct body mechanics.

If a student is dropped or falls while transferring independently, the student will need to be checked for injury and receive appropriate medical treatment, if needed. If the student hits his head during the fall, the parents should be immediately contacted and the student should be observed for any signs of head injury (e.g., drowsiness, confusion, unequal pupil dilation). Documentation of a fall should be done, including when the fall occurred, how the injury occurred, what body part hit what objects, any first aid given, and when the parents were contacted.

Back Pain

In certain circumstances, adults may injure their backs when lifting incorrectly or when surprised by a sudden movement the student

makes. If the adult feels pain in the back, he should immediately gently put the student down and get someone to help with the student. The back injury should be reported to the appropriate school personnel and documented. The adult should seek medical attention if it is severe. No further lifting should occur until the back has improved or the physician gives the OK for the adult to lift. The adult should also analyze what happened to result in back injury and learn how to avoid the same mistake in the future.

Student's Weight: _____

Type of Lift to Use with Student When Adult Weighs 100 Pounds or More

_____ One-person lift
_____ Two-person lift: side-to-side method
_____ Two-person lift: top-bottom method
_____ Mechanical lift

Preparation for Lifting

_____
_____
_____

Student's Participation in Lifting

_____ Assists with transfers
_____ Assists with holding onto adult
_____ Assists by using trunk support
_____ Other (specify)

Directions for Problems and Emergencies
Student is dropped: _____

_____
_____
_____

FIGURE 5-8 Specialized areas to include in an IHP on lifting

MANAGEMENT ISSUES FOR LIFTING AND TRANSFERRING

Individualized Health Plan and Individualized Educational Program

The various assistive strategies being used with an individual student to facilitate transfer from place to place should be written in that student's individualized health plan (IHP) and also posted so that all adults assisting the student can be using the same procedures. This will not only prevent injury to the adult and the student but also can provide learning opportunities for the student to improve independence during transfer. In addition, emergency procedures should also be included in the event that the student is accidentally dropped and injured. Figure 5–8 presents sample specialized information to include in an IHP for lifting.

The student's individualized educational program (IEP) should contain objectives that teach the student to participate in her own transfer or objectives in which the student is learning to lift and handle items herself. Areas of instruction may include (a) asking to be moved, (b) learning how the mechanical lift works to direct others in its use, (c) requesting the preferred two–person lift, (d) learning to partially or fully participate in her transfer, and (e) learning proper body mechanics and adaptations to lift and handle items herself. (See Figure 5-9 for sample objectives for an IEP.)

Planning for Multiple-Person Transfers

Some students will require two- or three-person lifts to be lifted safely. It is important that the teacher has planned ahead of time who will be responsible for assisting with these transfers. Sometimes the teacher or paraprofessional next door will be as-

---

Independent Performance of Task

The student will lift boxes at community-based vocational site using correct lifting techniques (as specified in one-person lift outline) with 100% accuracy on 8 out of 10 opportunities.

The student will independently transfer from the wheelchair to the toilet using the handrail with 100% accuracy on each occasion for 2 weeks.

Partial Performance of Task

When provided physical assistance to stand and maintain balance, the student will assist with transfers from the wheelchair to the toilet (and back) by moving feet and turning body to correct position to sit on the toilet (or wheelchair) with 80% accuracy on 100% of the opportunities for 2 weeks.

When a mechanical lift is used, the student will move to one side then the other as the lift sling is placed under the student with 80% accuracy on 100% of opportunities for 1 week.

Directing the Task

The student will direct another person in the steps for operating a mechanical lift with 100% accuracy on 100% of opportunities for 1 week.

The student will ask for assistance to be transferred from the wheelchair to the floor for circle time activity using his AAC device with 80% accuracy for 5 consecutive days.

Knowledge of the Task

The student will describe proper body mechanics, correct number of people required to lift an item, and steps of one- and two-person lifts each with 80% accuracy on 5 consecutive trials.

FIGURE 5-9 Sample IEP objectives for lifting

signed to assist when multiple-person transfers are needed; other times someone else is assigned. It is important that whoever helps with lifting and transferring has been trained on proper body mechanics and the best ways to lift the student. The persons assisting with transfers should also be readily available to assist, especially for bathroom transfers.

SUMMARY

Some students with physical disabilities will need adult assistance when being moved from place to place. To ensure that the students or adults are not injured during lifting, carrying, and transferring procedures, assistive transfer strategies need to be developed by the student's team. These strategies should include preparation activities, the type of transfer to be done, how the transfer is to be done, use of proper body mechanics during the transfer, and use of any assistive technology devices. In addition, the team should develop instructional strategies to teach the individual student to be as independent as possible in moving himself and in lifting and carrying items from place to place.

6

Proper Handling and Positioning

Students with physical disabilities have disorders of the body's motor system that result in limitations of posture and movement. Depending on the type and severity of their physical impairment, typical patterns of movement, such as crawling, sitting, or walking, may not develop. Over time, **contractures** (limitations in joint mobility) and other additional problems may occur due to a lack of normal **motor patterns** and proper positioning. This can result in a worsening of the student's current motor abilities. Therapeutic handling of students with physical disabilities, along with proper positioning, can help facilitate development of functional movement patterns and prevent many additional problems from occurring. Proper positioning and materials will also allow students to physically participate in self-help tasks, including health care procedures.

MUSCLE TONE AND PRIMITIVE REFLEXES

Before determining how to handle or position a child properly, the student's **muscle tone** and presence of primitive reflexes need to be determined. Muscle tone, also known as *postural tone,* is the state of tension that the central nervous system (CNS), composed of the brain and spinal cord, continuously exerts on all muscles of the body. This normal tension of the muscles enables the body to move against the force of gravity and provides the background for normal movement. This results in the muscles being ready for movement at any time. When communication breaks down between the brain and the muscles in the developing child due to damage in the communication pathway (in the brain, spinal cord, nerves, muscles, or sensory receptors), muscle tone and body movement will be atypical, and, as a result, motor development and functional movement patterns will be affected (Heller et al., 1996).

Students with physical disabilities may have muscle tone that is too high or too low. In some cases, the muscles of the body may exhibit a mixture of high and low tone (e.g., the trunk muscles may be low in tone while the arm and leg muscles may be high in tone). Muscle tone may also fluctuate with tone being too high one moment and too low the next. Atypical muscle tone may affect the student's whole body, only one side of the body, or one part of the body more than another (e.g., legs may be more involved than arms). Type and location of the atypical tone will depend on the location of the damage within the CNS. Disorders of muscle tone may also occur on a continuum from mild involvement that only minimally affects a student's movement and function, to severe involvement that makes independent movement and function very difficult. The level of involvement will depend on the extent of the damage within the sensorimotor system.

Hypertonia

Muscle tone that is too high is referred to as **hypertonia** or **spasticity.** It results in labored movement that often occurs in atypical patterns and within a limited range of motion. Because of the limited motion and the "tightness" of the muscles, students with hypertonia are at risk for joint contractures (i.e., limitations in joint mobility caused by permanent shortening of the muscle), orthopedic problems (e.g., hip dislocations), and skeletal deformities (e.g., curvature of the spine as seen in scoliosis).

Motor milestones and the development of functional independence are frequently delayed in students with hypertonia. Besides having difficulty assuming and maintaining positions that require working against gravity (e.g., sitting, crawling, standing), students with high tone may also have difficulty with breathing due to decreased movement of the ribs. Eating and speak-

ing may be adversely affected due to involvement of the oral and facial muscles. Using arm and hand muscles may also be difficult and result in the inability to independently perform the functional tasks of eating, dressing, washing, and toileting at an age-appropriate level. Additionally, once the child reaches school age, functional tasks necessary for classroom performance, such as writing, may also be impaired.

Hypotonia

Muscle tone that is too low is referred to as **hypotonia,** and students with hypotonia are sometimes referred to as being "floppy." Hypotonia results in decreased power to move the body against gravity, and it interferes with postural alignment. In some cases, joints may be overly flexible. Students with hypotonia are at risk for orthopedic problems such as dislocations (e.g., hip dislocations), skeletal deformities (e.g., scoliosis), breathing difficulties, feeding problems, and delays in reaching motor milestones. Delays may also occur in the development of functional skills.

Fluctuating and Mixed Tone

Students with physical disabilities may also display combinations of muscle tone problems. For example, a child may exhibit hypotonia in the head and trunk area while displaying hypertonia in the arms and legs. Additionally, damage to the parts of the brain controlling coordination of muscle function (e.g., the cerebellum) may result in uncoordinated movements and balance problems, sometimes referred to as *ataxia.*

Muscle tone that is at times too low and at other times too high is sometimes referred to as **athetosis.** Tone may change in various parts of the body as a result of the student's position (e.g., side lying vs. back lying) or attempts at active movement (e.g., resting quietly vs. trying to crawl or reach toward an object). Fluctuating muscle tone results in imprecise and uncontrolled movements. Breathing and feeding problems, delays in reaching motor milestones, and delays in developing functional skills are all possible outcomes for the child with fluctuating muscle tone.

Primitive Reflexes

At birth, the typically developing infant's movements are dominated by **primitive reflexes** or involuntary movements that are stimulated by various kinds of external sensory input (e.g., touch, pressure, vision, movement of fluid in the inner ear, stretch on muscle tendons, etc.). These reflexes are genetically programmed but are dependent on interaction with the environment. Some of the reflexes function to protect the baby; others form the beginning of motor skills. For example, a baby's initial grasp of an object placed in its hand in response to the tactile input (i.e., reflex palmar grasp) is important to the eventual development of voluntary grasp.

As the young student's CNS matures, these primitive reflex patterns of movement gradually fade by about 6 months of age and are replaced by higher-level, automatic postural reactions that continue throughout life. These automatic reactions allow the individual to function upright in space against gravity. For example, if an individual is standing on a bus, automatic postural reactions (i.e., righting, protective, and equilibrium [balance] reactions) allow the person to maintain an upright position, even though the bus is moving and making starts and stops. The individual does not need to think about standing: muscles adjust as necessary to hold the position (Heller et al., 1996). Table 6-1 lists some of the common primitive reflexes and postural reactions, including stimulus and response parameters.

Due to damage in the CNS, students with physical disabilities may exhibit persistence of the previously described primitive reflexive patterns of movement beyond when they would normally occur. Rather than promoting motor development, persistent primitive reflexes interrupt the student's ability to gain control over body movement. Attempts at functional movement may be interrupted by an obligatory motor response from a primitive reflex pattern. For example, an older child with an obligatory palmar grasp reflex would have difficulty releasing or orienting an object held in his hand, such as a pencil or spoon. In addition, higher-level postural responses, such as righting and protective and equilibrium reactions, which help develop upright control against gravity, cannot develop normally when persistent primitive reflexes are present.

PURPOSES AND GOALS OF PROPER HANDLING AND POSITIONING

Pediatric physical and occupational therapists employ various handling and positioning techniques with students with physical disabilities to decrease the effects of muscle tone problems and persistent primitive reflexes. Proper handling and positioning can also increase the potential for each student to learn normal movement patterns, increasing postural stability and functional movement at a developmentally appropriate level for the individual student. Many of these techniques can be taught to parents and teachers for carryover throughout the student's day. Sometimes adaptive equipment or devices are necessary to maintain optimal positioning or promote optimal functional independence. Therapists can also assist students, families, and teachers with securing appropriate adaptive equipment and training them in their use.

There are three main goals of therapeutic handling and positioning of a student with physical disabilities: (a) to bring muscle tone as close to normal as possible, (b) to minimize the occurrence of primitive reflexes, and (c) to facilitate active movement in typical patterns within the normal developmental sequence. The principles described here generally apply to handling and positioning students with physical disabilities, but the reader is cautioned that all students are individuals. Some techniques may work with some students and not with others. Some techniques

Table 6-1 Common Primitive Reflexes and Postural Reactions

Reflex	Stimulus	Response	Suppression
Primitive Reflexes: Present at Birth, Suppressed with Maturation			
Asymmetrical tonic neck	Head turning or tilting to the side	Extension of the extremities on the chin side, flexion on the occiput side	Suppressed by 6–7 months
Symmetric tonic neck	Neck flexion	Arm flexion, leg extension	Suppressed by 6–7 months
	Neck extension	Arm extension, leg flexion	
Moro	Sudden neck extension	Arm extension abduction followed by flexion-adduction	Suppressed by 4–6 months
Tonic labyrinthine	Head position in space, strongest at 45° angle to horizontal		Suppressed by 4–6 months
	Supine	Predominant extensor tone	
	Prone	Predominant flexor tone	
Positive supporting	Tactile contract and weight bearing on the sole	Leg extension for supporting partial body weight	Suppressed by 3–7 months and replaced by volitional standing
Rooting	Stroking the corner of mouth, upper or lower lip	Moving the tongue, mouth, and head toward the site of stimulus	Suppressed by 4 months
Palmar grasp	Pressure or touch on the palm, stretch of finger flexors	Flexion of fingers	Suppressed by 5–6 months
Plantar grasp	Pressure on sole just distal to metatarsal heads	Flexion of toes	Suppressed by 12–18 months
Automatic neonatal walking	Contact of sole in vertical position tilting the body forward and from side to side	Automatic alternating steps	Suppressed by 3–4 months
Placing	Tactile contact on dorsum of foot or hand	Flexion to place the leg or arm over the obstacle	Suppressed before end of first year
Postural Responses: Emerge with Maturation, Present throughout Life, Modulated by Volition			
Head righting	Visual and vestibular	Align face vertical, mouth horizontal	Emerge at
		Prone	2 months
		Supine	3–4 months
Body, head righting	Tactile proprioceptive vestibular	Align body parts	Emerge from 4–6 months
Protective extension or propping	Displacement of center of gravity outside of supporting surface	Extension-abduction of the extremity toward the side of displacement to prevent falling	Emerge between 5 and 12 months
Equilibrium or tilting	Displacement of center of gravity	Adjustment of tone and trunk posture to maintain balance	Emerge between 6 and 14 months

SOURCE: Based on *Pediatric Rehabilitation* by G. E. Molnar. Copyright © 1992 Williams & Wilkins. Used with permission.

may work better at one time than another with a particular student. The student's response to handling and positioning should be the indicator of whether a particular technique is used.

It is imperative that all handling and positioning of students with disabilities be done under the guidance of a pediatric physical and/or occupational therapist. Furthermore, all adults working with the child, including teachers, classroom aides, support staffs and family members should be using the same handling and positioning techniques. Within a transdisciplinary team model, therapists would teach the principles of handling and positioning to the other adults working with the child. Parents, teachers, and therapists would then share information about which methods they have found effective with the student. Finally, the whole team together would establish handling and positioning procedures that would become part of the student's daily routine at school and at home. If therapeutic handling and positioning are to be effective in promoting functional movement patterns and preventing secondary problems in the student with physical disabilities, consistency in handling and positioning throughout all daily activities is necessary (Orelove & Sobsey, 1996). To approach this topic, the chapter is divided into three major sections discussing handling, student positioning, and positioning of materials. The chapter will conclude with a section on instructional strategies, problems and emergencies, and management issues covering all three areas.

DESCRIPTION OF PRINCIPLES OF HANDLING

The presence of too much, too little, or fluctuating muscle tone is the result of damage to the student's sensorimotor system. Although this damage cannot be repaired, a variety of handling techniques can be used to alter muscle tone. However, the same techniques that alter muscle tone may

also affect a student's state of arousal. Activities that decrease muscle tone may also provide a calming effect, while activities that increase tone may be stimulating. Therefore, the techniques described here should be used carefully and under the supervision of a physical or occupational therapist to ensure that the desired effect is being achieved for each individual student.

Handling techniques should be used throughout an activity, as needed by the student, to facilitate optimal functional movement patterns. However, to use them effectively, four general guidelines should be followed. First, techniques that alter muscle tone are usually used to prepare the student's body before requiring active participation. Since initiation of active movement tends to increase muscle tone, this preparation is particularly important for the student with hypertonia (too much muscle tone).

Second, a student's body is usually handled at the head, shoulders, trunk, or hips. These key points of control, close to the center of the body, allow the person facilitating the student's movements to most accurately provide support or input and thereby have the greatest effect on the student's movement patterns.

Third, as the student's muscle tone changes through use of handling techniques, the facilitator should try to guide the student's body in typical patterns of movement. Typical patterns of movement tend to be **symmetrical,** with both sides of the body being positioned similarly and toward the midline of the body. For example, if a student with high muscle tone typically holds one arm in **flexion** (i.e., bent at the elbow, wrist, and fingers and rotated inward), handling procedures should be geared to guide that arm toward an extended and outwardly rotated position that is symmetrical and mirrors the functional position of the opposite arm. If a student with low tone usually lays on her back with arms and legs resting on the supporting surface held out to the side, handling/positioning procedures should be geared to bring arms and legs closer to the midline of the body so that a more functional position is obtained.

Fourth, handling techniques should be used to prepare and guide the student with physical disabilities to move in typical, functional ways, but they should not be overused. The ultimate goal of handling should be to have the student learn to move functionally, gradually fading out the handling support and requiring more independent movement on the part of the student.

Various other factors can affect a student's muscle tone. The student's physical health, mood, level of fatigue, medications, environmental factors (e.g., temperature, noise level), or activity level in a room can all influence the muscle tone of a student with a physical disability. These variables may need to be controlled if the student is to achieve optimal functional mobility during a particular task.

Before discussing physical handling techniques that can be used to alter muscle tone, it should also be noted that various medical procedures and medications have been developed in recent years that attempt to decrease hypertonia. Neurosurgery on the dorsal roots of the spinal cord (known as *selective dorsal rhizotomy*), surgical implantation of a pump under the skin that delivers a medication called Baclofen to selective areas of the spinal cord (Baclofen pump), and selective muscle injection with Botox (a derivative of the organism that causes botulism) all have been used on individuals with hypertonia to decrease muscle tone in specific parts of the body (Albright, 1995; Heller et al., 1996). These techniques have met with some success, but long-term study has not yet been possible. Since the techniques and medications lessen but do not eliminate hypertonia, proper handling and positioning techniques are still necessary to consider for individuals who have undergone these procedures.

ASSISTIVE STRATEGIES FOR THERAPEUTIC HANDLING

Inhibition Techniques

The following techniques can be used under a therapist's supervision to decrease muscle tone

that is too high and/or calm an irritable or over-aroused student. In general, activities that are slow, smooth, and repetitive usually inhibit (decrease) high muscle tone. These inhibition techniques include (a) gentle shaking or rocking, (b) relaxation techniques in the side-lying position, (c) relaxation techniques in the **supine** position (on the back), (d) slow rolling, (e) deep pressure, (f) neutral warmth, and (g) calming sensory stimuli.

Gentle Shaking or Rocking. A gentle shaking or rocking procedure can be performed to the total body or to a particular body part (e.g., an arm or leg). Slow and repetitive rocking can be performed to the total body in a rocking chair or while lying **prone** (on the stomach) over a therapy ball. Rocking is usually done in the forward/backward direction and with secure stabilization at the student's trunk or hips. To prepare a limb for a functional activity such as dressing, support should first be given close to the student's body (at the shoulder/elbow or hip/knee area). Then gentle, repetitive shaking or rotation of the limb can be performed until relaxation of the limb's muscle tone is felt. Typical postures and movements can then be facilitated.

Relaxation in the Side-Lying Position. To promote relaxation in the side-lying position, the student is placed in side lying on a comfortable, firm surface (e.g., mat) with a small pillow or folded towel under the head for support. The adult is in back of the student. One hand is placed over the student's upper shoulder and the other hand over the student's upper hip. The student's trunk is rotated by gently and slowly pushing the shoulder forward as the hip is pulled back and then reversing the procedure with the shoulder moving back as the hip is moved forward. This should be repeated slowly and rhythmically until the muscle tone relaxes and resistance to movement is no longer felt. As the muscle tone in the student's trunk relaxes, tone throughout the entire body should also relax, allowing easier passive and active movement of the arms and legs.

Relaxation in the Supine Position. A similar relaxation procedure can be carried out with the student in the supine, or back-lying, position. The student is placed in the back-lying position on a comfortable, firm surface with a small pillow or towel roll under the head. This position will flex the student's head slightly forward, thereby decreasing extensor tone in this area. A larger towel roll can be placed under the backs of the knees to flex the legs and decrease total body **extension.** The adult is at the student's feet. By lifting the student's legs, knees to chest, extensor tone can be further decreased. The gentle shaking or rocking procedure described earlier may have to be used first to relax the legs enough to allow them to be bent toward the chest. Trunk rotation can then be worked on by rolling the student's knees side to side, slowly and rhythmically, as the upper trunk is stabilized. This should be repeated slowly and rhythmically until the muscle tone relaxes and resistance to movement is no longer felt. As the muscle tone in the student's trunk relaxes, tone throughout the entire body should also relax, allowing easier passive and active movement of the arms and legs.

Slow Rolling. The student is placed in the back-lying position on a comfortable and firm surface with a small pillow or towel roll under the head. The adult is to one side of the student. One hand is placed on the student's hip and the other on the rib cage. The student is rolled away from the adult and then back onto the back. Gentle, repetitive slow rolling from back lying to side lying continues until the student's muscle tone is felt to relax. This technique is thought to provide a low-frequency vestibular stimulation that inhibits the CNS, producing relaxation and a calming effect (Fraser, Hensinger, & Phelps, 1990).

Deep Pressure. In this technique, deep pressure is applied to a muscle group through positioning or by placing the hands over the muscle. This provides tactile and proprioceptive input that is necessary to lengthen muscle fibers, resulting in relaxation of the muscles. The technique involves placing a hand(s) over the student's muscle group

that is to be relaxed and applying firm but gentle pressure with the whole hand into the muscle toward the supporting surface. This is done until relaxation is felt to occur. (This technique will also be discussed further under "Positioning.")

Neutral Warmth. Immersing the student in tepid (body-temperature) water or wrapping the body in a cotton blanket for 10 to 15 minutes as a preparation activity can relax general muscle tone. This technique obviously is more viable for home use than classroom use.

Sensory Stimuli. Various techniques using visual stimuli, auditory stimuli, taste, and smell may be used to promote relaxation. Cool colors, low lighting, and a reduced number of stimuli are inhibitory and aid in relaxation. Soft, regular rhythms of voice or music and a reduced amount of stimulation can help promote relaxation. Neutral temperatures and tastes of food and drink are also relaxing. Mild perfumes or other pleasant odors (e.g., vanilla) similarly have a relaxing effect.

Stimulation Techniques

Stimulation techniques can also be used under a therapist's supervision to increase muscle tone that is too low and/or arouse a lethargic student. In general, activities that are fast, irregular, and repetitive usually have a stimulating effect. Stimulation techniques include (a) relatively rapid, irregularly timed rolling, shaking, rocking, and bouncing; (b) joint compression; (c) quick stretch to a muscle; (d) resistance to a desired movement; (e) tapping; (f) vestibular stimulation; and (g) excitatory sensory stimulation.

Total body movement input that is fast and irregular needs to be given with caution. Due to the response of the vestibular system (in the inner ear), this type of stimulation may result in fearful, emotional, and physical reactions (e.g., nausea, dizziness) on the part of the student. In some students, seizures may also be caused as a result of this type of stimulation. As with any handling technique, supervision by a physical or occupational therapist and close observation of the student's response to the input are necessary to ensure that the technique is providing the desired outcome.

Relatively Rapid, Irregularly Timed Rolling, Shaking, Rocking, and Bouncing. This procedure can be performed to the total body or to a particular body part (e.g., arm or leg). Rapid rolling, rocking, or bouncing can be performed to the total body in a rocking chair or while positioned on a therapy ball. It can also be given in a number of different positions on a firm and comfortable surface, such as rolling from back to stomach on a mat, kneeling on all fours on a mat, lying on the stomach with support on elbows or hands over a wedge, sitting in a chair, kneeling up to a table, and/or standing. Rocking may be done in all directions while providing secure stabilization to the student where needed, depending on the student's position.

To prepare a limb for a functional activity such as dressing, support should first be given close to the student's body (at the shoulder/elbow or hip/knee). Then relatively rapid, irregular, but repetitive shaking or bouncing of the limb in space can be performed until an increase in the limb's muscle tone is felt. Typical postures and movements can then be facilitated.

Joint Compression. Joint compression, also known as *joint approximation,* provides input to the muscles on both sides of a joint, resulting in contraction of both sets of muscles. This lends stability to the joint and increases muscle power to work against gravity. Joint compression can be used on any body part where muscle tone needs to be increased. Proper positioning of the body part must first be achieved before the technique is applied. This is especially important at the head and neck, where use of this technique can cause spinal cord injury if cervical spine instability is present (as in some students with Down syndrome and other conditions). In these instances, joint compression to the head and neck area would be contraindicated.

Once the body part is properly positioned, either a series of quick, brief, and firm compressions or firm, continuous pressure can be applied through the joint(s) in the direction of the supporting surface. This technique is often applied during a weight-bearing activity to increase muscle tone and postural stability. For example, joint compressions may be given through the head and/or trunk to facilitate sitting, or they may be given through shoulders and elbows to facilitate maintaining a prone-on-elbows position.

Quick Stretch to a Muscle. This technique of applying quick stretches to a muscle needs to be used under a therapist's direction so as not to cause damage to the muscle or joint. The initial position of the body part and grading the stretch put on the muscle are critical to getting a desired response. Using a quick stretch of a muscle in one direction facilitates movement in the opposite direction. For example, if a student with low muscle tone has difficulty closing his mouth, a quick but gentle pull down on the jaw can facilitate jaw closure.

Resistance to a Desired Movement. As a student with low tone attempts to move actively, applying resistance to the movement can increase muscle tone and strength. How much resistance is applied and where it is applied on the student's body, as well as where in the movement pattern it occurs, should be under the direction of a therapist. For example, as a student with low tone begins to creep on all fours, slight resistance to forward movement might be applied at the shoulders to increase muscle tone. Care must be taken so that the resistance is not so much as to make movement difficult or impossible. Other examples of resisting a desired movement to increase muscle tone and strength would be to add weight to a walker for a student who is ambulating with such a device or to add a small, lightweight, weighted cuff to the arm of a student with low tone during certain fine-motor activities.

Tapping. Gentle, rapid tapping with flat fingers over a muscle can facilitate contraction of that muscle. For example, if contraction of the biceps muscle is desired to assist the student in bringing her hand to her mouth, gently tapping over the fleshy part of the muscle (on the inner aspect of the upper arm) may assist the movement. This technique, again, should be used only under the direction of a physical or occupational therapist.

Vestibular Stimulation. Fast rolling, spinning, tilting, and swinging can be used to arouse a student's general states and to increase muscle tone throughout the body. As has been already mentioned, the student should be monitored during these kinds of activities for signs of seizures, fear, emotionality (e.g., crying), and physical reactions (e.g., nausea, dizziness). If any of these signs occur, the activity will need to be stopped and, when attempted again, the rate, speed, or direction of movement evaluated and modified. Physical reactions such as nausea may even occur several hours after the stimulation is provided. This response should be recorded to adjust the amount provided during the next day.

Excitatory Sensory Stimuli. Visual stimulation, auditory stimulation, taste, and smell may be used to stimulate movement. For example, bright, warm colors and bright lighting are facilitory to general arousal and muscle tone. Fast, loud, irregular rhythms of voice and music are also stimulating. Cool or warm temperatures and strong flavors of food and drink are stimulating as well. Noxious or strong odors (e.g., ammonia, oil of cloves, etc.) also have a stimulating effect. Care should be taken that the odor is stimulating but not aversive to the student.

A Note on Fluctuating Tone. These activities have been described as techniques to inhibit tone in students with high muscle tone and to increase tone in students with low muscle tone. Activities for the student with fluctuating muscle tone will vary depending on the type of tone being exhibited at the time the student is being handled.

When the student is exhibiting high muscle tone, the inhibitory handling techniques should be used. When low tone is present, the stimulating handling techniques should be tried. The student's therapist will be an important resource, as the student with fluctuating muscle tone can be a challenge to handle and position appropriately.

PRINCIPLES OF POSITIONING

Proper therapeutic positioning of students with physical disabilities is an important adjunct to therapeutic handling. Therapeutic positioning can be defined as the placement of body parts in certain functional postures (Heller et al., 1996; Orelove & Sobsey, 1996). Once muscle tone has been altered through handling techniques, proper positioning of the student can maintain the positive effects of handling for a longer period and allow the student to use more functional independent movements gained through the changes in muscle tone. Proper positioning can also decrease the potential negative influence of primitive reflexes, thereby allowing more typical and functional movement patterns. Therapeutic positioning is also used to maintain symmetrical and/or midline alignment of body parts.

There are also several other goals of therapeutic positioning. Such positioning can maintain stabilization of body parts, readying the body to work against the effects of gravity, helping promote active participation in meaningful functional activities within a variety of different contexts. Therapeutic positioning can also provide a variety of experiences to enhance physical and cognitive development. Finally, it is also used to prevent secondary problems such as muscle shortenings, joint contractures, orthopedic problems, skeletal deformities, and health and medical problems (e.g., skin breakdown, infections, respiratory and digestive problems).

Positioning is dynamic in nature. Dynamic positioning occurs as the student is placed in or facilitated to move into, or through, a therapeutic position using appropriate handling. Static positioning may then be necessary to maintain the positive effects of the positioning. Static positioning includes the use of adaptive equipment to achieve the goals outlined earlier. However, since immobility is known to have adverse effects on cardiovascular, respiratory, urinary, gastrointestinal, metabolic, and motor functions, students with physical disabilities should experience a variety of positions (Heller et al., 1996; Orelove & Sobsey, 1991). Positions should be changed at least one time per hour, ideally every 30 minutes.

In selecting a position or positions for a student with physical disabilities, parents, teachers, therapists, and support staff should work together to answer the following questions: Is the position developmentally and/or task appropriate for the student? Does the position reinforce postures in which the student is currently developing greater control of active, functional movement patterns? Does the position discourage postures or movement patterns that the student should avoid? Does the position encourage social interaction and greater functional skill? Is the position a realistic alternative that will be used throughout typical home or school routines? For proper positioning, the answer to these questions should be yes. The next section will discuss positioning options in supine position (on the back), side-lying position (on the side), prone position (on the stomach), sitting, and standing, across adaptive equipment and assistive strategies. A section on instructional strategies will follow as it pertains to all of the positions.

SUPINE POSITIONING

Equipment and Adaptive Equipment

The supine (back-lying) position is a normal resting position. In this position, the young baby first develops control over the flexor muscles. However, for students with atypical tone and primitive reflexes, the position can promote abnormal tone,

abnormal movement patterns, and poor breathing patterns. This can result in the possibility of aspiration, limited environmental interaction, and **asymmetrical** body alignment. Students with physical disabilities should never be flat on their back in the supine position for any length of time due to the likelihood of abnormal postures. Even when sleeping, side lying or a supported supine position would be the preferred position. When the supine position is being used with individuals with physical disabilities, therapeutic handling and special positioning is needed to prevent abnormal positions and undesirable effects.

The student with physical disabilities usually requires a supported, somewhat elevated position to be functional in the supine position. To accomplish this, several types of equipment may be used, such as a mat with a firm but comfortable surface, pillows, rolled towels or blankets, bolsters (cylinder-shaped adaptive pieces of equipment used for positioning), wedges, and bath chairs. Each piece of equipment must be correctly positioned in key areas to achieve a functional supine position.

A rolled towel, blanket, or pillow may be used to position the student's upper body in a supine position. A lightweight towel (or blanket) can be rolled up into a cylinder and brought around the back of the head, just above the neck to bring the head into slight flexion. Placement of the towel on both sides of the head helps maintain a midline position of the head. If the towel ends are extended in back of the shoulders, or if additional towel rolls are placed in back of each shoulder, the arms are also brought forward somewhat toward midline.

The student's trunk and legs will also need positioning. To break up the extensor posturing seen with lower extremity hypertonia or to better position splayed, low-toned legs, a towel (or blanket) roll may be placed behind the knees. A bolster (a cylinder-shaped adaptive piece of equipment) may be used instead, but care should be taken that the appropriate size is used. Sandbags or rolls may also be required on both sides of the trunk/hips to align the body in midline.

A roll or pillow between the knees may also be needed if "scissoring" (i.e., extension, **adduction,** and internal rotation) of the legs is occurring. However, flexion at the hips and knees (obtained using the roll or bolster behind the knees) usually breaks up scissoring and other extension patterns.

These positioning suggestions can be improved upon for some students by using the suggested supports while the student is in the supine position on a wedge. A wedge is a triangular-shaped piece of positioning equipment. In this instance, the head would be on the elevated, high end of the wedge. This more elevated position allows for better environmental interaction and facilitates better breathing patterns.

Adaptive equipment such as bath seats may be used to support a student in the elevated supine position for specific functional activities such as bathing. Most bath seats have an elevating backrest that allows students to be comfortably and safely positioned at an angle that is optimal for their motor control and functional level. The seat sits on suction cups, low in the water to allow adequate washing and, for younger children, water play. Some bath seats have additional head and trunk side supports, to position the head and trunk in midline, and trunk, hip, or leg straps to further maintain an optimal body position while bathing.

Assistive Strategies

Parents, teachers, support personnel, and therapists should first determine whether the supine position is appropriate for the student with physical disabilities, answering the questions previously outlined. If the team decides that it would be an appropriate and therapeutic position for the student, the following assistive strategies should be followed.

First, a plan should be devised and documented that contains information on when, where, and how long the student will be placed in the supine position at home and at school. Inclusive in this plan should be consideration of

potential for interaction with other family members, peers, staff, and others as well as potential functional activities that the student can perform while supine.

Once the plan is devised, the adaptive equipment necessary to help position the student in the supine position should be obtained for home and school and stored in a convenient place close to where the positioning will occur. All adults working with the student then should be instructed by the student's PT or OT in setup and use of the adaptive equipment specifically required to assist the student with the supine position.

Before the student is actually placed in the adaptive equipment, he should be shown the equipment, and the rationale and plan for positioning should be shared with him. If the student is young, has sensory impairments, or has low cognitive abilities, he should still be allowed to "get acquainted" with the equipment (e.g., see and/or touch it). The student should always be informed when he is about to be moved into a piece of equipment, verbally; through object, movement, or touch cues; or through other forms of augmentative communication.

The next strategy consists of proper instruction in handling and positioning. All adults working with the student should be instructed by the PT or OT in handling techniques that are necessary to prepare/assist the student to move into and maintain the supine position. All adults will also need to receive instruction in correctly positioning the student in the necessary equipment. Correct alignment of each body part while the student is supine should be covered, beginning with head and trunk and including the desired position for arms and legs. Also, how frequently the student is placed in the supine position and a method of tracking this should be discussed and included in the plan. The adults should also be instructed in how to periodically check for maintenance of proper position while the student is supine. All adults working with the student then need to be instructed in proper setup of activities and materials that the student will use while supine and how to help the student access these activities and materials. Fine-motor activities requiring reach and grasp or visual motor coordination are good activities to perform in supine position since the shoulders are supported and working the arms in this position partially eliminates the effects of gravity. Adults need to be aware of the change in visual perspective that occurs while laying on the back, even in an elevated position, and choose activities with this in mind.

Finally, the adults should be instructed in correct handling methods to use with the student when he is being removed from the adaptive equipment to maintain the therapeutic benefits gained from the positioning. If indicated, the adults should also be instructed to check the student's skin for signs of pressure areas or circulatory problems once he is removed from the position. Follow-up procedures should be delineated and documented if such signs are observed.

SIDE-LYING POSITIONING

Equipment and Adaptive Equipment

Side lying is an excellent position for facilitating midline activities of the arms and hands. Many students with physical disabilities are unable to bring their hands together in the midline when lying on their backs or in a sitting position. By placing the student in the side-lying position, the arms are brought forward, and gravity assists in bringing the hands together (Hanson & Harris, 1986). The side-lying position is also useful for promoting a symmetrical and midline posture of the body and decreasing the effects of a persistent asymmetrical tonic neck reflex (ATNR) (see Table 6-1).

Side-lying positioning also can be used as a method to prevent or improve spinal curvatures (i.e., scoliosis) in students whose posture in other positions is asymmetrical. By positioning the student in side lying to both sides, the spine naturally undergoes range of motion, through gravity acting to pull the vertebrae in a straight line. For the student who already has a scoliosis, positioning in side lying, especially on the concave side of the curve, can help stretch out muscular tightness that may be contributing to the scoliosis.

Several types of equipment may be used to promote side lying: mats or other firm but comfortable surface, pillows, rolled towels or blankets, sandbags, upholstered furniture, and homemade or commercially made side-lyers. One example of a commercial side-lyer is in Figure 6-1.

Side lying should occur on a firm but comfortable surface. A padded carpet, mat, firm couch, or firm bed could all be appropriate for side lying at home or school. Too soft a support surface negates the benefits of side lying by allowing body misalignment and by not providing a stable surface off which to work against gravity.

For a small student or one without much independent mobility, pillows, rolled towels, rolled blankets, and/or sandbags can be used to help the student maintain a side-lying position. A small pillow under the head is usually used for comfort and to maintain the head in midline and in slight flexion. A pillow, rolled towel, rolled blanket, or sandbag may be used behind the student's back to

FIGURE 6-1 This student can easily move his hand to activate a switch to listen to music when he is positioned in a side-lyer.

prevent her from rolling onto her back. Sometimes the student's back may also be placed against a comfortable surface such as an upholstered chair or couch. If the student tends to roll forward, a roll may also need to be placed in front of the student's trunk. However, if a roll is used in this way, care must be taken to position the roll to allow the arms to come together in the midline so that the student can engage in a functional activity.

While in side-lying position, a pillow is also usually placed between the student's legs to separate the legs and allow the upper leg to be supported in flexion. This assists with comfort and helps decrease muscle tone in the legs. Side-lyers may be commercially made or homemade. The older or more severely involved student will probably need the support of the commercial type of device to be adequately supported in a side-lying position. These devices come in a variety of sizes and normally have a support with an adjustable angle at the student's back and either an adjustable support block at the student's abdomen or a cushioned harness or strap(s) to help maintain the student's position in the side-lyer. Additionally, the side-lyers also typically include a support cushion for under the head and between the legs.

Some students who experience breathing difficulties when laying flat on the floor may need to be positioned on their sides as described earlier (using either homemade or commercial side-lying adaptive equipment), but on an incline. In this case, the adaptive equipment can be placed on a wedge at a comfortable angle for the student.

Assistive Strategies

Parents, teachers, support personnel and therapists should first determine whether side lying is an appropriate position for the student with physical disabilities. If the team decides that it would be an appropriate and therapeutic position for the student, the physical or occupational therapist should give instruction on how to position the student correctly to all adults working with the student. Included in this instruction should be correct alignment of each body part during side lying, beginning with the head and trunk and continuing with demonstrations of the desired positions for each arm and leg (as these may differ, side to side). Also, how frequently the student is placed on one side versus the other side should be discussed, as well as a way of tracking the implementation of the positioning regime.

All adults working with the student then need to be instructed in proper setup of activities and materials that the student will use while in side-lying position and how to help the student access these activities and materials. Fine-motor activities requiring the use of two hands and transfer of objects from hand to hand are good choices for side-lying activities. Adults need to be aware of the change in visual perspective that occurs in the side-lying position and choose activities with this in mind.

PRONE POSITIONING

Equipment and Adaptive Equipment

In the typically developing newborn baby, **head control** in prone (on the stomach) is one of the earliest motor activities to develop. In the first 1 to 2 months of life, the baby learns to lift and turn his head while lying on his stomach. By the time he is 3 to 4 months old, he is able to support the weight of his upper body on his elbows, holding his head up in the midline at a 45- to 90-degree angle (Hanson & Harris, 1986). It is in the prone position that the muscles that extend the body against gravity are primarily developed. For the student with physical disabilities, these activities may be very difficult. However, working to achieve head control in the prone position is very important for gaining control over the body while upright in space.

Several different types of equipment may be used to position an individual prone. These include a mat or other firm but comfortable supporting surface, towel or blanket rolls, bolsters, half-rolls, and wedges.

Prone lying should occur on a firm, comfortable surface. A padded carpet, mat, firm couch or bed could all be appropriate for prone lying at home or school. As with other positions, too soft a support surface negates the benefits of prone lying by allowing body misalignment and by not providing a stable surface off which to work against gravity.

For a small student or one without much independent mobility, rolled towels or blankets can be used to help the student maintain a prone position. The towel or blanket should be rolled tightly, forming a firm roll. The roll should be just large enough to fit under the student's armpits while still allowing the elbows/hands to come into contact with the floor. The roll acts to support the student under the arms and in front of the chest. The student's arms are in front of the roll, elbows positioned under shoulders, ready to accept the weight of the upper body as the head is lifted.

A commercially available half-roll can also work well to support the young student in the prone position. A half-roll is usually covered in vinyl fabric and shaped like a cylinder cut in half. The flat bottom on a half-roll lends some extra stability to the support, but by not using a cylindrically shaped support, a dynamic aspect of the support is sacrificed (i.e., the support moving under the student as the student moves).

For the larger, older student, homemade or commercially made bolsters or wedges may be needed to provide adequate support in the prone position. Commercial bolsters come in a variety of diameters and are usually covered in washable vinyl material. Bolsters may be homemade by covering appropriately sized cans or newspaper rolls with a sheet of foam material and then making either a removable, washable fabric cover or a washable vinyl cover. The bolster is used just like a blanket or towel roll, placed under the student's armpits to provide support to the shoulders and trunk while maintaining the prone position. The bolster's diameter should just allow the student's elbows or hands to touch the floor, depending on whether elbow or hand support is desired.

Wedges can also be homemade by purchasing a block of foam and cutting the appropriate angle with an electric knife, then covering the wedge, as described earlier, with a removable, washable fabric cover or a vinyl cover. Commercially available wedges come in a wide variety of heights from the floor and are usually vinyl covered (see Figure 6-2). Some wedges are hollowed in the

FIGURE 6-2 A boy in prone position on a wedge

center with built-up sides to provide additional lateral support and to prevent the student from rolling off the wedge. Cushioned straps attached with Velcro are also sometimes provided to secure the student's position on the wedge. The student is positioned on the wedge with the head toward the high end and arms over the front of the wedge. Hands or elbows should touch the floor to allow for weight bearing.

Some students require additional supports (e.g., rolls, sandbags, etc.) to maintain the rest of their bodies in good alignment, once their arms are positioned over a roll, bolster, or wedge for prone lying. Supports may need to be placed on one or both sides of the student's hips or between the legs to keep the lower body in alignment and the legs from scissoring. A sandbag may also be placed over the student's buttocks while prone. This added weight can help "anchor" the student's pelvis on the supporting surface and provide a point of stability off which to lift the upper body against gravity.

Because of the influence of the primitive reflex (e.g., tonic labyrinthine reflex, tonic neck reflexes), students with hypertonia may build up tone while in the prone position, even after the most effective handling is done to relax the student prior to being placed in the position. Handling techniques to decrease the student's muscle tone may need to be used periodically throughout the time spent in prone position to facilitate typical, functional movement patterns.

Assistive Strategies

As with all positioning decisions, parents, teachers, support personnel, and therapists should first determine whether prone lying is an appropriate position for the student with physical disabilities. If they decide that it is, all adults working with the student should be instructed by the physical or occupational therapist in correctly positioning the student in prone position using the adaptive equipment. Correct alignment of each body part while the student is prone should be covered, beginning with the head and trunk, and progressing to the desired position for arms and legs. Also,

how frequently the student is placed in prone position and a way of tracking this should be discussed and included in the health plan.

All adults working with the student then need to be instructed in proper setup of activities and materials that the student will use while prone lying and how to help the student access these activities and materials. Visual activities (e.g., watching a movie, playing a visual game) will facilitate lifting the head up while supporting on arms/hands. Activities requiring reaching with one arm (e.g., to bat at an object) will also facilitate weight shift onto one arm while the opposite arm attempts to reach. Handling procedures may need to be performed during prone positioning to maintain relaxation or to assist the student to shift her weight over one arm. Adults will need to be instructed in these procedures. They should also be cautioned that this position can be very fatiguing for students and look for signs of tiring (e.g., head down on supporting surface).

SITTING POSITIONING

Equipment and Adaptive Equipment

The typically developing infant is able to sit up with slight support by the age of 3 to 6 months and usually can sit independently by 5 to 9 months. The student with physical disabilities may achieve independent sitting at a much later age or may never be able to sit independently without some type of external support. The student who is delayed in achieving independent sitting or who does not have enough control of the neck and trunk muscles to sit independently needs some type of adaptive positioning or equipment. Adaptive seating is particularly important in providing the student with physical disabilities the support needed in the trunk to enable him to free up his hands for functional activities such as self-feeding, play activities, and school-related tasks such as writing or using a communication device.

Table 6-2 Advantages and Disadvantages in Positioning

Position	Advantages	Disadvantages
Prone	Normal resting position; requires no motor control; promotes trunk and hip extension	Possibility of suffocation; stimulates asymmetry if head turned to side; may stimulate flexor tone; functional activities limited
Supine	Normal resting position; requires little motor control; no danger of suffocation; symmetry can be maintained	May stimulate extensor tone; prolonged position inhibits respiration; possibility of aspiration; ceiling view; functional activities limited
Prone on elbows	Encourages head, arm, and trunk control; allows improved view	May stimulate flexor tone; may stimulate excessive extension; tiring position; limits hand use
Side lying	Normal resting position; usually does not stimulate abnormal tone; improves alignment, brings hands together at midline	May require bulky equipment; sideward view; few functional activities; pressure on bony prominences (hips)
Side sitting	Easy to assume from lying, hands and knees, kneeling; promotes trunk rotation, range of motion in hips, trunk if sides alternated	May reinforce asymmetry; may require one or both hands for support; difficult with tight hips or trunk
Indian or ring sitting	Wide base of support; symmetrical position; easier to free hands	Difficult tansition to/from other positions; may reinforce flexed posture
Long sitting	May provide wide base of support; may prevent hamstring contractures	Impossible with tight hamstrings; may stimulate trunk flexion, flexor spasticity
Heel or W-sitting	Easy transition to/from other positions; stable base of support; frees hands	Reinforces hip, knee, and ankle deformity; reduces reciprocal movement, weight shifting, and trunk rotation; may stress hip joint
Chair sitting—standard chair	Normal position and equipment; easy transition to/from other positions; minor adaptations can be added to improve position	May not provide adequate position for feet, trunk, hips; may be overused
Chair sitting—bolster chair	Reduces scissoring at hips; may increase anterior pelvic tilt	Bulky equipment; difficult transition to/from other positions
Chair sitting—corner chair	Inhibits extensor tone in trunk and shoulders	May encourage excessive flexion; may rotate trunk and pelvis
Chair sitting—wheelchair	Allows for positioning and mobility simultaneously; adaptations can control most postural problems	Chairs may be expensive, complicated, easily maladjusted; may become overreliant on chair

SOURCE: From F. P. Orelove and D. Sobsey, *Educating Children with Multiple Disabilities: A Transdisciplinary Approach*, 3d ed. (Baltimore, MD: Paul H. Brookes Publishing, 1996), pp. 89–90. Reprinted by permission.

A number of commercially manufactured seating devices are available, as well as possibilities for homemade versions. The student's physical or occupational therapist is critical to assisting the student's parents and teachers in choosing a seating device that not only meets the student's current physical needs but also has the potential to grow and change with the student.

Equipment for proper positioning include the assisting adult's body, baby boppies (pillowlike rings), swim rings, rolls, bolsters, therapy balls, benches, Tumbleforms floor sitters, corner chairs, toddler chairs and other chairs with special supports for larger students, bolster chairs, and trays. The type of positioning equipment depends on whether sitting is occurring on the floor, in chairs, or on adaptive chairs.

Sitting on the Floor. The floor is a natural place for a young student or a student with physical disabilities to begin learning to sit independently. When a student is placed on the floor in sitting, a number of positions are possible: (a) Indian or tailor sitting (sitting with the knees bent and the lower legs crossed, (b) ring sitting (sitting with the hips and knees bent but legs apart), (c) long sitting (sitting with legs straight out in front), (d) side sitting (sitting with both knees pointing to the same side), (e) heel sitting (sitting on the heels), and (f) W-sitting (sitting in between the heels). Each of these sitting positions has advantages and disadvantages, as listed in Table 6-2. Positions of preference for students with physical disabilities are usually tailor, ring, and side sitting and possibly long sitting (if the student has enough lower extremity range of motion).

When sitting on the floor, the student's pelvis should be level and tipped slightly forward. Weight should be evenly distributed on the bottom, not to one side or shifted back onto the base of the spine. The trunk should be more or less straight, with shoulders level, head and trunk held in midline, and arms relaxed at the sides, supporting weight on the floor, if necessary.

If a student needs extra support to maintain sitting **balance,** she can be supported in sitting position between an adult's legs, straddling an adult's thigh, or on the adult's crossed legs. The adult's body in these cases can assist in controlling the position of the student's trunk and legs, with the adult's hands still free to assist the student in performing functional arm movements. Inflated swim rings or commercially available baby boppies (pillowlike rings) can also be used with smaller students to provide outside support during sitting. The student sits inside the ring with trunk supported by the ring and arms on top.

FIGURE 6-3 A girl on a therapy ball

For the student who is beginning to develop sitting balance (including righting responses, protective responses, and equilibrium responses), rolls, bolsters, and therapy balls can be used to practice sitting balance since they provide a moveable surface on which to sit (Figure 6-3). When the student reaches during functional activities, his weight shift causes the moveable surface on which he is sitting to shift slightly. This requires him to perform postural adjustments to maintain sitting balance. The student will need adult supervision in this situation to prevent falling and potential injury. These activities should be performed only under the direction of a physical or occupational therapist.

Low benches can also be used with students who are developing early independent sitting skills. The bench should be low enough to allow the student's feet to be supported on the floor. Reaching down for objects placed on the floor and coming back up to sitting and dressing/undressing while sitting on a bench would be two of many possible functional activities to engage the student in during bench sitting.

Getting into and out of sitting are also important skills for the student with physical disabilities to learn. The student's physical or occupational therapist can instruct the adults working with the student on the appropriate way to assist the individual student to accomplish this. Usually students assume sitting by pushing up to sitting from a side-lying position or use the hands-and-knees position as a transition position from lying prone on the floor to sitting.

Sitting in Chairs. In some instances, students with mild physical disabilities will be able to use regular chairs with some support. However, students with more involved physical disabilities will often require adaptive seating options (see Figure 6-4). Some seats, like the Tumbleforms floor sitter, require little control in sitting, basically cradling the student in a semireclining position the angle of which is adjusted by where the chair is Velcroed onto the base. Others, like a toddler chair, specially adapted armchair, or corner chair, require that the student have some ability to control his head and trunk upright in space. Toddler or special armchairs usually have flat backs and seats, like a standard chair, but are adapted to the student's special seating needs with add-ons that support the student's body at various points. Corner chairs have an angled back, with both back sections angled forward so that the student's shoulders/arms are brought forward and supported in this position. Still others, such as the bolster chair, require fairly developed postural reactions in sitting. Bolster chairs have a rounded, barrellike seat that the student straddles in sitting position.

Most special adaptive seating come available with trays to help with overall trunk support as well as to provide a surface for functional activities. Trays should be adjustable in height to facilitate optimal arm and trunk positioning. Usually chair arms or trays are positioned at the height of the elbows when the arms are relaxed at the sides. However, some students with atypical muscle tone may need the tray or arm supports to be elevated somewhat higher than elbow height to facilitate adequate trunk extension and a forward arm position. Many trays allow for an adjustable slant to the tray surface, which can be very important to allow for proper positioning of materials for the student with visual problems, as well as for optimal physical positioning for the student with motor disabilities.

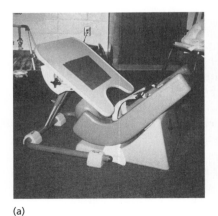
(a)

(b)

(c)

FIGURE 6-4 Different types of adapted chairs that promote correct positioning for sitting

SOURCE: Heller et al. (1996, p. 160).

The bath and shower chair are used to assist with hygiene activities. Bath chairs typically sit in the bottom of a bathtub, while shower chairs are typically elevated for shower use. These chairs are usually made of mesh fabric that enables water to pass through it. They usually come with adjustable seat and back angles, as well as additional support blocks or straps to allow for proper positioning of the individual student.

Toileting chairs may fit over a standard toilet or may include a pan within the unit that is easily removed for cleaning. One important feature of some toileting chairs is an adjustable back that allows both a reclining and forward-leaning position. Many students with physical disabilities and muscle tone disorders need to be able to lean forward somewhat to have a bowel movement. These toileting chairs usually also have (a) arms or a tray to provide support, (b) support blocks or straps and a footrest for appropriate positioning, and (c) a removable deflector for the seat for male students to use during urination.

Several general guidelines should be followed when placing a student in sitting, either in a regular chair or in special adaptive seating. The student's pelvis should be level, centered at the back edge of the seat, and tipped slightly forward. The seat itself should be firm and level and extend to approximately 1 inch short of the back of the knees. The student's hips and knees should be bent at 90 degrees, and the student's feet should be supported with ankles at a neutral, 90-degree position. The student's knees should in general be in line with the hips, and the student's trunk should be straight and shoulders level. The chair's backrest should be firm. The height of the backrest depends on the student's head and trunk control. Generally, the height should at least extend to shoulder blade level. The student's head and neck should be in midline and straight, and the student's arms should be relaxed at the sides or on a support.

These guidelines should begin with focus on the pelvis, because its position during sitting can influence the alignment of every other body part. Sometimes a simple readjustment of pelvic posi-

tion can radically improve a student's total body alignment in sitting. Proper pelvic and hip position in adaptive seating devices is, therefore, critical and should be controlled with at least a seat belt, placed at a 45-degree angle across the hips. Additional supports (e.g., lateral blocks, wedge seats, etc.) to control pelvic/hip position should be added as needed.

Sometimes other supports are necessary in adaptive seating to control a student's sitting position. These might include lateral trunk supports or an H- or X-shaped harness to help with trunk position, head supports to maintain a midline position of the head, an abductor post/wedge or straps to keep the legs apart, or foot straps or sandals to maintain the position of the lower legs and feet. These extra support devices can be very beneficial to maintaining a student in an optimal sitting position, but the reader is cautioned against overcontrolling the student's position or inappropriate selection of some support devices (e.g., use of X or V harness that may choke a student if he tends to "melt"). The student needs enough freedom of movement to be able to perform functional activities within motor limitations and to be able to develop new patterns of movement, if possible. Careful selection of supporting devices is needed.

Assistive Strategies

Parents, teachers, support personnel, and therapists should first determine whether sitting is an appropriate position for the student with physical disabilities. If they conclude that it would be an appropriate and therapeutic position for the student, all adults need to be properly trained in correctly positioning the student. Instruction should also include correct alignment of each body part, beginning with the pelvis and hips and continuing with the head/trunk, arms, legs, and feet. How the various positional supports (e.g., straps, abductors, lateral trunk or head supports) are used and the order in which they are applied should be made very clear, as this can affect the student's final position in the seating device.

All adults working with the student then need to be instructed in proper setup of activities/materials that the student will use while sitting and how to help the student access these activities/materials. All adults also need to demonstrate their understanding by positioning the student as the therapist watches. Many fine-motor, visual motor, or daily living tasks (e.g., eating) can be performed by the student in sitting position. Sitting also allows group and one-on-one interaction with peers (students with and without disabilities) that might not be available in other therapeutic positions. Sitting positioning should, therefore, be scheduled around times when this interaction can occur naturally.

STANDING

Equipment and Adaptive Equipment

The young student experiencing typical motor development will usually begin to pull up to standing at furniture between about 6 and 12 months of age. Independent standing, requiring no outside support, usually occurs by 9 to 15 months. Acquiring standing balance is an important prerequisite to independent walking (Hanson & Harris, 1986). The young student with a physical disability may learn to stand at a much later age or may never have adequate head and trunk control to stand without outside support. The previously mentioned positioning principles of attempting to achieve body symmetry, midline positioning, and utilizing minimal control at key points on the student's body are also important to consider when using adaptive equipment to help the student with a physical disability maintain supported standing.

Standing is important for students with physical disabilities because the position facilitates upright interaction with the environment, encourages head/trunk control, and promotes weight bearing, as well as functional use of the arms/hands. In addition, standing is thought to

encourage bone growth and density (due to the weight of the student being applied to the bones' growth plates). Finally, the upright position facilitates digestion and can help prevent respiratory and urinary tract infections. (Heller et al., 1996).

Several types of devices may be used to promote standing. These include lower extremity orthoses (braces), standing frames, prone standers, supine standers, and mobile standers. Proper positioning in a standing device is extremely important since all the joints of the legs are involved in bearing the student's weight while in standing. Therefore, a physical or occupational therapist must be involved in choosing the appropriate equipment for the individual student, adjusting the equipment for use by the student, and training all the adults working with the student in correctly positioning the student in the equipment.

For some students who are not used to standing, preparatory handling techniques may need to be used to prepare the student for standing. These could include relaxation techniques for the student with hypertonia or various stimulation techniques for the student with hypotonia. The soles of the student's feet may also need tactile preparation, using deep-pressure activities, as preparation for standing.

Orthoses. Some students with muscle tone that is too high or too low also require outside stabilization of the ankles/feet and, less frequently, knee position to enable them to stand in a well-aligned position. This stabilization is usually achieved by use of orthoses or braces. Orthoses are generally made of molded, rigid plastic and constructed by an orthotist or trained physical therapist. The orthoses fit very snugly, having been molded to the contours of the student's leg as it is stabilized in the desired weight-bearing position. For example, in Figure 6-5, this student has high muscle tone causing her to walk on tiptoe with poor balance. The use of an ankle-foot orthosis (AFO) allow her to bear weight on her foot and walk with stability.

Wearing time of orthoses must be gradually

(a)   (b)

FIGURE 6-5 A girl with (a) and without (b) ankle-foot orthoses

increased to eliminate the possibility of pressure injuries to the student's skin. Frequent adjustments and refitting are necessary, particularly in the growing student. Parents and professionals must, therefore, work closely together to ensure fit and usage of the orthoses (Heller et al., 1996).

Standing Frames. The type of standing equipment selected for use by an individual student depends on that student's level of motor control. Standing frames require the most motor control from the student (see Figure 6-6a). The student should have good head and trunk control and be able to bear weight on the legs in the upright, vertical position but may need assistance to maintain the position for any extended period. A standing frame usually provides support at the feet (to maintain foot position), knees (to maintain knee extension), hips (to maintain hip extension and midline position), and chest (to maintain trunk extension and midline position), by way of

(a)   (b)

FIGURE 6-6 A student using a standing frame (a) and prone stander (b)

various support blocks and straps. The standing frame can allow positioning of students in vertical standing while engaging in group activities (e.g., games) or during academic activities (e.g., classroom work on the blackboard).

Prone and Supine Standers. Prone standers allow students to be positioned on their stomach against the supporting surface while bearing weight through their feet at various angles from the vertical to about 55 degrees toward the horizontal (see Figure 6-6b). Because of the support provided up to the point of the student's armpits, the student does not need to be able to independently bear weight on the legs but should have ability to extend the head and upper trunk against gravity and maintain this position for some period of time. A prone stander usually provides support at the feet (to maintain foot position), knees (to maintain knee extension and keep legs apart in **abduction**), hips (to maintain hip extension and midline position), and chest (to maintain trunk extension and midline position). This support is provided by way of various support blocks and straps.

The prone stander may be placed against a surface, such as a sink, table, or elevated desk, to allow the student to participate in functional activities (e.g., washing dishes, brushing teeth, playing with toys, completing academic activities), either individually or in a group. Some prone standers are freestanding and come with wheeled bases with locking casters, facilitating moving the stander from place to place. These prone standers also usually come with detachable trays to provide a readily accessible work surface for the student.

The supine stander is similar to the prone stander, except instead of positioning the student forward on the chest and stomach, the person is tilted backward, allowing the student to assume the supine position (on the back) with support at all points of the body, including the head. The stander usually can be positioned at any angle from horizontal to vertical, thereby varying the amount of weight the student is required to bear

through the legs depending on motor control. This type of stander could be a possibility for the student who requires more support, because of poor control over the head and trunk against gravity and an inability to bear weight independently through the legs.

As with a prone stander, the supine stander usually provides support at the feet (to maintain foot position), knees (to maintain knee extension and keep legs apart in abduction), hips (to maintain hip extension and midline position), and chest (to maintain trunk extension and midline position). This support occurs through the use of various support blocks and straps. In addition, the supine stander also provides head support to keep the head in midline.

Most supine standers are freestanding and come with wheeled bases with locking casters, facilitating moving the stander from place to place. These supine standers also usually come with detachable trays to provide a readily accessible work surface for the student. Some commercially available standers allow the student to be positioned either prone or supine.

Mobile Standers. Mobile standers are similar to prone standers in the way that they position the student (in prone). However, they provide students who have the arm control with the added benefit of being able to propel themselves around the environment by means of large wheels attached to both sides of the stander, providing an alternative to wheelchair use. Even students without active use of their legs (e.g., in the case of myelomeningocele) can be positioned in the upright position in these devices, allowing them to access interaction with peers. The body support piece is usually padded and adjusts in height, width, and angle of tilt from the vertical. The wheels are also usually tilted inward to bring the top of the wheel under the hands for ease in propelling the stander. Wheels also detach for ease of transport. The footplate adjusts so that the student stands at the appropriate height to facilitate using the wheels. Brakes, trays, carriers (to transport books), support blocks, and straps that aid in positioning the student as outlined earlier are also available for these standers.

Assistive Strategies

Parents, teachers, support personnel, and therapists should first determine whether standing is an appropriate position for the specific student with physical disabilities. If they decide that standing would be an appropriate and therapeutic position for the student, all adults working with the student should be instructed by the physical or occupational therapist in correctly positioning the student in the standing equipment. Correct alignment of each body part should be covered, beginning with the feet and including the pelvis and hips, head/trunk, arms, and legs. How the various positional supports (e.g., straps, abductors, lateral trunk or head supports) are used and the order in which they are applied should be made very clear, as this can affect the student's final position in the standing device.

All adults working with the student then need to be instructed in proper setup of activities/materials that the student will use while standing and how to help the student access these activities/materials. Many fine-motor, visual motor, or daily living tasks (e.g., brushing teeth, handwashing clothes or dishes) can be performed by the standing student. Standing also allows group and one-on-one interaction with peers (students with and without disabilities, which might not be available in other therapeutic positions. Positioning in standing should, therefore, be scheduled around times when this interaction can occur naturally.

With any standing device, the student's time spent in the stander must be built up gradually, not to exceed about 30 minutes maximum at any given time. The student should also be examined for pressure points (i.e., excessive redness of the skin that does not disappear within 10 to 15 minutes) each time he is removed from the stander. If needed, adjustments should be made to the equipment to prevent excessive pressure from occurring while standing.

ASSISTIVE STRATEGIES FOR TRANSITIONING BETWEEN POSITIONS

In general, the adult who is facilitating movements from one position to another should use appropriate preparatory handling techniques, as directed by the student's physical or occupational therapist, prior to requiring the student to move. These techniques will help normalize tone and result in a better transition between positions. Facilitation of movement when changing from one position to another should occur using appropriate communication forms, using minimal control at the key body points, and encouraging the student to perform as much of the movement as possible by herself. These procedures would be individual for each student, but an example of such a transition procedure is given here.

To assist a student with high muscle tone to transition from back lying to sitting up, the adult could first relax the student's body by using trunk rotation achieved through rolling the student's legs side-to-side. Then the adult could indicate to the student (through speech, sign, cue, etc.) that rolling to the side was the desired movement. The adult could then help the student roll to the side using the hip as a key point, bending up one leg and bringing the leg across the student's body, facilitating rolling to the opposite side. A communication cue could then be used to indicate sitting, and the adult could provide support and facilitation (lifting under the student's under arm and pushing back on the upper hip) to assist in having the student push up on her arm into the sitting position.

Sometimes adaptive equipment is needed for transitioning from one position to another, especially when the student is large and heavy. Various types of electric or hydraulic lifts are available to assist in moving a heavy student from one position to another (e.g., from a wheelchair onto a mat). Slings are usually placed under the student's buttocks and behind his back, and these slings are attached to the lift. Then the lift is either turned on, if electric, or hand operated, if hydraulic, to lift the student off the supporting surface. The student can then be wheeled to the desired area and the procedure reversed to return the student to the new supporting surface. Use of lifts, especially when first initiated, can be very threatening to individuals with severe physical impairments; therefore, trust and good communication needs to be developed between adult and student.

POSITIONING MATERIALS

Positioning the student and positioning the material used in the instructional activity require careful consideration. When there are limitations in arm and hand movement, the student may not be able to manipulate the instructional material unless the student is properly positioned and the material is properly positioned. To facilitate access to the instructional material, the teacher will need to consider (a) object manipulation requirements, (b) object modifications, (c) positioning the student, (d) range of motion, (e) work surface modifications, (f) positioning devices, and (g) fatigue and endurance levels. Each of these may incorporate adaptive equipment and assistive strategies.

Object Manipulation Requirements

Various instructional goals will have different types of instructional material and motor requirements. Members of the educational team will need to examine each activity to determine the necessary objects and motor requirements. Objects' shape and size becomes important to note for students who are unable to pick up small items or have difficulty grasping. The motor movement required in the task is important in determining whether it is in the student's current ability. For example, pouring formula into a tube for tube feeding requires grasping a small tube, gripping a cup of formula, and being able to turn

at the wrist to pour the formula into the tube. Setting the table requires grasping and releasing silverware, as well as performing larger movements of placing silverware from side to side. Writing assignments require fine-motor movements and the ability to write from side to side. Using a task analysis to break down steps and identify motor movements and necessary objects will help pinpoint motor requirements. (See Chapter 2 for information on task analysis.)

Object Modifications

After determining the activity requirements, the educational team members needs to decide whether the items used in the activity should be modified when the student has difficulty manipulating them. Items can often be enlarged, have handles or straps added to them, have stiffer material added to them, be weighted, or be modified in numerous other ways. For example, some students will be able to hold items when they are enlarged by wrapping foam around them. For example, foam can be placed around a spoon or a tube-feeding syringe barrel to allow the student to hold it. In some instances, a strap or handle may be added to an object for students unable to grasp. Stiffening or thickening material by adding cardboard or other material to its back may promote better manipulation. Students who have tremors or coordination problems may benefit from weighting an object (by adding weight to it) or using wrist weights. In many instances, objects can be purchased already weighted such as spoons and pencils. The occupational therapist will often provide assistance to the teacher in determining possible object modifications.

Positioning the Student

As previously discussed in the chapter, the student needs to be properly positioned to allow for maximal access to the material. Incorrect positioning can decrease the student's range of motion and make it more difficult to access the material. The typical position used in the activity should first be considered using whatever positioning equipment is necessary for the student. In some instances, a different position may allow better manipulation of the material and will need to be considered for the activity. For example, the student may be able to perform more of the steps in changing a colostomy bag lying down with support rather than sitting. The physical and occupational therapist will be able to provide suggestions regarding positioning the student to access a particular task.

Range of Motion

After ascertaining the object manipulation requirements, possible object modifications, and optimal positioning, the student's range of motion needs to be determined for optimal placement of materials. Some students may have physical conditions that interfere with their ability to move through the entire movement pattern that the joint normally allows. The amount of movement available at a joint is referred to as *range of motion* (ROM). Limitations in range of motion can interfere with the student's ability to reach for objects and access material.

Range of motion can be divided into two categories: active and passive. Active range of motion is the range the student can achieve through her own movement by muscle activity. Passive range of motion refers to the range obtained by another person moving the involved joint within its full range while the student passively relaxes. Although more range can usually be obtained through passive range of motion, it is active range of motion that needs to be determined when positioning materials.

Within a student's range of motion, some areas may be easier to access than others. When the student is learning or being assessed on an instructional goal, it is important that the material be placed within an easy active range of motion for the student. This will allow the student to concentrate on the instructional goal, rather than struggling to access the material. If the student is working on a task that is already mastered, the material may be placed within areas that are in the outer ranges of the student's range of motion. This will allow the student the opportunity to maintain or improve his range of motion.

Many students with abnormal muscle tone may have muscle tone that fluctuates within the high to low ranges. In these instances, the student's muscle tone may impact the amount of active range of motion available throughout the day. For example, a student can sometimes easily access something in an upper right-hand corner of the tray in the morning but may not have the available range to reach this same area in the afternoon. Fluctuations in tone may be influenced by illness, excitement, fatigue, and the amount of time since the student last tried to extend the limb. Since the student's range of motion can fluctuate, the student may need to be quickly assessed prior to using the material to be sure he can access it.

In classroom situations, the student is often required to access material using the arm and hand that has the most movement. Often the range of motion of the shoulder, elbow, and wrist working together will help determine where materials should be placed. One quick method of assessing range of motion of the dominate arm is to construct an ROM grid. A ROM grid consists of a large piece of paper (e.g., 24 inches wide by 24 inches long) with 1- to 2-inch squares drawn on the paper. The grid is placed directly in front of the student. The student is asked to either point to various squares or items on the square or pick up items on the squares that are attached to the grid by Velcro, sticky tack, or tape. The student's range of motion is first assessed with the board flat on a table. The teacher records (by marking with one color on each square) how far the student is able to reach to the top, down, top left corner, middle left, bottom left corner, bottom right corner, middle right, and top right corner. Items that must be accessed flat on a surface should be positioned well within the determined range.

The student's ROM is also determined with the ROM grid being placed on a slant and at varying heights. Many students have increased ROM when the board is elevated, lowered, or slanted. During assessment, the height of the ROM grid can often be adjusted by placing books under it, using an adjustable table or board at varying heights, or just temporarily holding it in position. Whichever height and slant facilitates the best range of motion is typically used when possible, and items are placed well within the range of motion boundaries.

The last consideration that can be assessed using the ROM grid is the spacing of the items. Depending on the student's physical impairment, items may need to be spaced in such a way to allow clear indication of what the student is pointing to or allow the student to easily grasp without touching the other items. The items on the board can be placed at different distances from each other, and the student can be asked to touch or pick up the items. The student's ability to access a single select item will indicate the optimum spacing.

Sometimes the position required for good vision is not the ideal position to manipulate the materials. For instance, a student with cerebral palsy may be able to see items placed far out from the body but may only be able to manipulate the items if they are placed close to the body. In these instances, placement of the material will need to be determined on an individual basis. Sometimes the material will be shown then placed where the student can grasp it. Other times, the student may manipulate the material by feel or have someone else manipulate the material as the student visually accesses the material and directs the person on what to do.

Work Surface Modifications

Work surface modifications are often necessary for students with limited movement in their arms. These modifications may include the size, position, height, and/or slant of the surface. Cut-out tables with adjustable incline tabletops provide an adjustable work surface that can position materials for appropriate eye gaze and also sup-

port for the body to encourage erect trunk and head positioning. Tables also need to be adjustable in height to accommodate the student properly. For example, students with low muscle tone may perform better when the work area is higher, while those with high muscle tone may perform best if the work surface is lower (Bigge, 1991). Sometimes work surfaces are extended more to one side to benefit movement abilities. Work surfaces may also have boundaries or raised edges to prevent items from rolling off the table, out of the student's reach.

Positioning Devices

Positioning devices are used to assist with maintaining the correct position of materials. For students with physical impairments, the device may position the material to increase the student's access for manipulation or to stabilize the material. Once the appropriate position of the material is determined, positioning devices are then chosen. Positioning devices may be purchased commercially or may be developed by a local technician. Adjustable-angle easels often sit on the desk or table and can adjust the position of the materials while allowing the student to sit at a horizontal desk top. Static-angle easels provide positioning of material at one angle and can be made or purchased in a variety of materials including tri-wall cardboard, plywood, and plastic (see Figure 6-7). Acrylic angled picture frames are an inexpensive, easily available item that can provide temporary positioning for light-weight materials. Bookstands can be used to hold materials or books at the appropriate angle. Many book stands can vary the angle the item is placed in. Papers and materials may also be positioned on stenographer stands, clipboards, and easels. Card holders are also available to hold cards or items in a more upright position.

Placing items in the appropriate position is very important, but at times it may be difficult to maintain the items in the position, especially if the item is placed on an incline or repositioned accidentally by the student. Several different de-

FIGURE 6-7 This student uses a static angle easel to assist with writing.

vices may be used to assist with stabilizing an item in the appropriate position, including tape, Velcro, magnets, putty, nonslip matting, suction cup holders, putty, C-clamps, brackets, and straps. Clamping systems that attached the positioning device to the student's wheelchair are advantageous if the student uses the device in different environments but remains positioned in the wheelchair. When considering a positioning device on a student's chair, it is important that the device can be easily removed and replaced with minimal re-adjustment to the device. Development of a positioning system for the device when the student is placed in alternative positions such as the side-lyer or prone stander is ideal. Positioning devices with goose neck rods offer a variety of positioning possibilities especially during the evaluation and trial stages. These type of devices are also versatile for the students who are repositioned during the day in other positioning equipment.

Providing boundaries in the work area may assist the student in maintaining independent functioning on the school-related activity. Boundaries such as a raised lip on a wheelchair tray or a cut-out surface on a table or game board may assist the student in maintaining instructional items in the work space (Shepherd, Proctor, &

Coley, 1996). Texture, color, and picture boundaries may cue the student through their sensory system as to the physical limits of the activity. Boundaries with specific colors such as green on left and red on right may also cue students visually in how to organize the material within the boundaries (Shepherd et al., 1996).

Fatigue and Endurance Levels

The last factor that may contribute to determining functional positioning of the material in the classroom is the student's level of fatigue and endurance accessing the material. Sometimes a lot of energy is required for a student to access material, even when she is positioned optimally, the material is within her range of motion, and she have sufficient manipulation skills. As the student fatigues, she is less accurate and less able to continue with the activity. In these instances, alternate positioning of the material requiring a different movement pattern may be helpful. For example, if a student uses a switch to access an augmentative communication device by making a vertical pulling motion and is fatiguing, repositioning the switch so it can be accessed with a more horizontal pulling movement may decrease fatigue. However, it is important that the alternate position of the material still be easily accessible to the student and just as accurate as the original position. The student may also benefit from short rest breaks as needed throughout the activity.

INSTRUCTIONAL STRATEGIES FOR HANDLING AND POSITIONING

Students may be taught to participate in handling procedures, positioning themselves, or positioning items for them to access. Although students who are being positioned in supine, side-lying, prone, sitting, or standing positions are often so severely physically involved that they are unable to independently position themselves in the equipment or position the material once they are in position, several areas of instruction may be addressed. Some of these areas include learning about the equipment, choice making about when the equipment will be used, assisting with preparatory activities, participating in moving in or out of the positioning equipment, learning to check for correct positioning, and learning how to inform someone where to place certain items for ease of access.

The student should become familiar with the adaptive equipment prior to its use. He should also understand, to the best of his ability, why the position and equipment is being used, how he should be positioned in the equipment, and how long he is to be in the equipment. The student can become familiar with the equipment through sight, feel, verbal explanation, or demonstration with a doll. The student may be taught to assist with being placed in the equipment and may learn how each part of the equipment is adjusted or strapped on. He may also be taught to be responsible for determining whether he is correctly placed in the equipment. This knowledge can help if someone new needs to assist the student so that he can help direct his care. This also provides

the student with some control over his environment and an increase in self-esteem.

Choice making can also be incorporated into positioning and handling. If feasible, the student should be taught to determine where and when the positioning will occur. For example, for a young elementary student, a time when peers are on the floor (e.g., story time) might be the time when she would feel most comfortable being in the supine position. For a preschooler, rest time might be ideal. Standing in a prone stander for a high school student may occur when assisting with dish washing at a sink where the prone stander can be positioned, while use of the prone stander may be better during certain PE activities for a middle school student. If possible, the student should make choices of activities and materials to be used while in the positioning equipment.

Students may be taught certain skills prior to using positioning equipment. The student should be taught an appropriate form of receptive communication that adults use to indicate it is time to move to a certain piece of equipment (e.g., handling the student a piece of vinyl material similar to that used on the side-lyer to indicate it is time to be positioned in the side-lyer). This will help the student anticipate the event and prepare for it. Many students can be taught to follow a schedule and indicate when it is time to be positioned in certain equipment and when it is time to be removed. This helps teach students to direct their own care. Also, students with muscle tone problems can often be taught to assist with handling preparation activities by relaxing and by not resisting being moved. This should be encouraged when possible.

Some students will be taught to participate in moving in or out of the positioning equipment. If the student has a means of mobility (e.g., rolling, crawling, wheelchair use, etc.), he should move on his own to the positioning equipment. He may be taught to remove certain straps or move limbs in readiness for the transition to the equipment. He may be able to assist in moving limbs into or out of the equipment. While in the positioning equipment, the student should be taught to indicate discomfort at any time while positioned in the adaptive equipment, so that his position can be slightly changed.

When it is time to leave the positioning equipment, the student should be taught to assist with any functional movements that are possible when he is being removed from the adaptive equipment. After the activity, the student may be taught to perform a skin check, inspecting primarily bony areas that came in contact with the equipment for redness or injury.

Students should be taught to communicate to another person where material should be placed so it can be accessed. Teachers will often intentionally place material out of the student's range of motion to encourage the student to communicate that the material needs to be moved. For this strategy to be successful, the student needs ways to communicate about positioning needs and know how and when to ask for assistance. The teacher may need to model this several times and provide multiple opportunities for the student to practice this skill.

HANDLING AND POSITIONING PROBLEMS AND EMERGENCIES

Pain or Discomfort

Handling and positioning should never be painful, nor should handling or positioning ever be physically forced. School personnel, family, and others who are interacting with the student when positioned, or being positioned, in a piece of equipment should be alert to any indications of pain. These may include crying, grimacing, frowning, or otherwise giving the appearance of being in distress. The student should be taught to indicate pain or discomfort if possible. If the student complains of pain or discomfort, he may be repositioned or taken out of the equipment. The

student should be checked for areas of redness or any injury; if present, these should be reported and appropriate action taken. The therapists will need to be consulted to determine the course of action, even when no injury is present.

Dropping a Child

All adults who are responsible for assisting students into a position or positioning equipment should have been thoroughly trained on how to help a student safely and correctly into the position and/or the equipment. Adults should be careful not only to maintain support as needed but to prevent the student from falling or dropping the student upon handling. Proper training in and implementation of the principles of positioning, handling, and transferring (see Chapter 5) will assure the student's safety.

However, if a student should fall, first aid should be administered if needed. Students with movement problems may have more fragile bones and the student should be assessed for injuries or broken bones. If the student's head hits an object or the floor, serious injury could result, and medical personnel may need to assess whether any injury has occurred. Parents should be informed and appropriate action taken.

MANAGEMENT ISSUES FOR HANDLING AND POSITIONING

Individualized Health Plan and Individualized Education Program

An individualized health plan (IHP) may be constructed for handling and positioning. Specialized areas would include handling techniques and positioning equipment to be used (including length of time and frequency of use). Problems and emergencies would also be included such as dropping a student, appearance of poor fit with

Specific Therapeutic Handling Techniques Used with Student (specify activity)

Inhibition techniques: _____

_____

_____

Simulation techniques: _____

_____

_____

Adapted Positioning Equipment

Type	Length of Time	Frequency
_____ Wedge	_____	_____
_____ Side-lyer	_____	_____
_____ Adapted chair (specify)	_____	_____
_____ Prone stander	_____	_____
_____ Supine stander	_____	_____
_____ Other stander	_____	_____
_____ Other equipment	_____	_____

Directions for Problems and Emergencies

Pain: _____

Dropping child: _____

Appearance of poor fit with equipment: _____

Prevent skin breakdown by:

_____ repositioning student every _____ minutes

_____ having student do chair lifts every _____ minutes

_____ other

Detection of skin breakdown: _____

FIGURE 6-8 Specialized information to include in an IHP on handling and positioning

equipment, and skin breakdown. (See Figure 6–8 for an example of specialized information to put on an IHP for handling and positioning.) It may also be indicated on the IHP that the student is receiving physical or occupational therapy. Any special considerations or restrictions may also be included on the IHP.

A student who receives physical or occupational therapy will have objectives on the educational program that indicate positioning requirements to implement the educational objectives. It will be the responsibility of the educational team to determine the functional application of these objectives. IEP objectives for positioning may also include independent performance, partial performance, directing the task, and knowledge of the task. (See Figure 6-9 for sample objectives.) Besides objectives addressing student positioning, there may also be IEP objectives addressing material position-

Independent Performance of Task

Upon being transferred to the floor, the student will move onto a wedge and into correct position with 80% accuracy on 100% of opportunities for 5 consecutive days.

Partial Performance of Task

Upon being placed into a corner chair, the student will maintain an upright position for 20 minutes twice per day for 2 weeks.

Upon being placed into a side-lyer, the student will maintain her hands together at midline and manipulate a toy during playtime for 15 minutes, twice per day for 1 week.

Directing the Task

The student will inform an adult when it is time to change positions with 80% accuracy on 90% of opportunities for 2 weeks.

The student will tell an adult how she should be correctly positioned in the prone stander with 80% accuracy on 90% of opportunities for 1 week.

The student will inform an adult when she is not correctly positioned with 100% accuracy on 100% of occasions for 2 weeks.

The student will inform an adult when the material she needs to perform a task is not placed in an easily accessible area with 100% accuracy on 100% of occasions for 1 week.

Knowledge of the Task

The student will describe why positioning is important and what each piece of positioning equipment she uses is supposed to achieve with 80% accuracy on five consecutive trials.

FIGURE 6-9 Sample IEP objectives for handling and positioning

ing. These objectives may include having the student indicate proper positioning of material or adaptive equipment needed to access the material.

Although the physical and/or occupational therapist will be responsible for supporting the goals and objectives, they will need to be implemented by the teacher and other members of the educational team. This should only occur after proper training by the therapist. After the therapist provides training to the adults who will be assisting the student, pictures illustrating the student in correct positions may be provided for reference. The therapist will also periodically check that correct positioning and handling is being implemented.

Tracking Implementation

The activities and instructional objectives that the student is participating in throughout the day are typically organized through a student sched-

ule. To help assure that proper positioning and handling are occurring on a scheduled basis, part of the schedule should indicate the position and positioning equipment the student will use in each functional or academic activity. For example, if a student is supposed to be positioned prone for 20 minutes each day, as well as placed in other positions throughout the day, the educational team would look at the student's schedule of activities and determine during which activity prone positions (and other positions) would be optimally scheduled. In this example, this student has reading from 10:00 to 11:30 A.M. in a resource room, and part of that time is spent working on comprehension. The educational team may have determined that during 20 minutes of this time, he could be taken out of his wheelchair and positioned prone over a wedge. While prone over the wedge, the student looks at his reading book (which is positioned on an easel) as the teacher reads it, and they discuss the story. In this position, the student is more easily able to turn the pages and point to relevant pictures or targeted words. The student's schedule would indicate that during this reading time, he is to be positioned prone for 20 minutes over a wedge. Throughout the rest of the student's schedule, positioning plans would be attached to the student's planned functional, academic, or social activities.

Data should be taken to document that the student is being positioned in the specified equipment as planned. A data sheet should be used to keep track of the positioning schedule, as well as document that the positioning is occurring as prescribed. The data sheet should include the type of equipment, the length of time the student is positioned in the equipment, and when positioning occurred. On this data sheet may be instructional goals of coming to the equipment, assisting with transferring to the equipment, telling when time is up, or other determined goals.

SUMMARY

Assisting students with physical disabilities to transition from one position to another and maintain various functional positions is a very important goal for both home and school. To stay physically healthy, develop optimal functional movement patterns, and learn about their world, students with physical disabilities need to change their positions frequently throughout the day. They also need to have material positioned for optimal access and manipulation. Proper handling, body positioning, and positioning of materials is necessary to help maximize these students' abilities and potential.

7

Mobility

Providing a means of mobility for students with physical impairments can increase independence, provide a means to explore and interact with their world, and result in enhancing learning opportunities. When considering mobility options for students with physical disabilities, it is important to first evaluate the individual student's capability to move himself in space. Young, typically developing students move around the environment by rolling, **crawling** on their stomachs, **creeping** on hands and knees, scooting while in sitting position, cruising, and walking. All of these movements may be considered as mobility options for the student with physical disabilities, as long as their appropriateness to the situation and the physical environment is considered.

Some students with physical disabilities may have such severe physical impairments that they are unable to move themselves around their environments. In these cases, various mobility devices may be considered to help the student with mobility. Equipment used to assist mobility may include scooters, adapted bicycles or hand-driven devices, crutches or canes, walkers, or wheelchairs. In addition, various types of bracing, protective clothing (e.g., helmets), or other assistive devices (e.g., transfer boards) may also need to be used to promote optimal independent performance and safety.

Mobility in various environments and over various surfaces also will need to be considered. Often, a student with physical disabilities may need a variety of mobility strategies, depending on where, how far, and why he is moving. For example, an elementary student may be able to negotiate the school building using crutches, but may need to use a wheelchair when going out with the class on field trips due to the longer distance that she is required to move in the latter environment and resulting fatigue factors. At home, scooting on the floor may be an appropriate and efficient way for a middle school student to move from room to room in her house, but this would not be appropriate or efficient at school where a motorized wheelchair might be used. A high school student may be able to negotiate the school building without difficulty on his walker, but he may need other strategies or equipment when going outside on grass or uneven ground or to his job site where he may need to carry things from place to place.

As with all movement considerations for students with physical disabilities, choice of optimal assistive and adaptive equipment, assistive strategies, and instructional strategies for mobility should be done by a team consisting of the student (if possible), parents, teachers, physical and occupational therapists, and others who are significantly involved in the student's day. The movements required for independent mobility can be analyzed by the team, much like any other task. A program is then developed, citing specific strategies and equipment to be used in specific settings and situations, and then be carried out by all individuals working with the student.

When developing strategies to promote independent mobility, several goals should be kept in mind: (a) to help the student to move as normally as possible, (b) to teach the student to use movement to initiate interaction with and to control various aspects of his environment, and (c) to provide movement opportunities that are functionally based and allow the student to learn and gain as much independence as possible (Hanson & Harris, 1986).

DESCRIPTION OF MOBILITY CONSIDERATIONS

Not all students with physical disabilities will be able to gain independence in all areas of mobility, even using adaptive equipment/devices. However, all students, including those with severe/profound physical disabilities or multiple disabilities, should be able to at least assist with moving from place to place or making choices about movement. The following considerations should be made when making team decisions about an individual student's mobility (Bidabe & Lollar, 1990; Fallen & Umansky, 1985).

Readiness to Perform the Mobility Skill. Does the student have the motor ability to perform or learn to perform all or part of the required mobility skill? For example, a student with little head and trunk control could not be expected to crawl from place to place but might be able to roll or assist with rolling for mobility.

Goal Oriented and Functionally Based. Mobility should be goal oriented and functionally based. Movement does not occur in isolation but as a response to environmental stimulation or demands. For a student to be motivated to move, she must understand how her movement will affect the environment, and the resultant effect must be meaningful and important to her. For example, a small student is motivated to crawl to her high chair if she is hungry; associates the high chair with eating (from past experiences); sees, hears, and smells her mother preparing food; and wants to meet the goal of getting the food.

Interesting and Successful Experiences. Students are more likely to continue to practice a motor skill if they retain interest and achieve success. Each student's mobility program must be tailored to the individual capabilities, needs, and interests of that specific student, if it is to be successful.

Practice. Mastery of most mobility skills develops gradually through practice, with small improvements in parts of the skill over time and eventual total or partial elimination of extraneous and unpurposeful movements. If a whole skill is too difficult for a student to learn at one time, the skill may be task-analyzed and broken down into smaller increments, but the whole skill should still be kept in perspective as the final goal.

Prompt Use. Verbal, signed, visual, tactile, and/or physical prompts may be used to assist the student with physical disabilities to learn mobility skills. The student's specific disability(ies), learning style, and skill level should guide in determining which prompts are used. For example, a student with deafblindness and cerebral palsy who is learning to stand up from her wheelchair to assist with transferring would probably require tactile and physical prompts to learn the skill. Prompts should be faded as performance improves.

Across Environments. Mobility skills need to be taught across various environments where they may be used. For example, being able to transfer onto a toilet at school does not necessarily mean that the student can perform a similar transfer at home or on the job. Mobility skill generalization will only occur with practice across environments.

Energy Use. Optimal energy use needs to be considered when teaching mobility skills. All students will need to practice to increase skill, strength, and endurance when learning new movement skills. However, no mobility skill should leave the student too exhausted to complete routine activities. If a particular mobility skill is requiring too much energy on the part of the student every time it is performed or in certain situations, alternative strategies need to be devised.

EQUIPMENT AND ADAPTIVE EQUIPMENT FOR MOBILITY

Some students will be able to learn various mobility skills without the need for outside devices or equipment. However, when the physical disability is severe, various types of equipment may be used to assist with promoting mobility and allow these students to still gain independence in mobility skills. The following section will describe various types of assistive technology that can be used with students to assist in mobility. For each device described, the rationale for its use, the types of equipment available, and the correct use of and positioning in the equipment will be described.

Scooters

Students who have adequate head and trunk control to be able to bear weight on their arms and hold their head up while on their stomach and/or who can bear weight on their hands and knees may be ready for attempts at crawling or creeping. When a student appears to need additional support at the trunk to be able to practice the movements necessary for crawling or creeping, a scooter-type device is sometimes recommended by occupational and physical therapists to be used with the student (see Figure 7-1).

Scooter boards can be commercially purchased or easily made. The scooter board's base can be made of wood or plastic. It can be small and square to support just the trunk, allowing the legs and arms to be free to move, or longer to provide support to the whole lower body, allowing just arm movement. The scooter board's surface is usually padded to provide comfort while lying on the board. Four casters in each corner of the board provide movement in all directions. The scooter board usually has a strapping system to assist the student in staying on the board while moving arms and/or legs in attempts to crawl or creep. Some commercially available scooters are also adjustable in height from the floor to accommodate differences in arm and leg lengths. Some commercially available scooter boards also have curves built into the support surface to better accommodate supporting the body. Several commercially available scooter boards also provide multiple positioning functions, for example, adapting to become a prone stander. Use of a scooter board for mobility should be done under the direction of the student's physical therapist to ensure that the student is developmentally ready for the activity, to devise activities that are appropriate for the individual student, and to ensure the student's safety while on the piece of equipment.

For crawling activities, the student may be positioned with his chest, stomach, and lower legs supported on the board. A safety strap may be positioned at the hip area and, if needed, also at the

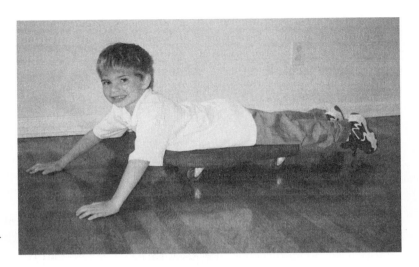

FIGURE 7-1 A boy using a scooter board

trunk. The board usually stops at about the level of the student's armpits, unless it is constructed with special extension areas to also support the student's head. The board should be just high enough so that the student can support himself on his hands on the floor, with a slight bend in the elbows.

To encourage the student to push on his hands, pressure through the student's shoulders into the hands while they are placed on the floor can initially be used to prepare the student for the scooter board activity. To give the student the idea of moving on the scooter board, the adult may hold onto the student's legs at the hips, knees, or ankles, as recommended by the student's therapist. Pushing the student forward and back on the board, or moving the board side to side or in a circle, giving the student time or assisting the student to adjust his hand/arm position, can help the student to experience the movements needed to initiate pushing and pulling with his arms/hands against the floor.

Many students will first be able to push backward or pivot around in a circle before they can pull themselves forward on the scooter board. All students should be encouraged to move to reciprocal use of their arms (using right, then left, in an alternating pattern) to move the scooter board, as this replicates the arm movements needed to crawl.

The same procedure can be used to facilitate creeping, using arms and legs, with the student positioned on a smaller square scooter board. A strap around the hips should still secure the student on the board, and the height of the board should allow the student's hands and knees to comfortably touch the floor. Adult guidance for moving the board should be provided at the student's hips or shoulders. Additional assistance may be given as needed for repositioning of the arms and legs to replicate reciprocal creeping movements (using opposite arm and leg). Refer to the assistive strategies sections on crawling and creeping in this chapter for ideas to assist the student with these movements.

Once the student can move on the scooter board, activities can be expanded to include pushing off a wall with feet or hands, going down a ramp, going through an obstacle course, and so forth to increase strength and endurance and enhance skill development in the position (Baker, Banfield, Kilburn, & Shufflebarger, 1991). Once the team decides the student is ready to use the scooter board to move from place to place in the environment, they then may determine which environments and situations are appropriate for this activity. Home, classroom, and physical education activities would probably be most appropriate locations for use of the scooter board to facilitate mobility in crawling or creeping. Use of the scooter board should not replace attempts at independent crawling or creeping but, rather, enhance these attempts.

Walkers

If a student with physical disabilities has the ability to bear weight on her legs, stand supported and take steps only while supported, her physical therapist may recommend a walker for mobility. The student needing a walker probably would require a significant amount of outside support to be able to move while upright on her feet. Use of a walker will allow such students independent mobility without tremendous energy usage, making walking a functional option.

Many different types of commercially available walkers provide different types and levels of support for the individual using them. The student's physical therapist would need to work with the rest of the team to determine what type of walker provides the most optimal performance for the student. A typical walker provides support in the front of the student, with hand grips for holding onto the walker on either side of the top of the frame. The walker may have four rubber tips on each of its legs, requiring the student to pick the walker up and move it forward after each step. Some forward support walkers are called *rollator walkers.* These walkers have wheels in the front and rubber tips in the back, allowing the student to push the walker in front of her as she walks, rather than picking it up between steps. Forward support walkers should be considered especially if balance and/or coordination is an issue.

Some walkers are open in the front and closed in the back (see Figure 7-2). These walkers are referred to as *posture control walkers.* This type of walker prevents the student from excessively leaning into the front of the walker, thereby helping decrease the student's tendency to use a "crouched" gait while walking. The closed back

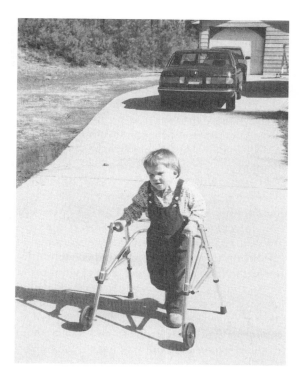

FIGURE 7-2 A child using a posture controlled walker at home

also may help give input to the buttocks muscles during walking, stimulating better hip extension and a straighter posture during walking.

Other walkers provide more support (e.g., trunk supports or "saddles" that allow the student to partially sit while attempting to walk), if needed, and have special add-ons available to prevent certain undesirable movement patterns. A type of walker called a *gait trainer* allows the student to lean partially forward on a trunk support and/or use a seat-type support to take some of the weight off of the feet and allow a better pattern of movement.

Special adaptations may also be put on any of the aforementioned walkers to improve body position. A foot board, attached to the walker between the student's feet, can keep the student from adducting his legs (i.e., pulling the legs together). Special straps attached to some walkers are also used to control this pattern at the student's hips. If the student has difficulty grasping the walker, arm troughs can be attached to the upper part of the walker so that the student can bear weight into his elbows/forearms. Special grips can also be attached to the walker to provide the student with handles to grasp the walker; these are adjustable to various angles, thereby accommodating for the individual student's limitations in range of motion or problems with muscle tone.

Use of a walker for mobility should be done under the direction of the student's physical therapist to ensure that the student is developmentally ready for the activity, to correctly select the type of walker and fit/adapt the walker to the individual student, to devise activities that are appropriate for the individual student, and to ensure the student's safety while using the piece of equipment. All walkers come in a variety of sizes and are adjustable in height, within a certain range. Once a particular walker is selected by the physical therapist, the therapist will need to adjust the height of the walker for the individual student. The walker is usually adjusted to be about waist high or somewhat below this level, allowing the student to grasp the walker with some bend to the elbows and stand with a straight trunk, hips, and knees and feet flat on the floor and slightly apart (if arm troughs are used for forearm weight bearing, the walker may have to be higher to accommodate this). Any additional add-on devices (e.g., grips, supports, straps, etc.) will then need to be adjusted by the therapist. The rest of the team members should be instructed by the student's physical therapist in maintaining these adjustments and/or utilizing the special add-ons before the student begins independent use of the walker.

The physical therapist then needs to train the student in safely getting into and out of the walker, taking steps forward and backward in the walker, maneuvering the walker around corners and in tight spaces, and using the walker on various surfaces (e.g., inclines; outside on grass, hills, uneven ground, etc.). The therapist also trains the rest of the team in these procedures. Alternative mobility strategies should be discussed and planned by the team, if needed for the individual student because of energy or skill considerations (e.g., use of a wheelchair for field trips).

Crutches and Canes

Some students with physical disabilities are unable to ambulate without outside support but do not require the level of support provided by a walker. For these students, the physical therapist may try crutches or canes as mobility aids, depending on the amount of support required. Students who are able to use crutches or canes for ambulation usually have fairly good arm function and control. Crutches usually provide more support to the individual than do canes. For every student, the goal for mobility should be to use as little adaptive equipment as possible, to promote maximal unaided functional independence. Crutches and canes provide the individual more independence than a walker because the individual can use both of these assistive devices to negotiate stairs, a skill not possible with a walker.

Depending on the individual student's support requirements during walking, the physical therapist may prescribe use of two crutches or canes or only one crutch or cane. One crutch or cane is usually used when there is asymmetrical weakness (as in the case of a hemiparesis), requiring support on only one side of the body.

There are basically two types of crutches: *axillary crutches,* which are full-length crutches that provide support under the armpits, and *Lofstrand crutches,* which are forearm crutches that basically provide support at the level of the hands/forearms (see Figure 7–3). Axillary crutches can be made out of wood or aluminum. They come in a variety of sizes, each size having a range of adjustability. The top of the crutch, which fits close to the armpit, is usually padded for comfort. The handgrip may also be padded. The bottom of the crutch has a replaceable rubber tip to grip the ground and prevent slippage of the crutch when in use. These tips need frequent monitoring and

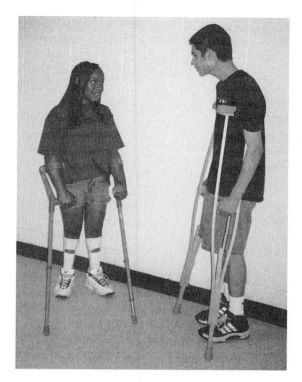

FIGURE 7-3 A girl using forearm crutches and a boy using axillary crutches

replacement when worn out to ensure safety for the crutch user.

Forearm crutches are usually made of aluminum. They also come in a variety of sizes, each size having a range of adjustability of height. The crutches have a grip for the hand and a cuff that encircles the forearm, holding the crutch in place. As with axillary crutches, there are replaceable rubber tips at the ends of the crutches. As with walkers, add-ons are available for crutches that allow the user to bear weight on the elbows/forearms and to grip the crutches using a variety of angles.

Canes are usually made of either wood or aluminum. The aluminum canes come in a variety of sizes, and each are adjustable within a certain range. The wood canes come in various lengths

but usually need to be cut with a saw to the appropriate length. Because of their lack of adjustability, wooden canes are not usually used with students.

The top of a cane typically has a curved handle or straight grip. The end can be either a single tip or a three-pronged tip, depending on the degree of stability required. Replaceable rubber tips, like those used on crutches, are placed on the end(s) of the cane to provide stability.

All crutches and canes come in a variety of sizes and are adjustable in height, within a certain range. Once a particular device is selected by the physical therapist, the therapist will need to adjust the height of the crutches or canes for the individual student. Crutches are usually adjusted so that the crutch tops are about two to four finger widths (depending on the student's size) below the student's armpits. This is done so that the student does not "hang" on the crutches, a habit that can cause skin irritation and nerve damage. The hand grips are set so that the student bears weight on the hands with a slight bend to the elbows and stands with a straight trunk, hips, and knees, with feet flat on the floor and slightly apart. Crutch tips should sit on the floor slightly forward and to the side of the student's feet (at about a 45-degree angle from the front of the foot). If arm troughs are used for forearm weight bearing, they are set somewhat higher to accommodate this. Canes are adjusted so that the student bears weight on the hands at about the hip level. The cane tip sits straight on the floor, close to the student's midfoot.

Use of crutches or canes for mobility should be done under the direction of the student's physical therapist to ensure that the student is developmentally ready for the activity, to correctly select the type of assistive device and fit/adapt the device to the individual student, to determine activities that are appropriate for the individual student, and to ensure the student's safety while using the device. The rest of the team members should be instructed by the student's physical therapist in maintaining these adjustments and/or utilizing the special add-ons before the student begins independent use of the crutches. The physical therapist will then need to train the student in (a) safely handling the crutches or canes, (b) standing up and sitting down safely using the devices, (c) learning where to place the devices, (d) taking steps forward and backward using the crutches or canes, (e) maneuvering corners and in tight spaces with the crutches or canes, and (f) using the crutches or canes on various surfaces (e.g., inclines; outside on grass, hills, uneven ground, etc.).

An additional training step will involve instructing the student in using the crutches or canes on stairs. When using crutches to ascend stairs, the stronger foot ascends the stair, followed by the crutches and the other foot. To descend stairs, the weaker foot is placed on the lower stair with the crutches, followed by the stronger foot. When using two canes or a single cane or crutch, the cane or crutch is placed on the opposite side from the limb it is assisting. For example, a student with a left-sided hemiparesis would hold a crutch or cane in the right hand and move the device at the same time he is moving the weaker limb (i.e., right crutch moves with left leg). A student requiring two canes to balance would move the right cane with the left leg, and the left cane with the right leg. The therapist will then need to train the rest of the team in these procedures. Alternative mobility strategies should be discussed and planned by the team, if needed for the individual student because of energy or skill considerations (e.g., use of a wheelchair for field trips).

Wheelchairs

Some students have such severe physical disabilities that standing and walking either are not physically possible or require so much energy that they are not physically practical. For these students, their main mode of assisted mobility may be a wheelchair. Especially important to consider before selecting a wheelchair for any student is the student's potential ability to gain independent mobility using the chair, including all of the settings and environments in which he will need to use the chair. This must be a team decision, with research on and consideration given to the many types of wheelchairs currently available on the market and a match made with the student's physical, sensory, and cognitive strengths and weaknesses. It should also be kept in mind that using the wheelchair for mobility should not preclude using other independent or equipment-assisted strategies for movement or other positioning for activities. Most individuals who use wheelchairs to get around require other types of strategies or equipment to use in different situations (e.g., transfer to a standard classroom armchair for tabletop activities, use of a prone stander for standing activities in PE, etc.).

The two basic types of wheelchairs are manual and motorized (see Figure 7-4). A manual chair requires the student or someone else to propel it. A motorized wheelchair allows the student to propel-herself by use of a switch device attached to a battery on the wheelchair. For the motorized chair to stay functional, the battery must be periodically charged.

For many years, standard wheelchairs featuring large rear wheels, caster-type front wheels, and soft sling-like back and seats were the only options commercially available. These wheelchairs were basically for use by individuals with good to normal head and trunk control who were capable of independent self-propelled transportation (e.g., individuals with paraplegia). In recent years, many different types of wheelchairs have come on the market, with many more options available to customize wheelchairs to meet different individuals' special physical needs (Fraser et al., 1990).

Wheelchair Frames. Wheelchair frames can be lightweight and foldable, allowing ease of movement and transport, or they can be heavy-duty to accommodate strong atypical movement patterns. The whole frame or the chair back alone on some models can recline, based on the individual's motor or health needs (e.g., for skin pressure relief). Some motorized wheelchairs even

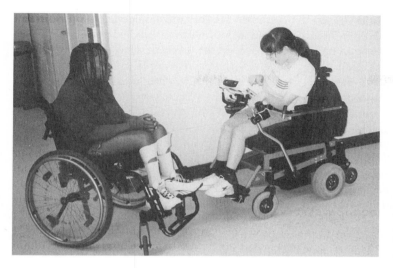

FIGURE 7-4 One student uses a manual wheelchair (on the left) that she can push herself, and another student uses a motorized wheelchair for independent mobility.

have special features that adjust the chair from a sitting to a standing position.

Wheelchair Backs and Seats. Chair backs and seats on any wheelchair should be firm, but some individuals require special supports to maintain an optimal sitting position. These supports can include head supports, trunk supports/harnesses, hip positioning supports/straps, leg positioning devices (e.g., abductors to keep the legs apart), and supports that hold the feet in place. Especially for young students, seat depth and back height should be somewhat adjustable to allow for growth. Some modular seating systems are also available that allow support pads of various lengths and thicknesses to be placed in the seating shell where needed for support. A seat cover is then placed over the pads. These modular pieces can be changed as growth occurs or support needs change.

For some individuals with postural asymmetries (e.g., scoliosis) and fixed skeletal deformities, custom contour seating can be formed that provides a firm surface that conforms to the shape of the individual's back and/or buttocks and thighs. A foam core molded to the individual's body, then dried and covered in cloth or vinyl, provides one of these custom options. A more sophisti-

cated process can also be used in which a mold is created of an individual's back, buttocks, and thighs by having the person sit in a sealed plastic bean-bag-type apparatus that contains small plastic particles while the air is extracted. A plaster cast is made of the impressions in the bean-bag and used as a guide to carve a foam shape that matches the body's contours. The foam is then dipped in a vinyl coating, and the seating system may be placed in a wheelchair frame (Fraser et al., 1990).

Armrests. Wheelchair armrests can be permanently attached to the chair, or they can be removable or swing away to allow for transfers out of the chair. Some armrests are also adjustable in height. For a student or for office work, armrest height should allow the chair to be placed under a table. Armrests should also accommodate a tray being placed on the wheelchair.

Wheels. Some wheelchairs have removable wheels to facilitate ease of transporting the wheelchair in a car. Spokeless wheels should be considered if the student is to be transported by bus because the tie-down systems used on buses to secure wheelchairs tend to break the spokes on wheelchairs with standard spoked wheels. Special rims or placement of the wheel might be necessary for the individual with physical disabilities who is self-propelling the chair. Some rims come with extensions that make it easier to grasp the wheels. Angling the wheel placement so that the top of the wheel slants inward can also make it easier to propel the wheelchair for some individuals. Toggle locks that act as wheel brakes may be sufficient, but some individuals require brake extensions to be able to get enough leverage to set the brakes against the tires. To help individuals negotiate the chair up a ramp or incline, devices are also available to keep the wheelchair from rolling backward.

Legrests. Wheelchair legrests usually allow the legs to remain in a position of 90 degrees of flexion at the knees and ankles. However, some legrests elevate to accommodate for orthopedic problems such as knee extension contractures. Legrests usually swing away to the side of the chair to allow forward transfers in and out of the chair, and some legrests also are removable. The footplate position is usually adjustable to accommodate for the individual student's lower leg length. Footplate angle is also sometimes adjustable to accommodate for ankle contractures or foot deformity.

Switch Selection and Placement for Motorized Wheelchairs. Most individuals with adequate upper extremity function use a toggle switch placed at some point on the wheelchair's armrest that is easily accessible to the more functional or dominant hand to operate a motorized wheelchair. Moving the switch in different directions causes the chair to move forward, backward, or to turn to the left or right and regulates speed of the chair's movement. Depending on the student's individual physical strengths and weaknesses and what part of the body has the most reliable movement ability, the occupational and physical therapist on the student's team, together with the rest of the team, can determine the type and location of the device needed for that student to operate the motorized wheelchair. Some stu-

dents use pressure on simple plate switches positioned as footswitches, headswitches, or switches placed near the knee or elbow. Other students with less control over body movement may use a sip-and-puff device that uses breath control to operate their wheelchairs. When determining placement of the switch for operating the chair, the team must also consider whether the student will need to use a laptray or an alternative augmentative communication device, as these devices may compete with switch placement.

Guidelines should be followed for proper positioning in a wheelchair and possible adaptations to achieve proper positioning. Figure 7-5 provides these guidelines. Use of a wheelchair for mobility should occur under the direction of the student's physical therapist to ensure that the student is developmentally ready for the activity, to correctly select the type of wheelchair to be used and fit/adapt the wheelchair to the individual student, to determine activities that are appropriate for the individual student, and to ensure the student's safety while using the wheelchair.

The physical therapist will then need to train the student in safely handling the wheelchair; transferring safely into and out of the wheelchair; managing add-on adaptations such as straps or supports, brakes, footrests, armrests, and so forth; wheeling forward and backward in the wheelchair; maneuvering corners and in tight spaces with the wheelchair; and using the chair on various surfaces (e.g., inclines; outside on grass, hills, uneven ground, etc.) and in different environments (e.g., through doorways, in bathrooms, etc.). The therapist will then need to train the rest of the team in these procedures. Alternative mobility strategies should be discussed and planned by the team, if needed for the individual student because of endurance, strength, or skill considerations (e.g., use of a walker for home, classroom, or other short distances).

Other Mobility Devices

Another independent mobility alternative to the wheelchair for the individual who does not have

Head and Neck
Midline position
Face forward (not pointed up or down)
Adaptations: Headrest (maintain head alignment); head strap (to hold head back in headrest)

Shoulders and Arms
Shoulders in midline and neutral position (not hunched over)
Elbows flexed about 90°
Adaptations: Shoulder straps (to hold shoulders back); shoulder pommels (to hold shoulder back); wheelchair tray (to maintain alignment)

Trunk
Midline position
Maintain normal curve of the spine
Adaptations: H-strap (to bring shoulders back and keep trunk up); scoliosis pads/side pads (to align trunk)

Hips and Pelvis
Midline position
Hips bent at 90°
Pelvis in back of the seat
Pelvis not tilted to one side
Adaptations: Seat belt across hips (to keep pelvis back of seat)

Legs
Thighs slightly apart
Knees slightly apart
Knees bent at 90°
Feet directly below or slightly behind knees
Ankles bent 90° with feet on footrest
Feet facing forward
Ball and heel of foot flat on footrest
Adaptations: Adductor pads (to keep knees aligned when knees are too far out); abductor pads (to keep knees aligned when knees are too close together); footrest straps

FIGURE 7-5 Guidelines for positioning in a wheelchair

active use of the legs but has fairly good upper extremity control is the dynamic or mobile stander. These devices allow individuals with physical disabilities to stand supported in a slightly forward-leaning position, freeing the arms for use. The individual can then propel herself forward in the device by pushing on the wheels. Hand brakes and a variety of special individualized body supports are also available to ensure optimal positioning and safety. The mobile stander allows eye-level, face-to-face contact with peers (potentially increasing self-esteem) and can be used in a variety of classroom, work, and recreational situations (see Figure 7-6a).

Sometimes other mobility devices are considered for students to provide movement options for specific activities or environments. Recreation is an important area to include in a mobility plan for any student. Specially adapted tricycles in a wide variety of sizes are commercially available for younger or older students. These special trikes provide extra supports to the student's trunk and hips, special straps that help the student to hold her feet on the pedals, special handlebars that assist the student to maintain grasp while steering, a hand brake system, and special transfer steps to assist getting on and off the device. A range of adjustability is usually built into all features of the tricycles to allow for individual adaptation and potential growth of the user. Such a recreational mobility device can allow a student with physical disabilities to participate in inclusive activities with his peers who are without physical disabilities.

Recreational mobility can still be an option for the student who does not have control of his legs but may have fairly good control of arm function by using hand-driven wheeled devices. In this device, the student sits low to the ground in a frame with a backrest and trunk/hip supports. The device requires that the student grasp handles on each of the wheels that he uses to turn the wheels, thus moving the device. Moving one wheel alone results in turning the device; using both wheels together propels the device in a straight line. As with the adapted tricycles men-

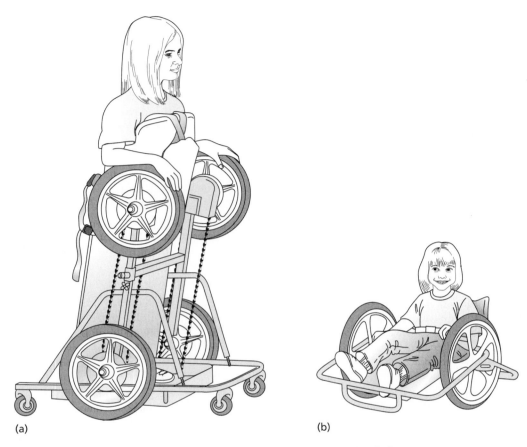

(a)   (b)

FIGURE 7-6 Students using a mobile stander (a) and a hand-driven wheeled device (b)

tioned earlier, these hand-driven wheeled devices can facilitate inclusive recreational activities. Figure 7-6b illustrates an example of this device.

Swimming is also a recreational activity that allows mobility for some students who otherwise would not be able to experience independent movement. The buoyancy of water supports the weight of the body, partially eliminating the effects of gravity and thereby allowing body movements that are not possible on dry land. Various devices to support the body, either partially or totally, are commercially available to assist in planning aquatic movement programs for individuals with physical disabilities. These devices, in partic-

ular, should only be prescribed and used under the direction of a physical, occupational, and/or recreational therapist because of the potential dangers of aquatic activity for the individual with physical and/or health disabilities (e.g., inability to regulate body temperature leading to hypothermia, ingestion of copious amounts of water leading to metabolic imbalance, and inhalation of water leading to pneumonia or drowning).

Swinging is also an enjoyable recreational movement activity that is important for stimulating and aiding in the development of typical responses in a student's vestibular system (i.e., the balance-control system located in the inner ear).

Adapted devices provide additional body support for the student with physical disabilities so that swinging can be safely enjoyed.

Mobility considerations also have to be made when moving the student with physical disabilities from place to place in a vehicle. Car seats providing adequate total body support are mandatory for young typically developing students who do not yet have control of body movement. If a wheelchair or other type of approved transport device is not being used with a student with physical disabilities when in a vehicle, then a special car seat may be necessary to provide enough support to the student to ensure comfortable and safe transport.

As with any positioning or mobility device, the student's physical and/or occupational therapist should be integral to the team in planning use of any of these devices for mobility strategies.

Other Assistive Technologies for Mobility

Various additional items of assistive technology can be used to facilitate an individual's independent mobility. Some of these items are assistive in nature; some are protective.

Weighted Vests/Cuffs. Some individuals, especially those with fluctuating muscle tone that is at times low and at other times high, or those with balance-related mobility problems (as seen in ataxic cerebral palsy) can gain better control over independent movements if additional weight is added to the trunk area or the arm/legs. This added weight is thought to provide additional proprioceptive cues to the body, resulting in increased muscle control and improved movement performance. Weight is added by applying either a snug-fitting weighted vest to the trunk or snug-fitting arm or leg cuffs usually to the wrists or ankles, respectively. The vests or cuffs attach by way of Velcro closures to attain a tight fit so that the weights remain stable and are not allowed to move around on the body part, and they vary in size and weight according to individual need. They are commercially available or can be easily

homemade, but they should be prescribed by the student's physical or occupational therapist to ensure their appropriateness for use and proper fit.

Splints and Braces. Various custom-made devices are available that physicians (usually orthopedists) may prescribe to hold a body part in a position that makes movement easier for the student. Due to students' rapid growth and the close fit of these devices, they must be monitored carefully and changed frequently.

Splints are usually made of molded, rigid plastic and are used to position arms and hands. Occupational therapists usually construct custom splints for a student. The splints are removable and may be worn for the whole day or for part of the day for certain activities. Splints can be important to mobility by providing consistent, functional hand positioning for an individual who may have atypical muscle tone but is pushing a manual wheelchair, operating a switch to drive a motorized wheelchair, and so forth. Correct splinting can make the difference in a student being able to move independently versus having to depend on others for mobility.

About 85% of students with atypical muscle tone use a lower-extremity brace, or orthosis, at some time (Geralis, 1998). Lower-extremity orthoses are made of molded, rigid plastic and are used to reduce tone and to position or stabilize the leg or foot. Ankle/foot orthoses (AFOs) control the position of the ankle and foot. (See Figure 7-7). Knee/ankle/foot orthoses (KAFOs) control the position of the knee, as well as the ankle and foot. Orthoses are typically prescribed by an orthopedist when the student with atypical muscle tone begins weight-bearing activities. They may be constructed by a specially trained physical therapist or an orthotist. Wearing time increases gradually, usually to include most of the student's waking hours (especially if the student is ambulating for mobility). Frequent adjustments and refittings are necessary. AFOs or KAFOs can provide the support and stability necessary in the legs to enable some students to walk independently who would otherwise not be able to do so.

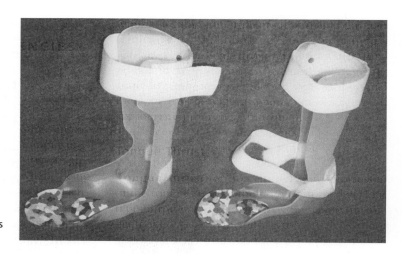

FIGURE 7-7 Ankle/foot orthoses (AFO)

The student's physical therapist is critical in determining when an orthosis should be tried, what type should be used, and in providing gait training to the student while using the orthosis.

A spinal orthosis is also sometimes needed to position or stabilize the trunk, thereby facilitating independent or assisted mobility. The jacket-type, molded plastic orthosis with a front opening is most commonly prescribed. The trunk brace provides total contact but may need padding in certain bony areas to prevent skin breakdown. Frequently small holes are made over the entire surface of the orthosis to provide ventilation to the skin. Bracing of the trunk in such a manner can provide proper positioning and enough central stability for some individuals to be able to operate a wheelchair independently who would otherwise be unable to do so. This is especially beneficial for students with severe weakness such as spinal muscular atrophy. The brace helps provide support in the trunk and prevent malformations such as severe scoliosis.

Some young students with no active control of their leg movements (as seen in myelomeningocele) may learn to walk independently using crutches and a parapodium brace. This brace has a solid bottom and extends to the student's chest. The student's legs are mechanically supported in the brace in an extended position. The student moves, using crutches, by either lifting her body together with the brace through space or rocking her body and the brace forward, one side then the other, by shifting weight and rotating her trunk. Use of this brace in older students is usually not seen because the energy eventually required to move the weight of the body plus the brace through space becomes too much for the task to be functional.

Transfer Boards. To be able to transfer independently in and out of a wheelchair safely and efficiently, some students will need to be taught how to use a transfer board. A transfer board is a lightweight, smooth board, usually with tapered ends and typically made out of wood or plastic. The board is used to "bridge the gap" between the wheelchair and a bed, toilet, chair, or other surface. To use the board, the individual places one end of the board under his buttock or thigh and the other end on the surface onto which he wants to transfer. Smaller, safer, more controlled sideways movements of the body can then be made to transfer over the gap between the wheelchair and the target area. (See Chapter 6 for more on transfer boards.)

Protective Head Gear. Some students who are able to independently ambulate are still at high risk for falling and hitting their heads. This is seen most often in students who have seizure disorders or who have slow or underdeveloped protective reactions in their arms and who therefore do not "catch themselves" when they fall. The team may determine that these students need to wear protective head gear (i.e., a helmet) when they are walking on their own to prevent head injury. Many styles and sizes of helmets are available, some with soft padded shells and others with hard plastic shells. Some helmets simply provide protection to the forehead and temporal areas, while others protect the whole head and face by way of a face guard. Various hats and caps are also available to fit over the helmets to make them more aesthetically appealing.

The student's team should work together to decide whether the student needs to use a helmet for protection, when he needs to use it, and what style he needs to provide adequate protection, based on the student's individual history. The student should be part of the team and have a part in the selection, if possible. Use of protective headgear can be a socially stigmatizing situation, and this should always be considered when deciding on its use, especially for an older student.

ASSISTIVE STRATEGIES TO PROMOTE MOBILITY

Students with physical disabilities will be able to optimally assist with movement or move independently if their muscle tone and initial body position are as near to normal as possible. The principles of handling and positioning discussed in Chapter 6 are important to use when assisting a student with mobility skills. For example, if a student with high muscle tone is going to be assisted to learn to progressively roll toward her wheelchair to facilitate transferring into the chair from the floor, the adult working with the student may need to first help reduce the student's general muscle tone through specific handling

techniques and then help her begin to roll from a relaxed, symmetrical initial body position. These handling and positioning principles and techniques should be kept in mind and used, when needed, throughout all assistive strategies used to promote mobility skills. The student's physical or occupational therapist should direct selection of specific techniques that will be used with individual students.

The MOVE (Mobility Opportunities Via Education) curriculum is a top-down, activity-based curriculum designed to teach students with disabilities basic, functional motor skills required for adult life in home and community environments. The curriculum is based on many of the basic mobility considerations outlined earlier and combines natural body mechanics with an instructional process, including a system of physical assistance/prompts, designed to help students acquire increased amounts of independence necessary to sit, stand, and walk. Using appropriate assistive technology is also a part of the curriculum (Bidabe & Lollar, 1990). As with any curriculum, the student's team should decide whether use of all or part of the MOVE curriculum for a particular student is indicated. The following sections will discuss various possible mobility skills and present sample assistive strategies to promote these skills.

Rolling

In the typically developing young student, rolling is the first mobility skill to be developed. Rolling allows young students to change their position and, therefore, their perspective on the world. It also enables them to move from place to place to interact with their environment (e.g., by attaining toys out of reach). Young students typically first roll from their backs to their sides at about 4 months of age, roll from stomach to side at about 5 months, roll from stomach to back next, and finally from back to stomach by about 7 months. As the student matures, there is more and more rotation seen in the trunk (around the body axis) during rolling. Each step in the rolling process requires more advanced control over sequential body movements. Progressive rolling for mobility—that is, rolling back to stomach, to back to stomach in sequence—is the most advanced movement pattern (Heller et al., 1996).

Many students with physical disabilities, even those with severe disabilities, learn to roll independently or at least assist with being rolled. The skill does not require a great deal of upright control of the body against gravity but does involve a sequence of coordinated body movements, as stated earlier. The following procedure provides a sample task analysis for rolling, showing movements to be performed by the student and the assistive strategies provided by the adult (Orelove & Sobsey, 1996; Diamant, 1992). It should be stated, however, that some students may initiate rolling with the leg, while others may initiate rolling with the arm, depending on their individual motor strengths. Input from the student's therapists would be needed to determine the assistive strategy that would best assist the individual student to initiate rolling for mobility.

Sample Procedure for Promoting Rolling

Student Movements	Adult Assistive Strategies
1. Lying on back, extend left arm overhead.	Verbal and touch cue to straighten left arm overhead with physical prompt or assistance to move at left upper arm. (Arm may also be kept close at the side of the body, if extending overhead is not possible.)
2. Bring right leg up and across body.	Verbal and touch cue to bend leg up and across with physical prompt or assistance to move at right thigh.
3. Rotate head and shoulders to left.	Verbal, visual, and/or touch cue to rotate head and shoulders to the left with physical prompt or assistance at head and/or right shoulder.
4. Extend right arm above head and bring arm up and across body, rolling onto stomach.	Verbal, visual, and/or touch cue to bring arm up and over with physical prompt or assistance at right upper arm.
5. Place left hand next to left shoulder, keeping right arm overhead.	Verbal and/or touch cue to place left hand next to shoulder with physical prompt or assistance at left elbow.
6. Turn face to left.	Verbal, visual, and/or touch cue to turn face with physical prompt or assistance at head.
7. Lift left leg up and across body and push off on left hand.	Verbal and/or touch cue to bring left leg back and across while pushing off on left hand with physical prompt or assistance at left thigh and left elbow.
8. Roll onto back, bringing head to midline.	Verbal and/or touch cue to roll onto back with physical prompt or assistance at head or left shoulder.

Visual, verbal, signed, or touch cues should be used from the beginning as assistive strategies to help the student anticipate and assist with the desired movement. These cues can be used in combination with physical prompts (here used to mean assistance with initiation of the required movement) or more general physical assistance at key points on the body (see Chapter 6), depending on the individual student's physical skills/needs. As physical assistance is faded, the cues can remain, if necessary, as reminders of the next movement in the sequence.

The student should also have a target goal to roll toward (e.g., a toy, the wheelchair, an activity set up at a table, etc.) to make the movement functional and meaningful to the student, providing motivation to move. If rolling on a flat surface is difficult, initial trials can be performed on a wedge of appropriate size. The student can be placed on the high end of the wedge and be facilitated to roll down the wedge to the lower end.

For the student with a physical disability, learning to roll can provide independence in changing position, help a caregiver with dressing, assist a caregiver by changing locations in preparation for a change in activity, and provide a safe way to move independently in the event of an emergency. For older students with severe physical disabilities, rolling may be the only truly independent mobility the student may be able to learn, without dependence on assistive equipment. However, use of rolling for mobility in the older student would need to be evaluated in the context of its social appropriateness to the situation and environment.

Crawling

By about 7 months of age, the typically developing student is able to crawl on his stomach and pivot around in a circle while on his stomach. The body movements used in these activities are precursors to the movements used later in creeping on the hands and knees and also allow the young student to move directly forward toward desired objects seen in the environment (Heller et al., 1996).

Before a student can crawl on his stomach, he must have first developed good head control while bearing weight on his elbows or hands in the prone position (on stomach). He must also have learned to shift his weight from one elbow or hand to the other as he frees the opposite arm from the supporting surface (as in reaching for toys). Once these skills are mastered, the young child or student with a physical disability is ready for crawling.

The following procedure may be used to assist with promoting crawling, demonstrating movements to be performed by the student and the assistive strategies provided by the adult (Baker et al., 1991; Hanson & Harris, 1986). It is assumed that the student has something or someone in front of him that he wants, motivating him to move forward. As with rolling, the task analysis provided is a sample. Input from the student's therapists would be needed to determine the assistive strategy that would best help the individual student to initiate crawling for mobility. Crawling down an inclined surface may also facilitate initial attempts at crawling, using gravity to assist the movement.

Sample Procedure for Promoting Crawling

Student Movements	*Adult Assistive Strategies*
1. Lying on the stomach, lift head and support weight on elbows.	Verbal, visual, and/or touch cue to lift head with physical prompt or assistance to move upward at the shoulders.

Student Movements	*Adult Assistive Strategies*
2. Shift weight onto the right side and pull left knee up.	Verbal or touch cue to shift weight to right with physical prompt or assistance to move by pulling upward under left hip (see Figure 7-8a).
3. With the desired object in front and out of reach, reach toward the object with left hand.	Verbal, visual, and/or touch cue to reach with left hand with physical prompt or assistance to move at the left upper arm.
4. Push down on left foot, propelling body forward.	Verbal and touch cue to straighten left leg with physical prompt or assistance to move provided by placing the flat of hand on sole of left foot and providing upward pressure (see Figure 7-8b).
5. Shift weight onto the left side and pull right knee up.	Verbal or touch cue to shift weight to left with physical prompt or assistance to move by pulling upward under right hip.
6. Continue as above, alternating sides.	Continue as above, alternating sides.

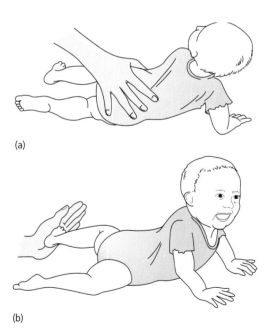

(a)

(b)

FIGURE 7-8 The adult is providing assistance for crawling by helping the child shift his weight on right side (a) and providing a hand against the child's foot for the child to push against (b).

Creeping

Once a young typically developing student has mastered the skill of crawling, she usually soon begins to push back from a stomach-lying position onto her hands and knees. From here she practices weight shift in this position by rocking back and forth and side to side while maintaining the position. She also becomes more skilled in the position by reaching for things while on her hands and knees, thereby improving her control in this position. By about 8 months of age, the typically developing student usually begins to use creeping on her hands and knees as a primary way of moving around (Heller et al., 1996). Creeping allows the student to move more quickly and to change the direction of movement more easily.

Before a student can creep, she must have first developed good head and trunk control while bearing weight on her hands and knees. She must have learned to shift her weight forward and back over her hands and knees, as well as from side to side. The student must also be able to free each limb (arm and leg) from the supporting surface (as in reaching for toys). Once these skills are mastered, the young child or student with a physical disability is ready for creeping. Creeping occurs when the student moves one hand and the opposite leg forward, alternating in sequence side to side.

The following sample procedure for creeping shows movements to be performed by the student and the assistive strategies provided by the adult (Hanson & Harris, 1986). It is assumed that the student has something or someone in front of her that she wants, motivating her to move forward. As with the other mobility skills, the task analysis provided is a sample. Students assume a hands-and-knees position in a number of ways. This procedure assumes pushing back onto the hands and knees from lying on the stomach. Students may also assume a hands-and-knees stance by rotating around from a sitting position. Input from the student's therapists is needed to determine the assistive strategy that will best help the individual student initiate creeping for mobility.

Sample Procedure for Promoting Creeping

Student Movements	Adult Assistive Strategies
1. Lying on the stomach, lift head and push up on straight arms, shifting the hips back over knees.	Verbal, visual, and/or touch cue to lift the head and push up on the arms with physical prompt or assistance to move upward at the shoulders first, then to move hips up and back with upward pressure at the student's hips or under the trunk (see Figure 7-9a).
2. With the desired object in front and out of reach, reach toward it with the right hand.	Verbal, visual, and/or touch cue to reach with the right hand with physical prompt or assistance to move at the right upper arm.
3. Bring the left leg forward.	Verbal, visual, and/or touch cue to move left knee forward, with forward pressure at left hip/thigh.
4. Reach toward the object with the left hand.	Verbal, visual, and/or touch cue to reach with left hand with physical prompt or assistance to move at the left upper arm.
5. Bring right leg forward.	Verbal, visual, and/or touch cue to move the right knee forward, with forward pressure at the right hip/thigh (see Figure 7-9b).
6. Continue as above, alternating sides.	Continue as above, alternating sides.

If the student needs additional support to creep, a folded blanket or towel may be placed under the student's trunk and used to support some of the student's body weight as he is gently helped to move forward. Using an inclined surface to creep down or placing the student prone on a scooter board may also facilitate initial attempts at creeping. The alternating, reciprocal movements used in creeping are important precursors to the movements needed for walking. Many students with high muscle tone and residual primitive reflexes learn to creep by bring-

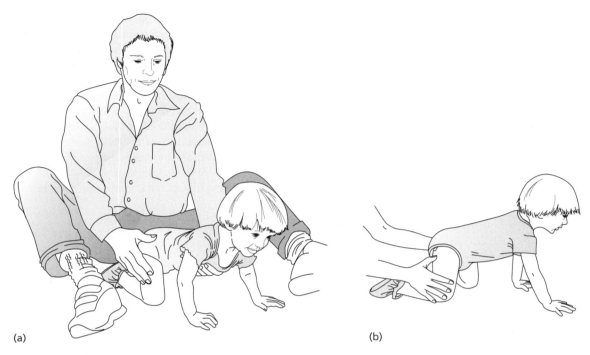

(a)   (b)

FIGURE 7-9 The adult is providing assistance for creeping by giving upward pressure at the child's trunk and stabilizing the hips (a). The adult is providing forward pressure at the right thigh (b).

ing both hands forward first, followed by both legs. This is sometimes referred to as "bunny-hopping." These students should be encouraged to develop a reciprocal creeping pattern, if possible, because of the need to establish reciprocal movement patterns and for movement efficiency. However, if development of such a reciprocal pattern is not possible, the alternative pattern should be allowed for the student to have independent mobility.

For the student with a physical disability, learning to creep can allow for independence in moving quickly and efficiently about the environment to obtain desired objects, assisting a caregiver by changing locations in an area in preparation for a change in activity, providing a safe way to move independently in the event of an emergency, and so forth. However, as with crawling, use of creeping for mobility in the older

student would need to be evaluated in the context of its social appropriateness to the situation and environment.

Scooting

Although not all typically developing students use scooting while in a sitting position as a means of mobility, it can be a viable mobility strategy for both typically developing students and those with physical disabilities. Usually, the typically developing student between 8 and 9 months of age has the postural skills in sitting to begin pivoting in a circle and scooting on his bottom to move about the environment without requiring arm support. By this time, the young student's protective reactions have sufficiently developed, as have his equilibrium reactions in sitting, to enable him to shift weight in all planes while maintaining sitting unsupported (Heller et al., 1996). Postural reactions, such as protective and equilibrium reactions, are explained in more detail in Chapter 6.

A sample procedure for promoting scooting follows, showing movements to be performed by the student and the assistive strategies provided by the adult and Figure 7-10 illustrates the assistive strategy. It is assumed that the student has some-

thing or someone in front of him that he wants, motivating him to move forward (see Figure 7-10a). As with the other mobility skills, the task analysis provided is a sample. Input from the student's therapists would be needed to determine whether the mobility skill is appropriate for the individual student and what assistive strategy would best help the individual student to initiate scooting for mobility.

Sample Procedure for Promoting Scooting

Student Movements	Adult Assistive Strategies
1. Sitting on the floor, with the legs in front and knees slightly bent, shift weight onto left hip.	Verbal, visual, and/or touch cue to shift weight onto left hip. Using a touch cue, the adult places her hand on the student's right hip and pushes toward the left, thereby displacing the student's weight onto the left hip.
2. Pick up right leg and extend straight in front, rotating trunk to left and pulling right hip forward.	Verbal, visual, and/or touch cue to pick up right leg and extend it straight in front, pulling right hip forward, with physical prompt or assistance to move by lifting and extending right leg at the thigh (see Figure 7-10b).
3. Reshift weight onto right hip.	Verbal, visual, and/or touch cue to shift weight onto right hip, with physical prompt or assistance to move by pushing left hip toward the right displacing the child's weight onto the right hip.
4. Pick up left leg and extend leg straight in front, rotating trunk to right and pulling left hip forward.	Verbal, visual, and/or touch cue to pick up left leg and extend leg straight in front, pulling left hip forward, with physical prompt or assistance to move by lifting and extending left leg at thigh.
5. Continue as above, alternating sides.	Continue as above, alternating sides.

The reciprocal, alternating weight shifts and leg movements made by the student during scooting in the sitting position can be viewed as precursors to walking. The weight shifts and equilibrium reactions required by scooting movements also can prepare the student to be ready to

make important transition movements between sitting and the hands-and-knees position, as well as pulling up from sitting, to kneeling, to half-kneeling (kneeling on one knee with the opposite foot flat on the floor), and, finally, to standing (Heller et al., 1996).

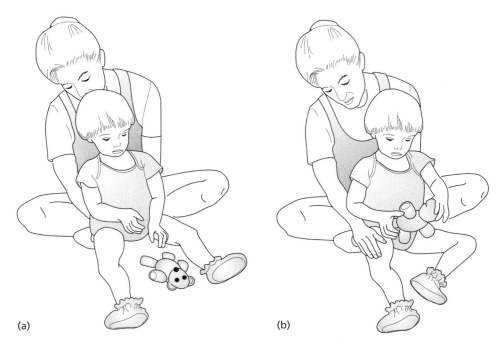

(a)   (b)

FIGURE 7-10 The adult places an interesting toy in front of the child (a), and after shifting the weight over to the left side, she assists the child to move her right leg forward (b).

For some students with physical disabilities, learning to scoot while in a sitting position can allow for independence in moving quickly and efficiently about the environment to obtain desired objects, assisting a caregiver by changing locations in an area in preparation for a change in activity, and providing a safe way to move independently in the event of an emergency, especially when other mobility patterns (e.g., creeping) are not possible. However, as with any mobility strategy, use of creeping for mobility in the older student must be evaluated in the context of its social appropriateness to the situation and environment.

Cruising

The typically developing young student begins to pull up from a hands-and-knees position to

kneeling, through half-kneeling, to standing at about 7 or 8 months of age. Cruising, or walking with the support of objects in the environment, usually begins in the sideways direction with both hands used for support and advances to cruising in the forward direction once trunk rotation increases, balance improves, and the need for outside support of both hands diminishes (Heller et al., 1996).

All students, including those with physical disabilities, usually must first have good head and trunk control, good sitting balance, and be able to bear weight on arms and legs before they can accomplish independent standing and cruising. However, weight bearing in a standing position is extremely important for all students with physical disabilities, even those who may not have the previously listed prerequisite skills for independent standing. Weight bearing in standing provides the needed pressure on the growth plates of the bones to stimulate bone growth. In addition to bone health, standing is critical to normal function of the internal organs, the circulatory system, the respiratory system, and the digestive system (Bidabe & Lollar, 1990). Learning to stand, then cruise, can also be a very important step toward learning to walk, whether independently or with adaptive equipment. If physically possible, upright mobility should be the ultimate goal for all students. These issues are important to consider when adaptive equipment is used to facilitate mobility.

Depending on the individual student's physical disabilities, assuming the standing position prior to cruising for mobility may be accomplished in a number of ways. If possible, the student should learn to come to standing from a kneeling, through a half-kneeling position. However, muscle tightness or weakness may prohibit this type of transition to standing. Standing up

from sitting on a raised surface, from squatting, or from other positions may also be used. The student's physical therapist should decide what is the best way for the student to transition to standing, based on the student's individual physical skills and limitations.

A sample procedure is provided for assisting students to cruise. It is assumed that the student has moved into the standing position (as described earlier) and has something or someone to either side of him that he wants, motivating him to move. The sample procedure is for cruising sideways to the left. The student should also be encouraged to cruise to the right. Once the student is able to cruise to each side, he should be encouraged to begin forward cruising. Input from the student's therapists is needed to determine whether the mobility skill is appropriate for the individual student and what assistive strategy would best help him initiate cruising for mobility.

Sample Procedure for Promoting Cruising

Student Movements	*Adult Assistive Strategies*
1. Standing on the floor with feet flat and slightly apart and with arms providing support against a table, couch, and so forth, shift weight onto right foot.	Verbal, visual, and/or touch cue to shift weight onto right foot, with physical prompt or assistance to move by pushing sideways (to right) at hips. Adult is behind student.
2. Take a step to the left by lifting left foot and moving it a step-sized distance to the left.	Verbal, visual, and/or touch cue to lift left foot and move it to the left, with physical prompt or assistance to move at left thigh (see Figure 7-11a).
3. "Walk" hands along support surface, first moving the left hand to the left, then moving the right hand to the left.	Verbal, visual, and/or touch cue to move the left, then the right hand to the left, with physical prompt or assistance to move at the shoulders or upper arms.
4. Complete step to the left, lifting right foot and moving it a step-sized distance to the left to meet the left foot (feet slightly apart).	Verbal, visual, and/or touch cue to lift the right foot and move it to the left, with physical prompt or assistance to move at right thigh.
5. Continue as above, repeating steps.	Continue as above, repeating steps.

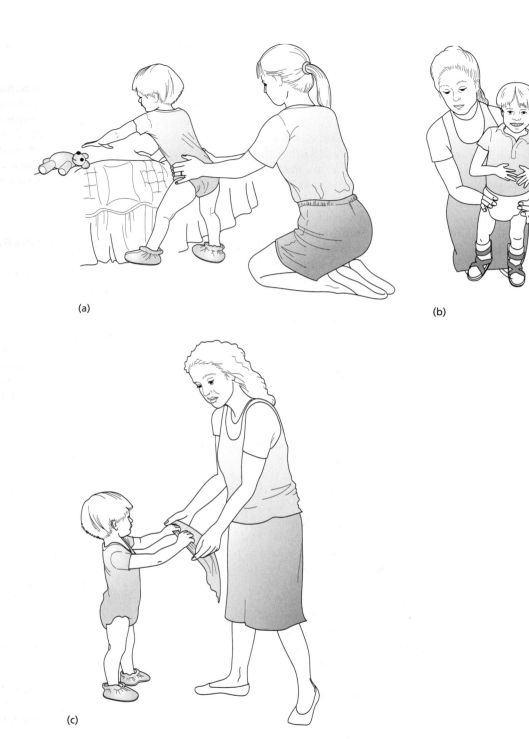

(a)

(b)

(c)

FIGURE 7-11 An adult assists the student to cruise to the left (a). She assists the student to walk by providing a physical prompt at the hips to shift weight to the left foot and raise the right leg to take a step (b), and by holding onto a towel for support (c).

Prior to learning to cruise, the student's independent world is basically on the floor. Cruising allows the student access to environmental stimulation and interaction which had previously been inaccessible. It is an important step toward independence. The above strategies may also be used with the student in a kneeling position. Knee-walking to the side while supporting against a surface is a precursor to cruising while in standing and is good practice for similar sets of muscle groups in the trunk and hips.

Walking

By the time the typically developing young student is about 10 months old, she is cruising along furniture in the forward direction using only one hand for minimal support. In the next month or so, increased control over balance and muscle coordination allows the child to cruise between pieces of furniture. Standing alone without support soon follows, usually by about 12 months. Over the next few months, between 12 and 18 months of age, the young student perfects her equilibrium and protective reactions in standing and gains progressively more control in walking. Initially when walking, the hands are held up and away from the body in a high guard position, and the feet are held wide apart to give a larger base of support. First steps are exaggerated high steps, flat-footed, and with little rotation of the trunk. As postural reactions in standing develop, through experience and practice, the student's arms lower, the legs move closer together, and the steps take on a more mature pattern, with heel strike and rotational movements in the trunk occurring during walking (Heller et al., 1996).

The student with physical disabilities may learn to walk independently, but walking may be significantly delayed, and the walking pattern may be somewhat atypical. Walking may also not be possible without adaptive equipment that lend external support. As stated earlier, however, walking should be a goal for all students who have the physical capability. Energy expenditure during walking will need to be considered across all surfaces (e.g., grass, uneven surfaces, hills, etc.) and across various situations and environments to determine whether additional mobility strategies are needed.

A sample procedure for walking is as follows, including taking initial steps and walking with support. It is assumed that the student has moved into the standing position (as described earlier), can stand without support, and has something or someone in front of her that she wants, motivating her to move. As with the other mobility skills, the task analysis provided is a sample only. Input from the student's therapists is necessary to determine whether the mobility skill is appropriate for the individual student and what assistive strategy will best help the individual student initiate walking for mobility, based on her individual physical skills and limitations.

As with cruising, some students benefit from initial attempts and practice with knee-walking before taking their first real steps. The steps to encourage walking on the knees are similar to those used for walking. Once the student has gained confidence in taking steps with less and less outside support, physical prompts or assistance should be gradually taken away, and the student should be prompted through visual, verbal, and/or tactile cues alone to walk independently for ever-increasing distances.

It should be noted that with walking, as with any other mobility skill that has been previously discussed, special considerations should be made for the student with visual impairment or deaf-blindness. Under the direction of an orientation and mobility (O&M) specialist, use of pre-cane or cane devices should be part of early attempts at walking, for the student to have a bumper between himself and environmental obstacles/hazards. It might also be necessary to incorporate trailing techniques or protective techniques (using the arm in front of the body) into early walking training. The individual student's team, including the O&M specialist, should decide which assistive strategies to use, based on the student's strengths and needs.

Sample Procedure for Walking

Student Movements	Adult Assistive Strategies
1. Standing on floor with feet flat, slightly apart and with body in good alignment, shoulders slightly forward of hips, shift weight onto left foot.	Verbal, visual, and/or touch cue to shift weight onto left foot, with physical prompt or assistance to move by pushing sideways (to left) at hips. Adult is behind student. If necessary, another adult may also stand in front of the student to offer support at the shoulders or hands.
2. Take step forward by lifting right foot and moving it a step-sized distance to the right front.	Verbal, visual, and/or touch cue to lift foot and move it forward, with physical prompt or assistance to move at right foot or knee, using the adult's foot or knee (as the student gains more skill, the physical prompts or assistance usually move higher on the body from the feet, to the knees, to the hips, to the shoulders). (See Figure 7-11b.)
3. Balance the body during the step by shifting the right shoulder back somewhat.	Verbal, visual, and/or touch cue to bring the right shoulder back with physical prompt or assistance to move at the right shoulder.
4. Shift weight onto the right foot, freeing left foot to move.	Verbal, visual, and/or touch cue to shift weight onto the right foot, with physical prompt or assistance to move pushing sideways (to right) and forward in a diagonal direction at hips.
5. Take a step forward by lifting the left foot and moving it a step-sized distance to the front, somewhat in front of the right foot.	Verbal, visual, and/or touch cue to lift the left foot and move it forward, with physical prompt or assistance to move at the left foot or knee, using the adult's foot or knee. Movement should be as rhythmic and continuous as possible.
6. Balance the body during the step by shifting left shoulder back somewhat.	Verbal, visual, and/or touch cue to bring the left shoulder back with physical prompt or assistance to move at the left shoulder.
7. Shift weight onto the left foot, freeing the right foot to move.	Verbal, visual, and/or touch cue to shift weight onto the left foot, with physical prompt or assistance to move by pushing sideways (to the left) and forward in a diagonal direction at the hips.
8. Continue as above, repeating steps.	Continue as above, repeating steps.

This procedure for walking was adapted from the MOVE Curriculum. As the student's skills improve, adult support can usually be moved from behind the student to the front of the student. Support can eventually be reduced from two hands to one hand. Sometimes, students can be reluctant to give up the security of support from another person. In this case, it is possible to provide support to the student without direct contact. The student can be placed with his back to a wall and encouraged to step away from the wall. Or steps can be taken by having the student push a weighted box or chair in front of him. The adult and the student can also practice taking steps as each hold onto a broom handle or a towel or rope. The adult should keep the support at about the student's shoulder level and walk backward slowly, as the student also holds onto the support and walks forward (Diamant, 1992). Figure 7-11c illustrates this strategy.

The student's team will also need to devise strategies to work on various other skills after the student learns to walk on his own, if he is to be truly independent in walking. Walking around, over, on or under obstacles, walking while carrying large objects, walking on uneven ground, walking backward, stopping and changing directions quickly, and stepping up onto and down from low objects (e.g., curbs) are examples of additional important skills to learn once walking is in place.

Wheeling

Some students with physical disabilities are involved significantly enough in their lower extremities that standing and walking is not possible. In many of these cases, especially if there is enough control of the upper extremities, the students can learn to operate a wheeled device with their arms that will allow them independent mobility. As seen earlier in this chapter, several different types of wheeled devices are available for students with physical disabilities. The sample assistive strategy presented in this section will assume that the student has good sitting balance in a chair-type device and adequate range of motion and strength in both arms to propel herself forward in a wheeled device. If this is not the case, a later section in this chapter on assistive technology will describe other available options to promote independent mobility through wheeled devices. A sample procedure to encourage propelling a wheeled device forward in a straight line is as follows.

Sample Procedure for Wheeling

Student Movements	Adult Assistive Strategies
1. Sitting in wheeled device, grasp top of both wheels with each hand, or place each hand at the top of each wheel (e.g., in a device with wheel extensions).	Verbal, visual, and/or touch cue to bring the hands to and/or grasp top of wheels, with physical prompt or assistance to move at elbows (the adult is behind child).
2. Apply force in forward and downward direction to both wheels at the same time.	Verbal, visual, and/or touch cue to push wheels forward and downward, with physical prompt or assistance to move at elbows or hands, depending on student needs.
3. Release grasp of wheels.	Verbal, visual, and/or touch cue to release the wheels, with physical prompt or assistance to move at the elbows or hands.
4. Repeat above.	Repeat above.

Once a student with physical disabilities has learned to maneuver in a wheeled device in a straight line, he needs to be instructed in how to turn the device to either side (by pushing forward on only one wheel at a time, the wheel opposite the direction he wants to turn, i.e., pushing on the left wheel results in a right turn; pushing on the right wheel results in a left turn). He also needs to learn how to push backward to back the wheeled device up, how to safely enter and exit the wheeled device, and how to negotiate obstacles such as tight spaces and curbs (if in a wheelchair). The latter is done by "popping a wheelie" or quickly pulling back on the main wheels as the individual adjusts his posture in the chair so that the small front wheels on the chair come off the ground. The individual's posture in the chair and forward pressure on the wheels then cause the front wheels to return to the ground, hopefully on top of the curb.

It should be noted that not all potential wheeled devices, especially those available for students, are wheelchairs. However, the general steps outlined here are useful in teaching use of any hand-driven wheeled devices.

INSTRUCTIONAL STRATEGIES FOR MOBILITY

For students who have severe physical disabilities that make independent mobility improbable even with the use of adaptive equipment, assistive strategies described earlier in the chapter can still be used with appropriate prompts to determine whether the student is capable of learning to at least assist with parts of the requisite movements necessary for mobility. If the student gains independence in any part of the movement, she should be required to perform these movements on her own and prompts should be faded, as possible. How, when, and where the student will be required to perform the specific movements should then be indicated on her IHP, along with

any contraindications for movement (e.g., rolling should not be performed on an uncarpeted surface because of the risk of the student hitting her head on the hard floor). A student receiving physical or occupational therapy will probably have mobility goals listed on her IEP, and the student's educational team must determine functional application of these goals. Although the physical or occupational therapist will be responsible for the goals, they will often need to be implemented by the teacher and other members of the educational team. This should only occur after proper training by the therapist. After the therapist trains the adults who will be assisting the student, diagrams or written instructions may be provided for reference. The therapist should also periodically check that correct assistance is being provided during mobility activities and document this.

Besides learning to assist with movement as much as possible, the more severely involved student should also be instructed in the purpose of the movement being required (e.g., when it is time to change activities from circle time on the floor to table activities, the student will be assisted to roll to the table). The student should also be instructed in how to direct caregivers to assist in movement when necessary due to pain or discomfort (e.g., through gesture, use of communication device, etc.). Once familiarized with the adaptive equipment to be used and why, when, and how it is being used, the student may be able to direct caregivers in using adaptive equipment when necessary (e.g., when someone new needs to assist him with his mobility).

Choice making should also be incorporated into mobility. If feasible, the student should be taught to help determine where, when, and how mobility will occur. For example, if several mobility options are available to a student when it is time to change activities (e.g., scooting on bottom to the table vs. walking with a walker), the student can be given options to choose how she wants to move to the table. However, care will need to be taken that, over time, all options will be practiced.

For the student who has achieved a level of independent mobility (with or without adaptive equipment) through the use of assistive strategies described earlier and eventual fading of prompts, mobility activities and instructional objectives related to these activities should be organized through a student schedule. To assure that the student is using mobility skills on a regular basis, part of the student schedule should indicate which mobility skill and mobility equipment the student will use during which functional or academic activity. For example, if a student is to be practicing mobilizing in his new motorized wheelchair and transferring out of the chair, his team might look at the student's schedule of activities and determine when this could best occur. If PE was followed by tabletop activities in the classroom on the schedule, the team might decide to schedule the student to use the wheelchair to go from the classroom to PE (where obstacles courses were being run), then back to the classroom where he would transfer out of his wheelchair to an adapted classroom chair for tabletop activities.

Sometimes use of task analysis will be necessary to instruct the student and the team appropriately in the process of a particular mobility skill (examples of task analyses have been given earlier in this chapter under the assistive strategies section). Figure 7-12 shows a task analysis of a mobility activity utilizing adaptive equipment. Written documentation of the task analysis can be kept in the student's file for reference and used for data collection.

Data should be taken to document that the student is performing mobility skills and using assistive devices, as planned. A data sheet should be used to keep track of the mobility schedule, as well as document that mobility activities are occurring as planned. The data sheet should include the mobility activity being performed, when the activity is occurring, in what context, the type of equipment being used, and any time or distance parameters. For example, John will use his mobile stander during PE class (volleyball) this week on Monday, Wednesday, and Friday for 30 minutes,

1. The student has the crutches appropriately placed on both arms with arm cuffs in place and is gripping both crutches firmly, with crutches placed at a comfortable 45 degrees from the front of feet.
2. The student is standing directly in front of the bottom of stairs, with her body straight.
3. The adult is standing behind the student with his right hand on the student's belt and his left hand on the student's left shoulder.
4. The student will bring her left (less involved) foot to the first stair, shifting her weight onto that foot and keeping her other foot and both crutches on the floor.
5. The student will bring both crutches and her right foot at the same time up to the first stair.
6. The adult will follow the student up the stairs, stabilizing the student at the shoulder and waist and being ready to assist if balance is lost.
7. The student will repeat the prior steps, continuing up the stairs.
8. The adult will repeat step 6, continuing up the stairs.

FIGURE 7-12 Sample task analysis for walking up stairs using forearm crutches

each day, and will push himself to and from class, a distance of 100 feet each way.

MOBILITY PROBLEMS AND EMERGENCIES

Falls

When students are learning to move, there is always a possibility that they may fall and injure themselves. It is therefore important to provide appropriate support and remain next to the unstable student when she is trying to move. The person who is watching or assisting the student should be prepared to catch the student should she fall. Some students will be much too large to catch fully. It will then be important to catch the head (and upper body) to prevent a head injury and protect the body from hitting any protruding objects.

If a fall occurs, the student needs to be checked for injury and receive appropriate medical treatment, if needed. If the student hits his head during the fall, the parents should be immediately contacted and the student should be observed for any signs of head injury (e.g., drowsiness, confusion, unequal pupil dilation). Documentation of a fall should occur, including when the fall occurred, how the injury occurred, what body part hit what objects, any first aid given, and when the parents were contacted.

Skin Breakdown from Mobility Equipment

Occasionally the student may have skin breakdown from using the adaptive equipment. This occurs when the equipment is not the correct size, the student is not placed correctly in the equipment, or the equipment is not used properly. Skin breakdown can occur with improper fit or use of many types of mobility devices or aids, such as poor-fitting splints (in which they are too tight or rub against the skin), improper use of crutches (in which the person leans on them with the armpits), and improper placement in the wheelchair (in which the person is not placed far enough back into the seat). Periodic skin checks should be done to monitor for skin breakdown, especially in the areas where there are bony prominences and where mobility equipment could rub or be too tight. Also, persons assisting the student in mobility needs should be thoroughly trained in proper use of the equipment to correct the student if he uses the equipment improperly, as well as to be sure they are placing the student in the equipment correctly. The physical therapist will be able to assist with this.

MANAGEMENT ISSUES FOR MOBILITY

Individualized Health Plan and Individualized Educational Program

When an individualized health plan (IHP) is used for mobility goals, it is important that the IHP include types of adaptive equipment used for mobility as well as any mobility restrictions. In some circumstances, it may not be advisable for the student to perform certain mobility activities, such as supported walking, due to a recent surgery or the student's specific medical condition (e.g., osteogenesis imperfecta, also known as "brittle bone disease"). This should be clearly placed on an IHP, and the educational team should be made clearly aware of the restrictions. The IHP may also include what to do for such problems as falls and skin breakdown. (See Figure 7-13 for an example of what to include in an IHP on mobility.)

Often a student with a physical impairment will have mobility objectives on their individualized educational program (IEP). These objectives can include any number of methods of mobility, such as crawling, creeping, cruising, walking, manipulating the wheelchair, or manipulating the walker. Although the physical therapist will typically determine the objectives, the team must be committed to assisting with the mobility objectives under the direction of the physical therapist. Some example IEP objectives are found in Figure 7-14.

Time Constraints Regarding Mobility

The team's commitment to achieve a mobility goal must be ascertained for the student to achieve success. Mobility goals are typically practiced when the student is going from one location to another, such as from the bus to the classroom, from the class to the lunch room, or between classrooms. Often it is much faster and easier to wheel a student down a hall in a wheelchair rather than have him slowly walk with the

	Length of Time (or Restrictions)

Type of Mobility Goals: _____

Type of Adaptive Equipment Being Used for Mobility

Type — Length of Time (or Restrictions)

_____ Canes — _____

_____ Walkers — _____

_____ Standard wheelchair — _____

_____ Electric wheelchair — _____

_____ Scooter — _____

_____ Adaptive tricycle — _____

_____ Adaptive bicycle — _____

Any Restrictions in Mobility: _____

Directions for Problems and Emergencies

Falls:_____

Skin breakdown:_____

FIGURE 7-13 Specialized areas to include in an IHP on mobility

Independent Performance of Task

The student will independently push her wheelchair from classroom to lunchroom within 10 minutes without running into walls or objects on 100% of opportunities for 2 weeks.

The student will walk using walker from the classroom to the playground area within 10 minutes.

The student will demonstrate the ability to change speed on her electric wheelchair with 90% accuracy on 8 out of 10 trials for three consecutive sessions.

Partial Performance of Task

The student will crawl across the room with an adult holding her feet for the student to push against to retrieve target item 7 out of 10 trials for four consecutive sessions.

When given partial support from an adult, the student will cruise from her desk to the circle time area with continual weight bearing, without falling for 6 consecutive days.

Directing the Task

When an adult is pushing her wheelchair, the student will tell the adult the route from the classroom to the lunchroom and back with 80% accuracy, daily for 2 weeks.

Knowledge of the Task

The student will describe proper wheelchair checks to assure proper functioning with 100% accuracy for three consecutive sessions.

FIGURE 7-14 Sample IEP objectives for mobility

walker or push his own chair. Mobility goals take up time. The team must determine the times of day that the student is to practice the mobility goals and make adjustments to carry them out successfully. For example, the student may need to leave a class early to propel herself to the next class. Balancing among not missing academic content, having personnel available to help her with mobility goals, and having sufficient time and practice to achieve the mobility goal must be worked out ahead of time. The team must then be committed to working on the mobility goal to help the student achieve optimal independence.

SUMMARY

Providing a means of mobility to a student with physical disabilities, whenever possible, is a very important goal for the student's health and well-being. Movement is important for personal safety, growth, and proper function of the body systems. It is also by moving about the environment that students gain independence, explore and interact with their world, and learn. When considering mobility options for students with physical disabilities, it is important to first evaluate the individual student's capability to move himself in space. A variety of movement options are available (e.g., rolling, crawling, creeping, scooting, cruising, walking, and wheeling). All of these movements may be considered as mobility options for the student with physical disabilities, as long as their appropriateness to the situation and the physical environment is considered. Some students with physical disabilities may have such severe impairments that they are unable to move themselves independently around their environment. In these cases, various mobility devices may be considered to assist the student with mobility. Mobility in various environments and over different surfaces also must be evaluated. The student with physical disabilities may need a variety of mobility strategies, depending on these environmental considerations.

As with all movement considerations for students with physical disabilities, choice of optimal assistive strategies, adaptive equipment, and instructional strategies for mobility should be done by a team consisting of the student (if possible) and her parents, teachers, physical and occupational therapists, and others who may be significantly involved in the student's day. The movements required for independent mobility should be analyzed by the team and a program developed, citing specific strategies and equipment to be used in specific settings and situations, which can then be carried out by all individuals working with the student.

Part III

Basic Self-Help Skills and Related Health Procedures

8

Eating and Feeding Techniques

Eating is one of the most basic and critical skills needed to sustain life. This seemingly simple skill actually consists of a complex series of processes that include moving the food to the mouth, accepting the food, manipulating the food within the structures of the mouth, and swallowing the food in a timely manner between breaths. Some students who have physical disabilities have difficulty eating due to a breakdown in one or more of these processes. Various strategies and adaptive equipment will be needed to help the student with this skill. The skill is referred to as *feeding* when another person gives the student food or liquids, concentrating on the sucking, chewing, and swallowing process. It is referred to as *eating* when the student is learning to take food or liquids independently. Eating includes not only the oral motor mechanics of eating, but also such areas as manipulating a spoon, eating finger foods, drinking from a cup, and drinking with a straw.

The ability to eat is a developmental process beginning before birth and developing as the student neurologically and physically matures. In a healthy infant, eating first consists of *sucking,* which is a rhythmic movement of the infant's mouth or tongue to obtain nutrition, typically occurring from a bottle or breast. By 6 months of age, the infant's oral motor skills are typically developed to the point that the baby can make vertical jaw movements to chew to assist with eating more solid foods. This type of chewing is known as *munching.* It is not until 9 months that the infant is able to make tongue movements that can move food between the teeth and are necessary to eating a wider variety of solid food. At this time, rotary chewing develops, which consists of circular jaw movements that allows an individual to grind food. As a person's oral motor system matures and allows him to make more complex oral motor movements, he will be able to eat more textured food. Initially, the student is only able to be fed pureed foods when a suck pattern is present (see Table 8-1). As the student has the ability to make more advanced jaw and tongue movements, food texture may progress from finely ground to eventually coarsely chopped

Table 8-1 Food Textures

Texture	Description	Example	Oral motor patterns
Pureed	No lumps, may have some fine grains	Cream of Wheat, pudding	Suck or suckle patterns, lips and jaw closure
Finely ground to coarsely ground	⅛" to ¼" pieces	Hamburger	Above, plus up-and-down (vertical) jaw and tongue movements (munching)
Finely chopped to coarsely chopped	¼" pieces to ½" chunks	Fruit cocktail	Above, plus side-to-side (lateral) movement of the tongue, vertical and diagonal jaw movements, enough strength to break up the pieces
Regular	Needs to be cut or bitten to be eaten	Apple	Above, plus rotary jaw movement and the strength to break up pieces

SOURCE: Adapted from *Beckman Oral Motor Assessment and Intervention,* Debra Beckman © 1995.
Reprinted by permission of Debra Beckman.

foods. When the student has the ability to make rotary jaw movements, he will be able to eat regular food. By 24 to 36 months, he will be able to eat independently using a spoon.

A student's ability to be able to eat regular food with mature chewing patterns depends not only on where the individual is developmentally in the eating process, but also on the integrity of the person's chewing and swallowing mechanism. A series of coordinated movements needs to occur for food to travel into the mouth and to the stomach. First, food enters the mouth and is moved between the teeth by the tongue for chewing to take place. Stimulation of the food on the mouth surfaces causes an automatic movement consisting of the jaw dropping and, in turn, rebounding. This causes the teeth to close around the food. As chewing continues, food is ground into a fine consistency. Chewing is important not only to make the food manageable to swallow, but because digestive enzymes only act on the surfaces of food particles. For this reason, food that is not well chewed (e.g., fruits and vegetables) will not be well digested. As the food is chewed and mixes with saliva, the food is formed into a **bolus** (rounded mass) that is ready to be swallowed.

Swallowing occurs in three stages. In the first stage, known as the *voluntary stage,* food is rolled into the back part of the mouth by the upward and backward movement of the tongue. In the second stage, known as the *pharyngeal stage,* food is involuntarily passed through the pharynx (the throat) and into the passage leading down to the stomach, known as the esophagus. This second stage involves: (a) the soft palate pulling upward to close off the nasal cavity to prevent food from entering that area, (b) the folds on either side of the pharynx pulling toward the middle to create a slip that prevents food too large from passing any farther, and (c) the epiglottis (a lidlike structure) swinging over the entrance to the trachea (descending tube leading to the lungs), preventing food from entering the lungs. In the third stage, known as the *esophageal stage,* passage of food occurs from the pharynx to the stomach by the involuntary process of *peristalsis* (which entails involuntary waves that move the food downward into the stomach and through the intestines) (Guyton, 1995). (See Figure 9–1 in the next chapter for a picture of the gastrointestinal system).

Difficulty with the eating process will often occur with students who have neurological or physical impairments that affect the muscles of the face, lips, jaws, tongue, or throat since these structures are involved in the eating process (Urbano, 1992). Eating may be affected in students who are developmentally delayed since they may not have achieved a more mature eating pattern. Students who have medical problems affecting some component of the eating process can also be affected. Several conditions predispose an individual to feeding and eating problems. As seen in Table 8-2, these may be due to physical abnormalities (e.g., cerebral palsy, cleft palate) or in some cases nutritional or hydration problems (e.g., short bowel syndrome) (McCamman & Rues, 1990).

Several warning signs indicate whether a feeding problem exists. Some of these include excessive drooling, excessive time needed to complete a meal, weight loss, frequent coughing when eating, and difficulty moving the food in the mouth prior to swallowing. Students with imperfect articulation (dysarthria) due to weakness in muscle control may also have eating problems since the muscles used for speech and feeding are similar (Groher, 1992).

Table 8-2 Select Medical Conditions Associated with Feeding/Nutritional Problems

Condition	Problems
Cerebral palsy	Possible oral motor feeding problems compromising ability to eat or be fed.
	Possible motor problems interfering with ability to eat independently.
	Possible need for increased caloric intake due to effects of spasticity on burning calories.
	Fatigue may occur with feedings that results in decreased oral intake.
	Possible vitamin and mineral deficiencies due to low intake of food or less variety.
	Constipation problems due to less motor movement and limited liquid intake.
Developmental delays	Feeding patterns may be delayed resulting in less mature feeding pattern. If this occurs, the student would also have limited ability to take foods of consistency commensurate with the student's chronological age.
	At risk for oral motor problems.
	At risk for tactile defensiveness.
Spina bifida	Often at risk for being overweight due to limited activity. May need restricted caloric intake.
Down syndrome	At risk for oral motor problems.
	Tendency for being overweight; may need restricted caloric intake.
	At risk for constipation; may need increased fluid intake.
	May have additional medical problems (cardiac).
Congenital heart defect	At risk for poor intake of food.
	May tire during eating.
	May have a restricted fluid intake due to heart complications (congestive heart failure). May require increased caloric intake due to increased work of the heart.
Chronic renal failure	May have fluid restrictions.
Insulin-dependent diabetes	Often has special dietary restrictions.
Prader-Willi syndrome	Poor tone and poor suck in infancy.
	Energy needs are often decreased.
	May have an extreme craving to eat (e.g., may eat trash).
Cleft palate, cleft lip	May have difficulties with sucking and swallowing.
	May not eat/drink sufficient quantities of food/liquid.
	May have hypersensitive mouth.

FACTORS AFFECTING EATING AND FEEDING

Seven different factors affect eating and drinking. Students with disabilities may have difficulties in one or more of these areas, affecting their ability to eat or be fed efficiently. These seven factors are (a) developmental readiness, (b) oral motor competency, (c) sensory awareness and discrimination, (d) medical stability, (e) positive practice, (f) environmental factors, and (g) motor control and position (Eicher & Kerwin, 1996). The feeder will need to consider whether the student is having difficulty in any of these categories and make the appropriate adaptations to facilitate feeding and eating.

Developmental Readiness

Eating skills follow a developmental progression. Students functioning at a low developmental level may not have developed more mature patterns of eating or drinking. For example, if a student is functioning at a 6-month level, she will not have the neurological ability to chew meats or other solid foods or drink through a straw (Eicher & Kerwin, 1996). Instead, she will probably function at a more basic level of eating, such as munching or sucking. When this is the case, the student may require food restrictions that limit the texture of the food. Some students may require soft food and be unable to eat regular food until they have been able to develop the necessary eating skills. Developmental readiness and motor control are important considerations when planning a student's feeding and eating program.

Oral Motor Competency

Problems in oral motor (oral-pharyngeal) competency are due to (a) difficulties with achieving the normal movements required for feeding or eating, (b) continuation of oral motor reflexes, and/or (c) the development of abnormal oral motor patterns. Feeding and eating require a complex integration of movements. Included in these movements are the lips (e.g., pursing, moving food off a spoon, closing the lips), jaw (e.g., closing the mouth, chewing), tongue (e.g., sucking, moving food to the back of the mouth and between teeth), and structures involved in swallowing. Some students have difficulties with these movements and need a variety of assistive strategies to help them eat. (See "Instructional Strategies and Modifications for Eating" and "Assistive Strategies for Drinking" later in this chapter for a description of how to address these areas.)

The second area affecting oral motor competency is the continuation of certain primitive reflexes that all individuals have as infants but that are typically integrated into other, more mature motor patterns within a few months of life. Some of these reflexes include biting, rooting, and sucking-swallowing. A **bite reflex** is biting that occurs when the gums or teeth are stimulated (not to be confused with the abnormal tonic bite pattern that is described later). When this is present, it is important that the feeder avoid touching the teeth or gums when feeding. A rubber-coated spoon may be used in case biting occurs. A **rooting reflex** is the movement of the head and mouth to the side, when that side of the mouth or the cheek is touched. When this is present, it is important to avoid touching the side of the student's mouth or face. However, in some instances the feeder may use a technique involving jaw control that uses the feeder's hand on the student's chin and face. If this causes a rooting reflex, the jaw control technique will need to be discontinued or modified so as not to give asymmetrical input. A suck-swallow reflex is the rhythmical movement of tongue upon touching the lips. In early infancy, this reflex helps liquids move to the back of the throat for swallowing (Fraser et al., 1990). The continuation of this reflex may interfere with voluntary and more advanced sucking and swallowing patterns and independent cup drinking. Progression of this reflex, as well as the other two primitive oral reflexes, may benefit from a treatment program developed by the occupational therapist or speech-language pathologist.

The third area affecting oral motor competency is the development of abnormal oral motor patterns. These include **tactile defensiveness** (increased response to tactile stimulation) or lack of response to tactile stimulation, tongue thrust, tonic bite and unsustained bite reflexes, and hypersensitive gag. Each one of these are described under the section "Eating and Feeding Problems and Emergencies," along with strategies to minimize their effect.

Sensory Awareness and Discrimination

As the student matures, more discriminating sensory processing skills are required to discriminate textures, temperature, shape, weight, taste, and placement of food within the mouth and to determine whether the food is ready to be swallowed. Students usually develop these discrimination skills through oral feeding and play (Morris & Klein, 1987). Feeding problems can develop if the student does not develop the discrimination skills required to provide information to assist with motor planning and if the student is hypersensitive or hyposensitive to food entering the mouth.

Medical Stability

Students will often have difficulty eating when one of the primarily organ systems is temporarily or permanently affected. This includes problems in the respiratory tract, the brain (or neurological tract), and the gastrointestinal tract (Eicher & Kerwin, 1996). Students who are mouth breathers or have respiratory congestion need to be assessed to determine whether they can breathe through the nose. This can be done by placing a mirror below the student's nostrils and seeing whether it fogs while using jaw control to close the mouth. For students who are mouth breathers or who have colds or congestion, procedures that cause the mouth to close (e.g., jaw control and lip closure) should not be used more than 10 to 15 seconds at a time so as to not interfere with breathing (Utley, 1991). One useful

way to keep track of this is for the feeder to hold her breath upon closing the student's mouth as a gauge as to when the student needs to breathe.

Problems affecting the brain may result in a lack of interest in eating, difficulty learning steps in the feeding or eating process, or physical disability affecting the oral motor mechanism. Each of these will need to be addressed by using reinforcing food, systematic instruction, and adaptive devices and assistive strategies.

Several problems may occur in the gastrointestinal tract. One of the most common problems found in students with physical disabilities is **gastroesophogeal reflux** (GER). Gastroesophageal reflex is the spontaneous backward flow of stomach contents into the esophagus (the passage from the pharynx to the stomach). Specific strategies to use with GER are discussed under "Eating and Feeding Problems and Emergencies."

Positive Practice

Development of mature feeding or eating patterns consists of sequentially progressing through increasingly refined and coordinated movements. For a student to perform these feeding and eating skills successfully, the new movements will need to be practiced until they are learned and have become incorporated into the student's regular pattern of eating or being fed. The amount of practice of these skills and the type of assistance given determines how quickly the student learns the skill (Eicher & Kerwin, 1996).

Environmental Factors

To facilitate a successful eating experience, the environment needs to be set up so that the student can focus on the feeding process and not on other stimuli, especially when the student is easily distracted. The environment should have minimal distracting noises to keep the student focused and relaxed. The environmental smells occurring at mealtime should be pleasant ones. The student, for example, should not be fed next to a trash can or bathroom. To promote visual attention, brightly colored spoons or place mats may be used. Using items, such as plates, that are high in color contrast to the table (or the food) can also be helpful with promoting attention to the meal. Some teachers will place a contrasting piece of construction paper under the plate for contrast or place the paper under the spoon as it travels to the student's mouth to make the spoon more visually noticeable. Placing bright or contrasting strips around the student's cup or utensil may also enhance its visibility and result in increased visual attending. It is also important that during the feeding process, the student is well positioned and no distracting movements occur while feeding, such as having the wheelchair frequently bumped as others pass by.

The feeding experience should be a pleasant, calm, and relaxing experience. The student should not be fed in a rushed manner. The appropriate amount of food should be on the spoon to avoid over stuffing the mouth and causing discomfort or gagging. The student should also be taught to communicate which food or drink he wants next. If food is refused, it should not be forced.

Positioning and Motor Control

How the student is positioned during feeding can impact the success of the feeding experience. It is important to achieve the proper position before determining any other intervention for feeding since many of the problems that occur in eating may be corrected once proper positioning is achieved. For example, when a student's head is incorrectly positioned in **hyperextension** (with the neck bending back), jaw closure will be more difficult and choking on the food is likely, with possible **aspiration** (food or liquid going into the lungs) (Campbell, 1993). Appropriate positioning for eating and feeding is a very individualized process that needs to consider the student's physical condition, oral motor skills, motor tone, respiration, and level of alertness. Additional considerations specific to eating include the student's motor abilities (including strength and range of motion) and visual abilities.

Appropriate positioning can occur in side lying, lying prone, reclining, sitting, or standing. What might be an optimal position for one student, such as facilitating the head tilted forward (chin tuck), may be harmful to another student with respiratory problems. Tilting the wheelchair backward 10 to 20 degrees may help an individual maintain head alignment when there is low postural tone (Campbell, 1993) but may be contraindicated in individuals with swallowing problems. Therefore, certain principles of positioning should be considered when determining the optimal feeding position for an individual that include (a) trunk support, (b) hip and pelvic position, (c) arm and shoulder positioning, and (d) head position.

The student's position should provide adequate trunk support for eating. If a student is struggling to support her trunk, she may compensate by increasing tension in parts of her body or by using her arms or legs to support herself. This may interfere with the student's ability to move her arms to grasp and move the feeding utensil. The student may also have difficulty supporting her head in an adequate position to accept and manipulate the food in the mouth.

The position of the hips and pelvis should be adequate in order for the curves of the spine to be positioned to provide support for adequate positioning of the head. In sitting, excessive backward tilting of the pelvis encourages a rounded flexed (bent) spine, which results in neck flexion and excessive chin tuck. To compensate, a student may then hyperextend the neck to see the food. Excessive forward tilting of the pelvis can encourage excessive extension (straightening) of the spine. This position may interfere with the student's ability to move his arms and may facilitate extension at the neck. If a student is sitting with more weight on one side of his hips than the other, the spine may curve laterally and cause compensatory head tilting. In general, the pelvis should be tilted slightly forward with equal weight distribution on both hips in sitting. Rolls or wedges may provide additional support if the student's current positioning device is not adequate.

The position of the shoulders should allow for movement of the arms and appropriate head positioning for feeding. Shoulders that are excessively rounded can make it difficult for the student to raise his head to accept food. It can also affect chewing, sucking, and swallowing. Shoulders that are adducted, with the shoulder blades pulled together, can tend to pull the neck into hyperextension. This can interfere with the student's ability to bring food to his mouth and to use lips, tongue, and jaw appropriately (Morris & Klein, 1987).

The position of the head as related to the neck, spine, and hips should allow for adequate movement of the jaw, lips, tongue, cheeks, and swallowing mechanism. When the head is positioned with the chin tipped downward, the tongue and lips are brought forward and can move more freely for eating and swallowing. However, when the neck is hyperextended (bent backward), a student may have difficulty closing her mouth, bringing her lips together, chewing, moving food in her mouth, and swallowing safely (Morris & Klein, 1987). Students with problems swallowing are placed at greater risk for aspiration with hyperextension at the neck, since swallowing is more difficult and since food can more easily enter the pharyngeal pathway and into the lungs (Wolf & Glass, 1992).

Spasticity. Some students with cerebral palsy will have increased tone in their muscles (spasticity) that results in the student assuming a position in which the neck and head are extended back. It is important to flex (tilt forward) the head slightly (to about 5 to 15 degrees) to reduce the chance of aspiration and to facilitate swallowing. Wheelchairs with headrest extension with additional neck or head support may be used for correct positioning. When severe spasticity is present, shoulders may be pulled back (retracted). In this instance, rolled towels may be placed behind the shoulders to bring the shoulders forward. If the shoulder's are rounded (protracted), the wheelchair may be adapted with devices that hold the shoulders back in proper position (Fraser et al., 1990).

Severe Extensor Thrusting. Students with severe spastic quadriplegia cerebral palsy may exhibit severe extensor thrusting, a total body movement that consists of neck hyperextension, bent arms, retracted shoulders, an arched back, and straight legs that are often pulled together. This total body movement interferes with feeding, since it hyperextends the neck, predisposing to aspiration, and results in a open jaw, jaw thrust, lip retraction, and tongue retraction. Proper positioning is crucial to inhibit the extensor thrusting. In a sitting position, the hips should be bent (flexed) in slightly more than a 90-degree angle by using a wedged wheelchair seat. The neck should be in a flexed position with the use of a headrest, and the shoulders should be brought forward with rolled towels under the shoulders or through the use of wheelchair adaptations (Fraser et al., 1990).

Hypotonic (Low) Muscle Tone. Some students with generalized low muscle tone have a lack of trunk and head control that results in the head falling to one side and food pooling between the cheeks and gums. First, the student's trunk and body need to be in the appropriate position, as previously described. When poor head control is present, the head may need to be supported by a headrest. In some situations, the wheelchair or adaptive chair may be slightly tilted back to prevent the head from falling forward. Feeders should be alert for signs of aspiration whenever backward tilting is required. The wheelchair or feeder tray may also be raised to about midchest to encourage proper positioning of the chest and to assist with arm use by providing additional elbow support when holding a spoon or cup.

Athetoid Movements. Some students with athetoid cerebral palsy will have continual nonvoluntary movement of their arms, legs, and head that interfere with feeding. In some cases, by restricting the involuntary arm and leg movement, the feeder can improve head control (Fraser et al., 1990). Padded straps may be used to secure the feet. The extraneous arm movement may be controlled by having the student hold onto dowels attached to the tray (if possible) or otherwise stabilizing the arms (e.g., with wrist weights). A headrest or neckrest may help keep the head in a midline position without movement. For students learning to drink and eat independently, weights on the wrists, a weighted cup or weighted utensils, and an elevated table height may be helpful.

Primitive Reflexes. Several reflexes that an infant has early in life are typically integrated into normal motor patterns early in life. However, for students with physical disabilities, these reflexes may continue and interfere with the feeding process. Two of these reflexes are the asymmetrical tonic neck reflex (ATNR) and symmetrical tonic neck reflex (STNR). In the *asymmetrical tonic reflex,* when the head turns to one side, the arm straightens on the face side and the other arm bends. To prevent this from occurring, it is important that food and drink be presented at midline. Head support devices that keep the head in midline with slight neck flexion may also be recommended. In the *symmetrical tonic neck reflex,* when the head flexes (chin toward chest), the arms flex and the legs extend. When the neck extends with the head going back, the arms extend and the legs flex. This interferes with stable sitting as well as with the student's ability to eat or drink. Achieving head stability by a headrest, a neck collar, or other head support will inhibit the reflex from occurring. Also, a tray is beneficial to support the arms in a relaxed symmetrical position and to help with sitting balance (Fraser et al., 1990).

EQUIPMENT AND ADAPTIVE EQUIPMENT FOR FEEDING AND EATING

Many different types of equipment and adaptive equipment are available for feeding and eating. Because of the differences between feeding and eating food versus drinking, the equipment de-

scribed in this section, as well as the following assistive and instructional strategies, will pertain exclusively to eating and feeding foods. The next section will discuss the equipment used in drinking liquids, as well as the assistive and instructional strategies for drinking.

Some of the adaptive equipment that the feeder or student may use to make eating and feeding more effective includes adaptive spoons, bowls and plates, Snack Caps, items used to enhance stability, and mechanical feeders.

Spoons

When teaching spoon feeding, the type of spoon used may directly affect the success of the process. Short-handled spoons are often more easy to control than long-handled ones. A deep bowl on the spoon helps the food stay on the spoon, while the flat-bowl spoon allows the lips to remove food from the spoon more easily. Spoons that have handles that are offset or bent may help students bring the food to their mouth if they do not have adequate wrist control. Spoons with built-up or wide handles may make it easier to maintain a grasp on the spoon if grasp is weak.

Gripping Utensils

When the student cannot hold the utensil, universal cuffs can be worn. These cuffs are made of Velcro strapping or more sturdy material and help hold the spoon in the student's hand, especially if the student has difficulty moving the arm and maintaining grasp simultaneously (see Figure 8-1).

Sandwich Holders

In some instances, the student cannot hold onto finger food or does not have the full range of motion to bring food to the mouth. In these cases, a sandwich holder may be used. Sandwich holders may be bought or adapted from other material such as a bag closer (chip clips) (Figure 8-2). Also, a disposable holder can be made from Popsicle sticks or tongue blades.

FIGURE 8-1 Examples of adaptive equipment used to promote eating (from top row left and across): scoop dish, two spoons with universal cuffs, bent spoon, two weighted spoons with built-up handles, and a sandwich holder (bottom left). Examples of adaptive cups (bottom row from left to right): cut-out cup (nosey cup), straw holder on cup, and cup with handle.

Bowls and Plates

The type of bowl should be considered when teaching spoon feeding. Bowls that have a higher edge will give the self-feeder something to scoop against. Wider bowls allow for adequate room to move and scoop the food. Scooper bowls and plates (or dishes) have a raised edge on one side to allow for extra surface area to scoop against and, frequently, a lowered opposite edge to allow access to the bowl (refer back to Figure 8-1). A plate guard may be attached to some plates that results in a raised edge.

Snack Cap

A Snack Cap is an assistive device that provides jaw support for the student who is finger- or spoon-feeding himself (see Figure 8-3). It has a supportive elastic strap that supports the chin; an additional strap can be attached to secure to the front of the chin to decrease slipping of the supportive strap toward the throat. This cap is helpful for students who are independent self-feeders but display oral motor difficulties such as tongue protrusion, decreased lip control, or decreased chewing skills due to jaw weakness or instability (Klein & Delaney, 1994; Morris & Klein, 1987).

Stability of Bowls and Plates

Another mealtime consideration is that the plate or bowl may move on the table when the student

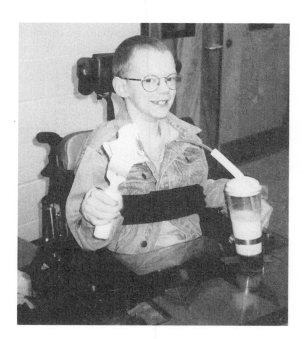

FIGURE 8-2 A student using a sandwich holder and an adaptive cup

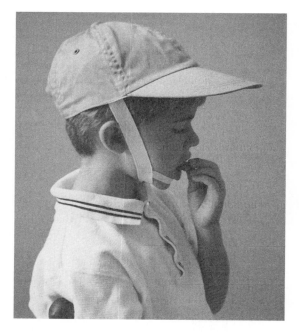

FIGURE 8-3 A boy using a Snack Cap to assist with self-feeding

example, works by pushing the switch in one direction to rotate the plate in order for the student to select which food he wants to eat. Upon pushing the switch in the other direction, a pusher (a rectangularly shaped piece of metal that scrapes across the plate) pushes food onto a spoon, which then is mechanically moved from the plate to the level of the student's lips. The student opens his mouth, brings his head forward to engulf the spoon, and takes the food off of the spoon. Upon hitting the switch a second time, the spoon returns back to the plate area. This requires good head control and the food must be prepared in bite size pieces or of a consistency that will fit on a spoon. Some feeders will also accommodate a bowl.

ASSISTIVE STRATEGIES FOR FEEDING

Several different oral motor problems may arise in the feeding process for a student with a physical disability. When oral motor problems are present, careful observation and assessment will be needed to determine which assistive strategies are needed to facilitate feeding. Assistive strategies for feeding a student food can be divided into six areas: lip movement, lip closure, jaw closure, jaw control, activating cheek muscles, and developing tongue lateralization.

Strategies for Lip Movement

Students who have tightness in the facial muscle may have difficulty actively moving their lips close enough to the spoon to remove food from the spoon. They may need to have their faces massaged or otherwise relaxed toward a closed mouth position prior to feeding to loosen the tight muscles (Klein & Delaney, 1994). (However, if the student is tactilely defensive, massaging the face is contraindicated. The student will first need to go through a controlled motor input program aimed at desensitizing the facial area and mouth.

is trying to eat from it. Some bowls have nonskid rings or suction cups on the bottom to help the bowl stay secured to the table. When that is not the case, material such as dycem, rubber matting, or rubber shelf liner can be put between the plate and table to prevent the plate from easily moving. The placement of the bowl or plate will also be crucial for many students in order for them to best access it. (See Chapter 6 for more on positioning material.)

Mechanical Feeders

Some students with severe physical impairments, such as a high spinal cord injury or severe cerebral palsy, will be unable to manipulate a spoon. For these students a mechanical feeder may be an option. Mechanical feeders are controlled by a switch that the student pushes with the chin, knee, hip, hand, arm, foot, or other body part. The Winsford Feeder by North Coast Medical, for

See the tactile defensiveness section under "Eating and Feeding Problems and Emergencies" for more information.)

Some students have low tone or weak facial muscles and have difficulty initiating contraction of these muscles for adequate lip movement required for lip closure. These students may need input to the facial muscles to alert or increase the tone of the muscles. Games that incorporate patting, tapping, and stroking such as patty cake and peek-a-boo can be done around the jaw, cheeks, and lips. Students can often tolerate this type of input when presented in a game or song manner (Morris & Klein, 1987).

Strategies for Lip Closure

Some students are slow to initiate lip movement toward the spoon to remove the food. The first intervention is for the feeder to pause with the spoon resting on the lower lip. This extra time may be all that is needed for the student to bring the lip down toward the bowl of the spoon (Klein & Delaney, 1994).

Using a sideways presentation of the spoon can also assist in facilitating active upper lip movement. In this technique, the feeder presents the spoon sideways with as much of the spoon as possible resting on the lower lip. The feeder should pause as described earlier. If no upper lip movement is noted, the feeder may then tip the spoon upward to touch the upper lip while still resting the spoon on the lower lip. The spoon is then returned to the initial position on the lower lip. Spoon tipping is repeated while verbally cueing the student, "This is where I want you to be. Come down and touch this spoon" (Klein & Delaney, 1994). Gradually more upper lip movement toward the spoon should be noted. When the student is not able to move the lip actively toward the spoon, assistance by the feeder can be provided by using the index finger to gently bring the upper lip down to meet the spoon while it is resting on the lower lip (Klein & Delaney, 1994; see Figure 8-4).

Another strategy for lip closure is applying a

FIGURE 8-4 A student achieves upper lip closure over a spoon through the assistance of an adult

quick stretch to the circular muscles around the mouth to promote active muscle contraction. The feeder uses index and middle fingers to stretch the muscle around the lips away from the mouth using a firm, quick, stretching motion repeated three or four times in succession. The feeder begins in the midline of the lips and moves to each corner executing the same movements. This is often used before taking bites of food (Utley, 1991).

Strategies for Jaw Closure

When preparation of the muscles prior to feeding is not enough to facilitate better lip closure and jaw support for feeding, external assistance to the jaw and lips may be necessary. The feeder can assist the student in achieving and maintaining jaw closure when the food is presented. This support can be provided in four ways.

The first two methods provide jaw support in front of the student. In the first method, the feeder is in front of the student and has the middle finger placed under the jaw behind the chin to assist with upward jaw movement and reduce tongue protrusion. The index finger is at the jaw joint (temporomandibular joint) to provide lateral stability to the jaw and stabilize the feeder's hand.

The thumb is then located on the chin below the lower lip to assist with downward movement of the jaw and to stabilize the lip (Morris & Klein, 1987) (see Figure 8–5a).

In the second technique, jaw support is provided in front of the student with the thumb under the jaw just behind the chin to assist with upward jaw movement (see Figure 8–5b). This technique is usually used instead of the first technique when the student is less physically involved and only needs jaw support. There is no lip support provided by this technique.

In the third technique, support is provided from the side or behind with the feeder's arm going around the student's nondominant side and the feeder's hand placed in a certain position (see Figure 8–5c). The feeder places the middle finger under the jaw behind the chin. The index finger is placed on the chin below the lower lip to assist with jaw movement and to stabilize the lower lip. The thumb is placed at the temporomandibular joint to stabilize the feeder's hand and lend lateral stability to the jaw (Morris & Klein, 1987). Besides assisting with jaw stabilization as do the first

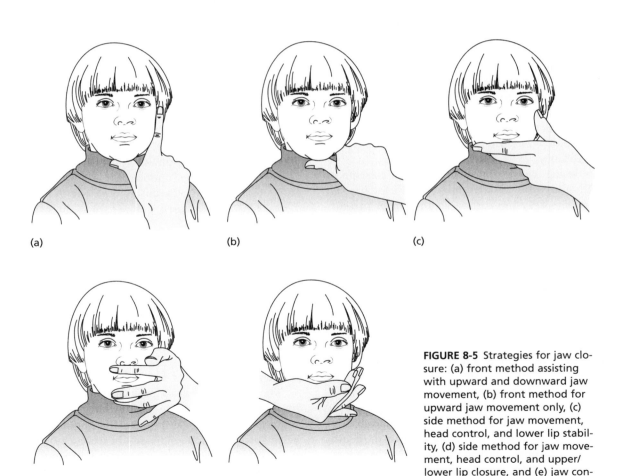

(a)   (b)   (c)

(d)   (e)

FIGURE 8-5 Strategies for jaw closure: (a) front method assisting with upward and downward jaw movement, (b) front method for upward jaw movement only, (c) side method for jaw movement, head control, and lower lip stability, (d) side method for jaw movement, head control, and upper/lower lip closure, and (e) jaw control for chewing.

two techniques, this third technique also assists with poor head control and neck hyperextension by having the feeder's arm placed gently around the back of the student's head (Wong, 1995).

A fourth technique is similar to the third technique but also provides additional upper lip control. In this technique, the feeder places her arm around the student, placing the ring finger under the chin, the middle finger under the student's lower lip, and the index finger over the upper lip. In this way, jaw control as well as lip closure can be assisted (see Figure 8-5d).

Strategies for Jaw Control While Chewing

To improve control of the jaw, the feeder can provide external support. The purpose of jaw support during chewing activities is to provide enough support for the student to move the jaw up and down, diagonally, and circularly. Light support is provided and should not restrict movements of the jaw for chewing. The technique used to provide support will depend on the feeder's comfort and the amount of support required by the student.

Chin cupping is provided by the feeder by cupping the chin with the thumb resting on the chin and the index and third finger supporting under chin. The feeder should be cautious not to place supporting fingers too far behind the chin, as it may interfere with tongue movement and cause gagging (see Figure 8-5e).

Strategies for Activating Cheek Muscles for Chewing

Active movement of the cheeks for chewing may be facilitated either by increasing the tone of the muscles if the cheeks have decreased tone or by relaxing or decreasing the tension in the muscles if the cheeks are tight. The strategy used depends on the specific limitations of the student. These strategies should be used prior to feeding to increase the likelihood that the student will be able to maintain food within the teeth region and to ensure that the food can be ground into small enough pieces for

safe swallowing. (However, if the student is tactilely defensive, these strategies may be overwhelming to the student, and a program to desensitize the student will have to be addressed first. Look under the section "Eating and Feeding Problems and Emergencies" for more information.)

Some of the strategies used with students who have low-tone cheeks include cheek tapping, NUK massage brush stimulation, and Infa-Dent finger toothbrush/gum massage. Cheek tapping is provided by the feeder putting the heel of the hands together and gently placing the fingers on the student's cheeks (see Figure 8-6a). Firm gentle tapping is provided on the student's cheeks on both sides at the same time or each side alternately, at approximately the same intensity as tapping on a typewriter. If the face becomes red, decrease tapping intensity (Klein & Delaney, 1994).

NUK massage brush stimulation is provide by placing the NUK massage brush inside the cheek and rolling it in an upward direction (Figure 8-6b). Continue the stimulation for approximately 5 to 10 seconds on each side. If the student tolerates this activity, repeat several times. Infa-Dent finger toothbrush/gum massage is performed by placing the Infa-Dent finger toothbrush over your index finger and inserting the finger into the student's mouth along the cheeks (Figure 8-6c). Stroking or massaging the inside of the cheeks is then provided in an upward direction. A back-and-forth stroke may also be attempted, depending on the student's response to stimulation (Klein & Delaney, 1994).

Some of the strategies used to relax tight muscles include facial molding, inner cheek finger massage, and Infa-Dent finger massage. Facial molding is performed by using finger tips and a gentle yet firm touch (Figure 8-6d). The student's cheeks and chin are massaged toward a closed-mouth position. This can also be done with a dry or warm, wet washcloth (do not use a cold washcloth or cold hands). Inner cheek finger massage is performed by using a straightened index and third finger. Place one finger inside the cheek and the other outside the cheek. The two fingers should

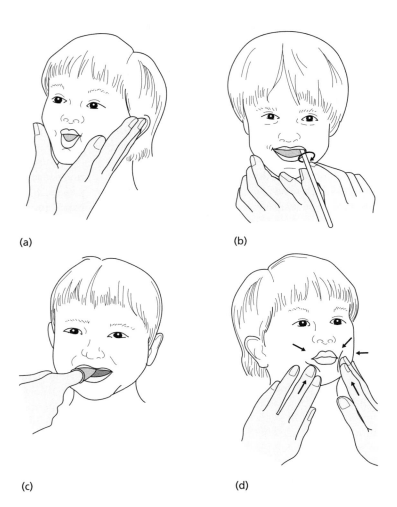

(a)

(b)

(c)

(d)

FIGURE 8-6 Strategies for activating or relaxing cheek muscles for chewing: (a) cheek tapping, (b) NUK massage brush stimulation, (c) Infa-Dent finger massage, and (d) facial molding

be parallel to each other. Gently shake or vibrate the cheek as the fingers are moved toward the lips. Infa-Dent finger massage is performed using the Infa-Dent toothbrush placed on an index finger. The finger is then inserted into the side of the mouth along the cheek. The cheek is slowly stroked toward the lips (Klein & Delaney, 1994).

Strategies for Developing Tongue Lateralization for Chewing

Delays in the ability to lateralize the tongue to move food within the mouth will affect the stu-

dent's ability to develop chewing. Delays in developing this skill may be due to the following reasons: oral hypersensitivity; low or increased tension in the muscles of the jaw, cheek, lips, and tongue; difficulty perceiving the location or texture of food in the mouth; or developmental skills that have not reached the developmental level of 6 to 9 months of age (Morris & Klein, 1987). As with other strategies, the feeding position needs to provide adequate support. Sometimes providing sensory input to the tongue can be helpful. This can be done by providing food that is more intense in taste or temperature (e.g., frozen lemonade, which combines a sour taste with cold) or using an NUK massage brush as instructed by the occupational therapist or speech therapist.

Food placement may help develop tongue lateralization by placing food on the side of the mouth since the tongue tends to move toward the side of the mouth the object is placed. Begin with foods that are soft and dissolve easily such as graham crackers, crackers, and small pieces of cereal. Alternate the side in which the food is presented in order for the tongue to practice moving to both sides, once lateralization of the tongue has begun. Have the student move the food to the middle and then to the other side in a game fashion. As chewing and tongue lateralization improves, food may be provided in long strips. This allows for a cycle of biting and chewing as the food moves into the side of the mouth (Klein & Delaney, 1994; Morris & Klein, 1987). Food items may include pretzels, bread sticks, toast strips, French fries, partially cooked carrot strips, and partially cooked potatoes. As the student's skill develops, strips of dried fruit, strips of chicken, or canned green beans may be introduced.

Lateral chewing can be practiced with food secured in organza or a gauze material (Beckman, 1994). Food is placed inside a piece of cloth and twisted in a bundle. The food bundle is placed between the molars on the side of the mouth, while the feeder holds onto the end. Upward pressure is provided to top molars to facilitate a chew, while the feeder observes for tongue lateralization toward the bundle while chewing occurs.

As the student's skills develop, a hide-and-seek game can be played to facilitate tongue lateralization. The game begins by placing food inside the cheek. The student then is instructed to find the food by touching the food item with the tongue before chewing and swallowing it. Food items such as a piece of Fruit Loop cereal with a stronger taste may be easier to locate in the beginning of such intervention.

Strategies to Develop Swallowing

To help facilitate swallowing, the feeder may first have the student position the head in midline with chin pointed toward chest. If the student can first smell the food, it will facilitate saliva production. After placement of the food in the mouth, deposited toward the back of the tongue, the student should hold the food in the mouth for a few seconds for the saliva to mix with the food. Food selection will play a key part in aiding the student to swallow. For individuals who have difficulty swallowing, food should be moist enough that it does not crumble or fragment in the mouth but dry enough to hold a shape (Suddarth, 1991).

Procedure for Feeding

After explaining to the student that it is mealtime, washing hands, going to an appropriate environment to be fed, and positioning the student, the feeder may begin to feed the student. Through the feeding process, the student should be given opportunities to make choices and communicate what she would like to eat next. Feeding should occur in a relaxed manner, providing the needed assistive strategies to help with oral motor functioning.

Steps in the Procedure for Feeding	Rationale
1. Explain it is time to eat, and position the student for feeding.	The student may be told it is time to eat or be given an object or symbol (e.g., a spoon) to communicate it is time to eat. Correct positioning is essential for successful feeding.
2. Place a napkin, towel, or padded T-shirt over the student.	These will protect the student's clothing. A bib should not be used unless the student is

Steps in the Procedure for Feeding	*Rationale*
	an infant since it is not age-appropriate. Sometimes T-shirts that are slit up the sides and have a towel sewn into the inside of the shirt are used since they look age-appropriate and are very absorbent.
3. Place one hand on the student's face to provide jaw or lip support, if needed.	Correct technique is important for success. (See the prior discussion for how to implement these strategies when needed.)
4. Scoop food on the first one-third of the bowl of the spoon.	This facilitates easy removal. It is important to only give the student small amounts at a time to avoid gagging.
5. Bring the spoon toward the student to the center of the mouth, with the spoon below eye level.	The feeder will want to avoid the spoon being presented from the side since that may elicit an ATNR reflex. Also, the spoon should be presented below eye level to prevent the student from looking up and possibly going into an extension pattern.
6. Place the spoon in the student's mouth, using assistive strategies as needed.	The feeder may need to assist with jaw control.
7. Remove the spoon using the student's lip to remove the food as the spoon is withdrawn straight out.	Do not scrape the food off the back of the teeth since this may elicit a reflex bite or cause hyperextension.
8. Continue the preceding steps, being sure that the student is fed slowly. Offer drink throughout the feeding process.	Rushing the feeding process should be avoided.
9. Blot food off the student's face as needed.	Do not wipe the face with a cloth or spoon since this can elicit oral reflex activity and mouth opening (Utley, 1991). Instead, blot the food off the mouth.
10. When finished feeding, wash the student's mouth and note how much the student ate.	Some students are poor eaters, and the parents will need to keep track of how much the student is eating to determine proper nutrition.

INSTRUCTIONAL STRATEGIES AND MODIFICATIONS FOR EATING

Students with physical disabilities should be taught the basic self-help skill of eating, if possible. A spoon is commonly the first utensil used.

Depending on the severity of the impairment, the student may be able to use a spoon independently or perform some steps in the eating process without assistance. Included in this process is providing the student with the opportunity to make food choices through oral, gestural, or augmentative communication.

Teaching Utensil Use

Students learning spoon use often require adaptive equipment (e.g., an adapted spoon) or modifications (e.g., raising the height of the table) to aid in skill acquisition. Also, the assistive strategies used by the feeder (e.g., jaw support) may need to be implemented while teaching the student independent feeding skills. Foods to be used first include those that the student likes and those that stick to the spoon (e.g., mashed potatoes). Identification of the proper adaptive equipment and assistive strategies to use in conjunction with the instructional strategies will be important for effective instruction to occur.

To teach the student independent spoon eating, it is important to identify the steps and break them into teachable parts. As discussed in Chapter 2, the steps may vary between students, based on their individual differences. After washing hands (yours and the student's), positioning the student, and explaining what is to occur, eating may begin. One possible task analysis for eating with a spoon is presented in Figure 8-7. The level

of assistance will depend on the student's current skills.

Considerations When Using Physical Guidance for Eating with a Spoon. In some instances, the student will need maximum support for initially learning the feeding process. When teaching spoon feeding beginning with full physical guidance, the teacher will want to include a few things to facilitate this process. One technique is the use of the utility hand hold. The utility hand hold helps guide and support the student's movements as he learns to feed himself (Klein & Delaney, 1994). The feeder should be positioned on the same side as the student's preferred hand. The spoon is placed in the student's preferred palm and held in place with the feeder's middle or index finger across the spoon (see Figure 8-8). The feeder's thumb is placed on the back of the student's wrist to help with wrist movement. (It is important that the thumb is not on the back of the hand since that pressure often releases a grasp.) The feeder's other hand is placed at the student's elbow, helping raise and lower the arm as needed to assist with the arm motion needed for the spoon to enter the mouth. As the student learns the necessary movements for manipulating the spoon, the feeder will gradually fade the physical assistance.

---

1. Wash hands.
2. Move hand to spoon.
3. Grasp spoon.
4. Pick up spoon.
5. Move spoon toward plate.
6. Put spoon in food.
7. Rotate wrist to scoop food onto spoon.
8. Lift spoon.
9. Open mouth.
10. Put spoon in mouth.
11. Close lips around spoon.
12. Move spoon out of mouth.
13. Chew food.
14. Swallow food.
15. Repeat steps 5 through 14.

FIGURE 8-7 Task analysis for eating with a spoon

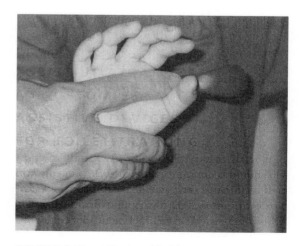

FIGURE 8-8 The utility hand hold

When using the utility hand hold, the teacher may want to include some antecedent prompts (or cues) in the teaching process as well as some additional physical support. These are as follows:

Steps in the Procedure for Spoon Feeding	Rationale
1. Assist the student to hold the spoon using the utility hand hold.	The utility hand hold provides support to the student's hand and wrist and allows the student to partially participate in directing movements.
2. Bring the elbow up to shoulder level and assist the spoon down to the plate. (The table should be at mid-chest level.)	The elbow in this position decreases the likelihood the student will turn the spoon and spill the contents.
3. Tap the plate with the spoon and pause.	This antecedent prompt increases the student's attention to the contents of the plate and transitions the student for the next step.
4. With the utility hand hold, help the student scooping the food onto the spoon and bring the spoon toward the mouth.	The scooping movement is a very difficult move to develop and requires assistance initially to develop the rotating forearm and wrist movement.
5. Pause in front of the mouth and wait for the student to pull the spoon the rest of the way toward the mouth and remove food from the spoon.	This allows the student to practice the final step of the procedure while also using good lip closure to remove food from the spoon.
6. Return the hand to the table to rest while the student chews and swallows.	This places the hand in ready position to begin the sequence again when ready and allows for the student to eat the food without movement distractions.

When starting with full physical guidance, assistance can be gradually faded through use of maximum prompts or graduated guidance. (See Chapter 2 for more information on instructional strategies.)

Using other utensils, such as a fork, is very similar to spoon use. The major difference is teaching the student the stabbing motion used to pierce the food onto the fork. Food must be large enough to easily pierce, but not too large that the student would be uncomfortable chewing and swallowing. For students using a universal cuff to hold the fork, place the fork in the cuff with the points pointing down. This allows the student to stab the food without rotating the fork in the hand. In some instances, fork use may not be taught when the student has jerky, uncontrolled arm movements that could result in the student piercing himself with the fork.

Use of a knife is usually the last utensil to be taught. The student should practice holding the knife with the index finger resting parallel on top of the knife blade while gripping the handle with the remaining fingers. The index finger helps to maintain a balance of the blade while moving the knife in a forward backward direction. Some students may be unable to move the knife in a back-and-forth motion while holding the food to be cut with a knife. In this case, a rocker knife may be used. The shape of this type of knife allows for stabilization of the food as the knife is rocked back and forth, cutting the food. In some instances, the student may need assistance with knife use, depending on the severity of the physical impairment.

Teaching Eating Finger Foods

Besides eating with a utensil, students also need to be taught to eat using their fingers. To help with this, proper positioning, food choice, and placement of the food will be crucial.

Positioning. To achieve an optimum sitting position, alternative seating devices may be used such as Tumble Form feeder seat, corner chair, or Rifton chair. (See the discussion on positioning devices described in Chapter 6.) Prone standers or standing frames are other positioning devices that may be used while a student is finger feeding. The upright position in these devices may allow for greater reach, grasp, and hand-to-mouth skills. Most of these devices come with trays that can be adjusted to assist with reach. Consultation with a physical and/or occupational therapist to determine optimum positioning is recommended.

Food Choice for Finger Food Eating. Providing the correct type of food that matches the student's hand and oral motor skills is also important when teaching finger feeding. At the developmental age of 5 to 6 months, when the student is beginning to transition from the sucking stage to the munching stage and is able to maintain a grasp on an item and bring it to her mouth, food items such as hard baby cookies and crackers may be used for finger feeding. As the student's oral motor skills develop in the areas of biting and chewing, foods such as cooked vegetable strips, fresh fruit strips, string beans, or pretzel sticks can be introduced. These items are large enough that the student can hold onto the food item and still have enough food exposed to munch or bite the item without actually releasing the item (Morris

& Klein, 1987). Cutting foods into strips is an excellent strategy to use with students who have the ability to bring the food to their mouth but have motor impairments that make release difficult.

As the student develops finer isolated finger movements, food items can be cut into cubes initially and eventually into smaller pieces. Food items that are small and round should be avoided as finger food trainers as they can easily get caught in the airway. These include popcorn, grapes, nuts, and hot dogs cut into circles.

Placement of Food Items. Some students demonstrate the ability to rake food items into their palms but have difficulty moving the food to the fingertips to develop the finer pinch skill. How and where small food items are located can influence the type of grasp a student uses. By spacing the individual pieces of food several inches apart or by presenting only one item at a time, the student can focus on using an inferior pinch grasp to pick up the food item. Use of the finer pinch skill may be more evident if the student picks up the small food item from shoulder level rather than tray level. The higher positioning of the food item encourages the student to extend the wrist, which allows for greater ease in isolating the thumb and index finger. This can be accomplished by an adult holding only one small piece of food between her finger and thumb at shoulder level and encouraging the student to take it. Other students may be better able to use their thumb and index finger to pick up small items if an adult assists in stabilizing the little finger side of the hand by holding the fourth and fifth fingers down in the palm.

In some instances, the student may not have learned to bring food to his mouth. Food may then be placed directly on the student's hand. The student's finger can be initially dipped into a reinforcing food item such as applesauce or pudding. The student's hand may then be guided to the mouth if needed. As the student learns to bring his hand to his mouth, this can be expanded to helping him pick up items to bring to his mouth. In some instances, the hand may not be able to reach the mouth due to the physical impairment. A sandwich holder may be used to provide extra extension of the item to reach the mouth.

Strategies for Changing Textures

The texture and consistency of food items are important dietary variables that can help or hinder a student's ability to manage the food safely. In general, the greater level of oral motor skill the student has developed, the greater diversity of texture and consistency of food the student can manage. It is important that the individuals preparing and providing food use the same terminology in describing food textures and consistency in order for the appropriate food to be prepared.

Textures of food can be described as pureed, finely ground, coarsely ground, finely chopped, coarsely chopped, and regular (refer back to Table 8-1 for descriptions). The consistency of food can be described as sticky, dry, wet (slippery), and runny. Depending on the student's oral motor problem, certain types of foods and consistencies may be difficult for the student (see Table 8-3).

Many students with feeding problems are given pureed foods at home or in the school. There may not be support for this since many students are able to eat soft, lumpy foods. It is important to increase the food texture, when possible, since this may assist with the development of more mature feeding patterns. Another common practice involves combining all the food and mixing it with milk. This should be avoided since it provides the student with less variety in the feeding experience and increases the production of mucous (Utley, 1991).

As the student develops greater postural and oral motor control, transitioning to foods with greater consistency and texture appears quite natural. However, some students have greater difficulty in making these transitions than others. This difficulty in transitioning to greater consistency and texture may possibly be due to oral hypersensitivity, difficulty collecting food into a bolus for swallowing, hypersensitive gag reflex, or underdeveloped oral motor skills to handle the new texture comfortably (Morris & Klein, 1987). Consultation with the student's occupational therapist or speech pathologist can assist in determining the cause of difficulty in food transition-

Table 8-3 Food Consistency

Consistency	Example	When this might be a problem
Sticky	Potatoes, rice, other starches	Weak or poorly coordinated tongue movements, thick saliva, dry mouth, hypersensitivity to pressure and movement. Sticky food can stick to the roof of the mouth or the back of the throat, leading to coughing or gagging.
Dry	Meats, bread, crackers	Weak or poorly coordinated tongue movements, thick saliva, dry mouth. If the person has any of these problems, dry food may wad in the roof of the mouth, leading to coughing or gagging.
Wet (slippery)	Chopped foods (okra, spinach, peach, banana)	Weak or poorly coordinated tongue movement, slow swallow. With these problems, wet food may come out of the mouth or move back too quickly, leading to coughing or gagging.
Runny	Pureed fruits or vegetables with lots of liquid	Weak or poorly coordinated tongue movement, slow swallow. As with wet foods, runny foods may move too fast for the person to control.

SOURCE: Adapted from *Beckman Oral Motor Assessment and Intervention*, Debra Beckman © 1995. Reprinted by permission of Debra Beckman.

ing and in developing a plan to progress to the next level.

Moving from Liquids to Puree (Strained Foods). For students who are primarily drinking from a bottle, new tastes can be introduced through the bottle first before introducing a spoon. The juice can be thickened with baby cereal or strained fruits to mimic the texture of the formula the student is accustomed to. A cross-cut nipple may be used to allow for the thickened liquids to pass through the hole in the nipple easily. The nipple may be dipped in strained foods, juice, or fruit nectar and presented to the student in small amounts to try new tastes.

Once the student becomes comfortable with the new taste, the item should be gradually thickened until the student is actually taking the strained food. Introduce a familiar taste in small quantities from a spoon. For example, give a thickened juice or watery strained item on the spoon. Then proceed with thickening the item until it becomes the texture of strained food.

Strained Food to Soft, Lumpy Food. The next step in changing textures is to transition the student from strained food to soft, lumpy food. The meal should begin with the comfortable strained food or food that the student likes before introducing the new texture. Thicken strained foods with baby cereal, instant baby cereal, dried pudding, or dehydrated baby food. If the student cannot handle thickening with texture, try just thickening the food with a commercially available thickener such as Thick-It or Thick & Easy. Introduce new textures with familiar foods. Give a spoonful of the familiar likable food followed by a spoonful of the familiar and new texture mixture. Continue to switch between the familiar food and the mixture until just the new texture alone is accepted. Once the student can tolerate thickened or ground foods, add lumps hidden in the thickened food. Lumps are less noticeable in thickened foods than in watery or strained foods. Use binder foods with lumpy foods such mashed potatoes with ground meat or canned beans.

Binder foods help keep foods together so that small pieces do not scatter in the mouth. Examples of binder foods include mashed potatoes, thickened sauces, and applesauce.

Lumpy Solids to Chewy Solids. The next step is to transition the student from lumpy solids to chewy solids by beginning to introduce foods that require chewing. Easy chewy solids such as raisins, chunks of cheese, canned green beans, or tuna may be enjoyed first. (See the chewing section to review strategies to develop chewing skills.) Gradually introduce foods that are more difficult to chew such as roast beef, pork chops, and raw vegetables. Foods that have a distinct difference in consistency such as noodle soup or dry cereal in milk require advanced oral motor skills as the student will need to coordinate swallowing of the liquid portion while chewing the solid portion.

Food Choice. The food chosen to teach spoon feeding should also be considered. The food should be something that the student likes and is motivated to work for. Foods that stick to the spoon such as mashed potatoes, pudding, mashed pasta meals, and flavored oatmeal are recommended.

EQUIPMENT AND ADAPTIVE EQUIPMENT FOR DRINKING

Several types of equipment or adaptive equipment may be used to facilitate successful drinking. These can be divided into cups and straws.

Cups

Different types of cups may be used with a student with a physical disability. Bell-shaped cups such as those made by Tupperware and First Years have a rigid rim that helps the beginning drinker achieve jaw stability either by positioning it close to the corners of the mouth or by achieving good contact with the lips against the rim. Cut-out, flex, or nosey cups are usually made of flexible plastic and have a curved cut-out area on one side of the rim. (Refer back to Figure 8-1.) The cut-out area allows for clear view of the speed of the liquid as it passes toward the lips. It also allows for view of the lips so that the feeder can see how the student is accepting the liquid. The flexible plastic also allows the feeder to have some control of the width of the cup on the student's lips. The width of the cup can help the student gain corner lip control. Finally, the cut-out area allows the cup to be tipped up without coming into contact with the nose, thereby facilitating a forward head position and decreasing the chance of an avoidance reaction and hyper-extension of the neck.

Some cups come with lids that offer the possibility of learning to drink from the cup with less mess when cups are overturned or dropped. These cups may have lids with spouts or without spouts. The lip and tongue control required to drink from a nonspout lid cup is more similar to that of a cup without a lid. This allows for an easier transition to drinking from cups without lids. When drinking from a cup with a spout, the student is more likely to treat the spout like a nipple and use a less mature sucking pattern when drinking. This may make the transition to drinking from a cup without a lid more difficult. However, some students need to have the more familiar spout to begin learning this new skill. There are also cups that have lids that can adjust the flow of the fluid by turning the lid. With the Infa-Trainer cup, the feeder can adjust the flow for slow, medium, or fast depending on the student's ability to tip the cup toward the mouth and intake the fluid.

The cup chosen for independent drinking will depend on the control of lips and jaw and the coordination of the student's arms. If a student is drinking from a cup with a lid already, the same type of lid should remain. However, if no lid is being used for assisted drinking from a cup, a lid without a spout may be considered to maintain

oral motor skills and to decrease spilling. A wide mouth or cut-out cup may be considered if the student needs extra assistance in maintaining chin tuck during cup drinking. A bell-shaped rim cup can be used to give the student extra jaw support to keep the tongue in the mouth (Morris & Klein, 1987).

To help the student move the cup to the mouth, cups may have handles or be weighted. Cups with handles may be helpful for students who are having difficulty achieving or maintaining a grasp on a cup. Students who have weakness on one side may prefer to hold onto a single-handled cup with the weak hand and stabilize the other side of the cup with the stronger hand. Cups that are weighted may help the student better control her movements of the cup. The weight provides extra sensory input to the joints and muscles that can increase the student's awareness of how she is moving.

Straws

The length and width of a straw can impact the skill required to suck liquid through it. Short, wide straws are helpful when learning straw drinking as they do not require as much suction to pull the liquid through. This is especially true if using thickened fluids. Flexible plastic straws that allow the top to be bent to 90 degrees provide easy access to the mouth. Long straws that are flexible throughout the length can provide a means to position a straw for students who cannot adjust their body toward the straw due to trunk instability or limited range of motion.

ASSISTIVE STRATEGIES FOR DRINKING

A person may use several strategies when feeding a student fluids that involve positioning, cup placement, lip control, jaw support, and thickness of fluid.

Positioning

As described earlier, proper positioning is crucial for a successful meal experience. When assisting with cup drinking, head positioning is crucial as the student is attempting to bring liquids in and swallow using new skills that are not well coordinated. The head should have a slight chin tuck, and the neck should never be hyperextended since it increases the possibility of liquids going into the lungs. A student may be verbally cued "Chin down" prior to initiating bringing the cup to the mouth, especially if the student tends to protrude her tongue when attempting to drink. If verbal cues and chin tuck are not enough to inhibit tongue protrusion, the student may be cued using the back of the hand to pat behind the chin at the base of the tongue. This input cues the tongue to return to a more normal resting position. An adaptive chair with a tray may be helpful to allow the student to rest her arms on the tray while bringing the cup toward the mouth.

Cup Placement

Cup placement is an important consideration when assisting a student to drink. The student may be able to more easily coordinate the lips, tongue, and jaw if the cup is placed snugly into the corners of the mouth and rests on the lower lip. The cup should then be tipped slightly to allow a small amount of liquid to pass toward the lips. The feeder should pause to be sure that the lips and tongue are moving in response to the fluid touching the lips and tongue. If lip and tongue movements are not noted, additional jaw support should be provided.

Lip Control

If the student has little movement of the upper lip, the cup can be slightly raised so that the liquid touches the lip. This often helps stimulate upper lip movement (Alexander, 1991). Another problem is leaking of liquids from the corners of the mouth. This is common when a student is

first learning cup drinking. However, if leaking continues even with the cup positioned toward the corners of the mouth and external jaw support, the feeder may want to provide lower lip support in conjunction with jaw support. This can be done by placing the index finger on the chin while providing slight upward support to the lower lip to move it toward the bottom rim of the cup. The third finger supports the jaw under the chin at the same time (Klein & Delaney, 1994; see Figure 8-5c).

Jaw Support

The student may be able to coordinate receiving liquids from a cup more easily when the feeder provides external jaw support. This is a critical strategy to use, especially if the student displays exaggerated or forceful tongue thrusting when attempting to drink. The least amount of jaw support to allow the student to coordinate sucking and swallowing of the liquid should be provided. As coordination of the suck and swallow increases, the amount of jaw support should decrease. (See previous discussion on jaw closure under "Assistive Strategies for Feeding" for more information.)

Thickness of Fluid

When teaching drinking from a cup, the consistency of the fluid can influence the student's ability to handle the fluids safely. Liquids that are thickened move out of the cup more slowly and allow the student more time to move lips and tongue to collect liquid in the mouth. Thickened liquids are also heavier and provide extra sensory information to the mouth to assist the tongue and lips to locate the liquid. Students who have delays in movement and timing may find drinking thickened liquids more successful as well. The thicker liquid does not flow as fast and will give the student more time to react to coordinate the flow. Strained foods with water added or formula thickened with cereal may be good fluids to try with beginning drinkers as the student is familiar with the taste. The liquid can be thinned gradually as the student's skills improve.

INSTRUCTIONAL STRATEGIES AND MODIFICATIONS FOR DRINKING

Cup Drinking

Students with physical disabilities should be taught the basic self-help skill of independent cup drinking, when possible. Depending on the severity of the physical impairment, the student may not be able to do parts of the cup drinking process. In these instances, it is important to have the student partially participate in the process. Included in this process is providing the student with the opportunity to make food and drink choices and promoting the student's form of communication during snacks and mealtimes.

As students are taught independent cup use, adaptive equipment (e.g., a nosey cup) and assistive strategies (e.g., jaw support) may be used in addition to teaching the student independent drinking skills. Identification of the proper adaptive equipment and assistive strategies to use in conjunction with the instructional strategies will be important for effective instruction to occur.

To teach the student independent cup drinking, it is important to identify the steps and break them into teachable parts. As discussed in Chapter 2, the steps may vary between students based on their individual differences. Once the steps are identified, the type of teaching strategy (e.g., time

1. Wash hands.
2. Move hand to cup.
3. Grasp cup.
4. Pick up cup.
5. Move cup to face.
6. Open mouth.
7. Put cup on lower lip.
8. Move upper lip down toward cup.
9. Tip cup up.
10. Liquid goes into mouth.
11. Swallow liquid.
12. Tip cup down.
13. Return cup to table.
14. Repeat steps 2 through 13.

FIGURE 8-9 Task analysis for cup drinking

delay, least prompts) will be determined, based on the student's individual needs (See Chapter 2 for a discussion of instructional strategies.) A typical task analysis for cup drinking is presented in Figure 8-9.

Considerations When Using Physical Guidance for Cup Drinking

In some instances, the student will need maximum support for initially learning to drink. When teaching cup drinking beginning with full physical guidance, there are a few things the teacher may want to include to facilitate this process. These are as follows:

Steps in the Procedure for Cup Drinking	*Rationale*
1. Assist the student to hold the cup with two hands.	Holding the cup with two hands helps the student to bring the cup to the mouth with the rim parallel to lips.

Steps in the Procedure for Cup Drinking	*Rationale*
2. Place the student's elbows on the tray while bending at elbow toward the mouth.	Placement of the elbows on a tray will provide stability for controlled arm movements (Klein & Delaney, 1994).
3. Place the rim of the cup on top of the bottom lip and close to corners of the mouth.	This provides stability for lip control of fluid (Klein & Delaney, 1994).
4. Tilt the cup so that the liquids flow over the lip into the mouth. Verbally cue the student, "Tip up."	Assistance is provided to ensure that the liquid moves slowly into the mouth. Verbal cues are provided to increase the student's awareness that liquid is beginning to flow.
5. Tilt the cup down to the original position with the cup resting on top of bottom lip and close to corners of the mouth. Verbally cue the student, "Stop tipping."	This stops the flow of the fluid before the cup is pulled away from the mouth. Verbal cues are provided to increase the student's awareness that the liquid flow has stopped.
6. Return the cup to the table and rest while swallow is completed.	This places the cup in a ready position to begin the sequence again when ready and allows the student to swallow the liquid without distraction.

Gradually, the level of assistance will be decreased following a system of maximum prompts or graduated guidance. (See Chapter 2 for a description of these instructional strategies.)

Straw Drinking

Some students will have severe physical impairments affecting the arms that will preclude independent cup drinking. However, if the cup is properly positioned and stabilized, many of these students will be successful independent drinkers using a straw. Typically, straw drinking is taught after the student has a fairly well-coordinated drinking ability with mouth closure and refined sucking and swallowing (Umbreit & Cardullias, 1980). Developmental checklists place this skill between 2 and 2½ years, but some students develop this skill earlier. Experience and oral skill development appear to impact when a student develops this skill (Klein & Delaney, 1994). Younger students tend to begin straw drinking using a suck similar to bottle drinking. The straw is placed more in the middle of the tongue, the tongue curls around the straw, and the student sucks. The more mature student will drink from a straw with only a small portion between the lips. The pressure created from the lips and cheeks pulls the liquid up the straw. For students with physical impairments, assistive strategies providing lower lip support, upper lip support, and/or jaw support may be used (see Figure 8-10).

A durable and flexible straw should be used with students with physical impairments to prevent it from breaking should the student bite it. A small-diameter straw is helpful since it is easier to suck and limits the amount of fluid, decreasing the possibility of choking. However, a wider-diameter straw may be helpful for students who have low muscle tone or difficulty closing their lips around a narrow straw. In some techniques, a short straw is recommended to begin straw drinking since less air is ingested before getting the fluid into the mouth. There is adaptive equipment that can be

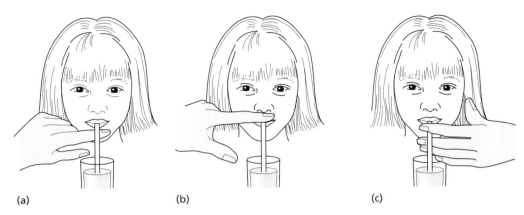

(a)   (b)   (c)

FIGURE 8-10 Strategies for straw drinking: (a) lower lip support, (b) upper lip support, and (c) jaw and lip support

used to help the straw stay upright in a cup; however, using a cup with a lid that has a place for the straw has the same effect. Also, adaptive straws are available that once sipped upon, the liquid remains near the top of the straw and does not return down to the level of the drink.

Shaping Straw-Drinking Procedure. Many techniques can be used to teach straw drinking. The first step is to teach the student to position his lips to pull the liquid through the straw. This can be done through a shaping technique using the end of the straw (Klein & Delaney 1994).

Steps in the Procedure for Straw Drinking	*Rationale*
1. Place a short straw into a half-filled glass of a reinforcing drink.	Starting with a shortened straw will allow less air to displace. Drink selection is important to assure the student's interest in drinking.
2. Put a finger over the top of the straw and remove the straw from the glass.	This will result in the liquid remaining in the straw.
3. Place the filled straw in the student's mouth and allow a small amount to drop into the mouth to allow the student to taste the drink.	Allowing the student to taste the reinforcing liquid enables the student to determine that it is something she wants.
4. Repeat step 3, but this time do not release the liquid until the student's lips are closed around the straw.	Only providing liquid when the lips are around the straw will help reinforce this behavior. If the student does not form her lips around the straw, some physical guidance may be necessary.
5. When the student has mastered step 4, begin to present the straw at an angle parallel to the floor or slightly higher.	By angling the straw, the student will need to begin to suck to get the fluid. When angling the straw parallel to the floor or slightly higher, the drink will also drip into the student's mouth very slowly.

Steps in the Procedure for Straw Drinking	*Rationale*
6. When step 5 is mastered, the straw should be gradually presented at lower angles until it is close to being vertical.	Slowly shaping the appropriate behavior will help the student learn the skill. Timing is important when using this technique since the feeder removing his finger too soon will result in the drink pouring into his hand.

Squeeze Bottle Technique. An alternative method for teaching straw drinking uses a squeeze bottle and a straw or clear plastic ice-maker tubing. The straw or tubing is placed through the opening of the top of a squeeze bottle (e.g., a mustard bottle or sport bottle). If the straw does not fit through the opening, carefully cut the top so that the straw can fit tightly through it. This tight seal creates a suction that will allow liquid to move up the straw when squeezing the bottle. By grading the squeeze of the bottle, the instructor can control the speed and the amount of fluid that passes through the straw. The squeeze bottle method may be beneficial for the student who needs to maintain a chin tuck to control the lips and tongue (Klein & Delaney, 1994). Assistance for jaw and lip support can be added to provide a tight lip seal. The procedure for squeeze bottle straw drinking is as follows:

Steps in the Procedure for Squeeze Bottle Drinking	*Rationale*
1. Place the straw between the lips or on the tongue of the student.	Placement of the straw will depend on the student's skill level.
2. Squeeze the bottle in order for a small amount of liquid to pass through the straw and into the mouth to let the student taste the fluid.	Squeezing should occur slowly to avoid squirting fluid to the back of the throat.
3. Repeat step 2, this time waiting for the student's lips to close around the straw.	Only providing liquid when the lips are around the straw will help reinforce this behavior. If the student does not form his lips around the straw, some physical guidance may be necessary.
4. When step 3 is mastered, present the straw, but this time stop the liquid approximately a $1/2$ inch from the end of the straw. Wait for the student to suck the fluid through the last $1/2$ inch into his mouth.	If the student is not sucking the liquid, it may be presented closer to the end of the straw.
5. Gradually stop the liquid farther away from the end of the straw until the student can suck the fluid through the entire length of the straw.	

EATING AND FEEDING PROBLEMS AND EMERGENCIES

Oral Tactile Defensiveness and Lack of Tactile Response

Some students have difficulty processing sensory input and are uncomfortable with the input provided. When the student is hypersensitive to this sensory input, he may overreact when being touched in or around the mouth. This hypersensitive reaction is referred to as *oral tactile defensiveness*. It may be so severe that touching around the mouth results in vomiting and any attempt at feeding is rejected. It may also be very mild and occur only when foods with more than one texture are presented. On the other extreme are students who are hyposensitive and have a lack of response to tactile input in their mouths. These students do not have sufficient feeling in their mouths. This also ranges from the more severe type, in which the student cannot determine where the food is in her mouth, to a more mild condition, in which the student does not know when food or saliva is on her chin.

In both oral tactile defensiveness and lack of tactile response, a controlled oral motor input program is needed throughout the day to desensitize or sensitive the student gradually to oral input. Usually the program for tactile defensiveness consists of gradually touching the student outside the mouth with a hand or toy using firm pressure (not a light touch) and gradually working to the point where the student can be touched inside the mouth. The student is usually first warned or prepared before touching the mouth by saying certain words or having the student's hands on the feeder's so the student can feel the hand moving toward the mouth. The amount of sensory information in the feeding environment is usually reduced. For students who lack tactile responses, the program is usually aimed at introducing the student to a range of types of touches and textures (Anderson, 1991). Two ways of providing more normal oral stimulation is through wiping/washing the student's mouth and through toothbrushing skills. Both of these skills can provide the student with firm and well-graded stimulation to the face and then to the gums, teeth, and tongue (Alexander, 1991). An occupational therapist can provide assistance in designing an appropriate program.

Tongue Thrust

Tongue thrust is a forceful outward protrusion of the tongue beyond the borders of the lips. This type of tongue movement may be seen with students who have high muscle tone such as those with cerebral palsy, students with low muscle tone such as those diagnosed with Down syndrome, and students who have stressed breathing. Tongue thrusting interferes with eating and drinking as it becomes difficult to insert food or liquid into the mouth. Tongue thrusting may also cause the food or liquid to be pushed out of the mouth. Tongue thrusting may be addressed by proper positioning, food consistency, jaw support, tongue pressure and/or vibratory input.

Feeding Position for Tongue Thrust. When feeding a student who displays tongue thrust, the feeder should first check the student's feeding position. The student's trunk and pelvis should be in alignment. The shoulder girdle should be forward with scapulas (shoulder blades) apart. The neck should be straight and the chin tucked. This approach is most critical with students who tend to move into an extensor pattern with head tipped back and chin up (Morris & Klein, 1987). Elevated side lying is also a possible positioning strategy for students who tend to move easily into an extensor pattern while sitting.

Food Consistency for Tongue Thrust. A change in food consistency may decrease the amount of tongue thrust a student uses to move food to the back of the mouth. A student who is having difficulty moving the jaw in an up-down pattern or moving the tongue laterally to move food toward the teeth may use exaggerated tongue protrusion or tongue thrust in an attempt to move the food to the back of the mouth. By decreasing the lumps in the food, the student may be able to manipulate the food without the thrust. Thickening liquids to allow for slow movement of the liquid toward the lips to facilitate sucking initiated by the lips may also decrease the exaggerated tongue protrusion (Morris & Klein, 1987). Jaw and cheek support may be provided as described earlier to provide stability for more mature lip and tongue.

Jaw Support for Tongue Thrust. The feeder can help the student achieve and maintain the tongue in the mouth by providing jaw support described earlier in this chapter while maintaining appropriate head and body alignment. The feeder can further decrease forward movement of the tongue by placing her finger directly under the chin and applying firm pressure. This technique should not be used if tongue protrusion is a compensation for respiratory distress (Morris & Klein, 1987).

Tongue Pressure for Tongue Thrust. One strategy for tongue thrust is to provide firm downward and inward pressure on the tongue for 2 or 3 seconds with the bowl of the spoon while feeding. This is most effective when the spoon is placed on the first third of the tongue, especially if there is also a hyperactive gag reflex. Food should be on the first third of the spoon to help with easy removal (Utley, 1991).

Vibratory Input for Tongue Thrust. Another strategy for tongue thrust is to provide vibratory input to the middle of the tongue. With infants, this can be achieved by placing the pad of a finger in the middle of the tongue and then shaking the finger in small rapid movements (Vergara, 1993). With students, a spoon can be used and placed horizontally into the student's mouth so that the spoon is parallel to the tongue. The spoon should rest in the middle of the tongue. Pressure is then applied evenly downward using a vibratory movement through the spoon. The spoon is

then slowly removed encouraging the lips to close and assist with food removal from the spoon. This technique should be used with caution with students who display a tonic bite or who become disorganized with the movement to their tongue (Morris & Klein, 1987).

Tonic Bite and Unsustained Bite Reflexes

Problems in biting can occur when a student does not have adequate jaw stability, strength, or sensory processing to develop a more mature, controlled bite and release. Students may become stuck at certain levels and not develop the control and release for functional biting. Two common problems are the tonic bite reflex and the unsustained bite. A student with a **tonic bite reflex** moves the jaw upward into a tightly clenched posture when the teeth are stimulated by a finger, spoon, or other object. The student then has difficulty releasing the tonic bite. The student who displays an **unsustained bite** can close teeth on the food but then hesitates prior to biting through the food. The student cannot bite through the food in a smoothly graded fashion. Several strategies may be used to address these bite reflexes, such as preparing the environment, tactile input, feeding strategies, and other techniques.

Preparing the Feeding Environment for Tonic Bite. Positioning and the sensory environment are key components to eliciting and preventing a tonic bite. Students who have a tendency toward tonic bite are much more likely to elicit this if the sitting positioning is poor. An overstimulating environment can also cause increased muscle tension and oral hypersensitivity, which will increase the likelihood for the student to elicit the tonic bite. (See the section on general positioning under "Description of Factors Affecting Eating and Feeding.")

Tactile Input for Tonic Bite. Tactile input to the face, gums, and teeth can help decrease hypersensitivity that occurs when contact is made with the teeth. This can be done while the student is in a calm, well-supported position prior to feeding. The feeder should begin by providing firm, sustained touch to the shoulder and back area and then gradually move toward the face and mouth. She should prepare the student by telling him where she will be touching and for how long. Incorporating this type of touch into a game format or song will make the experience much more enjoyable for the student and the caregiver. The feeder should not use tickling movement or touch as this can overstimulate and excite the tactile receptors. If the student can tolerate touch input to the jaw, cheeks, and lips, the caregiver will then want to provide input inside the mouth to gums and teeth. If a student shows signs of distress with this touch, such as an increase in tension in the face or body, gagging, or change in heart and/or breathing rate, tactile input to the oral area should be avoided until a calmer state for other facial input can be achieved. An occupational therapist or speech pathologist can assist the caregiver in developing a program that increases tactile input at the level of tolerance appropriate for the student.

Feeding the Student with Tonic Bite. The goal when feeding the student with a tonic bite reflex is to reduce the frequency in which the bite reflex occurs. This may be accomplished by developing a steady rhythm in which the spoon or cup is presented so that the item makes contact when the mouth is in an open position. The feeder should place the cup on the lower lip in order for the cup to come in contact with the lips, not the teeth. The student can then initiate suck of the liquids with the lips. This same strategy is used for removing food from the spoon. A soft coated spoon may be used so that the student is not harmed if any biting occurs. Jaw support as described previously in this chapter may provide stability in order for the lips to initiate the suck (Morris & Klein, 1987). If the student does not have the ability to suck foods from a spoon even with jaw support, the feeder may present food into the mouth by placing food or liquids be-

tween cheek and gums on the side of the mouth (Beckman, 1994).

Releasing Tonic Bite on a Utensil. There may be times when feeding a student with a tonic bite reflex that the student bites the utensil and cannot voluntarily release the item. Pulling on the utensil can increase the tension in the bite. The student may also become upset, which will increase the tension in the bite as well. The feeder should first check head position and be sure that the head is in midline with chin slightly pointed toward chest tuck (chin tuck). Next press slightly in on the utensil using a quick, firm movement. The jaw should then drop and the utensil should be removed immediately (Beckman, 1994).

Relaxing the facial muscles may also help release a tonic bite. Starting at both sides of the nose and moving toward the corners of the mouth, the feeder uses the thumb and index finger to provide firm pressure with slow, continuous movement. The feeder may also decrease the tension on the bite by providing gum massage as described previously (Beckman, 1994).

Another strategy uses upward pressure to release a utensil. First the jaws need to be aligned correctly. If they are not (as observed by teeth not meeting evenly, lower jaw protruding forward or backward), they need to be gently manipulated into place. When they are aligned, firm upward pressure is applied for 15 to 20 seconds with the hand in the position used for jaw control. An alternative is to provide three or four firm upward movements separated by a few seconds. This will usually result in the mouth opening (Utley, 1991).

Unsustained Biting Interventions. Students who have difficulty biting completely through an item may need to develop greater jaw stability and strength. This usually occurs naturally in development as the student mouths and bites onto play toys. Some students may need additional practice of this skill, beginning with holding toys, Popsicle sticks, or food items between their teeth and gums. If the student does not have the strength to hold the objects or food items between his teeth and gums, jaw support may be necessary. This can be provided with hand cupping the jaw (Figure 8-5e), supporting at jaw and cheeks (Figure 8-5c and 8-5d), or using a Snack Cap (Figure 8-3) (Klein & Delaney, 1994). As the strength of the jaw increases, the feeder can decrease the use of the external jaw support and increase the variety of textures the student can bite.

Hypersensitive Gagging/Choking

A **gag reflex** is a protective mechanism present at birth that prevents small particles from entering the trachea. In early infancy, a gag can be elicited when the tongue is touched halfway to the back. As the student's mouth comes in contact with nipples, toys, fingers, spoons, and other objects, the place on the tongue that elicits the gag moves farther to the back of the mouth. A **hypersensitive gag** is an exaggerated reaction compared to the response that would be expected and may be present in students with disabilities (Klein & Delaney, 1994). A hypersensitive gag can interfere with the feeding process, such as when a student gags when the food touches the tip of the tongue. It may also interfere with the transition to more difficult textures, such as when the student gags on lumpy foods even though she demonstrates the oral motor skills to handle the lumpy food. A hypersensitive gag may also be elicited with certain smell, tastes, temperature, and textures. Several techniques may be used to decrease a hypersensitive gag such as decreasing oral sensitivities, oral touch, and food transitions.

Decreasing Oral Sensitivities for Gagging/Choking.

Strategies that increase the student's ability to accept tactile input to the face and mouth may help decrease a hypersensitive gag. (See the previous section, "Tactile Input for Tonic Bite.") Tactile input to the body and face should be provided in a fun manner throughout the day, not just prior to feeding. Incorporating touch games with play items and songs can help lessen the tension the student feels and increase his tolerance to this type of sensory input (Morris & Klein, 1987). Touch input should start away from

the mouth and gradually move toward the more sensitive area as comfort and trust is established. Encouraging the student to provide his own tactile input through mouthing of toys and hands is very crucial in normalizing responses to oral sensations (Wolf & Glass, 1992).

Oral Touch/Pressure Input for Gagging/Choking.

Oral touch pressure input can be provided through gum massage, as described earlier in this chapter. It may also be provided on the tongue by applying firm downward pressure with a finger, toy, or spoon at the front of the tongue. This input is then progressively moved toward the back of the tongue by walking fingers or items back on the tongue until just in front of the point of triggering the gag response. The caregiver continues to move the item back and forth within the non–reflex-stimulating area. This can be done in a playful manner with music and games. If the infant or student can tolerate only brief tongue input, the caregiver starts at that point and works within the student's level of tolerance (Morris & Klein, 1987; Wolf & Glass, 1992).

Gradual Food Transitions for Gagging/Choking.

Some students have difficulty transitioning from liquids to strained foods and from strained foods to lumpy foods. They may overreact by gagging. A student may transition more easily from liquids to strained foods if the liquid is thickened in the bottle prior to using thickened cereal or strained foods by spoon. The same gradual transition may be necessary from strained to lumpy foods. Cereal, dehydrated baby foods, instant potatoes, instant pudding, and graham crackers may be used to thicken strained foods or blended foods to make the change in texture less noticeable to the hypersensitive mouth. Lumps are more obvious in strained foods than in thickened foods, especially to the hypersensitive mouth (Klein & Delaney, 1994).

When a student is having difficulty with dry foods, the type of food presented can be alternated. After a bite of the dry or lumpy food is provided, the feeder may then provide a spoonful of food that will bind the remaining dry particles and form into a bolus. Applesauce, cranberry sauce, or strained fruit or vegetables are good binder foods (Morris & Klein, 1987). As more mature chewing skills are developed, the student's ability to handle the dry foods should improve.

Intervention for Gagging/Choking. When a student coughs and is not turning blue, the head should be brought to midline with slight flexion. If the coughing does not end, the feeder should maintain the head in a slight flexion and use one hand to support the jaw while moving the head slowly from side to side to aid in clearing the irritating substance out of the pharyngoesophageal area. The feeder should then check to see that the food is being presented properly and that the student is positioned correctly (Beckman, 1994).

When a student gags, bring the head to midline with slight flexion. Additional flexion may be necessary by pressing against the sternum with the other hand. This position makes gagging uncomfortable and anatomically difficult. This technique lets the student know that a gag can be stopped before full vomiting occurs (Morris & Klein, 1987).

Certain foods should be avoided that are more likely to result in choking or gagging. These include carrots, peanuts, grapes, popcorn, hot dogs, and raisins. Any food that would fragment into the mouth instead of forming into a bolus (clump of food ready for swallowing) should not be given to the student with feeding problems. It is also important that students should never be left alone during feeding and eating, in case an emergency situation occurs. Additionally, students should never be force fed. Besides this technique being unpleasant, it can increase the likelihood of choking or gagging. When coughing occurs, the feeder should not pat the student's back since this is distracting and increases the likelihood of aspiration. If the student is choking, the Heimlich maneuver should be used.

Gastroesophageal Reflux

Gastroesophageal reflux (GER) is the spontaneous backward flow of stomach contents into the esophagus (passage from the back of the mouth to the stomach). When this occurs frequently, it can result in a constant burning sensation and/or inflammation of the esophagus. A common sign of GER is vomiting during or after a meal. Other signs may include crying during or after eating, eating inadequate amounts of food, or refusing to be fed. GER may be caused by general neuromuscular incoordination, allergy, medication, poor abdominal muscle control, oral hypersensitivity, and communication attempts (Morris, 1989). In some students with oral hypersensitivity, reflux may occur because of a strong gag reflex. When these students put their hands or objects in their mouths, vomiting occurs. In these instances, teaching the student to keep hands and objects out of her mouth may decrease vomiting.

Reflux can occur when the stomach is overdistended. One strategy to decrease reflux is to provide small, more frequent meals during the day. Also, when pressure is placed on the abdomen, abdominal pressure is increased, causing an increased likelihood of reflux. Because of this, diapers should not be tightly applied, and/or the student should not wear tight, restrictive clothing (Smith & Breen, 1991).

Proper positioning during and after meals is especially important to decrease the incidence of reflux. The student should be positioned at least 45 degrees upright. Prone standers and wedges often have these angles and may be used for positioning after meals (see Chapter 6 for more information on this adaptive equipment). Other options are side lying, especially on the right side since this facilitates emptying of the food from the stomach into the intestines. If positioning is not sufficient to decrease reflux, medication or surgery may be indicated. Controlling GER is crucial since students with this condition are at high risk for aspiration (Steadham, 1994).

Aspiration

Students with abnormal swallowing mechanisms are at risk for aspiration. Aspiration is the inhalation of food or liquids ingested by the mouth, secretions (saliva) from the mouth or upper airways, or regurgitated stomach contents into the lungs (Avery & First, 1994). It is rare that aspiration results in immediate death from asphyxiation. Instead, the inhalation of food results in aspiration pneumonia, which is pneumonia resulting from the inhalation of foreign matter. If aspiration occurs from regurgitation or vomiting, the amount of lung damage is determined by the amount of hydrochloric acid that has been regurgitated from the stomach and gone into the lungs. Typically, the symptoms of aspiration pneumonia occur within 1 hour and, in almost all instances, within 2 hours. Symptoms may include fever, fast breathing rate (tachypnea), coughing, and often cyanosis (turning blue, especially seen at the fingernails and around the mouth). The student may also stop breathing, and shock may occur (Behrman, 1992). If aspiration occurs, an ambulance should be called.

The best treatment for aspiration is prevention. Students with feeding and eating problems should avoid being overfed since this will overdistend the stomach and increase the likelihood of vomiting. Feeding should not occur with the head tilted back (hyperextension of the neck, also referred to as "bird feeding") since this increases the likelihood of aspiration. After feeding, it is important that the student be positioned with the head above the rest of the body. The student should *not* be positioned lying flat on her back. Also, if it is suspected that the student may be aspirating very small amounts of food or liquids when feeding, she should be referred to a physician for tests (e.g., physical exam, video fluoroscopy) and appropriate treatment. In some cases, the student may need a gastrostomy tube if aspiration is occurring. (See Chapter 9.)

Allergies

Some students will be allergic to certain foods. An allergy is a harmful immunological reaction due to hypersensitivity to a substance. Food allergies usually fall into three categories: intestinal (causing diarrhea, nausea), respiratory (causing sinus and/or breathing problems), and skin reactions (causing rashes) (Klein & Delaney, 1994). A food allergy reaction can occur immediately after eating the food or up to 48 hours after eating, although most occur within the first 2 hours. The student may have an allergy to a food that has not been eaten before or may develop an allergy to a certain food that has not caused a reaction in the past.

It will be important to identify the food substance that the student is allergic to and avoid giving it to the student. Elimination diets are often used to identify the food(s) that are causing the reaction. Elimination diets may begin by excluding a few suspected food items or by starting with a rigorous elimination diet in which the student can only have certain foods that generally do not cause allergies. Foods that are suspected to cause reactions are then slowly reintroduced, and the student is carefully monitored for reactions. Because these diets do not provide a full range of nutrition, they are used for only a short period of time and should be monitored by a registered dietitian (Klein & Delaney, 1994).

MANAGEMENT ISSUES FOR FEEDING AND EATING

Individualized Health Plan and Individualized Educational Program

Some students will have IHPs pertaining to feeding and eating. These health plans are used to specify any food or fluid restriction, any special diets, and any food allergies. It is important that everyone working with the student know what is on the health plan to avoid any unnecessary adverse health reactions. Specific assistive strategies used to promote eating and drinking are specified in the IHP, as well as problems and emergencies (e.g., eating insufficient amounts, choking, aspiration, tonic bite). See Figure 8-11 for sample eating and drinking areas to include in an IHP.

Special Diet: _____
_____

Food Is Given

_____ Liquid form

_____ Pureed

_____ Soft

_____ Regular but cut in small pieces

_____ Regular

Food allergies: _____
_____

Food restrictions: _____
_____

Fluid restrictions: _____
_____

Assistive techniques needed to promote eating: _____
_____

Directions for Problems and Emergencies

Eating insufficient amounts: _____

Drinking insufficient amounts: _____

Choking/gagging: _____

Aspiration: _____

Tongue thrust: _____

Tonic bite: _____

Unsustained bite reflex: _____

GER: _____

FIGURE 8-11 Specialized information to include in an IHP on eating and feeding

The IEP should include goals specific to eating and drinking. Also, it is important to note on the program the types of assistive and instructional strategies being used as well as any adaptive equipment. See Figure 8-12 for sample IEP objectives. Data sheets specifically tracking the student's progress should have the types of prompts used clearly marked.

Nutrition and Hydration

Maintaining proper nutrition and hydration is essential for health and growth. This entails a proper mixture of fats, carbohydrates, proteins, vitamins, minerals, and fluids (Batshaw & Perret, 1997). Nutritional problems may occur due to different disorders (e.g., short bowel syndrome) or abnor-

Independent Performance of Task

Using a weighted spoon and a scoop dish, the student will independently scoop food onto a spoon and eat it with no more than two occasions of spillage a meal during lunch for 3 weeks.

When given an adapted straw (which holds the liquid at the top of the straw), the student will drink half a glass of milk during snack and lunch for 3 weeks.

Partial Performance of Task

Upon being given jaw support and soft food, the student will close his mouth over a spoon, take food off the spoon, chew food, and swallow with 80% accuracy during lunch for 3 weeks.

Upon being given support at the elbow and soft food placed on a spoon, the student will move the spoon from the plate into his mouth with 80% accuracy on each opportunity during lunch for 3 weeks.

Directing the Task

Using her AAC device, the student will tell an adult when she is ready for the next bite of food and will select which bite of food or drink she wants with 80% accuracy during snack and lunch for 4 weeks.

Knowledge of the Task

The student will describe the operation of her mechanical feeder and explain its proper cleaning with 80% accuracy for three consecutive sessions.

FIGURE 8-12 Sample IEP objectives for eating and drinking

malities (e.g., GER), but they can arise because of other problems. Students who have severe oral motor dysfunction that results in long and strenuous feedings may not have the stamina to eat sufficient food. Some students have irregular appetites due to lack of activity, illness, or constipation, while some students may have no appetite (e.g., those with chronic renal failure) and eat insufficient quantities. Some parents and teachers may have inappropriate expectations of the amount of food the student needs, resulting in either providing too little food or too much food, which leads to vomiting. Abnormal feeding patterns may also occur when the student has strong preferences for only a few foods (e.g., certain types or textures), refuses to eat or drink for extended periods of time, eats and drinks too much, resulting in vomiting, or demonstrates a variety of behaviors that are disruptive to feeding (Munk & Repp, 1994). Approximately 25% of students with a disability have inadequate diets, and 90% have some kind of nutritional problem (Blackman, 1990). Also, it is estimated that 25% of individuals

with mental retardation are underweight, especially those with multiple disabilities and feeding problems (Simila & Niskanen, 1991).

Often, it is not enough to provide the regular amount of food intake that a nondisabled student would eat. Students who have high tone (e.g., those with spastic cerebral palsy) will need extra calories due to their physical impairment. This is because these students typically expend a great deal of energy performing tasks requiring movement, so their diet should include extra calories to meet their extra energy demands (Wong, 1995). Students who have low tone or who are not moving around much may need caloric restrictions to avoid becoming overweight.

Proper hydration is also important. Students with severe physical impairments are often at risk for not drinking enough fluids. In a student who is well hydrated, if the skin (on the stomach or inner thigh) is pulled away from the body, it will quickly recoil on release within 1 second. In a student with dehydration, the skin will remain raised (tented) for several seconds after. Times for providing liquids should be scheduled throughout the day, especially when the student is unable to clearly indicate when he is thirsty.

Students who take certain medications may be at risk of nutritional deficiencies. Many medications interfere with nutrition due to side effects interfering with vitamin absorption, mineral excretion, reduction of appetite, taste sensitivities, and hydration (Klein & Delaney, 1994). It is important to be aware of the nutritional side effects of the medication and find out from the student's doctor if there are special dietary requirements for the student due to the medication. Table 8-4 is a summary of general interactions that typically occur within medication groups.

It is important for the teacher and support personnel to observe for signs of malnutrition and report these to the parents. Some signs in-

Table 8-4 Select Medications Affecting Nutrition

Select medication group and example medications	Example of use	Possible effects on nutrition*
Antacids Maalox Mylanta	Stomach hyperacidity	Constipation Interferes with calcium and phosphorus absorption
Anticholinergics Artane Cogentin	Treat extrapyrmidal symptoms Parkinson's Several others	Constipation Dry mouth Slow stomach emptying GER
Antidepressants Elavil Tofranil	Depression	Loss of appetite Constipation
Antibiotics Amoxicillin Augmentin Erythramycin	Bacterial infections	Vomiting Decreased absorption of minerals, fats, and proteins
Anticonvulsants Dilantin Phenobarbitol Depakote	Seizure disorders	May affect vitamin metabolism Gum overgrowth Poor appetite Constipation Nausea and vomiting
Bronchodilators Theo-Dur Theophylline	Respiratory conditions	Stomach irritation, nausea GER
Cardiac medication Digitalis	Heart conditions	Nausea and diarrhea Urinary losses of minerals (e.g., calcium)
Corticosteroids Prednisone	Wide variety of uses (e.g., asthma, trauma, arthritis)	Decrease in child's growth Weight gain Swelling (edema)
Laxatives Mineral oil	Constipation	Interferes with vitamin absorption Electrolyte loss
Psychotropics Ativan Haldol	Anxiety disorders Psychotic disorders Tourette's disorder	Constipation Increase or change in appetite Dry mouth
Stimulants Ritalin Dexadrine	Attention deficit disorder Narcolepsy	Decreased appetite Weight loss Nausea or vomiting

*These vary by medication; check individual medication.

clude weight loss; tough, dry, scaly skin; rashes; brittle hair; red or bleeding gums; dark circles under the eyes; missing or damaged teeth; and dry cracked lips. Some students who are unable to obtain adequate nutrition through oral feeding will require tube feeding (see Chapter 9).

Special Diets and Restrictions

Students may have special diets depending on their medical condition. In some instances, the diet may need to include extra food component, such as the need for more fatty acids and vitamins and minerals in short bowel syndrome, or the diet may have restrictions, such as a restricted fluid intake for certain cardiac or kidney conditions. Some students may need diets that are pureed because they do not have the oral motor control to manage a diet with solid food. It is important to ascertain the specific dietary needs for each individual student from the student's physician and to be sure that all individuals working with the student are familiar with the special diet.

Students may eat specific types of food at meal and snack time based on oral motor feeding skills and nutritional requirements. It is important that the type of food that will be provided at mealtime be specified prior to initiating feeding, especially if the student has oral motor difficulties, gastrointestinal problems, and/or specific nutritional needs.

SUMMARY

For many students, feeding is a skill that develops naturally during the first 3 years of life, at which point they can feed themselves a variety of foods and textures with utensils. Students who have poor developmental readiness, oral motor competency, and medical stability, however, may have difficulties in feeding and eating. Teachers and caregivers need to encourage positive practice, arrange an environment conducive to eating, and provide appropriate positioning to encourage this skill. Use of adaptive equipment and provision of appropriate assistive strategies (e.g., jaw control) can help with feeding and eating. Instructional strategies should be used to encourage the student to eat and drink as independently as possible.

9

Tube Feeding

Proper nutrition is vital for growth, development, energy, and health. Some students, however, are unable to acquire proper nutrition by ingesting food orally (by mouth). In these instances, a tube may be inserted into the student's stomach or intestines, through which proper nutritional support can be delivered. This is called **tube feeding.** A tube feeding occurs during specific scheduled times in place of oral feedings or in addition to them.

Several conditions may necessitate tube feeding (see Table 9-1). In some neuromuscular conditions, such as cerebral palsy, inadequate oral feeding skills may occur. This condition can affect the student's ability to accept, ingest, and swallow food when weak oral–motor musculature or primitive oral reflexes such as a hyperactive gag reflex or strong tongue thrust are present (Luiselli & Luiselli, 1995). (See Chapter 8 for more information on these.) Some neurological conditions may result in an inability to take food orally due to a high incidence of aspiration (food going into the lungs). Other conditions, such as coma, pre-

vent oral feeding entirely. Tube feeding is often prescribed by a physician in these situations.

Students may be born with abnormalities (congenital anomalies) of the throat, esophagus, stomach, or intestines that can affect their ability to effectively take food orally. For example, in esophageal atresia there is an abnormal closing off of the esophagus that prevents food from traveling into the stomach; in tracheoesophageal fistula, there is an abnormal passage between the trachea (windpipe) and esophagus (passageway to the stomach) that may affect the ability to eat. In some instances, trauma, tumors, or burns may affect the face and throat and result in an inability to accept food orally. Individuals who need ventilators typically are unable to take food by mouth due to the tracheostomy tube and thus require tube feeding (Eisenberg, 1989; McCrae & Hall, 1989; Young & White, 1992).

In some instances, the student may be able to swallow but is unable to eat sufficient quantities of food to achieve proper nutrition. Tube feeding is then necessary to be certain the student is

Table 9-1 Select Conditions That May Require Tube Feeding

General body system	Example conditions	Possible reason for tube feeding
Congenital malformations of gastrointestinal tract	Cleft palate/lip Esophageal atresia Tracheoesophageal fistula	Malformation of part of the gastrointestinal tract makes oral feeding inadvisable
Gastrointestinal	Short bowel syndrome Inflammatory bowel disease	Conditions requiring supportive therapy for nutrition
Neurological	Coma	Inability to eat orally
Neuromuscular	Severe cerebral palsy	Persistence of excessive primitive reflexes result in inability to obtain enough nutrition
Metabolic	Burns Cardiac conditions Multiple trauma	Conditions requiring supportive therapy for nutrition
General	Anorexia Growth failure Malnutrition Weight loss	Requires extensive nutritional support that the person is unable to acquire orally

receiving adequate amounts. This may occur due to some gastrointestinal conditions, metabolic states, and conditions resulting in malnutrition or growth failure.

DESCRIPTION OF TUBE FEEDING

Tubes may be placed into the stomach for a variety of reasons, including administering medication, relieving distention by removing fluid and gas, relieving nausea and vomiting, removing gastric samples for testing, and providing nourishment (Oberc, 1991). The term **tube feeding** is used when a tube is introduced into the stomach or intestine for the purposes of giving fluids with high caloric value (*Dorland's,* 1994). Tube feeding is also known as **gastric gavage,** *gastric* meaning stomach and *gavage* meaning feeding. When the feeding tube is placed into the small intestine for the same purpose, it is referred to as **enteral gavage;** *enteral* means small intestine.

Description of Feeding Routes

Before discussing the various types of feeding routes used for tube feeding, an understanding of the anatomy of the gastrointestinal tract is needed. As seen in Figure 9-1, food enters the mouth, is chewed (when applicable), and is moved to the back of the oral cavity to facilitate or initiate a swallow. As swallowing occurs, the food enters the pharynx (the throat), and a series

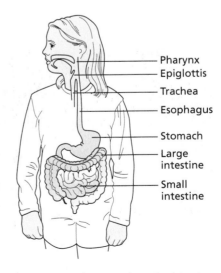

FIGURE 9-1 The gastrointestinal tract

of involuntary events occur: the soft palate pulls upward to close off the nasal cavity to prevent food from going into that area; folds on either side of the pharynx pull toward the middle, creating a slit that prevents food that is too large from passing any farther; and the epiglottis (a lidlike structure) swings over the entrance to the trachea, preventing food from entering the trachea where it would continue to the lungs (Guyton, 1995). Food continues from the pharynx into the esophagus. The esophagus is a tubelike structure that moves the food from the pharynx to the stomach by wormlike movements known as peristalsis. Upon entering the stomach, the food is mixed with gastric secretions until it forms a semifluid mixture. (At this point, very few nutrients are absorbed into the body from the stomach.) The stomach contracts, slowly emptying the semifluid mixture into the short upper portion of the small intestine known as the *duodenum*. Through peristaltic movement, the semifluid mixture next travels through the central portion of the small intestine called the *jejunum,* followed by the last part of the small intestine, referred to as the *ileum.* From there it empties into the large intestine. The nutrients in the semifluid mixture are absorbed into the body through the small and large intestines.

When a student requires tube feeding, a tube is placed directly into the stomach or into the small intestine (duodenum). The three most common forms of tube feeding are (a) nasogastric tube feeding, (b) gastrostomy tube feeding, and (c) feedings through a gastrostomy button (also known as skin-level device) (see Figure 9-2). A nasogastric tube feeding refers to a soft flexible tube being inserted through the nose (*naso-*) and the end of the tube being in the stomach (*gastro-*). In this case, as well as most other types of feeding routes, the type of feeding route and the general name of the tube refers to the entry and placement of the tube. Hence, the tube is referred to as a NG (*nasogastric*) tube.

Some feeding routes are created when an incision is made through the abdominal wall to the stomach or intestine. Depending on the procedure and the student's compliance, this surgery may occur under general anesthesia or by local anesthesia, sometimes taking only 10 to 30 minutes. The tube is placed through the abdominal wall into the stomach, often midway along the greater curvature of the stomach. The tube may be secured by a suture. The stomach is usually anchored to the peritoneum (a membrane lining the abdominal cavity) at the site of entry to prevent the formula (or liquefied food) from leaking into the abdominal cavity (Bockus, 1993; Wong, 1995). Operations resulting in artificial openings between two hollow organs or between an organ and the abdominal wall is loosely referred to as an **ostomy.** When the feeding tube is inserted through the abdominal wall into the stomach, it is referred to as a **gastrostomy tube** (or G-tube). Persons receiving gastrostomy tube feedings usually need tube feedings over a long period of time, making NG tube feedings not feasible. However, gastrostomies are not necessarily permanent.

In some instances, the student may not have a tube going through the abdominal wall but instead has a **gastrostomy button** (also known as a **skin-level device**). A gastrostomy button is a small, round silicon device that goes through the abdominal wall and is positioned at skin level. It continuously stays in place and is used for students on long-term gastrostomy feeding. It is closed off with a small cap. When it is time to give the formula, the cap is opened and an extension tube is attached to the gastrostomy button. The gastrostomy button usually has a one-way valve that prevents the formula from inadvertently coming out. The gastrostomy button has several advantages. It is cosmetically pleasing, is easy to care for, and can be immersed in water. However, a gastrostomy button requires a well-established gastrostomy site, is more expensive, and may become clogged. Also, the extension tubing can disconnect from the button, requiring the student to be still when feeding is occurring (Wong, 1995).

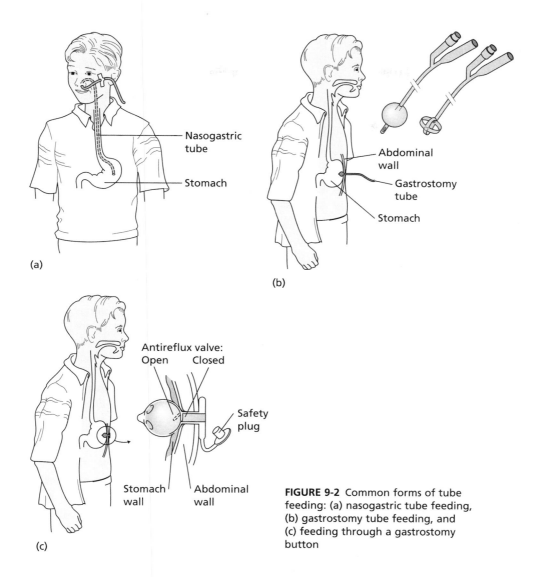

(a)

(b)

(c)

FIGURE 9-2 Common forms of tube feeding: (a) nasogastric tube feeding, (b) gastrostomy tube feeding, and (c) feeding through a gastrostomy button

There are other types of feeding routes, as seen in Figure 9-3. Sometimes a tube goes through the mouth instead of the nose. Placement through the mouth is usually uncomfortable due to the gag reflex, so placement through the nose is more common. Generally, students receiving tube feedings for a short period of time (approximately 6 weeks) have tubes that go through the nose or mouth and into the stomach (nasogastric, orogastric) (Bockus, 1993). Tubes may be placed through the nose (or mouth) and end in the small intestine instead of the stomach, or in some cases, the tube may go directly through the abdominal wall into the small intestine. In these cases, the term *duodenal* or *jejunal* is used to indicate that the tube is in the small intestine (e.g., nasoduodenal, nasojejunal, and jejunostomy).

Nasogastric = tube from the nose (*naso-*) to the stomach (*-gastric*)

Nasoduodenal = tube from the nose (*naso-*) to the first section of the small intestine (*-duodenal*)

Nasojejunal = tube from the nose (*naso-*) to the middle section of the small intestine (*-jejunal*)

Orogastric = tube from the mouth (*oro-*) to the stomach (*-gastric*)

Oroduodenal = tube from the mouth (*oro-*) to the first section of the small intestine (*-duodenal*)

Orojejunal = tube from the mouth (*oro-*) to the middle section of the small intestine (*-jejunal*)

Gastrostomy = tube through the abdominal wall into the stomach (*gastro-*) through an opening (*-ostomy*)

Jejunostomy = tube through the abdominal wall into the small intestine (*jejun-*) through an opening (*-ostomy*)

Prefix	*Suffix*
oro = oral (mouth)	*gastric* = stomach
naso = nasal (nose)	*duodenal* = small intestine (duodenum)
gastro = stomach	
	jejunal = small intestine (jejunem)
	ostomy = opening

FIGURE 9-3 Types of feeding routes

Types of Tube-Feeding Formulas and Their Delivery

Several different formulas may be given to the student as a tube feeding. The type and amount of formula as well as the frequency of delivery is prescribed by the physician. Formula selection will be determined by the medical diagnosis, the student's ability to digest and absorb nutrients, the feeding route, and the type of tube. There are five major categories of formulas. The most commonly used formulas are those that are lactose-free (e.g., Ensure). These contain casein or soy as the source of protein. A second type of formula are those that are milk based (e.g., Complete B). These formulas usually taste good and are often used as a supplement to additional feedings. The third type are elemental formulas (e.g., Vital HN) that are often used with individuals with limited or impaired gastrointestinal function. A fourth type of formula are modular formulas that supply a single nutrient such as protein, to supplement other formulas (e.g., Promide for protein). A fifth type of formula are specialty formulas that are used to meet specific needs of individuals with such medical conditions as renal (kidney) failure. For example, formulas may be made to decrease carbon dioxide production in individuals with certain respiratory diseases or made high in fiber to slow the passage of the nutrients so there can be a greater absorption in certain gastrointestinal conditions (Young & White, 1992). Formulas may come ready to be used, or they may need to be mixed with water. In some instances the physician may prescribe regular food (or baby food) that is pureed in a blender and mixed with water. Formula made of pureed food has the advantage of providing bulk for the intestines and helps with elimination (Plummer, 1983).

Regardless of the type of formula selected by the physician, the feeding may be given on an intermittent or continuous basis. Intermittent feedings are a set volume of feeding (e.g., 200 to 400 milliliters), given within a specific amount of time (typically within 30 minutes), by force of gravity, usually every 4 hours (Ciocon, Galindo-Ciocon, Tiessen, & Galindo, 1992). They may be given either by the **bolus tube-feeding method** or the **intermittent gravity drip method.** The bolus method uses a syringe barrel to deliver the formula by gravity over a short period of time (see Figure 9-4). The intermittent gravity drip method usually has the formula in a

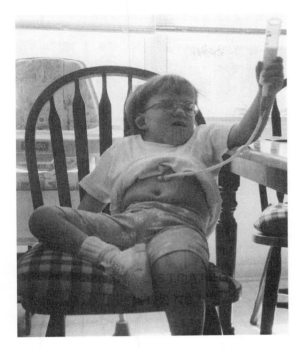

FIGURE 9-4 A girl feeding herself through her gastrostomy button using the bolus tube-feeding method

Whether an intermittent or continuous delivery method is used depends on what the student can tolerate. An intermittent method is usually used if the student can tolerate large amounts of fluid over a short period of time without discomfort or vomiting (Graff et al., 1990). However, diarrhea has been found to be significantly more frequent in some individuals receiving intermittent feeding versus continuous feeding (Ciocon et al., 1992). In these instances, the continuous feeding method may be selected.

Tubes used for feedings may be left in place between feedings or may be reinserted each time the formula is given. This applies to tubes that are going through the nose or mouth (i.e., nasogastric, orogastric tubes) as well as those going through the abdominal wall (i.e., gastrostomy tubes). Gastrostomy buttons are kept in place and not reinserted for each feeding.

EQUIPMENT AND ADAPTIVE EQUIPMENT FOR PERFORMING TUBE FEEDING

The type of equipment used in tube feeding consists primarily of the tube and a tube-feeding pump, when applicable. Feeding tubes are made out of a variety of materials and vary in length and diameter. For nasogastric (or nasojejunostomy) feedings, one of the most commonly used tubes for tube feeding students is the polyvinyl chloride tube (PVC tube). It may be used for continuous or intermittent feeding. The tube is firm enough to provide enough stability for insertion but also flexible enough to easily bend around the curves of the gastrointestinal tract during insertion. It may be left in place for several days or reinserted each time a feeding is scheduled.

Another type of nasogastric tube is a silicone or polyurethane tube. This tube is very soft and pliable and inserted using a guidewire (plastic or stainless steel stylet) to stiffen the tube during

bag and allows the formula drip more slowly, typically over 20 to 30 minutes (Graff et al., 1990). (In a few instances, a mechanical pump may be used to infuse the formula mechanically rather than using gravity. In these instances, it may be referred to as an *intermittent feeding method by pump*.)

When the student receives continuous tube feeding, a constant volume of formula is given over a specific unit of time (Ciocon et al., 1992). Continuous tube feedings may be given by the **continuous gravity drip method** or the **continuous infusion method by pump.** In these methods, the formula either is in a bag that is adjusted to drip at a certain rate by adjusting the clamp (as in continuous gravity drip method) or is delivered at a certain rate by setting a mechanical pump (as in the continuous infusion method by pump) (see Figure 9-5).

FIGURE 9-5 Tube feeding being delivered through an NG tube by the continuous gravity drip method (a) and the continuous infusion method by pump (b)

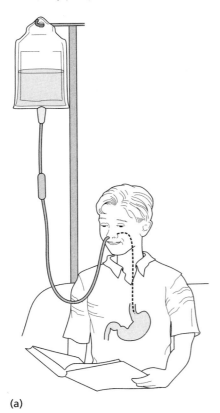

(a)

(b)

insertion. It is often weighted at the bottom to assist with proper placement. It is used for intermittent or continuous nasogastric or nasojejunal feeding on a long-term basis. Regular replacement of this tube is not needed because it is less irritating than PVC tubes (Oberc, 1991).

Tubes are made in a variety of sizes. The diameter of a feeding tube is often referred to by a term called "French." For example, the student may have a size 8, 10, or 12 French tube, and it may be 15, 36, or 42 inches long. Some tubes may have an additional port (another end with an internal tube that usually runs the length of the

feeding tube) for administration of medication. The physician decides which tube and size of tube is most appropriate.

There are several different types of gastrostomy tubes. The Malecot and Pezzar are two types of gastrostomy tubes that are designed to stay in place by having expanded tips to keep the tubes from dislodging. Some tubes have balloons on their ends that are inflated with water through a port after the tube is inserted (refer back to Figure 9-2b). The inflated balloon helps keep the tube in place. Some types of tubes that may have these balloons are the Foley, MIC, and Flow-

Thru tubes. In some instances (e.g., when a permanent tunnel gastrostomy is surgically created), a straight Foley catheter (one without the balloon) may be used and inserted each time that a feeding is scheduled (Deacon & Beachy, 1991).

Several types of gastrostomy buttons (or skin-level devices, as they are generically called) are available, too. Two devices commonly used with students are the Bard Button and the MIC-KEY. Although they differ in shape, they essentially function in a similar manner. The Button is a small, flexible silicone rubber device that is mushroom-shaped under the skin and above the skin has small retention flaps. The MIC-KEY is more slender and uses a balloon inflation system. Skin-level devices usually have a one-way valve that prevents leakage of the stomach contents and a safety plug that is closed after feeding to provide a secondary measure to prevent leakage of stomach contents (Deacon & Beachy, 1991). Special tubing attaches to the skin-level device. For the Button, there is a bolus feeding tube (for intermittent feeding), a continuous feeding tube (for continuous feeding), and a decompression tube (used to allow excess air to escape the stomach, since the one-way valve prevents this without the special decompression tube). The MIC-KEY only requires one extension tube that is used for both feeding and decompression. The MIC-KEY extension tube also has a medication port on it. Extension tubing used for feeding usually is replaced weekly and is cleaned after each intermittent feeding (Gaas-Beckert & Heyman, 1993). The skin-level devices vary as to when they need replacement. The button is recommended to be replaced every 6 months.

Often decisions need to be made regarding whether a gastrostomy tube or a skin-level device is going to be used. Skin-level feeding devices are associated with less skin breakdown, less risk of moving out of position, and more cosmetic appeal. However, skin-level devices require a well-established gastrostomy site, are available in only certain sizes, cost more than gastrostomy tubes, present a risk of the valve clogging, and, when certain operations have been performed, are contraindicated.

The second type of equipment that may be used to give tube feeding is the electric pump. Several models may be used. Essentially, a bag of liquid food is attached to special tubing designed to be used with the pump. The tubing attaches to the pump, which is set to deliver the feeding at a certain rate. Tubing leaves the pump and is then attached to the student's own feeding tube. Depending on the type of pump, several alarms may go off to indicate that the feeding is over or that the feeding is meeting resistance (e.g., when the tubing is kinked). The teacher should be familiar with the types of alarms and what needs to be done if one goes off. Also, it is important to find out how long the battery can run. In some instances, the pump is plugged into an electric socket when feasible, and the battery is used in locations not near an outlet.

ASSISTIVE STRATEGIES FOR PERFORMING TUBE FEEDING

Preparing for Tube Feeding

The student should be prepared for the tube feeding by being given an explanation of what is going to occur. For students who do not have good receptive communication skills, the student may be handed a syringe barrel or tube as a cue that tube feeding is about to occur.

Prior to beginning tube feeding, the location of the tube feeding needs to be determined. Infants receiving tube feedings should be held in a similar manner as when receiving a bottle and be offered a pacifier to suck on. This will assist the student to associate these activities with the feeling of having hunger satisfied and make the transition to oral feeding easier, when the tube is no longer necessary (Kuntz, 1996c). Toddlers should be fed in a high chair (or up to the table) and offered foods to taste (with the physician's approval) or to play with. Young students may take their food at the table with the family during mealtime. In school, some students prefer to have their tube feeding with the rest of the class during lunchtime, while others prefer the privacy of a classroom or nurse's office. In each case, it is important to have the feeding occur with oral stimulation and in a location where feeding typically occurs. An exception is when the student prefers privacy for tube feeding. If the tube feeding is continuous, the student may move about and perform his usual activities.

Prior to tube feeding, the person performing the procedure should thoroughly wash her hands, prepare the formula, and gather all needed equipment. Hand washing will help prevent bacterial contamination of the food as well as the spread of any infection. Nonsterile gloves may be used, but students who are allergic to latex should not come in contact with latex gloves; gloves made of other material (e.g., plastic) may be used. (See Chapter 1 for more information on latex allergies.)

In some cases, the formula needs to be prepared by mixing it with water. If food is given, it often needs to be pureed in a blender and mixed with water to get it to a consistency that will go down the tube. Use of baby food may require more water added than usually used. The food or formula typically needs to be given at room temperature. The exact amount of formula needs to be measured out, as prescribed by the physician. The remaining may be stored in the refrigerator. Finally, all necessary equipment should be gathered and placed in easy reach of the individual performing the procedure.

Also before the feeding begins, the student should be positioned in either a sitting or lying position. If lying down, the student should at least be elevated 30 to 45 degrees to decrease the risk of vomiting and aspiration. Also, besides being elevated in a lying position, being placed on the right side is most desirable since it aids emptying food from the stomach to the small intestine.

Inserting the Tube

In some instances, the feeding tube needs to be inserted prior to every feeding and is taken out when the feeding is complete. Although some gastrostomy tubes may be reinserted prior to each feeding, this technique is more common with nasogastric tubes. If this is ordered, the physician's step-by-step procedure should be followed. (This procedure will vary based on the type of tube.)

Nasogastric tube insertion requires a skilled, trained professional (e.g., a nurse) for proper tube insertion. When inserting nasogastric tubes, the length needed for the tube to reach the stomach is roughly determined by measuring the tube from the nose to the ear lobe to halfway between the end of the breastbone (sternum) and the navel. (If the tube is inserted through the mouth or ends in the small intestine, the measurement is adjusted accordingly.) This length is often marked with a pen. The tip of the tube is lubricated with water-soluble jelly and gently inserted into the nostril and slowly pushed straight back. When the tube reaches the pharynx (throat), it is helpful to have the student tilt her head forward or swallow sips of water to help it go down the esophagus, rather than the trachea (windpipe). When the tube reaches the pen mark, it is stopped and taped in place (with tape on the nose or cheek). Care must be taken that the tube does not coil in the mouth or go down the trachea. If resistance is met, the tube is withdrawn slightly then reinserted. If the student turns blue or begins choking, the tube should be withdrawn immediately (Kuntz, 1996d). In some cases, a wire guide inside the tube may be used to insert the tube, and this is withdrawn when the tube is in place.

Verifying Placement and Residual Volume

Before each feeding, the placement of the feeding tube that has been inserted through the nose or mouth needs to be verified to be sure it is not positioned in the trachea. This may be determined using several different techniques. In the aspiration technique, a syringe is attached to the end of the tube with the plunger depressed. The plunger is pulled back, resulting in the stomach contents coming up the tube into the syringe barrel. The presence of stomach contents confirms its placement in the stomach. (The stomach contents are then returned.) Sometimes there may be no stomach contents because the tube is not low enough in the stomach, the tube is lying against the wall of the stomach, or the stomach is empty. Sometimes the fluid aspirated to the gastrointestinal area looks almost identical to fluid aspirated from the respiratory system (Metheny, Reed, Berglund, & Wehrle, 1994). Because of this, and the possibility of no fluid being aspirated, it is suggested that more than one method be used.

Another method is the auscultation method, in which 5 cubic centimeters of air are drawn into a syringe and injected into the NG tube while listening with a stethoscope over the stomach. A gurgling sound should be heard as air enters the stomach (similar to blowing bubbles in a glass of water). However, since the sound may be heard when the tube is displaced in the respiratory tract, it is sometimes not viewed as reliable in differentiating between gastric and respiratory placement (Metheny, McSweeney, Wehrle, & Wiersema, 1990). Another method includes checking the pH of the secretions. If there is any doubt as to the placement, the feeding should be withheld and the proper person notified of the problem.

In some instances, the physician may have ordered that residual volume (the amount of food left in the stomach) be checked prior to giving a feeding, or every 4 hours when feeding is continuous. If the stomach is digesting the food too slowly, another feeding or continued feeding would be contraindicated until a certain amount of food had been digested. Giving too much food can result in nausea, vomiting, and discomfort. Checking residual volume is performed by withdrawing the stomach contents and measuring the amount. Typically, if the residual volume is greater than half the volume of the feeding, the next feeding (or continued feeding) is delayed (Kuntz, 1996d). In some instances, the physician orders the amount of residual volume to be subtracted from the next feeding. After checking residual volume, the stomach contents are returned by gravity to the stomach, since they contain vital electrolytes.

When a student has a gastrostomy tube, its placement and residual volume may also be checked. In this situations, a syringe is attached to the gastrostomy tube, without the plunger above the level of the stomach. The tube is unclamped and is moved below the level of the stomach (Kuntz, 1996c). Stomach contents should move into the tube and plunger. It is important to try this without use of the plunger, since the suction may irritate the lining of the stomach wall and cause bleeding or perforation (Deacon & Beachy, 1991). In some cases, the plunger may need to be used gently. To check the residual volume using a gastrostomy button, a special "venting" tube is used to attach to the button and then to the syringe. The syringe is then gently withdrawn to measure the stomach contents.

Equipment and Supply List for Intermittent Tube Feeding

Liquid feeding solution or formula

Syringe barrel

Clamp

Adapter and extension tubing (if using a button)

Water

Equipment and Supply List for Continuous Feeding

Liquid feeding solution or formula

Bag for formula

Infusion pump (sometimes used)

Clamp

Adapter and extension tubing (if using a button)

Water

Procedure for Intermittent Feeding

After explaining the procedure to the student, washing hands, gathering equipment, preparing the formula, positioning the student, and verifying placement of the tube, the person performing the tube-feeding procedure is ready to begin.

Steps in the Procedure for Intermittent Feeding	*Rationale*
1. Attach the syringe barrel.	
a. For an NG tube or G–tube, attach the syringe barrel to the feeding tube, keeping the tube clamped by either using a clamp or kinking or pinching the tube.	Keeping the tube clamped will inhibit air from entering the tube and going into the stomach. Excess air in the stomach can create discomfort.
b. For a gastrostomy button, first attach the adapter and extension tube to a syringe barrel. Put water into the syringe barrel and allow it to fill the extension tube. Clamp the extension tube so it remains filled with water. Open the plug of the gastrostomy button and attach the adapter and extension tube to the gastrostomy button.	An adapter allows the extension tube to fit into the gastrostomy button. The extension tube should be filled with water prior to connecting it to the gastrostomy button to prevent excess air from entering the stomach (Sale, 1992).
2. Pour fluid/formula into syringe barrel.	Water may be initially poured into the tube and allowed to flow into the stomach to check that the tube is not clogged.
3. The syringe barrel should be held approximately 6 inches above the stomach. Unclamp tube to allow the formula to flow into the stomach.	Be sure that there is some slack in the tube and the person holding the syringe barrel does not accidentally move the syringe barrel away from the student, causing the tubing to be pulled out or displaced.
4. Monitor the flow of the formula, allowing the fluid to flow slowly through the tube by gravity. Rate of flow for premature or small infants is usually no faster than 5 cubic centimeters every 5 to 10 minutes and for older infants and students, no faster than 10 cubic centimeters a minute (Deacon & Beachy, 1991).	The higher up the syringe barrel is held, the faster the formula will flow and the lower it is held, the slower the formula will flow. Do not force feed with a syringe plunger, unless instructed by a physician. Allowing the fluid to flow slowly prevents vomiting, diarrhea, or stomach cramping. Also, forcefully feeding using a plunger may cause reflux and increase the risk of aspiration (Perry, Johnson, & Trump, 1983).
5. Monitor the student.	If the student vomits during feeding or the NG tube slips, feeding should be *stopped immediately* by clamping or kinking the tubing. The tube feeding may be delayed when vomiting occurs. If the tube has slipped, placement must be verified before continuing.

Steps in the Procedure for Intermittent Feeding	*Rationale*
6. As the level of the formula nears the bottom of the syringe barrel, add more formula. This should be done in such a way that the syringe barrel is never empty. This is repeated until all of the formula is given.	By never completely emptying the syringe barrel, excess air does not enter the stomach.
7. When nearing the completion of the formula, add 20 to 50 cubic centimeters of water to the tube to rinse the tube of all formula, and be sure all formula has been given.	Rinsing the tube with water prevents dried formula from obstructing the tube.

8. Discontinue intermittent feeding.
   a. When the tube remains in place after feeding, some of the water should remain within the tube by plugging the tube with water in it.
   b. For gastrostomy buttons, remove the adapter and extension tube and close the plug.
   c. If the tube is to be removed when feeding is complete, pinch it firmly and withdraw it.
	By allowing some of the water to remain in the tubing, air will not be introduced into the stomach at the next feeding. In some instances in which the student forms a lot of gas, the tube may be left open and elevated for 15 to 20 minutes before plugging it to allow gas or air to escape from the stomach. (This is called "venting.")

9. The student should remain elevated after feeding for approximately 30 minutes.	This helps prevent vomiting or aspiration.
10. Document that the procedure has been done as well as any reactions to being tube fed.	Restlessness, color change, distended abdomen, nausea, vomiting, or discomfort should be reported to designated personnel and appropriate action taken.

Procedure for Continuous Feeding

This procedure is similar to the intermittent feeding but uses a larger container than a syringe barrel and occurs over a longer period of time. After explaining the procedure, washing hands, collecting the equipment, preparing the formula, positioning the student, and verifying placement, the person performing the tube feeding is ready to begin.

Steps in the Procedure for Continuous Feeding	*Rationale*
1. Attach the tubing to the prepared bag or container of prescribed formula.	Different types of tubing may be used, depending on whether there is a pump.

Steps in the Procedure for Continuous Feeding	*Rationale*
Hang the bag or container on an infusion pole or pump.	

2. Have the formula flow through the tubing.
   a. This may be done by unclamping the tubing, or
   b. When an infusion pump is used, the pump may be set to allow the formula to be drawn through the tubing.
	It is important to expel all of the air from the tubing by first having the formula flow through the tubing.

3. Insert tip of feeding bag tubing into the NG tube, G-tube, or gastrostomy button.	The tip should easily go in. If an extension tube and adapter are needed for the gastrostomy button, have the formula (or fluid) flow through these prior to attaching them to the gastrostomy button to prevent air from going into the stomach.
4. Begin feeding. a. For the continuous gravity drip method, open the clamp of the feeding bag tubing and adjust to the proper rate prescribed by the physician.	Adjusting a clamp to achieve a certain rate requires knowledge of the diameter of the tubing in the drip chamber.
b. For an infusion pump, open the clamp and adjust the rate on the infusion pump.	To set an infusion pump to a certain rate, the desired cubic centimeters per minutes are entered into the infusion pump.
5. Monitor the flow of the formula.	Flow of formula should occur at a constant rate. Be sure no changes in flow occur by changes in student's activity or position.
6. Monitor the student.	If any signs of distress occur during feeding, the feeding should be stopped by clamping the tube. Restlessness, color change, distended abdomen, nausea, vomiting, or discomfort should be reported to designated personnel and appropriate action taken. If the flow of formula is obstructed, check whether the tubing is kinked and straighten it out to resume flow. Adjust the flow to maintain the proper infusion rate, or contact designated personnel.

Steps in the Procedure for Continuous Feeding	*Rationale*
7. Add formula or discontinue. a. If a continuous feeding is being given, add more formula to the bag when the bag is close to being empty.	By adding more formula to a bag that is nearly empty, uninterrupted feeding is allowed and the chance of introducing air into the stomach is decreased. Rinsing the tube with water prevents dried formula from obstructing the tube.
b. If continuous feeding is to be discontinued, clamp the feeding tube (the G-tube, NG tube, or extension tubing for a gastrostomy button). Disconnect the feeding bag and flush tubing with 20 to 50 cubic centimeters of water. Follow the procedure on how to discontinue intermittent feeding (step 8 there).	
8. The student should be in an elevated position. (If continuous feeding was stopped, the student should remain elevated for approximately 30 minutes.)	This helps prevent vomiting or aspiration.
9. Document occurrence of the procedure and any abnormal reactions or encountered problems.	Restlessness, color change, distended abdomen, nausea, vomiting, or discomfort should be reported to designated personnel and appropriate action taken.

Care of Equipment

If the equipment is to be reused (e.g., the syringe barrel), wash and rinse the equipment with soap and water after each feeding. Cleaning the equipment prevents buildup of formula and helps decrease the likelihood of infection. Equipment should be stored in a clean area and should not come in contact with other student's equipment. Old equipment should be discarded after a certain period of time as set by the medical personnel. Bags and tubings are often replaced every 3 days in the home. Gastrostomy tubes may be replaced on a monthly basis, and gastrostomy buttons may be replaced approximately every 6 months. Plastic NG tubes are often changed every 3 to 5 days, while silicone NG tubes may be changed every month (Kuntz, 1996c).

Daily Care

The skin around the tube (whether an NG tube, G-tube, or button) should be cleaned daily and as needed (e.g., if site becomes dirty). Often soap and water is used for cleaning, although a particular cleaning solution may have been recommended. A protective skin barrier may have been prescribed to decrease the irritation of the tape and a special tape is usually used to hold the NG tube or G-tube in place. A mild antibiotic ointment may be prescribed to protect the skin from irritation. Skin should be carefully inspected for signs of irritation or redness. The gastrostomy button should be rotated each time it is cleaned to help the skin remain intact.

If irritation is present with the NG tube, the tube may be withdrawn and placed through the other nostril. If the G-tube site is open or draining, it may be cleaned with half-strength peroxide and sterile water, rinsed with sterile water, and allowed to air-dry. The appropriate person needs to be notified. Also, the adult must be alert to signs of infection and contact the appropriate person if it is suspected. If the area is draining stomach contents, a physician needs to be notified in case a larger tube is needed. A dressing may be placed around the tube to absorb the drainage (Kuntz, 1996c).

INSTRUCTIONAL STRATEGIES AND MODIFICATIONS FOR TUBE FEEDING

Students who require tube feedings should be taught to perform the procedure as independently as possible. Depending on the student's physical status, age, and cognitive status, the student may partially participate by performing only a few steps, such as holding the syringe barrel, to executing all the steps. It is as important to teach the student to perform the tube feeding as any other self-help skill to promote independence.

To teach students to tube-feed themselves, it is important to identify the steps of the procedure and break them down into teachable parts. As discussed in Chapter 2, the steps of the task may vary among students based on the individually prescribed procedure (i.e., steps differ based on the type of tube feeding, site, and physician's preference) and the student's physical capabilities. The teacher will need to write down the steps of the exact procedure prescribed by the physician. Also, the team will need to do a discrepancy analysis (see Chapter 2) to assess the student's ability to perform the procedure and determine whether adaptations are needed to assist the student in performing specific step(s). This may result in additional steps in the task analysis procedure. If a step is physically impossible for the student, the student may direct another person verbally or using an AAC device to perform the step. A typical

task analysis is found in Figure 9-6. The task analysis can be placed on a data sheet and used to document the student's progress with the procedure (refer back to Figure 2-8). Documentation should also include feeding tolerance, skin condition, and any problems encountered with the feeding.

Sometimes the student will have a physical impairment that does not allow the use of both arms and hands effectively. Several different adaptations may be used depending on the level of physical involvement. When one hand is primarily affected, making a holder to hold the tube-feeding barrel may be helpful. In some

---

1. Wash hands.
2. Prepare formula.
3. Prepare equipment.
4. Clamp or kink tube.
5. Remove plug.
6. Attach syringe barrel.
7. Pour prepared fluid/formula into barrel.
8. Hold barrel 6 inches above stomach.
9. Allow formula to flow by gravity.
10. Add more formula before barrel completely empties.
11. Continue to add formula until all is added.
12. Add water when formula nears bottom of barrel.
13. Kink or clamp tube before water empties completely from barrel.
14. Take off syringe barrel.
15. Put plug in tube.

(May have a separate task analysis for preparing formula and putting water in a cup to prepare for tube feeding.)

FIGURE 9-6 Sample task analysis of intermittent tube feeding for G-tube

cases, a block of wood with a hole (or a wire bent in a circle) is attached to a stand (e.g., music stand) or table to hold the syringe barrel. This frees up a hand and may allow the student to do other steps. Care must be taken that the adapted holder grips the syringe barrel at the appropriate height. Often one that is adjustable and allows the student to stop the feeding and move the barrel farther down to add the formula is ideal. This can be accomplished by using a gooseneck or flexible stand to attach the holder. The student should also be positioned close to the equipment so tubing is not pulled out.

In some instances, the syringe barrel is too small for the student to pour the formula. A funnel may be attached to the syringe barrel to enable a student to pour the formula into the syringe barrel. Also, a pitcher with an adapted handle may help the student hold the formula and pour it in. In some cases, the physical impairment may be so severe that the student is unable to perform the procedure physically. In these situations, the student should learn the steps of the procedure and what to do if a problem occurs to be able to direct others in the procedure. The student may do this verbally or through the use of augmentative and alternative communication.

The student can be taught to perform the procedure utilizing a number of different instructional strategies. Some students benefit from a picture prompting system showing the steps of the procedure or, if the student can read, having the steps listed out for the student to follow. Students with more severe cognitive impairments need a response prompt strategy such as the system of maximum prompts. The teacher will select the best instructional strategy to use with each specific student.

Time-Limited Steps and Caution Steps

Many instructional strategies allow a certain amount of time to pass before a prompt (or more intrusive prompt) is given, such as in the system of least prompts and time delay procedure. For most steps of the task analysis, that is appropriate. However, certain steps must be completed within a certain time frame. These are known as **time-limited steps.** For the tube-feeding procedure, this occurs when more formula needs to be added to the syringe barrel before it empties or when the tube needs to be clamped at the end of the procedure before the water completely empties. On these steps the teacher will need to assist the student should he not respond quickly enough to avoid air getting into the stomach and causing discomfort. For a high-functioning student, this may be done by modeling the step and then shadowing the student. (In shadowing, the teacher keeps her hand within an inch of the student's until the step is complete.) A lower-functioning student may require a full physical prompt and move to shadowing. Shadowing allows the teacher to intervene quickly to prevent errors.

Teachers needs also to identify which steps of a procedure are **caution steps,** meaning steps during which the student could injure himself by making a quick, jerking, or incorrect movement. For the tube-feeding procedure, the caution step is attaching the syringe barrel when the student has a G-tube, because the student could inadvertently pull out the G-tube. On caution steps, the educational team must determine whether the step is appropriate for the student to perform. If the student is to learn the step, then it may be modeled first and then shadowing may be provided, or, for lower-functioning students, full physical guidance may be provided and then shadowing. Teachers should highlight time-limited steps and caution steps on their data sheet as a reminder to provide shadowing. (See Chapter 2 for more information on instructional procedures and a sample data sheet.)

TUBE-FEEDING PROBLEMS AND EMERGENCIES

Several problems and emergencies may occur while tube feeding. Some of these include aspiration, tube displacement, nausea and vomiting, diarrhea, site infection, and a clogged tube. Of these problems, aspiration is considered an emergency situation requiring immediate treatment.

Aspiration

When discussing tube feeding, the term **aspiration** refers to inhaling the formula. When this occurs and is accompanied by respiratory symptoms, increase of white blood cells, and changes on an X-ray (showing infiltrates), aspiration pneumonia is present (Fox et al., 1995).

Aspiration can occur when the NG tube is misplaced into the lung instead of in the stomach or is not placed completely down into the stomach. This is why verification of proper tube placement prior to each feeding is essential. However, aspiration can occur even when the tube is correctly placed. Aspiration occurs when the student vomits or has **reflux** (backward flow of the stomach contents) and the formula goes from the stomach up the esophagus and down the trachea into the lungs. The chance of this response occurring increases when the student is fed lying flat on his back instead of being properly positioned on his side with his head elevated or in a sitting position.

Subtle signs of aspiration include a fast heart rate (tachycardia), breathing quickly (tachypnea), shortness of breath or difficulty breathing, coughing, fever, and wheezing. If subtle signs are present, the parent and physician need to be notified, and the emergency plan must be followed. A chest X-ray will be needed to confirm aspiration. If a large amount of tube feeding has been aspirated, acute respiratory failure can occur with severe breathing difficulty (stridor) and cyanosis (turning a blue color, especially seen around the mouth and fingernail beds). This can be a life-threatening situation and is associated with a high mortality rate (Fox et al., 1995). If any of these symptoms are present, *the feeding should be stopped immediately.* If respiratory distress is present, an ambulance should be called. While waiting for the ambulance, the student should be suctioned by qualified personnel and positioned on his right side (Bockus, 1991). After treatment, the student may be prescribed antibiotics to prevent or combat infection.

Tube Displacement

Some gastrostomies are constructed in such a way that gastrostomy tubes are introduced each time a feeding is to occur and are removed when the feeding is over. However, many gastrostomies are constructed with the gastrostomy tube or button remaining in place. In these gastrostomies, when the tube or button comes out, immediate action is needed. This is because many gastrostomies can close unless the tube is replaced within a few hours (Gauderer & Stellato, 1986). If the tube comes out, a clean, dry dressing should be taped over the opening and the person designated to replace the tube contacted immediately. (Depending on the student's individualized health plan, the designated person may be a nurse, parent, or hospital personnel.) The tube or button that has come out should not be thrown away; it should be placed in a clean cloth or container and given to the designated person for possible reinsertion (Urbano, 1992). Also, it needs to be inspected to determine if any part of it came off and has been left in the stomach.

Displacement can occur in several different ways. Most commonly, the student may pull the tube out, or the end of the tube may catch on something. To prevent displacement, it is important that the tube be properly taped. For a gastrostomy tube, the tube should be looped in a circle, and a special tape used to adhere to skin (e.g., paper or elastic tape) should go across it. The loop helps prevent dislodgment, since if the end is pulled, the loop may come undone and not pull directly on the part of the tube going into the person. Additional dressings, waist bands, or clothing may be needed over the site to help prevent a student from pulling it out. Behavior modification techniques may be used to teach the student not to pull out the tube. A special polyethylene body jacket with a special S-shaped tunnel for the feeding tube to exit has been successfully used to prevent the removal of the feeding tube (Tamler & Perrin, 1992).

Nausea, Vomiting, and Cramping

Nausea, vomiting, and cramping may occur with tube feeding due to several different causes. Whatever the cause, if the student has nausea, vomiting, or cramping while the tube feeding is being given, the tube feeding should be stopped to prevent further symptoms (or the IHP should be followed if different from this). The parent(s) should then be contacted.

In some cases, nausea, vomiting, or cramping may occur when the tube feeding has been delivered too rapidly, and the rate needs to be decreased. Nausea and vomiting may also occur if too much air has been allowed to enter the tubing and go into the stomach. This can be avoided by following proper tube-feeding procedures and preventing air from entering into the tube by kinking the tube and refilling the syringe barrel before it empties. In some cases, the physician may order the tube to be vented after feeding to allow air to escape.

Nausea, vomiting, or cramping may also occur if the stomach is not digesting the food quickly enough or if too much formula is being given. It is important that the volume of formula that has been prescribed is closely adhered to; otherwise, overfeeding can occur. Overfeeding can be assessed by checking for residual volume as previously discussed. When residual volume is greater than half the volume of the feeding, the feeding may be withheld under physician's approval to prevent overfeeding. A distended abdomen also gives an indication of overfeeding.

Nausea and vomiting may occur because of problems with the formula itself, and the formula may need to be modified. Formula that is given too cold may result in abdominal cramping, so it is important that the formula be given at room temperature. Contaminated formula may also cause nausea, vomiting, or cramping. Correct storage of the formula and infection control procedures should be in place. In some cases, nausea, vomiting, or cramping may occur and have nothing to do with the tube-feeding procedure or the formula. Nausea, vomiting, and cramping need to be reported to the parent who can do further follow-up with a physician to determine etiology.

Diarrhea

Diarrhea may occur from many of the same reasons that cause nausea and vomiting. Although the tube-feeding procedure or the formula are usually the first things attributed for causing diarrhea, tube feedings are often not the cause (Campbell, 1994). Sometimes medication effects or illness are the causes. Unlike nausea and vomiting that can result in aspiration, diarrhea does not create an immediate threat to the student (except for dehydration or electrolyte imbalance if severe). Unless it is specified in the student's own health plan, it is important that the tube feeding not just be stopped or slowed down under the assumption that it is the problem. This results in the individual not receiving the needed nutrients. The parents need to be notified, and the individualized health care plan should already have guidelines as to what should be done when this occurs.

In some cases, diarrhea is caused by the rate of delivery of the formula. If delivery is too fast, the rate may need to be decreased, as prescribed by the physician. In one study (Ciocon et al., 1992), diarrhea occurred significantly more frequently in individuals receiving tube feeding intermittently than those receiving tube feeding continuously. Because of this, some individuals may begin with continuous tube feedings and move to intermittent tube feedings once the feedings are more tolerated.

The content of the formula itself may cause the diarrhea, and the dilution of the formula may need to be altered (by physician's order). Formulas with fiber may need to be prescribed. Another possible cause of diarrhea is bacterial contamination of the formula or the feeding equipment (Bockus, 1991; Bussy, Marechal, & Nasca, 1992). This can be a life-threatening problem in the student with a condition that suppresses the immune system (e.g., AIDS, cancer). It is imperative that proper hand washing occurs and that the equipment is properly cleaned and stored (Bockus, 1991). The manufacturer's (or physician's) guidelines in reconstituting and storing the formula need to be followed. Some formulas can only be used within a certain number of hours.

Site Infection

Skin infection of gastrostomy sites occurs frequently when there is prolonged use of a gastrostomy tube (Brook, 1995). Students who are at risk of developing a gastrostomy site infection also include those who have neurological impairments, are malnourished, or are susceptible to serious infections. These infections may complicate an existing medical condition, making the use of the gastrostomy tube more difficult, and may result in serious local and systemic infections (Brook, 1995; Gallagher, Tyson, & Ashcraft, 1973).

Prevention of infection is important to avoid serious complications. Proper daily cleaning and drying of the gastrostomy site and of the equipment is essential to prevent infection. The person performing the tube feeding should follow infection control procedures (see Chapter 1). It is also important when taping the gastrostomy tube that the end of the tube not be going down into the diaper.

Close observation of the site is important to detect irritation or infection. The skin should be observed for redness, drainage, bleeding, or foul odor near the tube. If any of these are detected, the parents should be contacted. Sometimes a lubricant is used on the nostrils when irritation is present from the NG tube.

When an infection is present, the physician may prescribe local or systematic antibiotics to fight the infection. Careful and consistent administration of the medication as it is prescribed is important in order for the medication to be effective. The medication must be given until it is completed since stopping the medication before the entire dose in completed may result in a return of the infection.

Leaking of Stomach Contents

A feeding tube may leak if it is not securely clamped. Checking the clamp and reclamping is usually the first step taken when a leak is detected. Occasionally a gastrostomy button's antireflux valve may not work. Close the button with the cap, and report this to the parents. Sometimes a gastrostomy tube may leak because the balloon or the flange that holds the tube in place is not against the stomach wall. Gently pulling the tube until resistance is met and taping it in place may stop the leak. If a leak continues, the parents will need to be contacted to notify the physician (Urbano, 1992).

Clogged Tube

Clogging of the tube is another problem that may occur when giving tube feeding. Clogging has been attributed to formula residue, pill fragments, and physical incompatibility of medications in solutions (Kohn & Keithley, 1989; Galindo-Ciocon, 1993). Often this occurs when the tube has not been properly flushed with water after feeding or between giving different solutions. Flushing the feeding tube with water at room temperature before and after administration of medications has been found to produce the fewest occlusions (Scanlan & Frisch, 1992). Clogs also seem to develop more frequently for individuals receiving continuous feeding rather than intermittent feedings (Ciocon et al., 1992). For students receiving continuous feeding, the tube may need to be flushed with water every 4 hours (Galindo-Ciocon, 1993). A physician should be consulted regarding the need to flush the tube. Occasionally a clog may occur when the formula is too thick. Proper dilution of the formula is important to avoid this. Students with jejunostomies are at higher risk of tube blockages due to the smaller diameter of the tube (Bockus, 1993).

Several methods may unclog the tube:

1. If the obstruction is occurring in the extension tube, the extension tube may be disconnected, flushed with water, and reattached.

2. The tubing may be "milked," which is a procedure in which the tubing is pulled in short segments and rolled by hand (taking care not to pull it out of the student) to try to break up the clog.

3. Another technique involves using water to clear the obstruction. First, empty the syringe barrel (if it is full) into a clean container if you are performing intermittent tube feeding. If you are doing a continuous tube feeding, stop it and attach a 50–cubic centimeter syringe barrel to the student's tubing. Next, 25 to 30 cubic centimeters of water is poured into the syringe. The plunger is then gently pushed and pulled back and forth in an alternating manner, pushing water in or aspirating the clog out. It is important that this is done gently—never force the water in. Also, a 50–cubic centimeter syringe is needed since a smaller syringe may cause too much pressure and rupture the tube (Bockus, 1993). After the clog is cleared, the contents that were in the syringe barrel may be reintroduced.

4. Another method is similar to the third one but uses fizzing colas, cranberry juice, or meat tenderizer in addition to water. There is some disagreement as to the effectiveness of this method. Some claim that these agents are more effective than water (Webber-Jones et al., 1992); others argue that water is equally effective or, in some instances, that these alternate products can cause further clogging (Bockus, 1993). When using these agents, the procedure is similar as the one already outlined. However, it is often suggested that as much of the formula as possible should be withdrawn first above the clog. This is done by connecting the syringe barrel (with the plunger pushed completely into the syringe barrel) to the feeding tube and slowly pulling back on the plunger. (If nothing comes out, do not force it; just continue to the next step. Otherwise, the tube may close if done too strongly.) If some contents of the tube come up into the syringe barrel, the contents are emptied into a clean cup to be given after the clog is cleared. After trying to clear all of the formula above the clog, 5 cubic centimeters of the cola, juice, or tenderizer are poured into the syringe barrel and into the tube. The tube is clamped for about 15 minutes for the solution to work. Water is then added, and the tube is flushed or aspirated in a similar manner as with water alone (Webber-Jones et al., 1992). Use of these agents should be checked with the physician and indicated in the health plan.

Whichever method is used, it is most important that the clog never be forced by pushing strongly down on the plunger. In some instances, the person performing the procedure may be unable to unclog the tube. In these situations, the parent and physician will need to be contacted. a doctor may pass a special long-line catheter (tube) or a special brush through the tube to break up the obstruction. In some cases, a new tube may need to be inserted (Webber-Jones et al., 1992).

MANAGEMENT ISSUES FOR TUBE FEEDING

Individualized Health Plan and Individualized Educational Program

When constructing an individualized health care plan (IHP) for the student, several specialized areas need to be included for tube feeding, in addition to the general information in IHPs (see Figure 9-7). The doctor's precise orders for the tube feeding should be included and specify frequency (times), type of formula, and amount of formula. Student-specific guidelines with approved step-by-step directions on performing the tube feeding should be included in the IHP. The IHP also should describe emergency guidelines for aspiration and tube dislodgment. Guidelines should also be provided for other problems such as nausea and vomiting, diarrhea, and tube clog-

Tube-Feeding Route

_____ Orogastric   _____ Gastrostomy tube   _____ Nasojejunal
_____ Jejunostomy tube   _____ Nasoduodenal   _____ Nasogastric
_____ Gastrostomy button

Type of Tube Feeding

_____ Bolus method

_____ Intermittent gravity drip method

_____ Intermittent feeding method by pump

_____ Continuous gravity drip method

_____ Continuous infusion method by pump

Tube size: _____   Type of pump: _____

Formula: _____

Preparation of formula: _____

Schedule of feeding: _____

Positioning during feeding: _____

Positioning after feeding (and any positioning constraints): _____
_____

Amount of food or drink student can take by mouth (if any): _____

Student-specific procedure attached? _____ yes _____ no

Latex allergy present? _____ yes _____ no

Directions for Feeding Problems and Emergencies

Aspiration: _____

Tube displacement: _____

Nausea, vomiting, and cramping: _____

Diarrhea: _____

Infection: _____

Leaking of stomach contents: _____

Clogged tube: _____

FIGURE 9-7 Specialized areas to include in an IHP for tube feedings

ging. Information regarding the type of formula, its frequency of administration, exact times of administration, and how to reconstitute it (when applicable) should be included.

The individualized educational program (IEP) should include whether the student is being taught the procedure and in what manner (e.g., verbally to direct someone, partial participation, independent in all steps). Areas of instruction may include (a) understanding the purpose of tube feedings; (b) identifying the type of feeding tube and tip location; (c) demonstrating formula preparation; (d) demonstrating how to give the tube feeding (which may include checking residual volume, checking tube placement, assuming the correct position for feeding, flushing the tube, administering the formula, connecting the tube, closing the cap or clamping the tube); (e) demonstrating proper tube care (e.g., how to secure the tube, daily cleaning of site); (f) demonstrating proper equipment operation, cleaning, and storage; (g) understanding how to monitor nutritional status (e.g., weight taking, reporting of bloating or nausea); (h) demonstrating how to prevent and treat problems and emergencies (Young & White, 1992). See Figure 9-8 for sample IEP objectives.

Moving to Feeding

Many students who are tube fed will progress to feeding by mouth. This decision is made by the physician and must be closely coordinated with the physician and other specialists (e.g., nutritionist, gastroenterologist) who may be involved in

the student's care. The method for moving to oral feeding is to gradually eliminate one tube feeding at a time and provide an oral feeding in its place. This method helps evaluate whether the student will be motivated to eat orally when hunger occurs from a decrease in tube feeding. The quantity of calories consumed orally should ideally approximate the amount taken by tube. If this does not occur, an increase in calories may need to be provided at times that tube feeding is occurring (Luiselli & Luiselli, 1995).

Moving from tube feeding to oral feeding must also take into consideration food texture and composition. Students may go through a texture-change sequence beginning at liquids (e.g., water, milk, juice) or liquids with thickening agents to semisoft foods (e.g., yogurt, pudding), strained baby foods (infant cereals, vegetables), pureed foods (vegetables, fruits), thicker foods (e.g., cottage cheese, oatmeal), soft table foods (scrambled eggs, mashed potatoes), then ground foods (e.g., poultry) (Luiselli & Luiselli, 1995). Students may

---

Independent Performance of Task
The student will independently gather supplies and self-perform the tube-feeding procedure according to the prescribed step-by-step procedure with 100% accuracy for 2 weeks.

Partial Performance of Task
When given the equipment for tube feeding, the student will prepare the formula for tube feeding with 100% accuracy for 2 weeks.
The student will assist with performing the tube feedings by holding the syringe barrel at the proper height when the adult is pouring the formula with 100% accuracy for 1 week.

Directing the Task
The student will direct another person in gathering the correct materials listed on a checklist for tube feeding with 100% accuracy for 1 week.
The student will direct another person to perform each step of the prescribed procedure for tube feeding with 100% accuracy for 2 weeks.

Knowledge of the Task
The student will list the signs of infection at the tube feeding site with 80% accuracy for four consecutive sessions.
When asked what to do if he has nausea or abdominal cramping, the student will demonstrate how he will use his AAC device to alert another person to these problems with 100% accuracy on 10 of 10 opportunities.

FIGURE 9-8 Sample IEP objectives for tube feeding

then progress to foods that require more chewing to regular table food.

Food presentation, quantity, temperature, and preferences also must be considered when moving to oral feedings. Food presentation focuses on presenting food in a positive manner and not forcing the student to eat. In some situations the presentation may need to include oral motor stimulation for students who cannot tolerate the physical contact of a utensil and reject food and liquid. In these situations, a training sequence may begin with stimulation of the lips with a finger, to stimulation of lips with a spoon, to placement of the spoon between lips, to eventually having the student tolerate stimulation of spoon against the tongue and inner surface of the mouth. Students may refuse food when there is too much food on the utensil or the pace of the food presentation is too fast. Both food quantity and pace need to meet the individualized needs of the student (Luiselli & Luiselli, 1995). Student may also dislike certain foods, and appropriate alternatives may be given instead. The occupational therapist or speech-language pathologist will usually determine feeding program needs and activities.

Another consideration for moving to oral feeding is the location of the feeding and using reinforcement to encourage eating. Students who are learning to take food by mouth often need to be placed in a location where positive interaction can occur with a minimum of distractions. Sometimes being placed in a noisy, distracting area interferes with learning to feed orally. Over time, the location can be changed as feeding habits are established.

Some students moving from tube feeding to oral feeding demonstrate a strong dislike of oral feeding. In these instances, reinforcing items or activities need to be used to encourage oral eating. In a study by Luiselli (1994), two students with multiple disabilities who enjoyed rocking were allowed to sit in a rocking chair and were rocked noncontingently with no feeding demands in the area that would become the setting for mealtime. Using the same location and rocking chair, the students were presented with food to take and were contingently rocked only upon accepting the food. In this way the students received reinforcement (i.e., rocking) for accepting food. Another method simply uses positive reinforcement contingent upon the student's acceptance of food. Initially, reinforcement is provided after acceptance of each spoonful (1:1 ratio), and gradually the reinforcement is systematically thinned to a more intermittent schedule. Behavior programs such as these should be used after it is determined that there are no oral motor skill deficits interfering with transitioning to oral feeding (i.e., if a student lacks adequate jaw control, he may refuse oral feedings).

SUMMARY

Students who are unable to take food orally may receive nourishment through a feeding tube that goes into the stomach or small intestine. Some of the most common tube placements include (a) a nasogastric tube (NG tube), which is a tube going from the nose into the stomach; (b) a gastrostomy tube (G-tube), which is a tube going directly into the stomach; and (c) a gastrostomy button, which is a skin-level device going directly into the stomach. The student with these or other types of tubes may receive feedings on an intermittent or a continuous basis. It is important that the person performing tube feedings knows not only the student-specific steps of the procedure but what to do in emergencies such as aspiration or vomiting. Students should be taught to perform the procedure themselves whenever possible.

10

Toilet Training

ELISABETH T. COHEN,
PAUL A. ALBERTO,
KATHRYN WOLFF HELLER,
PAULA E. FORNEY,
AND TRUDY GOECKEL

Toileting is one of the most important self-help skills that can be taught to a student, because it is, by definition, an intensely private action. For students with physical disabilities, learning to use the toilet may be difficult due to positioning problems, communication problems, and sensory and motor abnormalities affecting the toileting process. Toilet-training students with physical disabilities often requires patience, consistency, adaptive equipment, assistive techniques, and systematic instruction.

Learning to use the toilet for urination and defecation is one of the basic developmental tasks typically acquired in early childhood. A student's ability to control these processes depends on several factors. First, the urinary and intestinal systems need to be intact. In an intact urinary system, kidneys extract water and waste products of metabolism from the blood, which are secreted as urine. Urine travels from the kidneys down the ureters to the bladder, a hollow organ made up of three layers of muscle (Rous, 1996). The bladder serves as a storage facility for urine. When the bladder is full, sphincter muscles at the base of the bladder release the urine. The urine then travels through the urethra to be expelled (see Figure 10-1a). A student's ability to control the release of urine from the body depends on having not only an intact system but also voluntary control of the sphincter muscles. These muscles are located at the base of the bladder and help retain urine in the bladder. Typically, a child without a disability gains voluntary control of the sphincter muscles between 2 and 3 years of age. The child must also be able to perceive when the bladder is full. The ability to detect a full bladder typically develops between 1 and 2 years of age (Frauman & Brandon, 1996).

In the intestinal tract, digestion and absorption of food occur primarily in the small intestines. The remaining unwanted waste material travels from the small intestine to the large intestine where further absorption occurs. Waste material travels slowly through the ascending colon, transverse colon, descending colon, and sigmoid colon of the large intestine and may be stored

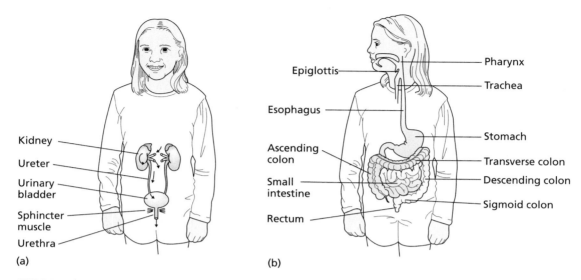

FIGURE 10-1 Anatomy of the urinary system (a) and the gastrointestinal tract (b)

there for up to 24 hours (see Figure 10-1b). Following meals, a marked increase in movement of waste material may occur. This increased movement, known as the *gastrocolic reflex,* may lead to a mass movement through the large intestine (colon). This causes the end section of the large intestine, known as the *rectum,* to expand. The expansion of the rectum with waste matter, or feces, automatically causes one set of muscles encircling the anus (the internal sphincter) to relax. The second set of muscles encircling the anus (the external sphincter muscles) will then relax, and defecation occurs. Typically, a child gains voluntary control of the external sphincter muscles of the anus and the sphincter muscles of the bladder at approximately the same time. As with the urinary system, the intestinal tract must be intact, and the child must be able to sense a feeling of fullness to control this process.

Several physical and health impairments can affect a student's ability to be toilet trained (see Table 10-1). Some students with cerebral palsy may have spastic bladders and sphincter abnormalities that affect continence. Additional difficulties with movement may make positioning on

the toilet difficult, even with adaptive equipment. Constipation is a frequent problem. Conditions such as spina bifida or spinal cord injury may result in an inability to sense bladder fullness, and control of urination may be lost due to a spastic or flaccid bladder. Bowel dysfunction is common in both of these conditions. Finally, students may have congenital abnormalities of the urinary or intestinal tract that make normal elimination impossible.

Some degenerative disorders cause a gradual loss of functional skills, including toileting ability. In conditions such as Duchenne muscular dystrophy, there can be abnormal bladder functioning and problems with constipation when the condition is in the end stages. In some situations, the increased dependence on others for assistance with toileting due to lack of ability to transfer independently to the toilet can be emotionally difficult for the student (Koehler & Loftin, 1994). This can result in the student not drinking adequate fluids or postponing going to the bathroom to avoid requesting help, which in turn may lead to accidents, constipation, or dehydration (Heller, Alberto, Forney et al., 1996).

Table 10-1 Medical Conditions That Can Affect Toileting Ability

Condition	Effects
Neuromotor conditions	
Cerebral palsy	Decreased sensitivity and muscle control may prevent a student from effectively controlling sphincter muscles; constipation possible due to lack of movement, dietary deficiencies, and dehydration; contractures can affect a person's ability to transfer to or sit on a toilet seat.
Spina bifida (myleomeningocele)	Can cause loss of bowel and bladder control.
Skeletal conditions	
Scoliosis, kyphosis, lordosis	Severe curvature of the spine can affect a child's ability to attain a seated position or maintain that position for sufficient time to allow a bowel movement to occur.
Congenital abnormalities	
Short bowel syndrome	Increased frequency of diarrhea due to malabsorption of water and other nutrients.
Fetal alcohol syndrome	Can result in multiple and varied congenital abnormalities, some of which can affect the urinary and intestinal tracts.
Degenerative disorders	
Muscular dystrophy	Progressive muscle weakness results in increasing need for assistance with toileting.
Spinal muscular atrophy	Progression of disease results in increasing need for assistance with toileting and transfers.
Major health conditions	
Cystic fibrosis	Causes poor digestion and chronic diarrhea; more frequent bowel movements, often accompanied by foul odor due to undigested fat.
Chronic conditions	Conditions resulting in hospitalization, or requiring certain medications and treatments, can interfere with consistency needed for toilet training.
Mental retardation	
Down syndrome	May result in constipation; if congenital heart defects are present, fluids may be restricted, exacerbating constipation.
Cognitive impairment	May result in postponement of toilet training by 1–2 years and longer training period.
Sensory impairment	
Visual impairment and deafblindness	Severe visual impairment or deafblindness do not affect a student's ability to learn toileting skills but do result in a loss of information that slows down the training process.

Several conditions may delay the student's acquisition of toileting skills. This includes having a sensory impairment, mental retardation, or chronic physical or health impairment. Students with visual impairments or deafblindness may have difficulty taking in information about the bathroom environment and the task. Often the student will need to be oriented to the position of the toilet, sink, towels, and soap. Students with cognitive impairments may lack an understanding of the components of toileting and have delays in obtaining necessary skills. Systematic instruction and consistency are critical in teaching toileting skills when cognitive impairments are present. Chronic conditions that involve hospitalizations, immobility, and certain medications or treatments may interfere with the consistency needed in teaching toileting. Also, if a student has had a colostomy (see Chapter 12) that has recently been closed, the student may have difficulty sensing fullness because of inexperience (Rushton, 1995).

DESCRIPTION OF
TOILET TRAINING

A toilet-training program consists of teaching numerous skills and a program of some design should be developed for all students. The outcomes of these programs will vary from student to student. For some students, the goal will be complete independence. Others will strive to achieve a maximal degree of participation in the toileting procedure. Partial outcomes may include some, but not all of the steps in a toileting procedure. For example, a student may learn to wash his hands after a diaper change, pass necessary toileting articles to a caretaker, or assist during transfers to and from a wheelchair. Some students may never achieve independence in toileting. In some instances, the nature of their physical disabilities may preclude independent toileting. For example, a student may not be able to tolerate a sitting position (Fraser et al., 1990). This might be due to severe torsion of the spine and contractures of the extremities. Thus, she will not be able to sit on a toilet seat long enough or with enough stability to urinate. However, this same student may learn to signal a need to use the toilet. Others may become independent by using external urinary catheters, clean intermittent catheterization, or ostomy management, when medical reasons indicate their use (see Chapters 11 and 12).

Many teachers and parents assume that students must have certain prerequisite skills before learning to use the toilet. For example, toilet training is sometimes unnecessarily postponed if a student cannot independently remove pants, undo buttons, or verbally indicate a need to go to the toilet. Rather than postponing, these skills should become part of the toilet-training program itself. Others may delay toilet training if the student does not have the ability to reach complete independence. This denies the student training in an essential skill that is chronologically age-appropriate, allows access to a greater number of environments, and enhances the perceptions of the student and others that he is capable (Baumgart et al., 1982).

Although toilet training should not be postponed due to some prerequisite skills, toilet training should occur when the student is maturationally ready. When bowel training is attempted too early, a student may hold back feces, leading to constipation and compaction (Connor, Williamson, & Siepp, 1978). Conversely, the student who holds in urine has an increased risk of urinary tract infections. The age at which students are ready to learn toileting skills is generally between 2 and 4 years (Honig, 1993). However, the age varies widely and needs to be individualized for each student. Students have different-sized bladders and different tolerances for sitting still. Males tend to have more difficulty with toilet training and may continue to have accidents for longer periods of time.

Collaboration is essential for developing a successful toileting plan, and a number of appropriate professionals should be included. First, the student's physician must be consulted to rule out any medical problems that might impede the progress of a toileting program. Students with multiple and severe disabilities are less healthy than their peers, with more urinary tract infections and other problems, such as intestinal parasites, that can hinder the student's toileting (Thompson & Guess, 1989; Orelove & Sobsey, 1991). The physician can screen and treat these problems. The physician will also be able to determine whether there is a medical problem that would inhibit independent toileting use such as the presence and extent of nerve or musculature problems. The physician can also prescribe stool softeners, bulk fiber, or dietary changes that will aid with the toileting process. Also, the student's physician should be consulted about side effects of medications that might inhibit toilet training. As seen in Table 10-2, several medications can interfere with the toileting process, and knowledge of their impact will help guide the construction of the training program.

The physical therapist, occupational therapist, and speech-language pathologist will also be able to contribute important information to assist with effective toilet training. The physical thera-

Table 10-2 Examples of Medications That Can Affect Toilet Training

Drug	Possible side effect
Over-the-counter	
Aspirin	Gastrointestinal tract irritations
Maalox	Constipation, passage of fat in feces
Antibiotics	
Neomycin	Decreased appetite, diarrhea, nausea
Chloramphenicol	Vomiting, malabsorption of nutrients
Tetracycline	Diarrhea, nausea, vomiting
Anticonvulsants	
Phenobarbitol	Gastrointestinal distress, constipation
Dilantin	Gastrointestinal distress
Laxatives	
Mineral oil	Abdominal cramps, gastrointestinal distress, excess fat in feces
Ex-Lax	Abdominal cramps due to hyperperistalsis
Corticosteroids	
Prednisone	Gastrointestinal distress
Diuretics	
Diamox reserpine	Increased urine output, gastrointestinal distress
Stimulants	
Ritalin	Decreased appetite resulting in decreased bulk in large intestine, nausea
Dexedrine	Decreased appetite resulting in decreased bulk in large intestine, nausea
Tranquillizers	
Mellaril	Increased appetite resulting in increased bulk in large intestine, dry mouth resulting in increased water intake, constipation, gastrointestinal distress

pist can recommend the most appropriate adaptive equipment to ensure effective positioning and stabilization on the toilet seat. The occupational therapist can recommend the use of needed devices to assist students in accessing and using toilet paper, flushing the toilet, and turning on faucets to wash hands. If the student is nonverbal, the speech-language pathologist can assist in providing information on various means and devices to allow the student to indicate a need to use the toilet or request assistance while in the restroom. Adaptations and devices used at school should be duplicated in the home for consistency and generalization.

Orelove and Sobsey (1991) suggest that a dietitian should be included on any transdisciplinary team. Dietitians can be contacted through the school system or the Department of Public Health. Many students with disabilities have modified diets. For example, students with disorders such as cerebral palsy with oral involvement may

be given pureed foods. However, pureed foods often lack fiber, protein, and certain vitamins (Sobsey, 1983); an unbalanced diet, especially one lacking fiber, will certainly have an effect on a student's stool and thus on the ability to eliminate waste. Similarly, the student dependent on tube feedings for nutrition may encounter problems due to the liquid diet or the type of formula being used (see Chapter 9).

ASSISTIVE DEVICES FOR TOILET TRAINING

Innumerable assistive devices are commercially available today that may assist the student with a physical impairment in the toileting process. These devices include adaptive toilets as well as assistive devices that may be used in the bathroom. Other devices may include those required for transferring the student from the wheelchair to the toilet, as well as adaptive clothing to assist with easier access for toileting.

Adaptive Toilets

A regular toilet may not provide the proper positioning or support for some students with physical impairments. In these instances, an adaptive toilet is necessary (see Figure 10-2). However, since there are several types of adaptive toilets, it is important to select one that provides the correct support and positioning. If the student is tense due to improper positioning or feels that he may fall off the adaptive toilet, he will unlikely be able to relax his muscles to urinate or defecate voluntarily.

Adaptive toilets fall into two categories: (a) stand-alone toilets and (b) devices that fit over the existing toilet. There are several different types of stand-alone toilets. Some are simple box-style potty chairs that typically have back support and/or armrests. For students who are more physically involved, some stand-alone chairs have additional side supports, head support, foot-rests, and a pad between the knees (abductor pad) to provide proper support. Straps are typically used to keep the student in the proper position.

For some students, the second category of using a seating frame that fits over the regular toilet may be appropriate. As seen in Figure 10-2c, seating frames may provide back support and armrests and can easily fit over the existing toilet to provide some support. Other devices include a toilet seat attached to a metal or plastic frame that fits over the existing toilet seat (Figure 10-2b). Simple devices such as a toilet seat riser that fits on the toilet seat to increase the height of the toilet seat may allow for easier lowering and rising of ambulatory students. For smaller students, adaptive seats with reduced hole size may assist the student in staying correctly positioned on the seat may be used.

(a)

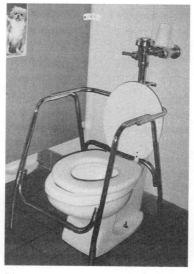
(b)

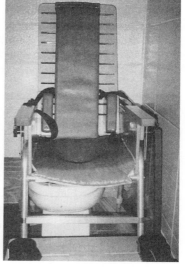
(c)

FIGURE 10-2 Examples of adaptive toilets: (a) a standard toilet with extra handrails attached to the wall for additional support, (b) a simple metal frame that fits over the toilet to provide a smaller toilet seat and extra handrails, and (c) a seating frame that fits over the existing toilet to provide trunk, head, and arm support.

Devices that fit over the regular toilet to provide support may not be as appropriate as stand-alone toilets for some small students who are severely physically involved. When appropriate, devices that fit over the regular toilet take up less room and can make cleanup easier. The physical therapist will be an essential member of the team to help determine the most appropriate adaptive toilet. Ongoing assessment is important since the adaptive toilet typically will need to change as the student grows.

Other Adaptive Devices

Other devices may be used for toileting. In some instances, students may be able to use a male or female urinal from their wheelchair or move into a position to use these devices easier than to an adaptive toilet (see Figure 10-3). Another option includes the use of a bedpan (or fracture bedpan) for urination or defecation. Some students have special wheelchairs with a removable portion of the seat and an attachable container that the student can directly use for toileting. In these instances, the student may use adaptive clothing for easier undressing and dressing.

General adaptive equipment is often needed in the bathroom as well. Bathroom handrails and widened stalls often assist with independent or semi-independent transfers for students with

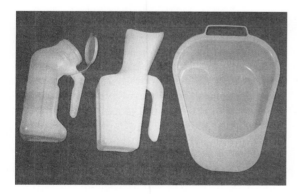

FIGURE 10-3 From left to right: A male urinal, a female urinal, and a fracture bedpan.

physical disabilities. Sometimes students with sensory impairments may feel unsafe or unbalanced on the toilet and require handrails or a foot stool to provide added stability and a sense of safety. Adapted sinks allow wheelchairs underneath. In addition, handles may be needed for the student to wash hands after toileting. The occupational and physical therapists can assist in modifying the bathroom for easier use.

Students may also require adaptive equipment for transfers. A pivot disc allows the student to easily pivot from the wheelchair to the toilet by standing on the rotating disc. For students requiring more assistance, transfer boards may be used in which the student sits on the board and moves along the board from the wheelchair to the toilet. In other instances, a lift system may be used in which the student is placed on a lift and moved from the wheelchair to the toilet. (See Chapter 5 for more information on transferring equipment.) The physical therapist will assist in selecting the most appropriate transfer devices.

ASSISTIVE STRATEGIES FOR TOILET TRAINING

Toilet-training the student with physical disabilities presents unique problems. Often, sitting and staying comfortably and securely on the toilet seat must be dealt with before training can begin. Furthermore, the process of transferring to the toilet and the position achieved on the seat must enhance relaxation for toileting to occur. The teacher and parents will need to work closely with the physical therapist to achieve correct positioning and transfers to and from the toilet.

Environmental Arrangement

Learning to use the toilet requires the student to relax enough to release the muscles used to control urination and defecation. Having a calm environment may be helpful, especially one free of sudden noises that may result in the student with cerebral palsy suddenly tensing (or going into a startle reflex). Some environmental noises, such as having a faucet running, or a book or toy may assist the student in relaxing to urinate. However, the bathroom should not become a playroom. If toys and books are distracting from the task, they should not be available.

Transfers

Although it may seem easier to simply carry the small student to the toilet who could otherwise assist in transferring, it will become more difficult as the student grows larger and heavier. Part of learning how to use the toilet is teaching the student how to transfer to and from the toilet. It will be important that the adult learn proper handling, carrying, and transferring techniques to properly assist the student and teach the appropriate skills. Proper transferring is important not only for correct instruction of the student but also for the student's safety and to prevent back injury to the individual who is assisting the student.

Numerous techniques may assist with proper transferring from a wheelchair to a toilet. The selection of the technique will partially depend on the extent to which the student can assist with the transfer. Techniques range from having the student correctly position the wheelchair next to the toilet for students who can support weight on their legs and require minimal or no assistance, to using a one- or two-person lift (or mechanical lift) for students who are unable to physically participate in the transfer process. Although there are multiple transfer techniques, the teacher should have knowledge and skill in the following areas: (a) proper lifting and handling techniques, (b) proper positioning of the equipment, (c) determining which aspects of the transfer the student can participate or learn, (d) determining how to safely monitor the student when she is independently or semiindependently transferring, (e) knowing how to break a fall to minimize injury, and (f) proper positioning of the student on the assistive equipment. For specific information, see Chapter 5, which contains detailed information on each transfer technique, as well as lifting and handling techniques to promote safe transfers for the student and teacher.

Positioning

The goals to be achieved in positioning a student on the toilet are to maintain normalized muscle tone, to maintain the alignment of the body, and to ensure that the student is stable (Orelove & Sobsey, 1991). To achieve these, the physical therapist may suggest certain handling techniques to use prior to the student being seated on the toilet. Handling and positioning techniques may also be suggested to assist the student to remain properly seated. (See Chapter 6 for descriptions of the various techniques.) In addition to handling techniques, special equipment may be required to attain a proper sitting position. Fortunately, there is a wide range of adaptive toilets, toilet seats, and other aids commercially available.

The student who cannot hold himself in an erect sitting position will need to be placed so that his hips, knees, and ankles are flexed to 90 degrees, his head and shoulders are in midline, his arms are relaxed, his trunk is stable, and his feet are supported. Appropriate positioning with the body in a flexed, supported position can facilitate elimination (Reid, 1996). Even when the correct adapted toilet is selected, it is important that the student be properly positioned on the adapted toilet. Often if the student's buttocks are not placed far enough back on the toilet seat and the hips are not in the correct position, the student will start to slide out of the chair. This will inhibit relaxing to use the toilet. Also, it is very important that the straps of the adapted toilet are placed correctly to keep the student in the proper position. Typically straps are placed across the lower hip area (rather than across the stomach) to keep the hip at a 90-degree angle and allow the student to be securely seated on the toilet. Straps should not be used as a means to keep an active student from leaving a place in which he has no interest. A physical therapist will provide information and demonstration for proper positioning and use of the adaptive equipment.

Abdominal Massage

The physical therapist may suggest and demonstrate certain exercises or other activities prior to the student's toileting time. These can help relax the student, thus facilitating bowel movements. One such assistive strategy is abdominal massage in which the individual gently massages the abdominal area, going along the path of the large intestine. This can help relieve stress, constipation, and abdominal muscle tension.

Medications

In some instances, a physician may prescribe medication to assist with bladder or bowel management. Some medications may be used to improve bladder storage capacity (e.g., anticholinergic medications). Stool softeners, laxatives, or an enema may be used on a periodic or regular basis to assist with elimination (see the section "Bowel Training" for more information).

INSTRUCTIONAL STRATEGIES FOR TOILET TRAINING

Toilet training involves two different systems: the urinary system and the gastrointestinal system. Typically the student will be taught simultaneously to use the toilet for both urination and defecation, although most students will learn bowel training more quickly than bladder training because it is usually more predicable and there is a stronger sensation for defecation than urination (Wong, 1995). When considering a toileting program, it is important to remember that if a student cannot be trained to use the toilet for one system (e.g., has a colostomy), training can still occur for the other system.

General Techniques for Toilet Training

When teaching a student to use the toilet, several general principles may be followed to assist with learning this skill, as seen in Figure 10-4. One of the first principles is to familiarize the student with the toilet he will be using. If the student has a visual impairment, he should be allowed to explore a clean toilet under supervision to aid in understanding the experience (Heubner, Prickett, Welch, & Joffee, 1995).

A second principle is associating toileting activities with the bathroom. Toilet training should be focused on the bathroom, whenever possible, so that the student learns the purpose of this room. Since toileting is considered a personal act, toileting should occur in such a manner that affords the student privacy, dignity, and respect. Besides giving explanations to the student regarding the toileting process, a parent of the same gender as the student may wish to demonstrate toilet use.

A third principle of toilet training is establishing times to use the toilet. The student should be taken to the toilet during student- and time-directed intervals. Accidents often occur because the student is distracted by an enjoyable activity. Students may be asked or taken to the bathroom at certain times to avoid these accidents. Having the student placed on the toilet during scheduled times will help establish a routine (see "Trip-Training Method"). Also, when the student shows signs of needing to use the toilet, such as crossing legs, acting fidgety, acting agitated, facial reddening, or grimacing, he should be placed on the toi-

1. Familiarize the student with the toilet.
2. Associate toileting activities with the bathroom.
3. Establish times to use the toilet (student-directed and time-directed).
4. Decide if boy will stand or sit to urinate.
5. Reinforce successes.
6. Teach child to perceive feelings of fullness.
7. Teach proper wiping and hand washing.

FIGURE 10-4 General principles of toilet training

let. When the student is seated on the toilet, he should be well positioned and relaxed.

A fourth principle is determinating if a boy stands or sits to urinate. The parents should make this decision and coordinate it with the school. Although most boys are taught to stand, boys who fatigue easily or are unsteady may need to sit to urinate. Later, he may switch to standing if this is preferred and physically possible. If the boy is sitting, he will need to be taught to point the penis downward into the toilet. A urine guard that prevents the urine from spraying out may be helpful.

A fifth principle for toilet training is reinforcing successes. When the student is successful, he should be praised for the accomplishment. However, before emptying the adaptive toilet or flushing the toilet, it is important that the adult explain what is about to occur first. Some students become upset upon seeing their accomplishment flushed down the toilet or seeing what they consider to be part of their body disappear. In some instances, it is helpful to reinforce the student for flushing or dispose of the wastes after the student has left the bathroom.

A sixth principle for toilet training is teaching the student to perceive feelings of fullness. Students typically develop the ability to perceive the sensation of bladder fullness between 1 and 2 years of age. However, some students with physical impairments or health impairments may have alterations in sensation making it more difficult to perceive this sensation. For example, a student with chronic renal failure who just received a renal transplant may never have experienced the sensation of the bladder filling (Frauman & Brandon, 1996). In these instances, it is important to teach the feeling of fullness. First, it needs to be determined that there is a full bladder. This may be accomplished through a nurse teaching the teacher or parent to percuss the bladder. (Percussion of the bladder involves tapping a certain way on the lower abdomen over the bladder and the sound will provide information if the bladder is full or not). Another method is by using an external bladder device (e.g., Bladder Manager) that

uses ultrasound to give information on the amount of urine in the bladder. The third way is to select times that the student is most likely to have a full bladder (e.g., after lunch). After ascertaining that the bladder is full, the student may be placed into a prone position to allow the weight of the student on the bladder to enhance the student's ability to perceive a full bladder. Gently pressing on the lower abdomen while giving an explanation of this feeling may also help the student learn to respond to the body's sensation of fullness (Frauman & Brandon, 1996).

Students often take a longer period of time to detect a full bladder when sleeping. Accidents are common at night and should be expected. Giving decreased fluids near bedtime often helps decrease these accidents, as well as waking the student around midnight to use the toilet (Wong, 1995). Some students may be taught through the use of a wet-bed alarm. A wet-bed alarm typically has auditory, vibration, and/or flashing light settings that are meant to wake the student when moisture is detected. Over time, the student usually learns to wake up when the bladder is full instead of the alarm waking him up after urination has taken place.

A seventh principle of toilet training is teaching proper hygiene. One part of this is teaching the student to wipe when physically possible. It is important that girls are taught to wipe from front to back to avoid any feces on the urethra. This can result in an infection. After each wipe, the paper should be disposed of and new paper obtained. Students who cannot wipe themselves due to physical impairments may be able to use an adaptive device or partially participate by tearing the amount of toilet paper needed. Afterward, both the student and the adult should wash hands using proper hand-washing techniques (see Chapter 1 for hand-washing techniques).

As with any skill, toilet training can be broken down into smaller parts. The task analysis will vary greatly according to each student's physical and cognitive capabilities as well as the student's specific procedure. Table 10-3 illustrates two different task analyses.

Table 10-3 Task Analyses for Students with and without Physical Impairment

Ambulatory	Physical impairment—wheelchair user
1. Request to use restroom.	1. Request to use restroom.
2. Go into restroom into stall.	2. Move into restroom.
	3. Position chair.
	4. Lock brakes.
	5. Undo seat belt.
	6. Move to edge of seat.
	7. Assist with assisted standing.
	8. Hold onto handrail.
3. Unfasten pants and pull down.	9. Help unfasten pants and pull down.
3.1 Unfasten belt.	
3.2 Undo zipper.	
3.3 Pull down pants.	
3.4 Pull down underwear.	
4. Sit on toilet.	10. Sit on toilet.
5. Urinate.	11. Urinate.
6. Wipe self.	12. Wipe self.
6.1 Take toilet paper.	
6.2 Pull off roll.	
6.3 Wipe self from front to back.	
	13. Call for assistance.
7. Stand up.	14. Hold handrail and assist with standing.
8. Pull up clothing.	15. Assist in pulling up pants and fastening.
8.1 Pull up underwear.	
8.2 Pull up pants.	
8.3 Zip up zipper.	
8.4 Fasten belt.	
	16. Assist with turning and sitting on wheelchair seat.
	17. Move back into seat.
	18. Put on seat belt.
	19. Unlock brakes.
9. Flush and go wash hands.	20. Flush and go wash hands.

Trip-Training Method

In the late 1960s and early 1970s Azrin and Foxx developed a method of toilet-training adults with severe and profound cognitive delays that has had a profound impact on subsequent toilet-training programs. Their method uses positive reinforcement for appropriate toileting behavior, positive practice to inhibit inappropriate toileting behavior, immediate feedback for inappropriate urination using an alarm system attached to the undergarments of the trainee, and increased quantities of liquids to increase the frequency of urination. Other self-help skills were taught in conjunction with the toileting program, including dressing and hygiene skills. The goal of the program was self-initiation and, if pos-

sible, complete independence (Anderson, 1982; Foxx & Azrin, 1973). Since Azrin and Foxx first published their program, numerous studies have attempted to replicate their results by either following their program or making various adaptations.

The most successful toilet-training programs involve some form of the **trip-training method.** A trip-training method is one that primarily uses scheduled times for the student to go to the bathroom, based on when the student typically urinates. Timing of the toileting sequence is based on three factors. The first factor is student request; nonverbal students will need an attention-getting device such as a buzzer labeled with a toilet symbol. The second factor is the presence of student cues. Student cues include clutching the crotch or crossing the legs for urination and reddening of the face or grimacing for defecation. The third factor involves basing toileting times on data collection taken before beginning trip training.

Pretraining Data. Before beginning any toileting program, the teacher must collect data on incidences of elimination. These pretraining (baseline) data are essential for two reasons. First, they provide a baseline with which to compare latter results and assess the success of the toileting program. Second, pretraining data allow prediction of patterns of elimination. Those times determined to be the most frequent for elimination become the preset times for trips to the toilet. Predicting successful toileting times for the student will save hours of unsuccessful training and prevent the student from becoming frustrated by unsuccessful attempts in the bathroom.

Pretraining data collection occurs by checking the student every half hour and recording the results on a data sheet. Although data may be collected from 3 days to 1 month (Snell, 1993), 2 weeks is usually recommended. Ideally, data should be taken both at home and school so that the trip-training program can occur in both environments. When this can occur, the student will have been checked every half hour from the time the student wakes up, until he goes to bed at night. During this data collection, the student's routine should not be changed in any way. If he is in diapers, he should remain in diapers. He should not be taken to the toilet during this pretraining baseline phase unless that is already a part of his routine.

The data collection form should be quick and easy to complete. The form in Figure 10-5 holds 7 days of data and has a column along the left to be filled in with the times that the student will be checked for accidents. The teacher or parent fills the chart out as follows: (a) enter *D* if the student is dry when checked; (b) enter *U* if the student has urinated; (c) enter *BM* if the student has had a bowel movement; (d) enter *U/BM* if the student has both urinated and defecated. If the student has not yet been put on the toilet, all data will be

recorded beneath the "Pants" column (as all accidents will have occurred in the student's pants). If the student is sometimes put on the toilet, data will be recorded beneath the column indicating where the student urinated or defecated. For instance, if the student was checked at 2:00 P.M. and had urinated, a *U* would be placed in the column under "Pants" across from that time. If he was placed on the toilet at 10:00 A.M., half an hour after his snack, and he urinated and had a bowel movement, a *U/BM* would be placed in the column under "Toilet" across from that time.

Toileting patterns may be related more to activities occurring in the classroom and home than to exact times. For this reason, data sheets should reflect times when the student eats, drinks, and participates in physical activity or rests (if this entails a change in position from upright to prone). This can easily be achieved by highlighting the times for various activities. For example, if the student eats lunch at 11:30 and has a snack at 2:00, use a green highlighter to indicate those two times on the data sheet.

Finally, Snell (1993) recommends recording whether toileting behavior is student or teacher initiated. Student-initiated behavior is marked with a "+"; teacher-initiated behavior is marked "—." For example, a *U+* would represent a student requesting a trip to the bathroom to urinate. This is especially useful when working with students with cognitive impairments. For these students, initiating the sequence may be a related skill that the teacher can include in the task analysis. Furthermore, on subsequent data forms the number of pluses can be counted and compared to baseline to record levels of increasing independence.

Setting the Trip-Training Schedule. Upon completion of 2 weeks of data, the teacher and parents should analyze the data and identify patterns of elimination to formulate a toilet-training plan. To establish the times when the student is most likely to urinate or have a bowel movement, the teacher need only add across the columns and enter the totals in the last column. A pattern

ELIMINATION RECORD

CHILD'S NAME:_____

DATE BEGUN:_____

KEY

D=Child is dry
U=Child has urinated
BM=Child has had bowel movement
U/BM=Child has had both

Time	Day 1		Day 2		Day 3		Day 4		Day 5		Day 6		Day 7		Total
	Pants	Toilet	Pants	Toilet	Pants	Toilet	Pants	Toilet	Pants	Toilet	Pants	Toilet	Pants	Toilet	
Total															

FIGURE 10-5 Data collection form for the trip-training method

should emerge. To set a trip-training schedule, the teacher should look at those times during the day when the student most frequently has accidents and schedule bathroom trips approximately 10 minutes before that time. Data collection should continue. If at the end of the 1 week, the student is still wetting outside the bathroom, the schedule can be adjusted by moving the toileting time forward another 10 minutes. Typically a student's schedule will consist of four to eight trips per day, with at least 1½ hours between each trip (Baker & Brightman, 1989).

As mentioned earlier, toileting times may be more dependent on the student's daily activities than on the time of day. For example, teachers may find that a student urinates midmorning on some days and late morning on others. Closer inspection may reveal that juice was given at different times on these days. If the student urinated 30 minutes after receiving fluids, the teacher has probably discovered the student's urination pattern. This example makes apparent the need to set a consistent daily schedule of activities that the student will follow for the duration of the toileting program. In addition, teachers and parents must be both consistent with the trip-training schedule and alert to signs that the student needs to use the restroom at unscheduled times. These signs vary from student to student but can include clutching at the crotch, crossing legs, squatting, and turning red in the face.

Instruction. Once the trip-training schedule is set, instruction can begin. The teacher will need to write out a detailed task analysis to be followed by all staff at school and by the parents at home (refer back to Table 10-3 for a sample task analysis). Since each student has differing impairments and problems, task analyses must be student-specific and therefore will vary among students.

Initial toileting behaviors may need to be shaped. For instance, the teacher may encounter a student who cannot sit still for a long period of time. Toilet training for this student would include reinforcing the student for sitting on the

toilet for 20 seconds, and then 30 seconds, and then 45 seconds, and so on, until the student is able to sit long enough to eliminate. Conversely, the teacher may encounter a student who falls asleep as soon as she is placed on the toilet. This student should be engaged in a running monologue describing exactly what she should be doing, keeping her awake and on task. She should be reinforced for staying awake and on task for successively longer periods of time. Usually the student should be on the toilet no longer than 5 minutes for urination and no longer than 5 to 10 minutes for defecation.

Toileting behavior is a complex chain of behaviors; each behavior is dependent on the previous behavior to act as a stimulus for the next link in the chain. Toileting can be taught using a backward chaining procedure or as a whole task (Alberto & Troutman, 1999). When a backward chaining procedure is used, instruction is provided on the last step of the procedure first. The teacher gives the student a prompt, such as "Time to go to the bathroom," and then helps the student undress, sit on the toilet, clean herself, pull up her pants, and flush. Instruction begins with the last step in the chain: hand washing. Once she reaches criterion for the last step, the next to last step is taught and so on. Backward chaining, while teaching the toileting steps in reverse order, ensures that the student completes the task and is reinforced for doing so.

When teaching the toileting procedure as a whole task, the teacher gives instruction on those steps listed in the task analysis that the student cannot presently accomplish. The teacher can use verbal or physical prompts to achieve each step, according to the student's needs. At the start of instruction, each step of the task should be reinforced. As the criterion is reached, reinforcement is faded to every other step, every third step, and so on. (See Chapter 2 for more information.)

The teacher should be very consistent both with the schedule and with expected behavior in the bathroom. If the student has not urinated after 5 minutes, she should be removed from the toilet and returned to class. She should not be reprimanded if she does not use the toilet at the scheduled time. Neither should the student be reprimanded for accidents. Scolding will only cause the student to become tense at toileting times and may cause more frequent accidents.

As the student's proficiency increases, the teacher should slowly withdraw from the bathroom. The teacher can begin by cleaning the sink or filling out the toileting data form near the door of the restroom, eventually moving into the hall and finally away from the restroom altogether. This ensures that the student has privacy and does not become overly dependent on the teacher for guidance. The student should not be left alone for longer than 5 minutes and should be supervised. Upon reentering the bathroom, the teacher should remember to give verbal praise for appropriate behavior.

Finally, data should be taken throughout the toilet-training process. This gives the teacher a means by which to evaluate progress in the toilet-training program. Periodic adjustments, adaptations, or changes in instructional strategy may be necessary. Changes in the student's schedule, health problems, or other sources of stress may periodically cause an increase in accidents. However, consistency on the teacher's part will lead to a successful outcome.

Bowel Training

The goal of **bowel training** is for the student to empty the bowel completely on a regularly scheduled basis. Training the bowel to empty routinely at a specific time helps establish reflex assistance as well as avoid many bowel problems such as overloading the bowel and incomplete emptying (Reid, 1996; Suddarth, 1991). Teaching a student to empty his bowel on a schedule may occur in conjunction with the toilet-training program used for emptying the bladder.

Before beginning a bowel program, it is important to examine the student's exercise and diet. Physical movement, exercise, and changes in position will aid in bowel evacuation. Also, the diet should contain sufficient fluid and fiber to promote a healthy bowel habit.

Selection of the time to target for bowel evacuation should be based on the student's and family's routine. Usually bowel training is targeted in the morning or about 30 minutes after a meal to take advantage of the natural gastrocolic reflex (which stimulates bowel emptying after a meal). The timing must also occur when the student is not rushed and can relax on the toilet. At the determined time, the student is taken to the restroom and encouraged. Techniques such as leaning over a rolled-up towel may also be used.

In some instances, digital stimulation (using a finger in the anus to stimulate elimination) or the use of a suppository (e.g., Dulcolax) may be used along with the natural gastrocolic reflex to initiate having the bowel movement. Digital stimulation or suppositories can relax the anal sphincter and promote the reflex contraction of the rectum that results in bowel evacuation. Sometimes these are an essential part of the daily bowel-training program for students with certain physical disabilities. Other students may require stool softeners or mild laxatives as a part of their bowel-training program to achieve bowel continence (Reid, 1996). It is important that digital stimulation, suppositories, or medication be directed for use by the appropriate health personnel. The total bowel-training program should be part of the student's individualized health plan, although it is typically performed at home.

Success in achieving bowel continence is dependent not only on the consistent implementation of a bowel-training program but also on the presence of an anal wink (ancutaneous reflex). The anal wink is a reflex closing of the anal sphincter. When this reflex is absent, as may be the case in some students with spina bifida (myelomeningocele), the anal sphincter has less tone, which affects the ability to retain and expel the feces. In some instances the feces may ooze out of the anus continually or be expelled with movement, coughing, or laughing. Before beginning bowel training, it will be helpful to ask medical personnel whether an anal wink is present because its presence indicates that total bowel continence is more likely to be achieved (Reid, 1996).

TOILETING PROBLEMS AND EMERGENCIES

Several different toileting problems and emergencies may interfere with the toileting process or occur because of improper toileting. Some of these include urinary tract infections, constipation, impaction, diarrhea, overhydration, intestinal parasites, skin breakdown, pica, and fecal smearing.

Urinary Tract Infections

Students with cerebral palsy develop urinary tract infections at three times the rate of their peers (Geralis, 1998). Students with spina bifida or other problems affecting the spinal cord may depend on catheterization (see Chapter 11), which also increases the risk of urinary tract infections. Students with severe and profound intellectual disabilities also contract these infections at a higher rate, partially due to their inability to properly clean themselves after a bowel movement.

Symptoms of a urinary tract infection may include frequent urination, cloudy urine, foul-smelling urine, and/or a burning sensation during urination. Related symptoms may include fever, vomiting, abdominal pain, and increased toileting accidents (Wong, 1995). It is vital that these infections be identified and treated by the student's physician as quickly as possible because untreated urinary tract infections can lead to more serious infections of the kidney. Urinary tract infections will also interfere with the success of a toilet-training program because of frequency of urination and a burning sensation that makes toileting uncomfortable.

Constipation

Constipation is having difficult or infrequent bowel movements. It can result from an insufficient amount of movement, lack of physical exercise, inadequate hydration, inadequate diet, or psychogenic reasons. To help decrease the occurrence of constipation, the student who uses a wheelchair should be taken out of the wheelchair and positioned in alternate positions several times per day. Also, participation in adaptive physical education is important. To determine whether constipation is occurring from dietary problems, a journal of the quantity and type of food and liquid given to the student should be kept. This record can give the parents and teacher insight into this problem and serve as a reference if the problem persists and a physician is consulted. Constipation resulting from psychogenic causes may occur when a student begins a toilet-training program too soon or resists going to the bathroom (Connor et al., 1978). Gentleness and understanding during the toileting program is essential. If constipation occurs, it will be important to determine the cause to intervene properly. Medical personnel are important in helping to determine the cause and intervention.

Impaction

A fecal impaction is the collection of hardened stool in the rectum or lower sigmoid that occurs from prolonged retention and accumulation of stool. Symptoms of a fecal impaction include an inability to have a bowel movement (although the student may have a desire to defecate), rectal pain, and abdominal cramping. Sometimes there is diarrhea or liquid seepage around the impaction. Individuals with neurological disorders (e.g., cerebral palsy, spinal cord injury) are at increased risk of fecal impaction (Suddarth, 1991).

Because a fecal impaction may appear as diarrhea, it is important that the possibility of a fecal impaction be ruled out before any treatment be given. This is imperative since the treatment for diarrhea may be contraindicated for a fecal impaction. Medical personnel should be contacted for appropriate diagnosis and treatment.

Diarrhea

Diarrhea is an excess loss of water and electrolytes that occurs with the abnormal elimination of frequent liquid stools. Diarrhea may be caused by any number of problems, including infections (e.g., bacterial, viral, fungal, parasitic, protozoal), allergies to certain foods, metabolic disorders, irritation of gastrointestinal tract by foods, mechanical disorders (e.g., incomplete small bowel obstruction), and congenital anomalies. Although symptoms will vary depending on the intensity and type of diarrhea, some of the symptoms are fever, loss of appetite, loose fluid stools, increased frequency of stools (ranging from 2 to 20 a day), behavior change (e.g., irritability, weakness, stupor), abnormal respirations (e.g., fast or decreased), and dehydration (e.g., decreased urinary output, poor skin turgor, dry skin, eyes sunken) (Suddarth, 1991).

The parent or guardian should be contacted if diarrhea is occurring at school and the student sent home. The parent or guardian should contact the physician for additional instructions. Providing the student with additional liquids is beneficial while waiting for the student's parent or guardian to pick up the student from school. However, when diarrhea is severe, a severe loss of fluid and electrolytes can be life-threatening. If the student shows signs of distress (e.g., rapid heart rate, difficult respirations, blue- or gray-colored skin, changes in responsiveness), emergency personnel should be called.

Overhydration

Students with physical disabilities, especially those with oral involvement, frequently do not drink enough liquids during the day. They are at risk of dehydration unless fluids are scheduled throughout the day. However, students can be given too much fluid. This sometimes occurs when increased liquid intake is used to encourage students to urinate. In some instances, this can lead to overhydration and water poisoning. Students with a severe or profound cognitive impairment who cannot indicate when they have had enough liquid are at greater risk for water poisoning. Symptoms may include nausea, vomiting, and muscular twitching. Severe overhydration can lead to seizures, coma, and death (Thompson & Hanson, 1983). Increased liquids should be used only after consultation with the student's physician.

Intestinal Parasites

There are several different types of intestinal parasites that individuals may acquire, including amoebas, hookworm, roundworm, and *Giardia lamblia* (protozoan). Contraction of these parasites may result in enteritis (inflammation of the intestine), with symptoms such as abdominal pain or distension, diarrhea, constipation, or related gastrointestinal complaints. If the teacher or parent notices changes in toileting behavior, the student should be taken to his physician to rule out parasitic infection or other conditions.

Skin Breakdown

Urine and fecal matter are caustic to the skin and can quickly cause the skin to become irritated. If not kept clean, skin cells will begin to break down leading to infection and ulceration (decubitus ulcers). Red or swollen skin, rashes, itchy skin, or skin sores are all signs of skin problems. Because of the location of these infections and the increased level of moisture and lack of air circulation, infections can take weeks to heal. Students who wear diapers and who spend a majority of their day sitting in a wheelchair are particularly prone to this problem. It is vital to prevent these infections before they occur.

Students with physical disabilities must learn to cleanse themselves thoroughly. This can be difficult if the student has contractures in the groin area. If possible, the student should help perform this task. Students wearing diapers or who have had an accident should be cleaned with warm water and a mild soap each time they are toileted. Skin should be completely dry before the student pulls up his pants or puts on a fresh diaper. Powder, easily available from the local pharmacy, can help keep the student dry.

Pica and Fecal Smearing

Two problematic behaviors that may arise during toilet training are pica and fecal smearing. *Pica* is the consumption of inedible or nonnutritive objects, including feces. *Fecal smearing* is the act of smearing feces on oneself or the walls and floor of the bathroom. These behaviors occur more frequently among students with severe or profound cognitive impairment. However, students with normal intelligence can develop these problem behaviors as well. It is patently obvious that both of these behaviors can lead to major sanitary and health problems.

Pica is especially hazardous in that the ingestion of feces (or other objects small enough for the student to swallow, including dirt, rocks, sticks, coins, etc.) can lead to poisoning, infection, intestinal obstruction, and even death (Foxx & Martin, 1975). Intestinal obstruction occurs when indigestible objects become lodged in the intestine. Liquid will pass around the obstruction, giving the student watery stool. As more material becomes impacted behind the obstruction, the abdomen becomes extended and tender. The student will have abdominal cramps and may run a fever as infection sets in. Surgery may be required to remove the obstruction.

A behavior management program aimed at complete extinction of these behaviors should be instituted if either behavior is observed. For pica or fecal smearing to occur, feces must be present, the student must see the feces, and the student must have access to the feces. Students who exhibit these behaviors should not be left unattended in the bathroom. When they have a bowel movement, they should flush the toilet immediately.

Fisher et al. (1994) list nine procedures found to be effective in reducing pica. Among them is facial screening. Facial or lower body screening can be used to prevent the student from seeing or reaching for the feces. Facial screening can be accomplished in the bathroom by tying a scarf loosely around the student's neck. The student attempting to reach into the toilet should have his hand gently redirected away from the toilet. The scarf can then be lifted over his eyes to screen his view. Lower body screening works in much the same way. A skirt of fabric is tied around the waist of the student so that the material drapes loosely over the student's legs, obstructing his view of the toilet. This will also prevent him from reaching into the toilet. The teacher should make sure that the student does not remain on the toilet too long and that he has something else to hold, such as toilet paper or a token for a reinforcer.

MANAGEMENT ISSUES FOR TOILET TRAINING

Individualized Health Plan and Individualized Educational Program

As an individualized health care plan is prepared, several areas should be included for the student's toileting program (see Figure 10-6). First, any physical problems that might adversely affect the student's ability to be toilet trained should be noted. Any medications that are used to improve continence or that may affect the toileting process should be recorded with their purpose and side effects. If the student is on a bowel-training program, the type should be recorded. A general toilet- or trip-training method should be noted. Student-specific procedural guidelines should also be included, containing the method of transfer from the wheelchair to the toilet and any adaptive equipment that the student will need. The IHP should contain guidelines for handling problems such as constipation and diarrhea and who should be contacted if questions or problems arise. Any creams, ointments, or powders used for skin care should be noted. Finally, a copy of the proposed toilet-training program, signed by the student, staff, and parents, should be included.

The individualized educational program should include the proposed training program and the level of participation of the student (e.g., verbal direction, partial participation, or independence). Besides the actual toileting procedure, areas of instruction may include (a) indicating when need to use the toilet, (b) assisting with transfers, (c) dressing and undressing, and (d) proper hand-washing technique. Figure 10-7 shows some sample IEP

Medical Problems That Will Affect Toilet Training: _____

_____

Medications That Are Prescribed to Enhance Continence: _____

_____

Medications That Will Interfere with Continence: _____

_____

Type of Adaptive Equipment and/or Assistive Strategies to Be Used: _____

_____

_____

Child-Specific Procedure Attached? _____ yes _____ no

Is the child on a trip-training schedule? _____

Is there a specific bowel-training program? _____

Other: _____

Directions for Problems and Emergencies

Suspected urinary tract infection: _____

Diarrhea: _____

Constipation/impaction: _____

Skin breakdown: _____

Change in urinary or bowel habit: _____

Fluid and Diet Considerations

Special diet: _____

Activity

Restrictions: _____

Positioning plan: _____

Adaptive PE: _____

FIGURE 10-6 Specialized information to include in an IHP for toileting

objectives across three levels of participation, as well as knowledge–based objectives.

Augmentative Communication

The nonverbal student will need to be provided with some means to indicate a need to use the restroom. This can be accomplished using a sign or gesture, picture symbol, bell, buzzer, or augmentative communication device placed within easy access of the student. Further, the nonverbal student will need some way to call for assistance from the bathroom. A bell or buzzer can be attached to the wall or toilet paper dispenser.

Independent Performance of Task

The student will tell the teacher when he needs to use the restroom and go to the restroom independently as needed with 100% accuracy for 2 weeks.

Partial Performance of Task

While using the trip-training method, the student will urinate in the toilet, when positioning on the toilet is assisted, with 100% accuracy on each occasion for 2 weeks.

With the use of stabilizing handrail, the student will adjust his pants, with minimal assistance, with 100% accuracy on each occasion for 2 weeks.

Directing the Task

The student will indicate on his AAC device when he needs to go to the restroom and will indicate to the adult that he is correctly positioned on the toilet after being placed on it with 100% accuracy on each occasion for 3 weeks.

The student will indicate on an AAC device to the adult when he has finished urinating on 100% of occasions for 3 weeks.

Knowledge of the Task

The student will list five signs of a urinary tract infection with 100% accuracy on four consecutive sessions.

The student will indicate when a urinary tract infection may be present with 90% accuracy on each occasion during the school year.

FIGURE 10-7 Sample IEP objectives for toileting

Diet

Many students with physical impairments, especially those with neuromuscular disorders such as cerebral palsy, have constipation (Geralis, 1998; Morris & Klein, 1987). A variety of factors contribute to this problem, including insufficient liquid intake and insufficient fiber and texture in the diet. Liquids and fiber are essential for urinary and bowel health as well as a successful toileting program. Care should be taken that the student is receiving enough liquids, not only for toileting purposes but for general health. Students who have difficulty swallowing liquids can have the liquid thickened with natural ingredients. For example, applesauce can be added to apple juice or ice cream to milk. Baby cereal also makes a good thickener. Commercial products such as Thick-It™ can be added to juices or punch-type drinks. (Do not use with water, since the taste is unpleasant unless used with something with flavor. Before using a product such as this, it is recommended that the teacher and parents try it for themselves.) The occupational therapist should be consulted for suggestions of appropriate adaptive cups and other appliances to help this endeavor. A nurse can be consulted for proper liquid intake.

Fiber and texture in the diet are important for regular bowel movements. However, students with liquid or pureed diets may not get the fiber or bulk that they need. This problem is frequently encountered with students who are tube fed or who have oral motor involvement. Bulk and fiber can be added to the diet with many easily obtainable foods such as high-fiber cereals and certain vegetables. Prunes (or prune juice mixed with a more palatable food) and bran will work as a natural laxative for those students suffering from constipation. Over-the-counter bulk fiber products such as Metamucil can also be used to promote regularity. However, these products along with laxatives should not be used unless recommended by the student's physician.

Activity Level

Immobility adversely affects all students. The medical community has long understood the need for activity to promote health. Both the urinary tract and the gastrointestinal tract are dependent on movement and repositioning for healthy functioning. The student who has participated in recess or physical education, rather than watching from the side of the gym, will be more easily toilet trained because exercise stimulates bowel and bladder movement. The student forced to live a sedentary lifestyle may not have sufficient muscle tone for proper elimination (Graff et al., 1990). Also, pressure from continual sitting, especially when aggravated by urine in an unchanged diaper, can lead to skin irritation, infection, and pressure sores. Students should change positions once every 1 or 2 hours, and a positioning plan should ensure that this occurs regularly.

Sex of Personnel Assisting the Student

Frequently, teachers are faced with the problem of toilet-training a student of the opposite gender. This problem is magnified as the student becomes older. Two conflicting issues come into play in this situation. First, school systems generally cannot hire teachers based on gender due to rights established in the Civil Rights Act of 1964. However, the Developmentally Disabled Assistance and Bill of Rights Act of 1975 ensures humane care and privacy, especially during activities such as dressing, bathing, and toileting, for persons with disabilities.

School systems can hire additional staff if need is documented and gender can be shown to be a bona fide occupational qualification (Rotegard, Hill, & Lakin, 1983). School systems may look for teachers of both genders and assign toileting responsibilities accordingly, or hire a male paraprofessional to assist a female teacher with these duties. This is especially important in a high school setting, as teachers cannot enter restrooms designated for students of the opposite gender. Also, the question of one-on-one training must be addressed. Some school systems require that more than one staff member be present during skills training and caretaking involving privacy issues for the student. Whatever decision is made, it is up to the teacher to assure the dignity and privacy of the student.

Toilet Training in Inclusive School Settings and the Community

There are special considerations when implementing a toilet-training program in a public school today. These include toilet training in an inclusion setting and during community-based instruction or vocational instruction. The logistics of toilet training in these settings will create the need for careful planning and coordination between teachers and staff.

Many students are now placed in an inclusive setting with their same-age peers, which makes it extremely difficult for a general education teacher to pause every 30 minutes for 2 weeks to take baseline data. Furthermore, it is not seemly for this work to be done in front of the student's classmates. Instead, baseline data may be collected in conjunction with standardized testing, usually in the spring and fall. Most students with physical or multiple disabilities are moved to a special education room during testing. This provides the perfect opportunity to take baseline data. At the end of 2 weeks the student can be reintegrated into his regular education classroom.

Providing the appropriate equipment during community-based instruction can be a difficult proposition. The answer to this problem depends, in part, on the amount of equipment needed by the student. Transfer boards can easily be taken into the community if the student is able to maintain a stable sitting position on the toilet. Students requiring equipment that is easily portable, such as hand-held urinals, fracture bedpans, or certain adaptive toilet seats, can discretely carry these in a backpack. At the community-based vocational instructional site, arrangements can be made for the student's toilet to be discretely transported and stored at the site. Students requiring bulky equipment that cannot be transported might have a shortened vocational training session to return to the school for their toilet needs. If at all possible, however, toilet training should occur in as many different environments as possible. Dunlap, Koegel, and Koegel (1984) found that students with severe intellectual disabilities and autism who were toilet trained across a variety of settings learned those skills more quickly. Generalization of any skill requires that it be taught in more than one setting.

SUMMARY

The ability to toilet oneself is an essential self-help skill. Dependence on others for assistance can prevent a student from fully participating in school outings and community-based instruction. Several types of adaptive equipment and assistive strategies can aid in successful toileting. Students may be taught using general toileting methods with adaptations or use a trip-training method. Teaching a student the additional skills associated with toileting such as dressing, undressing, and hand washing should be included in the toileting program.

11

Urinary Catheterization and Urinary Collection Devices

The ability to urinate properly has tremendous physical and social consequences. Urine must be eliminated from the body to assure physical health, and urine elimination needs to occur at socially appropriate times and settings to avoid embarrassing social situations. However, some students have abnormal urinary systems that makes normal urine elimination unfeasible. Some of these students will need **urinary catheterization,** the process of inserting a tube into the bladder to eliminate urine. Other students will benefit from using a device to collect the urine when it naturally exits the body. In both instances, the goal is to prevent damage to the urinary system and allow the student to achieve social continence (the ability to contain urine until a time when it is socially appropriate to dispose of it).

In an intact urinary system, the kidneys filter out impurities from the blood, resulting in the waste product known as urine. As seen in Figure 11-1, the urine flows from the kidneys down the ureters where it collects in the bladder. A sphinc-

ter is located at the bottom of the bladder and it remains contracted at rest, retaining the urine in the bladder. As the bladder fills with urine, the person receives the sensation of bladder fullness. When the person is ready to urinate, the bladder sphincter relaxes, the bladder outlet opens, and the detrusor muscle (muscle pushing against the bladder) contracts. This allows the urine to exit through the urethra (Kaplan, 1994).

Urinary incontinence, an involuntary elimination of urine, may occur from (a) urinary filling and storage problems or (b) bladder-emptying problems (see Table 11-1). Proper urine filling and storage requires the bladder to hold increasing volumes of urine at low pressure with normal sensation, have an absence of involuntary bladder contractions, and have a bladder outlet that is closed at rest and remains closed during stress (Wein & Barrett, 1988). One of the most common urinary filling and storage problems in persons with physical disabilities is involuntary bladder contractions. These occur when the detrusor muscles contract the bladder without vol-

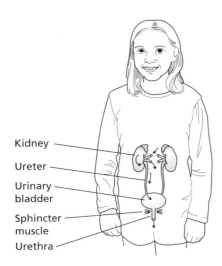

Kidney

Ureter

Urinary
bladder

Sphincter
muscle

Urethra

FIGURE 11-1 The urinary system

untary control, resulting in urine being forced out of the bladder. Other urinary filling and storage problems resulting in incontinence include a small-capacity bladder, sensory urgency (a need to urinate frequently), and sphincter abnormalities.

To empty urine properly, the bladder needs to contract sufficiently to allow complete emptying of urine, and the outlet needs to open sufficiently to allow urine to exit the bladder and leave the body. The bladder may be unable to contract correctly when there are conditions affecting the nerves of the bladder (neurogenic causes), such as in spinal cord injury. The bladder may be unable to empty because of problems with the muscles of the bladder (myogenic causes), psychological reasons (psychogenic causes), or unknown reasons (idiopathic causes). The outlet may also be abnormal, not allowing the urine to empty, such as when there is an obstruction or narrowing of the urethra (Kaplan, 1994; Wein & Barrett, 1988).

Several conditions may affect bladder storage and/or emptying of the urine. Some of these include brain tumor, Parkinson's disease, stroke, spinal cord injury, multiple sclerosis, diabetes, and congenital abnormality of the urethra. Spina bifida (myelomeningocele) is one of the most common neurological conditions that can result

in urinary elimination problems. This condition results in a neurogenic bladder, since the nerves going to the bladder are damaged. The damaged nerves result in an inability to sense when the bladder is full and an inability to control bladder emptying. Depending on the extent of the nerve damage, incontinence may result from non-coordination of the detrusor and sphincter muscles (resulting in a failure of the bladder to empty effectively), bladder contractions (resulting in urine being expelled involuntarily), and/or stress incontinence (leakage from physical exertion). The muscle tone of the sphincter may also be affected. These problems may result in the bladder overdistending (overstretching) and/or contracting irregularly or frequently. Urine may constantly dribble or not completely empty from the bladder (Taylor, 1990; Wong, 1995).

Problems in bladder storage and/or emptying may be serious if not treated. If the bladder does not empty when full, it becomes overdistended. The increase in pressure may result in a backflow of urine into the kidneys, possibly resulting in kidney infection and damage to the kidneys. In cases in which the bladder empties, but not completely, infection may occur and travel through the urinary system. Serious kidney infections or prolonged increases in pressure can damage the kidneys and impair their functioning. Impaired kidney functioning can be life-threatening.

Several different treatment options are possible, depending on the type of incontinence problem and the underlying cause (see Table 11-1). For individuals with impaired bladder contractility, the treatment of choice is clean intermittent catheterization. However, to be eligible for this procedure, the student must typically have sufficient bladder capacity and some sphincter tone. Students who have involuntary bladder (detrusor) contractions may also respond to catheterization or a collection device may be used (Kaplan, 1994). In other cases, medications may be effective in controlling incontinence by controlling involuntary bladder contractions, causing tightening of the bladder sphincter, or in promoting urine retention. Medication may be used alone or

Table 11-1 Sample Urinary Problems and Treatments

Problems	Possible treatments
Urinary filling/storage problems	
Involuntary bladder contractions	Medication, surgery, collection devices, indwelling catheter, clean intermittent catheterization
Small-capacity bladder	Surgery (e.g., balloon hydrodistention, augmentation cystoplasty)
Sensory urgency	Behavior modification
Sphincter abnormalities (stress incontinence, sphincter failure)	Surgery (e.g., suspension operations, artificial urinary sphincter)
Bladder-emptying problems	
Impaired bladder contractility (from neurogenic, myogenic, psychological, or idiopathic origins)	Clean intermittent catheterization, Credé, medications, surgery
Bladder outlet obstruction	Surgery

in conjunction with clean intermittent catheterization. When urinary continence can not be achieved by these conservative measures, more intrusive procedures or surgery may be indicated (e.g., creation of an artificial urinary sphincter, enlarging the bladder, use of bladder stimulation) (Cheng, Richards, & Kaplan, 1996; Kaplan, 1994; Levesque et al., 1996). However, in the school setting, teachers will be more involved with the use of catheterization and/or collection devices.

Many types of catheterization and collection devices may be used to control incontinence. This chapter will first describe clean intermittent catheterization (CIC) and the equipment and adaptive equipment, assistive strategies, instructional strategies, and problems and emergencies pertaining to CIC. This will be followed by describing the same areas as applied to Credé, external urinary catheters, and indwelling catheters. Various management issues of all four procedures will be addressed at the end of the chapter.

DESCRIPTION OF CLEAN INTERMITTENT CATHETERIZATION (CIC)

In the 1940s, Sir Ludwig Guttmann and his coworker started the use of sterile intermittent catheterization in the treatment of individuals with spinal cord injury (Guttman & Frankel, 1966). Sterile intermittent catheterization is the introduction of a sterile **catheter** (a long, thin tube) through the urethra and into the bladder on an intermittent basis to allow urine to empty from the bladder. In this procedure a sterile catheter and sterile technique are used. This implies that the equipment used either has never been touched and is aseptic or has been sterilized (e.g., by autoclave). Sterile gloves are worn, and the technique is performed in such a way that the catheter remains sterile until it enters the urethra.

In the 1970s Dr. Jack Lapides introduced the idea that a clean catheter and clean procedure could be used instead of a sterile one without a significant increase in infections (Lapides, Diokno, Silber, & Lowe, 1972). In **clean intermittent catheterization** (CIC), a clean catheter is introduced through the urethra and into the bladder. The catheter remains in place long enough to allow urine to be released from the bladder and then the catheter is removed. The catheter may be washed and reused. Traditionally, CIC is performed on a schedule, typically every 4 hours. However, new equipment is becoming available that will allow the procedure to be performed as needed rather than scheduled. (Refer to the section on equipment and assistive equipment for more information.) Also, CIC is now used for a variety of conditions and has successfully resulted in continence (Bakke & Hoisaeter, 1994).

The catheter used in this procedure is a narrow tube with a hole running through the middle of it for the entire length of the catheter (like a miniature garden hose). Catheters come in different sizes and are made of a variety of materials. Most are constructed of a rigid but flexible type of plastic material. For students who have sensation, passage of these catheters through the urethra is considered uncomfortable, not painful.

EQUIPMENT AND ADAPTIVE EQUIPMENT FOR CIC

Often, the only equipment that the student may use to perform CIC is the catheter itself. The catheter can be made out of plastic or rubber and comes in different sizes. The person buying the catheter will need to know the type and size that the physician has recommended. An additional extension tube may be purchased to attach to the end of the catheter so that it will reach the toilet

when a student is sitting in a wheelchair performing the procedure.

The newest adaptive equipment available that may be used by the student to determine the optimum time to catheterize is known as a Bladder Manager (by Diagnostic Ultrasound Corporation) (see Figure 11-2). The Bladder Manager is a portable device consisting of a sensor (placed over the bladder) and a monitor that provides a read out of how much volume of urine is in the bladder. Catheterization then occurs based on the volume of urine in the bladder rather than on a specific time schedule (e.g., every 4 hours). Volume-based intermittent catheterization avoids the problems that have been found with time-based catheterization. Time-based catheterization can result in a high percentage of unnecessary early catheterization, which increases the chance of infection or trauma. Also, time-based catheterization can result in late catheterization occurring when the bladder is already distended. In one study 21 individuals with neurogenic bladders were able to successfully use the device and perform volume-directed catheterization, thereby avoiding the problems seen with time-based catheterization (Binard, Persky, Lockhart, & Kelley, 1996).

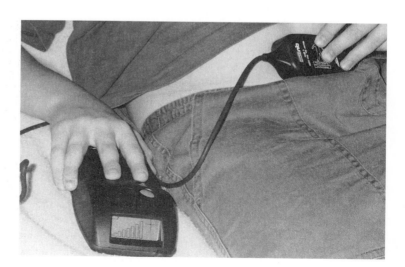

FIGURE 11-2 Student using a Bladder Manager to determine how much urine is in the bladder

ASSISTIVE STRATEGIES FOR CLEAN INTERMITTENT CATHETERIZATION

Preparing for CIC

The student needs to be prepared for the procedure by being given an explanation of what is going to occur. For students who have poor receptive communication skills, the student may be handed the container (or part of the container) that the catheter is kept in as a symbol representing the CIC procedure.

A very private location needs to be selected for CIC to be performed. Part of this selection process will depend on whether it can be done sitting or standing by a toilet. For female students, sitting on the toilet is usually the easiest position, if the student is able physically to do so. Some female students prefer to stand by placing a foot on the floor and the other foot on the rim of the toilet or a chair. Most male students prefer to stand by the toilet, when possible. Sitting by the toilet and using an extension tube attached to the catheter so the urine can flow into the toilet is another possibility.

Some students, however, who have severe physical impairments may be unable to sit or stand to perform the procedure, and they may not be able to be catheterized in a bathroom. In these instances, a location needs to be selected that allows privacy and permits the student to lie down. If using a lying position, some protective absorbent material (e.g., Chux, towel, diaper) is placed under the student's buttock to catch any leaks. The end of the catheter drains the urine into a container for disposal. A lying position is effective, but it is more difficult for the student to perform the procedure in this position.

Before and after performing CIC, the hands of the person performing the procedure and the student's hands should be washed. Hand washing prior to the procedure will help decrease the possibility of a urinary tract infection and afterwards will aid in lessening the spread of infection. Even if the student is not assisting with the procedure, learning appropriate times to wash one's hands is important. Since this is an intensely private procedure, nonsterile gloves should be worn by the person assisting with the procedure. The student does not need to wear gloves. It is important that the student be checked for a latex allergy or susceptibility to a latex allergy. If an allergy is present (or in some cases if the student is in a high-risk group such as those with spina bifida), latex gloves cannot be worn and an alternative (e.g., plastic gloves) must be selected (see "Latex Allergy Alert" in Chapter 1, page 23).

It is important for the person performing the procedure to know whether the catheter used by the student is used once and discarded or whether it is reusable. This is a decision by the physician and parents. If it is reusable, it is important that the proper cleaning procedure of the catheter is followed to decrease the chance of infection. Sometimes, reusable catheters are not only cleaned after use but cleaned with soap and water prior to the procedure. This information needs to be clarified before performing the procedure.

Equipment used in CIC should be easy to carry and discretely contained. The reusable catheter may be carried in a clean toothbrush holder, a pencil container, makeup bag, or other discrete container, with all the supplies in a side pack, bag, or purse. For students who will be completely independent with this procedure, a decision needs to be made as to how the equipment will be placed. Some individuals prefer to have a small table or counter to place the equipment. However, students who are independent and will be performing this procedure in public bathrooms will need to learn to manage their equipment without the use of a table. Often the equipment can be placed in a small hiking pack that opens up and attaches to the wheelchair.

Equipment and Supply List for CIC Procedure
Catheter (size _____)
Catheter storage bag (e.g., baggie, toothbrush container)

Water-soluble lubricant (e.g., K-Y Jelly, Lubrifax)

Cleansing supplies (e.g., disposable towelette or cotton balls, soap)

Container to collect urine (or a toilet, when applicable)

Protective pad (if not using toilet, pad may be placed under student in case of spills)

Procedure for CIC

After the student has had the procedure explained, gone to a private location, washed her hands, and been positioned and the person performing the procedure has assembled the equipment and put on nonsterile gloves, the student is ready for the procedure.

Steps in the Procedure for CIC	Rationale
1. Lubricate approximately the last 2 inches of the catheter with a water-soluble lubricant, such as K-Y Jelly. Place catheter on a clean surface (e.g., paper towel).	Lubricant helps the catheter slide in easier and minimizes trauma and discomfort (for those students whose physical impairment has not impaired their ability to sense discomfort in the genital area). Water-soluble lubricant (not petroleum-based lubricant such as Vaseline) is necessary so that the lubricant remaining in the urethra after the procedure will properly dissolve.
2. Clean the genital area:	
For Females: a. With the nondominant hand, separate the labia.	If the student is performing this step, she should hold the labia apart using her thumb and middle finger.
b. With the other hand, wash the genital area from front to back (first wiping inner labia folds, then down the middle) using clean cotton balls with soap and water or a designated cleansing agent for each area cleaned (see Figure 11-3a).	Never use the same wipe twice to decrease the chance of infection.
c. Keep the labia separate until the procedure is complete.	Keeping the labia separate (instead of allowing to return to the closed position) will minimize the risk of introducing microorganisms into the bladder with the passage of the catheter.
d. Locate the urethral opening.	If the student is doing this part of the procedure, she may locate the urethra opening by touch using the index finger. Occasionally, students may be taught using a mirror to help locate the opening, but this should be eliminated since a mirror may not always be available. Sometimes the urethral

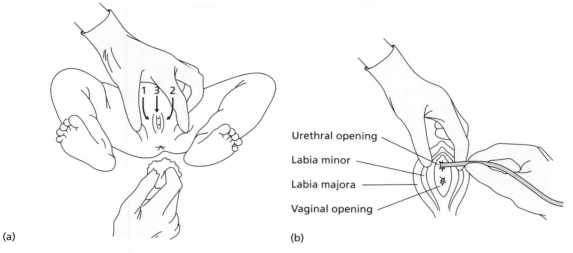

Urethral opening

Labia minor

Labia majora

Vaginal opening

(a)

(b)

FIGURE 11-3 Washing the inner labia folds, then down the middle (a), and catheterizing the female urethra (b)

Steps in the Procedure for CIC	*Rationale*
	opening is difficult to locate and may appear as a small dimple.
For Males:	
a. Hold the penis below the glans with the nondominant hand and gently pull back the foreskin in the uncircumcised male to expose the urinary opening (i.e., urinary meatus).	Holding the penis gently but firmly (instead of using light touch) will decrease the likelihood of an erection (Skale, 1992). However, do not hold the penis too tightly since you may block the urethra. Be sure to return the foreskin to the original position when the procedure is completely finished. Never use the same wipe twice to decrease the chance of infection.
b. With the other hand, wash the glans of the penis in a circular (or spiral) motion, starting at the center and going to the periphery of the glans, using clean cotton balls with soap and water or a designated cleansing agent (see Figure 11-4a). This is typically repeated three times, with a new cotton ball each time (Urbano, 1992)	
c. Continue to hold the foreskin back for the duration of the procedure.	By continuing to hold the foreskin back during the procedure, the risk of infection is minimized.

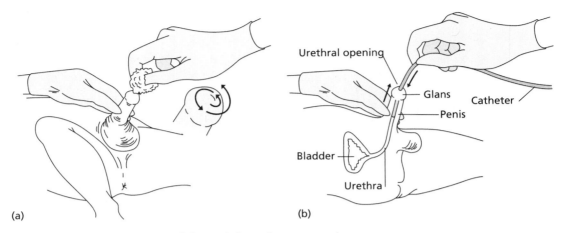

(a)   (b)

FIGURE 11-4 Washing the glans of the penis from the center to the periphery of the glans in a spiral motion (a) and catheterizing the male urethra (b)

Steps in the Procedure for CIC	*Rationale*
3. Insert the catheter into the urinary opening (meatus). *For females:* tip the catheter slightly upward when first inserting the catheter.	Should the catheter enter the vagina by mistake, use a second catheter and start again. The first one will need to be recleaned.
For males: hold the penis at a 90-degree angle for the entire procedure.	For males, holding the penis straight out will straighten the urethra.
4. Gently insert the catheter. It should easily slide in. *Never force the catheter.* (See Figures 11-3b and 11-4b.)	For males, there may be slight resistance as the catheter reaches the bladder. If this occurs, apply gentle steady pressure on the catheter until the muscle relaxes. Asking the older student to bear down may also relax the muscle.
	If the catheter will not easily advance or the procedure is painful, move the catheter back or twist it a little since it may have hit an obstruction or a tissue fold. If the catheter will not easily advance again (or is painful or there is no urine flow), remove the catheter and immediately notify appropriate personnel.

Steps in the Procedure for CIC	*Rationale*
5. When urine begins to flow, the catheter is usually advanced another ½ to 1 inch.	Presence of urine indicates the catheter is in the bladder. Advancing the catheter assures that the catheter is in the correct position for optimum drainage.
6. After the urine stops flowing, the physician may have ordered Credé to be performed at this time. (See Credé procedure.)	
7. Slowly remove the catheter. Stop removing the catheter if urine begins flowing again. Then resume removing catheter when urine flow has stopped.	Change in catheter position may result in draining some residual urine that was earlier unable to flow out the catheter.
8. The student may wipe the genital area with toilet paper after the catheter is removed. (If a male student is not circumcised, pull the foreskin back over urinary opening.) Have the student dress and wash hands. The person assisting should take off gloves and also wash hands.	A little bit of urine may be in the student's urinary opening, so wiping with toilet paper may be desired. Proper hand washing decreases the chance of infection.
9. Document the occurrence of the procedure and any problems encountered.	The person performing the procedure should observe for any problems or abnormalities and contact appropriate personnel when necessary. (See the later section on problems.)

Care of CIC Equipment and Daily Care

If the catheter is reusable, clean the catheter with soap and water or other specified cleaner, such as a mixture of 1:4 bleach and water, 1:2 providone-iodine and water or 0.6% hydrogen peroxide (McLaughlin, Murray, Van Zandt, & Carr, 1996). Clean the inside of the catheter by allowing soapy water or another cleansing agent to flow through it. A syringe may be used to squirt soapy water through the catheter. Rinse the catheter and allow it to air dry. Store the catheter in a clean, covered container until next use. Reusable catheters should be replaced approximately every 4 to 6 weeks (Heller et al., 1992).

INSTRUCTIONAL STRATEGIES AND MODIFICATIONS FOR CIC

Students who require CIC should be taught the procedure. Depending on the student's age, physical status, and cognitive abilities, the student may partially participate by performing only a few steps in the procedure, such as washing hands and cleaning the genital area, to performing all the steps. Teaching this important self-help skill will aid the student in becoming as independent as possible.

Just as with any other procedure, it is important to break down the procedure into small teachable steps. As discussed in Chapter 2, the steps of the task analysis may vary between students, based on the individually prescribed procedure (i.e., steps differ based on physician preference) and physical capabilities. The exact approved procedure will need to be adhered to in the task analysis. A typical task analysis is presented in Figure 11-5. The steps of the task analysis should be placed on a data sheet for evaluation purposes (see sample data sheet in Chapter 2).

Students as young as 2 and 3 are encouraged to participate in the procedure by learning to wash their hands properly and to hold and open the equipment. Students as young as 5 years of age often learn to correctly perform the proce-

1. Wash hands.
2. Take out catheter and supplies.
3. Undress.
4. Move into correct position for CIC.
5. Unscrew top of K-Y Jelly.
6. Put K-Y Jelly on catheter.
7. Clean genital area.
8. Insert catheter into urinary opening.
9. Gently advance catheter.
10. When urine flows, advance catheter $\frac{1}{2}$ inch and stop.
11. Wait until urine stops flowing.
12. Pull out catheter.
13. Wipe genital area and dispose of toilet paper.
14. Flush toilet.
15. Dress.
16. Wash catheter.
17. Wash hands.
18. Put top on K-Y Jelly.
19. Put away equipment.

FIGURE 11-5 Sample task analysis of the CIC procedure

dure totally independently. The use of pictures, model dolls, and demonstrations often aid the student in learning the procedure and result in a skill in which the student can experience success and take pride (Skale, 1992).

Consideration needs to be given to the student's developmental stage before determining when the student should begin to do the actual procedure. Typically, independent CIC is started when the student understands the need for the procedure; can describe the procedure, equipment, and supplies; can identify aspects of a "clean" procedure; and has initiated assisting in the procedure (Kuntz, 1996a). For a student who has no cognitive abnormalities, these guidelines are applicable. For a student who has mental retardation, this information may be learned while teaching the procedure itself.

Teaching self-catheterization to a student with mental retardation requires using systematic instructional strategies to teach each step in the task analysis. Six-year-old students with mild mental retardation have learned to self-catheterize successfully using a system of least prompts (Tarnowski & Drabman, 1987). In this study, the students had years of catheterization experience prior to being taught the procedure. However, they benefited little from their early experience. This was thought to be a result of the way the students were catheterized. Typically, no or minimal student participation was required. Although there was repeated exposure to the procedure, the student was shaped into a passive role where all aspects of the procedure were "done to" the individual. To prevent this type of learned helplessness (dependence), it is important to encourage the student to take an active role by systematically teaching the student specific steps of the procedure.

Students with physical impairments, including problems in postural control and fine-motor coordination, present unique challenges to learning self-catheterization. Students with spasticity, fixed joint contractures, severe scoliosis, and other structural problems may be able to achieve successful self-CIC when careful assessment and appropriate modifications are provided (McLaughlin et al., 1996). Careful assessment of the student's hand use, stability in the wheelchair, muscle tone of the arms and legs, and motivation needs to occur. Modifications may be used in the following categories: (a) modifications to the catheter, (b) modifications to the collection device, (c) positioning modifications, and (d) clothing modifications. For students who have difficulty holding the catheter, an attachment may be placed on the catheter that enlarges the grasping surface, angles the surface differently, or uses a grasping aid. An extension tube may also be placed on the end of the catheter to increase its length so that it may reach the toilet.

When reaching the toilet is not feasible, several different types of collection devices may be used in CIC. In some instances, a urinary collection bag is used with an extension tube. Urine runs through the catheter, through the extension tube, and into the urinary collection bag. When catheterization is completed, the urine is emptied from the urinary collection bag. It is important that the extension tubing and urinary collection bag be thoroughly cleaned after each use to maintain clean technique. Other items used to collect the urine may be a cup stabilized to the wheelchair or a plastic Ziploc bag.

Positioning of the student and the equipment is important for success. Female students who have impaired leg movement may benefit from learning to catheterize from the wheelchair since it may be more convenient when in the community. When the lower extremities have low tone, it may be helpful to elevate one leg onto the toilet rim, a low table, a chair, or over the side of the wheelchair to have access to the genital area. A thigh abductor or spreader (with or without a mirror) may be used to separate the thighs for those with low tone, high tone, or obese thighs to assist with access to the genital area. For privacy, a towel, newspaper, or article of clothing may be draped over the armrests of the wheelchair when performing the procedure. Students who are catheterizing from a toilet may need an adapted toilet for increased stability (see Chapter 10). Positioning of the equipment for easy access will be important when there is a phys-

ical impairment. (See Chapter 6 for information on positioning material.)

Clothing may be modified for easy access to the genital area. Often males may need adapted zippers or buttons for ease of opening the pants. For females who are wearing slacks, Velcro may be placed in the crotch for easy access. Velcro or zippers may also be placed at the side seams for easier access. If the student is too physically involved, the student may perform parts of the procedure. For the remaining steps that the student is unable to physically perform, the student should be able to verbalize or communicate them, as well as to know what steps to take if problems occur.

Time-Limited Steps and Caution Steps

When determining the type of instructional strategy to use with a student, it is important that each step of the task analysis is carefully examined for any time-limited steps or caution steps. *Time-limited steps* are steps in the task analysis that must be completed within a certain time frame. Since certain instructional procedures such as least prompts and time delay allow for a certain amount of time to pass before a prompt (or more intrusive prompt) is given, these strategies may not be appropriate for certain steps of the procedure. For the CIC procedure, the student should stop inserting the catheter at about ½ to 1 inch after urine begins flowing. This is a time-limited step since the student needs to stop insertion at the appropriate time and not continue to insert the entire catheter. On this step, the teacher will need to assist the student should she not stop inserting the catheter. For a high-functioning student, this may be done by modeling the step on a doll (or training device) and then shadowing the student. (In shadowing, the teacher keeps her hand within an inch of the student's hand until the step is complete so she can intervene if necessary.) A lower-functioning student may require a full physical prompt and move to shadowing.

Caution steps are steps in the task analysis in which the student could injure herself by a quick, jerking, or incorrect movement. For the CIC procedure, the caution step is inserting and advancing the catheter through the urethra. On caution steps, the educational team must determine whether the step is appropriate for the student to perform and, if so, be sure shadowing is provided (after modeling or physically prompting the student) to be able to quickly stop the student should an incorrect movement occur. Teachers should highlight time-limited steps and caution steps on their data sheet as a reminder to provide shadowing. (See Chapter 2 for more information on shadowing and a sample data sheet.)

Student Guidelines

One student learning a CIC program, made a list of cautions and encouragements that she found helpful in learning CIC (McLaughlin, Murray, van Zandt, & Carr, 1996). They are as follows:

> *Gretchen's List of Do's and Don'ts*
>
> Do always wash your hands before and after using your catheter.
>
> Do always wash your catheter before and after using it.
>
> Don't leave it wherever you happen to be, but put it away.
>
> Don't put it in places it shouldn't be (e.g., nose, mouth).
>
> Don't be afraid to tell someone if your urine smells or you are bleeding.
>
> Do change all catheters you have used if you have an infection, and get new ones.
>
> Do always have one handy in a purse or pocket if you are going somewhere.
>
> Don't let friends or anyone else use them for any reason.
>
> Don't stick anything in the catheter.
>
> Do keep spare catheters handy in case of emergencies.
>
> Don't let anyone tell you your arms are too short to cath.
>
> Don't get frustrated if it takes time to learn.

> Do remember that your parents and school nurse can and will help.
>
> Do be aware that although it is a private thing, you will need help in the beginning.
>
> Do know that when you learn you will be more free when staying overnight with friends or at camp.

CIC PROBLEMS AND EMERGENCIES

Several possible problems may occur during CIC that the student and person assisting with the procedure should be taught to identify. These include infection, inability to pass the catheter, omission of catheterization, no urine on catheterization, urine between catheterizations, soreness, swelling and discharge, and bleeding. Although it is rare to have emergency problems during CIC, excessive bleeding is a complication that requires immediate attention, and skipping catheterization may cause permanent damage to the kidneys.

Infection

When the urine exits the catheter, the person performing the procedure should observe the color, clarity, and odor of the urine for signs of a urinary tract infection. Cloudy and/or foul-smelling urine are the primary signs of an infection. Color changes may signal infection as well. Students who can experience sensory input may also have a burning or pressure sensation or flank pain (Kuntz, 1996a). Any of these symptoms need to be documented and reported to the parents.

Inability to Pass the Catheter

As discussed, firm, constant pressure may be needed for the catheter to pass through the bladder sphincter in males. If the catheter does not advance, other techniques such as trying to get the student to relax by taking a deep breath or bearing down as if to urinate may be helpful. If the catheter still does not pass, the catheter may be slightly withdrawn and twisted since it may have hit a fold in the tissue. If this is not successful, the procedure needs to be discontinued and the appropriate person notified. For female students, the same techniques of trying to get the student to relax and twisting the catheter should be tried. However, it is important to check that the catheter is inserted into the urethra and not the vagina. If it is inserted into the vagina, another catheter should be obtained and the procedure started again. A catheter that entered the vagina needs to be cleaned. It is imperative that someone be notified and action taken since complications can occur if the procedure is not performed.

Omission of Catheterization

Skipping a catheterization can be a serious problem. Although there is typically a little leeway in catheterization times (when using time- or volume-based methods), omitting a catheterization can result in an overdistended bladder in some students. Depending on the urinary system dysfunction the student has, urine may reflux back into the kidneys. In some situations, a serious kidney infection can result that could possibly lead to damage to the kidneys. It is important that the schedule be closely followed. Any omission of catheterization needs to be documented and reported to the appropriate personnel and parents.

If omission has occurred because the student has not followed the schedule or not complied in other ways, the student may need to be reevaluated as a candidate for CIC. For students who are being taught to do the procedure independently, motivation and student compliance is essential to avoid complications from not catheterizing when needed or incorrectly performing the procedure (Chai, Chung, Belville, & Faerber, 1995; Oakshott & Hunt, 1992). It should be noted that in one study, 30% of the people experiencing CIC found the procedure difficult, and about 33% of the individuals found the procedure aversive (Bakke & Hoisaeter, 1994). Stu-

dent support or counseling is recommended in these situations. Students who are motivated to do the procedure but have difficulty remembering when to catheterize due to age or cognitive ability may benefit from having a watch with a timer or following a schedule (e.g., picture or written schedule) that indicates when it is time to catheterize.

No Urine on Catheterizations

If there is no urine draining from the catheter when catheterizing, the catheter is probably improperly placed. For female students, check that the catheter is not placed in the vagina by mistake. For male students, it is possible that the catheter has not been inserted far enough. Recheck position of the catheter and try the procedure again.

Urine Between Catheterizations

Urine leaking between catheterizations may be a sign of a urinary tract infection or a change in bladder status. This condition needs to be reported to the parent and appropriate personnel.

Soreness, Swelling, and Discharge

When there is soreness, swelling, or discharge at the urethra, it is often attributed to incorrect technique (Lozes, 1988; Urbano, 1992). These symptoms should be documented and reported to the appropriate personnel. Retraining of the person performing the procedure is usually indicated.

Bleeding

A small amount of bleeding at the urethra may indicate that more lubrication is needed upon catheterization. If blood appears in the urine, this should be documented and reported to the parents and appropriate personnel. Excessive bleeding or pain is considered an emergency situation, and paramedics should be called to take the student to the hospital (Urbano, 1992).

DESCRIPTION OF CREDÉ

Credé is a procedure that may be used in conjunction with clean intermittent catheterization, or it may be used alone. Credé is also referred to as *manual compression of the bladder*. In this procedure, the student or person performing the procedure presses on the abdomen over the bladder using an inward and downward pressure with the heel of the hand to assist with eliminating urine. Typically, this procedure is used with individuals with decreased bladder tone who have decreased or borderline outlet resistance (Wein & Barrett, 1988). This procedure is prescribed by a physician since it may be harmful to use on individuals with certain bladder conditions.

Equipment and Adaptive Equipment for Credé

Typically no equipment is used in the Credé procedure. At times, a folded towel may be used to press on the area above the pubic bone (Wein & Barrett, 1988). However, most of the time, using the heel of the hand is sufficient.

ASSISTIVE STRATEGIES FOR CREDÉ

Preparing for Credé

The student will need to receive an explanation of what is going to occur. A student with poor receptive communication skills may be handed a part of the absorbent material or urine container as a symbol that Credé will occur.

Credé may occur as part of the catheterization procedure or it may occur alone. If it is occurring as part of the catheterization procedure, whatever position the student uses for that procedure will be satisfactory for Credé. When it is occurring alone, Credé may be performed with the student sitting on the toilet or lying down, depending on the student's physical status. As with all urinary procedures, it is important that the student have the procedure performed in a private location, with dignity and respect.

The hands of the student and/or person performing the procedure should be washed before and after the procedure. Since this is an intensely private procedure, nonsterile gloves should be worn by the person assisting with the procedure. If the student performs the procedure, gloves are not necessary.

If Credé is being performed without catheterization, how the urine will be collected needs to be determined. If the female student can sit on the toilet or the male can stand by the toilet, urine will go into the toilet for disposal. In some instances, males may aim the flow of urine into a container or a urinal (refer back to Figure 10-3). Occasionally, an external urinary catheter may be temporarily placed on the student. Female students may use a collection device designed for females, a bedpan, or absorbent material.

Procedure for Credé

After explaining the procedure to the student, going to a private location, washing hands, positioning the student, putting absorbent material under the student (if applicable), and putting on nonsterile gloves, the student is ready for the procedure.

Steps in the Procedure for Credé	*Rationale*
1. Visually locate navel and pubic region. Find the pubic bone and place the heel of the hand on the lower abdomen area, directly above the pubic bone.	It is important that the correct position is used so as not to damage any internal organs.

Steps in the Procedure for Credé	Rationale
2. Gently apply firm, downward, and inward pressure with the heel of the hand, and then release.	Using the heel of the hand usually provides the most effective results. Sometimes the fingers or fist may be used (Wein & Barrett, 1988).
3. Repeat step 2 until urine ceases to be expelled.	Cessation of urine indicates that the bladder is empty.
4. Empty urine from the container and clean it (if applicable).	The container may be cleaned with a disinfectant. The absorbent pad will need to be discarded properly (if used).
5. Remove gloves and wash hands.	Refer to Chapter 1 on proper hand-washing technique.
6. Document the occurrence of the procedure and any problems encountered.	The person performing the procedure should observe for any problems or abnormalities and contact appropriate personnel. (See the later section on problems.)

INSTRUCTIONAL STRATEGIES AND MODIFICATIONS FOR CREDÉ

Students who require Credé should be taught the procedure to promote independence. The procedure may be broken down into small steps and systematically taught (see Figure 11-6 for a task

analysis of Credé). Any number of instructional strategies may be used to teach the procedure (see Chapter 2). Often it is helpful for the teacher to place her hand over the target area and have the student push on the teacher's hand to assess how hard the student is pushing.

As with any other health procedure, it is important to identify any time-limited steps or caution steps in the task analysis so the teacher can use the instructional procedure of shadowing during that step to prevent the student from doing the step incorrectly. In the Credé procedure, there are not any time-limited steps, but there are caution steps. Correct hand placement and application of pressure are caution steps that could result in injury if done incorrectly. The educational team will need to determine whether these steps are appropriate for the student. The student may be taught by modeling the step and then providing shadowing. Lower-functioning students may require a full physical prompt and move to shadowing. Teachers should highlight these caution

---

1. Wash hands.
2. Undress.
3. Locate the correct area for Credé.
4. Put heel of hand on area.
5. Apply firm, downward, and inward pressure with heel of hand and release.
6. Repeat step 5 until urine is emptied.

FIGURE 11-6 Sample task analysis of Credé procedure

steps on their data sheet as a reminder to provide shadowing.

If the student is unable to perform the procedure due to physical disability, the student should be able to verbalize or communicate the procedure to others and know what problems could occur and what to do if they are present. Students may also learn to partially participate by washing hands, positioning themselves, undressing, or other aspects of the procedure.

CREDÉ PROBLEMS AND EMERGENCIES

Infection

Although infection should not occur from the Credé procedure, since the student has an abnormal urinary system, the person performing the procedure and the student need to be alert for signs of a urinary infection. Refer to "CIC Problems and Emergencies" for a description.

Injury

If Credé is performed incorrectly, such as using incorrect placement of the hand, internal injury may result. If the student complains of pain or other signs of injury are evident, the student should be taken to the hospital.

DESCRIPTION OF THE EXTERNAL URINARY CATHETER

Several types of collection devices may be used to collect urine for individuals who completely empty their bladder but are unable to achieve continence. The most common device for males is an external urinary catheter, also referred to as a *condom catheter* (see Figure 11-7). An external urinary catheter consists of a condomlike

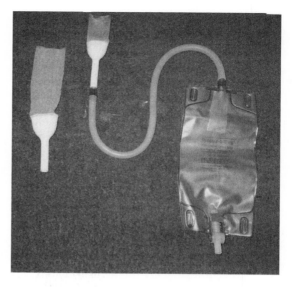

FIGURE 11-7 An external urinary catheter (on the left) and an external urinary catheter attached to a leg bag used to collect the urine (on the right)

device that goes over the penis. Attached to the bottom of this device is a long tube that attaches to a urinary collection bag (usually fastened to the student's leg). Urine is emptied from the bag when full. Unlike the catheter described in the CIC procedure, an external urinary catheter does not enter the urethra but is externally worn.

External catheters are often preferred over diapers because they provide better odor control, prevent accidents (when the diaper does not fully absorb the urine), make it easier for the student with disabilities to empty the bag rather than change the diaper, and decreases the risk of skin breakdown from extended contact with urine on the skin (Heller et al., 1992). However, irritation and severe pressure sores may occur at the site of the penis if the use of an external catheter is not carefully monitored (Wein & Barrett, 1988). If there are any signs of irritation or pressure sores on the penis, the external urinary catheter should be taken off and replaced with a diaper or absorbent padding.

At this time, there is still no satisfactory external catheter for females, primarily because of difficulties with fixation and leak-proof collection. Absorbent padding is the last resort for many individuals. The goal of absorbent pads is to keep the clothing dry and the skin as dry as possible to reduce chafing, rashes, or skin breakdown.

EQUIPMENT AND ADAPTIVE EQUIPMENT FOR EXTERNAL URINARY CATHETERS

Many types of external urinary collection devices are available. The most common type that was described in this section are those that use a soft rubber sheath, or condom, placed over the penis. These condom catheters come in different sizes. It is important that the correct size is selected to assure the best fit.

Urinary collection bags come in different sizes and attach in different ways. Leg bags often attach around the leg using stretchable straps. The drainage port may open and close differently depending on the type of urinary collection bag used. Some have a clamp on a short piece of tubing. This short tube is usually placed into a protective cover when not in use. Other urinary collection bags may have a plastic valve that is twisted or pulled for the urine to exit.

ASSISTIVE STRATEGIES FOR USING AN EXTERNAL URINARY CATHETER

Preparing for Using an External Urinary Catheter

When a teacher has a student using an external urinary catheter, the only care that the teacher or student will typically need to perform is to periodically empty the urinary collection bag. Changing the catheter usually occurs in the home setting. However, the external urinary catheter may accidentally come off and need to be replaced. If replacing an external urinary catheter, the person performing the procedure will need to explain to the student what is going to occur. For students with poor receptive communication skills, a piece of tubing may be given to the student as a symbol of the procedure.

A private location needs to be selected for putting on the external urinary catheter. As with all procedures involving the urinary system, both the student and the person performing the procedure should wash hands. The person performing the procedure should wear gloves (mindful of a possible latex allergy), unless that person is the student. This procedure may be performed with the student sitting or lying down.

Equipment and Supply List for Putting on an External Urinary Catheter

Condom-type catheter

Tubing

Urinary collection bag (leg bag)

Tape

Adhesive remover

Soap and water and washcloth

Paper towels

Adhesive

Procedure for Putting on an External Urinary Catheter (Condom Type)

After explaining the procedure to the student, going to a private location, washing hands, assembling equipment (e.g., opening the bag that contains the new external urinary catheter), positioning the student, and putting on nonsterile gloves, the student is ready for the procedure.

Steps in the Procedure for Putting on an External Urinary Catheter	*Rationale*

1. Empty the urine from the leg bag or other urinary collection device.
  a. Take a clean cup designated to collect the urine and place under the bottom of the leg bag.
  b. Twist or unclamp the tubing from which the urine exits.
  c. Allow the urine to drain from the bag.
  d. Reclamp the tubing.
  e. Empty the cup into toilet and clean (or throw out) the cup.
	The urinary collection bag is usually emptied first to avoid any accidents where the urine could spill.

2. Completely remove the previously applied catheter.
  a. With scissors, carefully cut the tape (if applicable) and part of the external urinary catheter under the tape.
  b. Gently pull off the external urinary catheter.
	Sometimes tape is not used. Some external urinary catheters have an additional waistband to help them stay in place (Bigge, 1991).

3. Inspect the skin on the penis for any redness, irritation, or skin breakdown. If any of these are present, do *not* put on an external urinary catheter until skin returns to normal.	Notify appropriate personnel if any skin irritation is present. Medical treatment may be needed. Disposable diapers, padded underwear, or other urine-absorbing material may be used to collect urine until the skin improves.
4. Clean the penis with soap and water. If needed, adhesive remover may be used to remove old adhesive from the shaft of the penis.	Cleaning the penis will decrease possible irritation, odor, and risk of infection. A new external urinary catheter will not stay on if the old adhesive is not removed.
5. If using adhesive, place the penis through a small hole in the center of a paper towel.	The paper towel is used to protect the pubic hair from adhesive spray.
6. Roll the condom-type external urinary catheter onto the glans of penis. A ¼- to ½-inch space should be left between the end of the penis and the bottom of the condom catheter (the end that attaches to the tubing).	It is important to leave a space at the bottom to prevent any irritation of the external urinary catheter against the penis.

Steps in the Procedure for Putting on an External Urinary Catheter	*Rationale*
7. If using adhesive spray, spray a thin layer of adhesive over shaft of penis, while keeping the glans of the penis covered with the condom-type catheter and the pubic hair covered with the paper towel. Wait a few seconds to allow the adhesive to become "tacky" before proceeding to next step.	Keeping the glans of the penis covered, protects it from the adhesive spray which would otherwise irritate the glans.
8. Unroll the rest of the condom-type external urinary catheter to cover the shaft of the penis.	
9. Keep the condom catheter in place.	
a. Place one strip of elastic nonirritating waterproof tape around the top of the condom-type external catheter, at the base of the penis. Do *not* wrap tape completely around the penis.	Completely wrapping the tape around the penis may cut off blood supply to the penis due to possible constriction.
b. Where the tape does not meet, place a small strip of surgical tape.	Surgical tape will help reinforce the area to keep the catheter in place, but it will not cause constriction of the penis.
c. If the condom catheter has a reinforced ring at the end of it, cut off the ring.	Leaving the ring on may cause skin breakdown.
10. Attach the external urinary catheter to the tubing and attach the tubing to the leg bag or other urinary collection bag.	The exact position of the bag may vary depending on the student's activity. The bag should be below the penis to prevent urine from running back into the external urinary catheter.
11. Dispose of the gloves. Wash hands.	Maintain proper infection control.
12. Document the occurrence of the procedure, the condition of the skin, and any problems encountered.	Person performing the procedure should observe for any problems or abnormalities and contact appropriate personnel when necessary.

Care of the External Urinary Catheter Equipment and Daily Care

The condom-type external urinary catheters are typically used only once then discarded. The tubing and the urinary collection bag should be cleaned with soap and water on a regular basis to control odor and prevent infection.

INSTRUCTIONAL STRATEGIES AND MODIFICATIONS FOR USING AN EXTERNAL URINARY CATHETER

Students who use external urinary catheters can often be taught to empty their own bag and put on their own external urinary catheter. For students without any cognitive problems, the procedure can easily be demonstrated and with a little practice, the student will easily be able to master the skill. For students with mental retardation, the steps of emptying the urinary collection bag and/or of putting on the catheter can be broken down into small teachable steps and systematically taught (see Figure 11-8 for a task analysis of emptying the urine bag). The task analysis should be put on a data sheet to effectively document and evaluate the data (see Figure 2-8 in Chapter 2).

Adaptations can be made to the outlet to allow students with physical disabilities to empty their urinary collection bag. Outlets that push to empty may be built up for a greater surface area to allow ease of opening the valve. Typically, to put on an external urinary catheter, there needs to be fairly good hand control. There are no time-limited steps or caution steps in this procedure.

---

1. Wash hands.
2. Get cup or container to collect urine.
3. Move clothing to see the leg bag.
4. Place a cup under the exit valve.
5. Pull the valve to open.
6. Wait for urine to drain completely from bag.
7. Close valve.
8. Empty cup/container.
9. Wash hands.

FIGURE 11-8 Task analysis for emptying a urine bag

EXTERNAL URINARY CATHETER PROBLEMS AND EMERGENCIES

Infection

The person performing the procedure should observe for any signs of urinary tract infection (described earlier). To help reduce the chance of infection, it is important to be sure that the outlet for the catheter bag does not touch the container into which the urine is draining. This helps prevents organisms from transferring from the container to the urinary collection bag, up the tubing to the penis.

Erection While Putting on the Catheter

Occasionally, the student may have an erection while the external urinary catheter is being put on. It must be remembered that this is a reflex and not under the control of the student, and it may be highly embarrassing for the student. If this occurs, the person performing the procedure will need either to wait to put the tape on when the erection is over or, if the tape is already on, recheck that the catheter has remained in place after the erection is over.

Skin Breakdown

This is the most serious complication of using an external urinary catheter. If the skin is not checked regularly, severe skin breakdown (tissue death) can occur down to and including the urethra, especially if the student has impaired sensation (Golz, 1981; Wein & Barrett, 1988). Anytime skin irritation is present, the catheter should not be put back on, and the appropriate person should be contacted.

DESCRIPTION FOR USE OF AN INDWELLING CATHETER

Indwelling catheters are catheters that go through the urethra into the bladder. The catheter remains in place to allow constant elimination of urine. It is placed into the bladder using sterile technique, usually by a nurse. Indwelling catheters are typically used on a temporary basis since there is an increased likelihood of urinary tract infection when they are used over an extended time period. They are most commonly used after surgical procedures or when the student is critically ill and needs constant monitoring of their urinary output (Skale, 1992). Individuals have been found to have higher rates of complications when chronically using an indwelling catheter than those using CIC (Chai et al., 1995).

Urine drains from the indwelling catheter into a urinary collection bag. The end of the catheter connects to tubing that then connects to the bag. The tubing may have a port (an opening) designed for withdrawal of urine for tests. As the tube enters the bag, there is usually a valve to help prevent urine from going back into the tubing from the bag. Most bags have measurements on them to allow for easy monitoring of urine output. At the bottom of the bag is an outlet to drain the urine from the bag. The outlet may consist of short tubing that is closed by a clamp and is kept in a protective sleeve when not in use or a plastic valve that turns to open. By releasing the clamp or turning a valve, urine exits out the bottom of the bag into a container or toilet. Emptying the urinary collection bag occurs on a periodic basis, when full or when prescribed by a physician, to measure the output regularly. It is important that the bag always be at a level lower than the student's urethra in order for gravity to help the urine to flow into the bag.

EQUIPMENT AND ADAPTIVE EQUIPMENT FOR INDWELLING CATHETERIZATION

The catheters used for indwelling catheterization are made of flexible material (e.g., rubber) and are longer than those used in CIC. Several types of catheters are available. Frequently there is a balloon port at the end of the catheter with a separate channel running the length of the catheter, in addition to the channel through which the urine flows. At the end of this channel, there is a balloon. Sterile water is usually injected into the port; as it flows to the end of the channel, the balloon inflates to help keep it in place. A variety of urinary collection bags may be used. (Refer to the preceding section on external urinary catheterization for further description.)

ASSISTIVE STRATEGIES FOR INDWELLING CATHETERIZATION

Inserting a sterile indwelling catheter is performed using sterile technique only by trained medical personnel. School personnel will have the responsibility of emptying the urinary collection bag and observing for complications. (Refer to the section on collection devices for the steps involved in emptying the bag.)

INSTRUCTIONAL STRATEGIES AND MODIFICATIONS FOR INDWELLING CATHETERIZATION

Since insertion of the catheter requires sterile technique, the student will not be catheterizing himself. However, the student may be taught to empty his own urinary collection bag. (Refer to Figure 11–8 for a task analysis.)

INDWELLING CATHETERIZATION PROBLEMS AND EMERGENCIES

Infection

School personnel need to inspect the urine before it is emptied to check for cloudiness, odor, or color change for indications of an infection. (Refer to "Infection" under CIC). To help decrease the likelihood of an infection, care must also be taken that the tube is not accidentally kinked or obstructed to allow the urine to flow out of the bladder. When moving the student, the bag must remain lower than the bladder, or the tubing needs to be clamped to avoid the problem of the urine flowing back into the bladder from the tubing, resulting in infection. In addition, to avoid the risk of infection, the catheter should not be disconnected from the urinary collection bag (Skale, 1992).

Accidental Removal of the Catheter

Indwelling catheters are taped in place to help prevent them from being pulled out. It is important that students in wheelchairs who have indwelling catheters be sure that the tubing does not get tangled in the wheels of the wheelchair and pulled out accidentally. If the catheter is pulled out, the designated personnel and the parents need to be notified. It is important that the catheter is kept so the balloon can be inspected to determine whether part of the balloon was left in the bladder. Pulling out the catheter with an inflated balloon may cause damage to the urethra, and the student may need to be seen by a physician.

MANAGEMENT ISSUES FOR URINARY CATHETERIZATION AND USE OF COLLECTION DEVICES

Individualized Health Plan and Individualized Educational Program

Several areas need to be included in an individualized health plan (IHP) for the student that are specific to the procedure and the individual student. Figure 11-9 includes the specialized areas for CIC, Credé, external urinary catheter, and indwelling catheter. Specific problems and emergencies for each procedure should be addressed as to what needs to be done if they occur.

The individualized educational program should include whether the student is being taught the procedure and in what manner (e.g., verbally to direct someone, partial participation, independence in all steps). Areas of instruction may include (a) demonstrating understanding of the purpose of the procedure, (b) identifying the equipment used in the procedure, (c) demonstrating the steps of the procedure, (d) demonstrating proper use of the equipment, including cleaning and storage, (e) understanding how to monitor fluid intake (if applicable), and (f) demonstrating how to prevent and treat problems and emergencies. Sample objectives for the IEP are found in Figure 11-10.

Diet and Fluid Intake

Sporadically drinking large quantities of water will cause the amount of urine in the bladder to vary. (Drinking such liquids as coffee will have the same effect.) When clean intermittent catheterization occurs on a time schedule, drinking excessive liquids is problematic since the bladder may overdistend before it is time to catheterize. Fluid intake is usually encouraged to be kept at a fairly constant level.

A well-rounded diet that includes fruits, vegetables, grains, and fluid is important to reduce the problem of constipation. Constipation can result in increased straining to have a bowel movement, which may result in the bladder releasing urine (Kuntz, 1996a).

Sex of Personnel Assisting Student

Consideration should be given as to who is selected to assist the student with the catheterization procedure. Adolescent girls may prefer to be catheterized by a female, and adolescent boys may prefer to be catheterized by a male (Gray, 1996). Some schools have the policy that catheterization occurs with someone of the same sex assisting. Other school systems have a policy of having a

Latex allergy? _____ yes _____ no, comment: _____

FOR CIC

Size of catheter: _____

Schedule of CIC (or if by volume, how it is set): _____

Child-specific procedure attached? _____yes _____no

Directions for CIC Problems and Emergencies

Infection: _____

Inability to pass catheter: _____

Omission of catheterization: _____

No urine on catheterization: _____

Urination between catheterizations: _____

Soreness, swelling, or discharge: _____

Bleeding: _____

FOR CREDÉ

Schedule of performing Credé: _____

Is it done in conjunction with CIC? _____yes _____no

Child-specific procedure attached? _____yes _____no

Directions for Credé Problems and Emergencies

Infection: _____

Injury: _____

FOR EXTERNAL URINARY CATHETER

If the external catheter comes off, do school personnel reapply another one?

_____ yes _____no

Child-specific procedure attached? _____yes _____no

Directions for External Urinary Catheter Problems and Emergencies

Infection: _____

Skin irritation: _____

FOR INDWELLING CATHETER

Directions for Indwelling Catheter Problems and Emergencies

Infection: _____

Catheter is accidentally pulled out: _____

FIGURE 11-9 Specialized areas to include in an IHP on urinary catheterization and collection devices

Independent Performance of Task

Using a designated time schedule, the
student will independently complete
all the steps of the task analysis for
catheterization with 100% accuracy
on each occasion for 4 weeks.

The student will empty the leg bag when
full, without spillage, with 100%
accuracy on each occasion for 3
weeks.

Partial Performance of Task

The student will gather equipment for
catheterization for the teacher to
perform procedure with 100%
accuracy on each occasion for 2
weeks.

The student will assume the correct
position for catheterization with 90%
accuracy on each occasion for 2 weeks.

After the teacher correctly places tube in
urethra, the student will help guide

the tube and stop moving the tube
into position when correctly
positioned with 100% accuracy for 4
weeks.

Directing the Task

The student will guide the adult in each step
of the catheterization procedure with
100% accuracy on each occasion for 2
weeks.

Knowledge of the Task

The student will identify and describe the
parts of the urinary system with 80%
accuracy for three consecutive sessions.

The student will identify three potential
problems that can occur with the
catheterization procedure and identify
what should be done for each, with
100% accuracy for four consecutive
sessions.

FIGURE 11-10 Sample IEP objectives for urinary catheterization and
collection devices

second assistant be present. Each school district
will need to determine how this type of situation
will be handled.

SUMMARY

Students who are unable to urinate using a toilet because of some physical problem may benefit from catheterization or using a collection
device. Some of the common procedures include

(a) clean intermittent catheterization, (b) Credé,
(c) use of an external urinary catheter, and (d) indwelling catheter. The student's physician decides
whether any of these procedures are needed to
help the student. The person performing any of
these procedures needs to remember to perform
these procedures in private and with dignity and
respect. The student should actively participate in
as much of the procedure as possible. It is important that the steps of the student-specific procedure are adhered to and that it is known what to
do if a problem occurs.

12

Colostomies and Other Ostomies

Elimination of feces and urine from the body is essential to maintain health by preventing the build-up of waste products in the body. Some students, however, may have an obstruction, disease, or trauma that prevents urine or feces from exiting the body through the normal anatomical route. These students typically have an artificial opening on their abdomens to allow urine or feces to exit. This artificial opening is known as an **ostomy** and is surgically created by connecting a section of the intestine or part of the urinary system to the outside of the body, typically through the abdomen.

There are different types of ostomies, named after the part of the urinary system or intestine used to make the ostomy. Ostomies can be divided into three major types: (a) ostomies of the urinary system, known as **ureterostomies** and **nephrostomies** (depending on the part of the urinary system); (b) ostomies of the small intestine, known as **ileostomies** and **jejunostomies;** and (c) ostomies of the large intestine, known as **colostomies** and **cecostomies.**

Ostomies have a long history. The earliest artificial openings were not performed by surgeons but by nature (e.g., strangulated hernia) or ancient warriors (e.g., abdominal wounds). The first purposeful creation of an ostomy occurred more than 200 years ago to treat abdominal trauma and bowel obstruction. This procedure has rapidly evolved over the years from a hastily constructed, conspicuous opening, covered by moss and leaves and held in place with a crude leather strap, to an odorless, inconspicuous opening that may not require a collection bag (Cataldo, 1993).

Several different conditions may result in the need for either a temporary or permanent ostomy. In some instances, an infant may be born with a congenital malformation of the intestines or bladder that requires an ostomy to permit elimination of feces or urine. Diseases, such as Hirschprung's disease (a congenital disease in which there is absent or abnormal intestinal movement, resulting in obstruction) or Crohn's disease (a chronic inflammatory disease of the intestines of unknown origin) can require an ostomy. Other types of conditions that may require an ostomy include intestinal cancer, trauma to the intestines or urinary system, diverticulitis, ulcerative colitis, and bowel or urinary tract obstruction (Borwell, 1996; Farr, 1991; Watt, 1985). If the ostomy is temporary, surgery can be performed to close the ostomy and reconnect the intestine or ureter when the intestine or bladder is repaired or returned to a functional state.

DESCRIPTION OF OSTOMIES

When a person has an ostomy, he can no longer eliminate urine through the urethra (when the ostomy pertains to the urinary system) or cannot eliminate feces through the anus (when the ostomy pertains to the intestines). Urine or feces will exit the visible part of the ostomy known as a **stoma.** The stoma is made with a section of the intestine, and it appears as a small donut-shaped hole, often pink in color. It is similar in color and texture to the inside cheek of the mouth. The stoma protrudes about ½ to ¾ inch above the skin surface. Although it may appear fragile, it can be rolled on or slept on without difficulty and washed with a washcloth. Since the stoma has no nerve endings, there is no feeling at the stoma, so care must be taken to prevent injury (Skale, 1992).

The stoma may be located in a variety of places in the abdominal area. Scars, skin lesion, obesity and other factors determine the site. Individuals with physical disabilities or obesity will often have the stoma placed slightly higher than usual for ease of access to the stoma. Some stomas may be made below the bikini line for cosmetic reasons. In very rare circumstances, the stoma may be located on a person's back. Depending on the type of operation, the person may have two stomas instead of one (Corman, 1993).

Different types of ostomies result in different types of elimination. Elimination may be continuous or intermittent. Most types of ostomies do not allow the person to control when urine or fecal material will be emptied. These ostomies will need an ostomy bag (also referred to as a pouch or collection bag) placed over the stoma to collect the waste material. The ostomy bag is emptied periodically throughout the day. Some ostomies do not require an ostomy bag, because feces can be eliminated through the stoma on a regular basis. The different types of ostomies will have different implications for the person responsible for assisting the student with ostomy care in the school setting.

Nephrostomies and Ureterostomies

Nephrostomies and ureterostomies are ostomies pertaining to the urinary system (see Table 12-1). In the urinary system, the kidneys filter out waste products that form urine. As the urine is formed, it flows from the kidney into the expanded upper end of the ureter, known as the *renal pelvis* of the kidney. Urine flow continues down the ureters and into the bladder where it is stored until it is time to urinate (see Figure 12-1). A *nephrostomy* is an opening made directly from the pelvis of the kidney through the abdominal wall. A *ureterostomy* is made by one or both ureters surgically moved to empty through the opening made on the abdomen (see Figure 12-2). In some instances, a ureter may surgically be connected to the intestine (known as an **ileal conduit**). Nephrostomies and ureterostomies drain urine constantly (Skale, 1992). To collect the urine, a collection bag is placed over the stoma and emptied when full.

Ileostomies and Jejunostomies

Ileostomies and jejunostomies are ostomies pertaining to the small intestine. In the digestive sys-

Table 12-1 Types of Ostomies and Their Placement

Type of ostomy	Placement
Nephrostomy	Urinary system
Ureterostomy	Urinary system
Ileostomy	Small intestine
Jejunostomy	Small intestine
Colostomy	Large intestine
Cecostomy	Large intestine

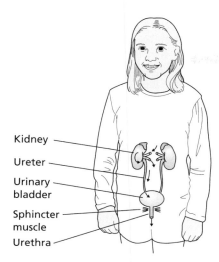

Kidney

Ureter

Urinary bladder

Sphincter muscle

Urethra

FIGURE 12-1 The urinary system

tem, food first enters the mouth and, after being swallowed, travels down the pharynx (throat) and through a passage leading down to the stomach, known as the *esophagus*. In the stomach the food is mixed with gastric secretions until a semifluid mixture is formed. As the stomach contracts, the semifluid mixture containing nutrients from the digested food and drink enters the short upper part of the intestine known as the *duodenum*. Through peristaltic movement (wormlike movements), the semifluid travels through the middle section of the small intestine, known as the *jejunum,* followed by the last part of the small intestine, referred to as the *ileum*. The contents then move into the large intestine (see Figure 12-3). While this semifluid makes its way through the intestines, nutrients and water are absorbed into the body from the intestines.

When the ostomy is made with the jejunum, it is referred to as a *jejunostomy*. An *ileostomy* is made from the ileum. Jejunostomies and ileostomies drain greenish brown or yellowish liquid stool almost continually through the stoma. An ostomy bag usually needs to be worn over the stoma. Proper fit of the bag is important to prevent the stool from coming in contact with the skin on the abdomen surrounding the stoma, because the stool from the small intestine contains digestive acids that are very irritating to the skin. If the stool comes in contact with the skin, skin breakdown can result (Graff et al., 1990).

Some individuals qualify for a special operation

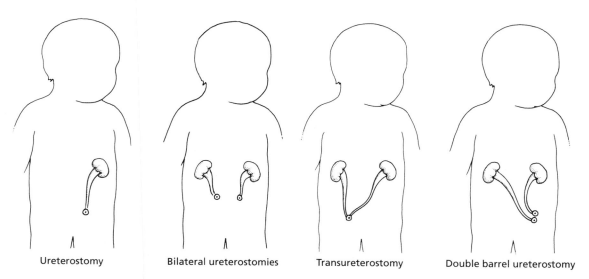

Ureterostomy   Bilateral ureterostomies   Transureterostomy   Double barrel ureterostomy

FIGURE 12-2 Different types of ureterostomies.

From Nedra Skale, *Manual of Pediatric Nursing Procedures*. Copyright © 1992 by J. B. Lippincott Company. Reprinted with permission of Lippincott, Williams, & Williams.

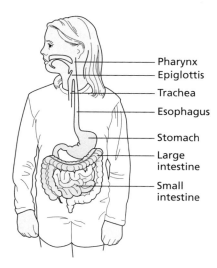

Pharynx
Epiglottis
Trachea
Esophagus
Stomach
Large
intestine
Small
intestine

FIGURE 12-3 The gastrointestinal system

that allows the individual to control the release of fecal material from the ileostomies. This is known as a *continent ileostomy*. Continent ileostomies are often made by making an internal pouch (reservoir) under the skin to hold the fecal material. To evacuate the internal pouch, a tube is introduced into the pouch about four times a day. A small dressing is put over the stoma between evacuation times. Individuals who are unable to put the tube into the pouch correctly due to cognitive or physical reasons are not considered appropriate candidates for this procedure (Gorfine, Bauer, & Gelernt, 1993). Other new procedures are currently being performed that eliminate an ostomy altogether and use internal pouches and sometimes artificial sphincter mechanisms in conjunction with the anus (Salter, 1996).

Colostomies and Cecostomies

Colostomies and cecostomies are ostomies pertaining to the large intestine. As the fecal material leaves the small intestines, it enters a large pouch at the beginning of the large intestine, known as the *cecum* (see Figure 12-3). From the cecum, the fecal material goes through the ascending colon, transverse colon, and descending colon. From the descending colon, it travels into the sigmoid

colon, then into the rectum, and out the anus. As stool progresses through the intestines, it becomes more solid as water is reabsorbed. Whereas the stool is liquid to semiliquid in the small intestine, cecum, and ascending colon, it is more formed in the transverse colon and more solid in the descending colon (Grotz & Pemberton, 1993).

There are several different types of colostomies. A *cecostomy* is the creation of an ostomy with the cecum. It is rarely used today and often temporary (Senagore, 1993). The most common ostomies are *colostomies,* which are ostomies of the large intestine. Typically, the student will have a single colostomy, composed of one stoma. When the colostomy is permanent, one end of the bowel is brought through an opening in the abdomen, and often the rest of the bowel is removed. Occasionally, a student may have a double-barrel colostomy or a loop colostomy in which there are two stomas (see Figure 12-4). These types of colostomies are easy to perform in emergency situations and are often temporary. By the surgeon bringing both ends of the bowel to the abdomen, the colostomy is easy to close once it is no longer needed (Pearl & Abcarian, 1993). When there are two stomas, one of the stomas will drain the stool. The second stoma that is located closer to the rectum (often called a mucous fistula) does not drain stool but mucus that is naturally made by the intestine. Some students with this type of colostomy may occasionally drain mucus from their rectum. Even if the colostomy is temporary, the length of time between the creation and closure of colostomies can range from 6 weeks to 6 months, making it likely that school personnel will come in contact with the student with the temporary colostomy (Khoury et al., 1996).

Colostomies drain less frequently, and the farther down the large intestine the colostomy is located, the more formed the stool tends to be. Typically the colostomy will intermittently drain stool into a bag, although colostomies of the descending colon may not need to use a colostomy bag. In some instances, these colostomies can achieve continence through **colostomy irrigation.** Colostomy irrigation is basically an enema that is given at the stoma. Often by irrigating the

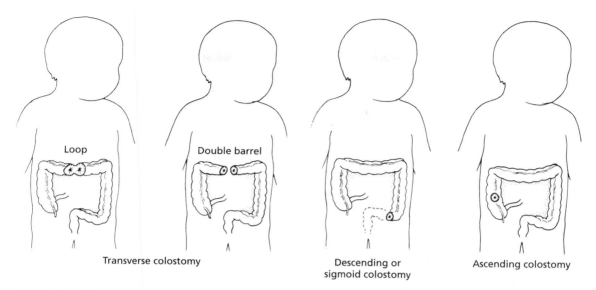

FIGURE 12-4 Different types of colostomies.

From Nedra Skale, *Manual of Pediatric Nursing Procedures.* Copyright © 1992 by J. B. Lippincott Company. Reprinted with permission of Lippincott, Williams, & Williams.

colostomy every day or every other day on a regular basis at home and by maintaining a controlled diet, the student can keep the stoma free of leakage between irrigations. The person may wear a colostomy bag (in case of leakage), a gauze pad or Band-Aid (for protection of the stoma), or nothing over the stoma. In some cases, new devices such as stoma plugs may be used to prevent accidental leakage for individuals who use irrigation to evacuate the colostomy. (See the section on adapted equipment for a description of the plug.)

Since colostomies are the most frequent type of ostomy, the term *colostomy* will be used primarily in the rest of the chapter. However, the information is applicable to most types of ostomies pertaining to elimination unless otherwise noted.

EQUIPMENT AND ADAPTIVE EQUIPMENT FOR OSTOMIES

Several different types of equipment are used in colostomy care. A colostomy system is typically composed of a skin barrier, a colostomy bag (with adhesive backing), and in some systems, a belt to help hold the colostomy bag in place. The skin barrier usually appears as a thin, flat, round (or square) wafer with a hole in the middle that fits around the base of the stoma. One side of the skin barrier attaches to the skin and the other side to the colostomy bag. The skin barrier protects the skin and prevents leakage of the stool or urine. The wafer-type skin barrier is often made of a rubbery type of material. However, some students may not use the wafer type of skin barrier but instead a skin barrier in a liquid or paste form.

Colostomy bags are typically one- or two-piece systems. One-piece colostomy bags have the skin barrier already attached to the bag as one unit. The unit is just attached to the skin (see Figure 12-5). Two-piece systems have the colostomy bag and skin barrier separate, so that the skin barrier is applied first, followed by the colostomy bag. In some two-piece systems, the colostomy bag and a barrier connect to each other with interlocking plastic rings that allow the colostomy bag to be taken on and off the barrier. In other two-piece systems, once the bag is at-

FIGURE 12-5 A child placing a one-piece colostomy bag system over a colostomy. The dark ring on the colostomy bag is the skin barrier, which is attached to an adhesive backing (clear, rectangular material). A plastic loop is sticking out from behind the adhesive backing, to permit a belt to be connected.

tached to the barrier, it cannot be taken off and then reattached. It should be noted that barriers are not always necessary for ureterostomies or nephrostomies. Skin barriers may be used for ureterostomies or nephrostomies since their use may increase the wearing time of the ostomy bag before a new one is needed. When a barrier is not used, the urinary ostomy bag may contain an antireflux valve that prevents the backflow of urine (Lavery & Erwin-Toth, 1993).

The skin barrier has a hole in the middle of it for the stoma to fit through. This hole needs to be large enough to easily fit over the stoma but small enough so that minimal skin is exposed to prevent the skin from coming in contact with the skin-irritating feces (or urine if it is a ureterostomy or nephrostomy). The hole is typically ⅛ to ¹⁄₁₆ inch larger than the stoma (Farr, 1991; Lavary & Erwin-Toth, 1993). In some systems, the skin barrier is precut to fit the exact size of the stoma. In other systems, the hole needs to be cut each time a new colostomy bag is used. A measuring guide with concentric rings outlining the different diameters is included with each new box of barriers. After determining the correct hole size with the measuring guide (unless it is already known), the hole is cut into the barrier. (The

back of the barrier usually has rings drawn as cutting guides, specifying the same diameters on the measuring guide.) Skin barriers for irregularly shaped stomas may be cut out by following a guide that may be made from a transparent piece of plastic and felt-tip marker by tracing the outline of the stoma. Since the size of the stoma decreases for the first 2 months after surgery, the size of the hole may change. Thus, the parents will need to measure the size every time they change the bag and regularly inform school personnel of the appropriate size.

The colostomy bag may vary in size, shape, and design. Some bags are disposable; some are reusable. Some colostomy bags open at the bottom to allow the contents to drain out. Depending on the type of colostomy bag, the bag may close using a plastic barrette-type clasp that pinches the bag closed. Some students may use a rubber band to close off the bottom of the bag. Some bags may open and close using a valve (usually for urinary system ostomies). Colostomy bags that open at the bottom are typically used when frequent emptying is needed. Other colostomy bags are not drainable (closed end) and are used for protection in case there is drainage at an unscheduled time (Figure 12-6).

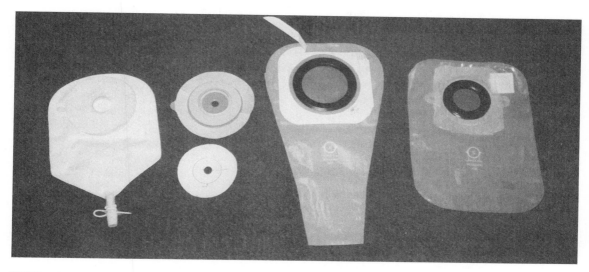

FIGURE 12-6 From left to right: A ureterostomy bag, a skin barrier that requires cutting (with a measurement guide under it), a colostomy bag that opens on the bottom and has paper backing starting to be removed to expose the adhesive backing, and a closed-end colostomy bag that has a small filter on the upper right-hand corner of the bag, which appears as a small square.

Some colostomy bags have a small filter to allow gas to escape (see Figure 12-6). If there is no filter, the colostomy bag may be opened at the bottom to allow the gas to escape. Another alternative is to make a small hole through the bag and cover it with tape. When gas occurs, the tape may be pulled back and the bag pressed by a hand to allow air to escape (Adams & Selekof, 1986). This is not always recommended since the odor usually contained in the bag can penetrate the tape and result in an odor outside the bag.

Some individuals who irrigate their colostomy and do not use a colostomy bag may use a **stoma cap** (also referred to as a *colostomy plug device*). This device is a disposable plug that fits into the stoma, preventing stool from leaking out but allowing gas to exit without odor or noise through a filtering system. It is typically used by individuals who are able to empty their colostomy on a regular schedule but may have some leakage from the stoma (Gorfine et al.,

1993; Soliani, Carbognani, Piccolo, Sabbagh, & Cudazzo, 1992). Other devices are also being used to try to achieve a continent colostomy. One new device under experimentation uses a colostomy tube that fits into the bowel and has an expandable inner ring that creates a barrier to fecal flow (Kosorok, 1995).

ASSISTIVE STRATEGIES FOR OSTOMIES

School personnel may be involved in emptying the colostomy bag or assisting the student in emptying the bag, or they may have no active role in colostomy care. Depending on the type of colostomy and the student's abilities, the student may be self-sufficient, or the colostomy may not need emptying at school. Typically the colostomy bag will be changed at home, approximately every 5 to 7 days (extending up to 10 days when there is a good seal and no leakage). Some bags may need to be changed more frequently on a daily or every other day basis to prevent leakage (Corman, 1993). However, if the colostomy bag leaks in school, it will need to be changed by the designated personnel to prevent skin breakdown. The following discussion includes two procedures: emptying a colostomy bag (of urine, stool, or gas) and changing a colostomy bag.

Preparation for Emptying a Colostomy Bag

When the colostomy bag is about one-third full, it should be emptied to prevent leakage. The student should be informed that it is time to empty the colostomy bag by being given an explanation of what is to occur. If the student has poor receptive skills, the student may be handed a clip similar to the one used to close the bag or a mounted rubber band (depending on what closes the bag) as a symbol that the bag is to be emptied.

Emptying the colostomy bag should occur in a private location, with dignity and respect afforded to the student. Sometimes there will be an odor as the contents are emptied. It should be kept in mind that this is normal for individuals who do not have ostomies and are having a bowel movement in the toilet. Room deodorizers can be kept in the location the bag is being emptied. Gloves should always be worn when emptying the colostomy bag.

Equipment and Supply List

Gloves

Container to empty contents of colostomy bag

Procedure for Emptying a Colostomy Bag

After explaining the procedure to the student, gathering equipment, going to a private location, washing hands, and putting on gloves, the person performing the procedure is ready to begin.

Steps in the Procedure for Emptying a Colostomy Bag	*Rationale*
1. Open the clamp or remove the rubber band. (If it is a colostomy of the urinary system, a valve may be opened).	The type of colostomy and the person's preference will determine what is used to close the bag.
2. Empty the contents into the toilet or other designated container. Empty the container contents into the toilet.	Often the student will be unable to be positioned on or by the toilet to empty the colostomy bag. It may be easier to empty the contents in a container first, then empty the contents of the container into the toilet.
3. Rinse the inside of the colostomy bag with lukewarm tap water using a small paper cup or squirt bottle with a small nozzle. The water should avoid the area near the stoma.	Water should be avoided near the stoma so that the seal between the barrier/colostomy bag and skin is not loosened, resulting in leakage (Skale, 1992). This step is optional and may not be part of the student's procedure.
4. Close the colostomy bag, remove gloves, and wash hands.	
5. Document occurrence of procedure and any abnormalities.	Feces should be observed for color, consistency, blood, or mucus. Urine should

Steps in the Procedure for Emptying a Colostomy Bag	Rationale
	be observed for color, amount, and odor. The stoma and skin should be examined (through the bag) for any signs of irritation or abnormality. If any abnormalities are noted, the appropriate person should be contacted, following the student's individualized health plan.

Preparation for Changing a Colostomy Bag

Typically the colostomy bag will be changed at home. If the colostomy bag leaks while the student is at school, however, the bag will need to be changed to prevent skin irritation. The procedure should be explained to the student. If the student has poor receptive skills, a symbol, such as part of a colostomy bag or the package of adhesive removal, may be given to the student as a symbol representing the procedure. As with emptying a colostomy bag, changing a colostomy bag should occur in a private location.

Equipment and Supply List
Gloves
Colostomy bag
Skin barrier

Measuring guide (if not precut)
Scissors
Skin preparation (see student-specific guidelines)
Belt (if applicable)
Soap and water
Washcloth (or other cloth or wipe)
Adhesive remover
Tape

Procedure for Changing a Colostomy Bag

After explaining the procedure to the student, washing hands, putting on gloves, gathering equipment, and going to a private location, the person performing the procedure is ready to change the colostomy bag.

Steps in the Procedure for Changing a Colostomy Bag	Rationale
1. Empty the colostomy bag. (See the prior procedure.)	Emptying the colostomy bag first (for those colostomy bags that open) will help avoid accidents.
2. Remove skin barrier and colostomy bag. a. Gently remove any tape. b. Apply a few drops of skin-safe solvent between skin and disc of appliance, if applicable.	Procedure may vary on how to take off colostomy bag, depending on type of colostomy bag and how it was applied. Some procedures will include the use of solvent to dissolve the adhesive.

Steps in the Procedure for Changing a Colostomy Bag	*Rationale*
c. Gently push skin away from bag instead of pulling the appliance off the skin.	Pushing skin away, rather than pulling, is less irritating.
3. Place toilet paper or other absorbent material over the stoma to absorb drainage.	Toilet paper will protect the skin from stoma drainage that can be irritating to the skin. Leave the toilet paper in place until it is time to put on a new bag.
4. If the bag is not open ended, empty its contents into the toilet. If the bag is reusable, rinse it out with water. (If the bag is disposable, empty it first, then place it in a plastic bag and tie it for later disposal.)	It is important to know whether the colostomy bag is reusable or disposable. If it is reusable, you may use it again or send it home in a proper container, depending on the student's procedure, availability of additional bags, and the bag's condition.
5. Remove absorbent material over the stoma while cleaning. Gently clean the stoma area, without scrubbing. (Typically it is cleaned with soap and water. Sometimes special soap may be used. In some procedures, solvent is used prior to cleaning on the skin.) Dry the area completely.	All adhesive needs to be removed from the skin in order for the new bag to adhere securely. Some procedures will include using skin-safe solvent to dissolve any remaining adhesive.
6. Inspect the skin and stoma for any irritation, skin breakdown, or abnormalities. Place new absorbent material over the stoma.	Careful examination of the area should routinely occur.
7. Prepare the colostomy bag for application. a. Cut a hole in the skin barrier (if not precut), using the guide.	Be sure the hole is cut to the prescribed size so it will fit over the stoma and minimize exposed skin.
8. If a skin preparation is prescribed, it would be applied at this time.	A liquid or spray skin sealant may be used to protect the skin from mechanical trauma. The "tacky" skin surface provided by the sealant promotes snug barrier adhesion (Farr, 1991).
9. Apply the skin barrier. a. For a wafer-type barrier, carefully place the adhesive side of the barrier over the stoma and gently press the barrier against the skin, being careful not to make any wrinkles in the barrier.	Wrinkles in the skin barrier will result in leaks and skin irritation. If this is a one-piece system, the absorbent material resting on the stoma is removed before applying the barrier with the preattached bag (see step 10).

Steps in the Procedure for Changing a Colostomy Bag	*Rationale*
b. If the skin barrier is a paste or powder, apply an even coat on the skin, up to edge of the stoma and covering about a 3-inch radius (Farr, 1991).	
10. Remove the absorbent material resting on the stoma, peel off backing from adhesive on pouch, center the hole of the colostomy bag over the stoma, and attach.	If using a two-piece system, the colostomy bag will attach to the barrier. If using a one-piece system, the colostomy bag with the preattached barrier will be applied to the skin around the stoma.
11. If the pouch is open ended, press out the air and close the opening with the provided clip or rubber band.	Pressing out the air will allow expelled gas to leave the bag. If this is not done, the colostomy bag can overinflate when gas enters it, causing the colostomy bag to partially detach from the barrier.
12. Place hypoallergenic tape around the edges of barrier that are against the skin, if indicated.	Tape may be additionally added for increased protection. Tape is applied in a "window pane" fashion (tape goes around edges).
13. If a belt is used to hold the colostomy bag in place, put the belt on.	
14. Put disposable items in a plastic bag and properly throw away.	
15. Take off gloves and wash hands. Document that the procedure was done and document any abnormalities.	Any skin, colostomy, or feces/urine abnormalities should be documented and the appropriate person contacted. Follow the student's individual health plan.

Care of Equipment and Daily Care

The stoma area needs to be kept clean, and the colostomy bag should be emptied as needed. Extra supplies should be kept in school in the event that the colostomy bag needs to be changed. Reusable colostomy bags should be thoroughly cleaned. If they are alternated, the one that was just used should be cleaned and allowed to dry. The parents may soak the bag in a deodorizing agent when it is sent home.

INSTRUCTIONAL STRATEGIES AND MODIFICATIONS FOR EMPTYING AND CHANGING A COLOSTOMY BAG

Students who have ostomies should be taught to perform the procedure as independently as possible. Depending on the student's physical status, age, and cognitive abilities, the student may perform only a few steps or the entire procedure. Teaching this self-help skill will increase the student's independence, cooperation, and self-esteem.

To instruct on properly emptying the colostomy bag, the procedure can be broken down into small teachable steps. As discussed in Chapter 2, the steps of any task will vary among students, based on the individually prescribed procedure and the student's physical and cognitive capabilities. A typical task analysis is shown in Figure 12-7.

A key element of emptying the bag, is to be sure the student is able to open the bag without pulling the bag off the skin barrier. Students with physical or cognitive impairments may be taught to rest their wrists on their abdomen. For students with physical impairments, this technique provides support; for students with cognitive impairments, it prevents the bag from being accidentally pulled away from the barrier. The type of closing device used with the colostomy bag will require some consideration when there is a physical disability. Rubber bands often require far more motor control than a simple clamp.

Students need to recognize when the colostomy bag needs to be emptied. For students who are very young or who have cognitive impairments, an antecedent prompt may be used as discussed in Chapter 2. In this instance, the an-

tecedent prompt is a mark (or tape) placed on the colostomy bag indicating that when the urine or feces reaches the mark, the bag needs to be emptied. Students should be taught to check their bag regularly to determine whether it needs emptying.

Putting on a new colostomy bag entails several steps, and students can gradually learn parts of the procedure until they can eventually do the entire procedure. Figure 12-8 shows a typical task analysis of the procedure. Some of the steps may need to be further broken down, depending on the student's capabilities. For example, step 7, cleaning the stoma area, may need to be ex-

---

1. Wash hands.
2. Open the clamp.
3. Empty ostomy contents into a container.
4. Empty the container contents into the toilet.
5. Close the ostomy bag.
6. Clean the container.
7. Wash hands.

FIGURE 12-7 Sample task analysis for emptying a colostomy bag

---

1. Wash hands.
2. Open the clamp.
3. Empty the ostomy contents into a container.
4. Empty the container contents into the toilet.
5. Remove the skin barrier and ostomy bag.
6. Place toilet paper over the stoma.
7. Clean the stoma area.
8. Dry the stoma area.
9. Peel the backing off a one-piece ostomy system.
10. Remove toilet paper over the stoma.
11. Put a barrier with the ostomy bag over the stoma.
12. Press the barrier to be sure it is adhering well.
13. Close the opening with a clip.
14. Clean out the container.
15. Put disposable items in a plastic bag and throw away.
16. Wash hands.

FIGURE 12-8 Sample task analysis for changing a one-piece colostomy bag

panded to include each step in the cleaning process. Different colostomy equipment will also affect the task analysis. Colostomy equipment selection should take into account the physical or cognitive abilities of the student. For example, thicker wafer barriers are easier to put on than thinner ones, which tend to wrinkle. It may also be easier to learn to apply a one-unit colostomy systems that has fewer procedural steps than a two-unit system. The person teaching the student this self-help skill may discuss equipment options with the parents and the nurse to determine whether other suitable equipment and supplies can be used that will allow the student to perform the procedure independently when there is a physical or cognitive impairment.

Time-Limited Steps and Caution Steps

Several different instructional strategies may be used to teach a student to empty or change a colostomy bag. For higher-functioning students, the teacher may model the steps and provide guided practice with the student, while lower-functioning students may benefit from a time delay procedure or multiple prompting strategy (e.g., system of least prompts). (See Chapter 2 for more information.) There are no time-limited steps in the colostomy procedures that require completion of a step within a certain time frame. However, cleaning the stoma can be considered a caution step since the stoma could be harmed by a quick, jerking movement resulting in poking the stoma or rubbing it very roughly. If the student is to perform this step, the teacher will need to model the step and then provide shadowing. For lower-functioning students, the teacher will often provide a full physical prompt and move to shadowing. Shadowing is performed by the teacher keeping her hands within an inch of the student's hands until the step is completed so that she can intervene quickly if necessary. As with all teaching procedures, the task analysis should be placed on a data sheet (like the one in Chapter 2) to chart progress. The caution step should be

highlighted on the data sheet as a reminder to provide shadowing.

COLOSTOMY PROBLEMS AND EMERGENCIES

Many problems may occur with a colostomy, such as gas and odor, leakage, and skin problems around the stoma. Depending on the severity of the problem, some emergency situations may include bleeding from the stoma, diarrhea, obstruction, and changes in appearance of the stoma.

Gas and Odor

As previously discussed, gas may be released from the colostomy bag through an opening in the bag or may escape through a filter. However, certain foods may produce a large amount of gas that the person may wish to avoid. Some of these gas-forming foods include apple juice, asparagus, cucumbers, dried beans and peas, eggs, fish, grape juice, melon, onion, sweet potatoes, and vegetables of the cabbage family (e.g., cauliflower) (Moffitt, 1992). For individuals with a colostomy, it typically takes about 6 hours from the time these foods are ingested to the time gas occurs. Some individuals may eat these foods at times when gas will not be an embarrassment, avoid them completely, or eat foods such as yogurt that decrease gas formation. Unacceptable amounts of gas may also occur from swallowing air. Since swallowed air is increased when chewing gum, using straws, or talking while eating, these activities may be eliminated or decreased.

Odor is primarily controlled through odor-proof colostomy bags and good hygiene (e.g., keeping the bottom of the bag clean) (Lavery & Erwin-Toth, 1993). Other means of odor control include the use of colostomy bag deodorants, which are tablets especially designed to be placed in the colostomy bag (when it is empty) to help eliminate odors. Certain oral tablets (e.g., Devrom), when taken consistently, may also reduce fecal odor. A persistent odor should not be present in a properly cared-for colostomy. If there is an odor, the bag needs to be checked for a leak or a poor seal.

Leakage

Colostomy bags that have been properly sized and correctly placed over the stoma should not leak. Leaks may be caused by a poor seal between the bag and the skin barrier. This can occur if the bag is not properly applied or when the bag is too full of feces, or urine, or gas that it pushes the bag away from the skin barrier. In these instances, the colostomy bag needs to be emptied and reapplied. It is important that leaks are not "patched" with tape or paste, because this approach usually does not work and can lead to skin irritation. Other possible causes of leakage include an incorrect bag size, improper care of the stoma, or diarrhea (Porter, Haynie, Bierle, Caldwell, & Palfrey, 1997). If this is the case, the appropriate person needs to be contacted and informed of the problem. Students should also be taught signs of an impending leakage. These include odor when the pouch is closed, visible wearing away of the skin barrier, or an itching or burning of the skin. When these occur, the ostomy bag needs to be changed promptly to prevent a leakage from occurring.

Skin Problems around the Stoma

The skin around the stoma may become irritated or actual skin breakdown may occur as a result of chemical, infectious, allergic, or mechanical causes. One of the most common chemical causes is the result of the skin coming in contact with urine or stool. This may occur when the hole in the colostomy bag around the stoma is too large or the colostomy bag is left on too long. The size of the colostomy bag and the barrier may need to be reevaluated.

Skin infections may occur from fungal or bacterial causes. Yeast infections are one of the most common types of infection in which the skin may appear patchy, reddened and scaly, or reddened and moist (Graff et al., 1990). Topical (on the skin) or oral medications may be prescribed by a physician to treat the infection. Good infection control procedures should be followed to decrease the possibilities of infection.

Allergic reactions may also cause skin irritation. Such reactions may occur from the products being used, such as the skin barriers, adhesives, and tapes. The precise product causing the reaction will need to be identified by the physician, and another product should be used in its place.

Mechanical skin irritation may occur when the tape or adhesive barrier is frequently removed from the skin (e.g., more than once a day). This can result in the skin pulling away as the adhesive is removed. The cause of frequent bag changes needs investigation, and the problem warrants correction to prevent skin irritation. Other mechanical trauma may occur when the stoma is injured from an improperly sized colostomy bag or the bag is applied incorrectly. If a belt is worn to hold the colostomy bag but is improperly placed, it may also injure surrounding skin. The procedure for applying the bag or belt may need to be retaught. If the colostomy bag is sized incorrectly, this situation needs to be corrected.

Careful examination of the skin surrounding the stoma for redness, irritation, or drainage should occur on a routine basis. Skin irritation should be reported to the appropriate personnel and intervention sought before it progresses to skin breakdown. Skin breakdown can be very serious if not treated and could result in infection and blood poisoning (septicemia).

Bleeding from the Stoma

Since there is no skin covering the stoma, it can easily bleed from being rubbed too hard or scratched by a fingernail. Fortunately, bleeding usually quickly stops. If it does not stop, applying pressure to the site should stop the bleeding. If the bleeding does not stop or bleeding is occurring from inside the stoma, a physician should be notified immediately.

Diarrhea or Vomiting

Students with ostomies may have an episode of diarrhea or vomiting, just as students without ostomies. Diarrhea and/or vomiting may occur because of illness or diet changes. When they do, the student must replace lost fluids and electrolytes. One way of monitoring when diarrhea is present is that for each bag emptied, the student should drink at least one glass of replacement fluid such as fruit juice, vegetable juice, broth, or sports drinks.

Individuals with ostomies of the small intestine or ascending colon are especially at risk for fluid and electrolyte imbalance when diarrhea or vomiting is present. School personnel and the student should know the warning signs of fluid and electrolyte imbalance: weakness, drowsiness, dry mouth and tongue, decreased urine output, stomach cramps, and/or dizziness when standing (Lavery & Erwin-Toth, 1993). If a fluid or electrolyte imbalance is suspected, a physician needs to be notified immediately, and the student often needs to be quickly taken to the hospital. Dehydration and severe electrolyte imbalance can lead to a life-threatening situation.

Obstruction

Passage of the stool may be blocked due to inadequately digested food. Food blockage may occur because of insufficient chewing of food or not eating enough foods with fiber. Certain foods have an increased incidence of blockage such as popcorn, peanuts, olives, string beans, and Chinese vegetables (Graff et al., 1990). Whatever the cause, personnel should be alert for signs of obstruction such as abdominal cramping, watery output (as the water seeps around the blockage) or no output, abdominal distention, stoma swelling, and nausea and vomiting. When an obstruction is suspected, the physician needs to be contacted immediately. If the obstruction is not treated, the pressure from the obstruction can result in tissue death in the intestine, possibly causing a hole that would require emergency surgery.

Changes in the Appearance of the Stoma

Personnel should be alert for any changes in the appearance of the stoma. Complications that could occur include (a) the stoma changing color (e.g., not receiving enough oxygen from the blood vessels); (b) the stoma retracting (sinking back into the abdomen); (c) stricture of the stoma (narrowing of the stoma opening due to inadequate blood supply to the stoma, skin irritation, or scarring); and (d) prolapse (the intestine connected to the stoma protrudes through the stoma) (Doberneck, 1991; Lazar, Kovalivker, Erez, & Motovic 1993; Londono-Schimmer, Leong, & Phillips, 1994). Since 20% to 30% of individuals with ostomies (specifically ileostomies) will have a complication relating to their stoma and 10% to 15% will require surgery to correct the problem, any changes should be immediately reported to the appropriate personnel (Nadler, 1992; Pemberton, 1988).

MANAGEMENT ISSUES FOR OSTOMIES

Individualized Health Plan and Individualized Educational Program

A student who has a colostomy (or other type of ostomy) will need several specific areas included in the individualized health plan (IHP) (see Figure 12-9). The plan should include the type of ostomy, how frequently it should be emptied, and the expected color and consistency of the output. Any dietary, fluid, or activity restrictions should be written on the plan. Student-specific guidelines, with approved step-by-step directions on changing the colostomy bag, if it comes off,

Type of Ostomy

_____ Ureterostomy

_____ Nephrostomy

_____ Ileostomy

_____ Jejunostomy

_____ Cecostomy

_____ Colostomy

Equipment

Is an ostomy bag used? _____ yes _____ no

Size of ostomy bag: _____

Size of barrier: _____

Expected frequency of bag emptying: _____

Typical color and consistency: _____

Fluid or dietary requirements: _____

_____

Activity restrictions: _____

_____

Child-specific procedure for emptying an ostomy bag attached? _____ yes _____ no

Child-specific procedure for changing an ostomy bag attached? _____ yes _____ no

Latex allergy? _____ yes _____ no, comment: _____

Directions for Ostomy Problems and Emergencies

Leakage: _____

Skin problems: _____

Bleeding from stoma: _____

Diarrhea or vomiting: _____

Obstruction: _____

Changes in appearance of stoma: _____

FIGURE 12-9 Specialized areas to include in an IHP on ostomy care

should be specified. The IHP should include guidelines for the following problems or emergencies: leakage, skin problems, bleeding, diarrhea, vomiting, obstruction, and changes in the appearance of the stoma.

The student's educational plan needs to address what aspects of care the student is learning for colostomy (or other type of ostomy) management. Areas of instruction may include (a) understanding the purpose of the colostomy; (b) identifying proper equipment; (c) demonstrating how to empty the colostomy bag;

(d) demonstrating how to change a colostomy bag; (e) demonstrating proper colostomy care; (f) demonstrating proper cleaning and storage of equipment; (g) understanding fluid, diet, and activity modifications; (h) knowing the signs of fluid and electrolyte imbalance and intestinal obstruction; (i) knowing the different potential problems and emergencies, how to identify them, and how treat them; and (j) practicing sound hygiene. Figure 12-10 contains some sample IEP objectives for colostomy and ileostomy management.

Diet and Exercise

When the intestinal stoma is newly constructed, the student will be placed on a special diet that first consists of clear liquids and progresses to a regular diet. Depending on the type of ostomy and surgery, the student may only need to eat a well-balanced diet and avoid foods that produce gas. In some instances, the physician may instruct the student to eat foods high in fiber to help prevent the development of food blockage. Any special diet needs to be documented on the health plan.

Students with ileostomies (and some colostomies) may be instructed to increase their fluid intake. Individuals with ileostomies often lose approximately 500 to 750 milliliters of fluid a day through the stoma, as compared to 100 to 200 milliliters a day by the average individual who has an intact intestinal system (Lavery & Erwin-Toth, 1993). It is especially important that teachers and the student are able to recognize signs of dehydration or electrolyte imbalance that can occur with periods of increased fluid loss (e.g., diarrhea). (See the section on emergencies.) Any fluid needs should be specified on the IHP.

Independent Performance of Task

After identifying that her colostomy bag needs to be changed, the student will empty the colostomy bag without spillage with 100% accuracy on each opportunity for 2 weeks.

The student will change her colostomy bag following the written procedure with 100% accuracy on each opportunity for 2 weeks.

Partial Performance of Task

After the adult pulls tape off, the student will gently pull off her colostomy bag and hand it to adult with 100% accuracy on each occasion for 2 weeks.

After the adult removes clip, the student will empty her colostomy bag into the designated container and hand the container to the adult to empty (and adult will reattach clip) with 100% accuracy on each occasion for 2 weeks.

Directing the Task

The student will identify proper equipment for the adult to obtain to change the colostomy bag with 100% accuracy for four consecutive sessions.

Using an AAC device, the student will guide the adult in each step of changing a colostomy bag with 100% accuracy on each occasion for 2 weeks.

Knowledge of the Task

The student will identify which foods may result in excessive gas in her colostomy bag or result in undesirable odors with 80% accuracy for four consecutive sessions.

With use of her AAC device, the student will identify potential problems that can occur with her colostomy and what should be done should the problem occur with 100% accuracy on four consecutive sessions.

FIGURE 12-10 Sample IEP objectives for colostomy and ileostomy care

Students with ostomies can participate in most physical activities, including swimming. However, the physician may advise the student against participation in contact sports due to the possibility of injuring the stoma (Lavery & Erwin-Toth, 1993).

Emotional Acceptance and Stoma Concealment

Students who acquire a colostomy (or other type of ostomy) in childhood or adolescence may have emotional difficulty accepting one. A colostomy represents a change in body image. Difficulty with coping, depression, and behavioral dysfunction have been found in individuals who have had a colostomy, months or sometimes years after the surgery (Alterescu, 1985; Keyes, Bisno, Richardson, & Marston, 1987). Teachers need to be supportive of the student and be willing to listen to concerns. In some instances, counseling may be indicated.

One management issue is maintaining privacy by concealing the stoma so it is not detectable to others. Clothing may easily conceal a stoma. When it is above the beltline, wearing a layer of knit clothing next to the body can help keep the colostomy bag secure and smooth. Wearing loose shirts or vests, sweaters, scarves, or jackets may also aid with concealment (Lavery & Erwin-Toth, 1993). When the stoma is below the belt line, snug undergarments over the colostomy bag can help conceal it. Girls may wear slacks or skirts with front pleats or that are loosely fitting. Bathing suits with patterns or draping may help with concealment. There are also specially designed underclothing for individuals with ostomies. Colostomy bag covers may also be used to conceal the bag contents as well as protect the skin from the plastic of the colostomy bag (Lavery & Erwin-Toth, 1993).

SUMMARY

There are three main types of ostomies: ostomies of the urinary system (ureterostomies and nephrostomies), ostomies of the small intestine (ileostomies and jejunostomies), and ostomies of the large intestine (colostomies and cecostomies). In the school setting, designated personnel will primarily be responsible for assisting the student to empty the ostomy bag when needed and observing for any skin or stoma abnormality or problem. However, if the ostomy bag leaks while at school, designated school personnel will need to apply a new one to prevent skin breakdown. Students with ostomies should be taught how to perform the procedure themselves as independently as possible, as well as the proper care and management of an ostomy.

Part IV

Instruction in Respiratory Procedures

13

Tracheostomies

Some students may have congenital abnormalities, medical disorders, or excessive respiratory secretions that result in an inability to breathe effectively through their mouth or nose. In these instances, the individual may need a tracheostomy. A *tracheostomy* is a surgical opening (from the suffix *-ostomy*) made in the lower neck into the trachea (windpipe). The individual primarily breathes through this opening instead of through the nose or mouth. A tracheostomy tube is usually inserted into the opening through which the individual breathes.

Tracheostomies have been described for thousands of years, with some accounts as far back as ancient Egypt (around 3000 B.C.). Their use became more common in children during the diphtheria and polio epidemics in the early to mid-1900s (Simma et al., 1994). Today, with the increased survival of very premature infants, tracheostomies are most commonly being performed for airway obstruction (subglottic stenosis) or prolonged mechanical ventilation and at much younger ages (Puhakka, Kero, Valli, & Iisalo, 1992; Schlessel, Harper, Rappa, Keningsberg, & Khanna, 1993; Shinkwin & Gibbin, 1996).

Tracheostomies are routinely used to (a) treat airway obstruction (at or above the larynx), (b) remove secretions that cannot be coughed out, and (c) provide an avenue for long-term artificial airway or mechanical ventilation (Skale, 1992). Airway obstruction may occur due to congenital malformation of the airway, tumors, narrowing of the airway (subglottic stenosis), foreign bodies, infections, and trauma to the upper face and neck (Simma et al., 1994; Tayal, 1994). Conditions such as pneumonia, hyaline membrane disease, and bronchopulmonary dysplasia may result in an inability to remove secretions (Skale, 1992). Neurological and neuromuscular conditions (e.g., spinal cord injuries) or conditions affecting gas diffusion may result in a need for a tracheostomy with mechanical ventilation (Biering-Sorensen & Biering-Sorensen, 1992; Gerber in Haas, 1993). Tracheostomies may be present for only a short time, such as until an infection clears or a foreign body blocking the upper airway is removed. In other instances, the tracheostomy may be permanent since the reason the tracheostomy was performed will not change but will stabilize the pulmonary condition (e.g., spinal cord injury, muscular dystrophy, chronic obstructive pulmonary disease).

DESCRIPTION OF TRACHEOSTOMIES

Several terms frequently arise when discussing tracheostomies. A **tracheotomy** is a temporary surgical incision made through the skin of the neck into the trachea (windpipe). A **tracheostomy** refers to a more permanent surgical creation of an opening in which the trachea is sutured to the skin incision (Tayal, 1994). However, these terms tend to be used interchangeably, with the term *tracheostomy* being used more frequently. The opening of a tracheostomy is referred to as a **stoma.** When a tube is inserted through the opening (as is usually the case), the terms **tracheostomy tube** or trach tube is used.

A tracheostomy is made by a surgical procedure in which an incision is made into the trachea. The incision point must be precisely located so as to not inadvertently cut a muscle (e.g., sternocleidomastoid muscle), vein or artery, or the thyroid. In adults, it is often necessary to remove part of the rings of cartilage surrounding the trachea to make the tracheostomy, while in children this typically is not necessary (Myers, Stook, & Johnson, 1985). There are some differences in the surgical procedure when the tracheostomy is only to remain for a maximum of a few months versus being permanent. When a permanent tracheostomy is anticipated, the procedure is modified to promote early

healing and maintenance of hygiene (Miller, Eliachar, & Tucker, 1995; Myers et al., 1985). A tracheostomy may also be created using a nonsurgical technique known as *percutaneous dilational tracheostomy.* This procedure involves inserting first a wire guide then a series of dilators over the guidewire until a tracheostomy tube will fit (Friedman et al, 1996; Toursarkissian et al., 1994).

A tracheostomy allows the person to breathe, exchange gases (e.g., oxygen and carbon dioxide), relieve obstruction, provide an avenue for suctioning, and allow administration of respiratory treatments and medications (including oxygen). However, a tracheostomy also results in several changes in the respiratory tract. Before discussing these changes, it is important to review some basic anatomy of the upper respiratory system (see Figure 13-1, and refer back to Figure 10-1b for upper airway).

The nasal airway is the primary pathway for breathing. As air enters the nostrils, some foreign particles are removed from the air as they come in contact with hairs located at the entrance of the nostrils. As the air flows through the winding nasal passages, air turbulence is created each time

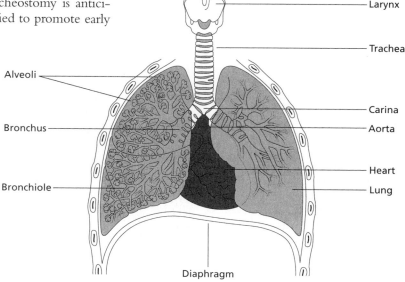

FIGURE 13-1 The respiratory system

the direction of air movement needs to change to make its way through the passages. This results in further filtering out foreign particles since these particles have more mass and cannot change their direction of travel as quickly as air. Particles then become entrapped in a mucous coating that lines the nasal passages. The nasal passages also result in warming and humidifying the air before it passes through the rest of the respiratory tract.

Oral breathing primarily occurs during speech or exercise. This is because oral breathing results in less resistance than nasal breathing. Due to nasal breathing resulting in air warming, humidification, and particle filtration, it is important that we breathe primarily through the nasal route even though it has a higher resistance (Motoyama, 1985). As the air leaves the nasal passages or mouth (if oral breathing is occurring), it flows to the back of the throat to a passage known as the *pharynx*.

From the pharynx, air flows to the entrance to the trachea (windpipe), known as the *larynx*. The larynx plays a key role in maintaining the airway and phonation and is often known as a person's "voice box." To maintain the airway, there is a lidlike structure known as the *epiglottis* that over-hangs the entrance to the larynx. When swallow-ing, it closes over the larynx to prevent food from entering the larynx and the rest of the respiratory tract. When open, air travels past the epiglottis and through the rest of the larynx. Within the larynx, there are vocal cords (technically referred to as *vocal folds*) that are stretched and positioned by several muscles of the larynx. When the cords close together, air travels across the vocal cords, causing them to vibrate and result in phonation (i.e., the ability to make sound). During breath-ing, the vocal cords are wide open, allowing air to pass freely.

After passing through the larynx, the air trav-els through a tube known as the *trachea* (wind-pipe). The trachea has multiple rings of cartilage extending about five-sixths of the way around the trachea to prevent it from collapsing. As air leaves the trachea, some travels down a tube leading to the left lung (left bronchus), and the rest travels down a tube leading to the right lung (right bronchus). From there the bronchi branch several times into smaller tubes known as *bronchioles*. At the end of the bronchioles are multiple air sacs (alveoli) from which gas exchange occurs.

In a tracheostomy, an opening is made directly through the lower neck into the trachea, bypassing the nasal cavity, pharynx, and larynx (see Figure 13-2). This results in several changes in the respira-tory tract. Without the filtering that usually occurs in the nasal cavity, foreign objects (e.g., powder, particles) are more likely to enter the trachea and lower respiratory tract through the tracheostomy, resulting in increased respiratory infections. Also, the loss of the natural humidification and warm-ing that typically occurs in the upper airways can lead to thick and dry secretions (Tayal, 1994) and a lung infection (Guyton, 1991). Coughing is weakened in individuals with tracheostomies. In a typical cough, the epiglottis briefly closes before coughing, raising the pressure in the abdominal and pleural spaces. With a tracheostomy, the epiglottis cannot close. Also, some research has shown that the ability of the epiglottis to close when swallowing may be compromised with prolonged tracheostomy, leading to more aspira-tion of food particles and resultant pulmonary

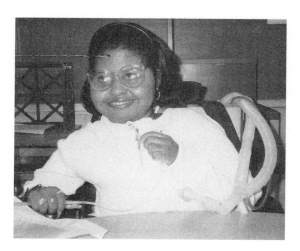

FIGURE 13-2 A student with a tracheostomy in her lower neck. She is in the process of removing secretions through her tracheostomy tube by inserting a suction catheter (tube) into the trache-ostomy tube.

infections (Sasaki, 1977). Phonation is often affected due to the lack of air through the vocal cords, resulting in a weakened voice or inability to speak (McDonald, Wilson, Turner, & Ault, 1988). The sense of smell and taste is also affected since air is not being inhaled through the nose. There may also be increased secretions from having a tracheostomy, especially when it is a new one.

EQUIPMENT AND ADAPTIVE EQUIPMENT FOR TRACHEOSTOMIES

Most individuals who have tracheostomies will require the use of a tracheostomy tube. Many different types of tracheostomy tubes are possible, with different lengths, angles of curvature, and diameters. They can be made of plastic (silicon or nylon) or metal. Semiflexible plastic tracheostomy tubes conform to the person's anatomy during movement. Rigid plastic tracheostomy tubes are usually selected when there is neck swelling to prevent the tube from collapsing. The newer silicone tubes can be used long term since they are durable and do not usually cause tissue irritation. Metal tracheostomy tubes (stainless steel or sterling silver) can also be used long term (Weilitz & Dettenmeier, 1994). However, metal tubes are not used as much as in the past, because of the advances in the construction of the plastic tubes.

As seen in Figure 13-3, most tracheostomy tubes have several main components. All tracheostomy tubes have a main curved shaft, known as a **cannula,** that fits down into the tracheostomy. The cannula connects to a neck plate. Each side of the neck plate is also known as a *flange*. The flanges have holes on their ends that are used to attach the **tracheostomy ties** (trach ties) that go around the neck to help hold the tracheostomy tube in place. Plastic tracheostomy tubes usually have a hub or an adapter at the end of the tube that is visible from the outside. It allows respiratory therapy equipment or a ventilator to attach easily to the tracheostomy.

Tracheostomy tubes may have a single or double cannula. A single cannula consists of one tube (Figure 13-3b). A double cannula consists of an inner cannula that fits into a second cannula, known as an *outer cannula* (Figure 13-3a). The inner cannula can be removed and cleaned or replaced, with the outer cannula remaining in place. A double cannula is often preferred when there are excessive secretions or difficulty clearing the secretions (Weiltz & Detternmeier, 1994). Most pediatric tracheostomy tubes do not have an inner cannula but use a single cannula, although adolescents who have tracheostomies may use double cannula tracheostomy tubes.

Some tracheostomy tubes are cuffed, while some do not have a cuff. Cuffed tracheostomy tubes have an inflatable cuff around the bottom of the tracheostomy tube. This cuff prevents air from escaping around the tracheostomy and into the upper airway. Cuffed tracheostomy tubes usually have a small thin tube with a small plastic balloon (pilot balloon) that hangs on the outside. The pilot balloon has an opening through which air can be inserted to fill the cuff. An inflated pilot balloon indicates that there is air in the cuff. Children under the age of 8 years rarely have a cuffed tracheostomy tube, since the child's tracheal cartilage is narrow and serves as a natural cuff. Cuffless tubes are changed less frequently and rarely cause tracheal irritation (Mizumori, Nelson, Prentice & Withey, 1994; Motoyama, 1985).

Some tracheostomy tubes are *fenestrated*. A fenestrated tube has a large hole or several small holes in the outer cannula, located on the outer curve of the tube. When the inner cannula is removed, the tracheostomy tube opening can be plugged using a special tracheostomy plug or a finger (but only with the physician's permission). Instead of the air going out of the tracheostomy tube, air goes through the hole(s) in the fenestrated tube and through the vocal cords, allowing the person to speak. Another alternative for speech is using one-way speech valves. (See the management section of this chapter for more information.)

There are alternatives to having a tracheostomy tube. Some students may have a **stomal stent** (also known as *silicone tracheal cannulas*) in-

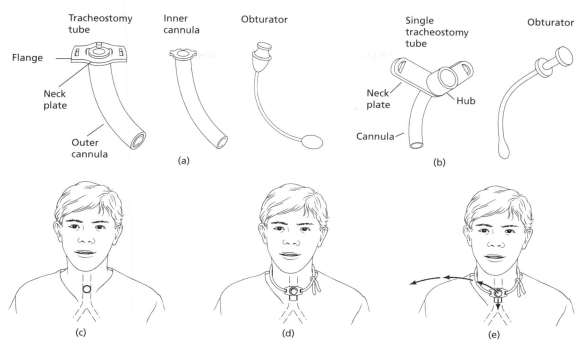

FIGURE 13-3 (a) A tracheostomy tube with an inner cannula and obturator, (b) a single tracheostomy tube with an obturator, (c) a stoma, (d) a tracheostomy tube in place, and (e) placement and removal of an obturator.

stead of a regular tracheostomy tube. A stomal stent is a short, straight tube that goes through the stoma but does not continue down the tracheostomy as tracheostomy tubes do. It is intended to minimize any damage to the tissue that could occur when there is pressure of the curved cannula on the inner walls of the trachea, and it maintains the patency of the stoma as well (Miller et al., 1995). Some individuals may have a **tracheostomy button.** Sometimes the individual may no longer require the tracheostomy but may need it in the future (or need it available for emergency ventilation). In these instances, a tracheostomy button is inserted into the stoma to keep the shape and patency of the stoma. However, the person is not breathing through the stoma (Mizumori et al., 1994). In some instances, individuals who have had a stoma for a while may still need to breathe through the stoma and have tracheal suctioning, but they may not need a tracheostomy tube. Instead, they may just have an

open stoma. Most individuals with a tracheostomy, however, will have a tracheostomy tube.

Some individuals may use an artificial nose, also known as an *in-line condenser* (see Figure 13-4). Artificial noses are used when the air needs to be humidified. They are filterlike devices that trap moisture from exhaled air. During inhalation, the air passes through this moisturized filter, warming and humidifying the air. The artificial nose needs to be changed daily or more frequently if there are secretions trapped in it (Mizumori et al., 1994). Humidifiers may be used to warm the air instead of an artificial nose. Tubing fits over the tracheostomy to provide humidified air (see Figure 13-4).

Obturators are thin, narrow devices used for insertion of the tracheostomy tube (refer back to Figure 13-3). Before inserting the tracheostomy tube, the obturator is placed inside the tracheostomy tube. It extends several millimeters out of the end of the tracheostomy tube, creating a smooth, angled surface to easily insert the tra-

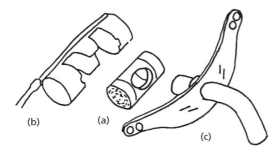

FIGURE 13-4 An "artificial nose" (a), which may have an optional oxygen attachment (b). The artificial nose attaches to the tracheostomy tube (c).

From J. Turner, G. L. McDonald, and N. L. Larter, *Handbook of Adult and Pediatric Respiratory Homecare.* Copyright © 1994 by Mosby-Year Book, Inc. Used with permission.

cheostomy tube into the stoma. When the obturator is in place, the person will be unable to breathe, so it must be immediately removed after insertion. (See the section on accidental removal of tracheostomy for emergency obturator use under "Tracheostomy Problems and Emergencies").

Care of the tracheostomy usually involves cleaning the stoma, cleaning the inner cannula, changing the tracheostomy ties, cleaning/changing the tracheostomy tube, and suctioning the tracheostomy. The physician will determine how often they are to be done, how often the tracheostomy tubes are changed, and whether these procedures are done with clean technique or sterile technique. In a sterile procedure, all of the supplies are sterile (aseptic, free from living microorganisms), and sterile gloves are worn. Utmost care is taken that nothing contaminates the sterile items. In a clean procedure, the supplies are clean and often reusable. Clean gloves are worn. It is always important to know the type of procedure that has been prescribed.

ASSISTIVE STRATEGIES FOR TRACHEOSTOMY STOMA CARE

Preparing for Tracheostomy Stoma Care

The tracheostomy stoma requires daily care to prevent infection or skin breakdown. Although routine stoma care is usually performed at home, the stoma may need to be cleaned more often if secretions are soiling the area. To maintain proper hygiene of the stoma and prevent infection or skin breakdown, the stoma will need to be kept clean and dry. Careful observation of the stoma site needs to occur at least when the stoma is being cleaned to detect any possible problems with the site, such as infection. The appropriate person will need to be notified if any of these problems are present.

Prior to cleaning the stoma, the hands of the person performing the procedure and the student's hands should be washed. Hand washing will decrease the possibility of introducing infection as well as prevent the spread of infection. Even if the student is not assisting in performing the procedure, learning appropriate hand washing is important. To perform the procedure, the student can be positioned in a sitting, standing, or lying position. However, if the student will be learning the procedure, a sitting or standing position in front of a mirror is recommended.

Equipment and Supply List for Cleaning the Tracheostomy Stoma

Water (in some instances, sterile water)

Half-strength hydrogen peroxide (half water and half hydrogen peroxide)

Small cups to hold water and hydrogen peroxide

Cotton-tip applicators (or similar application device)

Barrier cream or Vaseline (if ordered)

Dressing (if ordered)

Procedure for Cleaning the Tracheostomy Stoma

After explaining the procedure to the student, washing hands, assembling equipment, positioning the student, and putting on nonsterile gloves (if applicable), the person performing the procedure is ready to begin.

Steps in the Procedure for Cleaning the Tracheostomy Stoma	*Rationale*
1. If a dressing is present, gently remove the dressing.	Some students may have a small piece of gauze between the flanges of the tracheostomy tube and the neck to absorb excessive secretions. Dressing needs to be kept clean to prevent infection or irritation.
2. Closely inspect the stoma, skin surrounding the stoma, and skin under the tracheostomy ties.	Skin should be inspected for any skin irritation, redness, skin breakdown, cuts, bruises, swelling, or signs of infection. If present, the appropriate personnel should be notified.
3. Clean stoma with cotton-tip applicator (or gauze pad) with half-strength hydrogen peroxide. Cleaning motion should start at stoma and move away from stoma (Kuntz, 1996b).	Cleaning motion going away from stoma minimizes chance of moving unclean material into stoma. New gauze or applicator may be used with each wipe.
4. Rinse cleaned area with applicators that have been moistened in water. Use the same cleaning motion of wiping away from the stoma.	This will minimize chance of contaminating the stoma.
5. Pat area dry area with gauze pads.	Drying the area will help prevent skin breakdown.
6. If ordered, apply a thin layer of Vaseline or barrier cream, or a barrier wafer. (In some instances, a medication may be ordered to be applied topically due to irritation. This would occur at this step.)	Barriers come in creams or solid thin wafers that fit between the flanges of the tracheostomy tube (or neck plate) and the skin. Barriers (or Vaseline) are used to decrease the irritation caused by secretions against the skin or the dressing rubbing against the skin (if one is used).
7. If a dressing is used, replace a clean dressing under the flanges. Dressing may be a cut or folded piece of gauze (see Figure 13-5).	Dressing may be used to absorb secretions and prevent infection or irritation.
8. Check the tightness of tracheostomy ties. One finger should fit between the tracheostomy ties and the neck.	It is important to check that the fit is neither too tight or loose, thereby avoiding irritation, accidental decannulation, or obstruction of blood flow around the neck.
9. Discard used supplies. Record the cleaning procedure.	

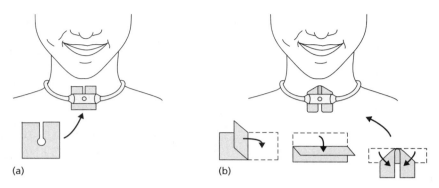

(a)   (b)

FIGURE 13-5 Tracheostomy dressings. The gauze pad may be cut to fit under the neck plate (a) or folded (b).

ASSISTIVE STRATEGY FOR CHANGING THE TRACHEOSTOMY TIES

Preparing for Changing Tracheostomy Ties

Tracheostomy ties (trach ties) are typically changed everyday when performing daily care at home. If they become wet or dirty, however, they will need to be changed at that time as well. It is not advisable to leave them wet or dirty since it can result in skin irritation and skin breakdown.

There are different types of tracheostomy ties. Some ties are known as *twill* or *trill tape* tracheostomy ties that are made of nonfraying material and usually need to be cut to length. Typically these are disposable. Some students may use tracheostomy tube holders instead of twill tracheostomy ties. Tracheostomy tube holders are usually cotton-lined adjustable neck bands with Velcro fasteners. They are usually washable and reusable. Tracheostomy tube holders can only be used with students who are cooperative or unable to undo the fasteners (Testi, 1991). Some individuals may also use foam or a special collar that goes around the neck between the tracheostomy ties and the neck to protect the neck from irritation (see Figure 13-6a) (Kuntz, 1996b). It will be im-

portant for the person performing the procedure to be familiar with the type of ties the student uses, as well as how the ties are secured.

As with all procedures, the student needs to be given an explanation of what is going to occur and, if possible, assist with the procedure. This procedure, however, has the potential of resulting in an accidental dislodgment or removal of the tracheostomy tube since the tracheostomy ties are being changed. This is especially problematic with tracheostomies that will close upon removal of the tracheostomy tube. Because of this, equipment should be available to reinsert the tracheostomy tube in case it comes out (decannulation). To minimize the risk of decannulation, either two people should be present to assist with tracheostomy tie changing, or a strict procedure should be followed in which the old ties are not removed until the new ones are in place.

Prior to beginning the procedure, the student and adult need to wash their hands. Gloves may be used for infection control; however, in some cases it is acceptable not to wear gloves, especially due to the difficulty of tying the tracheostomy ties correctly with gloves on. The student may lie down for the procedure, but it is better if the head if slightly flexed rather than extended to assure a snug fit when the ties are being tied (Wong, 1995). However, it will be difficult for the student to learn the proce-

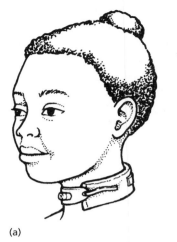 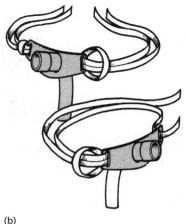

(a)   (b)

FIGURE 13-6 A student wearing a tracheostomy collar (a) and two methods used for tying and securing tracheostomy ties (when a collar is not used) (b).

SOURCE: (a) Copyright © 1996, Mark L. Batshaw. Used by permission. (b) Copyright © 1995 by Mosby-Year Book, Inc. Used by permission of the publisher and Dr. Donna Wong.

dure in this position. The procedure may also be performed with the student sitting up to a mirror.

Equipment and Supply List for Changing Tracheostomy Ties

New tracheostomy ties

Bandage scissors (scissors with one blunt end to avoid cutting the student)

Tweezers (optional)

Gloves (optional if clean procedure)

Obturator (in case of accidental decannulation)

Extra tracheostomy tube (in case of accidental decannulation)

Procedure for Changing Tracheostomy Ties

After explaining the procedure to the student, washing hands, assembling equipment, positioning the student (sitting or lying down), and putting on nonsterile gloves (if applicable), the person performing the procedure is ready to begin.

Steps in the Procedure for Changing the Tracheostomy Ties	*Rationale*
1. If they are not precut, cut the tracheostomy ties to the correct length.	Typically two tracheostomy ties are cut, one for each side of the trach tube. One trach tie is cut shorter than the other since they should be tied to the side of the person (not directly behind the neck). The health plan should state the premeasured length for ease of determining how long they should be.
2. Slide the old tracheostomy ties from the center of the hole on the flanges to top of the hole.	This will allow room for the new tracheostomy ties.

Steps in the Procedure for Changing the Tracheostomy Ties	*Rationale*
3. Insert the new tracheostomy ties through the hole under the old tracheostomy ties. Tracheostomy ties should be looped through the flanges (see Figure 13-6b).	Looping the tracheostomy ties through is a safer method than tying the ties at this location, since there is always the possibility that the ties could come loose. Tweezers may help bring the tracheostomy ties through the holes.
4. Tie new ties in a triple knot at the side of the neck. As the knot is being tied, be sure that one finger can fit between the tracheostomy ties and the neck for a good fit.	Be sure that the knot will not slip but is secure. By having the knot at the side of the neck, it can be more readily visualized to determine whether it is intact. The position of the knot should be changed each time to protect the skin (Kuntz, 1996b).
5. A piece of gauze or foam may be placed between the knot and skin.	This prevents skin irritation.
6. Cut the old ties with bandage scissors, and remove the old ties only after the new ties are in place (Wong, 1995).	Cutting the old tracheostomy ties after the new ones are in place will decrease the risk of accidental removal of the tracheostomy tube.
7. Recheck the tightness of the tracheostomy ties.	One finger should fit between the tracheostomy ties and the neck. This is usually considered an ideal fit that will not be too tight or too loose.
8. Discard used supplies. Wash hands and record changing of tracheostomy ties.	

ASSISTIVE STRATEGY FOR CLEANING/CHANGING AN INNER CANNULA

Preparing for Cleaning/Changing an Inner Cannula

When secretions stick to the sides of the inner cannula and cannot be suctioned out, they may result in difficulty breathing or respiratory distress. It will then become necessary to clean the inner cannula, if the student has a double cannula tracheostomy tube. Typically, cleaning the inner cannula is performed routinely at home; however,

if the student has frequent secretions, the cannula may be scheduled to be cleaned several times during the day. Also, if the inner cannula is becoming blocked, it will need to be removed and cleaned.

This procedure may be done as a sterile or a clean procedure, depending on the physician's orders. In a sterile procedure, all of the equipment is aseptic, free from living microorganisms. Sterile items are used and a sterile procedure is followed, taking the utmost care that nothing contaminates the sterile items. It will be important to know what type of procedure has been prescribed.

As with the other procedures, the student will need an explanation of what is going to occur and should be allowed to participate, if possible. Proper infection control should be followed, including washing of the adult's and student's hands.

(All of the following supplies will either be clean or sterile depending on what is prescribed.)

Equipment and Supply List for Cleaning/Changing an Inner Cannula

Hydrogen peroxide

Water

Containers

Brush or pipe cleaners

Temporary inner cannula (optional)

Procedure for Cleaning/Changing an Inner Cannula

After explaining the procedure to the student, washing hands, assembling equipment, positioning the student (sitting or lying down), and putting on gloves, the person performing the procedure can begin.

Steps in the Procedure for Cleaning/Changing an Inner Cannula	*Rationale*
1. Fill a container with hydrogen peroxide and fill a second container with water.	The container of hydrogen peroxide is used to clean the inner cannula. It may be half- or full-strength depending on what is ordered. The container with water will be used later to rinse the inner cannula.
2. Remove the inner cannula. This is usually accomplished by turning the hub and gently pulling the inner cannula in an outward and downward motion.	Be sure that the outer cannula is staying in place. One hand may gently hold the outer cannula at the hub while the other hand removes the inner cannula.
3. If a second cannula is to be placed in the outer cannula while cleaning occurs, it should be placed in the outer cannula at this time.	
4. Place the inner cannula in the hydrogen peroxide and soak for 1 to 5 minutes.	The bubbling action of the hydrogen peroxide will help clean the cannula.
5. Clean the inner cannula in the hydrogen peroxide with a pipe cleaner or a brush.	It is important to scrub all of the surfaces of the inner cannula and be sure all of the dried secretions are removed.
6. Rinse the inner cannula in the water.	If sterile technique is being used, the sterile water in the sterile container will be used to rinse the inner cannula. Then sterile water will be poured over the cannula. If clean technique is being used, the inner cannula may be rinsed over running water.
7. Shake dry.	

Steps in the Procedure for Cleaning/Changing an Inner Cannula	Rationale
8. Replace the inner cannula (or store the inner cannula if the replacement inner cannula is to remain in place). Replace the inner cannula by holding the hub of the outer cannula and gently putting the end of the inner cannula into the opening and sliding it into the outer cannula with a forward and downward motion. *Be sure to lock the inner cannula in place* by turning the hub.	If the inner cannula is not locked in place, it may come out accidentally.
9. Remove all used items, wash hands, and record that cleaning of the inner cannula took place.	

ASSISTIVE STRATEGY FOR CHANGING/CLEANING THE TRACHEOSTOMY TUBE

Tracheostomy tubes need to be changed and/or cleaned regularly. Regular changing and cleaning is important because tracheostomy tubes can become narrowed or clogged with secretions, and granulation tissue can form on the outer part of the tracheostomy tube, resulting in complications. Changing or cleaning the tracheostomy tube should be performed at home on the schedule prescribed by the physician. The caregiver should be taught by a nurse at the hospital (or visiting home nurse) about the care and maintenance of the student's particular type of tracheostomy tube and the student-specific procedure.

Although all tracheostomy tubes need to be periodically changed, not all tracheostomy tubes are cleaned to be reused again. Some are reusable and cleaned on a regular schedule at home, while others are disposable. The exact procedure for changing the tracheostomy tube and cleaning it will vary depending on the type of tracheostomy tube and the student-specific procedure. For cuffed tracheostomy tubes, for example, the cuff will need to be deflated prior to removal. Many students will need to be suctioned prior to removal of the tracheostomy tube before changing or cleaning the tube. In some cases, the changing or cleaning of the tracheostomy tube will be a sterile procedure, while for others it will be a clean procedure. (Since this procedure is done at home and the procedure varies depending on the type of tracheostomy tube and the student, only general guidelines will be provided.)

There are some general guidelines regarding changing and cleaning a tracheostomy tube. The person responsible for cleaning the tracheostomy tube will need to know how to remove and reinsert a tracheostomy tube. Typically, the tracheostomy tube is removed and a new one is inserted so that the student does not have a period of time without a tracheostomy tube in place. Although the cleaning procedure can vary, cleaning the tracheostomy tube is similar to cleaning an inner cannula. Typically, the tracheostomy tube and obturator are soaked in hydrogen peroxide (sometimes for an hour, depending on the procedure being used). A small brush is used to remove the secretions. The tube and obturator are rinsed in water. The tube and obturator are then air dried and stored for later use.

ASSISTIVE STRATEGY FOR SUCTIONING A TRACHEOSTOMY

When a student has a tracheostomy, it is vital that the person responsible for the tracheostomy knows how to properly suction it. Although the student may be able to cough the secretions through the tracheostomy tube, there is always the possibility that some secretions can become lodged in the tracheostomy tube, obstructing breathing. Chapter 14 discusses how to suction a tracheostomy as well as other procedures for removal of secretions.

INSTRUCTIONAL STRATEGIES AND MODIFICATIONS FOR TRACHEOSTOMIES

Students who have tracheostomies will need to participate in care of their tracheostomy as much as possible. Depending on the student's physical status, chronological and developmental age, cognitive abilities, and safety issues, student participation can vary from performing a few steps of each procedure to performing the entire procedure independently under adult supervision (Barnes, 1992). Some students are taught how to care for the stoma, change tracheostomy ties, clean the inner cannula, clean the tracheostomy tube, suction themselves, and change the tracheostomy tube (Grundfast & Hennessy, 1985). Additional areas to be addressed include equipment and supplies management and emergency management of the tracheostomy. Teaching these self-help skills will increase the student's independence.

When a student is old enough to understand verbal explanations and directions, he should be taught about the tracheostomy. Explanations typically begin with teaching some aspects of physiology and anatomy, gearing the explanations to the student's developmental level. For some students, the explanation may be as simple as discussing how the student breathes through the tracheostomy tube. Other students may learn more complex information regarding the anatomy of the respiratory system. It is important not to frighten the student or make the student feel atypical but instead to stress how the tracheostomy makes breathing easier and that it is very manageable. A doll with a tracheostomy may be used to demonstrate and practice certain skills. If the student has a physical impairment, it may be difficult for the student to perform these skills. However, it is important for the student to learn the steps of each skill and be able to communicate how it is performed to others.

Teaching tracheostomy self-care can be done via several techniques. One system uses five steps. First, the procedure is performed on the person with the tracheostomy by another person. Second, the person with the tracheostomy is shown how to perform the task. Third, they perform the procedure together. Fourth, the person with the tracheostomy performs the task under supervision, and, fifth, the person performs the task independently without supervision (Mason, Murty, Foster, & Bradley, 1992). For students, the procedures should always be done under supervision, and since there are many steps to each self-care task, the task usually needs to be broken down into smaller parts. Any of the instructional strategies may be used to teach the student (see Chapter 2).

Each of the skills can be broken down into a task analysis. Two of the easier skills to begin teaching is cleaning the inner cannula (or the tracheostomy tube) (Figure 13-7) and cleaning the stoma (Figure 13-8). When the inner cannula (or tracheostomy tube) is cleaned, the student can first participate by putting the tracheostomy tube into the hydrogen peroxide and later scrubbing it with a brush and rinsing it off. As the student gains competence, other parts of the task analysis can be taught. There are no time-limited steps in cleaning an inner cannula. (These are steps that must be completed within a certain time frame.) However, there are caution steps, which are steps during which the student could injure himself by

1. Wash hands.
2. Fill a container with hydrogen peroxide.
3. Fill a second container with water.
4. Remove inner cannula and put replacement inner cannula in place.
5. Put the inner cannula in hydrogen peroxide.
6. Set a timer to allow to soak.
7. Scrub the inner cannula with a brush in hydrogen peroxide.
8. Put the inner cannula in water.
9. Rinse with water.
10. Shake off excess water.
11. Put the inner cannula tube away (to later replace the other inner cannula when cleaning occurs again).
12. Clean/rinse the brush and containers.
13. Discard used items.
14. Wash hands.

FIGURE 13-7 Sample task analysis for cleaning an inner cannula using clean technique

1. Wash hands.
2. Identify any problem areas around the stoma.
3. Wet applicators with half-strength hydrogen peroxide.
4. Put the applicator on the skin by the stoma and wipe away.
5. Get a new applicator and repeat steps 3 and 4.
6. Continue the cleaning motion around the entire stoma.
7. Wet the applicator with water.
8. Put the applicator on the skin by the stoma and wipe away.
9. Get a new applicator and repeat steps 7 and 8.
10. Continue rinsing the entire area around the stoma.
11. Take a dry gauze pad.
12. Pat-dry the area.
13. Apply a barrier (if ordered).
14. Check the tightness of the trach ties.
15. Discard used supplies.
16. Wash hands.

FIGURE 13-8 Sample task analysis for cleaning the stoma around a tracheostomy

a quick, jerking, or incorrect movement. For cleaning an inner cannula, the caution step is removing the inner cannula and putting in an inner cannula (step 4 on the task analysis). The educational team must decide whether this step is appropriate for the student to learn. If so, the teacher may model the step and then provide shadowing (in which the teacher keeps her hands within an inch of the student's hands until the step is complete). If the student is lower functioning, the student may require full physical prompts and move to shadowing. Shadowing allows the teacher to intervene quickly should the student make an incorrect movement. As with all identified time-limited or caution steps, they should be highlighted on the data sheet as a reminder that shadowing should occur. (See

Chapter 2 for more information on shadowing and a sample data sheet.)

Learning what the stoma and skin surrounding the stoma should normally look like is important, as is identifying areas that need cleaning or have skin breakdown or a rash. Cleaning the stoma area needs to be gently performed with care taken that all of the secretions are cleaned off and the area is well dried. Cleaning the stoma area is often taught using a backward chaining model since the more difficult aspects of the task (e.g., cleaning around the stoma) occur early in the task sequence, and the easier parts (e.g., drying) occur near the end of the task sequence. Although there are no time-limited steps in a task analysis of cleaning the stoma, the actual cleaning and rinsing around the stoma are considered caution steps. On the task analysis (Figure 13-8), the caution steps are 4, 6, 8, and 10. This is because the area needs to be cleaned gently away from the opening, with care not to move unclean material into the stoma. If a barrier is ordered (step 13) that is in a cream form, it becomes a caution step since it would be inadvisable to have the barrier inadvertently placed into the stoma opening. The educational team will need to determine the appropriateness of teaching the student to perform these caution steps. If they are going to be taught, the teacher may model the step and then provide shadowing (in which the teacher keeps her hands within an inch of the student's hands until the step is complete). If the student is lower functioning, the student may require a full physical prompt and move to shadowing.

Checking the tightness of the tracheostomy ties is something that the student should be taught to do along with the adult throughout the day. The adult can check it first and then have the student put one of her fingers (or two fingers if her fingers are small) under the tracheostomy to check for proper fit. It is also important to ask the student how it feels.

Teaching a student to change tracheostomy ties is more difficult (see Figure 13-9) because of the fine-motor skill required to get the tie through the hole and loop it. It is also difficult for many students to tie the knot so that the tracheostomy ties are of the proper tightness. Having repeated practice checking the tightness of tracheostomy ties will help the student determine whether the fit is correct, but untying the knot to begin again when tied incorrectly can also be frustrating. Also, if the knot is not tied correctly, then it can come undone, resulting in possible decannulation. There are no time-limited steps in this procedure. However, tying the new tra-

1. Wash hands.
2. Cut trach ties to the correct length.
3. Slide old trach ties to the top of the hole.
4. Insert new trach ties through the right hole.
5. Make a loop at the hole.
6. Insert new trach ties through the left hole.
7. Make a loop at the end.
8. Tie new trach ties together in a triple knot.
9. Check the tightness of the trach ties.
10. Determine whether it is the correct tightness.
11. Cut old ties.
12. Remove old ties.
13. Recheck the tightness of the trach ties.
14. Discard used supplies.
15. Wash hands.

FIGURE 13-9 Sample task analysis for changing tracheostomy ties

cheostomy ties together in a triple knot is considered a caution step (step 8 on the task analysis of Figure 13-9) since it is possible that the student could pull the ties forcefully, resulting in very tight tracheostomy ties and choking. If the student is performing this step, the adult assisting the student will need to provide instruction using modeling then moving to shadowing, or full physical guidance then moving to shadowing. In some cases, the adult may elect to hold the tracheostomy ties as an added measure to prevent the student from pulling too hard.

Proper scissors use is also an important skill that requires close supervision. Only bandage scissors should be used, which are specially constructed to minimize the risk of cutting oneself inadvertently. However, since scissors are being used, cutting the old tracheostomy ties becomes a caution step that requires a decision as to whether the student will learn this step of the task analysis (step 11 of Figure 13-9). Depending on the student's motor skill and cognitive level, this skill may be postponed, or the student may only partially participate until he has the ability to do this procedure with minimal risk.

Other procedures that the student will need to learn are changing the tracheostomy tube and suctioning. To be fully independent adults, it is important that the skills be eventually taught. However, changing a tracheostomy tube can be a difficult procedure and is not recommended until the student has the motor control, cognitive ability, and emotional maturity to perform this skill. (Emergency tracheostomy tube change is described under "Tracheostomy Problems and Emergencies"; suctioning is discussed in Chapter 14.)

Students will also need to know how to recognize when there is a problem and what to do when a certain problem arises. Students need to be able to communicate with an adult that a problem exists. If possible, students should also be able to communicate the appropriate action to take. For students who do not have physical impairments, they may be taught to take the appropriate action themselves.

TRACHEOSTOMY PROBLEMS AND EMERGENCIES

Dislodgment of the Tracheostomy Tube

The tracheostomy tube can accidentally come out if the tracheostomy ties are loosened. It is important to check the ties periodically to be sure they are not coming undone. A good policy is to check the tracheostomy ties upon the student arriving at school, once during the middle of the school day, and before the student leaves for home.

To check the tracheostomy ties, the teacher determines whether one finger can easily slide between the tracheostomy ties and the student's neck. It should remain at this level of fit. The ties should also be visually inspected to be sure they are appropriately tied in a knot. When ties are

being changed, the student should never be left unattended with the ties untied or removed to avoid accidental tracheostomy tube removal.

Obstruction

The tracheostomy tube can become blocked by mucous secretions or foreign objects. If this occurs, the student will show signs of distress (see Figure 13-10): agitation, anxiety, difficulty breathing, and cyanosis (turning blue) (Buzz-Kelly & Gordin, 1993; Haynie, Porter, & Palfrey, 1989). Airway obstruction can be a life-threatening emergency and needs to be cleared immediately. The first step is to remove any obvious foreign

Abnormal breathing
- Difficult, labored breathing
- Decreased air exchange or inability to move air (through tracheostomy or airways)
- Shortness of breath, rapid breathing
- Wheezing, gasping for breath, abnormal breath sounds

Retraction of chest
- Pulling in of the chest and neck muscles (which occurs to help with breathing)

Cyanosis
- Dusky or blue color, especially at nailbeds and around mouth

Neurologic signs
- Agitation, anxiety, restlessness
- Confusion, inability to concentrate
- Dizzy
- Drowsiness
- Unconscious

Cardiac
- Fast heart rate (pulse)

FIGURE 13-10 Signs of respiratory distress

blockage at the tube opening that could be causing the obstruction (e.g., plastic bib). If this is not present, the next step is to suction through the tracheostomy tube. If the mucus is dry, then 1 to 2 milliliters of saline may be instilled prior to suctioning a second time (see Chapter 14's discussion on suctioning).

If the suction catheter cannot advanced into the tracheostomy tube, the inner cannula of the tracheostomy tube should be removed if this type of tracheostomy has an inner cannula (Tayal, 1994). Removal of the inner cannula should allow the student to breathe through the outer cannula. (If successful, the inner cannula can then be cleaned and put back into place.) If that is unsuccessful or if the tracheostomy has no inner cannula, the tracheostomy tube (or outer cannula) should be immediately removed and replaced with one of similar size (Grundfast & Hennessy, 1985). If respiratory distress continues after a new tracheostomy tube is inserted, the problem is not due to an obstruction in the tracheostomy tube. There could be an obstruction below the tracheostomy, in the trachea or bronchi (e.g., tracheal stenosis), or some other problem causing respiratory distress. The paramedics need to be called immediately. If the student stops breathing, CPR must be initiated.

CPR

Cardiopulmonary resuscitation (CPR) is a basic skill required to assist an individual who has become unconscious and is not breathing (respiratory arrest) and whose heart may not be beating (cardiac arrest). The basics of CPR consist of airway management, rescue breathing, and circulatory support. When the person has a tracheostomy, there will be some modification in the area of airway management and use of tracheostomy tubes and respiratory support equipment. School personnel and caregivers should take a basic CPR course and also learn how to provide CPR to a student who has a tracheostomy to provide assistance if an emergency occurs.

As with typical CPR, the neck should be extended (using the same method taught in CPR class). Sometimes the cause of respiratory distress may become evident by just doing this, such as when the tracheostomy tube is displaced. If this is the case, the tube will need to be immediately placed back in position. If tube displacement is not evident, manual respiration should be given. Manual respiration involves the rescuer giving breaths into the tracheostomy (instead of mouth-to-mouth resuscitation). This may occur by mouth–to–tracheostomy tube or mouth-to-stoma breathing. In these cases, the rescuer places her mouth over the student's tracheostomy tube (or stoma), forming a seal, and breathes into the tracheostomy or stoma according to standard rescue breathing procedures learned in CPR class. If air leaks out of the student's mouth or nose instead of filling the lungs, the mouth and nose need to be covered (Graff et al., 1990).

If available, a resuscitation bag (also known as a *manual resuscitator* or an *Ambu bag*) may be used instead (Figure 13-11). The resuscitation bag will need to have a special adapter to attach to the tracheostomy tube. When attaching the bag, the person should hold the tracheostomy tube with one hand so that it will not accidentally dislodge. The bag is then squeezed to give breaths. Whether breaths are given by mouth to tracheostomy tube, mouth to stoma, or using a resuscitation bag, they will need to be given at a regular prescribed rate. The rate is typically 20 breaths a minute (one breath every 3 seconds) for infants under 1 year old, 15 breaths a minute (one breath every 4 seconds) for students between 1 and 8 years old, and 12 breaths a minute (one breath every 5 seconds) for students over 8 years old (Buzz-Kelly & Gordin, 1993). If Ambu bags are available, proper training in its use must be taught to avoid over pressurizing the student which can cause problems. There are pressure gauges on the Ambu bags to assist with proper use.

If the rescuer cannot get air through the tracheostomy tube, there is an obstruction. If the individual has a tracheostomy with an inner cannula, it should be removed to allow breathing to occur through the outer cannula. However, if the

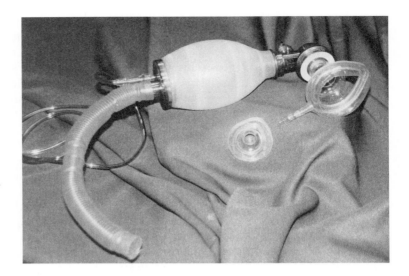

FIGURE 13-11 A manual resuscitation bag with a mouth/nose attachment that can be replaced with an attachment to fit onto a tracheostomy tube. After putting it over the nose/mouth or tracheostomy tube, the adult presses on the bag to deliver a breath.

student has a tracheostomy with a single cannula, it is recommended that an emergency tracheostomy change be performed immediately. Since a respiratory arrest has occurred and the person is unconscious and not breathing, an emergency tracheostomy change is considered the first step to take along with suctioning. Oxygen should be administered as well, if available. However, if there was a partial obstruction and obvious bubbling of secretions at the tracheostomy, suctioning may be an appropriate first step. After clearing the obstruction (by changing the tracheostomy tube, suctioning a partial obstruction, or repositioning one that is displaced), manual respirations will need to be given if the person is not breathing (Buzz-Kelly & Gordin, 1993). The rest of the steps in CPR should then be followed.

Emergency Tracheostomy Change

An emergency tracheostomy tube change will need to occur if (a) the tracheostomy tube is blocked (or significantly partially blocked) and will not clear after suctioning, (b) respiratory arrest has occurred with a blocked tracheostomy tube, or (c) the tracheostomy tube has accidentally come out or has been pulled out by the student. Upon taking out the old tube, a new one must be reinserted. If a new tube is unavailable, the old tube can be reinserted after cleaning, and a new tube should be inserted as soon as possible.

The following is a procedure for an emergency tracheostomy change (Ashcroft & Smith, 1993; Porter et al., 1997). Routine tracheostomy changes should not occur at school. The following is performed at school only in an emergency situation. Although one person can perform an emergency tracheostomy change, two people are more efficient.

Equipment for Emergency Tracheostomy Change
Tracheostomy tube of student's size
and type
Bandage scissors (or blunt scissors)
Tracheostomy ties
Gloves
Towel

These supplies should be available in the tracheostomy kit that should always be accessible to the student. (See the management section.)

Steps in the Procedure for Emergency Tracheostomy Change	*Rationale*
1. Explain what you are about to do to the student.	Although this is an emergency situation and must be quickly performed, the person doing the procedure can give quick explanations to help the student understand and cooperate with the procedure.
2. Wash hands and put on gloves.	Hand washing helps prevent infection. However, excessive time should not be taken if the student is not breathing.
3. Position the student on his back with the neck extended. If available, a rolled-up towel can be placed under the student's shoulders to help position the neck.	Another person may need to restrain the student to perform the procedure.
4. Prepare the new tracheostomy tube. Remove the tube from the sterile package, when sterile tracheostomy tubes are used. Reusable tracheostomy tubes will be clean, not sterile.	When removing the tracheostomy tube, hold it by the flanges. Avoid holding the tracheostomy by the cannula (curved tube) to maintain sterility (or cleanliness) of the tracheostomy tube.
5. Insert the obturator into the tracheostomy tube. (The end of the tracheostomy tube with obturator may be lubricated with sterile saline or sterile water if readily available.)	The obturator will make insertion easier. Some brands may not have an obturator to aid with insertion. In some emergency situations, a suction catheter may be used as a guide. The catheter is inserted into the stoma with the end cut off. The tracheostomy tube is slid over the catheter, then the catheter is removed. Do not let go of the catheter since it can be inhaled (Haynie et al., 1989).
6. Remove the old tracheostomy tube. Cut the old tracheostomy ties and gently remove the blocked tube. (This is best done by a second person while the first person is ready to proceed with inserting the new tracheostomy tube as soon as the old one is removed.)	Gently pull outward and downward. Remember that the tracheostomy tube is curved in a downward direction. (If this was not an emergency situation with a blocked tube, the student could receive two to four breaths with an Ambu bag prior to removal.)
7. Spread the stoma open with the index and middle fingers of the nondominant hand.	Many stomas will close when the tracheostomy tube is removed or comes out.

Steps in the Procedure for Emergency Tracheostomy Change	*Rationale*
8. With the dominant hand, gently insert the new tube. First, the tube is inserted straight back, and then an inward and downward motion is used, following the curve of the trachea. If there is no obturator, insert the new tube at right angle to the stoma and rotate it downward as it is inserted (Porter et al., 1997).	The direction is changed to accommodate the curve of the tracheostomy tube and how it needs to be finally positioned, with the cannula going vertically down the trachea until only the hub and flanges are visible.
9. Once the tracheostomy tube is in position, the obturator needs to be *immediately* removed.	Immediate removal of the obturator is necessary to allow the student to breathe. As long as the obturator is in place, no air can go through the tracheostomy tube.
10. Listen and look for air movement.	It is important to check for breathing. If there is no air movement, CPR needs to be initiated.
11. The tracheostomy tube will need to be held in place until a second person can assist in placing the tracheostomy ties.	Two people are required to put on tracheostomy ties safely. The tracheostomy ties should be tied on the side of the neck with the ties loose enough that one finger can be easily placed between the ties and neck. (In nonemergency situations, trach ties would have been attached to one side of tube prior to insertion.)
12. Depending on why the tracheostomy tube is being changed in the emergency situation, the person will next proceed with what is indicated.	If the tracheostomy was replaced because it had accidentally been removed, no further treatment may be necessary. If there was a blockage, suctioning may be indicated. If the person is not breathing, CPR would be indicated. Oxygen may need to be administered if available.
13. Remove gloves and wash hands.	

If the tracheostomy tube will not go into the closed stoma:

1. Try to reposition the head/neck, and try again to insert the tracheostomy tube carefully. (Blind reinsertion may result in incorrect placement in a new tissue plane, anterior to the trachea.)

2. If repositioning is unsuccessful, try to insert a tracheostomy tube of the next smaller size if one is available.

3. If the student is conscious and trying to breathe and a smaller tube cannot be inserted, some physicians recommend using a suction catheter as an airway. Put a suction

catheter into the stoma, hold the catheter in place, and cut off approximately 6 inches above the stoma. Do not allow the catheter to slip in accidentally (Ashcroft & Smith, 1993). Call 911. Continue to hold the catheter until help arrives. The student should be able to breathe temporarily through the catheter (until a skilled medical person can intubate from above).

4. If the student is unconscious with a respiratory or cardiac arrest and a smaller tube cannot be inserted into the closed stoma, begin CPR with mouth-to mouth breaths. If air leaks through the stoma, cover the stoma with your thumb (Haynie et al., 1989). Call 911.

Aspiration

If a student with a tracheostomy places an item into the tracheostomy or accidentally gets something into it, it may obstruct the tracheostomy tube or travel down the tracheostomy tube into the trachea or bronchi. If an obstruction in the tracheostomy tube occurs, follow the procedure for obstruction and emergency tracheostomy tube change. If the item or fluid goes down into the trachea or bronchial airways, this may result in partial blockage of the airway and/or respiratory distress. The student should be suctioned to try to remove the item or fluid. If the student continues to have difficulty breathing, the paramedics should be called. In situations where something was placed into the tracheostomy but the student appears unharmed, the student will often need to be seen by a physician to determine whether the item needs to be removed.

When a student takes something by mouth and it goes into the airway rather than to the stomach, the food or foreign object will usually rest on top of the tracheostomy tube and need to be removed. Choking interventions that are traditionally used when food has become lodged in the airway are typically not used with students with tracheostomies. Back blows for the infant and abdominal thrusts for the student will typically not be effective. Since breathing is occurring though the tracheostomy, respiratory distress is unlikely to occur. However, if it is suspected that the student has inhaled food or a foreign object, it is recommended that the student go to the emergency room. If there is respiratory distress, the tracheostomy will need to be treated as if there is an obstruction rather than viewed as "choking" (Buzz-Kelly & Gordin, 1993).

Falling Underwater

If the student is inadvertently submerged underwater by slipping underwater in a bathtub or falling into a swimming pool, water will enter the tracheostomy tube, resulting in an emergency situation. The student should be immediately suctioned. If the student is not breathing, CPR should be started immediately. The student will need to be seen by a physician, even if she appears unharmed in case some water has gone into the lungs.

Irritation or Bleeding at the Stoma

If the stoma appears irritated, inflamed, or has a rash, the appropriate health care personnel in the school and the parents should be notified. This can be caused by any number of reasons, including irritation from the cleansing agent used around the stoma, too much humidification, or irritation from frequent secretions at the stoma. The health personnel will make the appropriate recommendation on how to manage this problem.

Occasionally, mucus may be blood tinged, due to too frequent suctioning or the suction machine having too much pressure. More humidity may also need to be provided to the student (Graff et al., 1990). Again, the health care worker and parents will need to be informed. However, in the unlikely event that bright red mucus or overt bleeding occurs, the student's physician will need to be notified immediately, and the emergency plan in the IHP should be followed. (Bright red bleeding may occur as an uncommon long-term complication of the tracheostomy tube causing tissue damage and eroding into a blood vessel.)

Respiratory Infections

The school personnel and caretakers need to carefully observe for signs of respiratory infection so early treatment can occur. If the amount of respiratory secretions changes, the thickness or color changes, or an unpleasant odor exists, an infection may be present. If a fever is present, this will be another indication of a respiratory infection (or aspiration), and the parents will need to call the physician.

MANAGEMENT ISSUES FOR TRACHEOSTOMIES

Individualized Health Plan and Individualized Educational Program

A student who has a tracheostomy will need an individualized health plan (IHP). Besides the general items that are included in a health plan, the IHP will also need to include several areas specific to the care of the individual student. As presented in Figure 13-12, the type and brand of tracheostomy tube needs to be specified. Student-specific procedures for cleaning the stoma, cleaning the tracheostomy tube, changing tracheostomy ties, suctioning, and doing an emergency change of the tracheostomy tube should be available and approved by the physician. Each procedure should specify whether it is a clean or sterile procedure. Although many of the procedures are done as needed (p.r.n.), some are performed routinely at specific times and should be noted. The IHP should include guidelines for the following problems or emergencies: dislodgment of tracheostomy tube, obstruction, CPR modifications, emergency tracheostomy tube change, falling underwater, skin irritation or bleeding, and respiratory infection. Activity restrictions need to be specified as well.

The student's educational plan needs to address what aspects of care the student is learning for tracheostomy management. Areas of instruction may include (a) the purpose of the tracheostomy; (b) simple anatomy and physiology; (c) alternate communication; (d) demonstrating how to clean the tracheostomy tube or inner cannula; (e) demonstrating stoma care; (f) demonstrating tracheostomy tie changes; (g) demonstrating other procedures (e.g., suctioning, changing tracheostomy); (h) identifying when tracheostomy ties are at correct tightness; (i) identifying problems; (j) knowing the different potential problems and emergencies, how to identify them, and how to treat them; (k) knowing activity restrictions and restrictions regarding having small things near the stoma; (l) hygiene and clean or sterile technique; and (m) breathing techniques. Sample IEP objectives are found in Figure 13-13.

School Environment

To minimize tracheostomy problems, it may be necessary to modify the school and home environment. Anything that can go down the tracheostomy tube or obstruct it should be avoided. This includes plastic bibs and fuzzy blankets. The student should not play in sandboxes or boxes filled with small pellets or rice. Toys with small removable parts that the student could put into the tracheostomy tube need to be removed. Aerosols, powders, dust, and smoke should also be avoided (Porter et al., 1997; Wong, 1995). The student cannot go swimming (underwater). It is important that water not be allowed to enter the tracheostomy. If this occurs, the tracheostomy must be suctioned immediately, and medical care is usually necessary.

Clothing should not have a tight collar. When the student goes outside, an artificial nose or a thin cloth such as a bandana can go over the tracheostomy to help prevent cold air, dust, or dirt from entering the tube (Wong, 1995). Some covers are also made for older students and adults that cover the tracheostomy to give a more normalized appearance.

Type of Tracheostomy Tube

_____(brand) _____(size)

_____Cuffed   _____Uncuffed

_____Fenestrated   _____Not fenestrated

_____Single cannula   _____Double cannula (inner & outer)

_____Reusable   _____Not reusable

Humidification?_____yes, using_____   _____no

Activity restrictions:_____

How Does Student Communicate?

_____Has a speaking valve on tracheostomy

_____Uses larynx training

_____Artificial voice device (electrolarynx, tracheostomyeosophageal prostheses)

_____AAC device; specify type:_____

_____Other; specify:_____

Student-Specific Procedures

Student-specific procedure for stoma cleaning attached?_____yes_____no

　　　Procedure is:_____clean_____sterile

Student-specific procedure for cleaning inner cannula attached?_____yes_____no

　　　Procedure is:_____clean_____sterile

Student-specific procedure for changing tracheostomy ties attached?_____yes_____no

　　　Procedure is:_____clean_____sterile

Student-specific procedure for suctioning tracheostomy tube attached?_____yes_____no

　　　Procedure is:_____clean_____sterile

Student-specific procedure for emergency changing of tracheostomy tube attached?

_____yes_____no

　　　Procedure is:_____clean_____sterile

Latex allergy?_____yes_____no, comment: _____

Directions for Tracheostomy Problems and Emergencies

Dislodgment of tracheostomy tube:_____

Obstruction:_____

CPR modifications:_____

Emergency tracheostomy tube change:_____

Falling underwater:_____

Skin irritation or bleeding:_____

Respiratory infection:_____

FIGURE 13-12 Specialized areas to include in an IHP on tracheostomy care

Independent Performance of Task

The student will demonstrate how to clean the stoma following the steps of the task-analyzed procedure with 100% accuracy on each opportunity for 3 weeks.

The student will demonstrate how to clean the inner cannula of her tracheostomy tube following the steps of the procedure with 100% accuracy on each opportunity for 3 weeks.

Partial Performance of Task

The student will help hold the tracheostomy tube in place when trach ties are being changed by an adult with 100% accuracy on each occasion for 3 weeks.

The student will gather equipment for stoma cleaning (which will be performed by an adult) with 90% accuracy on each occasion for 2 weeks.

Directing the Task

The student will direct an adult in the steps of properly cleaning the tracheostomy with 100% accuracy on each occasion for 1 week.

The student will demonstrate the ability to signal an adult if a problem occurs with the tracheostomy or breathing with 100% accuracy on each occasion for 1 month.

Knowledge of the Task

Using her AAC device, the student will identify potential problems that can occur with the tracheostomy and tell an adult what should be done should the problem occur with 100% accuracy for four consecutive sessions.

The student will identify the type of tracheostomy she has, explain proper care of the tracheostomy, and explain precautions in its use with 80% accuracy for four consecutive sessions.

FIGURE 13-13 Sample IEP objectives for tracheostomy care

Activity Restrictions

Students with a tracheostomy have some activity restrictions. Water sports such as swimming or diving are dangerous and not allowed. Contact sports are often limited since sliding in the dirt increases the risk of aspiration and injury to the stoma and tracheostomy (Grundfast & Hennessy, 1985). Additional activities restrictions may be in place because of the student's respiratory and/or physical condition.

Communication

Speaking with a tracheostomy has only recently become a reality with the development of fenestrated tracheostomy tubes, cuffless tracheostomy tubes, and deflation of cuffed tracheostomy tubes (as previously discussed). In addition to these, speaking may occur with the use of one-way speaking valves, talking trachs, and electrolarynges. Speaking valves are one-way valves that permit air to enter through the tracheostomy tube, but then redirect air through the upper passages, across the larynx, and through the mouth and nose. The speaking valve may attach to the hub of the tracheostomy tube (e.g., Passy Muir valve) or be built into the inner cannula (e.g., Tucker valve). Speaking valves also have the advantage of allowing secretions to be coughed into the mouth, which will decrease the amount of suctioning necessary. Also, the senses of smell and taste are improved due to the redirection of air (Wong, 1995).

In some instances, the use of a speaking valve may not be appropriate. This is often the case in students with cuffed tracheostomy tubes, severe narrowing of the tracheostomy (tracheostenosis), excessive secretions, laryngectomy, or a critical illness (Wong, 1995).

Other possibilities include the use of talking trachs or electrolarynges. Talking trachs are specially designed cuffed tracheostomy tubes that have an extra air tube. The person's exhalations are typically directed out through the tracheostomy tube opening. For talking to occur, the extra air line is regulated by closing off an opening on the side of the catheter. Electrolarynges are external sound sources. Depending on the type, they either are placed on the neck where there is good sound resonation or have a tube that is placed in the mouth. On both types, a button is pushed on the electrolarynx to generate vibrations for phonation and speaking (Glennen, 1997).

In some instances, the student is unable to use any of these devices to talk. When the student cannot talk, it will be imperative that a form of communication be established to communicate desires, thoughts, questions, and needs (Adamson & Dunbar, 1991). Communication may take several forms, including facial expressions, gestures, sign language, objects, electronic or nonelectronic graphic communications systems (e.g., pictures or symbols, including letters), natural voice using larynx training, and artificial voice devices (e.g., electorlarynx, tracheostomyesophogeal prostheses) (Tayal, 1994). It will be important for the communication system to address emergency situations, as well as wants and needs and conversational topics (see Chapter 3 for more information). The use of these communication systems may be a temporary or permanent adaptation. Students who have tracheostomies before learning to speak have been found to develop speech with some differences in articulation when the tracheostomy was removed (Kamen & Watson, 1991).

Emergency Tracheostomy Kit for School and Travel

An emergency kit should always be available for use for individuals with a tracheostomy. This kit should be readily available at school as well as when the student is on a field trip or participates in community-based instruction. Individuals with the student should be well acquainted with this emergency kit and how to use it.

Several basic items should be in the emergency kit, including a replacement tracheostomy tube of the same size and type as the student's, tracheostomy ties, and bandage scissors. These items can be used if the tracheostomy comes out by accident or needs to be replaced. Suction equipment should be available, including suction apparatus, suction catheters, normal saline solution, and sterile water. These are used in case of a blockage or if the student requires suctioning. Resuscitation equipment should also be included, such as a resuscitation bag (Ambu) and an endotracheal tube that is slightly smaller than tracheostomy size (Buzz-Kelly & Gordin, 1993). Although medical personnel will be needed to insert the endotracheal tube, it will be helpful to have one of the correct size with the student.

SUMMARY

Students may have several different types of tracheostomies: single or double cannula, cuffed or noncuffed, or fenestrated or not fenestrated. Many procedures are associated with tracheostomy care. In the school setting, cleaning the stoma and suctioning the tracheostomy as needed are procedures typically the responsibility of designated school personnel, whereas cleaning the tracheostomy tube(s), changing the tubes, and changing the tracheostomy ties are typically the family's responsibilities and occur in the home setting. However, these procedures may be performed in the school setting on an as-needed basis or in an emergency; therefore, school personnel need to learn how to perform these procedures as well. It is important that the student fully or partially participate in these procedures when possible, to increase her independence and assist others. Knowledge of possible problems and emergencies and what to do if they occur also needs to be known by the student and all teachers working with the student.

14

Managing Respiratory Secretions

Some students have respiratory or physical conditions that result in difficulty moving secretions out of the respiratory tract, because of excessive secretions, thickened secretions, or an inability to cough effectively to clear the airway. Respiratory secretions that students are unable to clear on their own must be cleared by external means. They may be loosened and drained through techniques such as postural drainage, clapping, and vibration. Respiratory secretions may also be removed through one of several different suctioning procedures. These techniques have the common purpose of keeping the airway open and free of secretions that may block the airway.

Secretions may accumulate in several places along the respiratory tract. The respiratory tract begins at the nose (and mouth) where air is first inspired. Air travels next to the pharynx (throat), which connects the nasal airway and the oral airway. From the pharynx, air flows into the larynx (voice box), which has a lidlike structure (epiglottis) that overhangs the entrance to the larynx to

prevent food from entering. After air passes through the larynx, it goes through the trachea (windpipe) into the bronchi (large airways). From there the respiratory tract branches into multiple smaller airways known as *secondary bronchi* and *bronchioles.* Eventually, small airways end in multiple air sacs, know as *alveoli,* in which the exchange of gases to and from the bloodstream occurs (see Figures 10-1b and 13-1 from previous chapters). Secretions that need to be removed may be anywhere from the nose and mouth to the smaller airways in the lungs.

The entire surface of the respiratory passages, from the nose to the bronchioles, is coated with a layer of mucous secretions. These mucous secretions keep the airway moist and also trap small particles that are inhaled when a person breathes. The surface of the respiratory passages is also lined with epithelium cells that contain hundreds of hairlike structures, known as *cilia,* on each individual cell. These cilia move rapidly back and forth at about 10 to 20 beats a second. Cilia below the pharynx beat more strongly in an upward direction, while cilia in the nose beat more strongly in a downward direction. This results in the mucous secretions flowing toward the pharynx where they can be swallowed or coughed out (Guyton, 1991).

When secretions are thick or excessive, the cilia may not be able to move the secretions to the pharynx effectively. Further congestion will result if the student has a weak or ineffective cough, resulting in an inability to expel the secretions or move the secretions to the pharynx. This may occur when the person has certain neuromuscular conditions, spinal cord injury, condition or illness that results in a lack of strength to use muscles effectively, condition in which there are fewer cilia, or tracheostomy.

When these secretions are present in the airway, they may need to be loosened through various techniques or removed through suctioning. The beginning part of this chapter will discuss several techniques used in loosening and moving secretions from the respiratory tract. The remainder of this chapter will discuss different methods for removing the secretions through suctioning.

CHEST PHYSIOTHERAPY: MOVING AND LOOSENING SECRETIONS

Chest physiotherapy, also known as chest physical therapy (CPT) or chest percussion and postural drainage (CPPD), is the application of several specialized techniques, used singularly or in combination, that promote effective coughing, removal of secretions, and unobstructive breathing. Techniques that may be used in chest physiotherapy are (a) postural drainage, (b) percussion, (c) vibration, (d) coughing using several positions, and (e) other airway clearance techniques. Although these techniques may seem simple to perform, it should be pointed out that they require specific training and a doctor's order. For some students, these procedures are contraindicated or

extremely modified (e.g., students with increased intracranial pressure, osteogenesis imperfecta, end-stage renal disease) (Wong, 1995). Sometimes mobilizing secretions may cause problems if the secretions cannot be successfully removed.

Some state medical review panels have recommended that chest physiotherapy should not be performed at school, even by the school nurse (Ashcroft & Smith, 1993). Also, the use of percussion and vibration is controversial due to a lack of data demonstrating their effectiveness by some professionals, yet it is commonly prescribed with reports of good results.

Postural Drainage

Postural drainage is a technique in which the student is placed in specific positions during the day for specified periods of time. By positioning the student in certain positions, mucus is forced by gravity to move from the various sections of the lungs down the bronchioles and bronchi and into the trachea where they can be removed by coughing or suctioning. Postural drainage is used when there are excess mucous secretions. Its use is sometimes dramatically effective in students with chronic lung disease with thick mucous secretions (e.g., asthma, cystic fibrosis) (Wong, 1995).

As seen in Figure 14-1, several different positions may be used, depending on the area of congestion. When trying to drain the upper segments of the lungs down into the main bronchi, the student is usually placed in a sitting position. When trying to drain the anterior segments of the lungs into the main bronchi, the student may be positioned flat (with a pillow under the knees for comfort and support). The remaining positions have the student tilted downward to drain secretions from the lower lung segments up toward the trachea. How the student is placed, on his side or stomach in a head-down position, will depend on the section of lung being drained.

Postural drainage should not be scheduled immediately before or after a meal. Some students will have a loss of appetite if scheduled prior to a

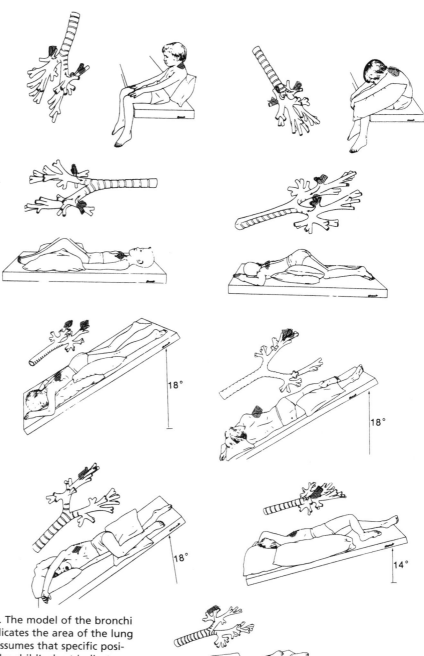

FIGURE 14-1 Postural drainage. The model of the bronchi and lungs beside each child indicates the area of the lung that drains when the student assumes that specific position. The area highlighted on the child's chest indicates the spot to be cupped or vibrated by the therapist.

SOURCE: From V. Chernick, ed. *Kendig's Disorders of the Respiratory Tract of Children, 5th ed,* (Philadelphia, PA: W. B. Saunders, 1990). Reprinted with permission.

meal. Waiting 1 to 1½ hours after a meal will decrease the possibility of vomiting. If the student is receiving continuous tube feedings, the feeding should be discontinued 30 to 60 minutes prior to treatment. Typically, the treatment will last approximately 20 to 30 minutes. The student will usually be placed in a maximum of 4 to 6 positions, although up to 10 positions are sometimes ordered.

Percussion. Sometimes a technique known as **percussion,** or clapping, is performed during postural drainage. Clapping typically uses a cupped hand (or sometimes a special percussion cup or mechanical percussion) to gently strike the person's chest in specific places over the underlying lung to hasten drainage by shaking secretions from the sides of the respiratory tract. When the cupped hand makes contact with the student's chest, an air pocket is created to cushion the blow and transmit a shock wave into the lung (Skale, 1992). Wrist action is used to make the striking motion rather than the arm. A hollow sound is heard, rather than a slapping sound. It is not a painful technique. Typically the student is percussed for 1 to 2 minutes at a time, then encouraged to cough (Mackay, 1993; Skale, 1992). It is important that personnel and students understand that the student is not being hit, but is having a special health care technique performed.

Vibration

Vibration is a technique to further help move secretions into the main airways. It is the application of fine shaking motions during exhalation over specific areas of the chest with a flat hand. Vibration may be performed manually or with a hand-held vibrator. In hospital settings, a more powerful vibrator may be used. Vibration may be ordered to be given after postural drainage and percussion, after postural drainage in place of percussion, or used independently. When it follows postural drainage and percussion, it is usually delivered 1 to 2 minutes after percussion is completed.

Coughing

Following any of the previous techniques, coughing should be encouraged. Ideally the person should be in a sitting position when coughing. Several deep breaths should be taken, and the last breath should be followed with a deep cough. Upon coughing, students 3 or 4 years of age and older are encouraged to spit out the secretions, rather than swallowing them. Although swallowing the secretions is not harmful, they may upset the stomach and result in vomiting. Spitting out the secretions also allows the caretaker to monitor the amount, color, and consistency of the secretions—important information when monitoring for respiratory infection. Typically it is expected that small students will swallow the mucous secretions (Mackay, 1993). If the student cannot cough effectively, then suctioning is usually ordered.

DESCRIPTION OF SUCTIONING

Some students may have oral secretions pool in the mouth and be unable to spit or swallow the secretions. Other students may be unable to effectively cough the secretions up from the trachea to the point that they can be swallowed or spit out through the mouth (or tracheostomy). To remove these excess secretions from the respiratory passages, **suctioning** may be required. Suctioning is aspiration of secretions by mechanical means. Typically, a suction catheter (specialized tube) is placed into the student's respiratory passage (i.e., mouth, trachea) to suck out the unwanted secretions. Removal of excess secretions will help promote efficient breathing.

Suctioning usually occurs on an as-needed basis, referred to as **p.r.n.** (an abbreviation from the Latin phrase meaning "according to circumstances required"). It is important that the student is carefully assessed to determine when suctioning is needed. Signs of needing suctioning include auditory noises such as gurgling or wheezing sounds or visual signs such as visible secretions in the nose or at the tracheostomy. Lack of oxygen may also be present with cyanosis (bluish color) at the nailbeds or around the lips and difficulty breathing. (Refer to "Preparing for Suctioning" for a complete list of signs.) When signs are present that indicate suctioning is needed, the procedure will need to be carried out immediately. Not suctioning when it is needed can result in blocked airways and respiratory distress, which can lead to lowered oxygen levels and possible respiratory arrest.

It is also important that suctioning does not occur too frequently or for too long a time. When suctioning is occurring, the person is not breathing, and oxygen is being sucked from the respiratory airways. To counter this, the suctioning procedure may include using oxygen, having the student take deep breaths, and/or waiting between repeated suctioning. However, even with this in place, if suctioning is occurring too frequently or for too long a time, damaging situations can occur, ranging from irritation to damage to the respiratory passages. On a more severe level, oxygen levels can drop (hypoxia), and there is a danger of a drop in heart rate (bradycardia) (Oberc, 1991). This condition has the potential of resulting in an emergency situation. It is important that proper procedures are implemented, with suctioning occurring only when needed. An exception to this is when the student has excess secretions, and the physician has ordered suctioning to occur as needed, as well as before naptime and bedtime and upon awakening (Mizumori et al., 1994).

There are several different suctioning procedures, based on where suctioning is to occur. Suctioning may occur singularly or in combination in the following locations: (a) the nose, (b) the mouth, (c) the pharynx (throat), (d) the trachea (windpipe), and/or (e) the bronchi. Suctioning of the upper airway usually consists of suctioning the nose or the nose and pharynx. Sometimes the mouth is to be suctioned as well. In these types of suctioning procedures, the suction catheter tube

in introduced only into the nose, the back of the nose, or the mouth.

Lower airway suctioning refers to suctioning the trachea and/or bronchi. This type of suctioning involves introducing a suction catheter into the trachea or bronchi and may occur by suctioning through a tracheostomy or by nasotracheal suctioning (see Figure 14-2). A tracheostomy is a surgical opening made in the lower neck into the trachea. A tube (tracheostomy tube) is usually inserted into the tracheostomy through which the person breathes (see Chapter 13). Suctioning through a tracheostomy involves passing a suction catheter through the tracheostomy tube, into the trachea to remove secretions. For students who do not have a tracheostomy, tracheal suctioning can still occur by nasotracheal suctioning. Nasotracheal suctioning involves inserting a catheter through the nostrils and nasal passages, down the pharynx and larynx, and into the trachea. (Rarely, the suction catheter may be passed through the mouth, but this is usually avoided due to the gag reflex and possibility of being bit.) Both tracheostomy and nasotracheal suctioning will remove secretions from the respiratory passages and may also stimulate coughing, which helps loosen and mobilize secretions (Suddarth, 1991).

If bronchial suctioning is ordered by the physician, the catheter will need to be inserted farther into the right or left bronchus. This often involves positioning the head in certain positions to facilitate correct placement of the suction catheter (e.g., turning the head to the extreme right with chin up to access the left bronchi) (Suddarth, 1991). Bronchial suctioning, however, is rarely performed in the school setting.

Suctioning may be ordered by the physician using sterile or clean technique. Sterile technique implies that the items have been specially prepared and packaged to be aseptic (free of living micro-organisms). Sterile technique requires the use of sterile gloves, sterile catheters, sterile water, and a sterile container to hold the water. During the procedure, care must be taken that only sterile items touch other sterile items in order for

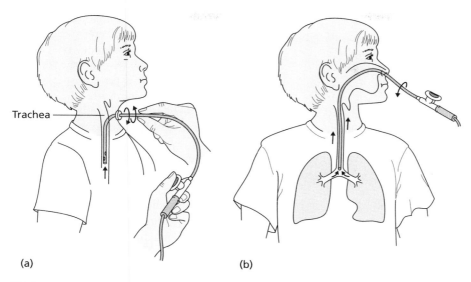

Trachea

(a)   (b)

FIGURE 14-2 Lower airway suctioning occurring through a tracheostomy (a) or by nasotracheal suctioning through the nose (b). When the catheter is withdrawn, it is turned back and forth to prevent it from clinging to the sides of the trachea (windpipe).

them to remain sterile (e.g., only a sterile glove would touch the sterile catheter). After completing the technique, all used supplies are discarded since they have been used and are no longer sterile. Other students may have the physician's permission to use a clean technique. In clean technique, the equipment and supplies are clean, not sterile. In some cases, some of the supplies, such as suction catheters, may be reused after cleaning. Clean technique is often acceptable for home and school care, but the physician makes the decision based on the student's needs (Mizumori et al., 1994).

EQUIPMENT AND ADAPTIVE EQUIPMENT FOR SUCTIONING

One of the essential pieces of equipment used in suctioning is the suction catheter. Depending on the type of suctioning being performed, most

procedures will require a straight **catheter** (see Figure 14-3). A straight suction catheter is a long, narrow, flexible tube that comes in various lengths and diameters. At one end are small holes into which the student's secretions can be drawn. On the other end is a connecting hub that allows the suction catheter to be connected to a connecting tube that attaches to a suction machine. Most suction catheters will have a suction thumb port (or suction vent) next to the connecting hub (see Figure 14.3). A *suction thumb port* is an opening in the catheter. When the suction thumb port is open and the suction machine is on, air will be sucked through the port instead of through the end of the catheter. When the suction thumb port is open, the suction is considered "off," since it is not sucking air through the suction catheter. The suction thumb port is closed by the adult putting a thumb over the suction thumb port and closing it. When this occurs, the air is sucked through the end of the suction catheter. When the suction thumb port is closed, the suction is considered

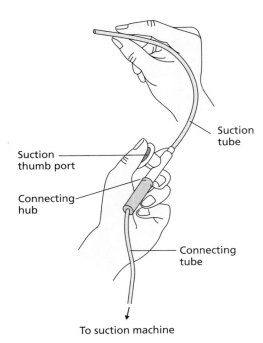

FIGURE 14-3 A typical suction catheter used for suctioning.

"on." The suction thumb port is an important feature. It allows the suction catheter to be placed into proper position in the respiratory tract without suction being on (by having the suction thumb port open), until it is time to suction (by closing the suction thumb port with the thumb).

Most students will be suctioned by having the suction catheter attach to a **suction machine.** There are many different types of suction machines (see Figure 14-4). Some are small and portable, fitting into a small suitcase container, while others are larger and fit on top of a table. Although suction machines vary in construction, they all have a collecting bottle into which the secretions go, a connecting tube to which the suction catheter attaches, a connecting hub (or rubber stoppers) that attach the connecting tube to the suction machine, and a motor. Often there is a second bottle (the same size as the collecting bottle) used to create suction. Most suction machines will have a power cord and require an electric outlet, but some will use batteries.

Most suction machines will also have a knob and gauge to set the amount of suction. The settings for the amount of suction will vary. Precise

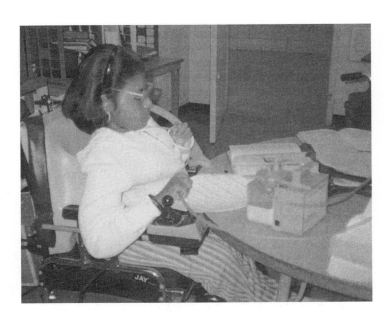

FIGURE 14-4 A student suctioning her tracheostomy. The suction machine is located on the table, and the student is holding the thumb port with her right hand as she inserts the suction catheter with her left hand.

settings for each student should be specified by the physician and take into account the student's age. Typical settings for portable suction machines are as follows: infants, 3 to 5 millimeters of mercury (mmHg); students, 5 to 8 (or sometimes up to 10) mmHg; and adults, 8 to 15 mmHg (Mizumori et al., 1994). It is important that the prescribed amount of suction be used. If the suction is too weak, it will be ineffective in removing the sections. However, excessive pressure can cause trauma, slow heart rate (bradycardia), spasms, cyanosis (blue tinge to skin due to lack of oxygen), and cardiac arrhythmias (Oberc, 1991).

Additional equipment may include the use of a resuscitation bag, also known as an Ambu bag (see Figure 14-5). In some suctioning procedures, the student is given a few breaths with the resuscitation bag prior to suctioning. The bag may fit over the mouth and nose, or may have an adapter to fit onto a tracheostomy. Oxygen may be connected to the bag to provide not just breaths of air but oxygen as well.

The main types of suctioning techniques are (a) tracheostomy tube suctioning, (b) nasotracheal suctioning, (c) nasal suctioning, and (d) oral suctioning. Individuals requiring suctioning may have one or multiple procedures prescribed. In all

of these procedures, a straight catheter and suction machine may be used. However, in some instances, other types of catheters (e.g., Yankauer) may be connected to the suction machine instead of a straight catheter. Alternate devices not requiring a suction machine may also be used (e.g., bulb syringe, DeLee catheter). In some instances, the student may use a straight catheter and suction machine to suction the trachea and a different device to suction the mouth. These alternative devices will be described later in this chapter, after discussing the procedures for suctioning with a straight suction catheter and suction machine.

ASSISTIVE STRATEGIES FOR TRACHEOSTOMY OR NASOTRACHEAL SUCTIONING

Preparing for Tracheostomy or Nasotracheal Suctioning

Before beginning suctioning, it is important that the person performing the procedure understands

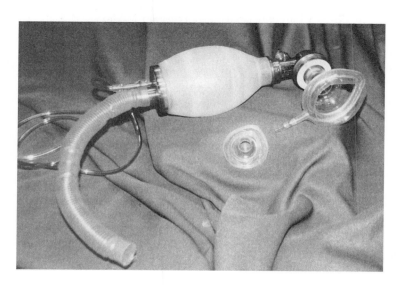

FIGURE 14-5 A manual resuscitation bag with a mouth/nose attachment that can be replaced with an attachment to fit onto a tracheostomy tube. Oxygen is attached to this bag with the small tube coming out of the back of the bag.

whether the trachea or the bronchi are being suctioned and how far the catheter should be inserted. This is important in both tracheostomy and nasotracheal suctioning. When a physician orders suctioning of the trachea through a tracheostomy, the physician may have prescribed shallow suctioning or deep suctioning. *Shallow suctioning* is a procedure of putting the suction tube briefly within the tracheostomy tube at a premeasured length of approximately 1 to 2 centimeters longer than the tracheostomy tube (Berry, 1993). *Deep suctioning* usually uses a procedure of advancing the suction catheter until resistance is met and then slightly withdrawing it and applying suction at that time (Mizumori et al., 1994). Although deep suctioning may be more effective in obtaining secretions that are at the lower levels of the respiratory tract, studies have indicated that deep suctioning may result in more damage to the tissue of the trachea (including tissue death, inflammation, loss of cilia, and increased mucus production) (Bailey, Kattwinkel, Teja, & Buckley, 1988; Kleiber, Krutzfield, & Rose, 1988). The person performing the procedure should understand the physician's directions regarding the depth the catheter should be advanced.

Not only is the depth of suctioning important, but accuracy in placement of the suction catheter is vital for proper suctioning to occur. In nasotracheal suctioning, errors can arise in catheter placement. The pharynx branches off into the larynx and trachea for the respiratory tract and the esophagus for the digestive tract. Therefore, it is imperative that the suction catheter be placed into the larynx and advanced into the trachea. Special techniques, such as having the student cough or say "Ahhh," may be used when the catheter is being advanced since these open the epiglottis, promoting correct placement into the airway. Advancing the catheter when the student is inhaling may also assist with proper placement. It is important that the catheter not be advanced when the student swallows because this will typically result in the suction catheter advancing into the esophagus. If the person performing the procedure has mistakenly advanced

the catheter into the esophagus, it will need to be removed and the procedure restarted.

Several procedural variations are possible based on the student's status, condition, and the type of procedure. Some procedural considerations are whether breaths are to be given prior to suctioning, whether saline is used when secretions are thick, and whether the procedure is a sterile or clean one. Also, if the student has a tracheostomy with an inner cannula, it must be determined whether the inner cannula is to be removed before suctioning (see Chapter 13 for more information on inner cannulas).

Identifying the Need for Suctioning

The student must be assessed to determine whether suctioning is needed (unless it is ordered at specific times). One of the most overt signs indicating a need for suctioning is hearing secretions bubbling in the airway or gurgling, wheezing, or whistling breath sounds. Other signs of possibly requiring suctioning include coughing, agitation, and fast breathing with no change in activity, or seeing secretions at the opening of the tracheostomy tube. In some cases, the student may show signs of difficulty breathing (labored breathing, complaints of inability to breathe, muscle retraction), low oxygen (restlessness, fast heart rate, flaring of nostrils, dusky or blue color around mouth or at nailbeds), or no air exchange (see Figure 14-6). When this occurs, due to secretions obstructing or blocking the airway, suctioning will be needed to unblock the airway (Ashcroft & Smith, 1993).

Upon determining that suctioning is needed, it is important to prepare the student for the procedure. Some students may be learning some of the procedure and be very cooperative. Others may not understand the procedure, find it very aversive, and need to be restrained through the procedure. If the student is not cooperative, restraining the student is important to avoid injury. Explanations are important prior to starting the procedure, as well as praise and reassurance to the student after the procedure is finished.

Both the student and adult will need to wash their hands before the beginning of the proce-

Abnormal Breathing
Difficult, labored breathing

Decreased air exchange or inability to move air (through tracheostomy or airways)

Shortness of breath, rapid breathing

Wheezing, gasping for breath, abnormal breath sounds

Retraction of Chest
Pulling in of the chest and neck muscles (which occurs to help with breathing)

Cyanosis
Dusky or blue color, especially at nailbeds and around mouth

Neurological Signs
Agitation, anxiety, restlessness

Confusion, inability to concentrate

Dizzy

Drowsiness

Unconscious

Cardiac
Fast heart rate (pulse)

FIGURE 14-6 Signs of respiratory distress

dure. Sterile gloves are always worn if sterile technique is used, and clean gloves are often worn when clean technique is being used. If the procedure is performed using sterile technique, it will be important that strict sterile technique is main-

tained with only the sterile gloves touching what is to remain sterile (e.g., all of the catheter except the suction thumb port). This precaution is for infection control purposes. During the procedure, the student is usually positioned with the head elevated in a sitting or reclined position.

Equipment and Supply List for Tracheostomy and Nasotracheal Suctioning

Suction machine

Gloves (clean or sterile, depending on ordered procedure)

Suction catheters (clean or sterile)

Water (clean or sterile)

Container (clean or sterile)

Lubricant (if nasotracheal suctioning and if ordered)

Resuscitation bag

Saline drops (if ordered)

Procedure for Tracheostomy and Nasotracheal Suctioning

After verifying that the student needs suctioning, explaining the procedure to the student, and obtaining the supplies and equipment, the person performing the procedure is ready to begin. In the case of a tracheostomy, the inner cannula is removed if applicable. Positioning will depend on the student's condition and the physician's instructions. However, the student's head should be elevated. The following procedure is for both tracheostomy and nasotracheal suctioning.

Steps in the Procedure for Tracheostomy and Nasotracheal Suctioning	*Rationale*
1. Wash hands and put on a sterile or clean glove on the dominant hand that will handle the suction catheter. (A second glove may be worn on the nondominant hand, if desired.)	A glove is used to keep the catheter sterile or clean and the hand clean. (If a sterile glove is used, care must be taken that the package is opened without contaminating glove or contents. A sterile glove is put on by holding the inside of the cuff with nondominant hand and pulling glove over dominant hand.)

Steps in the Procedure for Tracheostomy and Nasotracheal Suctioning	Rationale
2. Pour water into a cup.	Note for sterile technique: Some catheter packages come with the sterile cup inside.
Sterile technique: Remove the sterile cup from the package with the sterile gloved hand, and pour sterile water into it with the nonsterile gloved hand.	The designated person will usually put on a sterile glove then remove the sterile container. However, some equipment comes separate. The designated person may have to first open the suction catheter, sterile container, and gloves before putting on the sterile glove.
3. Pick up the suction connecting tube that is attached to the suction machine with the nondominant hand. Pick up the suction catheter with the dominant hand (sterile hand, if sterile technique is being used) and attach the catheter to the suction tubing.	If sterile technique is being used, the catheter should only be touched at this point with the sterile gloved hand.
4. Turn the suction machine on and verify the pressure setting with the nondominant hand.	Proper pressure setting should be given by the physician. Pressure is checked by kinking the connecting tube and reading the gauge.
5. Hold the end of catheter about 3 inches from the end with the dominant hand (that is wearing a sterile glove, if using sterile technique). Hold the suction thumb port with the other hand. Place the tip of the catheter in a cup of water and cover the suction thumb port with the thumb for a few seconds.	The water left on the catheter will lubricate it and decrease tissue damage and prevent secretions from sticking to the inside of the catheter (Berry, 1993). This step also verifies that the suction machine is working.
6. *Nasotracheal suctioning only:* The tip of catheter may have sterile lubricant applied at this time to decrease trauma and assist in its passage.	
Tracheostomy suctioning: If the physician ordered saline to loosen thick secretions, put 1 to 2 milliliters of sterile saline solution into the tracheostomy tube.	Instillation of saline into the airway assists with removal of secretions by lavage effect or coughing (Berry, 1993: Mizumori et al., 1994). Sterile saline comes in a very small container, ready for the top to be taken off and the sterile saline to be squirted into the tracheostomy.
7. Encourage the student to take deep breaths, or, if ordered, give the student	Hyperventilating the student (by encouraging deep breaths or providing

Steps in the Procedure for Tracheostomy and Nasotracheal Suctioning	*Rationale*
the prescribed number of breaths (e.g., three breaths) with manual resuscitator bag or ventilator. Breaths should be given in synchrony with the student's own breaths. (The physician may order a manual resuscitation bag to be connected to oxygen when giving breaths.)	breaths) helps increase the oxygen concentration that suctioning decreases. However, if very thick secretions or a mucous plug is suspected, the student should be suctioned prior to hyperventilating so that the secretion is not forced farther down the airway.
8. *Tracheostomy suctioning:* If the physician has ordered removal of inner cannula during suction, remove it temporarily until suctioning is over.	
9. *Tracheostomy suctioning:* With the finger off the suction thumb port, gently insert the catheter straight back into the tracheostomy tube.	Never insert the catheter with the suction thumb port on since this can result in irritating the tissue lining the trachea.
Nasotracheal suctioning: With the finger off the suction thumb port, gently insert the catheter straight back into the nostril. As the catheter advances into the pharynx area, have the student cough or say "Ahhh" to help it enter the trachea. If the student cannot do this, move the suction catheter forward on inspiration.	When advancing the catheter during nasotracheal suctioning, there is always the possibility that it will enter the digestive tract (esophagus) instead of the trachea. Having the student cough or say "Ahhh" will help direct the catheter into the trachea.
10. Insert catheter to premeasured length.	
Tracheostomy suctioning: This will typically be 1 centimeter below the tracheostomy tube. If deep suctioning is being performed, be sure that the catheter is withdrawn by 1 to 2 centimeters when resistance is met before applying suction (Berry, 1993).	It is important to minimize damage to the tissue of the trachea, so the procedure will need to be carefully followed inserting the catheter the proper distance.
Nasotracheal suctioning: The depth of insertion will vary depending on the student's size and how deep suctioning is to occur.	
11. Begin suctioning by placing the nondominant thumb over suction thumb port.	When the thumb is over the suction thumb port, suction is being applied. When the thumb is up and not over the suction thumb port, air is not being sucked into the distal

Steps in the Procedure for Tracheostomy and Nasotracheal Suctioning	*Rationale*
	end of tube and hence suction is considered off. Depending on the procedure, the thumb may be constantly over the suction thumb port for a few seconds until the procedure is complete, or suction may be applied intermittently with the thumb being intermittently applied on and off the suction thumb port for the few seconds that the procedure is being performed (Kuntz, 1996b).
12. With (sterile) gloved hand, rotate the catheter between the thumb and forefinger while withdrawing catheter, keeping the suctioning on with the thumb over the suction thumb port.	Rotating the catheter is important to prevent tissue from being drawn against the catheter and causing injury to the tissue. (If a pulling is felt, tissue may be caught and the suction should be released.)
Suctioning should never exceed 5 to 10 seconds. Pediatric tracheostomy suctioning should usually not require more than 3 to 4 seconds for withdrawal of the catheter (Chameides, 1988).	The person performing the procedure may want to hold his breath and count to be sure that the procedure is not taking any longer than recommended. Tracheostomy suctioning should take a shorter time since the artificial airway is shorter. Suctioning longer periods can decrease the student's oxygen levels.
13. If the airway is not clear after suctioning, put the suction catheter in the cup of water and apply suction to clean the suction catheter and relubricate it.	The suction catheter should have water go through it every time between suctioning attempts.
14. If applicable, repeat instilling saline, encouraging deep breathing or providing breaths, and repeat the suctioning procedure.	Allow 30 to 60 seconds between suctioning attempts with the catheter to allow oxygen levels to return to baseline (Wong, 1995). The physician may have ordered the student to be hyperventilated between suctioning.
15. When suctioning is completed, place the suction catheter in the cup of water and suction sufficient water through the catheter to clean out the suction catheter and connecting tube. If the physician ordered additional breaths after the suctioning procedure, they would occur at this time.	Respirations should be quiet and relaxed.

Steps in the Procedure for Tracheostomy and Nasotracheal Suctioning	*Rationale*
16. If needed, the mouth or nose may be suctioned at this time. (See the next procedure.)	
17. When completed, hold the catheter in the gloved hand and pull the glove off, encasing the catheter in the glove. Throw out both in a plastic bag in an appropriate container. (Some physicians allow catheters to be reused. If this is the case, the catheter will need to be cleaned following the physician's recommendations for cleaning and then stored.)	When performing a sterile procedure, always throw away the catheter when finished. Some clean procedures treat the catheter as sterile and also require discarding it after a single use.
18. Throw away used supplies and put away reusable supplies.	
19. Wash hands and document the procedure, including approximate amount, color, and consistency of secretions.	
20. After allowing the student to rest for a few minutes, resume the regular routine.	

Care of Equipment

The suction machine should be checked each day to be sure it is properly functioning. There are several different types of suction machines, so the manufacturer's instructions should be read for specific information. However, in general, the machine can be checked by turning on the suction machine and kinking the connecting tube or occluding the end of the connecting tube with a clean thumb. The pressure gauge should easily rise past 15 when the suction is on. If there is no gauge, the person should determine whether the machine is producing enough suction by looking, listening, and feeling the amount of suction being produced (Ashcroft & Smith, 1993).

The suction machine will need to be cleaned at least daily when used. The suction bottle should be emptied into the toilet. The bottle and connecting tube may be cleaned one of two ways, depending on the equipment and physician's orders. The bottle, connecting tube, and rubber stopper can be rinsed with clean warm soapy water in a sink and rinsed with water. A second method is putting the end of the connecting tube into a jar of warm soapy water and turning on the suction machine to suck the water through the connecting tube into the bottle. After emptying the bottle, this is repeated with warm water to rinse the equipment. It is important that hot water is not used since hot water can cause the mucous secretions to stick in the tubing (Ashcroft & Smith, 1993).

On a weekly basis, all of the parts of the suction machine need to be thoroughly cleansed with equal amounts of water and white vinegar, or another cleaning solution. Typically, the bottle, connecting tube, and rubber stoppers are soaked for 20 minutes, then rinsed with water. The bottle and rubber stoppers are dried, and the tubing is allowed to air dry. After reassembling the equipment, the suction should be checked. The rubber stopper should fit tightly, and the suction pressure should be functioning well (Ashcroft & Smith, 1993).

For students who have their physician's permission to reuse catheters, the catheters will need to be thoroughly cleaned after each use. When the catheter is reusable, it may be cleaned with a half cup of vinegar in a quart of water or other cleaning agent, as specified in the student's individual procedure.

Other material should be properly discarded. Gloves should not be reused, even if clean technique is being used; they should be discarded after each use. Open bottles of sterile water (or sterile saline) should be dated and discarded after a specified period of time. Bacteria can grow in these bottles (especially in saline), and they may need to be discarded daily.

ASSISTIVE STRATEGIES FOR NASAL AND ORAL SUCTIONING WITH A STRAIGHT CATHETER

Preparing for Nasal and Oral Suctioning

Nasal and oral suctioning are typically performed on an as-needed basis. The person responsible for the procedure will need to assess that nasal or oral suctioning is necessary. Indications for nasal suctioning can include difficulty breathing, restlessness, anxiety, noisy breath sounds, secretions coming from nose, or color change (paleness or cyanosis). Indications for oral suctioning include secretions in the mouth or pharynx or

when food has been aspirated (Urbano, 1992). The student should be encouraged to cough or blow the secretions out prior to suctioning. In some cases, nasal or oral suctioning will be unnecessary if the student has success coughing or blowing.

Suctioning the upper airway of the nose, mouth, and/or pharynx is typically a clean procedure, but the physician may have ordered a sterile one. Clarification of the type of procedure is essential. If both suctioning of the nose and mouth are ordered using clean technique, the same suction catheter may be used for both procedures. However, it is important that the nose is suctioned before the mouth. The mouth contains more bacteria, and it is important to avoid introducing this bacteria into the nose after suctioning the mouth (Haynie et al., 1989). Care should be taken that hands are properly washed and reusable supplies are kept clean for proper infection control.

Equipment and Supply List
for Nasal and Oral Suctioning

Suction machine

Gloves

Suction catheters

Water

Container

Saline (if applicable)

Resuscitation bag (if applicable)

Procedure for Nasal and Oral Suctioning with a Straight Catheter and Suction Machine

After verifying that the student requires suctioning, explaining the procedure to the student, and getting all supplies and equipment ready for use, the person performing the procedure is ready to start. Sterile technique procedure should be followed, if ordered.

Steps in the Procedure for Nasal and Oral Suctioning	Rationale
1. Wash hands and put a glove on the dominant hand that will handle the suction catheter. (If sterile technique, the dominant hand wears a sterile glove.) A second glove may be worn on the nondominant hand if desired.	A glove is used to keep the catheter and the hand clean. (If a sterile glove is used, care must be taken that the package is opened without contaminating the glove or contents. A sterile glove is put on by holding the inside of the cuff with the nondominant hand and pulling the glove over the dominant hand.)
2. Pour water into a cup.	Note for sterile technique: Some catheter packages come with the sterile cup inside.
Sterile technique: Remove the sterile cup from the package with the sterile gloved hand and pour sterile water into it with the nonsterile gloved hand.	The designated person will usually put on a sterile glove then remove the sterile container. However, some equipment comes separate. The designated person may have to first open the suction catheter, sterile container, gloves, and lubricant before putting on the gloves.
3. Prepare lubricant. *Clean technique:* Open lubricant package. *Sterile technique:* The lubricant package may be opened and lubricant squeezed onto the sterile inner surface of the package (e.g., opened sterile package that contained the sterile glove, catheter).	When using sterile technique, only the nonsterile hand can touch the outside of the lubricant package. If two hands are needed to open the package, it should be opened prior to donning the sterile glove.
4. Pick up the suction connecting tubing that is attached to suction machine with the nondominant hand. Pick up the suction catheter with the dominant gloved hand.	If sterile technique is being used, the catheter should only be touched at this point with the sterile gloved hand.
5. Turn the suction machine on with nondominant hand and verify the pressure setting.	The physician should have given the proper pressure setting. This is checked by kinking the connecting tube and reading the gauge.
6. Hold the end of the catheter (with the dominant gloved hand). Hold the suction thumb port area with the nondominant hand. Place the tip of the catheter in a cup of water and cover the suction thumb port with the nondominant thumb for a few seconds.	This will lubricate the catheter and further verify that the suction machine is properly working. However, for nasal suctioning, additional lubrication may be ordered.

Steps in the Procedure for Nasal and Oral Suctioning	*Rationale*

Nasal suctioning: If water-soluble lubricant is ordered, at this time apply lubricant on the catheter tip.

7. *Nasal suctioning:* Measure the length of the catheter for nasal suctioning from the tip of the nose to the earlobe (Ashcroft & Smith, 1993). Do not let the catheter touch the student (see Figure 14-7a). Mark the position by placing the thumb of the dominant gloved hand at the proper length.

    Measuring will give the proper length to insert the catheter for nasal suctioning. Typically for infants and small students, this is 4 to 8 centimeters; for older students, 8 to 12 centimeters (Perry & Potter, 1990). If the student begins gagging or coughing, it indicates that the catheter has advanced beyond the pharynx.

8. Encourage the student to take deep breaths, or, if ordered, give students the prescribed number of breaths (e.g., three breaths) with manual resuscitator bag. Breaths should be given in synchrony with the student's own breaths. (The physician may order manual resuscitation bag to be connected to oxygen when giving breaths.)

    Hyperventilating the student (by encouraging deep breaths or providing breaths) helps to increase the oxygen concentration which suctioning decreases. However, if very thick secretions or a mucous plug is suspected, the student should be suctioned prior to hyperventilating so that the secretion is not forced farther down the airway.

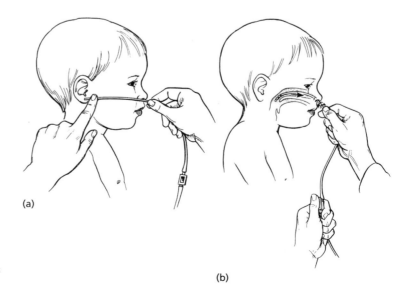

FIGURE 14-7 To determine how far to insert the catheter for nasal suctioning, measure from the tip of the nose to the earlobe (a). Nasal suctioning occurs through the nose (b).

(a)

(b)

SOURCE: From Donna Wong and Lucille S. Whaley, *Nursing Care of Infants and Children* (St. Louis, MO: Mosby-Yearbook, 1995). Reprinted with permission of Mosby-Yearbook and Donna Wong.

Steps in the Procedure for Nasal and Oral Suctioning	Rationale
9. *Nasal suctioning:* With the finger off the suction thumb port, gently insert the catheter into one nostril. *Oral suctioning:* With the finger off the suction thumb port, insert the catheter into the mouth.	Never insert the catheter with the suction thumb port on since this can result in irritating the tissue lining the trachea. Do not force the catheter if it will not advance.
10. *Nasal suctioning:* Gently advance the catheter along the base of the nasal membrane. Resistance may be met 2 to 3 centimeters into the nostril. Slightly rotating the catheter or having the student inspire air should remove the resistance. Continue to insert to premeasured length (Oberc, 1991) (see Figure 14–7b). *Oral suctioning:* Insert the catheter to the check area.	Never force the catheter. It should easily advance.
11. Begin suctioning by placing the nondominant gloved thumb over suction thumb port.	When the thumb is over the suction thumb port, suction is being applied. When thumb is up and not over suction thumb port, air is not being sucked into the distal end of tube, and hence suction is considered off. Depending on the procedure, the thumb may be constantly over the suction thumb port for a few seconds until the procedure is complete, or suction may be applied intermittently with the thumb being intermittently applied on and off the suction thumb port for the few seconds that the procedure is being performed (Kuntz, 1996b).
12. *Nasal suctioning:* With the gloved hand and suction on, rotate the catheter between the thumb and forefinger while withdrawing the catheter (see Figure 14–7b). The withdrawal of the catheter should be shorter than 5 seconds (Oberc, 1991). *Oral suctioning:* With the gloved hand, rotate catheter between the thumb and forefinger while suctioning the cheek area, under the tongue, and back of the	Rotating the catheter is important to prevent tissue from being drawn against the catheter and causing injury to the tissue. (If a pulling is felt, tissue may be caught and the suction should be released.) The person performing the procedure may want to hold her breath and count to be sure that the procedure is not taking any longer than recommended.

Steps in the Procedure for Nasal and Oral Suctioning	Rationale
throat. The withdrawal of the catheter should be shorter than 5 seconds (Oberc, 1991).	
13. If further suctioning is needed, encourage deep breathing, and clean the suction catheter by putting it into water and applying suction between each suctioning. *Nasal suctioning:* Repeat this procedure with the other nostril. *Oral suctioning:* Repeat this procedure if secretions are still present in cheek area, under the tongue, or in the back of the throat.	Allow 30 to 60 seconds between suctioning with catheter to allow oxygen levels to return to baseline. The physician may have ordered the student to be hyperventilated between suctioning.
14. When suctioning is completed, suction sufficient water through the catheter to clean out the tubing. If the physician has ordered additional breaths after the suction procedure, they would occur at this time.	Respirations should be quiet and relaxed.
15. When completed, hold the catheter in the gloved hand, pull the glove off, encasing the catheter in the glove. Throw out both in a plastic bag or appropriate container. (Some physicians allow catheters to be reused. If this is the case, the catheter will need to be cleaned following the physician's recommendations for cleaning, and then stored.)	During sterile procedures, always throw away the catheter when finished. Some clean procedures treat the catheter as sterile and also require discarding it after a single use.
16. Throw away used supplies.	
17. Wash hands and document the procedure, including approximate amount, color, and consistency of secretions.	
18. After allowing the student to rest for a few minutes, resume the regular routine.	

Care of Equipment

See the earlier section under tracheostomy and nasotracheal suctioning for care of equipment.

SUCTIONING WITH OTHER DEVICES

Tonsil Tip Devices

Tonsil tip devices are usually narrow plastic items that attach onto the connection tubing of a suc-tion machine. Two common ones are the Yan-kauer tip and saliva ejectors. They resemble the instruments used to suction the mouth during a teeth cleaning at the dentist's office. They are de-signed to suction the mouth. They are reusable, and their use follows a clean procedure.

Procedure for Tonsil Tip Devices. After ver-ifying the student needs suctioning, explain-ing the procedure to the student, washing hands, assembling equipment, and putting on gloves, the person performing the procedure is ready to begin.

Steps in the Procedure for Tonsil Tip Devices	Rationale
1. Wash hands and put on gloves.	Clean technique requires good infection control.
2. Pour water into a basin or cup.	
3. Connect tonsil tip device to connecting tubing.	
4. Turn suction machine on and verify the pressure setting.	Always verify the pressure setting. This is done by kinking the connecting tube between thumb and forefinger and noting the amount of pressure registered on the gauge. Adjust if necessary (Oberc, 1991).
5. Place the tip of the tonsil tip device in a cup of water. If there is a suction thumb port, cover it with the thumb for a few seconds.	This step will also verify proper functioning of the suction machine.
6. Insert the tip into the mouth, along the base of the tongue. If there is a suction thumb port, apply suction when the device is in place. For devices that do not have a suction thumb port, continuous suction occurs, and suctioning begins immedi-ately upon the device entering the mouth.	Inserting along the base of the tongue helps prevent spasms (Oberc, 1991).
7. Move the device continually around the mouth.	Continual movement helps decrease the possibility of damaging the tissue (mucous membranes) of the mouth.

Steps in the Procedure for Tonsil Tip Devices	*Rationale*
8. Withdraw the device before 5 seconds.	The person performing the procedure may want to hold his breath and count to avoid suctioning for too long.
9. Repeat steps 5 to 8 until the mouth is clear of secretions.	
10. When finished, clean the equipment. Remove and discard the gloves and wash hands. Document the procedure and color, consistency, and amount of secretions.	

Bulb Syringe

A bulb syringe is a simple device, typically made out of rubber, that has a round bulb area and a pointed end. When the bulb is squeezed then released, suction is created at the opening. Secretions will be drawn into the opening and into the inside of the bulb (see Figure 14-8). A bulb syringe may be used to clean the nostrils, mouth (under tongue, in cheek area), or the opening of a tracheostomy. It is typically reusable and follows a clean procedure.

Procedure. After verifying the student needs suctioning, explaining the procedure to the student, washing hands, assembling equipment, and putting on gloves, the person performing the procedure is ready to start. In some instances, the student will have both nasal and oral suctioning ordered. In this case, nasal suctioning is done first, followed by oral suctioning.

Steps in the Procedure for Bulb Syringe	*Rationale*
1. Grasp the bulb syringe with the index and middle finger around the tip end of syringe, and place the thumb over the rounded part of the bulb.	

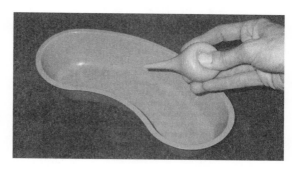

FIGURE 14-8 A bulb syringe used for suctioning the nostrils, mouth, or secretions that have been expelled from the tracheostomy. The contents of the bulb syringe are being expelled into a pan.

Steps in the Procedure for Bulb Syringe	*Rationale*
2. Compress the rounded part of the bulb syringe by pushing inward with the thumb and continue to hold it there.	It is important to compress the bulb before placing the bulb syringe into the mouth, nose, or opening near a tracheostomy so that air is not forced into the opening, moving secretions farther down.
3. Place the bulb syringe in the appropriate location. *Nasal suctioning:* Place the tip of the bulb syringe into one nostril. *Oral suctioning:* Place the tip of the bulb syringe into the side of the mouth.	If mouth and nose suctioning are both ordered, the nose should always be suctioned prior to the mouth because of the amount of bacteria in the mouth.
Tracheostomy opening suctioning: Place the tip of the bulb syringe beside the visible secretions.	The tip is never placed inside the tracheostomy tube. This catheter is only used for suctioning visible secretions.
4. Apply suction by slowly releasing the thumb, drawing secretions into the bulb syringe.	Gradually releasing the bulb syringe will help prevent injury to the tissues (Oberc, 1991).
5. When the bulb is reinflated, remove it.	The bulb will return to its natural shape.
6. Take a tissue and point the tip toward it. Push down with the thumb, expelling secretions into the tissue.	The secretions may be expelled into a small pan or cup instead of a tissue. The pan or cup will need to be cleaned or thrown away when finished.
7. Let the bulb syringe refill with air, and repeat the procedure if needed.	The procedure is finished when there are no visible secretions and none are heard on expiration.
8. Clean the bulb syringe in warm soapy water and rinse with water. Allow to air dry.	Proper cleaning of the bulb syringe is important since bacteria can grow inside.
9. Dispose of tissues and wash hands. Document the procedure and the color and amount of sections.	

DeLee Suction Catheter

The DeLee suction catheter is a device with two tubes and a small collection bottle (also referred to as a "mucus trap"). One tube goes into the student's respiratory airway. The other tube is connected to an adapter that the person performing the procedure puts into her mouth. The adult gently sucks on the tube, creating suction in the other tube (see Figure 14.9). Secretions are drawn through the student's tube and collect in the collection bottle. (The secretions will not go into the adult's mouth). DeLee catheters may be used to suction the nose and mouth. They have been used to suction tracheostomies, especially when suctioning is required when traveling and a suction machine is not available (Graff et al., 1990).

FIGURE 14-9 A DeLee suction catheter being used to remove secretions through a tracheostomy tube

SOURCE: Reprinted by permission of the University of Kansas Medical Center.

Procedure for Suctioning with a DeLee Catheter

After verifying the student needs suctioning, explaining the procedure to the student, washing hands, assembling equipment, and putting on gloves, the person performing the procedure is ready to start. In some instances, the student will have both nasal and oral suctioning ordered. If this is the case, nasal suctioning should be performed first, followed by oral suctioning.

Steps in the Procedure for Suctioning with a DeLee Catheter	Rationale
1. Wash hands and put on gloves.	This procedure usually follows clean technique.
2. Encourage the student to take deep breaths. The physician may have ordered that the student receives three breaths with resuscitator bag.	This is to promote good oxygenation.
3. Place the adapter in the adult's mouth. Do not suck.	Do not apply suction until the student's tube is in place.
4. Place the catheter into the student's nose, mouth, or tracheostomy tube, depending on the type of suctioning being performed.	
5. Suck on the adapter to remove the student's secretions into the collection bottle.	

Steps in the Procedure for Suctioning with a DeLee Catheter	Rationale
6. Rotate the student's catheter tube between the thumb and forefinger while withdrawing the catheter with the suction on.	Rotating the catheter prevents it from sticking to the sides of the respiratory tract.
Suctioning should usually not require more than 3 to 4 seconds.	It is important not to suction longer than recommended to avoid complications.
7. If the airway is not clear, wait 30 to 60 seconds and repeat the procedure.	Waiting 30 to 60 seconds allows time for oxygen levels to return to normal.
8. When finished, clean the DeLee catheter in soapy water and rinse or throw away.	A DeLee catheter is usually reusable, but in some instances it is discarded after use.
9. Take off gloves and throw away used supplies. Wash hands and document the procedure and color, consistency, odor, and amount of secretions.	

INSTRUCTIONAL STRATEGIES AND MODIFICATIONS FOR SUCTIONING

Suctioning typically occurs on an as-needed basis and must occur without delay to avoid respiratory complications. For students who require suctioning over a long period of time or on a permanent basis, consideration needs to be given regarding teaching the student to self-suction. Depending on the student's physical status, chronological and developmental age, and cognitive abilities, as well as the type of procedure and safety issues, the student may perform only a few steps or perform the entire procedure independently under adult supervision. Students as young as 5 to 8 years, with cognitive abilities ranging from 4 years to 5.25 years and fine-motor skills of at least a 4-year-old, have been taught to suction their tracheostomies (Derrickson, Neff, & Parrish, 1991). However, some authors advocate waiting until about 12 years of age or until the student has the physical and emotional maturity to perform the procedures on themselves

(Mackay, 1991). (Refer back to Figure 14-4 showing a student in high school who does her own suctioning.)

Training should include some aspects of anatomy and physiology. It is important that the student understand that the suctioning will only suck up secretions and not some internal body parts. Four separate skill areas may be taught: (a) gathering and assembling equipment, (b) performing the actual suctioning procedure, (c) cleaning up, and (d) doing daily and weekly care of equipment. Instruction may begin with teaching the student to clean up and provide daily and weekly equipment care. As the student cognitively matures and develops good fine-motor control, teaching the actual procedure may begin. Students with physical disabilities with poor fine-motor control may be unable to perform the suction procedure, but they should know the steps in the procedure. Students with low cognitive ability may not be able to self-suction but may be able to participate in some aspects such as cleaning and getting the materials.

The most difficult of the areas to teach is the actual suction procedure. In one study (Derrickson et al., 1991), training was initially performed on dolls, with the dolls sitting on the student's lap facing forward, to simulate conditions for suctioning. These skills were later transferred to self-suctioning. Using dolls provided the opportunity for mass practice on difficult steps and allowed the students to verbalize each step of the procedure while performing it on the doll. Allowing errors to be detected and corrected on a doll resulted in a safer situation to learn the procedure prior to performing the procedure on themselves.

The skills for self-suctioning can be broken down into a task analysis (see Figure 14-10). This procedure can be taught using the whole task technique or backward or forward chaining. Additional prompts may be necessary such as a stamp on the dominant hand to help the student know which hand holds the catheter. A string may be placed around the student's thumb to help the student remember to keep the thumb up (off) the catheter when it is being inserted. Later these prompts can be faded.

Students will also need to know how to recognize a problem and what to do when a certain problem arises. However, if the problem involves difficulty breathing, the student may become incapacitated and an emergency situation may result. An adult must always be present when the student is performing self-suctioning in case a problem arises.

Time-Limited Steps and Caution Steps

Procedures for suctioning contain both time-limited and caution steps. Time-limited steps are steps that must be completed within a certain time frame. In all suctioning procedures, there is a restricted amount of time that suctioning can occur. It is inadvisable for the suctioning to occur longer than is specified. If is student is going to learn this step, it is important that the adult teaching the student models the step and then provides shadowing. A lower-functioning student requires a full physical prompt and then a move to shadowing. When shadowing, the adult keeps her hand within an inch of the student's hand until

1. Wash hands; put on gloves.
2. Pour water into the cup.
3. Connect the suction catheter to the connecting tube.
4. Turn on the suction machine.
5. Put the suction catheter in water and cover the port.
6. Take deep breaths.
7. Take the thumb off the suction thumb port.
8. Insert the catheter to the specified length.
9. Cover the suction port.
10. Twirl the suction catheter while removing it.
11. Remove it in less than 5 seconds.
12. Repeat steps 5 to 11 if needed.
13. When finished, put the suction catheter in water to rinse.
14. Wrap the suction catheter around a glove.
15. Take off the glove with suction catheter inside and discard.
16. Wash hands.

FIGURE 14-10 Task analysis for suctioning a tracheostomy

the step is complete. This allows the adult to intervene should the student take too long or make an incorrect movement. Shadowing may be used on time-limited steps, and other instructional strategies may be used on other steps of the task analysis (e.g., system of least prompts or time delay). (See Chapter 2 for more information on shadowing and other instructional strategies.)

Caution steps are steps in the task analysis during which the student could injure herself by a quick, jerking, or incorrect movement. In the suctioning procedures, this can occur upon inserting, advancing, and withdrawing the suction catheter during tracheal, nasotracheal, or nasal suctioning. The educational team must determine whether these are appropriate steps for the student to learn. If so, the teacher may need to model the step and then provide shadowing. For lower-functioning students, the teacher may provide a full physical prompt and move to shadowing to avoid errors and injury. Teachers should highlight time-limited steps and caution steps on their data sheet as a reminder to provide shadowing. (See Chapter 2 for a sample data sheet.)

SUCTIONING PROBLEMS AND EMERGENCIES

Ineffective Suctioning

Suctioning is required for some students who are unable to clear their respiratory secretion. However, it is possible that suctioning may not be effective, especially if there are excessive thick secretions or if respiratory distress is not due to secretion obstruction. When suctioning is not effective, respiratory distress may occur. If any signs of respiratory distress are present and continue after suctioning, such as labored breathing, cyanosis, or rapid pulse or respiratory rate, 911 should be called (see Figure 14-6 for signs of respiratory distress).

When ineffective suctioning is due to a respiratory infection resulting in excessive, purulent secretions, the best measure is prevention. School personnel and parents should contact a physician immediately if there are yellow or green secretions, foul or unusual odor to the secretions, abnormally thick secretions, or a temperature over 100 degrees Fahrenheit. The student may need medication and respiratory treatments to treat the infection and permit effective suctioning.

Obstruction

The tracheostomy tube can become blocked by mucous secretions or foreign objects. If this oc-

curs, the first step is to remove any obvious blockage at the tube opening that could be causing the obstruction. If this is not the case, the next step is to suction. If the catheter cannot be advanced, the inner cannula of the tracheostomy tube should be removed, if one is present. If there is not one, an emergency tracheostomy tube change must occur. (See the previous chapter for how to perform an emergency tracheostomy tube change.)

CPR

If the student stops breathing, cardiopulmonary resuscitation (CPR) needs to implemented and 911 called. CPR is a basic skill required to assist an individual who has become unconscious and is not breathing and whose heart may not be beating. The student's teachers, as well as other support personnel, should be certified in CPR in case this is needed. (See Chapter 13 for specifics of CPR when the student has a tracheostomy.)

Reaction to Suctioning

It is possible that the student may adversely react to being suctioned because of prolonged coughing during the suctioning process or inadvertent stimulation of the vagus nerve, which can result in a drop in blood pressure and heart rate. Also, if too large a catheter is used for suctioning in a small-diameter artificial airway (tracheostomy), a vacuum can be created due to inadequate space for air to enter and the lung could collapse (atelectasis). If the student becomes cyanotic (blue) or mottled, or if she develops slow heart rate, pallor, or other signs of distress, suctioning should be immediately stopped. The student should be given breaths through the use of a resuscitation bag with oxygen (if available) until stable, and the appropriate personnel should be immediately contacted (Berry, 1991). In some cases, the paramedics will need to be called. These reactions can be avoided by using oxygen before suctioning when ordered by a physician and by limiting suctioning to 10 seconds or less.

Bleeding

When suctioning, bright red blood should never be present. If it is, the physician should be contacted immediately (Urbano, 1992), or the student may need to go to the hospital if bleeding is profuse. If a small amount of blood-tinged secretions are present upon suctioning, the machine pressure may be too high and may need to be decreased. Other possibilities are that suctioning is occurring too frequently and the lubricant (sterile water or sterile saline) is not being used prior to suctioning. Close examination of how the procedure is being implemented is important to avoid trauma to the sensitive tissues of the respiratory tract.

Emotional Response to Suctioning

Suctioning is not a comfortable procedure, and some students may become upset when being suctioned or fight with the person performing the suctioning. Explanations and reassurance are important to help calm the student. Some students may need to be gently held and reassured by another adult as the suctioning takes place. This may help calm the student and prevent the suction catheter from becoming contaminated by the student grabbing it.

MANAGEMENT ISSUES FOR MANAGING RESPIRATORY SECRETIONS

Individualized Health Plan and Individualized Educational Program

A student who requires suctioning or chest physiotherapy should have an individualized health plan (IHP). Besides the general items that are included in the health plan (discussed in Chapter 1), several areas are specific to these procedures.

As presented in Figure 14-11, the type of chest physiotherapy needs to be specified in the IHP, including the various postural drainage positions and times they should occur. For students who are suctioned, the IHP will need to include the type of suctioning procedure and whether it uses clean or sterile technique (see Figure 14-12). Student-specific procedures for suctioning should be attached and approved by the physician. Although suctioning is typically done as needed, in some instances it may done routinely at certain times, and this should be noted. The IHP should include guidelines for the problems or emergencies previously mentioned: ineffective suctioning, obstruction, CPR, averse reaction to suctioning, and bleeding.

The student's individualized educational program needs to state what parts of the procedure the student is learning. It will need to specify whether the student is learning to communicate the procedure (when he cannot physically perform the procedure) or actually implement all or part of it. Areas of chest physiotherapy include (a) assisting with getting into proper positions for postural drainage; (b) knowing the purpose of clapping, vibration, and other airway clearance techniques; and (c) demonstrating effective coughing when possible. Areas of instruction for suctioning may include (a) determining when suctioning is necessary, (b) understanding simple anatomy and physiology, (c) using alternate communication to communicate steps, (d) demonstrating setup and assembly of equipment, (e) performing all or part of the suctioning procedure, (f) cleaning up after suctioning is over, (g) performing daily or weekly care of equipment, and (h) following good hygiene and clean or sterile technique. Sample IEP objectives are in Figure 14-13.

School and Community Environment

For students who require suctioning, it is important that suction equipment always be available and easily obtained when needed. This typically includes a suction machine, catheter and supplies,

Type of Chest Physiotherapy

_____ Postural drainage

Specify type of positions: _____

_____

Duration of postural draining: _____

Frequency of postural draining: _____

If not all positions are to be used at one session, specify schedule: _____

_____

_____ Percussion

_____ Use hand in cupped position   _____ Use percussion cup

Duration of percussion: _____

Frequency of percussion: _____

Locations where percussion should occur: _____

_____

_____ Vibration

_____ Use of hand providing vibration _____

_____ Use of vibrator, type:

Duration of vibration: _____

Frequency of vibration: _____

Locations where vibration should occur: _____

_____

_____ Coughing

Coughing should be encouraged at the following times: _____

_____

FIGURE 14-11 Specialized areas to include in an IHP on chest physiotherapy

emergency oxygen, and manual resuscitation equipment (Ambu bag). Back-up equipment should also be available in case the suction machine is not working properly (Urbano, 1991); it may be a DeLee suction catheter. It is important that plenty of catheters and supplies are available to avoid not having enough when needed. This equipment should accompany the student when she participates in field trips or community-based instruction.

Type of Suctioning

_____ Oral   _____ Nasal   _____ Pharynx

_____ Tracheal   _____ Bronchial

Point of Entry for Tracheal/Bronchial Suctioning

_____ Through nose

_____ Through mouth

_____ Through tracheostomy

If tracheostomy suctioning, inner cannula is removed while suctioning:

_____ Yes   _____ No   _____ Not applicable

How far should the catheter be inserted (e.g., 1 cm below trach tube)? Explain: _____

_____

Oral/nasal suctioning procedure: _____ clean   _____ sterile

Tracheal/bronchial suctioning procedure: _____ clean   _____ sterile

Setting for amount of suction on suction machine: _____

Child-specific procedure attached? _____ yes   _____ no

Latex allergy? _____ yes   _____ no, comment: _____

_____

Suctioning occurs: _____ p.r.n. and _____ specified times, specify when: _____

Directions for Suctioning Problems and Emergencies

Ineffective suctioning: _____

Obstruction: _____

CPR: _____

Adverse reaction to suctioning: _____

Bleeding: _____

FIGURE 14-12 Specialized areas to include in an IHP on suctioning

SUMMARY

Some students will be unable to clear their airway of excess respiratory secretions effectively. To help mobilize the secretions, the physician may have ordered postural drainage (which consists of positioning the student in certain ways) and/or percussion or vibration to certain parts of the chest and back. Some students may also have suctioning ordered. Suctioning may assist with removal of se-

Independent Performance of Task

The student will suction herself as needed following correct task-analyzed procedure with 100% accuracy on each opportunity for 1 month.

Partial Performance of Task

The student will allow an adult to suction her trach tube without grabbing the suction catheter on each occasion for 1 month.

When provided arm support and a suction machine, and the catheter is set, the student will suction her mouth when needed with 100% accuracy on each occasion for 3 weeks.

Directing the Task

The student will tell an adult with her AAC device that she needs to be suctioned when needed with 100% accuracy on each occasion for 4 weeks.

The student will tell an adult how to position her for postural drainage for each position and monitor how long she is maintained in each position with 100% accuracy on each occasion for 3 weeks.

Knowledge of the Task

The student will identify four potential problems that can occur when clearing secretions and what should be done should the problem occur with 100% accuracy for four consecutive sessions.

The student will identify parts of suction machine, demonstrate proper care and cleaning of the machine, and explain how it works, each with 80% accuracy for four consecutive sessions.

FIGURE 14-13 Sample IEP objectives for managing respiratory secretions

cretions in the nose, mouth, pharynx, trachea, or bronchi. Suctioning may be a clean or sterile procedure and may use a suction machine or other equipment. The person performing any of these procedures needs to know how to manage emergency situations. Close observation of the students for signs of respiratory distress is also important to detect when certain procedures are needed, as well as to know what actions to take should some problem occur in implementing the procedures.

15

Oxygen Management

Some students require more oxygen than can be obtained through breathing room air, as a result of certain health conditions. In these instances, the student may require the use of supplemental oxygen to provide a sufficient amount of oxygen to the body. School personnel must be familiar with the operation of the student's oxygen system as well as basic management and modifications needed to meet the student's health needs.

Oxygen is necessary to sustain life and provide the body's cells and tissues with the energy they need to properly function. When air is inhaled, it travels through the nose or mouth, down the trachea (windpipe), and into the lungs through two large tubes known as *bronchi*. The bronchi branch into a series of tubes (secondary bronchi and bronchioles) and end in numerous air sacs, known as *alveoli*. In the air sacs, gas exchange occurs between the alveoli and the capillaries surrounding them. (See Figure 13-1 in an earlier chapter.) Oxygen is transported from the alveoli to the red blood cells in the capillaries. From there, the heart pumps the newly oxy-

genated red blood cells throughout the body. As oxygen is transported to the cells of the body, the cells use the oxygen and release carbon dioxide as a waste product. The blood cells then transport the carbon dioxide back to the capillaries surrounding the alveoli of the lungs. Carbon dioxide is transported into the alveoli and is expelled when the person exhales.

In some cases, the amount of oxygen in the blood is not sufficient. This decrease in the oxygen supply to the tissues is known as **hypoxia.** When hypoxia is present, the body is not getting enough oxygen. Symptoms will vary depending on how low the oxygen level is, how quickly it dropped, and how long it has been at a low level. When hypoxia is not severe, symptoms may be initially subtle. A person may only have muscle fatigue and reduced mental activity (e.g., drowsiness, confusion, sometimes euphoria) and occasionally a headache and nausea. (Guyton, 1991). Infants may show subtle signs such as irritability, lethargy, poor feeding, lack of weight gain, or mottling (Louch, 1993). Over time, however, this condition can progress to a coma if hypoxia is severe. When hypoxia occurs quickly or severely, the person will typically have respiratory distress, attempting to breathe harder and faster in an effort to get more oxygen into the body. A rapid pulse is usually present since the heart beats faster to try to transport oxygen to the body tissues more quickly. Cyanosis (bluish discoloration of the skin, especially seen in finger nailbeds and around the mouth) is often present. Other symptoms may include difficulty breathing, shortness of breath, retractions (skin sucks inward above the breast bone and between or under the ribs when inhaling), stridor (noise when breathing in), dizziness, confusion, or headache. If severe hypoxia continues, the person can become unconscious, and cell death can occur. The organs that typically will be damaged first by a lack of sufficient oxygen are the brain, heart, kidneys, and lungs. Eventually the person can die from hypoxia.

Several different conditions may cause hypoxia (see Figure 15-1). First, hypoxia may be caused by insufficient amounts of oxygen being inhaled, because of a lack of oxygen in the air (e.g., high altitudes) or certain diseases or conditions that can result in insufficient breathing (e.g., certain neuromuscular diseases). In some cases, enough oxygen is inhaled, but the oxygen is unable to make its way to the blood stream. This can occur in certain lung diseases due to restricted airways or lung damage from disease (e.g., cystic fibrosis). Hypoxia may be unrelated to getting enough oxygen into the lungs. Certain heart conditions can also cause hypoxia. Certain congenital heart defects (e.g., tetralogy of Fallot) cause some unoxygenated blood to be pumped through the body, because of defects in the heart itself. Hypoxia may also be caused by conditions that result in inadequate delivery or transport of oxygen such as circulatory deficiencies or anemia (decreased number of red blood cells to transport oxygen). In the last category, the cells of the body may be unable to use the oxygen when there is poisoning of the cells or diminished cellular metabolic capability (e.g., cyanide poisoning, vitamin deficiency) (Guyton, 1991).

Students typically have supplemental oxygen

Lack of Oxygen in Air
High altitudes

Neuromuscular Disease
Advanced muscular dystrophy

Central Nervous System Depression or Damage
High spinal cord injury
Coma

Lung Disease or Condition
Cystic fibrosis
Acute asthma attack
Pulmonary embolus
Chronic obstructive pulmonary disease

Congenital Heart Diseases
Tetralogy of Fallot
Transverse great vessels

Anemia
Sickle cell anemia

General and Localized Circulatory Deficiencies
Stroke
Myocardial infarction

Poisoning of Cells
Cyanide poisoning
Severe vitamin deficiency

Figure 15-1 Sample conditions at risk for hypoxia

---

prescribed to increase low oxygen levels, decrease the effort required for breathing, or lessen the work of the heart (Skale, 1992). However, supplemental oxygen will only be effective with some of the conditions resulting in hypoxia. Providing oxygen when there is an insufficient amount in the air would be of obvious benefit. Supplemental oxygen is also beneficial in conditions in which the person is not breathing adequately because of inefficient or damaged muscles or nerve control (neuromuscular diseases) or when the oxygen is not reaching the circulatory system (lung diseases). This is because a person who is being provided 100% oxygen can move five times as much oxygen into the alveoli with each breath than when breathing regular air. With increased levels of oxygenation, more oxygen can be provided to the body. When hypoxia is caused by congenital heart defects or transportation defects, small amounts of oxygen may be beneficial, but it is less effective than with other types of hypoxia since there is sufficient oxygen in the alveoli already. Supplemental oxygen for hypoxia due to poisoning of the cells or problems in their metabolism is not considered effective since oxygen is available, but the cells cannot utilize it (Guyton, 1991).

DESCRIPTION OF OXYGEN THERAPY

Oxygen is considered drug therapy. It may be prescribed for a short period of time (e.g., during a seizure, acute asthma attack) or for a long period of time (e.g., chronic lung disease) depending on the cause of the hypoxia and the need of the person. As with all drugs, it is important that it is given at a certain prescribed amount. If oxygen is needed and not enough is given, cell damage or death could occur. If too much oxygen is given, the lungs could collapse (pulmonary atelectasis), unconsciousness could occur (from oxygen induced carbon dioxide narcosis), red blood cells could be destroyed, and brain damage could occur (Jamerson, 1991; Wong, 1995). Depending on the person's needs, oxygen may be prescribed for a short or long period of time, continually or during certain times.

EQUIPMENT AND ADAPTIVE EQUIPMENT FOR OXYGEN DELIVERY

Delivery Systems

Supplemental oxygen may be delivered to the individual in several different ways. The most common administration of oxygen are by (a) nasal cannula, (b) oxygen mask, (c) face tent, (d) tracheostomy collar, and (e) oxygen tent and oxygen hood. Each of these delivery systems come in different sizes to fit the student appropriately and can vary as to how much oxygen is delivered. The physician selects the one most beneficial to the student.

As seen in Figure 15-2, a **nasal cannula** is a vinyl tube with two small prongs that fit into the nostrils. An appropriately sized nasal cannula should allow air to flow in and out of the nostrils around the prongs. If the prongs are not well tolerated, the physician may allow the prongs to be trimmed or removed (Jamerson, 1991). The tubing is usually looped behind the ears and then comes underneath the chin and is connected to the oxygen source. The student must have unblocked nasal passages and breathe through the nose for this to benefit him.

Oxygen masks are soft vinyl masks that should fit snugly over the nose and mouth (see Figure 15-3). They come in different sizes to assure a snug fit. Several different types deliver varying oxygen concentrations and flow rates of oxygen. The four main types of oxygen masks include the simple face mask, partial rebreather mask, nonrebreathing mask, and the venturi mask.

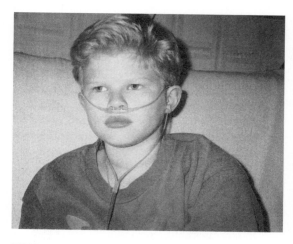

FIGURE 15-2 A boy wearing a nasal cannula that provides oxygen

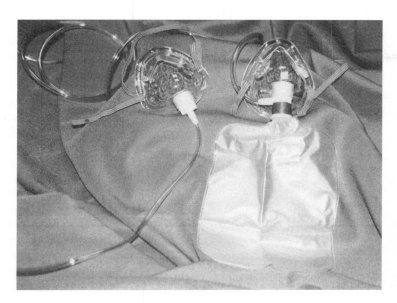

FIGURE 15-3 Two types of oxygen masks that fit over the person's mouth and nose and deliver oxygen: a simple face mask (on the left) and a partial rebreather mask (on the right)

All masks contain a nose clip that can be tightened to fit better over the bridge of the nose and a connection tube that connects the oxygen mask to the oxygen source. A simple face mask also has vent holes to allow carbon dioxide to escape upon exhaling and room air to be inhaled (in addition to the oxygen being delivered). A partial rebreather mask has the same vent holes and an additional reservoir bag to allow partial rebreathing of the gases. It can provide a higher concentration of oxygen than the simple oxygen mask. A nonrebreathing mask is similar to a partial rebreather mask but has one-way valves between the bag and the mask, preventing inhalation of gas that has been exhaled and additionally has valves (or flaps) over the vents that prevent inhalation of room air but allow for exhalation. This type of mask can provide one of the highest levels of oxygen concentration. The last type of mask, the venturi mask, is similar to a simple face mask, but also has an additional tube on the connecting tube that adjusts by percentages the amount of room air allowed into the mask to mix with the oxygen (Jamerson, 1991). The physician selects the type of mask based on the percentage of oxygen needed, how fast the oxygen needs to be delivered (flow rate), and the student's specific condition.

Oxygen may also be delivered through aerosol masks, such as **face tents** and **tracheostomy collars** (masks) or through a catheter (Figures 15-4 and 15-5). A face tent is a soft vinyl mask that fits loosely around the chin and neck. Students more easily accept it than a face mask. It can provide a wide range of oxygen concentrations as well as high humidity. The tracheostomy collar is designed for individuals with tracheostomies. It is a plastic cup with ports that are contoured to fit around the tracheostomy tube opening. Also, a

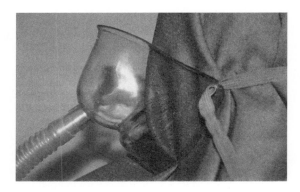

FIGURE 15-4 A face tent

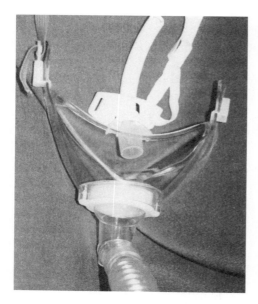

FIGURE 15-5 A tracheostomy collar placed over a tracheostomy tube

new technique using a catheter into the trachea (transtracheal oxygen therapy) may be used to deliver oxygen.

Oxygen tents and **oxygen hoods** are not usually found in school settings. An oxygen tent is a large canopy (or tent), while an oxygen hood is a Plexiglas box or hut that surrounds the upper portion of the student. They provide an oxygen-rich environment for the student to breathe in. They both require monitoring the temperature to prevent cooling, overheating, hypoxia (lack of oxygen), or hyperoxia (too much oxygen).

Oxygen Sources

The oxygen delivery system is connected to one of several possible oxygen sources: (a) compressed oxygen, (b) liquid oxygen systems, (c) oxygen concentrators and enrichers, and (d) wall oxygen. They all have flow meters that are adjusted to deliver so many liters per minute (L/min) of oxygen, as prescribed by the physician. However, each type of oxygen source stores oxygen differently and has different features. Selection of the oxygen source will be decided by the physician

based on the student's needs, amount of oxygen used, frequency of use, need for portability, cost, and ease of use.

Compressed Oxygen. Compressed oxygen uses steel or aluminum cylinders to store the oxygen that has been compressed under high pressures. This allows a large amount of oxygen to be stored in a small space. A regulator fits over the top of the tank to convert the high pressure to a lower pressure that is safe for the student. The extension oxygen tubing connects directly to the regulator. Typically there are two dials: a pressure gauge that shows how much oxygen is in the tank and a flow meter that shows the rate the oxygen is being delivered. The large tanks are called *H tanks* and are usually used at home (see Figure 15-6a). They have high flow capabilities but are heavy and cumbersome. The small portable tanks are called *E tanks,* and they are usually strapped to a stand with wheels for easy portability. A smaller portable unit that can be carried over the shoulder may also be used (see Figure 15-6b). Compressed oxygen is most commonly used for intermittent or infrequent use, although this may be the delivery system selected for continuous use. It can be stored indefinitely. However, it should be stored in its stand or secured to a wall. The oxygen tank should be well secured to prevent it from falling over. The tanks need to be handled carefully to avoid a rapid release of oxygen, which can dangerously propel the tank and possibly hit something.

Oxygen Concentrators. Oxygen concentrators filter out oxygen from the carbon dioxide, nitrogen, and water molecules in room air and deliver the oxygen to the student. They are electrically powered machines that are not portable and are primarily used with students at home. They typically consist of a power switch, an on light, a flow meter, an alarm (to inform of power interruptions), and a humidification bottle. They are ideal in rural, isolated areas as well as urban areas since they require no routine delivery of compressed or liquid oxygen. They are often more economical than oxygen reservoirs, and they can look like a

(b)

(a)

FIGURE 15-6 Oxygen tanks. A larger tank is usually used at home (a), while a small portable unit may be used in the community (b).

piece of household furniture for aesthetic purposes. When a student uses an oxygen concentrator, a back-up tank (usually of compressed oxygen) should be available in case of a power failure (McDonald, 1994). Disadvantages also include the need for routine maintenance, lower flow capabilities, and a tendency to be noisy.

Liquid Oxygen Systems. Liquid oxygen systems are the most concentrated form of oxygen. Oxygen is supercooled into a liquid, which decreases the volume of oxygen. At home, a **reservoir container** is used to store the oxygen. A reservoir container is like a large Thermos that keeps the oxygen cold and typically contains 3 to 5 days of oxygen, depending on the size of the reservoir and its use (McDonald, 1994). The reservoir may be used directly to obtain oxygen or as a device to fill a smaller portable unit. This smaller unit can be filled from the reservoir

through a filling connector. The smaller unit can be carried over the shoulder and usually contains 6 to 12 hours of oxygen (Moffit, 1994). Care must be taken that the student does not injure her skin (freezer burn) since some portable units can become cold. The liquid oxygen systems usually have a contents indicator (to indicate how much oxygen is left), flow meter, and optional humidifier bottle. This type of oxygen system is typically used for ambulatory individuals (individuals who can walk). However, liquid oxygen tends to be expensive, and oxygen is lost due to evaporation.

Wall Oxygen. The last type of oxygen container is a wall outlet of oxygen. This is found in hospitals or special care settings in which oxygen is pumped through the wall. A flow meter attaches to the wall to adjust the amount of flow, and the connecting tube of the oxygen mask connects directly to the wall unit.

Humidification

Some students will have humidification added to their oxygen delivery system to help counteract the drying effects of oxygen. Several types of humidification systems are available (e.g., pass-over humidifiers, diffusion-head humidifiers). Depending on the type, the humidifier will often connect between the oxygen delivery system (e.g., mask, cannula) and the oxygen source to provide humidification to the oxygen that is being inhaled. Humidification is typically used with students with tracheostomies or sometimes with students receiving high levels of oxygen (greater than 4 to 5 liters).

ASSISTIVE STRATEGIES FOR OXYGEN DELIVERY

Preparing for Emergency Oxygen Delivery

Some students will have oxygen ordered when certain conditions arise. For example, a student with tonic-clonic (grand mal) seizures who typically becomes cyanotic may have oxygen prescribed when this type of seizure occurs. A student who develops respiratory distress (see Figure 15-7) may have oxygen prescribed for use while waiting for an ambulance. School personnel must understand when oxygen is prescribed, how to administer it during these times, the amount of oxygen given, and the length of time for administration.

Understanding and recognizing the conditions under which the student is to receive oxygen is important. Since oxygen is a drug, the physician will have prescribed a certain amount. The dosage is specified as liters per minute, and the condition under which oxygen is to be given should be specifically defined (e.g., during a tonic-clonic seizure, during exercise). The minimum amount of oxygen is usually prescribed that will benefit the student to avoid problems result-

Abnormal Breathing
Difficult, labored breathing

Decreased air exchange or inability to move air (through tracheostomy or airways)

Shortness of breath, rapid breathing

Wheezing, gasping for breath, abnormal breath sounds

Retraction of Chest
Pulling in of the chest and neck muscles (which occurs to help with breathing)

Cyanosis
Dusky or blue color, especially at nailbeds and around mouth

Neurological Signs
Agitation, anxiety, restlessness

Confusion, inability to concentrate

Dizzy

Drowsiness

Unconscious

Cardiac
Fast heart rate (pulse)

FIGURE 15-7 Signs of respiratory distress

ing from too much oxygen. Length of time may be prescribed under certain conditions.

It is important that in an emergency, personnel are already familiar with how to manage the oxygen delivery system and give the student needed oxygen. Personnel should practice using the equipment prior to needing the use of it.

Equipment and Supply List of Oxygen Delivery Using Concentrated Oxygen

Concentrated oxygen tank

Regulator

Key (if not knob operated)

Appropriately sized mask, nasal cannula, tracheostomy collar, or face tent

Oxygen tubing

Procedure for Emergency Oxygen Delivery Using Concentrated Oxygen

After verifying that the student requires oxygen, obtaining the supplies and equipment, and quickly telling the student that he is receiving oxygen to help him breathe, the person performing the procedure is ready to begin.

Steps in the Procedure for Emergency Oxygen Delivery	Rationale

1. If the regulator is not on the tank, put it on the tank:
  a. Slide the regulator over the pointed metal valve on the top of the oxygen tank.
  b. Tighten the regulator with the thin metal knob on the side.
	The oxygen tank should be kept with the regulator left on the tank. (The regulator connects the oxygen tank to the oxygen tubing and has gauges on it).

2. Turn on the oxygen flow into the regulator by (a) turning knob on top or (b) for models without a knob, sliding the hole of the metal wrench (key) over the metal valve on top of the oxygen tank, and turn clockwise (see Figure 15-8).	Turning the knob or valve lets oxygen flow from the tank into the regulator. The pressure gauge will show a reading indicating how much oxygen is left in the tank.

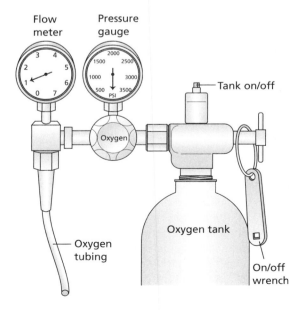

FIGURE 15-8 An oxygen tank. The on/off wrench (far right) fits over the tank on/off metal valve to turn on the tank. When the oxygen knob (in the middle) is turned, the pressure gauge indicates how much oxygen is in the tank. The flow of oxygen will be indicated on the flow meter and can be increased or decreased by adjusting the oxygen knob. Oxygen flows out of the oxygen tubing.

Steps in the Procedure for Emergency Oxygen Delivery	*Rationale*
3. Turn the flow meter knob (also known as the oxygen knob) to set the amount of oxygen prescribed.	It is important to set it for the correct amount.
4. Check that oxygen is coming out of the oxygen tank.	Place fingers under oxygen spout to be sure oxygen is coming out. If not, turn the knob on the oxygen tank more (step 1).
5. Attach the connecting tube to the oxygen tank by pushing the end of the connecting tube onto the regulator output nipple.	
6. Set the oxygen concentration on the mask valve if it is present.	Some masks have oxygen concentration valves that will need to be set to get the proper concentration of oxygen.
7. Have the student double-check that oxygen is coming out of the mask, cannula, tracheostomy collar, or face tent.	Tubing can become kinked and prevent the flow of oxygen. If oxygen is not coming out, check the tubing and unkink it.
8. Place oxygen on the student.	The student will have a specific type of oxygen delivery device ordered.
Oxygen mask: Put the mask snugly over the student's nose and mouth. Adjust the nasal band to fit. Adjust the strap around the back of the head for good fit. (If necessary, gauze or cotton may be placed under the elastic band against the cheeks to decrease irritation.)	The mask needs to be snug to allow for the proper concentration of oxygen.
Nasal cannula: Insert each prong into each nostril. Put tubing over each ear and then under the chin. Adjust fit by sliding the clasp upward (refer back to see Figure 15-2). (If necessary, the nasal cannula may be secured with special tape.)	The nasal cannula prongs can be trimmed if needed; this should be determined ahead of time. Placing the nasal cannula under the chin decreases the possibility of strangulation. If the ears cannot support the tubing, the tubing may be put on another way.
Tracheostomy collar: Place the front of the collar over the tracheostomy. Attach by wrapping the band around the neck and reattaching to the end of the collar.	The tracheostomy collar should not be too tight. If a humidification device is ordered, place it on as described in the IHP's student-specific guidelines (since there are many types and ways of setting them up).
Face tent: Place the front of face tent over the chin and the elastic band around the back of the head.	

Steps in the Procedure for Emergency Oxygen Delivery	Rationale
9. Stay with the student and observe for further difficulty breathing.	Since the oxygen is being used in emergency situations, personnel will need to monitor the student to be sure breathing improves. If breathing difficulties continue, an ambulance should be called (if not called already). If the person stops breathing, CPR will be needed.
10. Document procedure.	

Daily Care and Care of Equipment

The inside of the oxygen mask or face tent may be wiped dry as needed. Leaving moisture will promote skin breakdown. Skin should be checked regularly (every 8 hours) where straps and tubing come into contact with skin to assess for skin breakdown. Nostrils should be inspected to assure that nasal cannula is not causing irritation. If irritation or skin breakdown is present, the parents and appropriate medical personnel should be informed.

Oxygen masks, nasal cannulas, tracheostomy collars, and face tents are for one-person use. The oxygen mask, tracheostomy collar, and face tent should be routinely washed with soapy water. They may be cleaned with a nonirritating disinfectant. The outside of the nasal cannula and the prongs are cleaned as well, but the cannula is usually not completely submerged in water due to the difficulty of drying the interior of the tube. All parts are thoroughly rinsed with water and then air dried. For students who continually need oxygen, a second delivery system setup should be available for use while the used setup is being cleaned. The system should be replaced as ordered, sometimes being replaced on a monthly basis. Routine cleaning should occur at home, although if it becomes dirty with secretions at school, the system should be cleaned at that time. The physician's specific recommendations for cleaning should be followed.

The oxygen cylinder will need to be turned off after use. Turning off the oxygen cylinder means not just turning the flow meter down to zero but turning off the flow of oxygen from the oxygen tank to the regulator. Turning off the oxygen cylinder will prevent possible seepage of oxygen and also leads to safer storage. The oxygen tank will need to be checked periodically to be sure an adequate amount of oxygen is in the tank for use. If the oxygen level is low, the tank will need to be refilled.

INSTRUCTIONAL STRATEGIES AND MODIFICATIONS FOR OXYGEN DELIVERY

Some students may be prescribed oxygen delivery under certain conditions such as exercise or during sleep, while others may receive oxygen continuously. When at all possible, students who require oxygen should participate in the delivery of their oxygen. Participation in this skill will depend on the student's age, cognitive abilities, and physical abilities. For students who have a severe physical disability, they may check for appropriate amounts of oxygen and check that the correct flow is set and communicate this to the personnel responsible for monitoring them. Students with cognitive impairments may learn to do part of this skill, such as putting on the mask, cannula, or tracheostomy collar correctly.

Understanding and tolerating the use of the oxygen delivery system typically comprise the first step in teaching proper oxygen delivery. For young students, accepting an oxygen mask may be difficult due to a smothering or uncomfortable feeling of the mask. Sometimes playing that the mask is an airplane pilot's mask can be helpful. Some young students will accept the use of a nasal cannula instead of an oxygen mask. However, it is important to use whatever has been prescribed.

Training should include some aspects of anatomy and physiology and explanations of how the body requires oxygen. Explanations should be made on the level the student can understand. Five skill areas may be taught: (a) putting the equipment together; (b) caring for equipment; (c) identifying when oxygen is needed; (d) adjusting the correct flow of oxygen; and (e) putting on the face mask, cannula, tracheostomy collar, or face tent.

Assembling equipment will vary depending on the type of equipment used. An early step is teaching the student how to attach the oxygen tubing to the oxygen source (or humidifier that is attached to oxygen source). More complex steps would include how to put a regulator on an oxygen tank or how to transfer liquid oxygen from a reservoir container to the small portable container. Learning proper care of the equipment includes not only cleaning the oxygen mask (cannula, tracheostomy collar, or face mask) but more complicated tasks such as determining when more oxygen needs to be ordered and how to go about getting more.

The student should learn when oxygen is needed. If students only require oxygen during sleep or exercise, they can be taught to put on the mask and adjust the correct flow of oxygen at that time. If the student uses an oxygen mask, she may switch to a nasal cannula during eating (Jamerson, 1991). During that time, she can be taught to take the mask on and off. Learning how to check that the oxygen is at the correct flow rate can be done at select times during the day. The following is a procedure for teaching the student to provide oxygen to herself at select times during the day.

Steps in the Procedure for Self-Provision of Oxygen	Rationale
1. Identify that it is time to put on oxygen.	If oxygen is given at certain times or the mask is changed to a cannula at select times, the student needs to identify when this is to occur. Use of object calendars or a time schedule may be helpful.
2. Wash hands.	Washing hands helps prevent the spread of infection onto the oxygen equipment.
3. Turn on the oxygen with the flow meter knob.	For this procedure, the oxygen is already turned on from the oxygen tank to the regulator. This step is needed to turn the oxygen on from the regulator to the student. Students will learn how to turn the oxygen on from the tank to the regulator later.
4. Adjust the flow meter to the proper oxygen level.	Place a piece of colored tape or colored mark at the level prescribed to help the

Steps in the Procedure for Self-Provision of Oxygen	Rationale
	student find where the oxygen level should be adjusted. Use of the colored mark may be faded later.
5. Check that oxygen is coming out of the oxygen source.	Place fingers under oxygen spout to be sure that oxygen is coming out.
6. Attach the connecting tube to the oxygen source.	This takes a little strength to perform to be sure that the tubing is completely on. The student may only be able to partially participate in performing this step.
7. Set the correct oxygen concentration on the mask valve if present.	Some masks have oxygen concentration valves that will need to be set to deliver the proper concentration of oxygen.
8. Have the student double-check that oxygen is coming out of the mask, nasal cannula, tracheostomy collar, or face tent.	Tubing can become kinked and prevent the flow of oxygen. If oxygen is not coming out, check the tubing and unkink it.
9. Have the student put on oxygen as prescribed.	The student may use a mirror initially to assist with learning how to put on the oxygen device. However, over time, the mirror will need to be eliminated since a mirror may not always be available.
Oxygen mask: First, put the mask over the nose and mouth. Then, put the strap behind the head. Adjust the straps for a good fit.	The mask needs to be snug to allow for the proper concentration of oxygen.
Nasal cannula: First, insert each prong into each nostril. Put the tubing over each ear and then under the chin. Adjust the fit by sliding the clasp upward.	The nasal cannula prongs can be trimmed if needed. This should be determined ahead of time. Placing the nasal cannula under the chin decreases possibility of strangulation.
Tracheostomy collar: Place the front of the collar over the tracheostomy. Attach by wrapping the band around the neck and reattaching to the end of the collar.	The tracheostomy collar should not be too tight. If a humidification device is ordered, place it on as described in the IHP's student-specific guidelines (since there are many types and ways of setting them up).

A task analysis that can be put on a data sheet is in Figure 15-9. This example shows the steps for putting on a nasal cannula. This student has good fine-motor skills. Students with motor impairments may need adaptations to the equipment or to only partially participate in the procedure. To help put on an oxygen mask, the student with a physical impairment may need an extra loop of material attached to the back of the strap to facilitate pulling it over the back of the head.

---

1. Wash hands.
2. Turn on the oxygen with the flow meter knob.
3. Adjust the flow meter to the oxygen level.
4. Check the oxygen coming out of the source.
5. Attach the connecting tube to the oxygen source.
6. Check the oxygen coming out of the nasal cannula.
7. Insert each prong into each nostril.
8. Put the tubing behind each ear.
9. Slide the clasp upward under the chin to adjust fit.

FIGURE 15-9 Sample task analysis for putting on a nasal cannula

Students will also need to know how to recognize a problem and what to do if one occurs. However, if the student is having difficulty breathing, the student can become incapacitated. An adult should always be present when the student is putting on oxygen.

Several different instructional strategies may be used to teach students to manage their own oxygen and equipment. The teacher will select the most appropriate strategy based on the individual student's needs. (See Chapter 2 for a description of instructional strategies.) The teacher also needs to consider whether there are any time-limited steps (steps that must be done within a certain time frame) or caution steps (steps in which injury could result by a quick, jerking, or incorrect movement). Oxygen management typically involves no time-limited steps unless oxygen is needed in an emergency, and in these cases, the adult is usually providing the oxygen in a quick manner. There is only one caution step, and that involves putting the regulator on the oxygen tank. If the student incorrectly put the regulator on the oxygen tank and quickly turned it on, oxygen would leak into the room—

a dangerous and undesirable situation. If the student is going to learn to put on the regulator, the teacher needs to model the step and then provide shadowing. For lower-functioning students, the teacher must provide a full physical prompt and move to shadowing. Shadowing is keeping her hands within an inch of the student's hand until the step is complete to prevent an error. The teacher should highlight time-limited steps and caution steps on the data sheet as a reminder to provide shadowing (see the sample data sheet in Chapter 2).

OXYGEN PROBLEMS AND EMERGENCIES

Poor or No Oxygen Flow

Several problems can occur with the oxygen equipment that can require immediate attention. One problem that may occur is that the oxygen is not flowing or is flowing poorly through the oxygen delivery system (see Table 15-1). A common cause for this is obstructed tubing. The tubing needs to be visually inspected for kinks, leaks, or obstructions. If there is no visible obstruction, temporarily disconnect the tubing from the oxygen source to determine whether oxygen is flowing from the oxygen source well. If oxygen is flowing well from the oxygen source but not through the tubing, the problem is with the tubing and the tubing needs to be replaced.

If the tubing is disconnected from a humidifier and the oxygen is flowing poorly, the problem is with either the humidifier or the oxygen source. Temporarily disconnect the humidifier from the oxygen source. If the oxygen comes out well from the oxygen source, the humidifier may be dirty or plugged. If the humidifier is reusable, throw away the water and refill with new sterile or distilled water. If it is disposable, replace it with a new humidifier bottle (American Family Health Institute, 1986). If oxygen does not flow well through the oxygen source, the problem is the oxygen source itself.

Table 15-1 Lack of Oxygen Flow: Causes and Solutions

Oxygen equipment	Equipment check	Result	Solution
Tubing	Disconnect tubing and check if oxygen is flowing from oxygen source	Yes No	Change or unkink tubing Check humidifier or source
Humidifier	Disconnect humidifier and check if oxygen is flowing from oxygen source	Yes No	Change humidifier or if reusable, change water Check source
Oxygen source	Oxygen not flowing from source	Yes	Check if oxygen is on Check if regulator is on Check if source is empty Check if plugged in (if concentrator) Replace oxygen source

Check that the oxygen source is turned on, including oxygen flow from the tank to the regulator for systems using oxygen tanks. Also, check the level of oxygen remaining. The tank may need to be refilled.

Alarms

Some oxygen sources, such as the oxygen concentrators, have alarms. If the alarm goes off, it indicates that there is a disruption in the power source. The unit may not be plugged in securely and may need to be plugged into the electrical outlet. If there is a power failure, the back-up oxygen tank should be used.

Oxygen Leak

The oxygen tank should not make any noise. However, if there is a hissing sound, the tank is leaking oxygen. The windows in the room should immediately be opened, and the IHP directions for emergencies should be followed. The leaking could be caused by the regulator not being properly attached, a missing washer, or a malfunction in the regulator. Typically, the parents or the oxygen supply company will need to be called.

Hypoxia

The student should be closely observed for symptoms indicating that he is not receiving sufficient oxygen (hypoxia): restlessness, anxiety, fatigue, drowsiness, confusion, inability to concentrate, dizziness, headache, blue finger nailbeds or lips, and/or difficulty breathing (e.g., shortness of breath, retraction, increased respiratory rate, stridor) (refer back to Figure 15-7). If the student is showing signs that he is not getting enough oxygen, the equipment should be checked to be sure the oxygen is flowing and everything is properly attached. If everything is in working order, the emergency plan should be followed to address hypoxia, which often entails going to the emergency room. The oxygen flow level should *not* be turned up without a doctor's order. Assuming that more oxygen will help can be erroneous, especially with certain lung diseases in students.

Overoxygenation

The student should also be observed for symptoms that indicate that the student is receiving too much oxygen. People breathe because their bodies require oxygen. If there is too much oxygen, the person could actually stop breathing. Warning signs of too much oxygen include headaches, slurred speech, drowsiness, or shallow, slow breathing and increasing cyanosis or bluing. (This can occur with certain chronic lung diseases.) The emergency plan should be followed, which usually requires going to the emergency room. The oxygen flow rate should not be changed without the doctor's orders.

CPR

If the student stops breathing, cardiopulmonary resuscitation (CPR) should be implemented and an ambulance called. CPR is a basic skill required to assist an individual who has become unconscious and is not breathing and whose heart may not be beating. The student's teachers, as other support personnel, should be certified in CPR as well in case this is needed. (See Chapter 13 for specifics of CPR when the student has a tracheostomy.)

Other Complications

Personnel will need to be alert for other types of complications that may occur to the student receiving oxygen. Nasal cannula and oxygen masks can result in skin irritation (ear and nose), recurrent nosebleeds, loss of sense of smell and taste, blockage of tear ducts, sore throat, and septal perforation. The physician may choose to change the mode of delivery and may need to medically treat the problem. Other complications can occur from other types of delivery systems such as bronchospasm, pneumothorax, infections, and bleeding. Personnel should be alert to the color and amount of nasal or tracheal discharge for signs of infection or bleeding, as well as any indications of respiratory distress.

MANAGEMENT ISSUES FOR OXYGEN DELIVERY

Individualized Health Plan and Individualized Educational Program

A student who uses oxygen should have an individualized health plan (IHP). The health plan should contain several areas specific to oxygen therapy. As seen in Figure 15-10, some of these include the type of oxygen system, the amount of oxygen prescribed, and when oxygen should be given. It is also important to include baseline in-

formation such as the student's typical color (e.g., dusky, cyanotic), usual respiratory rate, and pulse. The IHP should also specify signs to look for that indicate respiratory distress and the steps to take should respiratory distress occur. The student's ability to request oxygen should also be noted. The IHP should include guidelines for problems and emergencies related to oxygen delivery, such as problems with the oxygen delivery system, not enough oxygen, and too much oxygen.

The student's IEP should specify what aspects of the procedure the student is learning. The student may learn to completely manage his own oxygen therapy independently (when not in acute distress) to partially participate on certain steps. Some areas may include (a) partially or completely assembling oxygen equipment, (b) identifying the need for oxygen, (c) communicating the need for oxygen and information about the oxygen system, (d) demonstrating knowledge of when oxygen is to be used, (e) donning the oxygen delivery system, (f) identifying when more oxygen is needed in the tank or container, and (g) partially or completely taking care of oxygen equipment (including how to get more oxygen ordered). Sample objectives are in Figure 15-11.

Environmental Arrangement for Oxygen

Oxygen can be a dangerous substance if not handled properly. First, it is a flammable substance. Concentrated oxygen, for example, can make smoldering objects (i.e., cigarettes) burst into flames. Also, pressurized oxygen will explode if it gets too hot. Second, oxygen tanks can be dangerous if the oxygen tank opens without the regulator, causing the tank to fall or be propelled into something or someone. Third, tubing needs to be visible, not under clothes or adaptive equipment where it can get kinked. To avoid any problems, there are certain rules that should be followed. As seen in Figure 15-12, these rules include avoiding having the oxygen around heat, direct sunlight, or material that can easily become ignited; being sure that the tank is secured in an upright position; and turning oxygen off when

Type of Oxygen Source

_____Oxygen tank   Type of tank:_____

_____Liquid oxygen   Type of liquid oxygen system:_____

_____Oxygen concentrator Type of oxygen concentrator:_____

Type of Oxygen Delivery System

_____Nasal cannula   Size:_____

_____Oxygen mask   Size:_____

_____Tracheostomy collar Size:_____

_____Face tent   Size:_____

Humidification?_____yes   _____no

Oxygen flow setting:_____

Oxygen use:_____continuous   _____intermittent   _____emergency

When oxygen is to be used:_____

_____

Student-specific procedure attached?_____yes   _____no

Latex allergy?_____yes   _____no, comment:_____

_____

Baseline Information

Skin coloring:_____

Pulse:_____

Respiratory rate:_____

Blood pressure:_____

Directions for Oxygen Delivery Problems and Emergencies

Machine malfunction

   No flow or inadequate flow of oxygen:_____

   Alarms go off:_____

   Leakage of oxygen:_____

Insufficient oxygen (hypoxia) (including symptoms to observe for):_____

Too much oxygen (including symptoms to observe for):_____

CPR:_____

FIGURE 15-10 Specialized areas to include in an IHP for oxygen delivery

---

Independent Performance of Task

The student will correctly put on the nasal cannula and pull the oxygen tank to the desired location without displacing the nasal cannula with 100% accuracy on each occasion for 1 month.

The student will attach the oxygen tubing, turn on the oxygen, adjust the oxygen to the correct rate, and put on the oxygen mask, each at 100% accuracy for 1 month.

Partial Performance of Task

The student will indicate with AAC device when inside of the oxygen mask needs to be wiped dry and upon adult taking off mask, student will wipe mask dry with 80% accuracy on each occasion for 3 weeks.

Upon the adult handing the student the oxygen mask, the student will place the mask in the correct position (while the adult puts the elastic strap behind the student's head) with 100% accuracy on each occasion for 3 weeks.

Directing the Task

The student will direct another on how to turn on and off the oxygen tank and how to adjust oxygen flow to the correct rate with 100% accuracy on each occasion for 1 month.

The student will direct another on how to check that there is enough oxygen in the tank and who to contact should more oxygen be required with 100% accuracy for five consecutive sessions.

Knowledge of the Task

The student will state five safety rules for oxygen management and demonstrate proper care of the oxygen tank with 100% accuracy for five consecutive trials.

The student will show how to alert an adult with her AAC device when there is a lack of oxygen flow on 8 out of 10 trials for five consecutive sessions.

FIGURE 15-11 Sample IEP objectives for oxygen delivery

---

not in use. Also, the fire department should be notified when oxygen is in use in a school, home, or community setting. They can assist with oxygen storage and usage guidelines (American Family Health Institute, 1986; Aschcroft & Smith, 1993; Haynie et al., 1989).

Activity Restrictions

Some students' activities will be limited due to inability to tolerate an increase in exercise. Some may also become fatigued with prolonged movement. In these instances, the student may require modified PE. Spreading out activities that require a lot of energy can be helpful for some students on oxygen, as well as allowing the student to rest between activities. Some students will

have decreased endurance and may need to walk slowly and periodically stop to rest. It will be important to know the student's activity limitations and what to look for to determine whether the student needs to rest (e.g., fatigue, shortness of breath, difficulty breathing). This is especially important if the student cannot verbally tell you (or inform you through the use of augmentative communication) that he needs to stop and rest.

SUMMARY

Oxygen can be delivered by an oxygen mask, nasal cannula, tracheostomy collar, face tent, or oxygen

1. The oxygen supply should be kept at least 5 feet from a heat source.

2. The oxygen should not be near a stove, space heater, radiator, or open flame.

3. The oxygen should be at least 5 feet from electric appliances.

4. Electric blankets and heating pads should not be used.

5. All-cotton clothing and all-cotton sheets and blankets should be used to avoid static electricity.

6. The student should not use moisturizers that contain oil or alcohol.

7. No oil, grease, or flammable material should come in contact with the oxygen equipment.

8. Oxygen tank or liquid oxygen should be secured in an upright position. Be sure it cannot be knocked over.

9. Do not put anything over the oxygen source.

10. No smoking near oxygen source.

11. Do not put oxygen tubing under clothes or adaptive equipment or where it can be easily kinked, blocked, or disconnected.

12. Oxygen should be kept off when not in use.

13. Know the phone number of the oxygen supply company.

14. Extra tubing and tank equipment (e.g., key wrench) should be available at the school and in an easily accessible location.

15. Never transport oxygen in the trunk of a car, and transportation of oxygen on school buses needs special safety precautions to secure the tank.

16. The fire department should be informed that oxygen is being used at the school or home.

17. Post an "Oxygen in Use" sign.

18. Keep a fire extinguisher nearby.

19. Do not use toys that might spark.

FIGURE 15-12 Safety rules for oxygen management

tent (or hood), depending on the needs of the student. The student may use concentrated oxygen (oxygen tank), liquid oxygen, or an oxygen concentrator. Oxygen may be prescribed to be delivered continuously, intermittently, or in emergency situations. Teachers will need to be familiar with the oxygen equipment and its use, as well as what to do if problems arise. The IHP should provide information regarding the use of oxygen and steps to take should problems occur. Students may learn to manage their own oxygen treatment, depending on their age and physical, cognitive, and health abilities.

16

Ventilator Management

Over the past decade, students increasingly have used mechanical **ventilators** in the school setting to assist with their breathing. This use has become possible due to medical advances in treating chronic conditions, development of portable ventilators, and the trend to educate students in the least restrictive environment. Unfortunately, school settings have not always been prepared to meet the needs of students requiring mechanical ventilation (Jones, Clatterbuck, Marquis, Turnbell, & Moberly, 1996). Having a basic understanding of ventilator management will help meet these students' needs.

Breathing, also known as **ventilation,** is the movement of air in and out of the lungs. Air is drawn into the lungs by the contraction of the diaphragm and the intercostal muscles. When the diaphragm contracts, it descends and increases the vertical dimension of the chest. Intercostal muscles (muscles between the ribs) also contract and increase the chest circumference. This expansion results in a negative pressure in the lungs that causes air to be drawn into the lungs. When the muscles relax, they return to their normal position, and air leaves the lungs as an exhale (Guyton, 1991; Pilbeam, 1992). Within the lungs, a process called external **respiration** occurs in which inhaled oxygen moves from the lungs to the bloodstream and carbon dioxide moves from the bloodstream into the lungs. This process moves the needed oxygen into the body and the unwanted carbon dioxide out of the body.

In some medical conditions, this process of ventilation and respiration is impaired to the point that mechanical (artificial) ventilation is needed. Mechanical ventilation is indicated when there is (a) a progressive decrease in oxygen in the body with excessive work of breathing with abnormal respiratory patterns, (b) inadequate respiratory effort, (c) hyperventilation (too fast breathing) due to increased intracranial pressure, and (d) inadequate ventilation (hypoventilation) (Wong, 1995). Several medical disorders can result in these respiratory problems. Depending on the type of disorder and the student's requirement for ventilator usage, some students can receive mechanical ventilation in the home or school setting.

Two categories of disorders typically are eligible for home and school ventilation. As seen in Figure 16-1, the first category consists of those conditions in which the lungs are typically normal, but there is a neuromuscular or neurological disorder that results in respiratory weakness or abnormal control of breathing. Some of these are due to trauma to nerves that control the muscles for breathing (e.g., high spinal cord injury) or disorders affecting the muscles or nerves that control breathing (e.g., Duchenne muscular dystrophy). Often these conditions need a ventilator to provide a specific volume of air with each breath. The second category consists of individuals who have respiratory conditions resulting in abnormal lungs, such as cystic fibrosis or obstructive pulmonary disease. Often these individuals need a ventilator to provide a specific volume of air and sometimes additional oxygen and additional air pressure to keep the lungs properly inflated.

Neurological and Neuromotor Conditions
Abnormal control of breathing
    Brain lesions (e.g., tumor, stroke)
    Brain injury (e.g., trauma)
Spinal cord disorders
    Tumor
    Trauma
Neuromuscular and muscular disorders
    Muscular dystrophies
    Polio
    Myasthenia gravis
    Guillain-Barre syndrome

Lung Diseases
    Chronic obstructive pulmonary disease
    Cystic fibrosis
    Pulmonary fibrosis

FIGURE 16-1 Examples of conditions that may require mechanical ventilation in the home or school setting

DESCRIPTION OF VENTILATORS

A ventilator is a machine used to assist or control ventilation as well as modify the air that is breathed through it. It may be used intermittently or continuously. Ventilators inflate the lungs using either a negative or positive pressure machine. Negative pressure machines work by creating a subatmospheric pressure around the chest wall, which causes air to move into the chest. A full-body chamber (e.g., iron lung), half-body chamber (chest cuirass), "chest raincoat" (a poncho-type device worn around the chest), or pnuemosuit (a bodysuit device) is placed around the chest to create the negative pressure (Kacmarek & Hess, 1994). Negative pressure machines are not typically found in the school setting. However, negative pressure ventilators are used at home with individuals experiencing chronic respiratory failure due to such conditions as late-stage Duchenne muscular dystrophy and polio (poliomyelitis) (Hill, Redline, Carskadon, Curran, & Millman, 1992).

Positive pressure ventilators are the most common type of machines used for ventilation and most often encountered in the school setting. They create a pressure in the airways that is greater than the pressure in the lungs. This results in forcing pressurized air into the lungs. Air will exit the lungs passively as the person exhales. Individuals who use this type of ventilator will usually require a tracheostomy for long-term management. A tube going from the nose to the trachea (endotracheal tube) may be used temporarily in the hospital setting for short-term management. Tubing from the ventilator attaches to the student's tracheostomy tube, allowing the pressurized air to be delivered to the student (see Figure 16-2).

Students using ventilators may not have the ability to cough effectively to clear mucous secretions. These students need to be suctioned, which involves passing a catheter through the tracheostomy into the airway to withdraw secretions. To help loosen the secretions, postural drainage, clapping, or vibration may be prescribed, along with

FIGURE 16-2 A student using a ventilator that sits on the back of her wheelchair and is connected to her tracheostomy by tubing from the ventilator

aerosols and inhaled medications. In some instances, students who use a ventilator may require other health procedures such as bladder catheterization or gastrostomy feeding (Janz, 1993). (See earlier chapters for more information.)

EQUIPMENT AND ADAPTIVE EQUIPMENT FOR VENTILATOR MANAGEMENT

Many types of positive pressure ventilators are available, with a range of capabilities. These ventilators may be pressure-cycled ventilators, volume-cycled ventilators, or time-cycled ventilators. Pressure-cycled ventilators stop providing an inhalation when a certain preset inspiratory pressure is reached. Volume-cycled types stop providing an inhalation when a preset volume of air is delivered. Time-cycled models stop inspiration when a preset time is reached (Wong, 1995). Most portable positive pressure ventilators that are found in home and school settings are volume-cycled machines that can deliver 0 to 3,000

milliliters (mL) of air in each breath and respiratory rates from 4 to 35 breaths a minute (Gramlich, 1992). However, there have been reports of inadequate ventilation (hypoventilation) during sleep with volume-controlled ventilators and uncuffed tracheostomy tubes, resulting in the suggested use of a pressure-controlled ventilator in certain circumstances (Gilgoff, Peng, & Keens, 1992). The type of ventilator the physician selects will be based on the student's condition and ventilatory needs. Additional considerations for school ventilatory use include reliability, safety, versatility, portability, user-friendliness, and ease of delivery of ventilation. Ventilators used in the school setting are typically portable and easily fit onto the back of a wheelchair or on a movable cart (see Figure 16-3).

Additional equipment used with the ventilator should be available. The ventilator may use an external (or sometimes internal) battery that connects to a charger with a cable. The battery and cable are important items since many ventilators are designed to use the battery primarily when moving and to charge the battery and use electricity when stationary. Other items that should be available include a humidifier (if ordered), ventilator filters, and alarms (if not part of the ventilator). An Ambu bag (manual resuscitator) should be available in case of ventilator malfunction. The manual resuscitator should have an attachment to fit over the tracheostomy to provide breaths by squeezing the Ambu bag (see Figure 14-5 in previous chapter). Ideally, a second backup ventilator should also be available for emergency use.

For the ventilator's electrical needs, the school and home need to be able to accommodate the voltage drainage without effecting the ventilator's performance. Circuit breakers should be used rather than fuses. Internal and external batteries should have automatic switchover between the batteries and the electrical wall power. Ideally, a home generator should be available in case of power failure.

Airway management equipment also needs to be available. This would include a suction ma-

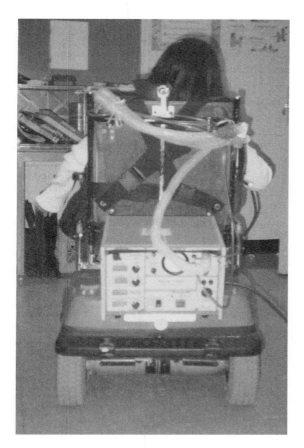

FIGURE 16-3 A ventilator mounted to the back of a student's electric wheelchair for ease of portability

chine, connecting tube, suction catheter, water or saline, container for water or saline, gloves, extra tracheostomy tubes, and obturator. Cleaning supplies and disinfectant solutions would also need to be available. (See Chapter 13, "Tracheostomies," and Chapter 14, "Managing Respiratory Secretions," for more equipment information.)

If the student is also using supplemental oxygen in the ventilator, oxygen equipment needs to be available. This equipment may include an E cylinder, concentrator, oxygen tubing, tracheostomy collar, and tubing. (See Chapter 15,

"Oxygen Management," for more information.) Depending on the student's needs, an air compressor may be needed for aerosolized medications (see Chapter 4 on medications).

ASSISTIVE STRATEGIES FOR VENTILATOR MANAGEMENT

General Student Care for Students Using Ventilators

Baseline information on the student should be available that includes the student's respiratory rate, pulse rate, skin color, level of alertness, blood pressure, and, if possible, typical levels of oxygen in the blood (i.e., blood gases or peripheral oxygen saturation levels). The student should be observed for any changes in baseline status and respiratory functioning. Personnel should be familiar with what action to take should any changes occur.

Other aspects of student care include suctioning and tracheostomy care. Many students on ventilators require suctioning on an as-needed basis (p.r.n.). Personnel should be alert to signs that the student needs suctioning and perform the procedure as indicated. The tracheostomy should also be periodically checked so that the tracheostomy ties are secure and that the tracheostomy tube is in place. Strict infection control procedures must be maintained in these procedures to avoid respiratory infections. Any signs of infection must be reported, and any problems with suctioning, tracheostomy placement, or student breathing should follow the student's specified emergency procedures.

Checking the Ventilator

The student's ventilator should be routinely checked every 1 to 2 hours, or more frequently if there is a change in the student's status (Haynie et al., 1989). Routinely checking the ventilator helps assure that the ventilator is properly functioning. Also, school personnel should know how to set the settings on the ventilator in case the settings are accidentally changed by another student or how to set them correctly if a physician orders a setting change in an emergency situation. (It is important that more people than the person designated to address the student's health needs be able to do this in case that person is temporarily unavailable when an emergency occurs.) Figure 16-4 shows a checklist that can be used to regularly check the functioning of the ventilator. However, ventilators vary as to their features, so only parts of the checklist may apply.

Power Source. The ventilator may operate with electricity or a 12-volt battery. The ventilator should have an external battery connected to the ventilator that operates approximately 12 to 18 hours. This can be used when the student is moving about or as an emergency backup should the electricity fail. Most ventilators also have an internal battery that operates in an emergency for approximately 1 hour (Mizumori et al., 1994). The school staff needs to know whether the battery is supposed to stay plugged in when the student is stationary or whether there are specific times when it is supposed to be charged. It is also important that accessible, functioning electrical outlets are always available for the ventilator. It is recommended that the school or home be mapped as to determine which electrical outlet is on which circuit. Should a circuit breaker trip, knowing the closest working electrical outlet is important. If the primary battery or power source fails, an emergency power supply or backup battery should be available.

Ventilator Settings. Ventilators will vary as to the different parameters available to the person being ventilated. Also, the student's specific condition, size, and uniqueness will determine how these parameters are set. The **respiratory rate** refers to how many breaths are delivered in a minute. It may be abbreviated as breaths per minute (bpm). The **tidal volume** setting controls how much air is delivered by the ventilator for each inhalation. The **peak inspiratory pressure (PIP)** setting controls the amount of pressure used to inflate the lungs to a prescribed tidal volume. **Flow rate** controls how quickly the gas (air/oxygen) flows into the lungs and is measured in liters per minute. If oxygen is being given, there will be an **oxygen control** knob adjusting the percentage of oxygen delivered to the student. Some ventilators will have **positive end expiratory pressure (PEEP).** Although PEEP is not as common with portable ventilators, when it is used, it provides a select amount of pressure to prevent the lungs from collapsing after exhalation. An **inspiratory time** (I time) refers to the amount of time in the ventilator's cycle that is used to deliver a breath (Porter et al., 1997). A **sigh volume control** adjusts the amount of milliliters (mL) of air that is intermittently pumped in to simulate a sigh.

The ventilator may also be adjusted to certain **ventilator modes:** controlled ventilation, assist-controlled ventilation, intermittent mandatory ventilation (IMV), or spontaneous intermittent mandatory ventilation (SIMV). In controlled ventilation, the ventilator typically provides breaths for a specific number of times regardless of the student's efforts to breathe on his own. It is usually appropriate only when the student is unable to make any effort to breathe. When the student makes an effort to breath, some assist-controlled ventilation may be used. In this mode, the ventilator is sensitive to pressure changes, and when the student attempts to take a breath, the ventilator gives a breath. Since a danger is that the student may not attempt to take a breath, there is usually a minimum minute ventilation setting (VE) that guarantees a minimum number of breaths delivered by the ventilator. The intermittent (IMV) and synchronized intermittent mandatory ventilation (SIMV) modes may be set if it is desirable for the student to breathe on his own without receiving a breath by the ventilator when

Directions:
   Settings: Fill in student's own prescribed setting. (For those not ordered, put an X.)
   Date, time: Ventilator should be checked every 2 hours.
   Check: Place a check in the box each time item is checked and is correct.
   Star: If setting is incorrect, star box, change to correct setting, and call physician.

Student: _____

Ventilator model: _____

Ventilator mode: _____ control _____ assist _____ IMV _____ SIMV

Ventilator hours: _____ continuous _____ other; specify: _____

If oxygen is in use, type of oxygen: _____ liquid _____ compressed (cylinder)

Ventilator check	Prescribed setting	Date and time										
Power	Battery charged											
Respiratory rate	bpm											
Tidal volume	mL											
Peak inspiratory pressure (PIP)												
Flow rate	L/min											
PEEP	cm H$_2$O											
Oxygen	More than _____ left											
Oxygen	L/min											
Alarms on	Type of alarms:											
Ventilator circuit	Connected and free of water											
Humidifier	Adequate water											
Ambu bag	Present											
Student respiratory status												

FIGURE 16-4 Ventilator checklist

he starts to inhale on his own. This helps the student retain some strength in the muscles used for respiration since every breath is not ventilator supported (Pilbeam, 1992).

Alarms

Ventilators differ as to the types of alarms present. Separate alarms may be purchased (or rented) and attached to the ventilator as needed. School personnel will need to be familiar with the student's own ventilator's alarms and what the alarms sound like (since different noises represent different alarms). Standard alarms include a power alarm and low-pressure alarms. A **power alarm** indicates that there is either a low battery or a loss of power. It is typically a continuous alarm. A **low-pressure alarm** indicates that there is little to no resistance when the ventilator is providing a breath. This can occur when the student is disconnected from the ventilator, an air leak is present, the exhalation valve is malfunctioning, the tracheostomy tube is dislocated or has come out, or the humidifier is not correctly attached or leaking. A low-pressure alarm is typically a continuous alarm (Haynie et al., 1989). Personnel will need to look for the problem immediately and correct it. This alarm can be periodically tested by removing the student from the ventilator and checking that the alarm loudly sounds in 10 to 15 seconds. (This check should only be done with the physician's permission.)

Other alarms are also available. Many ventilators will come with a **high-pressure alarm.** This indicates that when the ventilator is providing a breath, there is more resistance than normal to the air entering the lungs. This result can occur when the tubing is kinked, the tubing has water in it, the student needs to be suctioned, the exhalation valve is obstructed, or the tracheostomy tube is blocked or misaligned. Also, this alarm may occur when the student coughs or laughs but will then stop when the student finishes coughing or laughing. A high-pressure alarm is often an intermittent alarm. Some ventilators will have a pressure gauge to show the amount of pressure. This can be quickly checked to verify high pressure. Personnel will need to find the reason for the high pressure and correct it (e.g., unkink the tubing). Other alarms that may be included are an inspiratory flow alarm and inspiratory/expiratory ratio alarm or an apnea alarm. It is important that alarms are left on all of the time.

Oxygen. Only half of the current portable positive pressure ventilators are built to accommodate additional oxygen since most students using ventilators in the home and school use room air (Gramlich, 1992). If supplemental oxygen is being used, it is typically supplied in gas or liquid form. The gauge will need to be checked to determine whether an adequate supply of oxygen is available for the day. A spare tank should be available. Oxygen precautions need to be in place when oxygen is in use. (See Figure 15-12 in the previous chapter for a list of precautions to be followed.)

Humidifier. Some students have humidification attached to the ventilator to moisturize the air that they receive. It is important that the humidifier is checked to determine that sufficient water (sterile or distilled) is in the container. If not, more water will need to be added to the container or a new humidification bottle attached. Humidification can result in water collecting in the tubing going to the student. When this is the case, the water will need to be periodically emptied by quickly disconnecting the tube from the student and shaking the excess water out.

Ventilator Circuit. A ventilator circuit is the tubing, connections, and valves that connect the student to the ventilator. Typically the ventilator circuit consists of three main parts: a humidifier (which warms and moistens the air), an exhalation valve (which controls the direction of airflow) and tubing (which connects the student to

ASSISTIVE STRATEGIES FOR CHANGING THE VENTILATOR CIRCUIT

Preparing for Changing the Ventilator Circuit

The ventilator circuit should be changed and cleaned regularly, from daily to two to three times a week, depending on the physician's instructions. Changing and cleaning the ventilator circuit should occur in the home setting. However, it is possible in an emergency situation (e.g., a valve breaking or a hole being cut in the tubing), a new ventilator circuit would need to be applied. If the ventilator circuit needs to be changed, the student should be given an explanation. Hands should be washed and equipment assembled. It is important that the student be ventilated with an Ambu bag (with oxygen if indicated) if the student is completely ventilator or oxygen dependent since she will not be breathing without the ventilator circuit.

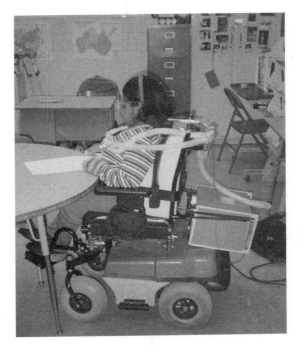

FIGURE 16-5 A student using a ventilator that is mounted to the back of her wheelchair. The ventilator circuit is visible, which includes the tubing, connections, and valves going from the ventilator to the student.

Equipment and Supply List for Changing the Ventilator Circuit

Ambu bag

Clean circuit (tubing, exhalation valve, humidifier)

Sterile distilled water

Tracheostomy connector

the ventilator) (Mizumori et al., 1994) (see Figure 16-5). Depending on the student's ventilator and needs, the ventilator circuit varies. It is important that school personnel trace where the tubing comes from and where it connects and memorize the tubing route. This is important in case some of the tubing becomes disconnected. If this occurs, school personnel need to be able to reconnect the tubing, without relying on one person (who could be unavailable at that particular moment). The tubing from the ventilator, to the humidifier, to the student's tracheostomy can become kinked or disconnected. When this occurs, the tubing should be unkinked or reconnected. Usually an alarm will go off signaling that there is a problem.

Procedure for Changing the Ventilator Circuit

After explaining the procedure, washing hands, and assembling equipment, the person performing the procedure may begin. (If an emergency, this will need to be performed quickly, and explanations will need to be short.)

Steps in the Procedure for Changing the Ventilator Circuit	*Rationale*
1. Place clean equipment on a clean surface (or towel), and be sure that the circuit is correctly assembled.	Personnel should be familiar with the student's own ventilator circuit. Typically, tubing extends from the ventilator to the humidifier, from the humidifier to the exhalation valve, and from the valve to the tracheostomy adapter. The tracheostomy adapter attaches to the student's tracheostomy. Having a circuit already assembled and kept in a new clean bag is sometimes done.
2. Fill the clean humidifier basin with sterile distilled water.	A second humidifier basin should be available with the rest of the ventilator circuit.
3. Check the current pressure gauge reading on the ventilator.	This reading will be used later. However, if the circuit is being changed due to a problem, knowledge of the usual pressure gauge reading is important.
4. Disconnect the tracheostomy connector (which has the rest of the ventilator circuit attached) from the student's tracheostomy tube, and have a second person provide the student with breaths with the Ambu bag.	The ventilator circuit should be already assembled prior to disconnection to limit the time off the ventilator.
5. Remove each part of the old circuit and immediately replace with the new/clean part.	This should be done in a quick, efficient manner. As the low-pressure alarm sounds, it may be reset by pushing the reset button (but only if this does not take away time from changing the circuit).
6. Slide the old humidifier container off the humidification unit and replace with a new one.	In some instances, humidification may not be used.
7. After the new circuit is in place, check for air leaks prior to connecting to student. This is done by occluding the tracheostomy adapter and observing the pressure setting move up to maximum (and/or the high-pressure alarm will sound).	If an air leak is present, check that the tubing is well connected at all sites. Recheck for air leaks and proceed when the maximum pressure limit is reached, indicating no air leaks are present.

Steps in the Procedure for Changing the Ventilator Circuit	*Rationale*
8. Reconnect the tracheostomy connector to the student with new circuit in place. Make sure if oxygen is used that it is connected immediately.	The student should now be back on the ventilator. Reset any alarms that are going off from the procedure.
9. Recheck the pressure gauge. The reading should be approximately the same before the procedure (or if there was a problem, it should be where it normally is maintained) (Mizumori et al., 1994).	If a problem continues, the appropriate person should be notified immediately.
10. Document the procedure and how the student is doing after procedure is complete.	The student should appear the same as baseline figures, without respiratory distress.

Care of Equipment

The ventilator circuit should be cleaned at home. This requires having a second set of tubing, connectors, valves, and humidification system to be used by the student while the first set is being cleaned. The ventilator circuit is first disassembled. Small tubing should be wiped with a clean, damp cloth and should not be submerged into water. The larger bore tubing, exhalation valve, tracheostomy connector, and humidifier should be washed in warm, soapy water using liquid detergent. To facilitate cleaning, it should be scrubbed with small brushes. Equipment is then submerged in disinfectant solution (or diluted vinegar) for approximately 15 to 20 minutes. (It is important that the equipment is not submerged longer since damage can occur.) Equipment must then be thoroughly rinsed with water and air dried. The valve and tubing should be checked for leaks, holes, or tears. The tubing, connectors, humidifier parts, and valves should be reassembled for use or for storage (in a clean plastic bag). Ideally, cleaning should occur every 24 hours (Gramlich, 1992; Mizumori et al., 1994). Another method for cleaning the ventilator circuit involves using the dishwasher. Specific recommendations for cleaning should be followed.

INSTRUCTIONAL STRATEGIES AND MODIFICATIONS

Students will not necessarily be able to respond to their own ventilator needs when a problem results, but some can assist with monitoring their own ventilator. This task is often limited by the ventilator's placement on the back of a wheelchair. However, having knowledge of the ventilator, its alarms, and ancillary procedures will enable students to assist others as well as participate in some aspects of their own care.

Training should be based on the student's chronological age, functioning level, cognitive abilities, and physical abilities. Typically, it should include some anatomy of the respiratory system and the principles of oxygen and gas exchange. How the student's disease interferes with the process should be simply explained to the level of the student's understanding. Information should be provided on how the ventilator assists the student and its basic operation. The ventilator settings and their meanings, as well as the meaning of the various alarms, should be explained.

Several skill areas need to be learned by the student when a ventilator is in use. These skill areas fall into four categories: ventilator management, tracheostomy management, managing secretions, and oxygen delivery. As see in Figure 16-6, ventilator management includes checking settings, checking and charging the ventilator's battery or power source, recognizing respiratory problems, using an Ambu bag, responding to alarms, responding to power/machine failure, changing and cleaning ventilator circuit (tubing, connectors, humidification), maintaining equipment, and controlling infection (Nissim & Sten, 1991). Depending on the students' physical condition, many students will be able to assist with checking settings and some aspects of cleaning and maintaining the equipment. Students should have a way of alerting others to any recognized respiratory or ventilator problems. Responding to alarms, machine failure, and use of Ambu will typically need to be performed by another person, should the student became incapacitated or not have the physical ability or strength to learn what to do should these problems occur. Finally, all students should learn the basics of infection control.

Tracheostomy management and managing secretions are basic skills that can be broken down into task analyses. If the student has supplemental oxygen given, in addition to room air, skills in this area will also need to be monitored. (See Chapters 13 through 15 for in-depth information in these areas.)

Ventilator care can be broken down into small steps in a task analysis and taught using any number of instructional strategies (see Chapter 2). As with all health-related procedures, it is important to identify any time-limited steps or caution steps of the task analysis. Any step involving an alarm going off or the ventilator not functioning in some way is considered a time-limited step, requiring an intervention to occur within a certain

Ventilator Management
Checking ventilator and settings
Checking and charging ventilator battery or
  power source
Response to alarms
Response to power/machine failure
Use of Ambu bag
Recognition and response to early signs of
  respiratory problems
Maintenance and care of equipment
Ventilator circuit changes and cleaning
Prevention of infection

Tracheostomy Management
Stoma care
Changing trach ties
Cleaning/changing inner cannula
Cleaning/changing tracheostomy tube
CPR with a tracheostomy
Emergency tracheostomy change
Maintenance and care of equipment
Prevention of infection

Managing Secretions
Chest physiotherapy
Hyperoxygenation with ventilator
Tracheal and nasopharyngeal suctioning
Using sterile technique (when ordered)
Maintenance and care of equipment
Prevention of infection

Oxygen Delivery
Checking oxygen supply
Checking oxygen delivery levels
Setting up oxygen delivery system
Putting on oxygen mask, cannula, trach collar,
  or face tent
Arranging safe environment for oxygen use
Maintaining and caring for equipment
Preventing infection

FIGURE 16-6 Skills for managing a mechanical ventilator and related procedures

time frame to assure the student's safety. Typically the adult must intervene to assist the student. However, in some cases, the student will learn an intervention, such as putting the ventilator tube back on the tracheostomy tube when it pops off and the low-pressure alarm sounds. If the student is learning to perform a time-limited step, it is important that the teacher provide modeling then move to shadowing, or for lower-functioning students, the teacher may provide a full physical prompt and move to shadowing. When providing shadowing, the teacher keeps her hands within an inch of the student's hands to be able to immediately assist the student if necessary.

Caution steps for ventilator management involve any steps in which the ventilator tubing needs to be attached to the tracheostomy tube. In caution steps, injury can result from a quick, jerking, or incorrect movement. The tracheostomy could be harmed if the student strongly hit the tracheostomy tube when trying to attach the ventilator tubing. The educational team must decide whether the student should perform this step. If the student is going to learn it, the teacher needs to model the step and then provide shadowing. For lower-functioning students, the teacher should provide a full physical prompt and move to shadowing. The teacher should highlight time-limited steps and caution steps on the data sheet as a reminder to provide shadowing (see the sample data sheet in Chapter 2).

VENTILATOR PROBLEMS AND EMERGENCIES

There is always the possibility that school personnel will encounter some problem or emergency with a student using a ventilator. Therefore, they should be familiar with not only ventilator problems but problems with ancillary procedures. Students using ventilators in the school setting typically have tracheostomies, require suctioning, and, in some cases, use supplemental oxygen along with their ventilator. Several problems and emergencies can occur with the management of these areas as well. The reader is referred to Chapter 13 on tracheostomies, Chapter 14 on managing secretions, and Chapter 15 on oxygen management for information on the specific problems and emergencies that can occur and the action to take. The following are problems specific only to ventilator use.

Ventilator Malfunction

As with any piece of machinery, there is always a possibility that the ventilator could malfunction or become disconnected. In one study (Nelson, Carroll, Hurvitz, & Dean, 1996), 3 out of 89 students who used ventilators in home and school settings died due to ventilator malfunction or disconnection. It is therefore critical that the ventilator be checked regularly and backup equipment is available. Also, ventilator alarms should never be turned off. Should the ventilator fail, it is important to already know whether the student is completely dependent on the ventilator and needs immediate help breathing. Some students may be able to breathe on their own for the short time that it takes for the backup system to be put in place. Others may need immediate assistance, and CPR will need to be initiated, preferably using an Ambu bag. The Ambu bag for providing breaths should always be kept with the student. Some students will have a backup ventilator for use. A backup ventilator is indicated for students who are not routinely off the ventilator for at least 4 continuous hours a day and when the replacement ventilator cannot be provided within 2 hours (Plummer, O'Donohue, & Petty, 1989). It will be important that a flashlight be kept near the ventilator in case of a power outage to assist with finding and hooking up the backup system.

Respiratory Distress

Even when the ventilator appears to be working properly, it does not necessarily mean that the student is being well ventilated (Wong, 1995). It is therefore critical that the student be assessed for any signs of hypoxia or respiratory distress. As discussed in Chapter 15, signs of insufficient oxygen can include restlessness, anxiety, fatigue, drowsiness, confusion, inability to concentrate, dizziness, headache, sweaty skin (diaphoresis), blue finger nailbeds or lips (cyanosis), or respiratory distress. Signs of respiratory distress include difficulty breathing, shortness of breath, chest retraction, increased respiratory rate, stridor, and cyanosis (see Figure 16-7). If the student is showing that he is not getting enough oxygen or experiencing respiratory distress, the emergency plan should be followed. This typically entails calling an ambulance. CPR should be initiated when needed and continuous oxygen given as prescribed.

CPR

If CPR (cardiopulmonary resuscitation) is needed, personnel should be familiar with how to perform it on a student with a tracheostomy. Manual respirations involve the rescuer placing her mouth over the student's tracheostomy tube, forming a seal, and breathing into the tracheostomy according to standard rescue breathing procedures learned in CPR class. However, most persons with ventilators should have a resuscitation bag (also known as a manual resuscitation or an Ambu bag). The Ambu bag should have an adapter to attach to the tracheostomy tube. When attaching the bag, the person should hold the tracheostomy tube with one hand so that it is not accidentally dislodged. The bag is then squeezed to give breaths. It can also be hooked up to oxygen to provide a higher level of oxygen than room air, if required. The resuscitation bag is typically squeezed once every 3 seconds for infants under 1 year old, once every 4 seconds for students between 1 and 8 years old, and once every 5 seconds for students over 8 years old (Buzz-Kelly & Gordin, 1993).

Obstruction and High-Pressure Alarm

A high-pressure alarm typically indicates some type of obstruction occurring between the lungs and the ventilator. This can occur from the student coughing or laughing, from mucous secretions in the respiratory passages, or from blocked tubing. If the student was coughing or laughing, the pressure will quickly return to normal. However, if the high-pressure alarm is occurring due to an obstruction in the airway from mucus, the student will need to be suctioned. Usually the student can be quickly assessed to determine whether suctioning is needed. Some of the indications that suctioning is needed are hearing secretions bubbling or gurgling in the airway, wheezing, or whistling breath sounds. Other signs include coughing, agitation, fast breathing, difficulty breathing, or change in color. If the problem appears to be with the tracheostomy, procedure for unblocking the tracheostomy or emergency replacement of the tracheostomy tube should be followed.

If the student does not appear to need suctioning, something may be wrong with the ventilator circuit. Typically this occurs due to a kink in the tubing or water from the humidifier accumulating in the tubing. The tubing should

---

Abnormal Breathing
Difficult, labored breathing
Decreased air exchange or inability to move
   air (through tracheostomy or airways)
Shortness of breath, rapid breathing
Wheezing, gasping for breath, abnormal
   breath sounds

Retraction of Chest
Pulling in of the chest and neck muscles
   (which occurs to help with breathing)

Cyanosis
Dusky or blue color, especially at nailbeds
   and around mouth

Neurological Signs
Agitation, anxiety, restlessness
Confusion, inability to concentrate
Dizzy
Drowsiness
Unconscious

Cardiac
Fast heart rate (pulse)

FIGURE 16-7 Signs of respiratory distress

be checked for any kinks, and these should be corrected. Any observable water in the tubing should be emptied (and routinely emptied when accumulation occurs). Water is emptied by disconnecting the tubing and allowing the water to drain from the tubing into a container. After draining the water for a few seconds, the tubing should quickly be reattached.

Air Leak/Low-Pressure Alarm

One of the most common problems with the ventilator circuit is an air leak. Air leaks will result in the low-pressure alarm sounding. The route of the tubing should be closely examined for any poor connections. Common sights of air leaks are tracheostomy connector coming off the tracheostomy tube, loose connections along the ventilator circuit, a leak in the valve (or a tear in the diaphragm of the valve), or a leak in the area around the tracheostomy tube (Mizumori et al., 1994). Any areas of a disconnection or loosened connection should be firmly reattached. A tear in a valve will require replacement. Leakage of air around a cuffed tracheostomy is not normal, and the cuff may have a hole in it. Emergency tracheostomy tube replacement (or an increase in tidal volume) may be indicated, and emergency plans should be followed and the physician contacted. In cuffless tracheostomies this problem is compensated for by the physician increasing the tidal volume to assure adequate ventilation.

MANAGEMENT ISSUES FOR VENTILATORS

Individualized Health Plan and Individualized Educational Program

A student who requires the use of a ventilator should have an individualized health plan (IHP). Besides the general information cited in the health plan, several specific areas should also be included. As presented in Figure 16-8, basic information about the type of ventilator and when ventilator support is needed should be in the health plan. The specific settings for the ventilator should be included. What should occur when the alarms go off should be specified. What to do in emergency situations such as ventilator malfunction and respiratory distress should be specified. Baseline student information should be available. Additional information for tracheostomy, suction, and oxygen delivery should also be included in health plans and attached to the plan for ventilatory management.

The student's educational plan should specify what the student is learning about his ventilator and its care. If the student is learning certain skills such as monitoring the ventilator or cleaning its tubing, these can be instructional objectives. Areas of instruction may include (a) anatomy and physiology, (b) communication strategies to indicate a problem and possible resolution, (c) how to check all parts of the ventilator equipment, (d) how to change and clean ventilatory equipment, and (e) steps to take in an emergency. Sample IEP objectives are listed in Figure 16-9.

Communication

Speaking with a tracheostomy has recently become a reality. One way this is accomplished is with the use of speaking valves. Speaking valves are one-way valves that permit air to enter through the tracheostomy tube, then redirect air through the larynx (voice box). These valves connect onto the tubing then to the tracheostomies and have been found to be successful in allowing speech in individuals using ventilators (Passy, Baydur, Prentice, & Darnell-Neal 1993). For students who cannot use valves, another technique involves deflating the cuff of the tracheostomy and augmenting the tidal volume of the ventilator. This results in a "leak" of air through the larynx to allow vocalization (Austan, 1992). This technique can only be done with the physician's permission. In some cases, the student can speak with the ventilator, but the voice is very quiet. In these

Ventilator Model: _____

Ventilator mode: _____ control _____ assist _____ IMV _____ SIMV

Ventilator hours: _____ continual _____ intermittent, specify: _____

_____

Ventilator Settings

Respiratory rate: _____

Tidal volume: _____

Peak inspiratory pressure (PIP): _____

Flow rate: _____

Positive end expiratory pressure (PEEP): _____

Inspiratory time (I time): _____

Oxygen: _____

Types of Alarms

_____ power alarm _____ low-pressure _____ high-pressure _____ other: _____

Power Source

_____ internal battery _____ external battery

Specify when to charge and when ventilator should be plugged into electric outlet: _____

_____

Humidification? _____ yes _____ no

Oxygen

_____ yes, type: _____ liquid _____ cylinder prescribed amount: _____

_____ no

Student-Specific Procedures

Student-specific checklist for monitoring ventilator attached:

_____ yes _____ no _____ N/A

Student-specific procedures for tracheostomy care attached:

_____ yes _____ no _____ N/A

Student-specific procedures for suctioning attached:

_____ yes _____ no _____ N/A

Student-specific procedures for chest physiotherapy attached:

_____ yes _____ no _____ N/A

Student-specific procedures for oxygen delivery attached:

_____ yes _____ no _____ N/A

Latex allergy? _____ yes _____ no, comment: _____

Directions for Ventilator Problems and Emergencies

Ventilator malfunction: _____

Respiratory distress: _____

Obstruction/high-pressure alarm: _____

Air leak/low-pressure alarm: _____

Student Baseline Information (respiratory rate, skin color, pulse, blood pressure): _____

_____

FIGURE 16-8 Specialized areas to include in an IHP on ventilator management

Independent Performance of Task

The student will change the ventilator circuit following an approved procedure checklist with 100% accuracy for five consecutive sessions.

The student will reconnect tracheostomy connector to tracheostomy tube when it pops off with 100% accuracy during five of five training trials for three consecutive sessions, and on 100% of opportunities for 1 month.

Partial Performance of Task

The student will assist with changing the ventilator circuit by reconnecting the tracheostomy connector to the tracheostomy (while an adult performs the rest of the steps) with 100% accuracy on five consecutive sessions.

Directing the Task

The student will direct another person on performing a ventilator check (using the ventilator checklist) with 100% accuracy on five consecutive sessions.

The student will direct an adult on the steps to take to change the ventilator circuit with 100% accuracy for five consecutive sessions.

Knowledge of the Task

The student will correctly identify ventilator settings and explain what each setting means to an adult with 100% accuracy on four consecutive sessions.

The student will identify what the ventilator alarms mean when they go off and explain using his AAC device what should be done when certain alarms go off with 100% accuracy for five consecutive sessions.

The student will demonstrate how he will alert an adult if he does not feel that he is being well ventilated using his AAC device with 100% accuracy on five consecutive sessions.

FIGURE 16-9 Sample IEP objectives for ventilator management

instances, an electrolarynx or voice synthesizer may be used to enhance the voice.

Some individuals will be unable to vocalize and cannot use a speaking valve or the technique of "leaking" air through the larynx. In these situations, alternative communication will be needed. Some communication options include lip speaking, writing, communication boards, sign language, and printed messages (Celli, 1994). No matter what approach used, the student must have the ability to quickly communicate when something is wrong.

Environment

Students with ventilators have been educated in a variety of settings including general education classrooms, resource special education rooms, self-contained rooms, self-contained schools, and homebound programs (Jones, Clatterbuck, Marquis, Turnbull, & Moberly, 1996; Levine, 1996). The setting needs to be selected based on the student's individual educational and health needs. Whatever setting is selected, the rooms should be accessible and provide enough room for the student to move about with the ventilator (whether it is mounted to a wheelchair or on a cart).

The school environment needs to be assessed in terms of appropriateness for a student using a ventilator. Ventilators are often plugged into an electrical outlet to conserve the battery whenever possible. Electrical outlets should be inspected to determine that they are grounded and that there are adequate 10- to 15-amp circuits in the student's classroom(s) and other commonly used school areas. Electrical outlets need to be accessible to where the student will be sitting. If an extension cord needs to be used, it should be grounded and heavy enough to accommodate the current load (Janz, 1993). Also, the phone and power company should be notified that a student is using a ventilator at school and a priority reinstatement request placed in case of power or phone outages. A plan should also be in place in case of a prolonged power outage.

Temperature is another environmental consideration. Some students on ventilators do not tolerate extreme temperatures without serious health problems. Rooms should be air-conditioned and heated to maintain a recommended temperature of approximately 68 to 72 degrees (Janz, 1993). If oxygen is in use, the student should not be placed near a space heater, and other precautionary measured should be followed (see Chapter 15's section on environmental considerations for oxygen use).

Should an emergency occur, a plan needs to be in place. How the office is notified that there is an emergency situation needs to be decided. Some schools place phones in the teachers' rooms or have emergency buttons. Others may designate a student to run to the office. Another consideration is the accessibility of the classroom(s) to emergency services. Some students' classes are moved to rooms near exits. In some situations this can be helpful for speed of delivery of emergency services, as well as for evacuation from the building for such emergencies as fire.

Emotional Issues

Students who use ventilators often have to deal with some emotional issues. Issues regarding social stigma can occur due to other students' and adults' reactions toward seeing a person with a ventilator in the school setting. There can be feelings of isolation due to diminished abilities to participate and decreased involvement in social activities. Students with ventilators may also have feelings of inadequacy or being unable to reach their potential. Feelings of dependency or being

tied to the machine may occur. Concern over an ambiguous future may also be present.

It will be important for the teacher to observe for these problems and address them (or find someone to help her address them). Often school personnel and students are afraid of the ventilator and react in a manner that increases social stigma. Although the alarms going off can be disconcerting, teachers and students will typically learn to become use to the alarms, such as most students with ventilators do, and immediately address the problems as they occur. It is important that the student is not overlooked in the maze of tubes and machinery. Social stigma issues should be directly confronted through inservicing school personnel and activities that will sensitize students. The teacher should also include the student in activities to decrease feelings of isolation. It is also important that the student is appropriately challenged and encouraged to perform his best. If the student appears to have serious emotional problems, counseling is often recommended.

SUMMARY

Students who are unable to breathe on their own require the use of a ventilator. Several types of ventilators may be used on a continuous or intermittent basis. The ventilator and its settings should be checked periodically throughout the day. Personnel should be familiar with the ventilator alarms and signs of respiratory distress and what to do if these occur. Some students may also receive supplemental oxygen through their ventilator. In these instances, oxygen precautions need to be in place. Since most students with ventilators have tracheostomies and may require suctioning, personnel must be familiar with tracheostomy and suctioning procedures. Students are encouraged to take an active part in their own care and may have educational goals to teach them to participate partially or independently.

References

Adams, D. A., & Selekof, J. L. (1986). Children with ostomies: Comprehensive care planning. *Pediatric Nursing, 12*(6), 429–433.

Adamson, L. B., & Dunbar, B. (1991). Communication development of young children with tracheostomies. *Augmentative and Alternative Communication, 7,* 275–283.

Alberto, P. A., & Heller, K. W. (1995). Multiple disabilities. In A. Dell & R. Marinelli (Eds.), *Encyclopedia of disability and rehabilitation* (pp. 476–478). New York: Macmillan.

Alberto, P., Sharpton, W., Briggs, A., & Stright, M. (1986). Facilitating task acquisition through the use of a self-operated auditory prompting system. *Journal of the Association for Persons with Severe Handicaps, 11,* 85–91.

Alberto, P., Sharpton, W., Sternberg, L., & Bowen, T. (1994). Components of instructional technology (pp. 297–332). In L. Sternberg (Ed.), *Individuals with profound disabilities.* Austin, TX: PRO-ED.

Alberto, P., & Troutman, A. (1999). *Applied behavior analysis for teachers.* Upper Saddle River, NJ: Prentice Hall/Merrill.

Albright, A. L. (1995). Spastic cerebral palsy: Approaches to drug treatment. *CNS Drugs, 4*(1), 17–27.

Alexander, R. (1991). Prespeech and feeding. In J. L. Bigge (Ed.), *Teaching individuals with physical and multiple disabilities* (pp. 175–198). Upper Saddle River, NJ: Prentice Hall/Merrill.

Alliance for Technology Access. (1996). *Computer resources for people with disabilities.* Salt Lake City, UT: Hunter House.

Alterescu, V. (1985). The ostomy. What do you teach the patient? *American Journal of Nursing, 11,* 1250–1253.

American Family Health Institute. (1986). *Oxygen therapy.* Springhouse, PA: Springhouse.

Anderson, D. M. (1982). Ten years later: Toilet training in the post-Azrin-and-Foxx era. *Journal of the Association for the Severely Handicapped, 7*(2), 71–79.

Anderson, S. (1991). Daily care. In E. Geralis (Ed.), *Children with cerebral palsy: A parent's guide* (pp. 91–132). Bethesda, MD: Woodbine.

Ashcroft, W. J., & Smith, S. C. (1993). *Take care: A transdisciplinary approach to the development of health and safety programs.* Nashville, TN: SCALARS.

Austan, F. (1992). Ventilator-assisted patient vocalization with positive end-expiratory pressure and tracheostomy cuff leak: A brief report. *Heart and Lung, 21,* 575–577.

Avery, M. E., & First, L. R. (1994). *Pediatric medicine* (2nd ed.). Baltimore: Williams & Wilkins.

Baer, D., Peterson, R., & Sherman, J. (1967). The development of imitation by reinforcing behavioral similarity to a model. *Journal of the Experimental Analysis of Behavior, 10,* 405–416.

Bailey, C., Kattwinkel, J., Teja, K., & Buckley, T. (1988). Shallow versus deep endotracheal suctioning in young rabbits: Pathologic effects on the tracheobronchial wall. *Pediatrics, 82,* 746–751.

Baker, B. L., & Brightman, A. J. (1989). *Steps to independence: A skills training guide for parents and teachers of children with special needs* (2nd ed.). Baltimore: Brookes.

Baker, M., Banfield, C., Kilburn, D., & Shufflebarger, K. (1991). *Controlling movement: A therapeutic approach to early intervention.* Gaithersburg, MD: Aspen.

Bakke, A., & Hoisaeter, P. A. (1994). Clean intermittent catheterization in lower urinary tract dysfunction: An overview. *Scandinavian Journal of Nephrology, Suppl., 157,* 55–60.

Bandura, A. (1969). *Principles of behavior modification.* New York: Holt, Rinehart & Winston.

Barnes, L. P. (1992). Tracheostomy care: Preparing parents for discharge. *MCN American Journal of Maternal Child Nursing, 17,* 293.

Batshaw, M. L., Blum, N., Borda, C., DaCosta, A., George, S. V., Mars, A. E., Starr, H. L., & Wang, P. P. (1996). Medications. In L. A. Kurtz, P. W. Dowrick, S. Levy, & M. L. Batshaw (Eds.), *Handbook of developmental disabilities: Resources for interdisciplinary care* (pp. 400–426). Gaithersburg, MD: Aspen.

Batshaw, M. L., & Perret, Y. M. (1997). *Children with handicaps: A medical primer.* Baltimore: Brookes.

Baumgart, D., Brown, L., Pumpian, I., Nisbet, J., Ford, A., Sweet, M., Messina, R., & Schroeder, J. (1982). Principle of partial participation and individualized adaptations in educational programs for severely handicapped students. *Journal of the Association for the Severely Handicapped, 7,* 17–27.

Beckman, D. (1994, September). *Oral motor assessment and intervention.* Continuing Education course sponsored by Milestones Seminars, Jacksonville, FL.

Beckman, D., Roberts, L., & Tencza, C. (1992). *Mealtime challenges: Eating assistance for individuals with severe oral motor challenges.* Produced for the Oklahoma Department of Human Services by Therapeutic Concepts, Winter Park, FL.

Behrman, R. E. (1992). *Nelson textbook of pediatrics.* Philadelphia: Saunders.

Berry, D. R. (1991). *Suctioning an endotracheal or tracheostomy airway.* In D. P. Smith, K. S. Nix, J. Y. Kemper, J. Liguori, D. K. Brantly, R. H. Rollins, N. V. Stevens, & L. B. Clutter (Eds.), *Comprehensive child and family nursing skills* (pp. 555–560). St. Louis: Mosby–Year Book.

Beukelman, D., McGinnis, J., & Morrow, D. (1991). Vocabulary selection in augmentative and alternative communication. *Augmentative and Alternative Communication, 7,* 171–185.

Beukelman, D. R., & Mirenda, P. (1992). *Augmentative and alternative communication: Management of severe communication disorders in children and adults.* Baltimore: Brookes.

Bidabe, L., & Lollar, J. M. (1990). *MOVE: Mobility opportunities via education.* Bakersfield, CA: Kern County Superintendent of Schools Office.

Biering-Sorensen, M., & Biering-Sorensen, F. (1992). Tracheostomy in special cord injured: Frequency and follow up. *Paraplegia, 30,* 656–660.

Bigge, J. L. (1991). *Teaching individuals with physical and multiple disabilities.* New York: Macmillan.

Binard, J. E., Persky, L., Lockhart, J., & Kelley, B. (1996). Intermittent catheterization the right way! (Volume vs. time-directed). *Journal of Spinal Cord Medicine, 19,* 194–196.

Blackman, J. A. (1990). *Medical aspects of developmental disabilities in children birth to three.* Rockville, MD: Aspen.

Bockus, S. (1991). Troubleshooting your tube feedings. *American Journal of Nursing, 91,* 24–28.

Bockus, S. (1993). When your patient needs tube feedings: Making the right decisions. *Nursing 93, 23,* 34–43.

Borwell, B. (1996). Colostomies and their management. *Nursing Standard, 13*(11), 49–53.

Bos, C. S., & Vaughn, S. (1998). *Strategies for teaching students with learning and behavior problems.* Boston: Allyn & Bacon.

Brook, I. (1995). Anaerobic infections in children with neurological impairments. *American Journal on Mental Retardation, 99,* 579–594.

Brown, L., Branston, M., Hamre-Nietupski, S., Pumpian, I., Certo, N., & Gruenewald, L. (1979). A strategy for developing chronological age appropriate and functional curricular content for severely handicapped adolescents and young adults. *Journal of Special Education, 13,* 81–90.

Brown, L., Falvey, M., Vincent, L., Kaye, N., Johnson, F., Ferrara-Parrish, P., & Gruenewald, L. (1980). Strategies for generating comprehensive, longitudinal, and chronological-age-appropriate individualized education programs for adolescent and young-adult severely handicapped students. *Journal of Special Education, 14*(2), 199–215.

Bussy, V., Marechal, F., & Nasca, S. (1992). Microbial contamination of enteral feeding tubes occurring during nutritional treatment. *Journal of Parenteral and Enteral Nutrition, 16,* 552–557.

Buzz-Kelly, L., & Gordin, P. (1993). Teaching CPR to parents of children with tracheostomies. *MCN American Journal of Maternal Child Nursing, 18,* 158–163.

Campbell, C. E. (1994). Diarrhea not always linked to tube feedings. *American Journal of Nursing, 94,* 59–60.

Campbell, P. H. (1993). Physical management and handling procedures. In M. E. Snell (Ed.), *Instruction of students with severe disabilities* (pp. 248–263). Upper Saddle River, NJ: Prentice Hall/Merrill.

Case-Smith, J. (1994). Self-care strategies for children with developmental deficits. In C. Christiansen (Ed.), *Ways of living: Self-care strategies for special needs* (pp. 101–156). Rockville, MD: American Occupational Therapy Association.

Cataldo, P. A. (1993). History of stomas. In J. M. MacKeigan & P. A. Cataldo (Eds.), *Intestinal stomas: Principles, techniques, and management.* (pp. 3–37). St. Louis: Quality Medical.

Cedar Rapids Community School District v. Garret, F., 67, U.S.L.W. 4165 (1999).

Celli, B. R. (1994). Home mechanical ventilation. In M. J. Tobin (Ed.), *Principles and practice of mechanical ventilation* (pp. 619–629). New York: McGraw-Hill.

Chai, T., Chung, W. D., Belville, W. D., & Faerber, G. J. (1995). Compliance and complications of clean intermittent catheterization in the spinal cord injured patient. *Paraplegia, 33,* 161–163.

Chameides, L. (1988). *Textbook of pediatric advanced life support.* Dallas: American Heart Association and American Academy of Pediatrics.

Cheng, E. Y., Richards, I., & Kaplan, W. E. (1996). Use of bladder stimulation in high risk patients. *Journal of Urology, 156,* 749–752.

Ciocon, J. O., Galindo-Ciocon, D. J., Tiessen, C., & Galindo, D. (1992). Continuous compared with intermittent tube feeding in the elderly. *Journal of Parenteral and Enteral Nutrition, 16,* 525–528.

Connis, R. (1979). The effects of sequential pictorial cues, self-recording and praise on the job task sequencing of retarded adults. *Journal of Applied Behavior Analysis, 12,* 355–361.

Connor, F. P., Williamson, G. G., & Siepp, J. M. (1978). *Program guide for infants and toddlers with neuromotor and other developmental disabilities.* New York: Teachers College Press.

Corman, M. L. (1993). Preoperative considerations. In J. M. MacKeigan & P. A. Cataldo (Eds.), *Intestinal stomas: Principles, techniques, and management* (pp. 52–59). St. Louis: Quality Medical.

Danella, E., & Vogtle, L. (1992). Neurodevelopmental treatment for the young child with cerebral palsy. In J. Case-Smith & C. Pehoski (Eds.), *Development of hand skills in the child* (pp. 91–110). Rockville, MD: American Occupational Therapy Association.

Deacon, J., & Beachy, P. (1991). Administering tube feedings. In D. P. Smith, K. S. Nix, J. Y. Kemper, R. Liguori, D. K. Brantly, J. H. Rollins, N. V. Stevens, & L. B. Clutter (Eds.), *Comprehensive child and family nursing skills* (pp. 418–428). St. Louis: Mosby.

Department of Education. (1992, September 29). Assistance to states for the education of children with disabilities program and preschool grants for children with disabilities, Final Rule, 57 (189). *Federal Register* (34 CFR Parts 300–301, pp. 44801–44802). Washington, DC: U.S. Government Printing Office.

Department of Education, Hawaii v. Katherine D., 727 F.2d 809 (9th Cir. 1983).

Derrickson, J. G., Neef, N. A., & Parrish, J. M. (1991). Teaching self-administration of suctioning to children with tracheostomies. *Journal of Applied Behavior Analysis, 24,* 563–570.

Deterding, C. (1996). Computer access options. In J. Hammel (Ed.), *AOTA self-paced clinical course: Technology and occupational therapy: A link to function (lesson 6).* Bethesda, MD: American Occupational Therapy Association.

Detsel v. Board of Education of the Auburn Enlarged City School District, 637 F. Supp. 1022 (NDNY, 1986).

Diamont, R. B. (1992). *Positioning for play: Home activities for parents of young children.* Tucson, AZ: Therapy Skill Builders.

Doberneck, R. C. (1991). Revision and closure of the colostomy. *Surgical Clinics of North America, 71*(1), 193–201.

Dorland's illustrated medical dictionary. (28th ed.) (1994). Philadelphia: Saunders.

Doster, S., & Politano, P. (1996). Augmentative and alternative communication. In J. Hammel (Ed.), *AOTA self-paced clinical course: Technology and occupational therapy: A link to function (Lesson 8).* Bethesda, MD: American Occupational Therapy Association.

Dowden, P., Beukelman, D., & Lossing, C. (1986). Serving nonspeaking patients in acute care settings: Intervention outcomes. *Augmentative and Alternative Communication, 2,* 38–44.

Doyle, P., Wolery, M., Ault, M., & Gast, D. (1988). System of least prompts: A literature review of procedural parameters. *Journal of the Association for Persons with Severe Handicaps, 13,* 28–40.

DPHD Critical Issues and Leadership Committee. (1999). Special report: Position statement on specialized health care procedures. *Physical Disabilities: Education and Related Services, 18*(1), 1–2.

Drabman, R. G., Cordua y Cruz, G., Ross, J., & Lynd, S. (1979). Suppression of chronic drooling in mentally retarded children and adolescents: Effectiveness of a behavior treatment package. *Behavior Therapy, 10,* 46–56.

Dunlap, C. I., & Marchionno, P. (1983). Help your COPD patient take a better breath with inhalers. *Nursing, 13*(5), 42–43.

Dunlap, G., Koegel, R., & Koegel, L. (1984). Continuity of treatment: Toilet training in multiple community settings. *Journal of the Association for Persons with Severe Handicaps, 9*(2), 134–141.

Eicher, P. S., & Kerwin, M. E. (1996). Feeding and nutritional concerns. In L. A. Kurtz, P. W. Dowrick, S. E. Levy, & M. L. Batshaw (Eds.), *Handbook of developmental disabilities: Resources for interdisciplinary care* (pp. 327–341). Gaithersburg, MD: Aspen.

Eisenberg, P. (1989). Enteral nutrition: Indications, formulas, and delivery techniques. *Nursing Clinics of North America, 24,* 315–337.

Elliott, M. (1991). Administering intradermal, subcutaneous, and intramuscular injections. In D. P. Smith, K. W. Nix, J. Y. Kemper, R. Liguori, D. K. Brantly, J. H. Rollins, N. V. Stevens, & L. B. Clutter (Eds.), *Comprehensive child and family nursing skills* (pp. 669–679). St. Louis: Mosby–Year Book.

Ellis, E. S., & Sabornie, E. J. (1986). *Teaching learning strategies to learning disabled students in postsecondary settings.* Unpublished manuscript, University of South Carolina, Columbia.

Epps, S., Stern, R. J., & Horner, R. H. (1990). Comparison of simulation training on self and using a doll for teaching generalized menstrual care to women with severe mental retardation. *Research in Developmental Disabilities, 11,* 37–66.

Fallen, N. H., & Umansky, W. (1985). *Young children with special needs.* Upper Saddle River, NJ: Prentice Hall/Merrill.

Falvey, M. (1989). *Community-based curriculum* (2nd ed.). Baltimore: Brookes.

Farr, K. S. (1991). Maintaining an ostomy. In D. Smith, K. Nix, J. Y. Kemper, R. Liguori, D. K. Brantly, J. H. Rollins, N. V. Stevens, & L. B. Clutter (Eds.), *Comprehensive child and family nursing skills* (pp. 450–457). St. Louis: Mosby–Year Book.

Fisher, W. W., Piazza, C. C., Bowman, L. G., Kurtz, P. F., Sherer, M. R., & Lachman, S. R. (1994). A preliminary evaluation of empirically derived consequences for the treatment of pica. *Journal of Applied Behavior Analysis, 27*(3), 447–457.

Fox, K. A., Mularski, R. A., Sarfati, M. R., Brooks, M. E., Wameke, J. A., Hunter, G. C., & Rappaport, W. D. (1995). Aspiration pneumonia following surgically placed feeding tubes. *American Journal of Surgery, 170,* 564–567.

Foxx, R. (1981). *Effective behavioral programming: Graduated guidance and backward chaining.* Champaign, IL: Research Press.

Foxx, R. M., & Azrin, N. H. (1973). *Toilet training persons with developmental disabilities: A rapid program for day and nighttime independent toileting.* Champaign, IL: Research Press.

Foxx, R. M., & Martin, E. D. (1975). Treatment of scavenging behavior (coprophangy and pica) by overcorrection. *Behavioral Research and Therapy, 13,* 153–162.

Fraser, B. A., Hensinger, R. N., & Phelps, J. A. (1990). *Physical management of multiple handicaps: A professional's guide* (2nd ed.). Baltimore: Brookes.

Frauman, A. C., & Brandon, D. H. (1996). Toilet training for the child with chronic illness. *Pediatric Nursing, 22,* 469–472.

Friedman, Y., Filder, J., Mizock, B., Samuel, J., Patel, S., Appavu, S., & Roberts, R. (1996). Comparison of percutaneous and surgical tracheostomies. *Chest, 110,* 480–485.

Fried-Oken, M., Howard, J. M., & Stewart, S. R. (1991). Feedback on AAC intervention from adults who are temporarily unable to speak. *Augmentative and Alternative Communication, 7,* 43–50.

Gadow, K. D. (1986). *Children on medication* (Vols. 1 & 2). Boston: College-Hill.

Galindo-Ciocon, D. J. (1993). Tube feeding: Complications among the elderly. *Gerontological Nursing, 19,* 17–22.

Gallagher, M. W., Tyson, K. R. T., & Ashcraft, K. W. (1973). Gastrostomy in pediatric patients: An analysis of complications and techniques. *Surgery, 74,* 536–539.

Gauderer, W. L., & Stellato, T. A. (1986). Gastrostomies: Evolution, techniques, indications, and complications. *Current Problems in Surgery, 23,* 661–719.

Geralis, E. (1998). *Children with cerebral palsy: A parent's guide.* Bethesda, MD: Woodbine.

Geyer, L. A., Okino, S. J., & Kurtz, L. A. (1996). Activities of daily living. In M. L. Batshaw, P. W. Dowrick, L. A. Kurtz, & S. E. Levy (Eds.), *Hand-*

book of developmental disabilities: Resources for inter-disciplinary care (pp. 449–458). Gaithersburg, MD: Aspen.

Gilgoff, I. S., Peng, R., & Keens, T. G. (1992). Hypoventilation and apnea in children during mechanically assisted ventilation. *Chest, 101,* 1500–1506.

Glennen, S., & DeCoste, D. C. (1997). *The handbook of augmentative and alternative communication.* San Diego, CA: Singular.

Glennen, S. L. (1997). AAC in the hospital setting. In S. L. Glennen & D. C. DeCoste (Eds.), *The handbook of augmentative and alternative communication* (pp. 603–628). San Diego, CA: Singular.

Golz, H. (1981). Complications of external condom drainage. *Paraplegia, 19,* 189.

Gorfine, S. R., Bauer, J. J., & Gelernt, M. P. (1993). Continent stomas. In J. M. MacKeigan & P. A. Cataldo (Eds.), *Intestinal stomas: Principles, techniques, and management* (pp. 154–187). St. Louis: Quality Medical.

Graff, J. C., Ault, M. M., Guess, D., Taylor, M., & Thompson, B. (1990). *Health care for students with disabilities.* Baltimore: Brookes.

Gramlich, T. (1992). Home mechanical ventilation. In S. P. Pilbeam (Ed.), *Mechanical ventilation: Physiological and clinical applications* (pp. 567–599). St. Louis: Mosby–Year Book.

Gray, M. (1996). Atraumatic urethral catheterization of children. *Pediatric Nursing, 22,* 306–310.

Groher, M. E. (1992). *Dysphagia: Diagnosis and management.* Boston: Butterworth–Heinemann.

Grotz, R. L., & Pemberton, J. H. (1993). Stoma physiology. In J. M. MacKeigan & P. A. Cataldo (Eds.), *Intestinal stomas: Principles, techniques, and management* (pp. 38–51), St. Louis: Quality Medical.

Grundfast, K. M., & Hennessy, P. A. (1985). Home care of the child with a tracheostomy. In E. N. Myers, S. E. Stool, & J. T. Johnson (Eds.), *Tracheotomy* (pp. 235–250). New York: Churchill Livingstone.

Guttmann, L., & Frankel, H. (1966). The value of intermittent catheterization in the early management of traumatic paraplegia and tetraplegia. *Paraplegia, 4,* 63–85.

Guyton, A. C. (1995). *Textbook of medical physiology.* Philadelphia: Saunders.

Haas, M. B. (1993). Individualized healthcare plans. In M. B. Haas, M. J. Gerber, K. M. Kalb, R. E. Luehr, W. R. Miller, C. K. Silkworth, & S. I. Will (Eds.),

The school nurse's source book of individualized health-care plans (pp. 41–44). North Branch, MN: Sunrise River.

Haas-Beckert, B., & Heyman, M. B. (1993). Comparison of two skin-level gastrostomy feeding tubes for infants and children. *Pediatric Nursing, 19,* 350–364.

Hanson, M. J., & Harris, S. R. (1986). *Teaching the young child with motor delays: A guide for parents and professionals.* Austin, TX: PRO-ED.

Harris, S. P., & Prudy, A. H. (1987). Drooling and its management in cerebral palsy. *Developmental Medicine and Child Neurology, 27,* 805–814.

Hart, V. (1988). Multiply disabled children. In V. Hasselt, P. Strain, & M. Hersen (Eds.), *Handbook of developmental and physical disabilities* (pp. 370–383). New York: Pergamon Press.

Haynie, M., Porter, S., & Palfey, J. (1989). *Children assisted by medical technology in educational settings: Guidelines for care.* Boston: Children's Hospital.

Heller, K. W., Alberto, P. A., & Bowdin, J. (1995). Interactions of communication partners and students who are deaf-blind: A model. *Journal of Visual Impairments and Blindness, 89,* 391–401.

Heller, K. W., Alberto, P. A., Forney, P. E., & Schwartzman, M. N. (1996). *Understanding physical, sensory, and health impairments: Characteristics and educational implications.* Pacific Grove, CA: Brooks/Cole.

Heller, K. W., Alberto, P., & Meagher, T. (1996). The impact of physical impairments on academic performance. *Journal of Physical and Developmental Disabilities, 8,* 233–245.

Heller, K. W., Alberto, P. A., Schwartzman, M. N., Shiplett, K., Pierce, J., Polokoff, J., Heller, E. J., Andrews, D. G., Briggs, A., & Kana, T. G. (1992). *Suggested physical health procedures for educators of students with special needs.* Atlanta: Georgia State University.

Heller, K. W., Fredrick, L., & Rithmire, N. (1997). Special health care procedures in the schools. *Physical Disabilities: Education and Related Services, 14,* 5–22.

Heubner, K. M., Prickett, J. G., Welch, T. R., & Joffee, E. (Eds.). (1995). *Hand in hand: Essentials of communication and orientation and mobility for your students who are deaf-blind.* New York: American Foundation for the Blind.

Hill, N. S., Redline, S., Carskadon, M. A, Curran, F. J., & Millman, R. P. (1992). Sleep-disordered breathing in patients with Duchenne muscular dystrophy using negative pressure ventilators. *Chest, 102,* 1656–1662.

Honig, A. (1993). Toilet learning. *Day Care and Early Education, 21*(1), 6–9.

Instructions for visual hygiene. (1996, Spring). (Available from Parents Active for Vision Education, 9620 Chesapeake Drive, Suite 105, San Diego, CA 92123.)

Irving Independent School District v. Tatro, 468 U.S. 883, 104S. Ct. 3371 (1984).

Jamerson, P. A. (1991). Administering and monitoring oxygen. In D. P. Smith, K. S. Nix, J. Y. Kemper, R. Liguori, D. K. Brantly, J. H. Rollins, N. V. Stevens, & L. B. Clutter (Eds.), *Comprehensive child and family nursing skills* (pp. 568–577). St. Louis: Mosby.

Janz, J. (1993). *Children with special health needs in school: Developing an individualized educational program (IEP) and an individualized heath care plan (IHCP).* Paper presented at the 71st Annual Convention of the CEC, San Antonio, TX.

Johnson, H., & Scott, A. (1993). *A practical approach to saliva control.* Tucson, AZ: Communication Skill Builders.

Jones, D. E., Clatterbuck, C. C., Marquis, J., Turnbull, H. R., & Moberly, R. L. (1996). Educational placements for children who are ventilator assisted. *Exceptional Children, 63,* 47–57.

Kacmarek, R. M., & Hess, D. (1994). Home mechanical ventilation. In M. J. Tobin (Ed.), *Principles and practice of mechanical ventilation* (pp. 111–154). New York: McGraw-Hill.

Kamen, R. S., & Watson, B. C. (1991). Effects of long-term tracheostomy on spectral characteristics of vowel production. *Journal of Speech and Hearing Research, 34,* 1057–1065.

Kaplan, S. A. (1994). The neurogenic bladder. In R. R. Bahnson (Ed.), *Management of urologic disorders* (pp. 9.1–9.11). London: Wolfe.

Kerr, D. L. (1991). Schools need to provide infection control training and supplies. *Journal of School Health, 61,* 106–107.

Keyes, K., Bisno, B., Richardson, J., & Marston, A. (1987). Age differences in coping, behavioral dysfunction and depression following colostomy surgery. *Gerontologist, 27*(2), 182–184.

Khoury, D. A., Beck, D. E., Opelka, F. G., Hicks, T. C., Timmcke, A. E., & Gathright, J. B. (1996). Colostomy closure. *Diseases of the Colon and Rectum, 39,* 605–609.

Kleiber, C., Krutzfield, N., & Rose, E. F. (1988). Acute histologic changes in the tracheobronchial tree associated with different suction catheter insertion techniques. *Heart Lung, 17,* 10–14.

Klein, M. D. (1983). *Pre-dressing skills: Skill starters for self-help development* (rev. ed.). Tucson, AZ: Communication Skill Builders.

Klein, M. D. (Ed.). (1990). *Parent articles for early intervention.* Tucson, AZ: Therapy Skill Builders.

Klein, M. D., & Delaney, T. A. (1994). *Feeding and nutrition for the child with special needs.* Tucson, AZ: Therapy Skill Builders.

Knight, D., & Wadsworth, D. E. (1994). Guidelines for educating students who are technology-dependent. *Physical Disabilities: Education and Related Services, 13*(1), 1–8.

Koehler, W., & Loftin, M. (1994). Visually impaired children with progressive, terminal neurodegenerative disorders. *Journal of Visual Impairments and Blindness, 88,* 317–328.

Koheil, R., Sochaniwskyj, A., Bablich, K., Kenny, D., & Milner, M. (1987). Biofeedback techniques and behavior modification in the conservative remediation of drooling by children with cerebral palsy. *Developmental Medicine and Child Neurology, 29,* 19–26.

Kohn, C., & Keithley, J. (1989). Enteral nutrition: Potential complication and patient monitoring. *Nursing Clinics of North America, 24,* 339–353.

Kosorok, P. (1995). Colostomy tube: New device for a continent colostomy. *Diseases of the Colon and Rectum, 38,* 760–763.

Kramer, L., & Whitehurst, C. (1981, December). Effects of button features on self-dressing in young retarded children. *Education and Training of the Mentally Retarded,* 277–283.

Kuntz, K. R. (1996a). Bladder catheterization. In L. A. Kurtz, P. W. Dowrick, S. E. Levy, & M. L. Batshaw (Eds.), *Handbook of developmental disabilities: Resources for interdisciplinary care* (pp. 395–397). Gaithersburg, MD: Aspen.

Kuntz, K. R. (1996b). Care of tracheostomy sites. In L. A. Kurtz, P. W. Dowrick, S. E. Levy, & M. L. Batshaw (Eds.), *Handbook of developmental disabilities: Resources for interdisciplinary care* (pp. 374–378). Gaithersburg, MD: Aspen.

Kuntz, K. R. (1996c). Gastrostomy care. In L. A. Kurtz, P. W. Dowrick, S. E. Levy, & M. L. Batshaw (Eds.), *Handbook of developmental disabilities: Re-*

sources for interdisciplinary care (pp. 378–383). Gaithersburg, MD: Aspen.

Kuntz, K. R. (1996d). Nasogastric tubes/feeding pumps. In L. A. Kurtz, P. W. Dowrick, S. E. Levy, & M. L. Batshaw (Eds.), *Handbook of developmental disabilities: Resources for interdisciplinary care* (pp. 378–383). Gaithersburg, MD: Aspen.

Lafontaine, L. M., & DeRuyter, F. (1987). The non-speaking cerebral palsied: A clinical and demographic database report. *Augmentative and Alternative Communication, 2,* 153–162.

Lapides, L., Diokno, A. C., Silber, S. L., & Lowe, B. S. (1972). Clean, intermittent self-catheterization in the treatment of urinary tract disease. *Journal of Urology, 107,* 458–461.

Lavery, I. C., & Erwin-Toth, P. (1993). Stoma therapy. In J. M. MacKeigan & P. A. Cataldo (Eds.), *Intestinal stomas: Principles, techniques, and management* (pp. 60–84). St. Louis: Quality Medical.

Lazar, L., Kovalivker, M., Erez, I., & Motovic, A. (1993). Simple method of dilatation for strictured colostomy in children. *Diseases of the Colon and Rectum, 36,* 199.

Levesque, P. E., Bauer, S. B., Atala, A., Zurakowski, D., Colodny, A., Peters, C., & Retik, A. B. (1996). Ten-year experience with the artificial urinary sphincter in children. *Journal of Urology, 156,* 625–628.

Levine, J. M. (1996). Including children dependent on ventilators in school. *Teaching Exceptional Children, 28*(3), 25–29.

Light, J. (1997). "Let's go star fishing": Reflections on the contexts of language learning for children who use aided AAC. *Augmentative and Alternative Communication, 12,* 158–171.

Londono-Schimmer, E. E., Leong, A., & Phillips, R. (1994). Life table analysis of stomal complications following colostomy. *Diseases of the Colon and Rectum, 37,* 916–920.

Louch, G. K. (1993). Chronic lung disease. In M. Krajicek & R. Tompkins (Eds.), *The medically fragile infant* (pp. 61–76). Austin, TX: PRO-ED.

Loumiet, R., & Levack, N. (1993). *Independent living: A curriculum with adaptations for students with visual impairments. Vol. II: Self-care and maintenance of personal environment.* Austin: Texas School for the Blind and Visually Impaired. Austin, Texas.

Lovaas, O. I. (1981). *Teaching developmentally disabled children: The me book.* Austin, TX: PRO-ED.

Lovell, W. W., & Winter, R. B. (1986). *Pediatric orthopaedics* (3rd ed.). New York: Lippincott.

Lozes, M. (1988). Bladder and bowel management for children with myelomeningocele. *Infants and Young Children, 1,* 52–62.

Luiselli, J. K. (1994). Oral feeding treatment of children with chronic food refusal and multiple disabilities. *American Journal of Mental Retardation, 98,* 646–655.

Luiselli, J. K., & Luiselli, T. E. (1995). A behavior analysis approach toward chronic food refusal in children with gastrostomy-tube dependency. *Topics in Early Childhood Special Education, 15*(1), 1–18.

MacDonald, S. (1992, May 27). Imperfect vision: 20/20 score no guarantee of problem-free eyesight. *Cincinnati Enquirer,* Section D.

Mackay, B. J. (1991). Administering medications by nebulization. In D. P. Smith, K. W. Nix, J. Y. Kemper, R. Liguori, D. K. Brantly, J. H. Rollins, N. V. Stevens, & L. B. Clutter (Eds.), *Comprehensive child and family nursing skills* (pp. 658–663). St. Louis: Mosby–Year Book.

Mackay, B. J. (1993). Performing chest physiotherapy. In D. P. Smith, K. S. Nix, J. Y. Kemper, J. Liguori, D. K. Brantly, R. H. Rollins, N. V. Stevens, & L. B. Clutter (Eds.), *Comprehensive child and family nursing skills* (pp. 560–568). St. Louis: Mosby–Year Book.

Macomb County Intermediate School District v. Joshua S., 715 F. Supp. 824 (E.D., Mich. 1989).

Martin, J., Rusch, F., James, V., Decker, P., & Trytol, K. (1982). The use of picture cues to establish self-control in the preparation of complex meals by mentally retarded adults. *Applied Research in Mental Retardation, 3,* 105–119.

Mason, J., Murty, G. E., Foster, H., & Bradley, P. J. (1992). Tracheostomy self care: The Nottingham System. *Journal of Laryngology and Otology, 106,* 723–724.

Matas, J. A., Mathy-Laikko, P. B, Beukelman, D. R., & Legresley, K. (1985). Identifying the nonspeaking population: A demographic study. *Augmentative and Alternative Communication, 1,* 17–31.

McCamman, S., & Rues, J. (1990). Nutrition monitoring and supplementation. In J. C. Graff, M. M. Ault, D. Guess, M. Taylor, & B. Thompson (Eds.), *Health care for students with disabilities* (pp. 79–118). Baltimore: Brookes.

McCrae, J. A., & Hall, N. H. (1989). Current practices for home enteral nutrition. *Journal of American Dieticians Association, 89,* 233–240.

McDonald, G. J. (1994). Home oxygen therapy. In J. Turner, G. J. McDonald, & W. L. Larter (Eds.), *Handbook of adult and pediatric respiratory home care* (pp. 247–272). St. Louis: Mosby.

McDonald, P. L., Wilson, R., Turner, R., & Ault, M. (1988). In L. Sternbrg (Ed.), *Educating students with severe or profound handicaps* (pp. 53–100). Rockville, MD: Aspen.

McDonald, P. L., Wilson, R., Turner, T., & Mulligan-Ault, M. (1988). Classroom-based medical interventions. In L. Sternberg (Ed.), *Educating students with severe or profound handicaps* (2nd ed., pp. 53–99). Rockville, MD: Aspen.

McLaughlin, J. F., Murray, M., van Zandt, K., & Carr, M. (1996). Clean intermittent catheterization. *Developmental Medicine and Child Neurology, 38,* 446–454.

Medcom Trainex. (1993). *Universal precautions: AIDS and hepatitis B prevention for healthcare workers.* Garden Grove, CA: Medcom.

Mercer, C. D., & Mercer, A. R. (1998). *Teaching students with learning problems.* Upper Saddle River, NJ: Prentice Hall/Merrill.

Metheny, N., McSweeney, M., Wehrle, M. A., & Wiersema, L. (1990). Effectiveness of the auscultatory method in predicting feeding tube location. *Nursing Research, 39,* 262–267.

Metheny, N., Reed, L., Berglund, B., & Wehrle, M. A. (1994). Visual characteristics of aspirates from feeding tubes as a method for predicting tube location. *Research Journal of the American Nurses Association, 43,* 282–287.

Miller, F. R., Eliachar, I., & Tucker, H. M. (1995). Technique, management and complications of the long-term flap tracheostomy. *Laryngoscope, 105,* 543–547.

Mitsuda, P. M., Baarsiag-Benson, R., Hazel, K., & Therriault, T. M. (1992). In K. M. Yorkston (Ed.), *Augmentative communication in the medical setting.* Tucson, AZ: Communication Skill Builders.

Mizumori, N. A., Nelson, E. J., Prentice, W. S., & Withey, L. M. (1994). Mechanical ventilation in the home. In J. Turner, G. J. McDonald, & N. L. Larter (Eds.), *Handbook of adult and pediatric respiratory home care* (pp. 273–295). St. Louis: Mosby.

Moffitt, K. (1992). *Special children, special care.* Florida Diagnostic and Learning Resource System, Tampa, FL.

Morris, S. E. (1989). Development of oral-motor skills in the neurologically impaired child receiving non-oral feedings. *Dysphagia, 3,* 135–154.

Morris, S., & Klein, M. (1987). *Pre-feeding skills: A comprehensive resource for feeding development.* Tucson, AZ: Therapy Skill Builders.

Motoyama, E. K. (1985). Physiologic alternations in tracheostomy. In E. N. Myers, S. E. Stool, & J. T. Johnson (Eds.), *Tracheotomy* (pp. 117–200). New York: Churchill Livingstone.

Mulligan-Ault, M., Guess, D., Struth, L., & Thompson, B. (1988). The implementation of health-related procedures in classrooms for students with severe multiple impairments. *Journal for the Association of Persons with Severe Handicaps, 13,* 100–109.

Munk, D. D., & Repp, A. C. (1994). Behavioral assessment of feeding problems of individuals with severe disabilities. *Journal of Applied Behavioral Analysis, 27,* 241–250.

Myers, E. N., Stook, S. E., & Johnson, J. T. (1985). Technique of tracheostomy. In E. N. Myers, S. E. Stool, & J. T. Johnson (Eds.), *Tracheotomy* (pp. 113–125). New York: Churchill Livingstone.

Nadler, L. H. (1992). General considerations and complications of the ileostomy. *Ostomy/Wound Management, 38*(4), 18–22.

National Council of State Boards of Nursing. (1995). *Delegation: Concepts and decision-making process* [On-line]. Available: http://www.ncshn.org/pfiles/delefati.html.

Neeley v. Rutherford County Schools, 68F. 3rd 965 (6th Cir. 1995).

Nelson, V. S., Carroll, J. C., Hurvitz, E. A., & Dean, J. M. (1996). Home mechanical ventilation of children. *Developmental Medicine and Child Neurology, 38,* 704–715.

Nietupski, J., & Hamre-Nietupski, S. (1987). An ecological approach to curriculum development. In L. Goetz, D. Guess, & K. Stremel-Campbell (Eds.), *Innovative program design for individuals with sensory impairments.* (pp. 225–253) Baltimore: Brookes.

Nissim, L. G., & Sten, M. (1991). A ventilator-assisted child: A case for empowerment. *Pediatric Nursing, 17,* 507–511.

Nix, K. S. (1991a). Administering eye, ear, and nasal medication. In D. P. Smith, K. W. Nix, J. Y. Kemper, R. Liguori, D. K. Brantly, J. H. Rollins, N. V. Stevens, & L. B. Clutter (Eds.), *Comprehensive child and family nursing skills* (pp. 664–668). St. Louis: Mosby–Year Book.

Nix, K. S. (1991b). Administering metered-dose inhalers. In D. P. Smith, K. W. Nix, J. Y. Kemper, R. Liguori, D. K. Brantly, J. H. Rollins, N. V. Stevens, & L. B. Clutter (Eds.), *Comprehensive child and family nursing skills* (pp. 653–658). St. Louis: Mosby–Year Book.

Nix, K. S. (1991c). Administering oral medications. In D. P. Smith, K. W. Nix, J. Y. Kemper, R. Liguori, D. K. Brantly, J. H. Rollins, N. V. Stevens, & L. B. Clutter (Eds.), *Comprehensive child and family nursing skills* (pp. 646–652). St. Louis: Mosby–Year Book.

Oakshott, P., & Hunt, G. M. (1992). Intermittent self catheterization for patients with urinary incontinence or difficulty emptying the bladder. *British Journal of General Practice, 42,* 253–255.

Oberc, M. C. (1991a). Clearing an oral or nasal airway. In D. P. Smith, K. S. Nix, J. Y. Kemper, J. Liguori, D. K. Brantly, R. H. Rollins, N. V. Stevens, & L. B. Clutter (Eds.), *Comprehensive child and family nursing skills* (pp. 547–555). St. Louis: Mosby–Year Book.

Oberc, M. C. (1991b). Inserting and maintaining a gastric or jejunal tube. In D. P. Smith, K. S. Nix, J. Y. Kemper, R. Liguori, D. K. Brantly, J. H. Rollins, N. V. Stevens, & L. B. Clutter (Eds.), *Comprehensive child and family nursing skills* (pp. 418–428). St. Louis: Mosby–Year Book.

Orelove, F. P., & Sobsey, D. (1991). *Educating children with multiple disabilities: A transdisciplinary approach.* Baltimore: Brookes.

Orelove, F. P., & Sobsey, D. (1996). *Educating children with multiple disabilities: A transdisciplinary approach* (3rd ed.). Baltimore: Brookes.

Passy, V., Baydur, A., Prentice, W., & Darnell-Neal, R. (1993). Passy-Muir tracheostomy speaking valve on ventilator-dependent patients. *Laryngoscope, 103,* 653–658.

Pearl, R. K., & Abcarian, H. (1993). Diverting Stomas. In J. M. MacKeigan & P. A. Cataldo (Eds.), *Intestinal stomas: Principles, techniques, and management* (pp. 107–126). St. Louis: Quality Medical.

Pellock, J. M. (1984). Efficacy and adverse effects of antiepileptic drugs. *Pediatric Clinics of North America, 36,* 435–448.

Pemberton, J. (1988). Management of conventional ileostomies. *World Journal of Surgery, 12,* 203–210.

Perry, A. G., & Potter, P. A. (1990). *Clinical nursing skills and techniques.* St. Louis: Mosby.

Perry, D., Johnson, S., & Trump, D. (1983). Gastrostomy and the neonate. *American Journal of Nursing, 83,* 1030–1033.

Physicians' Desk Reference. (1999). *Physicians' desk reference* (53rd ed.). Montvale, NJ: Medical Economics.

Pilbeam, S. P. (1992). *Mechanical ventilation: Physiological and clinical applications.* St. Louis: Mosby–Year Book.

Plummer, A. L., O'Donohue, W. J., & Petty, T. L. (1989). Conference report: Consensus conference on problems in home mechanical ventilation. *American Review of Respiratory Disorders, 140,* 555.

Plummer, N. (1983). *Tube feedings.* Bloomington, IN: Vocational Education Services.

Polloway, E. A., & Patton, J. R. (1993). *Strategies for teaching learners with special needs.* Upper Saddle River, NJ: Prentice Hall/Merrill.

Porter, S., Haynie, M., Bierle, T., Caldwell, T. H., & Palfrey, J. S. (1997). *Children assisted by medical technology in education settings: Guidelines for care.* Baltimore: Brookes.

Puhakka, H. J., Kero, P., Valli, P., & Iisalo, E. (1992). Tracheostomy in pediatric patients. *Acta Paediatrica, 81,* 231–234.

Radtka, S. (1977). Feeding reflexes and neural control. In J. M. Wilson (Ed.), *Oral-motor function and dysfunction in children* (pp. 96–105). Chapel Hill: University of North Carolina at Chapel Hill, Department of Medical Allied Health Professions, Division of Physical Therapy.

Rapport, M. J. (1996). Legal guidelines for the delivery of special health care services in schools. *Exceptional Children, 62,* 537–549.

Reid, S. R. (1996). Bowel and bladder function in neuromuscular disorders. In L. A. Kurtz, P. W. Dowrick, S. E. Levy, & M. L. Batshaw (Eds.), *Handbook of developmental disabilities: Resources for interdisciplinary care* (pp. 427–430). Gaithersburg, MD: Aspen.

Romski, M. A., & Sevcik, R. (1996). *Breaking the speech barrier: Language development through augmented means.* Baltimore: Brookes.

Rotegard, L., Hill, B., & Lakin, K. (1983). Sex as a bona fide occupational qualification for direct care staff in residences for mentally retarded people. *Mental Retardation, 21*(4), 150–152.

Rous, S. N. (1996). *Urology* (2nd ed.). Cambridge, MA: Blackwell Science.

Rushton, H. G. (1995). Wetting and functional voiding disorders. *Urologic Clinics of North America, 22,* 75–93.

Sale, N. (1992). *Manual of pediatric nursing procedures.* Philadelphia: Lippincott.

Salter, M. (1996). Advances in ileostomy care. *Nursing Standard, 11*(9), 49–53.

Sasaki, C. T., Suzuki, M., Horiuchi, M., & Kirchner, J. A. (1977). The effect of tracheostomy on the laryngeal closure reflex. *Laryngoscope, 87,* 1428.

Scanlan, M., & Frisch, S. (1992). Nasoduodenal feeding tubes: Prevention of occlusion. *Journal of Neuroscience Nursing, 24,* 256–259.

Schlessel, J. S., Harper, R. G., Rappa, H., Keningsberg, K., & Khanna, S. (1993). Tracheostomy: Acute and long-term mortality and morbidity in very low birth weight premature infants. *Journal of Pediatric Surgery, 28,* 873–876.

Schupf, N., Ortiz, M., & Kapell, D. (1995). Prevalence in intestinal parasite infections among individuals with mental retardation in New York State. *Mental Retardation, 33,* 84–89.

Senagore, A. (1993). Cecostomy. In J. M. MacKeigan & P. A. Cataldo (Eds.), *Intestinal stomas: Principles, techniques, and management* (pp. 127–134). St. Louis: Quality Medical.

Shephard, J., Procter, S. A., & Coley, I. L. (1996). Self-care and adaptations for independent living. In A. S. Allen, J. Case-Smith, & P. N. Pratt (Eds.), *Occupational therapy for children* (3rd ed., pp. 461–503). St. Louis: Mosby.

Shinkwin, C. A., & Gibbin K. P. (1996). Tracheostomy in children. *Journal of the Royal Society of Medicine, 89,* 188–192.

Simma, B., Spehler, D., Burger, R., Uehlinger, J., Ghelfi, D., Dangel, P., Hof, E., & Fanconi, S. (1994). Tracheostomy in children. *European Journal of Pediatrics, 153,* 291–296.

Simila, S., & Niskanen, P. (1991). Underweight and overweight cases among the mentally retarded. *Journal of Mental Deficiency Research, 35,* 160–164.

Skale, N. (1992). *Manual of pediatric nursing procedures.* Philadelphia: Lippincott.

Smith, D. P. (1992). Preventing transmission of infection in an acute care setting. In D. P. Smith, K. S. Nix, J. Y. Kemper, R. Liguori, D. K. Brantly, J. H. Rollins, N. V. Stevens, & L. B. Clutter (Eds.), *Comprehensive child and family nursing skills* (pp. 307–312). St Louis: Mosby–Year Book.

Smith, D. P., & Breen, M. (1991). Feeding techniques with gastroesophogeal reflux. In D. P. Smith, K. S. Nix, J. Y. Kemper, R. Liguori, D. K. Brantly, J. H. Rollins, N. V. Stevens, & L. B. Clutter (Eds.), *Comprehensive child and family nursing skills* (pp. 402–406). St. Louis: Mosby–Year Book.

Smith, R., Benge, M., & Hall, M. (1994). Technology for self-care. In C. Christiansen (Ed.), *Ways of living: Self-care strategies for special needs* (pp. 379–422). Rockville, MD: American Occupational Therapy Association.

Snell, M. E. (1993). *Instruction of students with severe disabilities* (4th ed.). Upper Saddle River, NJ: Prentice Hall/Merrill.

Snell, M., & Gast, D. (1981). Applying delay procedure to the instruction of the severely handicapped. *Journal of the Association for Persons with Severe Handicaps, 6,* 3–14.

Sobsey, R. (1983). Nutrition of children with severely handicapping conditions. *Journal of the Association for Persons with Severe Handicaps, 8*(4), 14–17.

Soliani, P., Carbognani, P., Piccolo, P., Sabbagh, R., & Cudazzo, E. (1992). Colostomy plug devices: A possible new approach to the problem of incontinence. *Diseases of the Colon and Rectum, 35,* 969–974.

Steadham, C. (1994). Health maintenance and promotion: Infancy through adolescence. In S. P. Roth & J. S. Morse (Eds.), *A life-span approach to nursing care* (pp. 147–169). Baltimore: Brookes.

Struck, M. (1996a). Assistive technology in the schools. In J. Hammel (Ed.), *AOTA self-paced clinical course: Technology and occupational therapy: A link to function (lesson 11).* Bethesda, MD: American Occupational Therapy Association.

Struck, M. (1996b). Augmentative communication and computer access. In A. S. Allen, J. Case-Smith, & P. N. Pratt (Eds.), *Occupational therapy for children* (3rd ed., pp. 545–562). St. Louis: Mosby.

Struck, M., & Corfman, S. K. (1994, September). Strategies for integration of adapted computer use. *School System Special Interest Section Newsletter, 1*(3), 3–4.

Suddarth, D. S. (1991). *The Lippincott manual of nursing practice.* Philadelphia: Lippincott.

Tamler, M. S., & Perrin, J. C. (1992). Use of a polyethylene body jacket to prevent feeding tube removal in an agitated patient with anoxic encephalopathy. *American Journal of Physical Medicine & Rehabilitation, 71,* 236–238.

Tarnowski, K. J., & Drabman, R. S. (1987). Teaching intermittent self-catheterization skills to mentally retarded children. *Research in Developmental Disabilities, 8,* 521–529.

Tayal, V. S. (1994). Tracheostomies. *Emergency Medicine Clinics of North America, 12,* 707–727.

Taylor, M. (1990). Clean intermittent catheterization. In J. C. Graff, M. M. Ault, D. Guess, M. Taylor, & B. Thompson (Eds.), *Health care for students with disabilities* (pp. 241–252). Baltimore: Brookes.

Testi, C. (1991). Maintaining a tracheostomy site and airway. In D. P. Smith, K. S. Nix, J. Y. Kemper, R. Liguori, D. K. Brantly, J. H. Rollins, N. V. Stevens, & L. B. Clutter (Eds.), *Comprehensive child and family nursing skills* (pp. 604–611). St. Louis: Mosby.

Thompson, B., & Guess, D. (1989). Students who experience the most profound disabilities: Teacher perspectives. In F. Brown & D. H. Lehr (Eds.), *Persons with profound disabilities: Issues and practices* (pp. 3–41). Baltimore: Brookes.

Thompson, T., & Hanson, R. (1983). Overhydration: Precautions when treating urinary incontinence. *Mental Retardation, 21*(4), 139–143.

Thorbecke, O., & Jackson, H. (1982). Reducing chronic drooling in a retarded female using a multi-treatment package. *Behavior Therapy and Experimental Psychiatry, 13,* 89–93.

Toursarkissian, B., Zweng, T. N., Kearney, P. A., Pofahl, W. E., Johnson, S. B., & Barder, D. E. (1994). Percutaneous dilation tracheostomy: Report of 141 cases. *Annuals of Thoracic Surgery, 57,* 862–867.

Traver, G. A., & Martinez, M. (1988). Asthma update. Part II: Treatment. *Journal of Pediatric Health Care, 2,* 227–233.

Umbreit, J., & Cardullias, P. J. (1980). *Educating the severely physically handicapped: Basic principles and techniques.* Columbus, OH: Council for Exceptional Children.

Urbano, M. (1992). *Preschool children with special health care needs.* San Diego: Singular.

Utley, B. (1991). Physical management, handling, and motor programming. In L. Sternberg (Ed.), *Educating students with severe or profound handicaps* (pp. 267–309). Rockville, MD: Aspen.

Vergara, E. (1993). *Foundations for practice in the neonatal intensive care unit and early intervention: A self-guided practice manual* (Vols. 1 & 2). Rockville, MD: American Occupational Therapy Association.

Wacker, D., & Berg, W. (1984). Use of peer instruction to train complex photocopying tasks to severely retarded adolescents. *Analysis and Intervention in Developmental Disabilities, 4,* 219–234.

Watkins, S. (Ed.). (1989). *The INSITE manual.* Logan: Utah State University: SKI★HI Institute.

Watt, R. (1985). The ostomy: Why is it created? *American Journal of Nursing, 85,* 1242–1245.

Webber-Jones, J., Sweeney, K., Winterbottom, A., Fontneau, L., Johnson, K., & Fradette, M. (1992). How to declog a feeding tube. *Nursing, 92,* 63–64.

Weilitz, P. B., & Dettenmeier, P. (1994). Test your knowledge of tracheostomy tubes. *American Journal of Nursing, 94,* 46–50.

Wein, A. J., & Barrett, D. M. (1988). *Voiding function and dysfunction: A logical and practical approach.* Chicago: Year Book Medical.

Weinstein, R. S., & Mayer, B. (1986). *Learning strategies.* In M. C. Wittrock (Ed.), *Handbook of research in teaching* (3rd ed., pp. 302–346). New York: Macmillan.

Westcott, M. A., Dynes, M. C., Remer, E. M., Donaldson, J. S., & Dias, L. S. (1992). Congenital and acquired orthopedic abnormalities in patients with myelomeningocele. *RadioGraphics, 12*(6), 1155–1173.

Wilcox, B., & Bellamy, G. T. (1982). *Design of high school programs for severely handicapped students.* Baltimore: Brookes.

Wolery, M., Ault, M. J., & Doyle, P. M. (1992). *Teaching students with moderate to severe disabilities.* New York: Longman.

Wolf, L. S., & Glass, R. P. (1992). *Feeding and swallowing disorders in infancy: Assessment and management.* Tucson, AZ: Therapy Skill Builders.

Wong, D. L. (1995). *Whaley & Wong's nursing care of infants and children.* St. Louis: Mosby.

Yorkston, K. M., Smith, K., & Beukelman, D. (1990). Extended communication samples of augmented communicators: A comparison of individualized versus standard single-word vocabularies. *Journal of Speech and Hearing Disorders, 55,* 217–224.

Young, C. K., & White, S. (1992). Tube feeding at home. *American Journal of Nursing, 92,* 46–53.

Glossary

Abduction. Movement out to the sides, away from the middle of the body.

Abductor pad. A pad used to move a limb away from the body.

Adaptive equipment. Devices that are used to assist the student to perform some function.

Adduction. Movement toward the middle of the body.

Adverse drug reactions. See *side effects.*

Aided AAC. A communication including any device that a student may use beyond her body to communicate to another person.

Alternative performance strategy. A manner of performing a behavior (form), other than that usually done by a nondisabled person, that achieves the same result (function).

Antecedent prompts. Alterations of, or additions to, the instructional material to focus student attention on the natural cue(s) for making correct responses.

Aspiration. The inhalation of food or liquids ingested by the mouth, secretions from the mouth or upper airway, or regurgitated stomach contents into the lungs.

Assistive strategies. Techniques that a person uses to help the student perform some task.

Asymmetrical. One side of the body being unequal or different than the other side.

Athetosis. Muscle tone that is at times too high and at other times too low (fluctuating tone).

Augmentative and alternative communication (AAC). The combination of all methods of communication available to an individual, including any speech, vocalization, gestures, and communication behaviors as well as specific communication strategies and communication aids.

Balance. The ability to maintain a steady position.

Bite reflex. Biting that occurs when the gums or teeth are stimulated.

Bolus. A round mass of food formed in the mouth.

Bolus tube-feeding method. A tube-feeding method using a syringe barrel to deliver the formula by gravity over a short period.

Bowel training. The process of teaching an individual to empty the bowel completely on a regularly scheduled basis.

Cannula. A tube for insertion into a duct or cavity. For tracheostomy tubes, it is the main curved shaft of the tracheostomy tube.

Catheter. A long, narrow, flexible tube that comes in various lengths and diameters and may be used for such procedures as suctioning and catheterization.

Caution steps. Steps in a task analysis in which injury could occur by a quick, jerking, or incorrect movement.

Cecostomy. The creation of an ostomy (surgical opening) with the cecum (part of the intestine) to empty fecal material.

Clean intermittent catheterization (CIC). A process in which a clean catheter is introduced through the urethra and into the bladder to empty urine.

Colostomy. Ostomy (surgical opening) of the large intestine to empty fecal material.

Colostomy irrigation. An enema that is given at the stoma.

Continuous gravity drip method. A tube-feeding method in which the formula is in a bag that is adjusted to drip at a certain rate by adjusting the clamp.

Continuous infusion method by pump. A tube-feeding method in which the formula is in a bag that is adjusted to drip at a certain rate by setting a mechanical pump.

Contracture. A limitation in joint mobility caused by permanent shortening of the muscle.

Crawling. Moving on one's stomach using the hands and knees to push forward.

Credé. Manual compression of the bladder to empty urine.

Creeping. Moving on hands and knees.

Decubitus ulcer. A skin breakdown that can occur when the student is in one position over an extended period of time. Also known as a *pressure sore*.

Discrepancy analysis. The format of direct observation of students performing functional skills to identify current performance capabilities and skills that require instruction and/or adaptation.

Drug interaction. An alteration in absorption, distribution, metabolism, and excretion of one drug by another.

Ecological inventory. An analysis of skills and activities identified by observing those necessary in community, home, school, and vocational settings in which areas of instruction may be determined for a student with a disability.

Enteral gavage. A process in which the feeding tube is placed into the small intestine for the purpose of giving fluids with high caloric value or nutritional feedings.

Equilibrium. The state or act of balance.

Errors. Incorrect responses can be organized according to the reason for the student's incorrect response. These include learning errors, physical errors, sensory errors, motivational errors, health errors, and communication errors.

Extension. Straightening a joint or a part of the body.

Face tent. A soft vinyl mask that fits loosely around the face and neck to deliver oxygen.

Flexion. Bending a joint or a part of the body.

Flow rate. The rate that gas (air/oxygen) flows into the lung. It is measured in liters per minute (L/min).

Gag reflex. A protective mechanism present at birth that prevents small particles from entering the trachea (windpipe).

Gastric gavage. A process in which the feeding tube is placed into the stomach for giving fluids. It is another term for *tube feeding;* from *gastric,* meaning "stomach," and *gavage,* meaning "feeding."

Gastroesophogeal reflux (GER). Spontaneous backward flow of stomach contents into the esophagus.

Gastrostomy button. A small, round silicon device that goes through the abdominal wall and is positioned at skin level. A connecting tube attaches to it for tube feedings to be given.

Gastrostomy tube. When a feeding tube is inserted through the abdominal wall into the stomach, it is referred to as a *gastrostomy tube.*

Generic name. The name of a drug's chemical compound.

Head control. The ability to control the head's position.

Health. A state of optimal mental, social, and physical well-being, not merely the absence of disease and infirmity.

High-pressure alarm. An alarm indicating that there is more resistance than normal to the air entering the lungs when the ventilator is providing a breath.

Hygiene. The science of health and the prevention of disease.

Hyperextension. Excessive extension of a limb or body part. *Neck hyperextension* refers to the neck bending back.

Hypersensitive gag. An exaggerated reaction compared to the response that would be expected.

Hypertonia. Increased muscle tone and increased resistance to passive stretching of the muscles. Also referred to as *high tone.*

Hypotonia. Diminished (or decreased) muscle tone and diminished resistance to passive stretching of the muscles. Also referred to as *low tone.*

Hypoxia. The decrease in oxygen to the tissues.

Ileal conduit. A ureter that is surgically connected to the intestine.

Ileostomy. An ostomy (surgical opening) made from

the ileum (part of the small intestine) to empty fecal material.

Individualized education program (IEP). A required program plan designed to specify the educational goals for the student that will be targeted for instruction.

Individualized health plan (IHP). A recommended health care plan designed to provide information on the student's medical status health needs, and individualized health care procedures.

Inspiratory time (I time). The amount of time in the ventilator's cycle that is used to deliver a breath.

Instructional strategies. Teaching techniques that are used to teach a student to perform a skill or learn targeted information.

Intermittent gravity drip feeding method. A tube-feeding method in which the formula is in a bag, and the formula is adjusted to drip more slowly over 20 to 30 minutes.

Jejunostomy. An ostomy (surgical opening) that is made with the jejunum (part of the small intestine) to empty fecal material.

Learned helplessness. The lack of persistence at tasks that could be mastered.

Learning, stages of. The cumulative levels of learning: acquisition (accurate performance of new skill), proficiency (accurate performance at an appropriate rate), maintenance (proficient performance over time), generalization (proficient performance across settings, materials, and persons), and application (applying the acquired skill to new situations).

Low-pressure alarm. An alarm indicating that there is little to no resistance when the ventilator is providing a breath.

Mechanical lift. A device used to lift a student from one location to another.

Multiple disability. The presence of two or more disabilities that usually creates an interactional, multiplicative effect rather than a simple, additive effect.

Muscle tone. The amount of tension of the body's muscles.

Nasal cannula. A vinyl tube with two small prongs that fit into the nostrils to deliver oxygen.

Nephrostomy. A opening made directly from the pelvis of the kidney through the abdominal wall.

Nonaided AAC. A communication system in which meaning has been assigned to some type of movement the person makes.

Nonsymbolic communication. The behaviors or expressions that a student displays to intentionally communicate with another person but that do not have a direct symbolic meaning.

Obturators. Thin, narrow devices that are used for insertion of the tracheostomy tube.

Orthopedic impairment. A skeletal system impairment that adversely affects a student's educational performance, including impairments caused by congenital anomalies and disease.

Ostomy. A term loosely referring to an operation resulting in artificial openings between two hollow organs or between an organ and the abdominal wall (e.g., made for a colostomy, tracheostomy, or gastrostomy).

Other health impairments. Impairments that result in limited strength, vitality, or alertness due to chronic or acute health problems (e.g., heart condition, tuberculosis, hemophilia, or diabetes).

Over-the-counter (OTC) drugs. Drugs that do not require a physician's order.

Oxygen control. A control that adjusts the percent of oxygen delivered to the student.

Oxygen hood. A Plexiglas box or hut that surrounds the upper portion of the student for the delivery of oxygen.

Oxygen masks. Soft vinyl masks that should fit snugly over the nose and mouth to deliver oxygen.

Oxygen tent. A large canopy (or tent) that delivers oxygen.

p.r.n. An abbreviation from the Latin phrase meaning "according to circumstances required."

Partial participation. The curriculum and instruction philosophy that students with disabilities for whom independent performance is not possible, should have objectives that target some type of participation within a task. It is believed that partial participation encourages active participation, self-esteem, and interaction with the environment and peers.

Peak inspiratory pressure (PIP). The amount of pressure used to inflate the lungs to a prescribed tidal volume.

Percussion. A technique using a cupped hand (or sometimes a special percussion cup or mechanical percussion) to gently strike the person's chest in specific places over the underlying lung to hasten drainage by shaking secretions from the sides of the respiratory tract.

Physical dependence. A condition in which a drug alters the physiological state of the body, and, to prevent withdrawal symptoms, the person must receive continued administration of the drug. Another term for this is *addiction*.

Positive end expiratory pressure (PEEP). A select amount of pressure to prevent the lungs from collapsing after exhalation.

Postural drainage. A technique in which the student is placed in specific positions during the day for specified periods of time to drain fluid.

Postural reaction. An automatic reaction that allows an individual to function upright in space.

Power alarm. A ventilator alarm indicating that there is either a low battery or a loss of power.

Prescription drugs. Drugs that require a physician's order.

Primitive reflex. An involuntary movement that functions to protect the baby or form beginning motor skills and that may continue abnormally in individuals with physical disabilities.

Prone. Lying on the stomach.

Reflux. Backward flow of the stomach contents.

Reservoir container. A container that keeps the oxygen cold and typically contains 3 to 5 days of oxygen.

Respiration. A process in which inhaled oxygen moves from the lungs to the bloodstream and carbon dioxide moves from the bloodstream into the lungs.

Respiratory rate. The number of breaths that are delivered in a minute; measured in breaths per minute (bpm).

Response prompts. Assistance provided by the teacher to initiate and/or guide student performance of a behavior. Types of response prompts include verbal, gesture, model, and physical prompts. The coordinated use of response prompts are used as instructional strategies, such as time-delay, system of least prompts, system of maximum prompts, and graduated guidance.

Righting. The ability to put head and body back to a vertical position when the body is shifted off center.

Rooting reflex. Movement of the head and mouth to the side when the mouth or cheek is touched.

Self-operated prompt. A form of antecedent prompt in which students are taught to self-manage performance by using picture sequences or tape-recorded instructions.

Shadowing. A type of graduated guidance in which the teacher keeps her hands within an inch of the student's hands throughout the trial until the behavior is completed. Therefore, if assistance is needed, it can be quickly provided.

Side effects. An effect of a drug or treatment that occurs in addition to the intended effect for which the drug or treatment was taken. Also referred to as *adverse drug effects* or *untoward effects*. Side effects may range in severity from being very mild and trivial to resulting in serious health concerns.

Sigh volume control. The amount of milliliters of air that is intermittently pumped in by the ventilator to simulate a sigh.

Skin-level device. A small, round silicon device that goes through the abdominal wall and is positioned at skin level. A connecting tube attaches to it for tube feedings to be given. (Also known as a *gastrostomy button*.)

Spasticity. Hypertonia or having increased muscle tone.

Stages of learning. See *Learning, stages of*

Stoma. An opening.

Stoma cap. A colostomy plug device that fits into the stoma preventing stool from leaking out.

Stomal stent. A short, straight tube that goes through the stoma into the airway but does not continue down the trachea.

Suction machine. A machine used to pull secretion from the airways through suction.

Suctioning. The aspiration of secretions by mechanical means.

Supine. Lying on one's back.

Symmetrical. Both sides of the body having equal size, shape, and alignment.

Tactile defensiveness. A greater than usual response to tactile stimulation.

Task analysis. The process of breaking down a complex task into its component steps, which allows for analyzing the student's competence in performing each step and for structuring instruction.

Tidal volume. The volume of air that is delivered by the ventilator for each inhalation.

Time-limited steps. Steps in a task analysis that must be completed within a certain time frame.

Titration. A process in which, to obtain the correct dosage of certain drugs, a small dose is given, then it is gradually increased until the desired effect occurs.

Tolerance. The loss of the characteristic effect of the medication after repeated administrations.

Tongue thrust. A forceful outward protrusion of the tongue beyond the borders of the lips.

Tonic bite reflex. Upward jaw movement into a tightly clenched position stimulated by touching of the teeth or oral area.

Tracheostomy. A permanent surgical creation of an opening through the neck to the trachea (windpipe) in which the trachea is sutured to the skin incision.

Tracheostomy button. A closed tube inserted to keep the shape and patency of the stoma when the tracheostomy is not being used.

Tracheostomy collar. A collar that goes around the neck between the tracheostomy ties and the neck to protect the neck from irritation.

Tracheostomy ties. Ties that go around the neck to help hold the tracheostomy in place.

Tracheostomy tube. A tube inserted through an opening into the trachea (windpipe). Also referred to as a *trach tube*.

Tracheotomy. A temporary surgical incision made through the skin of the neck into the trachea (windpipe).

Trade name. The name of the drug given by the pharmaceutical company that patented the drug.

Trip-training method. A method of toilet training that primarily uses scheduled times for the student to go to the bathroom, based on when the student typically urinates.

Tube feeding. A process in which a tube is introduced into the stomach or intestine for the purpose of giving fluids with high caloric value. Also known as *gastric gavage*.

Universal precautions. A method of minimizing contact with blood and body fluids to minimize the risk of acquiring or transmitting infection.

Unsustained bite. An incomplete closing of the teeth resulting in failure to bite through the food.

Ureterostomy. A procedure in which one or both ureters are surgically moved to empty through the opening made on the abdomen.

Urinary catheterization. The process of inserting a tube into the bladder to eliminate urine.

Ventilation. The movement of air in and out of the lungs. Also known as *breathing*.

Ventilator. A machine used to assist or control ventilation as well as modify the air that is breathed through it.

Ventilator modes. Settings on a ventilator to control how ventilation is delivered.

Index